WITHDRAWN FROM LIBRARY

THE POLITICAL WRITINGS OF
JEAN JACQUES ROUSSEAU

Volume I

The Political Writings of JEAN JACQUES ROUSSEAU

*Edited from the original MSS.
and authentic editions with*

INTRODUCTION & NOTES BY
C. E. VAUGHAN
M.A., LITT.D.

*In Two Volumes
Volume I*

JOHN WILEY & SONS, Inc.
NEW YORK
1962

First edition (Cambridge University Press) 1915
Reprinted 1962

PRINTED IN GREAT BRITAIN

ROUSSEAU'S PREFACE TO THE PROJECTED EDITION OF HIS COLLECTED WORKS.

* Avant de prendre, comme je fais maintenant, ce congé du public après lequel je soupirais depuis plusieurs années, j'ai voulu lui présenter un recueil complet et correct des mêmes écrits qu'il accueillit séparément, espérant qu'il voudra bien encore les accueillir réunis et purgés de ces multitudes de fautes et de contre-sens dont fourmillent toutes les éditions faites jusqu'ici par divers libraires, et qui n'ont pas laissé de s'épuiser avec facilité. C'est la première édition dont je me suis mêlé; ce sera la dernière. Elle contient tout ce qui me restait en manuscrit de présentable; et comme je ne la fais qu'en posant la plume....

[MS. Neuchâtel, 7871 (bis). It must refer to the collected Edition of his Works, planned by Fauche of Neuchâtel in 1764–5. This was dropped in consequence of the explosion caused by the *Lettres de la Montagne*. See Rousseau's letters to du Peyrou of Nov. 29, and Dec. 13, 1764.]

PREFACE

I HAVE attempted three things in the following volumes: to collect all the political writings of Rousseau in one body; to present a correct text of what he wrote; and to define his place in the history of political thought.

I.

In the current editions of Rousseau, the political writings are scattered over some four or five volumes. And to these must be added various pieces, separately issued within the last sixty years and never yet included in the collected *Works*: the *Projet de Constitution pour la Corse*, published by Streckeisen-Moultou in 1861; the first draft of the *Contrat social*, published by M. Alexeieff in 1887 and in 1896 by M. Dreyfus-Brisac; a variety of Fragments, some of great importance, published by the first and the last of the three scholars just mentioned and by M. Windenberger (*République confédérative des petits États*, 1900); and finally, some further Fragments, which have hitherto lain buried in the Library of Neuchâtel.

Such a scattering of material is certainly inconvenient. What is worse, it has probably tended to obscure the wide range of Rousseau's enquiry and, in particular, the practical object with which much of it was carried out. A glance at these volumes will suffice to shew that more than half of their contents were written with a directly practical purpose: for the sake of reforming evils which affected the whole of Europe, or some one of the States of which the European commonwealth is built up. The miseries of war and the remedy offered by Federation; the wrongs entailed by vast inequalities of wealth and inequitable methods of taxation, with the best means of striking at their root; above all, the overwhelming importance of a sound system of Education to the well-being of nations: these are some of the subjects to which he returns again and again, and on which he is full of fruitful suggestion. All this may accord ill with the picture which paints him as nothing but a theorist and a dreamer. But it is one side of his genius; and it is only when this aspect of his work has been fully realised that his greatness, even as a theorist, can be properly understood.

Of the pieces not included in the collected *Works* the most important are the fragment, *L'état de guerre*, the fragments relating to the earlier chapters of the *Contrat social*, and the earlier version of the *Contrat social* itself; but the treatise on Corsica, hitherto known only in a very faulty text, is not far behind. Their main significance lies in the proof they offer that the idea of Contract is, at most, no more than a secondary element in Rousseau's contribution to political theory; that he hesitated long before adopting it; and that, after he had done so, he again allowed it to be thrust into the background by the ideas of environment and historical tradition which, in the first instance, he drew from Montesquieu. A discussion of these questions will be found in the general Introduction and in that to the first version of the *Contrat social*.

The amount of matter now published for the first time is not very great: some five and twenty pages, all told, would probably exhaust it. But it covers the whole of Rousseau's literary life: from the *Réponse au Roi de Pologne* (1751), which was written in connection with his earliest notable piece, the *Discours sur les sciences et les arts*, to the *Dialogues* and the *Rêveries* (both in 1776) which bring us to within little more than two years of his death. Some of these fragments throw a significant light upon the gradual formation of his political theory; others are striking examples of a style which, in grave emotional appeal, has seldom been approached; others again—the autobiographical pieces printed in the Appendix to the second volume—add something to our knowledge of the frame of mind in which the *Confessions* were written and in which the last sad years of the author were too manifestly passed. If a single new letter of Cicero were brought to light, the discovery would be proclaimed in triumph upon the house-tops. Twenty-five new pages by Rousseau will probably go unnoticed. Yet what comparison is there between the two men, in genius or importance?

II.

I have done all that lies in me to provide the text which Rousseau actually wrote. And it is no easy task. Even the works published during the author's lifetime have suffered strange things from later editors; much more, those that have been brought out since his death. Both statements must be briefly justified.

More than half the matter contained in these volumes was seen through the press by Rousseau himself. And, though he took no direct part in any subsequent edition, he left revised copies and a few notes which were used by his 'universal trustee,' du Peyrou, in preparing the authoritative edition published at Geneva four years after the author's death (1782). Du Peyrou's work, upon this part of his material, was executed with extraordinary accuracy and fidelity. It is clear therefore that the sole duty of any subsequent editor of the treatises concerned is to take du Peyrou's text as it stands, merely recording the variations between it and the *editio princeps* of the work in question[1]. Unfortunately, this is not the sense in which many of the later editors have understood their obligation. They have made emendations on their own account to the right hand and the left; and have thus, generally without a word of acknowledgment, presented the world with a text very different from that which Rousseau actually left.

These 'emendations' are of two kinds. They are made either because the editor did not understand the author's meaning, or because he conceived that he could improve upon the author's French. In the former case, it may be that he could not help himself; and the only alternative was to surrender the task to some other man more fortunately placed. But it may be suggested that to put in, or leave out, negatives—the course frequently adopted—is a method which, however convenient, is hardly likely to be sound[2].

---

[1] Naigeon and others responsible for Bozerian's edition of 1801 claim to have used Romilly's copy, 'corrected by the hand of the author,' for the *Discours sur l'inégalité* and the *Contrat social*; and that of 'citizen Clos' (Choderlos de la Clos) for the *Lettres de la Montagne*, also corrected by Rousseau. I cannot say whether they did what they professed. But, to give them the benefit of the doubt, I have recorded the variations of this edition also. Rousseau's acquaintance with de la Clos is proved by a letter (à M. D. L. C.), containing a criticism of his *Épître à la Mort*, printed in Ed. 1782 (4°), XII. p. 513. I cannot find this letter in Ed. Hachette.

[2] One of the most flagrant instances of this, which I recall, is to be found in

x *Preface*

The second form of correction is more wanton, and therefore still less pardonable, than the first. The style of a great writer, even when not strictly obedient to the rules of the grammarians, ought under no circumstances to be garbled: least of all, when he avowedly holds 'the harmony of a sentence to be more important than anything except its clearness,' and boldly proclaims that there are cases when 'it is right to break the rules of grammar, for the sake of being more clear[1].' More often than not, however, the editors cannot even plead the poor excuse of grammar for their vagaries. A glance at the notes to these volumes will shew that they have habitually altered words because it suited their fancy, and for nothing else. What Rousseau would have said to such liberties is fortunately upon record; for his publisher, in the early days of their association, had ventured on exactly the same offence. Here is the outraged author's protest: 'The truth is, I am beginning to doubt whether I am an author you are printing, or a schoolboy you are correcting. Really, M. Rey, you must leave me to bear my own sins, without putting in more of your own making[2].' I have done my best to weed out these impertinences. But they are so thickly strewn—in the better known treatises, one at least for every second or third page—that it is possible some few may have escaped my spud.

It remains to consider the writings published since the author's death. These, again, fall under two heads: those published by du Peyrou in 1782; and those which successive editors, from Streckeisen-Moultou onwards, have given to the world during the last sixty years. It is necessary to make this distinction: because the former—which reduce themselves to the *Jugement sur la Paix perpétuelle*, the *Extrait* and *Jugement de la Polysynodie*, and finally the *Gouvernement de Pologne*—had been more or less carefully prepared by Rousseau himself, with a view either to publication or, at the least, to being read by others; while the latter, if we except the early draft of the *Contrat social*—and even that exception is only partial—are no more than rough drafts, the text

Firmin Didot's edition of *Émile*. Here (p. 61, in the paragraph beginning 'Tout sentiment de peine,' near the opening of Book II.) the editor has wrecked the argument by substituting *malheureux* for *heureux* and *au-dessus* for *au-dessous*; although Eds. 1762 and 1782, as well as the Manuscript (Geneva MS. f. 205), are all against him. For instances from Hachette's edition, which from its cheapness is the most familiar of all, see my notes to the text, *passim*.

[1] See letter to Rey of July 8, 1758 (Bosscha, p. 52), and to du Peyrou of April 12, 1765 (*Œuvres*, XI. p. 244).

[2] See letter to Rey of July 20, 1758 (Bosscha, p. 56).

of which it is extremely difficult, sometimes almost impossible, to make out.

The four writings of the former class have, in the main, been edited with great accuracy: the *Gouvernement de Pologne*, if we may judge from the Neuchâtel manuscript (which, however, was not that actually used for publication) and its pencilled corrections, quite remarkably so; the three others, when allowance has been made for one or two rather damaging blunders, almost as well. It is needless to say that here too, as in the writings published during Rousseau's lifetime, later editors have busied themselves with sowing tares among the wheat.

The writings of the latter class—the early draft of the *Contrat social*, the *Projet de Constitution pour la Corse*, and the fragments (including the crucial one, *L'état de guerre*)—manifestly stand on a different footing. The difficulty of deciphering them is so great that mistakes may reasonably be forgiven. Streckeisen-Moultou, who has done far more than any other editor in the working of this field, has also, at least in the case of the *Projet pour la Corse*, executed his task with considerably less of accuracy. In his defence it must be said that the manuscript of the *Projet* is perhaps the most crabbed of the whole collection. Certainly, his reproduction of the other pieces—the long series of fragments printed in the first volume of this edition (pp. 325—358)—is a far more faithful piece of work. And the same praise must be given to M. Dreyfus-Brisac and M. Windenberger.

It remains true that a certain number of mistakes have crept into the text of these *inedita*. I have spared no pains to remove them in these volumes. There is no fragment, however short, the manuscript of which I have not collated at least twice. And, with all the more important pieces (whether 'edited' or 'unedited'), I have repeated the process six or seven times. Yet, with the best will in the world, the attention will sometimes flag; and I should not be surprised if errors should here and there be detected by future workers. Each student, as I have the best reasons for knowing, profits by the labours of those who have gone before. One by one, the false readings are corrected. But, however slow the advance, the goal for which we have all striven will at length be reached; and a great writer will at last have come by his own: a text printed exactly as he wrote it, not marred by any of the 'guess-work' against which he warned his editors, or by the garbling, however involuntary, of which he always stood in dread.

Two points only remain to mention. I have deliberately refrained from any attempt to preserve either Rousseau's spelling, or his punctuation. To perpetuate the archaic spelling of a great writer—above all, of a philosopher—seems to me to be sheer pedantry; it simply distracts attention from the weightier matters of thought and of expression; while for the ordinary compromise, which consists in modernising such forms as *intérest* or *contract*, and at the same time retaining the *oi* of the imperfect and conditional, there is, so far as I can see, no possible defence. I have settled the question by modernising throughout. On the same principle, I have throughout rejected Rousseau's logical, but extremely complicated, system of punctuation; and have, in every case, adopted that which seemed likely to make his meaning as clear as possible to the reader.

The other matter concerns the text of the posthumous *Gouvernement de Pologne*. At the end of 1912, it was announced by the Marquis de Girardin in the *Bulletin du Bibliophile* that the Manuscript from which the treatise was printed by du Peyrou in 1782 had at last been unearthed at Cracow. In the *Annales de la Société J.-J. Rousseau* for 1913 this announcement was supplemented by a brief account of the manuscript from the hand of M. Olszewicz. Owing to a press of other business, which I now bitterly regret, I did not see either of these notices until the summer of last year (1914). I at once made arrangements for a journey to Cracow at the beginning of August. Meanwhile the war broke out; and the journey became impossible. Much against the grain, I am forced to content myself with simply reprinting the text of 1782, the accuracy of which is confirmed, as to two-thirds of the treatise, by the corrections pencilled in the hand of du Peyrou upon the Neuchâtel MS., and, as to three-quarters, by the Coindet Copy now in the Library of Geneva. As I have pointed out in the Introduction, there remain one or two questions which can only be settled by a careful collation of the manuscript at Cracow.

III.

As to Rousseau's place in the history of political philosophy, it would be idle to add anything to what will be found in the various Introductions. There are, however, some kindred matters which I have endeavoured to explain. These are, firstly, the historical circumstances necessary to the understanding of the several treatises, in particular those concerning Geneva, Corsica and Poland; secondly, the vexed question of the various Manuscripts, above all those of the *Contrat social* and the *Gouvernement de Pologne*; thirdly, the history of the controversy between Rousseau and Diderot on the subject of natural law—a controversy which, beginning as a friendly difference and eventually flaming out into a deadly feud, has left its mark upon the closing words of the *Confessions*; and lastly, the light in which Rousseau's philosophy presented itself to the men of his own generation and of that which immediately followed. The two first of these matters are discussed in the Introductions to the respective treatises; the third in that to Diderot's article, *Dròit naturel*; and the fourth in the Introduction to the final version of the *Contrat social*. Some further illustrations of the last point will be found in the Introduction to the extracts from *Émile* and in a note to the *Jugement sur la Paix perpetuelle*.

Nothing remains save to express my gratitude to those who have helped me in what has necessarily been a long task. I desire to pay my sincerest thanks to my former colleagues, Professor Mackenzie, of the University of Wales, and Miss Cooke, of the University of Leeds, who have aided me in numberless ways with criticism and advice; as well as to Professor Paul Barbier fils, of the latter University, who encòuraged me to undertake the task, helped me with his great and accurate knowledge of Rousseau's life and writings, and kindly revised the earlier proofs. Since August last, he has been serving his country against our common enemy, and has therefore been unable to render the same good offices to the later proofs. I fear their accuracy may have suffered accordingly. If, in spite of my efforts, errors of language or accentuation have slipped through, I must throw myself upon the indulgence of my readers; openly confessing that, if I had not counted upon thè help of my friend's scholarship, I should hardly have had the courage to shoulder a burden which it was perhaps, in any case, presumptuous for a foreigner to take up.

My warmest thanks are also due to the following friends: to Professor A. C. Bradley, to my former colleague, Professor Little, and to Lieutenant C. R. Sanderson, until lately of the John Rylands Library, who have been good enough to look up doubtful points at the British Museum, at times when it was impossible for me to make the journey myself.

I cannot close this Preface without also offering my best thanks to those who have helped me in the various Libraries where my work has lain: in particular, to the Librarian and staff of the Rylands Library; to M. Fernand Aubert, *sous-directeur des manuscrits* at Geneva, who has aided me in many difficulties; to M. Robert, Director of the Library at Neuchâtel, who has repeatedly permitted me to work in that Library when it was officially closed; and to his Assistants, M. Ganeval and M. Künzi who have, with ungrudging courtesy, made themselves responsible for me at such times and whose life, I fear, must often have been made a burden to them by my importunities. The British Museum is, I fear, too impersonal to thank.

C. E. VAUGHAN.

MANCHESTER,
    May, 1915.

TABLE OF CONTENTS

VOLUME I

	PAGE
Introduction: Rousseau as political philosopher	1
Discours sur l'inégalité:	
Introduction	118
Text	125
Author's Notes	197
Lettre à M. Philopolis	221
Économie politique:	
Introduction	228
Text	237
L'état de guerre:	
Introduction	281
Text	293
Fragments	307
Writings of Saint-Pierre:	
Introduction	359
Extrait de la Paix perpétuelle	364
Jugement sur la Paix perpétuelle	388
Extrait de la Polysynodie	397
Jugement sur la Polysynodie	413
Droit naturel (Diderot):	
Introduction	422
Text	429
Contrat social, first Version:	
Introduction	434
Text	446
Appendix I: Rousseau's reply to criticisms on the *Discours sur l'inégalité*	512
Appendix II: Contents of MS. Neuchâtel, 7840	514
Facsimile	*between* 302–3

LIST OF MANUSCRIPTS USED

BRITISH MUSEUM.

MSS. add. 4925: *Dialogue I*; Vol. II. Appendix I.

BIBLIOTHÈQUE NATIONALE, PARIS.

Nouvelles acquisitions françaises, 1183 (consulted only; see Introduction, Vol. I. p. 14).

BIBLIOTHÈQUE DE GENÈVE.

MS. français, 228: *Préface* (fragment); Vol. I. pp. 350–1. Fragment; Vol. I. p. 339.
MS. français, 225: first draft of *Contrat social*; Vol. I. pp. 446–511.
MS. français, 205: *Émile*; Vol. II. pp. 142–158.
MS. français, 229: *Projet de Constitution pour la Corse*; Vol. II. pp. 307–356.
MS. français, 246: *Gouvernement de Pologne* (Coindet's Copy); Vol. II. pp. 425–491.

BIBLIOTHÈQUE DE LA VILLE, NEUCHÂTEL.

MS. 7829: *Extrait de la Polysynodie* (rough draft and fair copy, with fragments of the rough draft of *Extrait du Projet de paix perpétuelle*); Vol. I. pp. 364–387, 397–412.
MS. 7830: *Jugement sur la Polysynodie*; Vol. I. pp. 413–422. Fragments; Vol. I. pp. 324, 358.
MS. 7836: *Lettre à M. Philopolis*; Vol. I. pp. 221–7.
MS. 7838: *Considérations sur le Gouvernement de Pologne et sur sa réformation projetée*; Vol. II. pp. 424–516.
MS. 7840 [for a complete list of its contents see Vol. I. pp. 514–6]: rough draft of *Économie politique* (Vol. I. pp. 237–280); Fragments (Vol. I. pp. 308–322, 323–4); rough draft of *Lettres de la Montagne*, vi.–ix. (Vol. II. pp. 197–291); close of *Lettre* v. (Vol. II. Appendix I.); Fragments on Art (Vol. II. Appendix I.).
MS. 7842: *addenda pour la grande Édition*; Vol. I. p. 410; Vol. II. pp. 25, 27, 29, 74, 77, 86.
MS. 7843: Fragments; Vol. I. pp. 325–7, 355–7.
MS. 7844: *Avant-propos du Projet pour la Corse*; Vol. II. pp. 306–7.
MS. 7849: Fragment; Vol. I. pp. 327–9.
MS. 7854: Fragments; Vol. I. pp. 307, 322, 341–350.
MS. 7856: *L'état de guerre*; Vol. I. pp. 293–307.
MS. 7858: Fragment on Saint-Pierre; Vol. I. p. 360.

List of Manuscripts used

MS. 7859: *Jugement sur la Paix perpétuelle*; Vol. I. pp. 388–396.
MS. 7867: Fragments; Vol. I. pp. 330–4.
MS. 7868: Fragments; Vol. I. pp. 334–9.
MS. 7871: Fragments; Vol. I. pp. 339–341.
MS. 7872: Fragments; Vol. I. pp. 358, 512–3; Vol. II. Appendix I.
MS. 7886: Letter to Mirabeau; Vol. II. pp. 159–162.
MS. 7893: Letter to Voltaire; Vol. II. pp. 163–5.
MS. 7894: Rough copy of the same.
MS. 7899: Correspondence with Buttafuoco; Vol. II. pp. 356–367.
MS. 7923: *État des écrits posthumes qui sont ici* (Ermenonville); Vol. II. pp. 422–3. Other quotations from this MS. in Vol. II. pp. 304, 400.

SHORT LIST OF BOOKS NECESSARY FOR THE STUDY OF ROUSSEAU'S POLITICAL WRITINGS AND LIFE

I. First editions of the works published in Rousseau's lifetime:

Discours sur l'inégalité: Rey, Amsterdam, 8vo, 1755.
Économie politique: in Vol. v. of *Encyclopédie*, Paris, Fol. 1755.
Extrait de la Paix perpétuelle: Amsterdam, 8vo, 1761.
Émile: Néaulme, Amsterdam (and Duchesne, Paris), 4 vols. 8vo, 1762.
Contrat social: Rey, Amsterdam, 8vo, 1762.
Lettres écrites de la Montagne: Rey, Amsterdam, 8vo, 1764.

II. Collected editions:

Collection complète des Œuvres de J.-J. Rousseau (ed. du Peyrou, and serving as the first edition of *Jugement sur la Paix perpétuelle, Extrait de la Polysynodie, Jugement sur la Polysynodie, Considérations sur le Gouvernement de Pologne*, as well as of the *Confessions, Dialogues II, III*, and the *Rêveries*): 17 vols., Geneva, 4to, 1782 sqq.; 33 vols. 8vo, 1782–4; 33 vols. 12mo, 1782–4.

Œuvres de J.-J. Rousseau (Bozerian and Didot aîné; edited by Naigeon, Fayolle and Bancarel): 25 vols., Paris, 12mo, 1801.

[These are the only editions which can claim any authority; and it is very doubtful whether the variations in Bozerian's edition are anything more than a capricious corruption of the text. In du Peyrou's Quarto edition, Vol. I. contains the *Discours sur l'inégalité, Lettre à M. Philopolis, Économie politique, Contrat social*, and *Gouvernement de Pologne*; Vol. VI., *Lettres de la Montagne*; Vol. XII., the two treatises on *La paix perpétuelle* and the two on *La Polysynodie*, and the Letters to Voltaire, Usteri (July 15, 1763), Mirabeau and Buttafuoco. The Dedication (Vol. I.) contains a passionate vindication of Rousseau against the calumnies of Diderot.]

III. Subsequent publications of Texts:

Streckeisen-Moultou, *Œuvres et Correspondance inédites de J.-J. Rousseau* (*Projet pour la Corse* and Fragments): Michel Lévy, Paris, 8vo, 1861.
Streckeisen-Moultou, *Rousseau, ses amis et ses ennemis* (Correspondence): Michel Lévy, 2 vols., Paris, 8vo, 1865.
Dreyfus-Brisac, *Du Contrat social* (Final version, earlier version, *L'état de guerre*, and other Fragments): Alcan, Paris, 1896.
Windenberger, *La République confédérative des petits États* (*L'état de guerre* and other Fragments; *Contrat social*, I. ii. (earlier version)). Paris, 8vo, 1900.

[I have been unable to get sight of M. Alexeieff's edition of *Contrat social* (earlier version), Moscow, 1887.]

IV. Other works:

Rousseau, *Correspondance* (Ed. Hachette, Vols. x.–xii.).
Abbé de Saint-Pierre, *La paix perpétuelle*, 2 vols. 8vo, 1712; *Discours sur la Polysynodie*, Amsterdam, 12mo, 1719.
Mably, *Du Gouvernement et des lois de la Pologne* (1770–1), in *Œuvres*, Vol. viii., Paris, 8vo, 1797.
Bernardin de Saint-Pierre, *Études de la Nature* (containing many reminiscences of Rousseau), 3 vols., Paris, 12mo, 1784.
Sébastien Mercier, *De J.-J. Rousseau considéré comme l'un des premiers auteurs de la Révolution*, 2 vols., Paris, 8vo, 1791.
d'Escherny, comte de, *Éloge de J.-J. Rousseau* (in *Philosophie de Politique*, 2 vols., Paris, 8vo, 1796); and *Mélanges* (containing reminiscences of Rousseau), 3 vols., Paris, 12mo, 1811. [*Éloge* written in 1789.]
Corancez, *Journal de Paris*, Vol. xlii. (Prairial 19 and 21, An vi.), Paris, 4to, 1798.
[The *Biographie générale* states that Corancez was married to a daughter of Romilly, Rousseau's friend, a Genevan watchmaker settled at Paris; also that Corancez first published his reminiscences of Rousseau in 1778 (only 50 copies), and again in an appendix to his volume of poems (1790). In the British Museum is an English translation of his articles in the *Journal de Paris*: *Anecdotes of the last twelve years of the life of J.-J. Rousseau*, London, 12mo, 1798.]
Dussaulx, *De mes rapports avec J.-J. Rousseau*, Paris, 8vo, 1798.
Marmontel, *Mémoires*, 4 vols., Paris, 8vo, 1804.
Grimm, *Correspondance littéraire* (1753–90), 17 vols., Paris, 8vo, 1813 (another edition, by Tourneux, 16 vols., Paris, 8vo, 1877–82).
Mme d'Épinay, *Mémoires et correspondance*, 3 vols., Paris, 8vo, 1818.
Musset-Pathay, *Histoire de la vie et des ouvrages de J.-J. Rousseau*, 2 vols., Paris, 8vo, 1821.
Bosscha, *Lettres inédites de Jean Jacques Rousseau à Marc Michel Rey*, Amsterdam, 8vo, 1858.
Lord Morley, *Rousseau*, 2 vols., London, 8vo, 1873.
T. H. Green, *Works*, Vol. ii., London, 8vo, 1886.
Höffding, *J.-J. Rousseau og hans Filosofi*, Copenhagen, 8vo, 1896.
Bosanquet, *The philosophical theory of the State*, London, 8vo, 1899.
Mrs Macdonald, *Jean-Jacques Rousseau, a new Criticism*, 2 vols., London, Chapman and Hall, 8vo, 1906.
Vallette, *Jean-Jacques Rousseau, Genevois*, Geneva and Paris, 8vo, 1911.
Annales de la société J.-J. Rousseau, Geneva, 8vo, 1905 sqq.

N.B. In referring to works of Rousseau, other than those included in this edition, I have always used Hachette's edition in 13 vols., Paris, 8vo, 1905; as being probably the most generally accessible. The text, however, is far from correct.

CORRIGENDA ET ADDENDA

p. 37, note 1, *for* '[204],' *read* '203.'
ib. note 3, *for* '[25],' *read* '161.'
p. 38, note 3, *for* '*Œuvres*, III. p. 204,' *read* 'Vol. II. p. 202.'
p. 278, l. 10, *for* 'avant qu'il y eut,' *read* 'avant qu'il y eût.'
p. 319, l. 5 from bottom, *for* 'put,' *read* 'pût.'
p. 409, note, *for* 'revolution,' *read* 'révolution.'
p. 451, l. 18, *for* 'legères,' *read* 'légères.'

---

pp. 379–80 (paragraph beginning 'En effet, dira-t-on'). To the phrases marked as wanting in Ed. 1772 add the two following: *c'est à dire le précieux droit*; and *à ces antiques prétentions qui tirent leur prix de leur obscurité, parce qu'on les étend avec sa fortune*. Neither these phrases, nor any of the other variants from Ed. 1782, are represented by equivalents in the English Translation of 1761, the year in which Rousseau's original was published. It may therefore be reasonably concluded that Ed. 1772 is a faithful reprint of Ed. 1761; and that the variants appeared for the first time in Ed. 1782. This conclusion is confirmed by the fact that Ed. 1764 (Neuchâtel, 13 vols. 8vo) agrees *verbatim* with Ed. 1772 and, so far as can be judged, with the English Translation of 1761. To this statement there are three trifling exceptions: *i.e.*

    p. 367, l. 6 from bottom, Ed. 1764 has *d'intérêt, de droits*.
    p. 378, last line, Ed. 1764 has *de conquêtes*.
    p. 386, l. 26, Ed. 1764 has *sujets de contestations*.

It must also be recorded that the Notes on p. 367 and p. 383 are entirely wanting in the English Translation of 1761.

I have unfortunately been unable to find any copy of the original Edition.

INTRODUCTION

ROUSSEAU AS POLITICAL PHILOSOPHER

THE work of Rousseau is little known in this country, and less understood. The title of the *Contrat social* is familiar. But to most men it suggests an extreme form of individualism. It stands, that is, for ideas which are either expressly repudiated by the author, or saluted hurriedly from afar. What the real argument of the book may be, or what its place in the history of political theory, few have troubled themselves to enquire. And fewer yet are aware that it forms but a small part of what Rousseau wrote upon this subject; or that, with one exception (the *Discours sur l'inégalité*), the remainder of these writings are based on ideas still further removed from the individualist—indeed, from any abstract—doctrine than the *Contrat social* itself.

Strike out the *Discours sur l'inégalité* with the first few pages of the *Contrat social*, and the 'individualism' of Rousseau will be seen to be nothing better than a myth. Strike out a few more chapters of the *Contrat social*, and his results, if not his methods, will be seen to be not abstract, but concrete. Even when sweeping principles are laid down, the widest possible latitude is left for their application. They are not imposed as a law. Rather they are held up as an ideal, the acceptance of which may quicken the sense of justice in the more favoured communities, but which even the most favoured community can never hope fully to attain.

That Rousseau himself is partly responsible for this misunderstanding, may readily be allowed. But it remains true that his readers have been singularly blind. Within the last five and twenty years light has doubtless begun to break in upon the darkness. It has so in this country; it has so, perhaps more generally, in Switzerland and France. But it may be doubted whether even professed students of the subject have yet grasped either the vast range of thought which Rousseau opened up, or the goal to which it pointed.

Before justice can be done to him, it is necessary that his work in this field should be studied as a whole. And it is the object of these volumes to remove the obstacles which have hitherto lain in the way of such a study. Here—as I believe, for the first time— the whole body of his work as political philosopher is collected and arranged in order of time: the practical part of it as well as the speculative; the writings which he published himself, as well as those which, until the last few years, lay buried in the Libraries of Neuchâtel and Geneva.

Three points at least will be made clear by a study of this collection. The first is that Rousseau, so far from supporting the individualist theory, is its most powerful assailant. The second, that he concerns himself with action no less than with theory; that he is at least as much a practical reformer as a political philosopher. And the third, which indeed is the natural consequence of the second, that his arguments, so far from being abstract, have the closest reference to conditions of time, place and historical antecedent; that to him, as to Burke, 'circumstances, which with some men pass for nothing, in reality give to every political principle its distinguishing colour and discriminating effect.' The first appears from the two main speculative treatises, the *Contrat social* and the *Économie politique*. The second, from the treatises upon the affairs of Geneva, Corsica and Poland; it might indeed be suspected by the reader of the *Contrat social* itself. The third is writ large on the later pages of the *Contrat social*; and the subsequent treatises are one long application of the principles there laid down. A doctrinaire, who deliberately shuts his eyes to circumstances and rides rough-shod over consequences—that is still apparently the Rousseau of popular belief. Can we honestly say that it is the Rousseau of the *Contrat social* or of *Le Gouvernement de Pologne*?

I

GENERAL POSITION OF ROUSSEAU

Like other men of his mark, Rousseau worked his way by slow stages to the point which he ultimately reached. He began as the pupil of Locke. In the crucial years of his growth he was the whole-hearted disciple of Plato. And towards the close—the first stages of the process may be plainly traced even in the *Contrat social*—he passed, and was indeed the first great thinker to pass, beneath the spell of Montesquieu.

The strongest influence of these three was undoubtedly that of Plato. And in at least one cardinal point, the doctrine of Sovereignty, it was reinforced, strangely enough, by reluctant respect for the masterful genius of Hobbes. But, either late or early, the other two influences also told strongly upon his work. The voice of Locke is heard plainly, and with results disastrous to the general tenor of the argument, in the opening chapters of the *Contrat social*. After that, though it is doubtful whether the pupil ever recognised how far he had drifted from his master[1], it silently drops out. Far more fruitful is the influence of Montesquieu; and, unlike that of Locke, it was strengthened, not weakened, by time. In the *Contrat social* it is not yet fully assimilated. It breathes through every page of the practical treatises which followed. It is not always easy to reconcile with the influence of Plato. It runs directly counter to the more abstract strain inherited from Locke.

The influence of Montesquieu was, from the nature of the case, first and foremost an influence upon method. That of the other two thinkers was in the first instance an influence of ideas. The ideas, in this case, may be summed up in one word—Right. That was the chief object of the search of Plato. In another and far narrower sense, it was the goal also of Locke. There is no sense in which the same could be said of Montesquieu. And, with all respect for present modes of thought, that is the one thing wanting to his achievement. 'He did not concern himself with the principles of Right. He was content to treat of the positive rights recognised by existing Governments. And no two studies in the world could be more different.' This is Rousseau's verdict on 'the one man of modern times who was capable of calling this great, but useless science into being[2].' And, however deep our admiration for Montesquieu—no man could have admired him more than Rousseau—it must be admitted to be just. The historical method, invaluable as a servant, is an ill guide when taken for master. It gives inestimable aid in the application of first principles. But it is powerless to discover them. In and by itself, it can never rise above considerations of circumstance and expediency. But beyond and above these lies

[1] Thus in *Lettres de la Montagne*, VI. he writes (with reference to the *Contrat social*): 'Locke a traité ces matières exactement dans les mêmes principes que moi.' Vol. II. p. 206.
[2] *Émile*, Liv. v.; Vol. II. p. 147. The 'useless science' is that of Political Right.

man's unconquerable craving for justice and for Right. And it is the lasting service of Rousseau that, with all the weight he allows to considerations of the former character, he never ceases to give the first place to the latter. The realisation of Right, in anything approaching to the full sense of the term, may, he holds, under given circumstances, be impossible. But he never falters in the faith that, wherever possible, it is and ought to be the ideal. That is the conviction which underlies the *Contrat social*. With a yet fuller allowance for circumstances, it is the faith also of his writings on Geneva, Corsica and Poland.

The first question, therefore, which Rousseau sets himself to answer is: What is the nature, and what the source, of Right? It is only when this is disposed of that he goes on to ask: Under what circumstances, with what limitations, is it to be realised in the given case? It is with the former question, and with that alone, that we are concerned at the present moment. And to this question the earlier writings of Rousseau—it must be remembered that this means no more than the two *Discourses*—suggest, though they do not explicitly give, a very different answer from the later. The earlier have commonly, and with some show of reason, been taken to plead for an extreme form of individualism. The *Contrat social* and the *Économie politique*, on the other hand, subordinate the individual ruthlessly to the community at large. The former find the ultimate base of Right in the will of the individual; the latter, in that of the community in which the individual is merged.

The fact is that two lines of thought meet and cross in the Politics of Rousseau. He is the champion of individual liberty. He is the champion also of the sovereignty of the State. He is the heir of Locke. He is the disciple also of Plato and, in this point though in no other, of Hobbes. That, in truth, is his historical significance. Standing at the parting of the ways, he embodies the results of the past; he prepares the ground for the wholly different ideals of the future. He sums up the instincts of revolt which had already shattered the medieval Church and were soon to lay the axe to the root of the still semi-feudal State. He points the way to the constructive principle which was once more to draw order out of chaos; to lift to a higher unity the elements which, in the world as he found it, were held together by nothing better than by blind custom or by force.

Such are the two strands which run through the political thought of Rousseau, the two threads which it is the business of the reader to hold carefully apart. In Rousseau himself they are apt to be entangled, rather than interwoven, with each other. He realises the vital conditions of the problem—the necessity of individual freedom, the equal necessity of collective control—with amazing clearness. That he is as successful in harmonising them, it is impossible to maintain. When all is said, the two rival elements, the individual and the community, are left not so much reconciled, as in ill-veiled hostility, to each other. In his earlier writings he asserts the freedom of the individual, but of an individual divorced from all communion—it is hardly too much to say, from all connection—with his kind. In his later work he reverses the process, and exalts the claims of the community to the utter 'annihilation' of individual interests and rights.

Both arguments are manifestly one-sided. But both are landmarks in the history as well of action as of thought. In his own day and in the generation which followed, it was the earlier argument which struck home. The later argument was either disregarded, or explained silently away. The 'principles of 1789' were universally supposed to be, and to some extent actually are, the principles of Rousseau. But it was the Rousseau of the second *Discourse*. And it is through them that Rousseau has left the deepest mark upon subsequent history; the history not only of France, but of the civilised world. Wherever, during the last century and a half, man has revolted against injustice and oppression, there we may be very sure that the leaven of the second *Discourse* has been working; there the spirit of the great liberator has without doubt contributed to the result.

To trace the working of this influence upon individual thinkers would be lost labour. It is manifest in such men as Paine and Godwin, Mill and Spencer, in this country. It is not to be mistaken in Kant and the earlier treatises of Fichte. During the first two-thirds of the nineteenth century it was probably, so far as English publicists are concerned, the strongest force at work. And though it may have been less strong upon the continent, even there it was a power to be reckoned with.

With the later argument, that of the *Contrat social* and the *Economie politique*, the case is curiously different. In the field of action, their direct influence is probably confined to the short period during which the ideals—which, for our purposes, must be sharply distinguished from the methods—of Saint-Just and Robespierre prevailed. Indirectly they may have told upon subsequent socialist movements. But, as Rousseau was no socialist in the economic sense, it can have been only in a vague and general manner. His doctrine of Sovereignty would, doubtless, find a ready welcome among socialists. Even his theory of Property, as we shall see later, may be held to have no distant affinity with theirs. But the glaring differences have probably blinded them to the few points of resemblance. And altogether it would be hazardous to expect from them any hearty acknowledgement of a debt which, for all that, it is impossible wholly to deny.

Nor again, when we turn to more distinctly speculative thought, is it any easier to gauge what the influence of the *Contrat social* has actually been. Those who have followed the same line of argument have been shy of acknowledging Rousseau for their master. For various reasons, of which the chief is probably the supposed taint of individualism in his doctrine (or again, his alleged responsibility for the excesses of the Revolution), one and all—Fichte, Hegel, Comte, Mazzini, above all Burke—have borne a grudge against his name[1]. All we can say is that he was the first to attack individualism face to face and in its speculative stronghold; the first also to take up and extend the assault directed against it by Montesquieu on what may conveniently be called historical grounds. It is difficult to believe that he has not influenced those who have followed him in this path. It is equally difficult to lay the finger upon any clear instance—still more, upon any explicit acknowledgment—of the debt. What Burke would have said, if the debt had been brought home to him, it is impossible even to imagine. It is a strange case of negligence, not to say ingratitude. But signs are not wanting that the father of modern collectivism, if the term may be used in a sense which has no reference to Economics, is at last about to come by his own.

So much by way of introduction. We now turn to consider the broad bearings of his work in the two—if we ought not rather to say the three—main stages of its growth.

[1] I do not refer to more recent thinkers. If I did, a marked exception must have been made in favour of Mr Bosanquet, whose *Philosophical Theory of the State* (1899) is full of recognition for Rousseau. The same is true, to take one other instance only, of Höffding's *J. J. Rousseau og hans Filosofi* (1896). Of the writers mentioned, Hegel is by far the most ready to do justice to Rousseau. See *Geschichte der Philosophie*, III. pp. 476—8.

II

THE *DISCOURSES* AND LONGER FRAGMENTS

It was as moral reformer that Rousseau first came before the world. And his earliest writing, the *Discours sur les Sciences et les Arts*[1], has no more than an indirect bearing upon political action. To political theory, in the strict sense, it has no reference at all. To an Englishman the position of the writer may best be expressed by saying that he anticipates—or rather, goes far beyond—Carlyle: that his main object is to assert the supreme —it would not be too much to say, the exclusive—importance of the active and moral virtues; to deny that they are in the slightest degree dependent upon man's intellectual or imaginative advance. Indeed, the author goes much further than this. He is ready to assert that the effect of the latter has always been disastrous; if Macaulay's phrase may be adapted, that 'as civilisation'—by which is here meant knowledge of the Arts and Sciences—'advances, moral virtue necessarily declines.' This was to open a deadly breach in the system of Voltaire and the Encyclopedists, and it is no wonder that they should at once have taken alarm. The first note of disquiet was sounded by d'Alembert in his Introduction to the *Encyclopédie*, which was published later in the same year (1751)[2]. Rousseau is here treated as a brilliant, but erring, brother who may yet be recalled from the error of his ways. But the next six years were to shew that the Encyclopedists were hopelessly mistaken in their man. The controversy, which had begun as a friendly difference, gradually widened into a breach which nothing could bridge over. And the mild protest of d'Alembert finally swelled into a cry of execration and contempt. For the moment, however, all this lay far in the future. It belongs, moreover, to the history rather of Rousseau's life than of his work.

With the deeper issues of Rousseau's work as moral reformer— and they are full of instruction—we have here no concern. For

[1] Written in 1749, crowned by the Academy of Dijon in 1750 and published at the beginning of 1751. Rousseau's argument is further developed in the group of writings which immediately followed (1751—3): *Lettre à Grimm, Réponse au Roi de Pologne, Réponse à M. Bordes, Préface de Narcisse*. Of these, the two last are the most important.

[2] See *Discours préliminaire à l'Encyclopédie*; *Mélanges de d'Alembert*, I. pp. 171—2 (ed. 1763).

us the crucial point is that, in assailing the moral perversity of his age, he was inevitably led on to attack its social institutions. To him the whole organisation of society is rotten to the core; and the vanity which leads men to despise the homely virtues is at once effect and cause of this corruption. Other causes, he fully admits, have been at work. But this is one of the most serious and far-reaching.

The vein of thought opened in the first *Discourse* is explored further, and with entirely fresh applications, in the second[1]. And in the interval the armoury of the writer had been strengthened out of all knowledge. The first *Discourse* is little more than an explosion of temperament. The second is a masterpiece of reasoning and eloquence. The title of this famous piece is *Discours sur l'origine et les fondements de l'inégalité parmi les hommes*; or in the still more significant wording of the theme, as proposed by the Academy of Dijon: *Quelle est l'origine de l'inégalité parmi les hommes, et si elle est autorisée par la loi naturelle?* The latter was the form of the question which Rousseau had before him when he thought out his answer. And, as will appear in the sequel, the very difference of titles is full of meaning.

Among the causes assigned in the first *Discourse* for the general corruption of mankind was 'the fatal inequality which springs from the exaltation of talent and the disparagement of virtue[2].' And in another passage the author had denounced 'the invention of the odious words *mine* and *thine*, the division of mankind into the cruel and brutal beings known as masters and the lying rascals whom we call slaves[3].' In the second *Discourse* both texts are again taken up. This time, however, the stress of the writer lies not on the former but the latter. His first thought is now not so much for the individual as the race. He speaks no longer as personal moralist, but as critic of social, and even political, institutions.

From this and other circumstances it has commonly been inferred that we have here the first draft of Rousseau's political philosophy, that the main object of the treatise is to trace the historical origin and, as a natural consequence, to enquire into the philosophical justification, of the State. To this interpretation there are, however, strong grounds of objection. And though there

---

[1] Written in 1753—4; published in June, 1755.
[2] *Œuvres*, I. i. p. 16 (ed. Hachette).
[3] *ib.* pp. 53—4 (*Réponse à M. Bordes*).

is something to be said for it, the balance of evidence would seem to be clear against it. The chief object of the author is, in truth, rather practical than speculative. As in the first *Discourse*, his results are not so much positive as negative. He is still concerned rather to expose the abuses of man's life—in this case, of his social life—than to lay down a theory either of origins, or of Right.

A brief sketch of the argument will put the reader in a position to judge for himself. Given an original 'state of nature'—and that assumption was implied in the question put before him—What form, Rousseau asks, is it likely to have taken? It was not the 'war of all against all' imagined by Hobbes; nor was it the state of 'peace, good will, mutual assistance and preservation' conceived by Locke. The one writer imports the vices, the other the virtues, of civilisation into a state which, *ex hypothesi*, is its very opposite[1]. The state of nature, if it existed at all, must rather have been a state of isolation; a state in which each man lived solely by and for himself[2]. Even the Family had not yet come into being. Male and female met casually, and casually parted. The mother reared her children till they were strong enough to fend for themselves, and then saw them no more[3].

Under these conditions, man was infinitely stronger and more adroit in body than he is now. He was in fact, all things considered, a match for any of the beasts that crossed his path[4]. In intelligence, again, there was little to distinguish him from them. The only mental gifts which set him above them were the capacity for pity and the capacity for development[5]. The former contained the germ of all that has since made him a moral being. The latter, both intellectually and morally, was ultimately to prove of supreme importance; and that, for evil at least as much as for good. But, in the beginning, its operation was both lingering and slight. Advance came mainly from the growth of his passions; and this, in turn, from the extension of his needs[6]. At first these were uncommonly simple; and, in a being whose perceptions were rudimentary and whose only passions were desire and fear, their

---

[1] Below, pp. 140, 144, 159—168; also Notes I, L. The following sentence sums up Rousseau's criticism both of Hobbes and Locke: 'Les philosophes qui ont examiné les fondements de la société ont tous senti la nécessité de remonter jusqu'à l'état de nature, mais aucun d'eux n'y est arrivé.' *ib.* p. 140.

[2] *ib.* pp. 148, 158—160. Compare Geneva MS. of *Contrat social*, Liv. I. Chap. ii. Below, pp. 447—450.

[3] *ib.* pp. 153—4.   [4] *ib.* p. 144.

[5] *ib.* pp. 150, 161—2.

[6] *ib.* pp. 150—1. Compare *Émile*, Liv. IV.; *Œuvres*, II. pp. 182—191.

development was slow[1]. It was the more so, because speech was as yet unknown to him; and without speech, thought in any true sense is impossible. How these twin faculties were wakened to life, is and will probably always remain a mystery. Ages may have passed before they came to birth. And until they did, it is evident that man must have remained, to all intents and purposes, cut off from his kind; though the converse is also true, that nothing but long intercourse with his kind could make speech, and with it thought, either necessary or possible[2].

The state of nature, then, is a state of solitude; of wants almost purely physical in character; of desires limited to the passing moment, and remaining the same from one generation to another. To call such a state 'miserable' is an abuse of terms; for misery implies a conscious craving for something other and better than what we have; and by the nature of the case such a consciousness is here excluded. Besides, are we really sure that man is worse off in the state here supposed than in that which we proudly term civilisation? To call it 'immoral,' again, is a pure confusion; for that likewise implies a consciousness of something higher, together with a recognised obligation to strive after it, of which there can obviously be here no question. Unmoral, no doubt, it is; a state neither of virtue, nor of vice. And who shall say that this is not better than the state of vice of which our vaunted civilisation is the fruit? But, above all, the state of nature is not, as Hobbes asserted, a state of war; nor are its 'cardinal virtues force and fraud.' For these things imply a power of calculation, a forethought, of which man in the state described is manifestly incapable. They imply also the absence of that pity which is natural to man even as we know him and which, if we may judge from the less educated classes of men at the present day, must have been far stronger in the state of nature[3].

Once more, however, we are confronted with the question: For what reasons, and by what stages, did man pass out of this state into one so radically opposed to it as the state of bondage with which, in one form or another, we are all familiar? To this question none but hypothetical answers can be given. It may have been

[1] Below, pp. 150—1.

[2] *ib.* pp. 153—7. Compare the *Essai sur l'origine des langues*, a highly suggestive writing, which may have preceded the second, if not also the first, *Discourse.* *Œuvres*, I. pp. 370—408. It is MS. Neuchâtel, 7835.

[3] *ib.* pp. 159—163. In what he says about pity, Rousseau skilfully appeals to the admissions of Mandeville. It should be noted that he finds traces of pity even in the beasts.

from the pressure of population which, under primitive conditions, is likely to have multiplied more rapidly than at present. It may have been owing to a change from the precarious livelihood, offered by the wild fruits of the earth, to that of hunting or fishing, which call for cooperation. Or it may have sprung from a series of accidental causes, which are now beyond our divination. In any case, the result is certain. The wandering life of primitive man was at some time exchanged for a home, more or less settled, and the first faint beginnings of property. His solitary existence was slowly replaced by the life of the Family. The Family insensibly grew into the Tribe and so brought with it the earliest forms of political association, loose enough at first but gradually tightening their hold, until they have now become the controlling law of our being. This, in turn, has brought about a revolution in the very character of man. It has brought dependence, rivalry, self-assertion, vanity: things unknown in the state of nature, but evil in themselves and destined to bring yet greater evils in their train[1]. Most savage races of the present day are still in the earlier stages of this process. And, though such a life lacks the innocence of the state of nature, it is probably the happiest that man has ever known. It is free at once from the discomforts of 'nature' and the full-blown vices and miseries of civilisation[2].

Of this intermediate state the leading characteristics, as has been said, are mutual dependence and the beginnings of property. And, as invention advances, each of these inevitably developes. The practical arts, one and all, depend on cooperation; and agriculture, the most important of them all, is inconceivable without some form of ownership. It is here that the true corner-stone of civil society is to be sought. It was to convert possession into property, an usurpation into a right, that Law was founded and the State called into existence. 'The first man who enclosed a plot of ground and bethought himself of saying *This is mine*, and found others foolish enough to believe him, was the true founder of civil society[3].'

But, before things could come to this pass, great disorders must already have arisen. And it was as an escape from these, in particular as they affected ownership, that the creation of Law and the formation of the State was proposed. Who had the adroitness to bring about this revolution? the poor, or the rich? The latter,

[1] Below, pp. 169—175.   [2] *ib.* pp. 173—5.
[3] *ib.* p. 169. These words form the opening of the second Part of the *Discourse*. They may have originally opened the whole treatise.

without a doubt. It was they who profited by it. The poor, expecting perhaps to gain by it, were in fact further impoverished and enslaved. The proposal was, in truth, a masterpiece of cunning, 'the most deeply calculated scheme which has ever entered into the wit of man.' And it was crowned with complete success. 'The whole world ran to meet its chains.' The rich had secured safeguards by which they stood to gain all that in equity would have been withheld from them. The rest were henceforth 'condemned to toil, slavery and misery.' And as the earth becomes covered with such communities, the same spirit of greed pollutes their dealings with each other. Open war without, veiled civil war within—that is the subsequent history of mankind[1].

The new order of things, it must be added, was confirmed by a contract which, like all other contracts, is dissolved *ipso facto*, directly its conditions are broken. And its dissolution necessarily carries with it a return to the state of nature. Hence it is that, whenever the despotism of the ruler becomes intolerable, his power is overthrown by a revolution; and the community starts afresh with another ruler, or another polity, of its own making. The contract is compatible with the most diverse forms of government; the particular form in each case being determined by the distribution of wealth and influence at the time of its conclusion[2].

So ends the formal argument of the *Discours sur l'inégalité*. The conclusion, however, yet remains to be considered. And it is strangely different from what the received interpretation of the author's purpose would have led us to expect. What we look for, as the practical moral, is a call to action: a demand that the false contract, the birth of fraud and deception, should be swept away, and the true contract, that of Right and equity, be put summarily in its place. What we find is a burning denunciation of the moral evils which are inseparable from *all* forms of civil government; which, in the long run, reduce even the best form, that in which the whole body of citizens is Sovereign, to a despotism of the rich over the poor[3]. What we find further is that man is powerless to stay this tide of corruption; that 'the vices which make social institutions a necessity are the same vices which, at a later stage, make the abuse of them inevitable[4].' Submission to an iron law is the conclusion of the whole matter. The second *Discourse*, like the first, points straight to fatalism and despair. It is not a call to political action. It is not a theory of political Right. It is the

[1] Below, pp. 170—9. [2] *ib.* pp. 184—191.
[3] *ib.* pp. 191—6. [4] *ib.* p. 191.

hopeless voice of the prophet crying in the wilderness; the despondent wail of the moralist denouncing evils which neither he, nor any other man, has the power to remove.

The conclusions suggested by the end of the treatise are borne out by the general tenor of the whole. No one, it may be assumed, after reading the above analysis will contend that Rousseau's object was to prepare the way for political reform. His attack throughout is directed not against any one form of Government, but against civil society as such. For a reformer, the only possible remedy, under these circumstances, would have been to demand a return to the state of nature. That, no doubt, is the course which popular opinion and lively critics supposed Rousseau to prescribe[1]. It is a remedy, however, which he himself expressly repudiates, as unthinkable and absurd[2].

Political action being thus excluded, can we suppose that the *Discourse* is intended for a statement of political theory? For this interpretation more, perhaps, is to be said than for the last. Yet here too the objections are too serious to be lightly put aside. It is manifest that the theory in question must be either a theory of historical origins, or a theory of Right. If it is a theory of historical origins, how does it happen that the author again and again insists upon the purely hypothetical character of his facts[3]? that the state of nature itself, the very first link in the chain, is admitted to be a state 'which may perhaps never have existed[4]'? If, on the other hand, it is a theory of Right, how can we account

---

[1] See Voltaire's amusing letter to Rousseau of Aug. 30, 1755, and *Les Philosophes* of Palissot (1760). Voltaire writes: 'On n'a jamais employé tant d'esprit à vouloir nous rendre bêtes; il prend envie de marcher à quatre pattes, quand on lit votre ouvrage.' And in *Les Philosophes*, a disciple of Rousseau enters on all fours, munching a lettuce. For Rousseau's generous treatment of Palissot's earlier skit (*Le Cercle*, 1755), see the closing paragraphs of *Confessions*, Liv. VIII. See also the letters to the Comte de Tressan of Dec. 26, 1755, and Jan. 7 and 23, 1756; *Œuvres*, x. pp. 108, 110, 112. Compare Palissot, *Œuvres*, II. pp. 68—86 (Liége, 1777).

[2] See *Dialogues*, III.; *Œuvres*, IX. p. 287. See also *Réponse à M. Bordes*; *Œuvres*, I. p. 65; and *Préface de Narcisse*; *Œuvres*, v. pp. 108—9.

[3] 'Commençons donc par écarter tous les faits, car ils ne touchent point à la question. Il ne faut pas prendre les recherches dans lesquelles on peut entrer sur ce sujet pour des vérités historiques, mais seulement pour des raisonnements hypothétiques et conditionnels, plus propres à éclaircir la nature des choses qu'à en montrer la véritable origine, et semblables à ceux que font tous les jours nos physiciens sur la formation du monde.' *Ib.* p. 141. I cannot agree with M. Morel (*Annales*, v. p. 136) that the *sole* reference here is to the facts recorded in *Genesis*. See below, pp. 168, 181—3.

[4] *ib.* pp. 136, 141.

for the fact that the course of events which leads up to the foundation of society is, as the author never ceases to insist, a tissue of injustice and of wrong? how, for the yet more damaging fact that, once founded, all forms of society lead with equal certainty, though some sooner and some later, to the 'slavery' of the many and the yet more hateful despotism of the few?

Once more. The theory of the *Discourse*, if there be any theory at all, can by no possibility be anything but a theory of individual rights. The conception of man implied throughout the first part of it is that of an isolated being. And such a conception, if applied to political speculation, could end in nothing but individualism run mad. How then is it conceivable that the man who wrote the *Discourse* should within a year and a half—it is an outside estimate—write and publish a work which is a negation of all the principles that individualism holds dear? that, at the very moment when he was correcting the proofs of the former, he should in all probability be meditating and composing the latter? Yet, on the interpretation we are now dealing with, that would be the case as between the *Discours sur l'inégalité* and the *Économie politique*[1].

For these reasons, the opinion that the *Discourse* is a treatise on political theory—a crude version of the *Contrat social*—must be rejected no less than the suggestion that it is a cry for political reform. And when these two interpretations are set aside, what alternative is left but to treat it as, in the first instance, the work of a moralist? as a return to the theme which, from another side, he had already handled in the *Discours sur les Sciences et les Arts*? Here, as there, the chief purpose of the writer is to expose the vices which for ages have poisoned the life both of the individual and the race: the eternal sacrifice of virtue to reputation, of the substance to the shadow of well-being[2]. Here, as there, he sees no hope of

---

[1] The second *Discourse* was written in the latter half of 1753 (*Confessions*, Liv. VIII.). It was revised, and the Notes and Dedication (probably the Preface also) added, in 1754 (*ib.*). It was published, after many delays which excited the wrath of Rousseau (see, in particular, his letter to Rey of May 29, 1755 [Bosscha, p. 25]), in June, 1755 (letter to Rey of June 19, 1755 [Bosscha, p. 27]) The *Économie politique* was published in the *Encyclopédie* (T. v.) in Nov. 1755 (letter to Vernes of Nov. 23, 1755 [*Œuvres*, T. x. p. 107]); and it is impossible that it should have been written later than the summer of that year—very probably, earlier. An interesting correspondence between Rey and Malesherbes, relating to the admission of the second *Discourse* into France, is preserved in the Bibliothèque Nationale (*Nouvelles acquisitions françaises*, No. 1183). These letters run between March 20 and June 2, 1755.

[2] See the closing paragraphs of the *Discours sur l'inégalité*; below, pp. 191—3. Compare Mercier's judgment, recorded in Vol. II. p. 14.

remedy; he is convinced that the disease is the inevitable consequence of steps long ago blindly taken but, once taken, never to be retrieved. This is the main thread of the treatise. But with it other threads are inextricably, and not very happily, entwined.

For the last dozen years, as we learn from the *Confessions*, Rousseau had thought deeply over the problems of political philosophy[1]. The idea of the state of nature, universally accepted in those days, had sunk into his mind and fired his imagination. He saw, as a man of his eloquence and dialectical genius could not fail to see, with what effect it could be used to drive home his ethical appeal. And the contrast between 'man's man and nature's man[2],' which forms the core of the whole argument, gave a force and sting to that appeal such as no other weapon could probably have supplied. At the same time it must be confessed that he gives more space to themes of history and philosophy than is easily to be justified in a moral argument. And this has served, more perhaps than anything else, to confuse the issue to his readers, not impossibly even to himself.

Nor is philosophy the only disturbing element. The moral zeal of the man was always winged with religious fervour; and the moral argument is here enlisted in the service of a religious idea. If he denounces the follies and vices of man, it is largely that he may justify the ways of God. 'Everything is good as it comes from the hand of the Creator. Everything becomes evil in the hands of man.' The thought expressed in these words is the central thought of *Émile*. Though seldom mentioned, it is never far from the surface in the second *Discourse*. It appears plainly, though not obtrusively, in the *Lettre à Philopolis*, which immediately followed. And when, long afterwards, Rousseau wrote the history of these years in the *Confessions*, it is on the moral and religious side of the argument that he lingers, while its political aspect is almost, if not entirely, ignored[3].

Yet the political argument is there, and it would be madness to overlook it. It bore little or no fruit for the moment; but it is of great importance in the history of the author's political ideas. It shews us where Rousseau stood at the moment when he had

---

[1] *Confessions*, Liv. IX. (1756). He dates his study of the subject from the time of his residence at Venice, 1743—4.

[2] The phrase is taken from the account of the *Discourse* given in the *Confessions*, Liv. VIII. (1753). Compare Kant's verdict (Vol. II. p. 20).

[3] *Confessions*, Liv. VIII. It is perhaps hardly necessary to say that the words quoted in the text—*Tout est bien*, etc.—are the opening words of *Émile*.

shaken off all but the last remnants of the theory inherited from Locke, and was about to enter, if he had not already entered, on the task of weaving a more valid theory for himself.

The knot of the whole question lies in his treatment of the state of nature. It is here that his speculative genius asserts itself for the first time and beyond all possibility of dispute. The more obvious points of conflict between him and Locke have already been noted. But there are other and yet more vital differences behind. To Locke, as we have seen, the state of nature is a state of 'good will and mutual assistance' between man and man; to Rousseau, a state in which each man is utterly isolated from the rest. To Locke, therefore, the state of nature *is* the civil state, *minus* only its political machinery. To Rousseau the one is the direct opposite of the other. It may be admitted that neither conception is anything better than a fiction. But it is the merit of Rousseau that, unlike Locke (or indeed any other previous writer), he has a lively consciousness that it is so. It is a further and still more striking merit that his fiction is by far the more plausible and fruitful of the two. The 'natural man' of Rousseau does at least answer to his name. The corresponding being of Locke's fiction is nothing less than a very good Christian in disguise. The one is a healthy animal. The other has pored himself pale over the Sermon on the Mount.

And here we come to the core of the whole matter. The corner-stone of Locke's theory is the assumption of a 'natural Law'—a law of admitted duty to others—'known and read of all men' in the state of nature. Rousseau is under no such illusion. He sees that the sense of duty must necessarily be a thing of slow growth; that to suppose it implanted as an 'innate idea' in the breast of man was not only inconsistent in Locke, but wholly unreasonable in itself; that for primitive man, even as he is conceived by Locke, much more as he must have been in reality, it is nothing short of an absurdity. For these reasons, he sweeps away the idea of natural Law, root and branch. It is conspicuously absent from the *Discours sur l'inégalité*. In the first draft of the *Contrat social*, which in all probability goes back to a date shortly before, or shortly after, the *Discours*, it is explicitly thrown aside. The chapter in which he demolishes this article of the faith is a monument of speculative insight[1].

[1] *Contrat social*, Geneva MS., Book I. Chap. ii. (*De la société générale du genre humain*). See below, pp. 447—455. See also M. Dreyfus-Brisac's edition of the *Contrat social*, pp. 246—255.

To his mind, the term *Natural Law*—or, as he rightly prefers to call it, the Law of reason[1]—is a legitimate term to denote the common sense of justice which has gradually formed itself in the minds of men during long ages of moral discipline and of positive Law. In this sense, it may, perhaps not altogether wrongly, be applied as a rule for testing the standards of ages other than our own. It may even, if we are careful to remember what we are doing, be applied in this fashion to the conditions—we cannot here say the standards—of the state of nature. But to suppose that in the state of nature it operated, or could by any possibility have operated, as a guide to conduct—and that is manifestly what Locke means by the Law of nature—is a fatal error.

The truth is that the meaning of the term 'natural Law' necessarily varies from age to age. It stands for nothing more than the code of morality commonly accepted in a given state of civilisation[2]. And in an essentially unmoral—not, it will be observed, immoral—age like that of primitive man—an age which is 'without moral relations' of any sort or kind[3]—it can have had no existence at all. It may be read into the mind of primitive man by descendants who are, or at least claim to be, civilised. But for primitive man himself it would have been utterly without meaning.

The argument is a striking proof of Rousseau's originality. The idea of natural Law had held the field since the days of the Roman Jurists. With the political philosophers of more recent times, it had been a commonplace since the days of Hooker and Grotius. None of them save Hobbes and Spinoza—the latter far more completely than the former[4]—had escaped its tyranny. The authority of Locke had given it a new sanction. And even apart from the almost unbroken tradition in its favour, there was much in it that could not but appeal strongly to the spirit of Rousseau. It is therefore the clearest proof both of his speculative genius and of his intellectual honesty that he should have decisively rejected it. And the chapter of the original *Contrat social*, which lays bare in detail the hollowness of the whole conception, is a masterpiece of philosophical criticism. Together with the illuminating Essay, *Que l'état de guerre naît de l'état social*, it is by far the most

[1] *Contrat social*, Geneva MS. ; below, p. 449.
[2] *ib.* pp. 452—3.
[3] 'Les hommes dans cet état, n'ayant entre eux aucune sorte de relation morale ni de devoirs connus, ne pouvaient être ni bons ni méchants et n'avaient ni vices ni vertus.' *Disc. sur l'inégalité*; below, pp. 159—160.
[4] See the curious letter (Ep. L.) in which Spinoza explains his relation to Hobbes ; *Opera* (ed. Tauchnitz), T. II. p. 298.

important of the Fragments here published[1]. And of the two it is decidedly the more original.

It is, therefore, one of the services rendered by Rousseau in the second *Discourse* that he leaves the idea of natural Law, so dear to the Academy of Dijon[2], entirely on one side and treats primitive man as the creature purely of impulse and of instinct. No doubt, there is a sense in which Spinoza, writing eighty years earlier, had done the same. Like Rousseau, he banishes the idea of duty, he bars out all moral relations, from the state of nature. But, unlike Rousseau, he credits the 'natural man' with a sagacity, a calculating power, which it is absurd to suppose that he possessed. 'A city of hucksters,' is Vico's criticism of Spinoza's civil state[3]. And, in a less degree, the criticism applies also to his state of nature. In this cardinal point, therefore, the work of Rousseau opens a new era in political philosophy. And it is a point for which he is entitled to more credit than he has received.

Another signal merit of the *Discours sur l'inégalité*—and this again applies to the two Fragments just mentioned—is the ruthless firmness with which the assumptions of the individualist theory are here pushed to their logical conclusion. All other forms of that theory seem pale and flaccid beside this. If the individual ever existed apart from his kind, we say to ourselves, it must have been as he is conceived by Rousseau, rather than by Hobbes or by Locke. Neither wolfish war with his neighbour, nor serviceable peace, is the natural outcome of the separate existence from which all forms of the theory take their start, and to which, so far as it can be realised, all of them tend as their consummation. Isolation—unbroken except by fleeting accident—that alone satisfies the unspoken cravings of the individualist ideal. No doubt, the very completeness of the individual's isolation in the state of nature makes it well-nigh inconceivable that he should ever pass into even the loosest possible form of the civil state. In this respect, the theory of Rousseau is exposed to the same objection which, on slightly different grounds, attaches to the corresponding argument of Hobbes. But this very objection throws a searching light upon the hybrid and watered individualism, which passes muster with the common herd of political critics and which ultimately goes

---

[1] MS. 7856 in the Bibliothèque de la Ville, Neuchâtel.
[2] See above, p. 8.
[3] 'Benedetto di Spinoza parla di Repubblica come d' una società che fusse di Mercadanti.' Vico, *Scienza nuova*, Versione seconda; *Opere* (ed. Ferrari), T. v. p. 138. The reference, of course, is to Spinoza's *Tractatus politicus*.

back to the *Civil Government* of Locke. It is the very half-heartedness of this theory which alone gives it plausibility. It is only because the individual is at every turn credited with acute social instincts and a burning desire for the public good—in other words, only because he is represented as something quite other than the individual—that he becomes a possible member of the 'individualist' State. And even so, it remains a mystery by what witchcraft he is induced to make vast sacrifices for ends which have nothing to do with his own welfare or even with his immediate neighbour's: for social reform, for national defence and independence, for foreign conquest—in a word, for all those ends which, so far from securing life and property, are likely to imperil them; so far from increasing the freedom of the individual, are certain to diminish it; and which only the wildest confusion of thought can reconcile with the premises on which the individualist theory, even in its least individualist form, is based. No State, which should cleave consistently to individualist principles, could hold together for a moment. And it is very certain that no State, of which this could truly be said, has ever existed. The 'noble savage' of the second *Discourse*—and he is your only thorough-bred individualist—must have run wild in his native woods to the end of time. He is the *reductio ad absurdum* of his tribe.

The last of the great services rendered by the *Discourse* has already been noticed. It is to have quickened beyond measure the hatred of injustice and social wrong which was already stirring at the time; to have sounded the charge for the Revolution which Rousseau himself seems at moments to have foreseen[1]. None of his works, not even the *Économie politique*, gives so burning an utterance to this side of his genius[2]. None so unmistakably bears the stamp of that 'inextinguishable hatred of oppression' which was among the strongest and noblest elements of his strangely blended nature[3].

[1] See *Émile*; *Œuvres*, II. pp. 9, 195—6: 'Nous approchons de l'état de crise et du siècle des révolutions.' Compare *Réponse au Roi de Pologne*; *Œuvres*, I. p. 46.

[2] See, however, *Économie politique*; below, pp. 267—8; and compare the Essay, *Que l'état de guerre naît de l'état social*, below, pp. 293—307. We learn from the *Confessions* (Liv. VIII.) that the most provocative passage in the *Discourse*, together apparently with others in a like vein, was not only inspired, but actually written, by Diderot. Compare the letter to Saint-Germain of Feb. 26, 1770; *Œuvres*, XII. pp. 187—8. Doubt has been thrown on these statements of Rousseau; not, I think, on any solid ground.

[3] See the characteristic anecdote told in *Confessions*, Liv. IV.; *Œuvres*, VIII. p. 116.

III

L'ÉCONOMIE POLITIQUE AND LE CONTRAT SOCIAL
(GENEVA MS. AND FINAL VERSION)

In the *Discourse on Inequality*, Rousseau had pointedly declined to 'enter on an enquiry into the nature of the social Contract,' and excused himself on the ground that the task 'needs to be done afresh from the beginning[1].' This was the problem reserved for the next group of his writings; and the *Contrat social*, in the two versions which have come down to us, contains, among many other things, the solution of it which he had carefully thought out.

Of the *Économie politique* (1755), which must have been written about the same time as the earlier parts of the first draft of the *Contrat social*, it is unnecessary to speak in detail; the more so, as the original Contract, though tacitly assumed as the foundation of all Government, is never explicitly defined. In all other respects—there is one exception which will be duly noted in its proper place[2]—the *Économie politique* anticipates step by step the argument of the more famous treatise which followed. The doctrine of the 'corporate self' (*le moi commun*[3]) and of the 'general will' which serves as its organ[4]; the doctrine of the Law as, in the strictest sense, the expression, the living voice, of the general will[5]; the doctrine of Sovereignty[6]; the analogy between the State and the animal organism[7]—in short, all the more abstract ideas which lie at the root of the *Contrat social* are here, summarily perhaps in some cases, but yet quite definitely, forestalled.

We may pass, therefore, at once to the *Contrat social*; and, except for special reasons, the difference between the two drafts of it—differences which, in fact, hardly extend beyond the cancelling of two important chapters[8]—will be rigorously ignored.

The *Contrat social* was published in 1762, seven years after the *Économie politique*. Much of it may have been—parts of it, including in all probability the two chapters finally suppressed,

---

[1] Below, p. 188.   [2] See below, pp. 104—5.
[3] Below, p. 241.   [4] *ib.* pp. 242—4.
[5] *ib.* pp. 243, 245. It may be noted that the passage reappears word for word in the first draft of the *Contrat social*. See below, pp. 62, 475.
[6] *ib.* p. 241.
[7] *ib.* p. 241. The analogy of the animal organism is not expressly brought forward in the *Contrat social*; but, throughout the more abstract part of the treatise, it is manifestly present to Rousseau's mind.
[8] Geneva MS. of the *Contrat social*, Liv. I. Chapters II. (*De la société générale du genre humain*) and v. (*Fausses notions du lien social*).

certainly were—written at a much earlier date[1]. But the exact truth on this point is now beyond our reach. And, with the exception of those two chapters, the question is fortunately of no great importance. Antiquarian discussions here sink into the background. The significance of the book lies entirely in its matter: in its speculative originality and in the vast influence which, both directly and indirectly, it has exercised upon the subsequent course of thought.

This influence, like that of the author's work as a whole, has told in two different, indeed in two contrary, directions. The opening chapters, with their assumption that no Government can be lawful which was not in the first instance set up with the free consent of each individual concerned, gave a fresh life to the individualism which the main argument of the book was destined to destroy. Until the Contract is made—such is the tenor of the opening pages—the individual, 'stupid and limited animal' as he is, is unchallenged lord of his own fate. And it is only by his own spontaneous act that his independence can be lost. But throughout the rest of the treatise all this is forgotten. From the moment the Contract is concluded, the individual ceases to be his own master. His life, his will, his very individuality are merged in those of the community. He is as much lost in the communal self as the member is in the body. He has no longer the independent value of an unit. He has become a mere fraction whose worth is determined solely by its relation to the whole[2].

That these doctrines are necessarily inconsistent with each other, there is no need to maintain. That is a question which will have to be considered later. All that concerns us here is that they are manifestly drawn from different sources and represent wholly different strains of feeling and of thought. The one is individualist in character, the other strongly, not to say defiantly, collectivist. But, different as they are, each has left its mark upon the upheaval which came after. The former of them prevailed during the opening phases of the Revolution. It was the ideal of the National Assembly and of the 'spontaneous anarchy'

[1] We have Rousseau's authority for this statement. 'Ce n'est pas qu'il n'y ait chez Rey un *Traité du Contrat social*, duquel je n'ai encore parlé à personne, et qui ne paraîtra peut-être qu'après l'*Éducation* (i.e. *Émile*); mais il lui est antérieur d'un grand nombre d'années.' Letter to Roustan of Dec. 23, 1761; *Œuvres*, x. p. 294.
[2] See *Contrat social*, I. vi., viii. See also the opening pages of *Émile*. (Vol. II. pp. 143—7.)

which gave that Assembly at once its irresistible strength and its incurable weakness. The later and more terrible phases of the struggle saw the triumph of the latter. It was the necessity, if not the ideal, of the Convention. In a distorted form, it was the ideal of the Jacobins. It was the ideal, above all, of Robespierre and Saint-Just.

Each of the two parties to that conflict, individualists as well as collectivists, appealed to the *Contrat social*. But the men who drew up the Declaration of Rights thought only of the opening pages of the treatise; they thought still more of the second *Discours*. The Jacobins, on the other hand, appealed to the body of the work. And, whatever their aberrations, they had at least the merit of grasping that here, and not in the preparatory chapters, was to be found the real message of the treatise, its true claim to originality. The glosses they put upon the text were unwarrantable. By no man would they have been repudiated more vehemently than by the author[1]. But the text itself was sound, as well as authentic. And it had the supreme importance attaching to a new principle; a principle in the light of which the whole fabric of European polity was to be recast.

When we turn to the book itself, the first thing to strike us is that we are at last face to face with the question of Right. In the earlier writings—and this applies even to the *Économie politique*—that question had either been left in the background, or deliberately set aside. Here for the first time it is put in the forefront of the argument. The very title of the work—*Du Contrat social, ou Principes de Droit politique*[2]—proclaims that the author has thrown away the scabbard and is ready to do battle for the Right. It is the former part of the title, in truth, which is open to objection; and it is a thousand pities that Rousseau did not replace it, as at one moment he intended to do, by the neutral phrase, *De la société civile*[3]. A 'Contract' could not fail to suggest

---

[1] See the striking denunciation of the doctrine of *le salut public* in *Économie politique*; below, pp. 252—3.

[2] Rousseau himself sometimes cites the work under the latter title, *e.g. Émile*, Liv. II.; *Œuvres*, II. p. 52. See also the letter to Rey of Aug. 9, 1761 (Bosscha, p. 116).

[3] The successive stages of the title in the Geneva MS. are: *Du contrat social* (cancelled); *De la société civile* (cancelled); and finally *Du contrat social* (restored). The sub-title is *Essai sur la constitution de l'État* (cancelled); *Essai sur la formation du corps politique*, with a variant *la formation de l'État* (both cancelled); and finally, *Essai sur la forme de la République*. A Facsimile is given in M. Dreyfus-Brisac's edition, p. 244.

to his readers, it has in fact universally suggested, that his theory is no more than a variant upon Locke's. And that is the very last inference that he should have desired to see drawn. So far from adopting the principles of Locke, he is in full revolt against them. The very Contracts of the two writers—not to speak of the ultimate consequences involved in each of them—are about as different as two things can possibly be. Yet the mischief, however fatal, is now done beyond recall. And the determined foe of individualism is still, after five generations, labelled as its champion through thick and thin. Other things, no doubt, have contributed to this misapprehension. But an ill-judged and picturesque title must bear no small part of the blame.

Principles of political Right—that, then, is the real subject of the *Contrat social*. And setting out to discover the foundations of Right, Rousseau naturally begins by sweeping away the false foundations laid by his predecessors, which can only end in wrong[1].

Civil society, he argues, is not an offshoot of the Family, though the Family may perhaps have served, in the first instance, for its model[2]. Still less is it the creation of force, whether that force take the shape of apparently peaceful influence (as in the *Discours sur l'inégalité*), or of actual conquest by the sword. Such force may exist in fact. It may form the basis of many Governments known to history or the experience of the present. But it can never constitute a Right, nor form the basis on which Right may subsequently be built up. Moreover, it is as shifting as it is unjust. And that being so, it cannot serve as a permanent foundation for anything, not even for a wrong. Nor, even when we confine ourselves to the region of fact, can it ever explain the formation of the most primitive societies; the transition, if for the moment we may anticipate matters, from the natural to the civil state.

So far, Rousseau is merely summarising the results he had already reached in the *Essay on the state of War*, and in one of

[1] In many respects the chapter which Rousseau devotes to this refutation in the first draft (I. v., *Fausses notions du lien social*) is more pregnant than the corresponding passages in the final draft.

[2] It may be noted that both in the *Économie politique* and in the Geneva MS. Rousseau is much more explicit in rejecting the Family than he is in the final version of the *Contrat*: 'Il est donc certain que le lien social de la Cité n'a pu ni dû se former par l'extension de celui de la famille, ni sur le même modèle.' Below, p. 466; compare *Éc. pol.*; below, pp. 237—240.

the two cancelled chapters of the first draft of the present treatise[1]. In what follows, except in so far as it coincides with the *Économie politique*, he is breaking entirely fresh ground[2].

These 'false bonds of social union' being thus disposed of, the only one that remains is the free consent of those who join to make it. In other words, civil society is the offspring of convention, or it is nothing[3].

Convention, however, in all its senses implies a contrast with what exists outside of it: in this case, a contrast with what may conveniently be called the state of nature. Of the state of nature Rousseau, who had known all about it when he wrote the second *Discourse*, can now tell us nothing. It has become a mere blank, the purely logical negative of the civil state. Even on the steps which led to the abandonment of it he is studiously vague. 'I suppose men brought to the point at which the obstacles which make it difficult for them to remain in the state of nature carry the day over the forces which each individual can bring to bear, so as to maintain himself in that state. That being so, it is impossible that the primitive state should continue; and mankind would perish, if their way of life were not entirely changed[4].' Clearly, that does not tell us much. And Rousseau was at least as well aware of this as we.

The resources of the individual being thus exhausted, it is plain that the only hope left lies in an association of many: an association so complete as to enable them jointly to overcome the disruptive forces against which each singly was powerless to contend. Hence the necessity of the civil state and of the social compact which, in right if not in fact[5], is the only possible foundation for it. But the question at once arises: How is it possible to reconcile the mutual concessions, indispensable to any joint action

[1] *i.e.* Geneva MS. I. v. The *Essay on the State of War* (Neuchâtel MS. 7856) is clearly an early work, by its handwriting, if nothing else. But it is also early in respect of style. It may be conjectured that it belongs to about the same period as the second *Discourse*, and possibly to a slightly earlier date.

[2] That is, so far as we can speak with certainty. It is impossible to date the composition of the greater part of the *Contrat social*.

[3] *Contrat social*, I. ii.—iv.

[4] *ib.* I. vi. It may be noted that the account given in the Geneva MS. is almost word for word the same. But the preceding Chapter (I. ii.) tells us more. See below, p. 441.

[5] For a discussion of the question whether, and in what sense, Rousseau regarded the Contract as a historical fact, see Introduction to the *Contrat social* (first draft). Below, pp. 436—8.

of the whole body, with the maintenance of the liberty which is essential to the well-being of the individual members? 'This difficulty may be stated as follows: How can we find a form of association which shall enlist the forces of the whole community for the protection of the person and goods of each associate? and in virtue of which each, uniting with all, shall in spite of this obey no one but himself, and remain as free as he was before? Such is the crucial problem, the solution of which is given by the social Contract[1].

'The clauses of this Contract,' Rousseau continues, 'are so completely determined by the nature of the act that the smallest deviation would make them null and void. Hence, although they may never have been formally declared, they are everywhere the same; everywhere tacitly admitted and recognised, until the moment when, the social pact being broken, each individual re-enters upon his primitive rights and resumes his natural freedom, thus losing the conventional freedom for the sake of which he had renounced it.

'These clauses, properly understood, reduce themselves to a single one; that is, the total surrender (*aliénation totale*) of each associate with all his rights to the community at large....If then we put aside all that is not of the essence of the Contract, we shall find that it reduces itself to the following terms: Each of us throws himself and all his powers into the common stock, under the supreme control of the general will; and, as a body[2], we receive each individual member as an inseparable part of the whole.

'At that very instant and in virtue of this act of association, the individual self of each contracting member is replaced by a moral and corporate body, composed of as many members as the Assembly contains votes. And from the same act this collective body receives its unity, its corporate self (*son moi commun*), its life and its will[3].'

---

[1] *C. S.* I. vi. Most of the modern editions that I have seen distort the sense by putting 'Contrat social' in italics. Rousseau, however, is not puffing his own wares; he is speaking of the social Contract, as a historical fact or as an idea of Right.

[2] *ib.* It may be observed that most modern editions read here, 'nous recevons *encore*' etc. The true reading—that of the Geneva MS. and the first edition (Rey, Amsterdam, 1762); that also of the corresponding passage of *Émile*, Liv. v. (Geneva MS. and first edition)—is, 'nous recevons *en corps* chaque membre comme partie indivisible du tout.' The meaning is not seriously affected by the false reading; but it is less correctly, and less pointedly, expressed.

[3] *ib.* I. vi.

All that is left is to provide a sanction for this formidable instrument. And the only sanction possible is force: the united force of the community as a whole. 'In order that the social compact may not prove an empty formula, it includes the tacit undertaking that, whoever refuses to obey the general will, shall be compelled to obedience by the whole body of citizens. But this means nothing more than that they will force him to be free[1].'

Such, according to Rousseau, is the fateful act upon which the whole subsequent destiny of man necessarily depends. The effects of it are far-reaching indeed. And they are at least as much moral as political. The paragraph in which Rousseau describes the former is perhaps the most crucial in the whole treatise: 'The passage from the state of nature to the civil state brings about a momentous change in man. In his conduct, it replaces instinct by justice, and gives to his acts a moral character which was wanting to them before. The voice of duty takes the place of physical impulse; right supplants appetite. Now for the first time, man, who hitherto had thought only of himself, sees himself forced to act on other principles, and to consult his reason before listening to his desires. It is true that, in the civil state, he deprives himself of many advantages which he holds from nature. But, in return, he gains advantages so great, his faculties are so trained and developed, his ideas so enlarged, his whole soul exalted to such a degree, that, if the abuses of the new order did not often degrade him below the level of that from which he has escaped, he ought without ceasing to bless the happy moment which tore him for ever from the old order, and which, of a stupid and limited animal, made him a reasoning being and a man[2].'

There is a page in the first draft which takes the same thought from the negative side, and expresses it yet more vividly and precisely. The author is here seeking to prove that there can at

---

[1] *C. S.* I. vii. The last sentence has sometimes been supposed to bear a sinister meaning. In reality, it does no more than state the commonplace that the ultimate sanction of every law is the penalty imposed for disobedience. Moreover, the 'freedom' here spoken of is clearly moral freedom, *i.e.* readiness to observe the moral Law. And the penalty for disobedience is supplied by the criminal Law. Is there anything sinister, or Jacobinical, in this? Compare: 'Les lois criminelles, dans le fond, sont moins une espèce particulière de lois que la sanction de toutes les autres.' *ib.* III. xii

[2] *ib.* I. viii. (*De l'état civil*). See also the following paragraph.

no time have been a 'general society of the human race'; a society, that is, not cemented by any civil bond or positive compact, but held together solely by mutual good will; the kind of society, in short, which is assumed in Locke's version of the state of nature. His conclusion is that such a society, even had it been possible, would have been wanting in the best things that civil society, as we know it, has to offer.

'More than that. This perfect independence, this unchartered freedom, even had it never ceased to go hand in hand with primitive innocence, would always have suffered from an inherent flaw, a flaw fatal to the growth of our highest faculties: namely, the lack of that bond between the parts which constitutes the unity of the whole. The earth might be covered with men, but among them there would be hardly any communication. We might touch each other at point after point, and find union in none. Each would remain isolated among the others; each would think only of himself. Our understanding could never develope. We should live without any feeling, and die without having lived. Our whole happiness would consist in not knowing our misery. There would be neither kindness in our hearts, nor morality in our acts. We should never have tasted the sweetest feeling of which the soul is capable: that is, the love of virtue[1].'

The upshot of both passages is that neither reason, nor the moral law, is to be realised by man except in and through the civil state. It is a conclusion which few readers can have expected from the author of the second *Discourse*.

But, if the moral consequences of the Contract are momentous, no less so are those which we are apt to regard as distinctively political. Henceforth the individual self of man is replaced by the 'corporate self'; his individual will by the 'general will' of the community as a whole[2]. By the 'general will,' Rousseau is careful to explain that he does not mean the sum of the individual wills taken separately; but the corporate will which, from the nature of the case, belongs to a body having a common life, an organised being, of its own[3]. It is not invariably—it is seldom most clearly—to be discerned by the mere process of counting

[1] Geneva MS. I. ii. (*De la société générale du genre humain*). Below, p. 449.

[2] *C. S.* I. vi.; *Émile*, Liv. I.: 'Les bonnes institutions sociales sont celles qui savent le mieux dénaturer l'homme; lui ôter son existence absolue pour lui en donner une relative, et transporter le moi dans l'unité commune.' Compare *Économie politique*, p. 241.

[3] *C. S.* II. iii. Compare *Économie politique*, pp. 241—2.

heads[1]. It implies a collective consciousness—more than that, a public spirit—leavening and giving unity to the whole mass. He may not always be consistent in working out this conception[2]. But it is clear that, when he is true to himself, this is what he is striving to express. Indeed, once accept the idea of the 'corporate self,' and that of the 'general will,' as at once the inward unity and the specific organ of this new self, necessarily follows.

But the will is no will unless it takes shape in act. And the act of the political will, as can be seen from the English term 'Act of Parliament,' is nothing more nor less than a law. The Law, accordingly, is the outward expression of the general will, or it is nothing. The moment it ceases to be so, the moment either the will which enacts it, or the end to which it is directed, ceases to be general, it becomes nothing better than a fraud[3].

From this conception of the general will and of the Law, as its embodiment, results a practical consequence of the last importance. It is that the right of framing the Law belongs of necessity to the whole body of citizens; that the smallest exclusion—there is no talk here of voluntary abstention—is enough to invalidate the result. In other words, no political society can be held legitimate which is not based on the sovereignty of the people. The sense in which Rousseau understood this principle must be held over for later consideration[4].

So far, we have spoken about the Law, as if the manner of its first establishment were self-evident. That, however, is far from being the case. Whatever time we may suppose to have passed between the making of the Contract and the first beginnings of

[1] *C. S.* II. iii. The Geneva MS. is still more emphatic on this point than the final draft: 'La volonté générale est rarement celle de tous.' Geneva MS. I. iv. Compare *Éc. pol.* p. 247.

[2] *e.g.* in the very next sentence he slips back into a virtual identification of it with the 'will of all.'

[3] It is clear that Rousseau, and quite justly, set great store by his doctrine of Law—'sujet tout neuf: la définition de la Loi est encore à faire' (*Émile*, Liv. v.). It is to be found in *C. S.* II. vi.; *Économie politique*, pp. 244—5; and Geneva MS. I. vii. and II. iv. (the former of which passages is a reproduction of that in *Éc. pol.*). One sentence may be quoted from Geneva MS. II. iv.: 'Comme la chose statuée se rapporte nécessairement au bien commun, il s'ensuit que l'objet de la Loi doit être général ainsi que la volonté qui la dicte; et c'est cette double universalité qui fait le vrai caractère de la Loi.' The passage in *Émile* (Vol. II. p. 152) is also of great importance.

[4] *C. S.* I. vii.; II. i., ii., vi. 'Pour qu'une volonté soit générale, il n'est pas toujours nécessaire qu'elle soit unanime, mais il est nécessaire que toutes les voix soient comptées; toute exclusion formelle rompt la généralité' (II. ii.). 'Tout Gouvernement légitime est républicain' (II. vi.).

settled Law, it is manifest that, until the latter step is taken, the community is still quite unformed; that its members cannot be very far removed from the 'stupid and limited animals' of the state of nature. How, then, can they hope to accomplish a task which would be none too easy for the wisest and most experienced of sages? 'How can a blind multitude, which often does not know its own mind because it seldom knows its own interest, carry out in its own strength an enterprise so vast and intricate as that of legislation?' The question seems to defy an answer. The terms of the problem appear to carry with them a contradiction from which it is impossible to escape. In order to solve it, 'the effect,' we are driven to say, ' would have to become the cause; the civic spirit, which is to be the result of the legislation, would have to inspire the legislation itself; all the associates would have to be before the Law that which they can only become by and through the Law.' Nothing short of a miracle can reconcile these contradictions. And for this miracle, Rousseau invokes the Lawgiver—a highly idealised version of Moses, Solon and Lycurgus; a Social Contract incarnate in the flesh[1].

'The Lawgiver,' he writes, ' must feel himself in a position to change the nature of man; to transform each individual, who in himself is a self-contained and isolated whole, into part of a larger whole, from which he receives, in some sense, his life and his being. He must feel himself able to alter the constitution of man, with a view to giving it greater strength; to put a dependent and moral existence in place of the independent and physical existence which we have received from nature. In a word, he must take from man his natural powers, in order to give him powers which are foreign to him, and of which he can make no use without the help of others. The more completely those natural powers are mortified and annihilated, the greater is the strength and durability of those which he acquires; the more solid and perfect, moreover, is the work of the Lawgiver. It follows that, if the individual citizen is nothing and can do nothing without the aid of all the rest, if the powers acquired by the whole body are equal or superior to the sum of the powers belonging by nature to all the individual members, then we are entitled to say that the legislation has reached the highest point of perfection which it can attain[2].'

[1] *C. S.* II. vi. and vii.; Geneva MS. I. vii.; II. ii.
[2] *C. S.* II. vii.; Geneva MS. II. ii. The opening sentences of this paragraph are preserved also in a very early Fragment, written in pencil on a small slip of paper, which has been accidentally shuffled in with the MS. of Rousseau's *Jugement sur la Polysynodie* (Neuchâtel MS. 7830). See below, p. 324.

This account of the matter presents two difficulties of which it is necessary to take notice. The first of them is this: What is the relation of the Lawgiver to the ordinary machinery of government? how are his functions to be reconciled with the sovereignty of the people? On the answer to this question Rousseau does not hesitate for a moment. The work of the Lawgiver, however commanding his genius, can never become law until it is freely accepted by the community as a body. The sovereignty of the people is a principle which can never be set aside, least of all at a moment when the whole future destiny of the people is at stake. The people has no power to lay aside or transfer its rights, even if it wished to do so. For by the original compact it is only the general will that can bind the individual. And there is no assurance that the general will is represented by the will of the Lawgiver, until the matter has been submitted to a free vote of the people, as a whole[1].' The Lawgiver, in short, is a kind of cross between a medieval Podestà and a modern constitutional minister, between one of Carlyle's heroes and an 'old parliamentary hand.'

The other difficulty is, at first sight, less serious; but it has an important bearing on the central idea of the whole treatise. At what time in the history of a people does the Lawgiver commonly appear? In what relation does his work stand to the original Contract? Rousseau assumes throughout that a long time, perhaps many ages, must pass between the Contract and the work of legislation[2]. But he tells us nothing of the conditions which prevail in the interval. And, but for his explicit statement to the contrary, we should naturally have supposed the one event to follow immediately upon the other. It is obvious, indeed, that the two things are inseparable from each other; that the earlier without the later is an empty form of speech. The very words in which the work of the Lawgiver is described are almost the same as those applied elsewhere to the Contract[3]. And on Rousseau's own shewing, he is there solely to bestow pith and substance on the Contract, to give reality to the changes which, as we now learn, the Contract was only able to foreshadow. 'The Contract,' he tells us, 'gave life and being to the body politic; it is for the Lawgiver to endow it with will and motion[4].' But, without will and motion, it is hard to say what 'life' a body can

---

[1] *C. S.* II. vii.   [2] *C. S.* II. viii.—x.
[3] Compare *C. S.* II. viii. ('Celui qui ose entreprendre' etc.) with *C. S.* I. viii. and *Émile*, Liv. I. (Vol. II. p. 146).   [4] *C. S.* II. vi.

claim. Again, Rousseau explicitly assures us that 'the laws, properly speaking, are nothing more nor less than the terms of political association[1].' And what are we to say of an association, the terms of which are drawn up centuries after the association itself has been formed? The truth is that this is one of the instances in which Rousseau has been led astray by the desire to square a theory, which in its essence was ideal and abstract, with certain concrete and historical facts. The *Social Contract*, so far at least as its fundamental principles are concerned, is a 'pattern laid up in the heavens[2].' It has nothing to do with considerations of time and place. Its argument is concerned not with what is, but with what ought to be. It does not gain, but lose, by reminiscences of Solon and Lycurgus, of William the Silent or of Calvin.

In one respect, however, the incongruity is significant. With the Lawgiver, as we shall see directly, Rousseau reaches the turning-point of his argument. In the Lawgiver he finds the wonder-working magician who takes command of the host at the parting of the ways; whose mission it is to lead man from the ideal to the actual, to guide him from the abstract principle to its practical application. With this necessity in his mind, he allows himself—most unfortunately, it must be admitted—to forestall the future, to introduce outward facts and circumstances at one stage earlier than, by good rights, the argument allowed. The new actor is brought upon the scene a moment or two sooner than his cue directed, and those who held the stage before him are inevitably thrown out.

In any case, with the appearance of the Lawgiver a new page of the argument is opened; a wholly new range of thought—that suggested by *Esprit des lois*—is spread before us. Up to this point, Rousseau had rigidly limited himself (as his title, if strictly interpreted, required that he should) to principles of Right. He now turns, though he by no means confines himself, to considerations of circumstance and expediency. Hitherto he had dealt solely with the abstract conditions of the problem. Henceforth he is ready to reckon with the qualifications imposed upon them by outward conditions of time and place, of racial character and historical tradition. The influence of Montesquieu is writ large upon the remainder of the treatise; but nowhere more clearly

---

[1] *C. S.* II. vi.
[2] See Geneva MS. I. v.: 'Je cherche le droit et la raison et ne dispute pas des faits.' Below, p. 462.

than in the chapters which define the task and methods of the Lawgiver.

'Before putting up a large building'—such are the opening words of this section—'the architect observes and tests the ground, to discover whether it will bear the weight. In the same way, the wise Lawgiver begins not by framing laws good in themselves, but by asking himself whether the nation for which they are destined is capable of bearing them[1].' It is not the business of the Lawgiver, he had said in an earlier writing, to lay down a code of abstract justice. 'If that were all, the veriest novice of a law-student could draw up a code of morals as pure as that of Plato. That, however, is not the only question. His real task is to adapt his code so completely to the nation for which it is framed' that obedience follows almost of itself. 'It is, as Solon saw, to impose on the nation not so much the laws that are best in themselves as those which are the best it can bear in the given conditions[2].' The conditions in question are partly those of soil and climate; partly the extent of the given territory and the size of its popula-tion; above all, the national character, whether inborn, or the outcome of present circumstances and of past history[3]. All these must be taken into account by the Lawgiver; and to do so requires consummate wisdom and insight, as well as an exalted ideal. It is for lack of these qualifications—particularly, perhaps, the two former—that so many rulers have gone wrong. Peter the Great, for instance, 'saw that his people were barbarous; he failed to see that they were not ripe for refinement (*la police*). He attempted to civilise them, when he ought to have rested content with hardening them to war. He strove to make Germans and English of them straight away, when he ought to have begun by making them Russians....His genius was imitative, not the true genius which creates a world out of nothing[4].' It is a shrewd thrust; and when we remember the adulation lavished first on Peter, then on Catherine, by the philosophers, it is one highly

---

[1] *C. S.* II. viii. For 'bonnes en elles-mêmes,' the Geneva MS. (II. iii.) has 'au hasard.' Below, p. 483.

[2] *Lettre à d'Alembert* (1758); *Œuvres*, I. i. p. 222.

[3] *C. S.* II. viii.—xi.; III. i., ii., vi.—viii.

[4] *C. S.* II. viii. This is wanting to the corresponding passage (II. iii.) of the Geneva MS. And, in general, it would seem that in the first draft Rousseau, for reasons which will appear in the sequel, dwelt less on considera-tions of circumstance than he does in the final version. It is impossible, however, to speak with certainty, seeing that no more than the first two books of the Geneva MS. have come down to us. Compare Vol. II. p. 434.

creditable to the sturdy bent of Rousseau's character and intellect[1].

There is no need to dwell longer upon the wider aspects of this argument; the less so, because the subsequent course of thought has made them common property to all. But this must in no way make us forget that more than one third of the *Contrat social* is devoted to this sort of consideration, and that to ignore the part which it plays in Rousseau's theory is a fatal error. We pass at once, therefore, to the special applications given to these principles by Rousseau; and in particular to what he says of the various forms of Government, and of the conditions by which the choice of the Lawgiver, in deciding between them, should be guided.

Before entering on the subject, it is well to remind the reader that Rousseau distinguishes sharply between Sovereignty and Government. Put baldly, it is the difference between the Legislative and the Executive. The former, according to Rousseau, belongs, and in all rightful forms of Government must necessarily belong, to the community as a whole[2]. The latter may be lodged in the hands of all, or of some, or of one—it may be a democracy, or an aristocracy, or a monarchy—as circumstances, or historical accident, may happen to decide[3]. In Governments originally founded on the feudal model, this distinction is unfortunately obscured. In England, for instance, the term 'Sovereign' is legally applied to the chief executive officer, and to him alone. But the question where the real Sovereignty—that is, the ultimate controlling power—resides in such cases, is left wholly untouched by such legal technicalities.

The distinction so drawn is enough of itself to prepare us for Rousseau's main line of argument in this crucial section of his work. So long as the sovereignty of the people is preserved—so long as the legislative power, which is the badge and seal of that sovereignty, is left solely in their hands—the specific form of Government, be it democracy, monarchy, or aristocracy, is a matter of indifference. It is a question to be decided by circumstances, and by nothing else. In theory, all alike are compatible with the sovereignty of the people. And though, as the conventional use of

---

[1] See the letters of Voltaire to Schouvaloff relating to Peter (*e.g. Corr. gén.* VI. 9), and the whole of his correspondence with Catherine. See also the amazing *Lettres de Grimm à l'Impératrice Catherine II*, in the publications of the Russian Academy, T. XLIV.; *e.g.* the letter of Nov. 24, 1776 (pp. 3—5), and that of July 9, 1782 (p. 231). See also Vol. II. Appendix II.

[2] *C. S.* II. vi.; III. i.—iii.   [3] *C. S.* III. i.—iii.

the term 'sovereign' implies, the monarch is in practice more often absolute than not, still there may be cases—in his softer moments, Rousseau might have been willing to admit that the England even of his day was such a case—in which the monarch himself has to bow to the legislative power of those who all the time are officially called his subjects[1].

All forms then being, at least in theory, alike legitimate, we are naturally led to ask: To which, if any, is the preference to be given? and, if given, on what grounds? The ground of Right, with the one limitation just mentioned, has already been excluded. To base our answer upon it is to misunderstand the first principles of the subject. And that being so, the only test left is expediency—adaptation to circumstances which inevitably vary from case to case[2].

Judged by this test, Democracy, in the unusual sense which Rousseau attaches to the term, is condemned as placing demands on human nature greater than, under ordinary circumstances, are likely to be made good. If Democracy means, as it is here taken to mean, that form of polity in which the actual administration is in the hands of all, where shall the wisdom be found equal to such a task? and where the public spirit? A multitude is liable to be swept by gusts of passion; it is almost certain therefore to commit acts of folly and injustice. It is still more certain to leave the actual management of affairs to a small handful of its members. In that case, the Government manifestly ceases to be a democracy in anything more than name. In all probability it becomes a shifting sea of factions, which struggle among themselves for mastery and ultimately plunge the community into civil war. The very theoretical virtues of this form of government are its practical defects. 'If there were a nation of gods, its form of Government would be democratic. So perfect a Government is not adapted for men[3].'

The dangers of Monarchy are even greater and more certain.

[1] *C. S.* III. i.—iii., vii.

[2] 'On a de tout temps beaucoup disputé sur la meilleure forme du Gouvernement, sans considérer que chacune d'elles est la meilleure en certains cas, et la pire en d'autres. Si, dans les différents États, le nombre des magistrats suprêmes doit être en raison inverse de celui des citoyens, il s'ensuit qu'en général le Gouvernement démocratique convient aux petits États, l'aristocratique aux médiocres, et le monarchique aux grands....Mais comment compter la multitude de circonstances qui peuvent former des exceptions?' *C. S.* III. iii.

[3] *C. S.* III. iv. Compare the description of Athens as 'not a democracy but a highly tyrannical aristocracy' (rather, 'oligarchy'): *Économie politique*; below, p. 243.

If elective, it will commonly lead to faction and corruption. If hereditary, the best of monarchs is always liable to be succeeded by the worst, the weakest and most foolish. Nay, in such a post even ability has its dangers. An ambitious king finds himself too big for the position he has inherited; 'he causes as much misery to his people by the abuse of his talents as a fool or sluggard by the want of them.' Even apart from the certain recurrence of these inconveniences, there are two evils of the first magnitude from which Monarchy cannot possibly escape. The first is that this form of Government is suitable only for large States. And large States are almost invariably ill-governed. The best of rulers in such a State is compelled to govern mainly by deputy; and we know what a monarch's deputies are likely to be. Moreover, large as his dominions may be, he always desires to make them larger yet. The result is that the evil is constantly on the increase; and the more it increases, the more does the control of the people—and that is essential not only to all good, but to all legitimate government—become an empty name. A further result is that the monarch is for ever plunging his people into war. 'And war is, with tyranny, one of the two worst scourges of mankind[1].'

The second evil is yet graver; it is also still more inevitable. Experience teaches us that all monarchs alike desire to make themselves absolute. And if a sage assures them that it is against their own interest to do so, they laugh him to scorn. 'Even the best king wishes to have the power of doing harm, if the whim seizes him, without ceasing to be master. His personal interest is always to see his people weak and miserable; in short, utterly powerless to resist him.' By the former evil, the sovereignty of the people is reduced to a mockery. By the latter, it is openly assaulted, and must eventually be destroyed[2].

For these reasons, it is impossible to award the preference either to Monarchy, or Democracy; though either of them may find ample justification in the circumstances of a given case. The only form of Government yet left is Aristocracy; and it is evident that here, if anywhere, the working ideal is to be found. 'There

---

[1] *Émile*, v.; Vol. II. p. 158; *C. S.* III. vi.; IV. i. Compare the following description of a well-ordered state: 'Ces esprits vastes, si dangereux et si admirés, tous ces grands ministres dont la gloire se confond avec les malheurs du peuple, ne sont plus regrettés; les mœurs publiques suppléent au génie du chefs; et plus la vertu règne, moins les talents sont nécessaires.' *Éc. pol.* p. 250. The dread of a military dictator, which haunted the dreams of Robespierre, was in part inspired by such passages as this.

[2] *C. S.* III. vi. Compare *Éc. pol.*; below, pp. 263—5; also pp. 389—391.

are three kinds of Aristocracy: natural (*i.e.* that of age), elective and hereditary. The first is suitable only to primitive communities. The third is the worst of all forms of Government. The second is the best; it is Aristocracy in the true sense of the term[1].'

Aristocracy, in this form, has the following advantages. It distinguishes sharply between the executive and the legislative power. It lodges the former in the hands of a few, chosen freely by their fellow-citizens on account of their talents and virtue. It retains the latter in the hands of the whole body of citizens; and in addition reserves to them a general, though not a detailed, control over the acts of the Executive. Few, if any, of these merits can be claimed either for Monarchy or Democracy. It is certain that all of them together meet in Aristocracy alone. It is to Aristocracy therefore that the Lawgiver will assign the preference, whenever circumstances permit[2].

It will be observed that by Aristocracy Rousseau means what we should commonly call Democracy[3]. It is, in short, nothing more nor less than Cabinet Government: with this difference, that the Cabinet is appointed not by Monarch or President, but by the whole body of citizens; that it is responsible not to an assembly of Representatives, but to the people as a whole; and that the people which conferred the power may revoke it at will[4]. What may have been his motive for this curious, and not very happy, use of terms, it is not possible to say for certain. It may have been a desire to veil the boldness of his conclusions from the arbitrary Governments of the day. It may have been a wish to humour the susceptibilities of the Genevan authorities, who might be shy of hearing their constitution described as 'democratic.' If these were his intentions, they were doomed to a speedy disappointment. The *Contrat social* was prohibited in France[5]. It was assigned as one of the grounds for the Decree of Arrest launched against the author by the Government of Geneva; and, with *Émile*, it was burned by the hands of the common hangman[6]. What is certain

---

[1] *C. S.* III. v.   [2] *ib.*

[3] It is significant that Rousseau himself admits Democracy, in *his* sense of the term, to be an impossibility. 'À prendre le terme dans la rigueur de l'acception, il n'a jamais existé de véritable démocratie, et il n'en existera jamais.' *C. S.* III. iv. Compare the passage quoted above from *Éc. pol.* p. 243. In defence of *his* use of the term *democracy* the authority of Plato and Aristotle might perhaps be cited; and, in more modern times, that of Kant and Fichte.

[4] *C. S.* III. v., xv., xviii.   [5] *Lettres de la Montagne*, VI. p. 204.

[6] *ib.* v.; *Œuvres*, III. p. 195; VI. p. 204.

is that, in the *Lettres de la Montagne*—written after he had renounced membership of his native city—he habitually describes the constitution of Geneva, his professed ideal[1], as a 'democracy[2]'; and that, in his notable letter to Mirabeau (July 26, 1767), he speaks of the principles of the *Contrat social* as being those of an 'austere democracy[3].' He would have avoided confusion, if he had used the same term in the *Contrat social* itself.

With the discussion of the various forms of Government, the main argument of the *Contrat social* comes to an end. The rest of this, the third Book, is taken up either with a reinforcement of first principles from particular points of view, or with a statement of certain practical consequences which Rousseau has specially at heart. With the former we need hardly concern ourselves. Of the latter, three may be taken out, not only on account of their intrinsic importance, but also for the searching light they throw upon the author's political ideas.

The first is that 'the institution of Government is not a contract' between the governors and the governed; that, on the contrary, it is a purely fiduciary act; and that, like the appointment of trustees under a private will, it may therefore be revoked at any moment, at the pleasure of the appointer. This is manifestly directed against Locke and his disciples[4].

The second conclusion is that government by Representatives is radically vicious and illegitimate; that it is an 'absurd' relic of the feudal system and, like the rest of that system, 'degrading to humanity'; that it involves a surrender of the popular sovereignty which no plea of convenience can justify. This is a direct blow at the English ideals which were already becoming fashionable among the amateur politicians of France[5]. It marks a rebellion also against the authority of Montesquieu[6].

[1] 'J'ai donc pris votre constitution (*i.e.* celle de Genève), que je trouvais belle, pour modèle des institutions politiques.' *Lettres de la Montagne*, VI.; Vol. II. p. [204.] Compare *C. S.* Liv. I., Introduction.

[2] *e.g. Lettres de la Montagne*, VII. pp. 209, 227; VIII. pp. 230, 237.

[3] Vol. II. p. [25.]   [4] *C. S.* III. xvi., xviii.

[5] 'Le peuple anglais pense être libre; il se trompe fort. Il ne l'est que durant l'élection des membres du parlement : sitôt qu'ils sont élus, il est esclave, il n'est rien. Dans les courts moments de sa liberté, l'usage qu'il en fait mérite bien qu'il la perde.' *C. S.* III. xv. For a curious illustration of English influence on the French political writers of the time, see Mably, *Droits et devoirs du citoyen* (1758).

[6] See Montesquieu, *Esprit des lois*, XI. vi.; and compare the close of Burke's *Appeal from the New to the Old Whigs*. The whole of *C. S.* III. xv. is devoted to an assault on Representative Government. Contrast *Ec. pol.* p. 273.

The third corollary—already anticipated in Rousseau's criticism of Monarchy, and further forestalled in the preceding argument—is that the small State is infinitely preferable to the large; that, 'so far as I can see, it is impossible, under present conditions, for the Sovereign to preserve its rights, unless its numbers are very small'; unless—as the Geneva Manuscript puts it still more trenchantly—'the State is limited to a single town, at the very most[1].' This leads straight to the doctrine of Federation, which the author had at one time intended to treat at length. But his views on this subject, if ever written, have now, by the treachery of a friend, been irrecoverably lost[2]. In this matter, as in his assault on individualism, Rousseau was a pioneer.

The fourth Book of the *Contrat social* is in the nature of an appendix. With the exception of the last Chapter, it is almost entirely devoted to historical illustrations of the ideas expounded in the main body of the treatise. And these are drawn, with few exceptions, from the history of the Roman Republic—'the best government there has ever been[3].'

The closing Chapter, which we know to have been an afterthought, is the famous—and, in one sense, most unfortunate—discourse on *Civil Religion*. But, however much we may deplore its practical conclusions, the ideas which lie behind them are full of significance and instruction. It is a misfortune that the inferences drawn from them by the author, and carried into act by Robespierre, should inevitably have tended to discredit them.

IV

LEADING IDEAS OF THE *CONTRAT SOCIAL*, AS AN ABSTRACT THEORY

We pass now to consider the leading ideas of the *Contrat social*; but the leading ideas only. All that is necessary to say may be grouped under three heads: the Contract itself, and the whole

---

[1] 'Tout bien examiné, je ne vois pas qu'il soit désormais possible au souverain de conserver parmi nous l'exercice de ses droits, si la Cité n'est très petite.' *C. S.* III. xv. 'Il suit de là que l'État devrait se borner à une seule ville, tout au plus.' Geneva MS. II. iii.; below, p. 487.

[2] See the account of the matter printed as a note to *C. S.* III. xv.; Vol. II. p. 134. Compare *Émile*, Livre v.; Vol. II. pp. 157—8.

[3] The transition to the history of Rome occurs at the end of IV. iii. The words quoted at the end of the above paragraph are taken from *Lettres de la Montagne*, VI.; *Œuvres*, III. p. 204. Compare *C. S.* III. xi.; *Émile*, Liv. v.; Vol. II. p. 153.

chain of ideas attaching to it; the relation of the principles of Right, as conceived by Rousseau, to considerations of expediency; and lastly—but this will be reserved for a separate section—the chief practical applications given by Rousseau to the speculative principles which lie at the root of the whole treatise.

The doctrine of Contract was a commonplace among the philosophers of the seventeenth and eighteenth centuries. But Rousseau, like Hobbes before him, gave it an entirely fresh turn. To his predecessors, with one exception, it had served as the cornerstone of individualism. To him—as, in an utterly different way, to Hobbes—it forms the porch to a collectivism as absolute as the mind of man has ever conceived. This is the assumption of the *Économie politique*. In the *Contrat social* he sets himself to prove it by every argument at his command.

With the opening sentence, indeed, we seem for the moment to be back again at the second *Discourse*; at no great distance, perhaps, from the *Civil Government* of Locke. 'Man was born free; and everywhere he *is* in chains[1].' What could promise better for an individualist theory than this? But the very next sentence is enough to dispel the illusion. 'Such an one believes himself to be the master of others, when all the time he is as much of a slave as they.' It is clear that we have passed suddenly from 'freedom' in the abstract and political sense to 'freedom'—or 'slavery'—in the concrete and moral sense; from mere naked independence to the state of the man who ought to be a 'law unto himself,' but is, in fact, a slave to his own passions and, by an inevitable consequence, to the will of others[2]. And this transition, however little we may defend its suddenness, furnishes the key to the whole treatise. Throughout, the idea of independence is replaced by that of freedom from ignorance and brutishness.

[1] It may be noted that, in the first draft of the treatise, this Chapter (which, thrown defiantly in the face of the reader, has done so much to create a false impression as to the scope and bearing of the whole work) does *not* form the beginning of the book. It does not occur until after a long chapter in which war is declared upon individualism and all its works, and in which the fundamental conceptions of Locke—in particular, his doctrine of the state of nature and of natural Law—are subjected to a most damaging criticism. The sting of this individualist outbreak is thus drawn in advance. See Geneva MS. I. ii. and iii.

[2] The key to this difficult passage is, I think, to be found in the following: 'La domination même est servile, quand elle tient à l'opinion; car tu dépends des préjugés de ceux que tu gouvernes par les préjugés.' *Émile*, Liv. II.; *Œuvres*, II. p. 50. Compare *Omnia serviliter pro dominatione* (Tac. *Hist.* I. 36)

Throughout, it is not a negative goal, the mere absence of restraint, but the positive one of moral discipline, of which Rousseau is in search. The freedom which he desires, as the result of the Contract, is in truth the very opposite of that which formed the ideal of Locke. And that is the reason why, when its terms are examined, his Contract is seen to have nothing but the name in common with the Contract of Locke.

The importance of this initial difference is hardly to be overrated. To Locke—still more, to later individualists—politics are entirely divorced from morals, or indeed from any spiritual need of man. The individual leads his life—moral, religious and intellectual—wholly to himself. All the State does is to provide the machinery which shall enable him to do so; or rather, to remove from his path the obstacles which might let and hinder him from doing so. The State is something wholly external to his life; it never touches the inner springs of his being. The result is that the life of the State is emptied of all that has any vital interest for man. All that makes his life worth living is rigidly excluded from its ken. All action on the part of the State, beyond the bare protection of life and property, is regarded with the bitterest suspicion. 'Government,' wrote Paine, 'even in its best state is but a necessary evil; in its worst state, an intolerable one[1].' And this accurately reflects the feeling which lies at the heart of every individualist.

Contrast this with Rousseau's view of the relation between the individual and the State. Here the conditions are exactly reversed. It is the individual who is here empty of all definite content; of all that saves man, as we know him, from being as 'stupid and limited' as the beasts. It is in the State alone that he acquires his intelligence, his sense of Right and duty: in one word, all that constitutes his humanity. It is there only that he 'becomes a reasoning being and a man.' And the Chapter from which this description is drawn closes with words which bring us back to the point from which we started. 'To the gains conferred by the civil state must be added that of his moral freedom. And it is this alone which makes him master of himself. For the promptings of mere appetite'—and he had just said that they are man's only motive in the state of nature—'are slavery; and obedience to the law which we impose on ourselves is what constitutes freedom[2].'

[1] Paine, *Common Sense*, p. 3 (ed. London, 1793).
[2] *C. S.* I. viii.

It needs but a slight acquaintance with the history of philosophy to see that these words involve nothing less than a revolution in political speculation. For the last two centuries, one thinker after another—all of them under the spell of individualist assumptions—had been in search of a principle which should make politics wholly independent of ethics. It is not the least of Rousseau's services to have abandoned this, as a false scent, and to have cast back to the sounder doctrine of Aristotle and Plato. Thirty years later, both Kant and Fichte—doubtless, in a spirit very different from that of their forerunners—were still engaged in the same unprofitable quest. Had they but taken to heart the teaching of the *Contrat social*, they might have spared themselves the trouble[1].

So far, then, the argument of Rousseau is beyond reproach. It is, in fact, a restatement, in his own terms and with his own implications, of the Greek principle: 'Man is by nature a political animal.' And it would have been well if the rest of the argument had been carried out in the same vein. The misfortune is that this was impossible for Rousseau. He brought to it a mind charged and clogged with ideas which no skill could reconcile with it. These were the idea of an original state of nature and the idea of a Contract as, both in fact and in Right, the only way of escape from it. Both ideas were a bequest from Locke and the individualists. Both entangled him once more in the individualist system from which he was struggling to shake free.

In handling these ideas, had he confined himself to the ground of fact, no great harm might have been done. Even granted that the 'civil state' is a state indispensable—and therefore, in a very real sense, natural—to man, it is not absolutely impossible that there may have been a stage in his history at which that state had not yet come into being, and during which there was no bond of connection, still less of fellowship, between one individual and another. In the *Discours sur l'inégalité*, Rousseau had already—avowedly as a mere hypothesis—indicated the steps by which this isolation of man from man might imperceptibly have passed into some rude form of political association. And other hypotheses of the same sort might readily be suggested; they might easily have found acceptance with Rousseau himself. Nor, so long as either accident or some form of force, veiled or open, is conceived as the

---

[1] See Kant, *Zum ewigen Frieden*; *Werke*, VII. p. 237 (ed. Rosenkranz); Fichte, *Grundlage des Naturrechts*; *Werke*, III. pp. 12—16. The date of the former is 1795; of the latter, 1796.

moving cause of such a change—so long, that is, as all ideas of Right are rigidly excluded—is there any great objection to such historical, or legendary, speculations. In the *Contrat social*, however, Rousseau is no longer content with grounds of fact, actual or hypothetical. Nothing will now satisfy him but that the change must be based on ideas of Right. It is to provide a foundation of Right for the State that he has recourse to the Contract. For the Contract is a guarantee of free consent on the part of the citizens; or, as Rousseau more accurately puts it, of the 'associates.' And from first to last the assumption is that, unless such consent be given at the outset, the State is for ever debarred from resting upon Right.

It is doubtless true, as Rousseau urges[2], that this account of the matter, if otherwise sound, does provide a solid basis for Right. The misfortune is that it raises many more difficulties than it solves. In the first place, it is at glaring variance with the facts, so far as we know them. In the second place, if the Contract is to have binding power—and unless that be the case, where is the use of making it?—there must obviously be some sanction behind it. But in this case, no sanction is possible except either force, or a sense of moral obligation. The former, as Rousseau himself insists, must be excluded at once. It is, in his view, the direct antithesis of Right; it is therefore impossible that it can ever serve as the basis of Right[3]. The only sanction left is that of moral obligation. And that too, as a little reflection will shew, has been effectually barred out by Rousseau.

In the first draft of the *Contrat social*, the conception of 'natural Society' and, with it, of 'natural Law'—the conception so dear to the individualists and so essential to their plea—had been expressly repudiated[4]. And though the Chapter in question is cancelled in the final version, there is nothing to shew that the author had withdrawn from this position. On the contrary, everything points to the opposite conclusion. When he speaks of man in

[1] *C. S.* I. vi.

[2] 'Indépendamment de la vérité de ce principe, il l'emporte sur tous les autres par la solidité du fondement qu'il établit; car quel fondement plus sûr peut avoir l'obligation parmi les hommes, que le libre engagement de celui qui s'oblige? On peut disputer tout autre principe; on ne saurait disputer celui-là.' *Lettres de la Montagne*, VI.; Vol. II. p. 200.

[3] *C. S.* I. iii., iv. This is not inconsistent with the account given on p. 26.

[4] 'Ce prétendu traité social'—*i.e.* la loi naturelle—'dicté par la nature est une véritable chimère.' Geneva MS. I. ii. (*De la société générale du genre humain*; originally, *Du droit naturel et de la soc. générale*; MS. Neu. 7854).

the state of nature as being entirely devoid of 'reason, duty, justice and humanity,' he is merely saying the same thing in other words[1].

Now it is obvious that any sanction on which the Contract is to rest must be acknowledged as binding at the moment of its conclusion. But we have it from Rousseau's own lips that, at the time when the Contract is made, man is entirely lacking in all that constitutes the moral sense. And that can only mean that he is incapable of recognising any moral obligation. The moral sanction, therefore, falls to the ground, as that of brute force had done before it. And the Contract is left with no sanction whatsoever. It might just as well have never been made.

The strange thing is that, in another of his writings, Rousseau virtually makes this admission; or rather, by doing so in a parallel case, he leaves us no choice but to apply his argument to the present instance for ourselves. The passage referred to occurs in *Émile*, where he denounces the folly of exacting promises from children, which he considers to be merely a means of entrapping them into 'le mensonge de droit.' 'This lie,' he continues, 'is still less natural than the last ('le mensonge de fait'). For all promises to do, or to abstain from doing, are acts of convention. They take us out of the state of nature; they are an infringement of liberty. More than that: all promises made by children are, by their very nature, null and void. The outlook of children is limited, and cannot reach beyond the moment. When they pledge themselves, they do not know what they are about[2].'

It will be noticed that two arguments are here brought forward against the validity of promises made under such conditions. One is that every promise is an 'act of convention,' and therefore cannot have any binding force on those who, when they make it, are in the state of nature. The other is that all promises made by those who 'cannot look beyond the moment are, by their very nature, null and void.' Each of these arguments applies, and applies with yet greater force, to the case before us. The social Contract is still more manifestly than the child's promise an 'act of convention,' and it is made by those who are still more manifestly in the state of nature. And if all promises made by children are, by their very nature, null and void, what are we to say of promises made by those whom the author himself describes as 'stupid and limited animals'? It is evident that the capacity

[1] *C. S.* I. viii.
[2] *Émile*, Liv. II.; *Œuvres*, II. p. 69. Compare *Fragments*, A; below, p. 324. See also *C. S.* III. xvi.; Vol. II. p. 99.

of such beings must be yet more limited than that of children; that they must be in a worse position even than children for 'knowing what they are about.' A contract made under such conditions is clearly no better than a fraud. And any state of things which results from it is a state founded not upon Right, but upon deception, and consequently upon wrong.

Thus on Rousseau's own shewing, the Contract and the state of nature are only disturbing elements in his theory of Right. There was nothing to gain, and everything to lose, by their importation. Historically, they are, to say the least, improbable. Logically, as he now admits, they are not only unavailing, but destructive. He was right in thinking that, unless the individual will is subordinated, and freely so, to the general will, the State, as we now know it, is impossible. He was wrong in supposing that this subordination could ever be the result of a single and conscious act; much more, the act of men who, up to the moment of its accomplishment, were wholly undisciplined and unhumanised. He was right in holding that the civil state, in some form, is essential to the moral life of man, to the existence of even the most rudimentary sense of duty. He was wrong in assuming that either the civil state, or the sense of duty, could ever have sprung to birth in a single moment; that it was possible for them to be anything but the slow growth of time.

Time, however, is just what he is not willing to give. And to him, as to Bacon, and, for that matter to Plato also, 'time is the great innovator, which impaireth all things.' The good is always, in his view, the birth of a single moment, the product of a single effort. Directly that moment is passed, that effort completed, time, the enemy, begins his insidious work; and there is nothing to look for but degeneration and decay. Thus all that is salutary in man's record—the Contract which gave him 'reason and humanity,' the Law which gave to that Contract reality and substance—lies wholly outside of the natural order. It is as much a miracle as any that staggered the faith of the Savoy Vicar in the sacred books of Christendom. Nature resumes her work only when the miracle is accomplished. And it is a work of ceaseless hostility and destruction. It is a strange result for the 'worshipper of nature' to have reached; an unhappy consequence of his refusal to recognise that if man, in his strength as well as in his weakness, is not a part of nature, he is nothing. Rousseau would have been the first to exclaim against any such judgment on the ways of outward nature; the first to insist that we have here a world of ordered growth, in which miracle has no place. Yet in the world of man, he steadily refuses to see anything but discord and confusion. Wherever these cease, there he traces the hand of some higher power, whose action is beyond reckoning; and whose work, directly his hand is withdrawn, falls a prey to the perversity of man and the corroding spite of time.

Thus, in the case before us, his difficulties are largely of his own making. They depend upon the sharp antithesis between Right and force, which he assumes from the beginning. And, so far as historical origins are concerned, that antithesis is false. In the earlier stages of man's history the two things are inextricably entangled with each other. Look merely at the outside of things, and it is probable that we shall see little beside brute force. Once get beneath the surface, and it may well be that, behind that brute force, we shall recognise the first crude beginnings of Right, the seed of what has since grown to be the 'civil state.' And when conditions are favourable, it has been the task of succeeding ages gradually to strip off the outer rind of force and allow the 'soul of goodness'—of Right and justice—to unfold itself from within. There is no need of Contract, of heaven-sent Lawgiver, or any other form of miracle. The whole thing is a natural process, brought about by human will and human wisdom, working with persistent stubbornness upon material that responds.

Once more, however, there is no one moment at which we can say that force has passed definitely into Right. It is the essence of the process to be imperceptible; and Right is an ideal to be striven for, not a fixed point that can ever be finally attained. In other words, the idea of development is essential to a true theory of Right. And it is because that idea was entirely foreign to his mind that the theory of Rousseau is so imperfect[1]. He persistently conceives of Right as belonging to a golden age—or rather, a golden moment—in the past, rather than as a thing to be slowly realised in the present and future. The advance of man, in his view, is not forwards, but backwards; not progress, but retrogression. We have already traced this tendency, on the moral and intellectual side, in the two *Discourses*. In the *Contrat social* it reappears, in application to the State.

The general tendency, then, of Rousseau is to fix an impassable barrier between might and Right; to deny that any community

[1] 'C'est là le vice inhérent et inévitable qui, dès la naissance du Corps politique, tend sans relâche à le détruire, de même que la vieillesse et la mort détruisent enfin le corps de l'homme.' *C. S.* III. x.

originally founded upon the former can ever hope to raise itself to the latter. And this means that, so far as he is true to his own principle, the test he applies to all governments is not their present beneficence, but their past orthodoxy; that, in Burke's words, he is always 'at war with governments not on a question of abuse, but a question of competency and a question of title[1].' There is, however, one passage in the first draft of the *Contrat social*—a passage unfortunately suppressed in the final version—which approaches, though it may not absolutely reach, the sounder view of the matter:

'All this dispute about the social Compact reduces itself, as it seems to me, to a very simple question: What but their common advantage can have induced men to join of their own will in corporate society? This common advantage, then, is the basis of civil society. That being granted, how can we distinguish between the rightful State and a mere forced aggregation which nothing can justify, but by asking what is the aim or end of the one and of the other? If the form of the community is such as to tend to the common good, then that community will live according to the spirit in which it was founded. If, on the other hand, it has in view nothing but the interest of its chiefs, then, by every right of reason and humanity, it is illegitimate[2].'

In this passage, if in this only, Rousseau explicitly makes public advantage, *l'utilité commune*, the end of the State, and he establishes the closest bond between it and Right. Not that he falls into the error, so common since his day, of asserting that, apart from expediency, Right has no existence. So gross a delusion was to him impossible. What he does is to hint, though it may be no more than hint, that Right and expediency stand in the nearest relation to each other. Both are virtually described as the 'end' of the civil state. But what the exact relation between them may be, is left wholly undefined. A little reflection might have shewn him that it could be nothing but the relation of the end to its necessary means; of the idea, considered as abstract, to its organic articulation in concrete facts and deeds. That, however, is an inference which he refrains from drawing in words. It is improbable, though not impossible, that it was ever present to his mind. Yet, had he followed out the vein of thought he had here struck upon, he must inevitably have come to this conclusion. And then it is safe to say that his theory of Right would, in some

[1] Burke, *Reflections on French Revolution*; *Works*, I. p. 403.
[2] Geneva MS. Liv. I. Chap. v.; below, p. 470.

crucial points, have been very different from what it is. The state of nature and the Contract, so far as they bear on the plea of Right, would have vanished from the argument. Had they remained at all, it would have been for the humbler purpose of providing a possible explanation of the way in which, historically speaking, society may have shaped itself out of chaos. So far as these preliminaries are concerned, he would have reverted, more or less closely, to the position of the second *Discourse*. He would have freed his argument from logical embarrassments of which he was apparently half conscious, but which, for fear of opening the door to tyranny, he never had the courage to face. That, it is only fair to remember, was the real cause which prevented him from following out the above line of thought to its logical conclusion. It was because the Contract seemed to him the one impregnable barrier against tyranny that he was prepared to stake all in its defence.

So much for the difficulties which beset the opening pages of the *Contrat social*. We now pass to the core of the treatise. We leave the preliminaries of the Contract behind us, and turn to consider the nature of the Contract itself.

The first thing to strike us is the gulf which parts the Contract of Rousseau from that of Locke. And this is no less true of its form than of its matter. The Contract of Locke is an absolutely free contract. Its terms may be indefinitely varied. It is capable, at least in theory, of taking as many shapes as there are communities to make it[1]. That of Rousseau, on the contrary, is a tied contract. Once men have decided to enter upon it, no choice is left as to its terms. 'They are so completely determined by the nature of the case that the smallest departure from them would make the whole act null and void[2].' This amounts to saying that, in the very act of making the Contract, the individual has already laid aside his 'natural' liberty, and exchanged it for the 'moral' liberty which, from the point of view of individualism, is no liberty at all.

The same difference holds good in respect of matter. To Locke, the Contract is essentially an instrument of individual freedom. Its terms may indeed vary indefinitely with the varying circumstances out of which it springs. But throughout it is taken for granted that the aim of the individual will always be to give as

[1] This would seem to have been the view of Rousseau himself at the time when he wrote the second *Discourse*. See below, p. 189.
[2] *C. S.* I. vi.

little power to the community, and to keep as much in his own hands, as he possibly can. It is further assumed as a fundamental principle that no powers belong to the community except such as have been expressly entrusted to it by the individual; that all which have not thus been passed over to it remain, both in fact and of right, in the hands of the individual. It follows from this that the Sovereignty of Locke's State is avowedly a limited sovereignty; or, to put the same thing otherwise, that in the last resort it is vested in the individual.

With Rousseau, all these conditions are reversed. To him, the Contract is the 'total surrender' of the individual. More than this; it is the 'mutilation,' the 'annihilation,' of his separate personality; its replacement by the corporate personality, the 'collective self,' of the community as a whole[1]. Again, in the act of forming the association, the individual reserves, and can reserve, no powers to himself. From the nature of the case, everything—his goods, his rights, his very will—is 'alienated' to the State. The Sovereignty of the State is therefore an absolute sovereignty. There neither is, nor can be, any constitutional limit upon its powers[2].

Thus, while the Contract of Locke is expressly devised to preserve and confirm the rights of the individual, that of Rousseau ends, and is intended to end, in their destruction. By the former, the individual contracts himself into the full exercise of his primitive freedom; or at least, of as much of it as, by the 'natural law,' he has any right to possess. By the latter, he deliberately, and for the sake of a greater and higher benefit, contracts himself out of it. The one is a charter of individualism. The other, with certain crucial qualifications to be noted shortly, is an extreme form of collectivism. A more complete contrast it is hardly possible to conceive.

Yet it must never be forgotten that Rousseau himself, like most men of his day, had been brought up on Locke's theory; and that as the champion of political liberty, as the sworn foe of political tyranny, there was much in it to which he must have been powerfully drawn. What, then, were the motives which impelled him to adopt conclusions so startling in themselves, and so deeply at variance both with his own prejudices and with the dominant convictions of his time?

[1] *C. S.* I. viii., II. vii.; Geneva MS. I. iii., II. ii.; *Émile*, Liv. I.; Vol. II. pp. 145—6.
[2] *C. S.* II. iv.

There can be little doubt that both political and moral causes were at work. And it is significant that, in his mind, the two things were inseparably interwoven. On the side of politics, he was convinced that such a community as is presented in Locke's *Treatise* was incapable of the keen public spirit, the strong communal life, which was to him the supreme good attainable in the State. Rome and Sparta, with their constant sacrifice of private to public interests, always hovered before his imagination[1]. The passionate intensity of their civic life never ceased to be his ideal. Nor was it only an imaginative impulse that drove him in this direction. It was also a reasoned distrust of all purely abstract theories of Politics; a deep conviction that no theory which does not rest itself upon the passions of men, as well as their calculating instincts, can hold water for a moment. This was his quarrel with the crazy theories of the Physiocrats[2]. It would be strange if it were not also one of the causes which weaned him from the principles of Locke. For apart from all logical inconsistencies—and they are glaring enough—that is one of the fatal flaws in Locke's theory, or indeed in any theory which bases itself upon the sovereignty of the individual. They reduce the State to a mere device of convenience; an institution which may be necessary, but can certainly never become an object of devotion.

When the State is stripped of all its moral aims, when it claims to be no more than the guardian of life and property, it is idle to hope that it can draw the love, or even the respect, of its members; still more idle to dream that it can enlist their passions in its service, or act as a quickening and controlling force upon their soul. 'To make us love our country,' said Burke, 'our country ought to be lovely[3].' And how can it be so, when all that appeals

[1] 'Un citoyen de Rome n'était ni Caius ni Lucius; c'était un Romain; même il aimait la patrie, exclusivement à lui.' *Émile*, Liv. I. See Vol. II. p. 145. The two following paragraphs give examples from Sparta.

[2] 'Mais supposons toute cette théorie des lois naturelles toujours parfaitement évidente,...comment des philosophes qui connaissent le cœur humain peuvent-ils donner à cette évidence tant d'autorité sur les actions des hommes? comme s'ils ignoraient que chacun se conduit très rarement par ses lumières, et très fréquemment par ses passions.' Letter to Mirabeau (July 26, 1767); Vol. II. p. 160. Compare 'Mille écrivains ont osé dire que le Corps politique est sans passions....Comme si l'on ne voyait pas, au contraire, que l'essence de la société consiste dans l'activité de ses membres, et qu'un Etat sans mouvement ne serait qu'un corps mort.' *L'état de guerre*; below, p. 298. And 'Un homme qui n'aurait point de passions serait certainement un fort mauvais citoyen.' *Éc. pol.*; below, p. 255.

[3] Burke's *Reflections*; *Works*, I. p. 410. Compare *Éc. pol.*; below, p. 251.

to the higher and nobler nature of man is rigidly banished from its ken? It is of the essence of individualism to disparage the State. And if the theory had ever been strictly carried out—a feat which no community on record has attempted, much less accomplished—all that is commonly understood by the State and the spirit of citizenship would have been destroyed. To no man of modern times would such a result have been so hateful as to Rousseau.

But, if political considerations were enough to drive Rousseau from the camp of Locke and the individualists, much more were the moral consequences with which, in his mind, they were inseparably bound up. One of these—doubtless, from another point of view—has already been mentioned; and we have seen that to him, as to Plato and Aristotle, the crowning value of the State lies in the specific influence it has upon the character of its members, the specific quality which it stamps upon their soul. It lies, that is, in the passionate public spirit which was fostered by such States as Rome and Sparta, and which he had caught himself, while yet a mere boy, from the glowing pages of Plutarch. Fabricius and Regulus, Agesilaus and Lycurgus—such were the characters that he reverenced beyond all others. And he did so, because they lived not for themselves, but for their country; because virtue itself was to them the same thing as love of country. It is for this reason that, in a striking passage of the *Économie politique*, he puts even Socrates below Cato. 'For Athens was already lost, and Socrates had no country left but the wide world; while Cato never ceased to bear his country in the inmost chamber of his heart; he lived for nothing but his country, and could not bring himself to outlive her[1].'

Behind this motive, however, there lies another yet more fundamental and more purely ethical: a motive which, just because it is purely ethical, goes to the very root of all political speculation. It is Rousseau's conviction—and once more he treads in the steps of the great Greek thinkers—that without organised society there can be no such thing as morality for man. And by organised society he, like Plato and Aristotle, understood the State. Of the two, it was obviously Plato who served as the

[1] 'Il est certain que les plus grands prodiges de vertu ont été produits par l'amour de la patrie: ce sentiment doux et vif, qui joint la force de l'amour-propre à toute la beauté de la vertu, lui donne une énergie qui sans la défigurer, en fait la plus héroïque de toutes les passions.' *Économie politique*; below, p. 251. Compare the passage quoted from *Émile* on p. 49.

source of his inspiration. And the argument of Socrates in *Crito* has stated for all time the plea which must have come home no less to his intellect than his heart[1]. The Laws, it is there written, watch over the birth, the rearing, the education of the citizen. They give him a share, with all other citizens, of all the blessings in their power. How shall he, then, turn round in after life and, repaying good with evil, do them all the harm that lies in *his* power, by defying or evading them?

It is not often that Rousseau puts such thoughts into words. But when he does so—as in his picture of the change wrought in man's nature by the Contract and the Lawgiver[2]—he speaks with a conviction that comes from the bottom of his soul. And the idea which prompts these passages forms the very key-stone of the argument which the *Contrat social* builds up. The truth that Plato taught had faded from the minds of men in the interval. And to rediscover it was hardly less of a service than to proclaim it at the first.

That society of some kind is the first condition of morality is, of course, admitted by all. Once grant that all, or nearly all, the acts we specifically describe as 'moral' are acts done from man to man, and that consequence follows of itself. So far, Locke is at one with Plato and Rousseau; and it would be impossible for any man who knows what he is talking about to dispute their conclusion. To Locke, however, a purely 'general society'—a society without organisation and without positive Law, a society which may fairly be described as in the 'state of nature'—is enough to meet the needs of the case. And he justifies his position, as indeed he was compelled to justify it, by the assumption that such a society, of itself and in default of all positive legislation, will be governed by 'natural Law'; that its members will, in the main, act on the 'golden rule'—Do as you would be done by. To him, therefore, a sense of the moral law is part of man's primitive endowment. All that it lacks in the state of nature is an outward and positive sanction.

To Rousseau, as we have seen, this hypothesis is incredible. The primitive, the 'natural,' state of man is a state not of society, but of solitude and isolation. And there is no halting-place

---

[1] ἡμεῖς [οἱ νόμοι] γάρ σε γεννήσαντες, ἐκθρέψαντες, παιδεύσαντες, μεταδόντες ἁπάντων ὧν οἷοί τ' ἦμεν καλῶν σοὶ καὶ τοῖς ἄλλοις πᾶσι πολίταις, ὅμως προαγορεύομεν,...ᾧ ἂν μὴ ἀρέσκωμεν ἡμεῖς, ἐξεῖναι λαβόντα τὰ αὑτοῦ ἀπιέναι ὅποι ἂν βούληται. *Crito*, p. 51 D. See the whole passage, pp. 50—4.

[2] *C. S.* I. vi., viii.; II. vii.

between this isolation and a 'civil state,' controlled by positive (though it may well be unwritten) Law, and based upon the 'absolute surrender' of its individual members. Between these two states there may have been a period of transition. If so, it was a period of misery; of misery so great that it could not possibly endure. For 'in proportion as we are severed by our passions, we are driven together by our wants; and the more we hate our kind, the less we can do without them'; so that, 'if such a state could endure, it would be an unfailing source of crimes and misery for men, each of whom would see nothing but his own interest, follow nothing but his own impulse, and listen to nothing but his own passions[1].' Thus, if the civil state is a necessity to man, it is not only because without it there is no external sanction to the moral law. It is also, it is far more, because, until this sanction is provided, until men have formed themselves into civil communities, the law itself does not exist, the moral sense is so utterly undeveloped as to have no influence upon their conduct. Hence it is not too much to say that the moral sense, the sense of duty and obligation, is, in Rousseau's view, the creation of the State. 'It is from the State that our first distinct notions of justice and injustice are derived. For the Law is anterior to justice, not justice to the Law[2].'

If this be an accurate statement of the case, it is clear that, on moral no less than on political grounds, Locke and Rousseau are diametrically opposed. Their views of the state of nature are directly contrary. So also are their views of the civil state. To Locke, the former is essentially a moral state; a state in which the rights of each are, at least in principle, recognised by all. It is, in fact, the rule of the Gospel enforced, so far as it is enforced, by the sanctions of the Gospel. To Rousseau, on the contrary, it is a state entirely without moral ties; a state equally without Law and without Gospel; a state, in the first instance, of 'bestial' isolation; and, as the isolation passes into neighbourhood, a state of active 'enmity, misery and crime.'

No less violent is the contrast between the two conceptions of the civil state. To Locke, the civil state is, in fact though not

[1] Geneva MS. I. ii.; below, pp. 447—8.
[2] *ib.* II. iv. (*De la nature des lois et du principe de la justice civile*): 'C'est ainsi'—*i.e.* from the relation of the citizen (*a*) to his fellow citizens, (*b*) to the citizens of other communities—'que se forment en nous les premières notions distinctes du juste et de l'injuste; car la Loi est antérieure à la justice, et non pas la justice à la Loi.' Compare the passage from *Histoire des Mœurs*, given below, pp. 335—6: MS. Neu. 7868.

by his own admission, less fully moralised than the state of nature. An outward sanction, unknown to the state of nature, has indeed been provided against certain acts of violence and fraud. But the distinction, which from the first was latent, between the sphere of social compulsion and the sphere of conscience has now become explicit. All that, on the narrowest construction, does not fall within the scope of the former is permitted, or at least tolerated, by the State. With the intrinsic justice or injustice of an act the community has no concern. That is a matter solely for the conscience of the individual. So long as certain outward forms are observed, the State is satisfied; it has no right to interfere. The result of this upon the life of the State has already been pointed out. There is a further, and corresponding, consequence to the life of the individual. When the State insists on deciding right and wrong by purely formal tests, when it asserts the right of each man to do what he will with his own, can we wonder that the individual should follow suit? Is it surprising if he pronounces the morality which is good enough for the community to be good enough also for himself? The distinction between justice and legality may have been made, in the first instance, for the benefit of the former. But once made, experience shews that it is but too likely to be pressed into the service of the latter. And a right pushed to its furthest limits—a right, that is, drained of all moral content—is the extremest form of wrong. That Locke himself never intended such an abuse, is absolutely certain. Theories, however, are to be judged not only by intentions, but by the consequences which may naturally be drawn from them. And the history of the individualist theory is one long proof that this consequence invariably results.

Few men have felt this so keenly, or so bitterly, as Rousseau. From the second *Discourse* to *Émile* and the *Contrat social*, his soul is burdened with the sense that oppression is abroad upon the earth, that the weak are everywhere sacrificed to the strong, that the forms of justice are universally employed to maintain and perpetuate injustice. And the chief aim of his political writings—above all, of the *Économie politique* and the *Contrat social*—is to discover a method by which this veiled conspiracy may be defeated, the rule of the 'general,' or corporate, will asserted and the supremacy of the Law established, in fact as well as in name, against the craft and violence of the individual[1]. It is to this end

[1] 'Voilà dans mes vieilles idées le grand problème en politique, que je compare à celui de la quadrature du cercle en géométrie et à celui des

that all his efforts are directed. And it is only when we bear this practical end in mind that the true scope of his theory is made clear.

What, then, are the leading points of that theory, as set forth in the more abstract chapters of the *Contrat social*? They are: firstly, that the moral sense, the sense of duty to others, begins only with the foundation of the State. Secondly, that this sense belongs directly to the community thus organised, and only by derivation to the individual member. Thirdly, that justice is to be secured only when the individual will has been totally 'surrendered' or 'annihilated,' and its place taken by that of the community at large. And lastly, that the Law, which is the voice of that 'general will,' is by its very nature concerned only with general objects; and that the moment it begins to distinguish between man and man, between class and class, it has destroyed the very purpose of its being and forfeited all title to respect. It will be observed that, the first step once granted, all the other steps follow logically, if not necessarily, in its train; that every step is deliberately calculated to bar out the intrusion of the individual; that, from first to last, the theory of Rousseau is, and is intended to be, the exact antithesis to that of Locke.

The first two points stand in the closest connection with each other and may best be taken together. At the outset it must be confessed that Rousseau himself is here responsible for some confusion. And it is necessary to strip the substance of his argument of the half historical form in which it is unfortunately clothed. The question is not whether man, as a mere animal, ever existed, or may be supposed to have existed, apart from some kind of civil organisation. That is a question for the biologist, or the anthropologist. And their results have little bearing upon political philosophy. It is whether some form of civil society is not essential to the life of man, as an intellectual and moral being. In his answer to this question, Rousseau is at one with the best thought of those who had gone before him: at one with Plato and Aristotle among the ancients, with Vico and Montesquieu in the generation just before his own. And subsequent thinkers, from Burke onwards, have followed in

longitudes en astronomie : trouver une forme de Gouvernement qui mette la Loi au-dessus de l'homme.' Letter to Mirabeau (July 26, 1767); Vol. II. p. 160. See also *Éc. pol.*; below, pp. 267—8: and the following from *Émile*, Liv. IV.; *Œuvres*, II. p. 206, 'L'esprit universel des lois de tous les pays est de favoriser toujours le fort contre le faible, et celui qui a contre celui qui n'a rien. Cet inconvénient est inévitable, et il est sans exception.'

his steps. They have given a depth and fulness to the argument, which would have been impossible to Rousseau. But, as for its speculative basis, they have added little or nothing to what was already contained in the *Contrat social*.

'Man is by nature a political animal....By nature (or ideally) the State is prior to the individual'—in these two sentences of Aristotle we have the root of the whole matter. Strip the individual of all that he owes to the teaching of the home and of the school, to the national tradition which, with different results in each country, has collected itself, age after age, in these two vital forces; strip him of all that he owes to the influences— religious, moral, social, political and intellectual—which surround him and are as the air he breathes every moment of his life: and you will leave him little more than the empty name of man; you will reduce him to something which defies both experience and imagination, and which can hardly be said to bear the mark of humanity at all.

To conceive of the individual as apart from a given society, a given community, is, in truth, a plain impossibility. If we attempt the task, we shall find that, in the last resort, we are defining him by a mere string of negatives, which offer nothing definite for the understanding to lay hold of. It is as member of a community that we know the individual, and as that alone. And, as member of a community, he has become something entirely different from what the imagination may conceive that he might have been, as the unsocial, naked individual, who may conceivably have existed in the remote past, and of whom we talk so glibly in the present. In each community, and by that community, he has been moulded to all that gives him any positive quality, to all that stamps him with distinctive character, to all, in short, that constitutes his individuality. It is the traditions of his particular race, his particular social order, his particular polity and religion, that have made him what he is. It is these that constitute his 'permanent reason' and his true self. Without them, as Burke said, 'men would be little better than the flies of a summer[1].'

Such is the thought which underlies the whole of the more abstract part of the *Contrat social*, and which comes to the surface in such chapters as those on the *Lawgiver* and the *Civil State*. At the time when Rousseau wrote, it was entirely original; it marked a wholly new departure in political philosophy. It was

[1] Burke's *Reflections*; *Works*, I. p. 417.

indeed a commonplace with the Greek philosophers; but since their time it had fallen dead in men's minds. It is doubtless presupposed—in the one case more, in the other less, vaguely—in the great works of Montesquieu and Vico[1]; the former of which preceded the *Contrat social* by more than a dozen, and the latter by nearly forty, years. But the bent of both these writers was rather for history than philosophy. And Rousseau was the first to lift this cardinal principle of Politics into clear consciousness; the first to give it speculative form and to grasp the full bearing of all that it involves. In this respect, even Burke—and that, quite apart from any direct debt he may have owed to Rousseau—must yield to his precursor. And before any further advance can be recorded, we have to look forward to Fichte and to Hegel. To find anything like it in the past, we have to go back, as Rousseau himself went back, to Aristotle and Plato.

The pity is that, in grasping this fundamental truth so firmly, Rousseau should have lost his hold on the opposite truth, which is necessary to supplement and correct it. However much the individual may owe to the State or the community, he owes much also to himself. However much the 'general will' may differ from the mere sum of individual wills, those individual wills are, after all, the material, and the only possible material, out of which the general will is to be shaped. The individual will is not only the evil principle which has to be 'mortified' and 'annihilated.' It is also the source, and the only conceivable source, of the good principle by which man is purified and elevated; by which, as we say, he is taken out of himself and made capable of the self-sacrifice, of the devotion to corporate aims and collective purposes, which is the essence of the State. More than that: the general will is not only compatible with the existence of strongly marked individual wills; it is infinitely poorer for the lack of them. It is not only none the worse, it is beyond all estimate the better, for their energy. There are moments when Rousseau recognises this as fully as could be desired. When he insists that the best State is that which enlists the passions of the citizens the most strongly in its service, he must mean this, or he means nothing. But there is no disguising the fact that he commonly ignores it. And the reason is too plain. For the purpose of founding the State, and as the indispensable condition of its foundation, he had reduced the individual to a cipher. How was it possible, then, that, at any

---

[1] The date of *Scienza nuova* is 1725 (that of the later draft, 1735); and the date of *Esprit des lois* is 1748.

later stage, the individual should recover the value which had thus 'absolutely' been taken from him? How, without resolving the State into its primitive atoms, could he regain the powers, the will, the self which he had deliberately given up? It was only when he made himself a 'fraction' that the State came into being. If he should once more become an unit, it must inevitably fall in pieces.

Thus the first step in overstatement could never afterwards be retrieved. The 'stupid and limited animal' of the earlier state could never, without the aid of a miracle, become the 'reasonable being, the man,' of the later. And, even granted the double miracle of Contract and Lawgiver, he could never attain to spiritual majority, never be fit to move without leading-strings, never be anything more than a puppet in the hands of the 'general will' and of the State. This is the conclusion which inevitably follows from the premisses. It is the conclusion which Rousseau himself, in his more abstract moments, unhesitatingly accepts.

This brings us at once to the third stage of Rousseau's argument, as it appears in the earlier and more abstract chapters of the *Contrat social*. Given that the 'natural man,' the individual, is, as such, incapable of recognising the moral bond which unites him to his fellows, it follows that the only means of establishing this bond is the 'annihilation' of the natural man 'with all his rights'; the 'total surrender' of the individual will to the 'corporate will' of the community which, from reasons into which there is no need to enquire further, he has been led to form. In this revolution, according to the *Contrat social*, lies the only hope either of calling out the moral and intellectual capabilities of the individual, or of maintaining the existence of the community which his needs have led him to create.

The leading idea of this section of the treatise is that of 'total surrender' and 'annihilation.' That carries with it the conception of the 'corporate self,' by which the mere individual and 'animal' self of the natural man has, in the civil state, to be replaced. And that, in its turn, unfolds itself into the doctrine of the 'general will' which, with more or less of alloy, has now passed into the common currency of political thought. For the moment, it is expedient to put aside all the limitations with which Rousseau subsequently surrounds this 'unconditional surrender,' and to consider the theory under the sweeping form in which it was originally laid down.

The analogy between the animal and the social organism, so elaborately worked out in the *Économie politique*[1], is conspicuous

[1] *Éc. pol.*; below, p. 241.

by its absence from the *Contrat social*[1]. But its spirit dominates the whole treatise. And, unless taken in the most vague and general sense, no analogy could be more misleading. It is of the essence of the animal organism in its healthy state that no one of its members has a separate life, a separate will, of its own; that all of them live and will solely in and through the whole body. Far otherwise is it with the body politic. There, the members have a double life: on the one hand, an intellectual and moral life, which is no doubt largely conditioned by that of the community, but which is always distinguishable—if not, in the strict sense, separable—from it and is capable of rising into the sharpest antagonism with it; and, on the other hand, a physical life which, in all but the most indirect manner, is absolutely independent of it. And there are moments when Rousseau himself is as keenly alive to this distinction as it is possible for any man to be. Thus in an early fragment he writes as follows: 'The difference between the work of man's art and the work of nature makes itself felt in the result. The citizens may call themselves *members* of the State. But they can never be united to it as closely as the members are to the body. No power on earth can prevent each of them from having an individual and separate existence, in virtue of which he is self-sufficient to his own maintenance. The nerves of the corporate body are less sensitive, the muscles are less powerful, the bonds which unite one member to another are looser; the smallest accident is capable of dissolving the whole frame[2].'

These considerations are obvious enough in themselves. But they are a notable admission on the lips of Rousseau. And it is to be wished that, when he came to write the *Contrat social*, he had given them greater weight. For though this is the most original part of the treatise, it is also the most exaggerated, and therefore the most open to question. A profound truth may, and does, lie at the bottom of the argument. But the precise form in which Rousseau clothes it justly provokes objection. That objection rests on two grounds: the one of logic, the other of the practical consequence which the whole argument involves.

As to the former, even though it be granted—as it certainly must be—that, for all that is most vital to his intellectual and moral life, the individual depends upon the community of which he is a member, it in no way follows that this dependence is absolute

---

[1] There is one exception: 'Comme la nature donne à chaque homme un pouvoir absolu sur tous ses membres, le pacte social donne au Corps politique un pouvoir absolu sur tous les siens.' *C. S.* II. iv.

[2] *L'état de guerre* (MS. Neuchâtel, 7856). See below, p. 298.

and unlimited; or that the ends of the community are to be attained only by the 'annihilation' of the individual, by the 'total surrender' of his will to that of the community as a whole. That, after all, is a purely mechanical way of conceiving the relation between the two elements in question; and as such, it is little likely to give adequate expression to what, from the nature of the case, must be a moral relation, or nothing at all. The union between the individual and the community must surely be not mechanical, nor even organic. It must involve not the absorption of the one in the other; but the reaction of each upon the other, the interpenetration of each by the other. And that is precisely what is barred out, on any strict interpretation of the passages before us. Or, to put the objection otherwise: when we say that the individual is dependent upon the community, this does not in the least imply that the dependence must necessarily be on one side only. It in no way excludes the possibility that it exists equally on the other. Between these two possibilities the facts—the facts, as interpreted by a just sense of relative values—alone can judge. And, in this instance, it is the latter construction which squares with the facts. The former flies straight in their face.

And this brings us direct to the other ground of objection. Not only is Rousseau's statement of the case at plain variance with the facts, as we know them. It also leads to consequences which would be fatal to the welfare of mankind. The relation of the individual to the State is, on his shewing, one of unmitigated slavery. 'Individuality is left out of their scheme of government[1],' was Burke's charge against France, as she was under the Directory. It is hardly less true of Rousseau. If we press his words, he is, in fact, the sworn foe not only of individualism, but of individuality. The individual is, for him, absolutely merged in the community, his freedom utterly lost in the sovereignty of the State. This is against all reason and all experience. A State of which this were true would be a State without freedom, without life, without hope of progress.

That Rousseau himself goes far to accept these consequences—including, as we have already seen, the denial of progress—can hardly be gainsaid. It appears from what he says of the individual. It appears also from his condemnation of all partial or subordinate societies—religious, political, industrial and others—such as custom has sanctioned within the borders of the State. He was doubtless right in holding that, whenever such societies either defy the

[1] Burke, *Letters on a regicide Peace*, II.; *Works*, II. p. 315.

sovereignty of the State or strive to withdraw themselves from its control, they have forfeited all right to forbearance, and that any concessions made to them under such circumstances are no more than concessions of grace. But he goes much further than this. He regards the very existence of such societies as a permanent threat to the rights of the community, a standing menace to the corporate life of the whole body. He denounces them as nests of faction and disloyalty. He holds that, by their very nature, they are bound to corrupt, and in the long run to destroy, the purity of the general will, upon which the welfare of the whole community depends.

On these principles, it is clear that the very right of association is called in question; or rather, peremptorily denied. Now it may safely be said that, without the right of association, the individual is left helpless in presence of the State. He can neither secure the redress of his own grievances, nor influence public opinion for the benefit of the whole mass. In fact, if the right of association is necessary to the freedom of the individual, it is no less necessary to the welfare of the State. Without it, the sovereignty of the State is likely to be nothing better than another name for tyranny. It is certain to end—as Rousseau, with characteristic fatalism, foresaw that it must end—in stagnation and decay.

As has already been stated, this must not be taken to mean that the right of association is absolute and unlimited. On the contrary, like all other rights, it is subject to the general control of the community, acting as the State. For the manner in which this control should be exercised, no rules are to be laid down. All we can say is that it should never be put in force save in extreme cases; and that, even when set in motion, it should be with leniency, and to an extent no greater than the circumstances manifestly demand. The guiding principle, in this as in all such matters, is expediency: expediency construed in a generous sense, and with a leaning towards mercy. Yet, when all is said and done, the rights of the community, thus interpreted, are above those of the association or the section; and in extreme cases there is no choice but to enforce them. To hold otherwise is a dangerous error. It bars the road to progress no less certainly than the doctrine of the *Contrat social* itself. The arguments by which it is commonly defended are its strongest condemnation. They are a survival of the feudal spirit—the spirit of separatism and obscurantism—against which Rousseau, whose name is an object of holy horror to the champions of ecclesiastical and other sectional ascendencies, waged inexpiable war. So far, it is right that we should go with him. It is equally right that we should part company with him, when he falls into the opposite extreme.

Up to this point, we have dealt with Rousseau's doctrine solely in its most abstract and uncompromising form. It is now time to consider the successive qualifications which it eventually receives. And in so doing, we pass to the fourth and last article of this section of the *Contrat social*: to Rousseau's conception of the 'general will' and of the Law. This, in its turn, will lead on to the latter part of the treatise: to the more sweeping qualifications—due to time, place and circumstance—which the influence of Montesquieu, an influence which in the first instance can hardly have been congenial, induced the great idealist to accept.

The main importance of these ideas—the General Will and the Law—lies in their bearing upon the relation of the individual to the State. But before entering on this subject, it is well to sift out the precise meaning which they conveyed to the mind of Rousseau, as taken by themselves.

And first, for his doctrine of the general will. From one point of view, the general will is to him simply the expression of the corporate self. It *is* that self, as directed to, and issuing in, action. It implies, therefore, the existence of the State as, in the fullest sense, a corporate body, with a life of its own quite apart from that of the individual members of which it is built up. Hence the distinction, already noticed, between the 'general will' and the 'will of all,' between *la volonté générale* and *la volonté de tous*[1]. It is a cardinal distinction: a distinction in which the whole of Rousseau's theory, on its more abstract side, is implicitly contained.

To Rousseau, however, the term *volonté générale* means a great deal more than this. It has not only a speculative, but also a practical, sense. It stands not only for a faculty of the corporate self, but also for a specific temper or habit of mind which, in any healthy condition of things, must be manifested both in the corporate self and in the individuals who compose it. This is the temper that we commonly call 'public spirit.' It is roughly equivalent to what Montesquieu, in a well known passage, describes as 'virtue,' and pronounces to be the distinguishing mark of a democracy[2]. Rousseau, justly enough, objects to this limitation, on the ground that the sovereign authority is the same in all good forms of Government, and that the animating principle must

[1] *C. S.* II. iii. See above, p. 27—8.   [2] *Esprit des lois*, Liv. III. cap. iii.

therefore—doubtless in varying degrees—be 'everywhere the same[1].' Of all the practical consequences which flow from his theory, this is at once the most far-reaching and that which lies nearest to his heart. His whole conception of the State assumes the existence of a public spirit which to modern ears may sound incredible, but which was intensely real to the student of Plutarch, to the spiritual child of Sparta and of Rome. To maintain this is the first duty, as to possess it is the first condition, of the State. To secure this, Rousseau is willing, in case of need, to sacrifice all other ends: even the sovereignty of the people, even the yet more sacred right of personal freedom. This once given, he is prepared, at least for the moment, to tolerate serfdom; he is prepared to tolerate that hereditary aristocracy which, of all rightful forms of Government, he had pronounced to be the worst[2].

Much simpler is his conception of the Law. That to Rousseau always means one thing, and one alone. It is invariably the 'voice,' the 'organ,' of the general will; the sole means by which that will can find expression. 'By what mysterious skill,' he asks, 'was the means discovered for bringing men into subjection, in order to make them free? for employing in the service of the State the possessions, the arms, the very life, of all its members, without constraining them and without consulting them? for enthralling their will with their own permission? for vindicating their consent against their refusal, and for forcing them to punish themselves when they do that which they have not deliberately willed? How can it come about that they obey while none commands them, that they are servants and yet have no master: all the more free in truth, because, under the appearance of subjection, no one of them loses any part of his liberty except that which runs counter to the liberty of another? These miracles are the work of the Law. It is to the Law alone that man owes justice and freedom. It is this beneficent organ of the will of all which reestablishes in the world of Right the equality which belongs to man in the state of

---

[1] *C. S.* III. iv.

[2] See *Gouvernement de Pologne*, Chaps. vi., xiii.; Vol. II. pp. 445, 497—9. It may be noted that the latter chapter is immediately preceded by these words: 'De l'effervescence excitée par cette commune émulation naîtra cette ivresse patriotique qui seule sait élever les hommes au-dessus d'eux-mêmes, et sans laquelle la liberté n'est qu'un vain nom et la législation qu'une chimère.' *Ib.* p. 492. See his views on hereditary aristocracy in *C. S.* III. v.; III. x. (note). In the latter passage he calls it 'la pire des administrations légitimes.' In Poland, the nobles held not only the Government, but the Sovereignty.

nature. It is this voice from heaven which dictates to man the commands of the corporate reason (*la raison publique*) and teaches him to obey the maxims of his own judgment and not to be for ever in contradiction with himself. The laws constitute the sole motive power of the body politic, which acts and feels only through them. Without them, the State would be nothing more than a body without soul, bare existence without action. For it is not enough that each should submit himself to the general will. In order to comply with it, he must know it[1].'

Not that Rousseau desires to see laws multiplied on the right hand and on the left. On the contrary, he regards such a multiplication as a sure sign of perversion or decay. The better the spirit of the community, the fewer—after the initial work of the Lawgiver—are the laws it will demand[2]. And if doubtful cases arise, he is willing to leave a large discretion in the hands of the Executive, which can always divine the decision of the general will by asking itself, What are the equities of the matter? and which is more likely to reach a just conclusion, because less likely to be swept by gusts of passion—more likely to see the facts as they are, because less liable to be blinded by ignorance—than the body of citizens, as a whole[3].

The Law then is the organ of the general will. And the only further condition to be observed is the obvious one that the will, of which it is the living voice, must be general in deed as well as in name. And that means, as we have already seen, that it must be general in two distinct senses: general, not only in respect of its source, but also, and no less, in its character and scope[4].

[1] Geneva MS. I. vii.; below, p. 475. The whole passage, down to 'in contradiction with himself,' appears also in *Éc. pol.* p. 245.

[2] 'Un État ainsi gouverné'—*i.e.* as in Appenzell and other pastoral Cantons of Switzerland, 'le plus heureux peuple du monde'—'a besoin de très peu de lois.' *C. S.* IV. i.

[3] See *Éc. pol.* p. 247. It may be objected that this rather startling passage does not represent the mind of Rousseau, as it was when he wrote the *Contrat social*. There is, however, a similar passage in *C. S.* II. vi.: 'La volonté générale est toujours droite, mais le jugement qui la guide n'est pas toujours éclairé. Il faut lui faire voir les objets tels qu'ils sont, quelquefois tels qu'ils doivent lui paraître.' Instead of 'mais le jugement...éclairé' the Geneva MS. (I. vii.; below, p. 476) has: 'il n'est jamais question de la rectifier: mais il faut savoir l'interroger à propos.' It is true that this is said of the Lawgiver. But it would be hard to establish any distinction on this point between his work and that of ordinary legislation.

[4] 'Comme la chose statuée se rapporte nécessairement au bien commun, il s'ensuit que l'objet de la Loi doit être général ainsi que la volonté qui la dicte.' Geneva MS. II. iv.; below, p. 492. Compare Vol. II. pp. 44—5.

And firstly, in respect of its source. The general will, if it is to be in fact what it claims to be in word, must not cancel—still less, must it formally exclude—the will of one single individual. On the contrary, it must take up all into itself. It may remould them, it may transform them; the more completely it does so, the better. But at least it must include them all, it must draw its mandate from them all. The will which does not base itself upon the consent of the whole community, upon the sovereignty of the whole people, is not general at all. That is what Rousseau meant by saying that the corporate will, and the Law as its expression, must be general in its source.

It is equally necessary that it should be general in its scope. The Law is no respecter of persons; nor again is it a respecter of classes or of sections. Directly it becomes so, directly it begins to discriminate between man and man, between class and class, it loses the universality which is essential to its being, and forfeits all title to respect. It is, in fact, no Law at all. By marks which are evident to all men, it is null and void.

This brings us at once to the bearing of the two conceptions, the Law and the general will, upon the relation between the individual and the State. Each of these two conditions, when we consider its practical effect, is seen to furnish, and is intended by Rousseau to furnish, a guarantee for the freedom of the individual, or of the social group, against the tyranny of the community: in other words, to restore to them some part at least of the independence which, on the author's first account of the matter, seemed to have been irrevocably withdrawn. The first of the two secures that the voice of each individual shall have the chance of making itself heard; that, in the spirit as well as in the letter, the Law shall represent the will of the community as a whole. In this connection, it is necessary to remember the secondary meaning which the term *volonté générale*, as we have already seen, bore to the mind of Rousseau: the 'public spirit,' the renunciation of all selfish or sectional interests, which to him it necessarily involved[1].

The second of the two conditions works still more powerfully in the same direction. By denying the right of the State to pass any law which does not, in theory at any rate, equally affect all members and all sections of the community, it is evident that Rousseau largely reduces the powers of the State and, in exactly

---

[1] 'En effet, la première loi, la seule véritable loi fondamentale, qui découle immédiatement du pacte social, est que chacun préfère en toutes choses le plus grand bien de tous.' Geneva MS. II. iv.; below, p. 493.

the same proportion, largely increases those of the individual; more than that, of the various social groups into which the community naturally, if not inevitably, falls. Once more, therefore, it is clear that a sweeping qualification is here grafted by Rousseau upon his original account of the matter; that, to a large extent, he gives back to the individual, and even to the section, with one hand what in the first instance he had taken, or seemed to take, away with the other.

The same result follows from yet another qualification, to which Rousseau evidently attached much weight, but which readers of the *Contrat social* are far too apt to overlook. By the terms of the Contract, as has again and again been insisted, the 'surrender' of the individual is 'total' and 'without reserve.' We are, therefore, hardly prepared for the following statement which occurs at a later point of the treatise: 'We are all agreed that the only part of his powers, his possessions and his liberty that the individual surrenders by the social compact is that part of them which is of service to the community. But we must also agree that the sovereign'—that is, the community—'is the sole judge of what that service demands[1].' Even when all allowance has been made for the closing sentence, it is clear that a fresh colour is here put upon the whole transaction. The intellectual and moral freedom of the individual receives a safeguard of which, on the first statement of the case, there had been no suspicion. The absolute right of the State is limited by a whole network of utilities and expediences. And, though the right itself remains in the abstract, in practice it is pared down to something far less formidable than could ever have been supposed. This is notably the case, as Rousseau himself points out, in the region of religious thought; a fact which must be borne in mind when we come to consider the Chapter on *la religion civile*[2].

It may be objected that all three safeguards are illusory; that they offer securities which are either mere words or, at the first

[1] *C. S.* II. iv. (*Des bornes du pouvoir souverain*). It is to be noted that the closing sentence is wanting in the Geneva MS. (I. vi.); below, p. 471.

[2] 'Le droit que le pacte social donne au souverain sur les sujets ne passe point, comme je l'ai dit, les bornes de l'utilité publique. Les sujets ne doivent donc compte au souverain de leurs opinions qu'autant que ces opinions importent à la communauté....Chácun peut avoir, au surplus, telles opinions qu'il lui plaît, sans qu'il appartienne au souverain d'en connaître; car comme il n'a point de compétence dans l'autre monde, quel que soit le sort des sujets dans la vie à venir, ce n'est pas son affaire, pourvu qu'ils soient bons citoyens dans celle-ci.' *C. S.* IV. viii.

temptation to override them, will be thrown to the winds. The objection is not captious; it deserves serious consideration. It is unfortunate that, for that purpose, each of the three conditions must be taken by itself.

As to the first condition, that relating to the general will, it must be owned that we have to do mainly with a question of words. The general will, says Rousseau roundly, can never err[1]. This is subsequently explained to mean that, whenever it does err, it ceases to be general. And that does not afford much practical help. Even this, however, is enough to clear Rousseau from the extravagance, sometimes attributed to him, of holding that whatever the majority wills is always sure to be just. He had already gone out of his way to deny this in relation to the dealings of one country with another; and on the explicit ground that the two communities stand to each other as two individuals in the state of nature[2]. He now makes the same admission with regard to cases which may easily arise within the bounds of the community itself. When they do arise, it is because individual or sectional interests, 'masquerading under the sacred name of the public interest,' carry the day, and the general will—which 'remains unvarying, incorruptible and pure'—'is reduced to silence[3].'

As against the two remaining checks, the objection is not so much that they are a matter of words as that, in practice, they would come to nothing. And first, for that which concerns Rousseau's conception of the Law. A law, he insists, must always be general in its scope. If it be aimed at any one man, or group of men, it is null and void. Now it is safe to say that, on any strict interpretation of this canon, a large number of the laws enacted in all States ought never to have been passed. An Act regulating the Liquor Trade or Limited Liability Companies, an Insurance Act, a Merchant Shipping Act—all these are directed against—at the least, they injuriously affect—particular classes or groups of men. All therefore are, on Rousseau's principles, so many violations of the Right. Yet without them, no State, especially under the enormous complexity of social and industrial relations at the present day, could hold together for a moment. Writing as he did, before the expansion of European industry had been born or thought of, Rousseau would doubtless have replied

[1] *C. S.* II. iii. (*Si la volonté générale peut errer*).
[2] *Éc. pol.*; below, p. 242.
[3] *C. S.* II. iii.; IV. i. (*Que la volonté générale est indestructible*). *C. S.* II. vi. Compare *L'état de guerre*; below, p. 304.

that these relations are wholly artificial, that there is no need for their existence, and that the sooner they are swept away, the better for the moral, and even the material, welfare of mankind. That is a subject to which some return must be made later. It is certainly true that the State which he has in view—the City State of the Greek world, or its counterpart in medieval and modern times—is largely, if not entirely, free from such embarrassments. And for the purposes of the present argument, he is perhaps entitled to the benefit of his assumption. Yet even the City State must raise taxes. And the whole aim of taxation is, or ought to be, to throw the burden upon the shoulders most capable of bearing it; to draw as little as possible from the poor, and as much as possible from the rich. No man could have proclaimed this duty more loudly than Rousseau himself[1]. Yet here is a plain instance of discrimination between class and class, between one section of the community and another.

When all is said and done, however, the principle which Rousseau lays down is a principle of the first importance. As a general principle, it lies at the root of all justice and all equity. And Rousseau did well to insist that, as a general principle, it offers a precious security for justice, an inestimable check upon injustice and oppression. His mistake lay in not recognising that, like most other principles, it is capable of perversion; that to apply it in all cases would be the surest means of giving a licence to the injustice, the tyranny of the rich over the poor, which he regarded with 'inextinguishable hatred.'

The last condition imposed by Rousseau is that the rights of the State over the individual extend no further than its own welfare and the needs of its own service demand; the State itself being the sole judge of what those demands actually are. Once again it may be said that this is a safeguard rather in theory than in practice; that there is no State which will not persistently interpret so vague a maxim to its own advantage, and to the disadvantage of its members. The answer to this is that from that danger there is no sound way of escape; that not only in Rousseau's State, but in all States where the sovereignty is undivided, the individual will sometimes be sacrificed without reason for the benefit of the community, or the prince. The only remedy is to divide the sovereignty. And that—as the experience of the United States shews—is a remedy worse than the disease. It puts the State at the mercy of the individual;

[1] *Éc. pol.* pp. 266—9.

and that is still more disastrous than to put the individual at the mercy of the State.

That Rousseau himself, in adopting the latter course, was keenly alive to the dangers besetting it, it is impossible to doubt. The qualification here placed on the original terms of the Contract is one proof. The following passage is another: 'The existence of the State is so closely bound up with the security of its members that, if allowance had not to be made for human frailty, the social compact would in strict right be dissolved if a single citizen perished when his life might have been spared, if a single man were wrongfully imprisoned, if a single action were decided in face of what was manifestly just....Has not the nation bound itself to watch over the life of the least of its members with the same care that it gives to all the rest? And is the community less concerned with the welfare of the individual citizen than with that of the whole State? Let them tell us that it is expedient that one man should perish for the sake of all the rest. I shall admire such a maxim on the lips of the patriot who devotes himself to death, of his own free will and as a duty, for the salvation of his country. But, if it be meant that it is legitimate for the Government to sacrifice an innocent man for the benefit of the multitude, then I hold that doctrine to be one of the most execrable that has ever been devised by tyranny, the most false that could be put forward, the most dangerous that could be admitted, and the most utterly opposed to the fundamental laws of human society[1].' Such were the principles of Rousseau when he wrote the *Économie politique*. And there is no ground for supposing that he had departed from them by one hair's breadth in the interval between that and the *Contrat social*. The practices of the Committee of Public Safety have sometimes been charged upon his name. Those who do so must have forgotten that they are here branded in advance.

On the whole, then, it must be said that the qualifications with which we have been concerned represent a marked advance upon the original statement of the theory. They are doubtless not so precise as some critics might desire. But it would be the height of injustice not to recognise the intention with which they were put forward, or refuse to credit the author with an honest effort to guard the rights both of individuals and minorities, and, by so doing, to meet the dangers which the doctrine of absolute sovereignty inevitably carries with it. It is quite true that, for the

[1] *Éc. pol.* p. 252.

accomplishment of this end, he trusts rather to the spirit than to the letter; that he rejects all attempts to limit sovereignty by statute, and relies solely upon the sense of equity without which no statute, no constitutional check, can have any value whatsoever. But in this it is by no means certain that he was wrong. Weak or impracticable as his securities may seem to some, it is, to say the least, doubtful whether any others, however promising in theory, would in practice prove more effective. The guarantees which he rejects are things of paper and of parchment. Was he not right in preferring the 'public spirit' which, to him at any rate, meant a passionate craving not merely for the general good, but for the welfare of every member, a conviction no less passionate that each of these is to be won only by and through the other[1]?

Such then, in its main outlines, is Rousseau's theory of the State. In his presentment of that theory, as we have seen, there are two stages which must be held carefully apart: the abstract form in which it is originally presented to us, and the more concrete and qualified form which it ultimately assumes. The former, the defiantly abstract presentation, is a theory of pure collectivism: a collectivism as uncompromising as that of Plato and, thanks to the doctrine of popular sovereignty, far more consistently carried out. In both writers, the burdens of citizenship are at least as conspicuous as its privileges. In both, the daily life of the citizen—it would not be too much to say, his every act—is subject to incessant direction and control. The difference is that, in the *Republic*, both burdens and privileges are confined to a small fraction; in the *Contrat social*, they are distributed equally over the whole mass. In the one, the bulk of the community is left, in the main, to follow its own course: to buy and sell, to marry and to give in marriage; and there is nothing to shew that, so long as a decent appearance is kept up, the rulers will trouble themselves to interfere. 'God careth not for such cattle'— that is the unspoken thought of a great part of the *Republic*. In the other, every member of the community is a member also of the sovereign. But every member of the sovereign is also subject to the sovereign's decrees. All his rights, we are expressly told, are held at the sovereign's discretion. It is true that the sovereign, on its side, has no right to require of him more than can be proved

[1] 'En effet, la première loi, la seule véritable loi fondamentale qui découle immédiatement du pacte social, est que chacun préfère en toutes choses le plus grand bien de tous.' Geneva MS. II. iv.; below, p. 493.

'of service to the community at large.' But it is equally true that 'the sovereign'—that is, the community—'is the sole judge of what that service demands.'

At this stage, the whole conception of Rousseau is manifestly determined by the unspoken analogy of the body and the members. The 'surrender' of the individual to the community is 'absolute and unreserved.' His 'powers, his possessions, his liberty, his very will and self' all lose their separate existence. They are all merged in the sovereignty, the will, the 'corporate self,' of the community as a whole. Such is the communal despotism which, at least in the first presentment of his theory, Rousseau is willing to accept.

At later points of the treatise the bonds are considerably loosened. In theory, the community is still absolute master of the individual. Its will has, once for all, absorbed and taken the place of his. In practice, however, we learn that there are, and ought to be, large remissions of his dependence. The sovereign is bound, so far as possible, to respect the individuality of its members. It has no right to demand of them more than it is for its own interest to obtain. Again, it is only by laws passed with every constitutional formality that any restriction on individual liberty can be imposed. And as the author spares no pains to discourage the passage of new laws, it is evident that, in his view, the number of restrictions will be comparatively small[1]. Lastly, no law, we are told, is to be justified which is not equally applicable to all. And Rousseau was convinced—far more deeply convinced than he had any right to be—that no community will pass a law, from the effects of which every member is liable to suffer[2].

The general upshot of all this, at least in the intention of the author, is to surround the original absolutism of the community

---

[1] 'Si l'on me demandait quel est le plus vicieux de tous les peuples, je répondrais sans hésiter que c'est celui qui a le plus des lois.' *Fragments divers*, p. 330. Compare *C. S.* IV. i.: 'Un État ainsi gouverné a besoin de très peu de lois'; 'Plus vous multipliez les lois, plus vous les rendez méprisables.' *Éc. pol.* p. 249. Compare Vol. II. p. 473.

[2] 'Il est impossible que le corps veuille nuire à tous ses membres; et nous verrons ci-après qu'il ne peut nuire à aucun en particulier. Le souverain, par cela seul qu'il est, est toujours tout ce qu'il doit être.' *C. S.* I. vii. Compare *ib.* II. iv. See also *Émile*, Liv. v.: 'D'où il suit qu'un particulier ne saurait être lésé directement par le souverain qu'ils ne le soient tous, ce qui ne se peut, puisque ce serait vouloir se faire du mal à soi-même.' It is doubtless impossible that a community should *wish* to harm itself. It is only too possible that it should do so, without wishing and without knowing it. Rousseau himself admits as much of the 'blind multitude.' *C. S.* II. vi.

with a whole network of limitations; to restore to the individual in practice a large share of the rights and liberties which, in theory, he had surrendered. The harshness of the primitive theory is thus considerably softened. The latter part of the theory opens the door for qualifications which, in the abstract statement of the earlier part, might well seem irrevocably barred out. And the same process—towards the concrete, and away from the abstract—is carried yet further in the still more startling qualifications which we are now about to consider.

V

LEADING IDEAS OF THE *CONTRAT SOCIAL*, AS MODIFIED BY THE INFLUENCE OF MONTESQUIEU. LATER WRITINGS

'Before putting up a large building, the architect observes and tests the soil, in order to see if it can bear the weight. In the same way, the wise lawgiver begins not by drawing up the laws which are the best in themselves, but by examining whether the nation for which they are destined is capable of bearing them[1].' 'Liberty is not a fruit which grows in all climates. It is therefore not within the reach of all nations. The more we reflect on this principle established by Montesquieu, the more its truth will be felt. The more it is disputed, the larger the opening for establishing it by fresh proofs[2].' If title-page and author's name were not there to prove it, who would ever have guessed that these sentences were written by Rousseau? Who would believe that more than a fifth part of the *Contrat social* is devoted to expounding them[3]? or that the whole of the author's subsequent work in Politics—the three treatises which close the present edition—is nothing more nor less than an application of the principle here summarily laid down?

For reasons which have already been given, and which moreover are sufficiently obvious in themselves, there is no need to explain these principles at length. It is enough to point out that we have

---

[1] *C. S.* II. viii.: Geneva MS. II. iii. (with the variant 'ne commence pas par rédiger des lois au hasard').

[2] *C. S.* III. viii. Montesquieu sums up his doctrine on this point in one sentence: 'L'empire du climat est le premier de tous les empires'—with reference to the ease with which Peter the Great carried through his reforms. *Esprit des lois*, XIX. xiv.

[3] *C. S.* II. vii.—x.; III. iii.—viii.

here a full acceptance of the 'historical method,' subject only to the limitations which the truth demands, but which the fanatical champions of the method—among whom Montesquieu himself is not to be reckoned—persistently disregard. It is a remarkable instance of the working of one great mind upon another: the more remarkable, when we remember how bitter was the general prejudice against which Montesquieu had to battle, and how strong the inner bias which Rousseau himself, as disciple both of Locke and Plato, had to overcome. The philosophers, whose ways of thought were nothing if not abstract, might speak scornfully of *Esprit des lois*[1]. Rousseau, unlike them in this as in most other things, was the earliest convert to its teaching. The influence of Montesquieu is, in truth, the dominant influence throughout the latter part of the *Contrat social*, as well as the practical treatises which followed. It is no less marked in Rousseau's treatment of the three traditional forms of Government—Democracy, Monarchy and Aristocracy—than in what he says of the 'empire' of soil and climate, of the moulding force exercised upon the ideals and destinies of nations by outward circumstance, by inherited character, by historical tradition.

There is no need for us to ask, what is the value of these principles and of the method which they carry with them? That is now universally acknowledged. Nor need we much concern ourselves with the detailed application given to them by Rousseau. That must be left to the reader to discover for himself. The sole question which, for our purposes, demands an answer is: How far are these principles—how far is this method—consistent with the method and principles of the earlier part of the treatise? Does Rousseau, or does he not, succeed in fusing what he had learned

[1] Both Voltaire and Helvétius wrote sarcastic commentaries on *Esprit des lois*. Neither of them understood more of it than to recognise that it cut dead against the cherished principles of the 'Enlightenment.' The following sentence from the letter of Helvétius to the author [Montesquieu, *Œuvres*, 8 vols. Paris, 1822, T. v. p. 423] is a fair specimen of both: 'Je finirai par vous avouer que je n'ai jamais bien compris les subtiles distinctions, sans cesse répétées, sur les différentes formes de Gouvernement. Je n'en connais que de deux espèces—les bons et les mauvais : les bons qui sont encore à faire ; les mauvais, dont tout l'art est, par différents moyens, de faire passer l'argent de la partie gouvernée dans la bourse de la partie gouvernante.' The well-known epigram of Mme du Deffand—'C'est de l'esprit sur les lois' —represents the verdict of the small fry of the party. It is quoted with approval by Voltaire, *Commentaire*, § xix. *ib.* p. 330. Elsewhere Voltaire speaks of *les saillies gasconnes*—the gasconnades—*de Montesquieu*. *Correspondance générale*, IX. p. 382 (letter to Servan of Jan. 13, 1768).

from Montesquieu with what he had beaten out independently for himself? Is the one element brought into organic unity with the other? or are they forced together at nothing better than the arbitrary *fiat* of the author?

Upon the abstract character of the opening chapters there is no need to insist further. For good or for evil, it has been felt by all readers from the first moment of publication[1]. The 'total surrender' of the individual is expressly said to be the first condition of the rational State. And that surrender is to be made not to any one man, or body of men, but to the community as a whole. The 'annihilation' of the individual and the sovereignty of the people—these are the two principles upon which all States, worthy of the name, are bound to rest. And the smallest departure from either of them is enough, in right if not in fact, to dissolve any community into its primitive atoms. If this line of reasoning is not abstract, it is nothing.

With the second Book, however, a change appears to come over the spirit of the treatise. In particular, we are met by two arguments which seem to tell in the opposite direction. These are, firstly, the argument which restores to the individual some at least of the independence which he had originally laid down; and secondly, the argument which asserts that the form of polity, and with it the national ideal, of each State must be largely determined by considerations of soil, climate, character and surroundings; and which, in the case of hereditary monarchy at any rate, seems to admit a form of Government not easily to be reconciled with the sovereignty of the people. In both arguments, the ground of discussion is shifted from the abstract to the concrete. Both appear to admit qualifications which the sweeping assertions of the opening chapters would certainly not have led us to expect. And the question at once arises: Are these qualifications, is this change of ground, inconsistent with the principles originally adopted by the author? or do they mean no more than that he is now recognising facts which from the first were present to his mind, but which, in a summary statement of first principles, might legitimately be ignored?

---

[1] 'On parle beaucoup du livre de Rousseau qui doit servir de cinquième volume à son *Traité de l'Éducation*: c'est le *Contrat social*...on le dit extrêmement abstrait.' *Mémoires secrets* (Bachaumont), June 25, 1762. See also entry for Sept. 3, 1762. Quoted in *J.-J. Rousseau raconté par les Gazettes de son temps*. P.-P. Plan (Paris, 1912). Compare Intr. to *C. S.*; Vol. II. pp. 10—17.

It is manifest that the two cases must be taken separately. And that of the relation between the State and the individual—the question so recently before us—will most conveniently be taken first.

On this point, by any fair construction of the matter, Rousseau must be acquitted. A glance at the *Économie politique* will shew that the conception of the general will and of the Law—and it is upon them that the qualifications in question depend—had taken complete shape in his mind some six or seven years before the *Contrat social* was published[1]. It is hardly conceivable, therefore, that, when he wrote the opening pages of the later treatise, the limitations, already sketched in the earlier one, should not have been present to his thoughts. That, of course, does not exclude the possibility that his method of statement was misleading. He was a born stylist and controversialist. His first instinct was always to arrest the attention of the reader, at the very start, by a sweeping assertion. And it is only when that end is attained that he begins to define, to limit, to suggest necessary qualifications. The effect, at any rate on some minds, may have been different from what he intended. It is a defect inseparable from the method. For the moment, however, we are concerned with his intentions. And to any practised reader these are plain enough. The qualifications at issue were not an afterthought. They were intended from the first.

On the other point it is impossible to speak with the same confidence. And there are two positions against which the assault may be directed, the admission that Monarchy is a legitimate form of government; and the admission that Right, as it is understood in the *Contrat social*, is by no means always to be realised—that 'freedom is no fruit for all climates, nor within the reach of all nations.' The latter admission is by far the more damaging of the two.

The recognition of monarchy, when fairly considered, does not raise any serious difficulty. It would do so, no doubt, if it were true that monarchy is always and necessarily the same thing as despotism. But it is notorious that, even in Rousseau's day, that was far from being the case. Poland among elective, England among hereditary, monarchies were striking instances to the contrary. And in our own time, not only has the example of

---

[1] *Éc. pol.* pp. 242—4: especially the paragraph beginning 'Il ne s'ensuit pas pour cela que les délibérations publiques soient toujours équitables.'

England been widely followed; but England herself, while retaining monarchy, has imposed far stricter limits upon its powers than were in force when the *Contrat social* was written. Now this is just the point upon which Rousseau fastens. To him a limited monarchy is legitimate. It is only when absolute that he will have none of it. And the reason is plain. In the former case, it is not incompatible with the sovereignty of the people; in the latter, it manifestly is. That is the distinction which his principles compelled him to draw; and that is the distinction which he draws in fact.

It may be objected that, in his day, all forms of monarchy, limited as well as absolute, were hostile to the popular sovereignty, as interpreted in the *Contrat social*, and that he ought therefore to have rejected them all. And it is to be wished that he had drawn more distinctions, and drawn them more carefully, than he does. But there are two things to be borne in mind. The first is that, treating as he was of first principles, he was bound to take account not only of what was, but what might be. And the experience of later times has shewn—the experience of the past had perhaps shewn already—that it is not impossible for monarchy to go hand in hand with the fullest measure of popular sovereignty. The second is that, with every motive for measuring his words, he makes no attempt to conceal his conviction that, as a matter of fact, monarchy does almost invariably end in despotism, and is therefore, even when apparently harmless, to be viewed with suspicion and mislike. 'All kings,' he writes, 'desire to be absolute[1]'; and when they are so, we know how he would desire to deal with them. From all this it is clear that, if he admits monarchy among the legitimate forms of government, he does so with reluctance; and that, in his heart, he regards it with suspicion, if not with contempt. He does not, and cannot, condemn the principle in itself. But he believes the use of it to be hardly separable from the abuse. Motives both of prudence and honour made it hard for him to speak out. But, if we construe his words fairly, there is little inconsistency in the letter, and none at all in the spirit.

The other line of attack is far more difficult to meet. In the

[1] *C. S.* III. vi. Compare the following: 'Toute l'occupation des rois, ou de ceux qu'ils chargent de leurs fonctions, se rapporte à deux seuls objets: étendre leur domination au dehors, et la rendre plus absolue au dedans.' *Jugement sur la paix perpétuelle*; below, p. 389. See also *L'état de guerre*; below, pp. 302—4.

opening chapters of the treatise there is no hint but that a 'free' government—that is a government based on the Social Contract—is open to all. Indeed, Rousseau expressly says that 'the terms of the Contract, though they may never have been formulated in so many words, are everywhere the same and everywhere tacitly admitted and recognised,' until the moment when they are broken, and chaos comes again. After this sweeping announcement, who would expect to hear that there are large tracts of the earth in which monarchy—which, in at least one passage, he contrasts with the 'free' forms of government[1]—is virtually a necessity? and others, still larger, in which no decent form of government—no form which, on the most liberal construction, can be squared with the Social Contract—is possible at all[2]?

In this case, the contradiction lies not only in the words, but in the thought. The former might, with some management, be explained away. The latter is inherent in the whole tenor of the argument. The earlier passage suggests, if it does not directly state, that the Contract is available always, everywhere and for all. Its terms are, in fact, 'dictated by the very nature of the case; and the smallest departure from them is enough to make the whole act null and void.' If this does not mean that it is within the power of all men, under all circumstances, to enter into the Contract, and that it is their duty to do so, it must be confessed that the author has not written with his usual clearness. It is certainly the sense which the words naturally bear; it is the sense which they have borne to the vast majority of his readers. And if this be the correct interpretation, how is it possible, at a later stage of the argument, to confine the benefits of the Contract to a small minority of mankind? to that part of it which is fortunate enough to live within the temperate zone, and lucky enough to have formed itself into communities of such a size that monarchy, with all its attendant evils, is not a necessity? In the first statement of his argument, Rousseau lays down sweeping principles which, on any natural construction, claim to be of universal application. In the sequel, if a phrase may be taken from Burke, he is driven to 'limit logic by despotism': the

[1] 'Plus on y réfléchit, plus on trouve en ceci de différence entre les États libres et les monarchiques.' *C. S.* III. viii. Compare *Éc. pol.* pp. 243—5.

[2] 'Les lieux ingrats et stériles...doivent rester incultes et déserts, ou seulement peuplés de sauvages: les lieux où le travail des hommes ne rend exactement que le nécessaire doivent être habités par des peuples barbares: toute *politie* y serait impossible.' *C. S.* III. viii.

despotism of outward circumstance and historical fatality. It is hard to see how the contradiction can be denied.

The truth is that in the theory of Rousseau, as his opponents have always seen, there is a hard core of abstraction which rebels against all qualifications, and stiffens itself against the touch of all outward circumstance and condition. It was under an abstract form—the form bequeathed to him by Hobbes and Locke—that the problems of political philosophy first presented themselves to his mind. And when, at a later period, he was led by Montesquieu to see that, in actual practice, there is no principle which is not modified by circumstances, the abstract bent had already been given; the unbending ply was already taken; and the new experience could never fit itself perfectly into the rigid framework which he had built up from the beginning.

The result is one of the strangest upon record. The two strands of thought, the abstract and the concrete, lie side by side in his mind, for ever crossing each other, yet never completely interwoven; each held with intense conviction, but each held in entire independence of the other. At one moment he is more abstract than Locke or Plato; at the next he is as ready to yield to circumstances as Montesquieu or Burke. At one moment he holds that all men are equal and, in respect of capacity for freedom, that all men are alike. At the next he assures us that there is no such thing as equality between one group of men and another; and that the differences are due not to their own doing, but to the tyranny of soil and climate and of the conditions, economic or political, which spring partly from these physical causes, partly from the inherited traditions of the past. He follows the one line of thought no less ardently than the other. He betrays not the smallest suspicion that the one runs counter to the other.

In the earlier chapters of the *Contrat social*, it is clear that the more abstract vein was that which lay uppermost in his mind. In the fierce ring of the opening sentences, who has not heard a call to battle, and a call which he hoped would reach every corner of the earth? And who can suppose that, when he put them there, he was not conscious of the thrill they were to send through every heart, of the answering shout they were to awaken from one nation after another? Here, at any rate, is no paltering with soil and climate, no balancing of circumstances, no quailing before the traditions of the past, no misgiving that one nation may be less born for freedom than another. The whole world is summoned to throw off its chains, to regain the heritage it had lost, to reassert the rights which no time can destroy and which, when boldly asserted, no force is able to withhold.

Pass on a few years—pass on even a few pages—and the relations are reversed. In the latter part of the *Contrat social*, still more in the *Lettres de la Montagne* and the *Gouvernement de Pologne*, the abstract plea has fallen into the background; a cautious, almost a timid, regard for national prejudice and historical tradition has taken its place; and the freedom for which Rousseau pleads is no longer a right common to all men, but a right strictly limited by time and place, by the circumstances of the present, by the habits and precedents formed under the pressure of a thousand accidents during the forgotten struggles of the past. In one word, it is a freedom specially calculated for Geneva, for Corsica, for Poland. It is no longer a freedom to be sought and won by all nations, by the united efforts of mankind.

More than that. Let it be proved that freedom, even in this limited form, is to be won only at the cost of civil conflict, and Rousseau will have none of it. No bondage, he now holds, however galling, can justify man in shedding one drop of his brother's blood. 'Regain your freedom, if you can,' he writes to the citizens of Geneva, 'but choose slavery before parricide. Shed the blood of the enemy, if need be, whatever your repugnance. But let that of your fellow citizens be sacred[1].' And a yet more staggering instance of the change which had come over him is to be found in the *Gouvernement de Pologne*, where he is willing to accept even serfdom, at least for the moment, as a hateful necessity inflicted by the dead hand of the past.

The change of spirit is, no doubt, partly due to a change of scope and purpose. The *Contrat social*—yet even there, as we have seen, the change makes itself strongly felt—is intended to deal with none but the general principles of the subject. It is, as the title tells us, a treatise on the *Principles of political Right*. And in the first draft, he apologises for introducing considerations of circumstance, on the express ground that matters of expediency have, strictly speaking, no place in an exposition of Right[2]. The

[1] 'Genevois, s'il se peut, redevenez libres; mais soyez plutôt esclaves que parricides. Versez en gémissant le sang ennemi, s'il est nécessaire, jamais celui de vos concitoyens.' *Lettres de la Montagne*, VIII. (MS. Neuchâtel, 7840, p. 45). It is fair to say that this, together with the striking passage immediately preceding it, was suppressed in the published version. See Vol. II. p. 245.

[2] 'Quoique je traite ici du droit et non des convenances, je ne puis m'empêcher de jeter en passant quelques coups d'œil sur celles qui sont

later works, on the other hand, are manifestly concerned with the affairs of particular States at a particular crisis of their history. And a difference of spirit and outlook was accordingly inevitable. But the differences which actually meet us go far deeper than this. They amount to nothing short of contradiction; and that, on those questions of principle and method which lie at the root of the whole matter. And we are driven to ask ourselves: Is this due to pure levity and infirmity of purpose? or is it because the mind of the author had, in the interval, gone through a great change?

The latter is the more charitable explanation, and it is also the more probable. The mind of Rousseau worked slowly. And with such minds, new ideas may be recognised long before they are fully accepted and taken to heart. At the first glance he had seen the importance, as well as the novelty, of the methods and principles of Montesquieu. But it took years of brooding before he made them thoroughly his own. And even then, it is doubtful whether they would have borne fruit, save for the call of outward circumstance and the demands made on him by the patriots of Geneva, Corsica and Poland. Thanks to this, he found himself suddenly summoned to test his theory by practice. And he had to make up his mind which of the two conflicting elements of that theory was the more helpful for his purpose. What his conclusion was, may be plainly gathered from the result. The abstract principles of the earlier part of the *Contrat social* are left entirely on one side. It is to the concrete principles and the historical methods of the latter part—in other words, to the methods and principles of Montesquieu—that he instinctively has recourse. The relative proportions of the two elements are now exactly reversed. What in the earlier treatise was all-important has now almost faded out of sight. What in the earlier treatise appears as little more than an afterthought has become the guiding principle of the whole. The ideas implanted in the first instance by Montesquieu are now almost more real to Rousseau than those

indispensables dans toute bonne institution.' Geneva MS. II. iii. (*Du peuple à instituer*). It will be observed that these words form the opening to the chapter in which considerations of expediency are for the first time definitely introduced. They are immediately followed by the words 'Comme avant d'élever un édifice' etc., quoted at the beginning of this section. It is fair to bear this in mind, in considering the abruptness of the transition from considerations of Right to those of expediency. This is, doubtless, partly due to the fact that the latter train of thought is properly no part of Rousseau's subject. It belonged rather to the *Institutions politiques* than to the *Contrat social*.

he had worked out for himself. But, in becoming his own, they have ceased to be what they were in the soil from which they were transplanted. They have none of the fatalism, none of that tendency to bow to the accomplished fact, which may be traced fitfully in Montesquieu, and persistently in most of his disciples. They do not exclude a faith in the power of man—under strict limitations, doubtless—to shake off the chains which have been forged for him by his past. For here too, as in the *Contrat social*, is a call to freedom. And the voice which utters the call, though cast in a lower key than formerly, is still unmistakably the voice not of Montesquieu, but of Rousseau.

Thus the political work of Rousseau, when taken as a whole, presents an unbroken movement from one position almost to its opposite. He starts as the prophet of freedom, in the most abstract sense conceivable. His ideal, in the second *Discourse*, is a state of things in which each individual is absolutely independent of the rest. And that ideal finds a ringing echo in the opening sentences of the treatise which marks the next stage of his advance. It is, however, no more than an echo. And, save for those opening sentences, the *Contrat social* represents a very different—and assuredly a less abstract, as well as a less individualist—ideal. Here freedom is no longer conceived as the independence of the individual. It is rather to be sought in his total surrender to the service of the State. It involves therefore a close network of concrete duties, a tissue of definite relations to other individuals and to the whole. Yet, here too, the abstract character of the conception is not to be mistaken. The individual is emptied, so far as may be, of all that gives him individuality. And, so far at least as the State is concerned, all individuals are equal, and all are assumed to be alike. More than that, each State is built on the exact model of every other State. All are founded on the same rigid principle, and the smallest deviation from that principle is fatal to their claims.

Such is the view presented in the main body of the *Contrat social*: the view which, at the time of publication, seems to have been dominant in the author's mind. Side by side, however, with that view—yet, for the moment, manifestly subordinated to it—is to be found the different and far more concrete conception, derived by Rousseau, as by all subsequent thinkers, from *Esprit des lois*. According to this view, the determining principle of the State is to be sought rather from without than from within; rather in external circumstances than in the will of men resolved at all costs to be free. It springs from conditions of soil and climate; from the economic needs and the national character, which in the main are their result. Thus, so far from identity of political type, we have endless variety; a variety very far from exhausted by the familiar division of monarchy, aristocracy and democracy.

In the *Contrat social*, little or no attempt is made to reconcile these different, if not opposite, conceptions. Nor is there any formal reconciliation, in the practical writings which followed. Yet, silent though it is, the change of tone and temper is complete. The abstract principles of the speculative treatise have dropped out of sight, and almost out of mind. Their place is taken by an appeal to outward circumstance and historical precedent, which might have come from Montesquieu or Burke. The abstract individualism of the second *Discourse*, the abstract collectivism of the *Contrat social*, are alike forgotten. We are in a world of concrete conditions, of interwoven relations, in which neither of them could find place. The long journey is at last ended. And Rousseau now stands at the opposite point of the compass from that at which he started.

But still the question forces itself upon us: Is there, then, no means of harmonising the two strains that we hear by turns in the *Contrat social*? Is it impossible for the reader to find the link, the absence of which the writer himself seems never to have discovered? A vague answer is all that can be expected in such cases, and it is all that will be offered.

The dominant principle of the *Contrat social* is the sovereignty of the people; the conviction that no Government which is not founded upon that principle can be either legitimate or 'free.' On the other hand, there are not a few passages in which Rousseau argues, apparently with no less conviction, that many communities—all, in fact, whose lot is not cast in the temperate zone—are incapable of realising that ideal; and consequently that the government of most nations can be neither legitimate nor free. The ideal, so far from being open to all alike, is to be attained by none but the favoured few. It is not the ideal, but an iron law of circumstance—physical, economic, historical—that forms the true principle of the State.

The resemblance between the latter doctrine and that of Montesquieu is too plain to be mistaken. It is avowed again and again by Rousseau himself. When closely examined, however, it is found to be a resemblance with a difference. And this is still more true of the occasional writings—those on Geneva, Corsica and Poland—than of the *Contrat social* itself. For here the author has passed from the bare statement of the doctrine to its practical application; and in so doing, he has restored some measure of the ideal element which, in the first instance, he had at any rate appeared to rule out. It is by following this vein of thought that we are most likely to discover that link between conflicting theories which Rousseau himself was too hasty, or too negligent, to seek.

The leading principle in all these occasional pieces is the necessity of reckoning with given circumstances and conditions; the conviction that, at every step, the life of the community is largely, if not wholly, determined by the outward needs of the present and the more inward, but no less urgent, traditions inherited from the past. And the zeal with which, in each case, Rousseau sets himself to master the intricate conditions of the problem is surprising in itself, still more surprising when we consider that all his instincts must have lain the other way. In the case of Geneva, the obstacles from without were comparatively small. The past history of the city had long been familiar to him[1]. The spirit of its life had entered into his very soul. Where his own knowledge was at fault, a score of friends were at hand to correct or guide him. But with Corsica and Poland it was another matter. There he had no previous knowledge; the information at his disposal was broken and uncertain; and he had no friend to help him in case of need. The difficulties of the task might well have staggered him. But, in the work on Poland at any rate, he triumphed over them all.

Compare it with Burke's writings on the affairs of France. The author of the *Reflections* started with everything in his favour. His genius lay in the patient unravelling of detail. His life had been one long discipline in the use of the historical method. The main facts of the case were accessible to all the world; and where there was any reasonable doubt, further information

---

[1] One of his Commonplace Books in the Library of Neuchâtel (MS. 7843) contains a History of Geneva written, or compiled, by himself (pp. 30—66). It is not dated. But it occurs immediately before some Maxims for *Émile*, which may have been written between 1758 and 1761, but *may* be as late as 1767. The rough draft of the opening passage of the sequel of *Émile*—'J'étais libre, j'étais heureux, O mon maître' (probably after 1762)—a letter about *La nouvelle Héloïse* (1761) and a letter about Voltaire's pamphlet, *Sentiment des citoyens* (1764), are the other chief pieces in the volume. It was probably written in connection with the *Lettres de la Montagne*.

might have been readily obtained. All these advantages, however, were thrown wantonly away. He made no effort to form an unbiassed judgment. He deliberately surrendered himself to prejudice and passion. And though his work in this field is a masterpiece of speculative genius, yet in practical insight, in breadth and wisdom, in power of marshalling and interpreting the facts of the case before him—in all that, on his own showing, is necessary to a sound judgment of political affairs—he is immeasurably inferior to the man of whom he never speaks but with scorn and loathing: to the despised theorist, the metaphysical 'madman,' of Geneva.

This, then, is the characteristic mark of the last group of Rousseau's writings: a patient use of the historical method, a determination to master all the known facts of the case, to bolt them to the bran, to interpret them in the light not of any preconceived theory, but of expediency and practical possibility. Is, then, the historical method, pure and simple, a sufficient guide to us in such matters? Is it true that the circumstances, when set in the dry light of reason, are enough to speak for themselves? It is clear that Rousseau at least did not think so. It is doubtful whether any man, who knew what he was doing, has ever thought so. An ideal of some kind—it may be conservative, it may be liberal—must be there to guide the enquirer from the first. A vital principle of some sort must be brought to bear, before the circumstances will speak. And it is to the lasting credit of Rousseau that, with all his fidelity to the facts, he never shrinks from acting upon this conviction; that he always views the facts in the light of an ideal; and that his ideal is always to secure the utmost pitch of liberty, the highest degree of national energy, that the circumstances will admit. The outward obstacles may be strong; the national spirit, crushed by a vicious tradition, may to all appearance be lamentably weak. But he is always on the watch for any sign of yielding in the one, always ready to catch any spark of life that may linger in the other. In the last resort, the latter is the one thing needful. There must be some token that in promise and potency, if not in actual energy, the corporate spirit, the 'communal self,' is there and is capable of development; that the members of the community feel themselves, however dimly, to be united in one body, and have the will to surrender their private interests for the benefit of the whole. If such tokens be present, Rousseau is willing to sacrifice all else. He is ready to lay aside his most cherished convictions. He is prepared to put up, at least for the moment, with serfdom, or with the oligarchy of privilege which the *Contrat social* had condemned; to waive, at least for the moment, doctrines so fundamental as the right of personal freedom, or the sovereignty of the people.

Thus at every turn the one tendency is controlled and modified by the other. If Rousseau bows to circumstances, it is only in pursuit of an ideal which no circumstances can reveal. If he seeks to realise that ideal, it is only through the means which circumstances—the circumstances of the given time and the given place—seem to put into his hand. The two strands of thought, which in the *Contrat social* are held jealously apart, are now woven, sometimes more and sometimes less completely, into one. And, in the process, each has lost something of the abstract, unbending quality which it bore in the earlier and more speculative treatise. The idea of an unvarying Right—the same always, everywhere and for all—is now definitely abandoned. On the other hand, the conception of an iron law of circumstance, overriding the will of man and setting impassable barriers to his action, has been manifestly softened. The gulf which the *Contrat social* had fixed between the two theories is now narrowed, if not actually bridged. And if the author himself does not attempt to pass it, he has at least put his readers in a position to make the passage in his name.

But, if this be a correct account of the matter, it is clear that the whole argument of the *Contrat social* has been silently recast. And before leaving the subject, it will be well to shew, as Rousseau himself had neither the will nor perhaps the power to do, how much of the original doctrine survives in the final form of his theory, and how much has been silently suppressed.

The crucial fact in the writings before us is the tacit abandonment of the abstract idea of Right. And when this, the corner stone, is withdrawn, the whole theory of the State, as built up in the *Contrat social*, is shaken to its base. To the author of the *Gouvernement de Pologne*, the perfect State, the 'pattern laid up in the heavens,' is still doubtless what it was in the more sanguine days when the *Contrat social* was written. The total surrender of the individual, the replacement of the personal by the corporate self, the corresponding right of every individual to an equal share in the government of the whole—there is nothing to shew that he had departed by one step from this ideal. But it is now no more than an ideal: an ideal which may and ought to 'regulate' or inspire action, but which is no longer imposed on all men, as an article of the faith. In the *Contrat social* it was an absolute standard, the infallible test of the legitimacy, or illegitimacy, of any State. In the later writings it has become merely a counsel of perfection: a model which all States will do well to keep in view, but to which few, if any, can be expected fully to attain. In the *Contrat social*, all that fail to conform to it are cast into outer darkness; they are branded as bastard growths which nothing can redeem. In the later writings, no such ban is passed upon them. So long as any sign of life can be traced in them, so long as any spring of energy remains to them, Rousseau is always ready to welcome them with encouragement and hope.

More than that. If the first efforts at reform are feeble and imperfect, he still has faith that the future may have better things in store. If he consents to tolerate serfdom, it is because he trusts that, at the first opening, it will be swept contemptuously away. If he puts education in the forefront of political duties, it is because he sees in the young the sole hope of the ultimate regeneration of the State. On the strength of such scattered hints, we might even be tempted to detect in his latest writings what none would claim for any of the earlier treatises: the first faint beginnings—at the highest estimate, it is impossible to go further than this—of a belief in progress. If that were indeed the case, there could be no stronger proof of the change which, as we know on other grounds, had come over the whole spirit of his creed.

And if we ask what is the principle to which this change of outlook may be traced, the answer comes at once. It is the principle which Montesquieu first threw upon the world; the conviction that the State is a natural, and largely unconscious, product; that not ideas, but circumstances, are the dominant factor in its growth. Of the writings of Rousseau, the *Contrat social* is the earliest in which this principle appears; and, as we have seen, with no very fortunate result. It is cast into the midst of an argument which, both in form and tenor, is nothing if not abstract and exclusive. And no attempt is made to remove, or even soften, the discord which inevitably results. The two principles are left to fight it out as best they may; and the more abstract of the two, lying as it does at the root of the whole treatise, naturally prevails.

In the years that followed, the balance was silently reversed. The abstract principle, the abstract method, of the *Contrat social* fade swiftly into the background. The concrete principle, the concrete method, of Montesquieu insensibly take their place. Yet the ideal which inspired the *Contrat social*, the ideal of a State self-governed and self-determined, is never wholly cast aside. It is no longer an ideal which is to be conquered in defiance of circumstances. It has become an ideal which is to be sought only through a given train of circumstances, to be attained only in so far as those circumstances will permit. The *Contrat social* may admit the principle of Montesquieu in words. But the main argument, rigid and unyielding, remains virtually untouched. The later writings go far to reverse the process. It is now the principle of Montesquieu that forms the groundwork of Rousseau's argument. His own principle, the principle of the *Contrat social*, is admitted only when he has bent and bowed it to a yoke which, as he first conceived it, it was never intended to endure.

Yet who will deny that the final form of the theory, as it may be pieced together from its practical application, marks a signal advance not only upon the *Social Contract*, but upon the *Spirit of the Laws*? And who will not regret that, by the time the new light dawned upon him, Rousseau had bade farewell to philosophy, and that the ripest fruits of his reflection were consequently never cast into speculative form? A new *Contrat social*, a *Contrat social* revised in the light of the *Gouvernement de Pologne*, would have been one of the most curious and instructive books on record[1]: more curious than the last Books of the *Confessions*, which were never written; more instructive than the *Institutions politiques*, which was ruthlessly destroyed. As it is, the *Contrat social* is left as the one systematic statement of Rousseau's political philosophy. And it is by the *Contrat social* that, in the main, he will inevitably be judged.

VI

CONTRAT SOCIAL. SOME DETACHED PROBLEMS

It remains only to return upon a few points which, standing apart from the main argument of the *Contrat social*, have hitherto been passed over. Three only of these will need to be considered: the chapter on the Civil Religion, the references to Federalism, and the position which Rousseau holds towards economic Socialism. The last subject will naturally lead to the Collectivism which lies at the core of the two capital treatises, the *Contrat social* and the *Économie politique*; and so, in a concluding section, to a general estimate of Rousseau's work in political philosophy, as a whole.

[1] 'C'est un livre à refaire,' he said himself of the *Contrat social*. See Dussaulx, *De mes rapports avec J.-J. Rousseau*, p. 102 (Paris, 1798).

(a) *The Civil Religion.*

The chapter on the Civil Religion formed no part of the original scheme of the *Contrat social*. It was an afterthought, added after the completion of the first draft and shortly before the second and final draft was sent to the press[1]. The rough version of it, which however was considerably altered before publication, is to be found scribbled on blank pages of the Geneva Manuscript[2]; and from the haste with which it is written, we can see that Rousseau was working under the spur of a first, fevered inspiration. The general conclusions, however, were reached much earlier in his life. They appear in the well-known letter which he wrote to Voltaire, after reading his poem on the Earthquake of Lisbon (Aug. 18, 1756)[3]. We may infer therefore that the closing chapter of the *Contrat social*, so far from being a caprice of the moment, represents, at least in sum and substance, the settled opinions of the author. The argument is as follows.

No State can exist without some form of religion; and it is of the last importance that the form adopted shall be both true in itself, and such as will serve the legitimate purposes of the State. The former test is enough to bar out Paganism; the latter is fatal to Catholicism, as well perhaps as to some varieties of Protestantism. For Paganism, in spite of its civic virtues, is not only demonstrably false; it also fans the flames of racial hatreds and barbarities. Catholicism, on the other hand, besides laying immoderate stress on the unessentials of belief, inevitably sets the believer at discord with the citizen, the Church at war with the State. This alone is enough to condemn it. 'To offer further proofs of its badness would be mere waste of time.'

The only other form of religion with which there is any need to reckon is Christianity—the Christianity not of the Churches, but of the Gospel, 'which is a very different thing.' At first sight, this may seem to satisfy both the tests which it is our duty to apply. It is intellectually true; it is also morally ennobling. How then can it fail to make better citizens, as well as better men? This, however, is just where Christianity fails. Its kingdom is not of this world, and for that very reason it can do nothing to

---

[1] 'Vous le trouvez (*le Contrat social*) petit pour un volume; cependant il est copié sur le brouillon que vous avez jugé en faire un, et même le chapitre sur la religion y a été ajouté depuis.' Letter to Rey of Dec. 23, 1761 (Bosscha, p. 126).

[2] Geneva MS., v° of pp. 46—51.   [3] See Vol. II. pp. 163—5.

strengthen the bonds that bind the individual to the State. Indeed, so far from strengthening, it positively weakens them. 'So far from binding the heart of the citizen to the State, it weans him from this, as from all other earthly ends.' If Paganism is the religion of the citizen and Catholicism that of the priest, Christianity is the religion of the individual soul; and nothing more hostile to the spirit of citizenship can easily be conceived. The very perfection of the Christian ideal is fatal to the State.

So far, our results are purely negative. Paganism, if favourable to intensity of civic life, is intellectually false and, in some points, morally degrading. Christianity, true and noble in itself, is not only no support to the civic spirit but, in essence and principle, violently opposed to it. It follows that neither of them can offer that of which we are in search. The problem is, therefore, to find a form of religion which shall exclude the drawbacks and embrace the merits of both; which shall unite the truth and nobility of Christianity with the civic fervour, the ardent patriotism, of the purer forms of Paganism. This is the end to which the rest of Rousseau's argument is avowedly directed.

At the first glance, the problem might well be thought insoluble. It is only when we recall the principles laid down in the more speculative part of the *Contrat social* that light begins to dawn. The State, it was there argued, has a right to demand of the individual everything that can serve its needs, but nothing beyond. Now that every citizen should have a religion which 'makes him love his duties' towards his neighbour and the community, is essential to the State. So far therefore as it is concerned with such duties, religion may justly be demanded of every citizen by the State. But in so far as religion deals with duties towards God, with the things of the other world—and the purely dogmatic, or theological, side of it clearly falls under that head—the State, from the nature of the case, has no interest in the matter, and consequently no right to interfere. With this clue in our hand, it is not impossible that the labyrinth may be threaded.

Christianity, as we have seen, is the religion of the individual. As a motive to the performance of individual duties—and even that is a matter in which the State is profoundly interested—it leaves nothing to be desired. But the duties of the citizen— and to the State that is a point of yet greater importance— lie beyond its ken. It regards them with indifference, not to say hostility. That being so, the course of the State is clear. Leave individual duties to the conscience of the individual and the care of the Churches. Let the State touch them only when the citizen has laid himself open to public penalties by their breach. Leave dogma to take care of itself. What a man affirms, or denies, in that region is no business but his own. But as to public duties, the State is in a very different position. It is essential to her that they shall be discharged, and discharged not only with strictness, but with zeal. She has therefore the right to demand that every citizen shall acknowledge them; the right to impose the only sanction effective for that purpose, the sanction of religion.

'There is, then, a profession of purely civic faith, the articles of which must be fixed by the sovereign. These must be regarded not strictly as dogmas of religion, but as sentiments of sociability, without which it is impossible for a man to be either a good citizen, or a loyal subject. It is true that no man can be compelled to believe them. But if he does not, he may be banished from the State: banished, not as irreligious, but as unsociable; as incapable of loving the Law or justice with sincerity and, in case of need, of sacrificing his life to his duty. Again, if, after publicly accepting these dogmas, he behaves as though he did not believe them, let him be punished with death. He has committed the most heinous of all crimes : he has lied in the face of the Law.

'The dogmas of the civil religion should be few and simple.... The existence of a God of power, reason, goodness and loving providence; the life to come, the happiness of the just and punishment of the wicked; the sanctity of the Social Contract and of the Law—such are the dogmas to be affirmed. As for the dogmas to be repudiated, I limit them to a single one—intolerance. It brings us back to the religions which we have already barred out....Now that the national and exclusive religions (Paganism and Judaism) have had their day, we are bound to tolerate all those which are tolerant themselves, in so far as their dogmas contain nothing contrary to the duties of the citizen. But whoever dares to say "Outside of the Church, none can be saved" ought to be driven out of the State; unless, indeed, the State *is* the Church, and the Pontiff the chief magistrate[1].'

Such is the doctrine which brought a thousand troubles on Rousseau in his life, and has never ceased to weigh upon his memory in death. The moral objections which it provokes are glaring. They may be summed up in one word—Persecution. A religious test is imposed on all members of the State. Those

[1] *C. S.* IV. viii.

who fail to satisfy it are to be driven out or, under certain circumstances, to be punished with death[1]. And the test is so framed as to strike equally at two opposite classes: atheists or agnostics, on the one hand; bigoted Catholics, upon the other. Can we wonder that both attacks should have been bitterly resented? Is it surprising that an age which was just beginning to learn the lesson of tolerance should have risen against this sudden revival of intolerance? that the persecutions, which had seemed odious in the Church, should have been none the more welcome when they were recommended in the name of the State? At the moment when Rousseau wrote, the tide of opinion was already beginning to turn against persecution in any form, political, intellectual, or religious. In the interval between his day and ours, it has set still more decisively in the same direction. To accept this has now, we may hope, become part of the moral heritage of mankind. It is grievous to think that a man like Rousseau should have done his utmost to fight against the light, to drive the world back into the darkness from which it was at last struggling to escape.

But, grave as are the moral objections to his argument, there are other objections which it is impossible to overlook. Let us grant that religion is as necessary to the welfare, to the very existence, of the State as Rousseau believes. Let us grant, if only for the sake of argument, that it is just for the State to impose a religious test upon its members. Admit both propositions: and is there the smallest proof that the test will do anything to secure the end for which it is imposed? is Rousseau one step nearer to the goal which he desires to attain? There are two unanswerable reasons which compel us to deny it.

In the first place, tests of the kind proposed are—and Rousseau ought to have known that they are—a premium on hypocrisy[2]. And the very reason he assigns for imposing them—that the atheist, having rejected the only possible sanction of duty, must of necessity be without the sense of duty—is in reality the strongest reason for renouncing them altogether. It is obvious that the man who has no sense of duty will not scruple to commit perjury. And to impose a test on such a man is no better than a farce.

[1] That Rousseau, when it came to the point, would have shrunk from carrying out his own precept, is shewn by the following: 'Si j'étais magistrat, et que la Loi portât peine de mort contre les athées, je commencerais par faire brûler comme tel quiconque en viendrait dénoncer un autre.' *Nouvelle Héloïse*, v., Lettre v. (Note); *Œuvres*, IV. p. 413.

[2] Compare what Spinoza says about the danger of *assentatio*: *Tract. theologico-pol.* xx. 36—7.

It is true that Rousseau meets this objection by a second test still more odious than the first: by the provision that 'whoever, having accepted the dogmas of the civil religion, behaves afterwards as if he did not believe them, shall be punishable with death.' This doubtless saves his intellectual consistency; but only at the cost of plunging him in a moral enormity, which is infinitely worse. Accept this solution, and we have accepted a principle worthy of the Inquisition at its height: a principle which would substitute rumour for evidence, vague suspicion for proved fact, and turn every Court of Justice into a whispering gallery of calumny and intrigue. And this from the man who claimed, and not altogether without reason, to be exceptionally tolerant: 'the only tolerant man I ever knew[1].'

The second objection cuts even deeper than the first. What Rousseau professes to seek in the civil religion is a living faith, a faith that shall issue not in words, but in deeds. Anything short of that, for his purposes, is nothing. Now that is just what no test can ever provide. Hypocrisy apart, the utmost a test can prove is that certain beliefs are accepted by the intellect. It can never shew that they are also welcomed by the heart; still less, that they are in the smallest degree likely to work themselves out into the life. And the last is the one thing needful. If that be lost, nothing that is worth having can possibly be won. It was not the least of Rousseau's services to remind the world that religion is nothing, if not a thing of the spirit and the heart. This was the truth that he braved all to proclaim to others. This was the faith in which his own soul found refuge, when all earthly hope had been torn from his grasp. And it is a bitter irony that the man whose life was one long witness to the spiritual nature of religion should have stooped for one moment to treat it as a matter of police. Yet this, and nothing else, is the conclusion to which the whole argument of the *Civil Religion* inevitably leads.

But, if a religious test has no positive value, it may be argued —and Rousseau himself argues—that it has a negative one: that at least it will serve to exclude avowed atheists, to save the State from harbouring a band of men on whose sense of duty no reliance can be placed. It may be that this plea presents more difficulty

---

[1] 'Hors moi, je n'ai vu que lui seul (Altuna) de tolérant depuis que j'existe.' *Confessions*, Liv. VII; *Œuvres*, VIII. p. 232. 'Je suis tolérant par principe, et je ne connais de vrai tolérant que moi.' Cancelled close of *Lettres de la Montagne*, V. See Vol. II. Appendix I. The last sentence occurs also in *Dialogue* II.; *Œuvres*, IX. p. 200.

than the others. But there are three grounds on which it must be set unflinchingly aside.

Firstly, whatever may be the philosophy of the matter and whether it be true, or no, that religion is the ultimate sanction of moral duty, there can be no doubt that some of the justest and most public-spirited men who ever lived have been atheists or agnostics. The author of the *Nouvelle Héloïse* should have been the last man to dispute this. And if that be the case, the test proclaims itself at once as an unjust test; a test which acts purely at haphazard; a test which, while professing to operate on moral grounds, may admit those who are morally worthless, and exclude those who are morally beyond reproach[1]. All that it can do is to bar out the conscientious atheist—which to the creator of Wolmar should hardly have seemed a gain[2]—and to let in those of less scrupulous conscience: which, if there is to be any discrimination at all in such matters, must surely be a loss.

Secondly, the conscience of mankind has come, and justly come, to be more and more against the imposition of penalties—let alone the death penalty—upon speculative opinion or belief. And the reason is plain; it is insisted upon elsewhere by Rousseau himself[3]. What I believe, or do not believe, is a matter not of the will, but of the intellect or of instinct. In either case, it is a matter entirely beyond my own control. On no theory of justice can it be a proper matter for punishment. And the man who makes it so throws himself violently against the barriers which the thought of the best men, Rousseau himself included, and the labour of many generations have built up.

Lastly, unless thought and speech be left absolutely unshackled, there can be no such thing as progress. And the man who persecutes for opinion is not only unjust to his victim, but a declared enemy to the freedom without which there can be no advance in vital knowledge and in truth. Rousseau himself spoke scornfully of science and philosophy. He had little or no belief in progress. But his deeds belied his words. Kant excepted, he

[1] Compare Spinoza, *Tract. theologico-pol.* xx. 30 : 'Sequitur leges quae de opinionibus conduntur non scelestos, sed ingenuos respicere, nec ad malignos coercendum, sed potius ad honestos irritandum condi, nec sine magno imperii periculo defendi posse.'

[2] The character of Wolmar was avowedly, at least in part, a portrait of d'Holbach, author of the *Système de la Nature* and perhaps the most extreme of the 'philosophers,' whom Rousseau sometimes calls 'les holbachiens'; *e.g.* letter to Saint-Germain of Feb. 26, 1770; *Œuvres*, xii. p. 193.

[3] See *Émile* and *Lettres de la Montagne*, i.

was richer in speculative ideas than any man of his century. And he gave an impulse to progress which, after a century and a half, has not yet spent its force. He himself would have received short shrift at the hands either of Rome or of Geneva. The author of *Émile*, if once in their clutches, would certainly have found his way to the prison, and not impossibly to the scaffold. It is true that he would have suffered, not as an atheist, but as an 'enemy of the Faith.' But once admit persecution, it is impossible to fix the limit where it is to stop. His own fate, the storm of persecution that broke on him with the publication of *Émile* and the *Contrat social*, was one more warning against the admission of a principle so fatal, as well as so capricious, in its results.

The proscription of bigoted Catholics rests, it need hardly be said, on different grounds. A double charge is brought against them: that their intolerance makes it impossible for them to live at peace with their fellow-citizens, and that they defy the sovereignty of the State. In both charges there is—it is more charitable to say, there was—too much of truth. The judicial murder of Calas took place in the very year when the *Contrat social* was published[1]. And the whole history of the Civil Constitution of the Clergy—whether that series of measures was wisely planned or no—shews how exorbitant the claims of the Church are capable of becoming, as against the authority of the State. It is impossible, therefore, to deny that Rousseau had some ground for the harsh treatment which he is prepared to deal out to the more fanatical of the Catholics.

Yet here again there is the fatal objection that he imposes penalties not for acts, but for opinions. And if it has sometimes needed great forbearance in the more civilised States to keep terms with their Catholic members, it must be remembered that here, as always, clemency has in the long run been justified by its fruits; that the Catholics, when treated reasonably, have shewn themselves to be reasonable beings. All honour to the statesmen who, in this and other countries, were wise enough to face the real dangers of Emancipation, to sacrifice all other considerations to their sense of justice. Once again, it is sad to think that Rousseau should have done his best to fan the flames of religious enmity:

[1] March 9, 1762. This event had not happened when Rousseau wrote the chapter on *Civil Religion*. Still less, of course, the enactment of the Civil Constitution of the Clergy, and the clerical resistance to it (1790—2). I take these instances because they are well-known examples of the temper which Rousseau had in view.

that he, of all men, should have ranged himself, on grounds however plausible, with the hosts of darkness.

How was it, we ask, that he let himself be drawn into this quicksand of reaction? What was it that led him to accept conclusions so alien both to his native tolerance and to some at any rate of his most deeply cherished beliefs? The answer is not difficult to find. It is to be sought partly in speculative causes, partly in a historical tradition which, almost to his own day, had gone virtually unchallenged.

The speculative ground of his action is obvious enough. It was part of his mission to stem the tide of materialism, then running strong in the western parts of Europe. This was at the bottom of his feud with the philosophers. It was at the root also of his daring attempt to strip Christianity of all that was doubtful or irrational, and so reconcile religion with the proved facts of science and history. It was a heroic task. But, in this instance, he suffered the zeal of the Lord's house to consume him.

In this error he was probably confirmed by the authority of a long line of enlightened thinkers. When Milton wrote his inspired plea for liberty of thought and utterance, he was careful to exclude both Catholics and atheists from its scope[1]. Locke, with whose writings Rousseau was certainly familiar, followed the same course[2]. Even Spinoza, the real founder of modern biblical criticism and, in many ways, of modern beliefs about religious freedom, admits the right of the State to establish a religion and to enforce at least outward conformity upon its members[3]. Thus the very fathers of religious tolerance seemed to support Rousseau in his conclusions. And, though he was too sturdy a thinker to rest his plea on authority, it may well be that, consciously or unconsciously, he was influenced by authorities so imposing. That, however, can hardly be said to constitute an excuse. In his own lifetime, a new light had dawned upon the better minds. And it is the lasting service of Voltaire and the Encyclopedists to have

[1] 'I mean not tolerated popery and open superstition, which, as it extirpates all religious and civil supremacies, so itself should be extirpate....That also which is impious or evil either against faith or morals no law can possibly permit.' *Areopagitica*; Milton, *Prose Works*, p. 118 (ed. 1835).
[2] 'That Church can have no right to be tolerated which is constituted upon such a bottom that all those who enter into it do thereby *ipso facto* deliver themselves up to the protection and service of another Prince.' 'They are not at all to be tolerated who deny the being of God.' Locke, *Letters on Toleration*; *Works*, II. p. 251.
[3] *Tract. theologico-polit.* XIX. 21—27, XX. 11—17; *Tract. politicus*, III. 10.

shamed the world, at least in theory, out of its long bondage to bigotry and intolerance. In this enterprise, Rousseau ought to have stood shoulder to shoulder with his enemies and slanderers. But, both on speculative and personal grounds, they were the last men in the world from whom he was likely to take a lesson. He fought them at this, as at all other points. And on this point it was they who were in the right, and he who was in the wrong[1].

One matter only remains over for consideration. Was he right, or was he wrong, in holding that Christianity is hostile to the civic spirit? So far as the experience of the past went, it would seem that he was justified in his judgment: that Christianity has, far too much, been the 'religion of the individual'; and that, except in those cases where 'the State *is* the Church,' the instinct of Christians has commonly been to look with indifference, or even hostility, upon the life and aims of the State. In the last generation, however, a great change has come over the temper of religious men in this matter. And the most devout Christians of the present are also those who are most deeply stirred by the civic spirit. Christianity, in fact, has—at least in this country and in Switzerland, among Catholics as well as Protestants—largely come to be a 'civil religion.' And the end which Rousseau strove to attain by force is in the way to be reached by peaceful means: by the natural growth of germs, the existence of which he denied, but which, as the Letters of Saint Paul might have shewn him, were in some sense present from the beginning. In this revolution—for it is no less—it is probable that the teaching of Rousseau himself has borne a decisive part. Certainly, he was among the first, if not the first, to demand it.

(b) *Federation.*

On the question of Federation there is much less to be said. And the reason is that the materials are scanty. It is almost certain that Rousseau wrote a Fragment of some length—sixteen chapters—on the subject. But the friend to whom he committed it took fright in the early months of the Revolution and destroyed it. We are left with a single sentence of the *Contrat social*—that in which we are told that Federation would have been one of the subjects treated in the *Institutions politiques*—and the light

[1] It may be remarked that Hegel imposes a requirement still more objectionable than that of Rousseau: viz. that 'every member of the State must belong to some religious body.' *Rechtsphilosophie* (ed. 1820), p. 330

thrown upon the matter by Rousseau's criticism of the *Paix perpétuelle* of Saint-Pierre.

There is, however, a further passage in *Émile*. This manifestly sketches the line of argument that the *Institutions politiques* would have followed; and it is so important that it must be given at length: 'After having considered each form of civil society in itself, we shall go on to compare them, with a view to discovering their various relations: some large, others small; some strong, others weak; each attacking, insulting, destroying the others; and in this incessant action and counter-action causing more misery, and costing the life of more men, than if they had all remained in their primitive liberty. We shall ask ourselves whether, in the foundation of societies, men have not done either too much or too little; whether the submission of the individual to the authority of the Law and of other men, while at the same time the several communities remain as regards each other in the state of nature, does not leave him exposed to all the evils of both conditions, without the advantages of either; whether, in fine, it would not be better to have no civil society at all than to have several[1]....Is it not this partial and incomplete association which is the cause of tyranny and war? And are not tyranny and war the two worst scourges of mankind?

'We shall examine finally the kind of remedy that men have sought against these evils in Leagues and Federations, which, leaving each State master in its own house, arm it against all unjust aggression from without. We shall enquire what are the means of establishing a good form of federal association, what can give it permanence, and how far we can extend the rights of the Federation without trenching on those of Sovereignty[2].'

[1] Compare: 'La première chose que je remarque en considérant la position du genre humain, c'est une contradiction manifeste dans sa constitution qui la rend toujours vacillante. D'homme à homme, nous vivons dans l'état civil et soumis aux lois. De peuple à peuple, chacun jouit de sa liberté naturelle: ce qui rend au fond notre situation pire que si ces distinctions étaient inouïes; car vivant à la fois dans l'ordre social et dans l'état de nature, nous sommes assujettis aux inconvénients de l'un et de l'autre, sans trouver la sûreté dans aucun des deux....En faisant trop ou trop peu, nous n'avons rien fait, et nous nous sommes mis dans le pire état où nous puissions nous trouver.' *L'état de guerre* [MS. Neuchâtel, 7856]. See below, p. 304. See also the opening paragraphs of the *Extrait du projet de paix perpétuelle*, below, pp. 365—8.

[2] *Émile*, Liv. v.; see Vol. II. pp. 157—8. From this detailed sketch, it seems to me more likely than not that Rousseau had already written down part, at least, of his views on the subject of Federation. If so, we have here an indirect confirmation of the curious story told by d'Antraigues. See Vol. II. p. 135.

From this sketch two inferences may with almost complete certainty be drawn: the one relating to the purpose for which such Federations are to be formed; the other, to the best means for securing that end—in other words, to the guiding principle which is to regulate their scope. Federation, as here conceived, has a double aim. It seeks to do for the whole community, and for all communities concerned, that which the Social Contract has already done for the individual himself; to complete the work of drawing man from the state of nature which the Contract had begun. It seeks further to free man from the scourge of war from without, and the no less cruel scourge of tyranny which war seldom fails to bring upon the community from within. And if we ask what are the States which are most likely to gain by adopting it, we see at once that the small State has more to fear from unjust aggression than the large; that tyranny, which is the natural destiny of the large State, is contrary to the whole end and being of the small. For this reason, Federation is, in a special sense, the interest of the small State rather than the large. It is the weapon with which both reason and experience teach the small State to arm itself against the greed and insolence of the large. That is the reason why Federation lay so close to the heart of Rousseau. In his view—and who shall gainsay him?—it is the only means of preserving the small State, which to him is the only State worth having, from being swept, as in a tempest, off the face of the earth.

So much for the ends which Federation is intended to secure. By what means, we go on to ask, may those ends be most readily attained? what is the best form of Federation? and what the principle on which it rests? Here again there can be little, or no, doubt about the intention of the author. A mere scrutiny of the alternatives will probably put this beyond question[1].

There are, it may roughly be said, three things that the term *Federation* might naturally cover: a simple treaty of alliance; a federal State such as the American Commonwealth, the Swiss

[1] In what follows, I owe not a little to the very ingenious essay of M. Windenberger, *La République confédérative des petits États* (Paris, 1900). I must confess that the author seems to me to press the analogy of the Social Contract further than the facts will warrant. Moreover, Rousseau is, to him, 'essentially an individualist' (p. 248); and, for reasons already given, this is, in my opinion, the very reverse of the truth. In spite of these qualifications, I consider that, both by his publication of MSS. and by his original work, M. Windenberger has done inestimable service to the study of Rousseau.

Federation, or the German Empire—all of the present day; and finally, a form of federation midway between the two, like the Achæan League of the Greek world, the 'Confederation of the United States' as it was between 1781 and 1789[1], or the Union of the Swiss Cantons as it existed in the days of Rousseau. No doubt, each of these groups offers considerable varieties within itself. The constitution of the German Empire is a different thing from that of the United States or the Swiss Federation. The Union of the Swiss Cantons before the French Revolution was not framed on the same principles as that of the thirteen States of America in the years immediately following their liberation from the rule of the mother country. Even a treaty of alliance may impose obligations of very varying degrees. Still, for our purposes, the threefold division is accurate enough. And for the sake of shortness, we may distinguish the three groups, in a descending scale, as a Federal State, a Confederacy, and a treaty of alliance.

Now it is quite clear that Rousseau contemplates something much closer and more permanent than a mere treaty of alliance. Else, why should he insist on 'guarding the Sovereignty' of the individual States concerned[2]? It would be unusual, though certainly not impossible, that a treaty should result in 'trenching upon Sovereignty.' From the same phrase we may draw the inference that he was not in favour of the Federal State. For such an association can hardly exist without 'trenching,' and trenching rather deeply, 'upon the Sovereignty' of the individual States composing it.

But, if we exclude the Federal State after the fashion of the American Commonwealth upon the one hand, and the mere treaty of alliance upon the other, we are left with nothing but that form of union which lies midway between the two: closer than the treaty of alliance, looser than the Federal State: that form which, for reasons deeply scored in the history of the American Commonwealth, has come to be known as Confederation. And on every ground, that is the form of union which we should have expected Rousseau to prefer.

Affection for the small State breathes from every page of the *Contrat social*. It is clear that, to Rousseau's mind, this was the

---

[1] The two successive Constitutions of the United States (that of 1781 and that of 1788—9) are given *in extenso* in Bryce's *American Commonwealth*, Vol. I. pp. 569—587.

[2] See the last sentence of the passage from *Émile*, as given above.

only soil in which that ardent patriotism, which he valued above all things, is capable of growing. It was in the hope of preserving and strengthening the small State—so he tells us expressly in the *Dialogues*[1]—that all his writings, moral as well as political, were undertaken. How, then, could he be expected to look with favour upon any scheme which, by providing a second country, would have the inevitable effect of weakening the love of the citizen for the first? of distracting his civic affections, only in order to water them at every outlet they can find?

If any further argument be needed, we have only to glance at the closing paragraphs of the *Lettres de la Montagne*. He sees clearly that, apart from civil war, there is no choice for his former countrymen but either submission, or 'mediation[2].' He recognises that the latter necessarily means a surrender of the full Sovereignty which was theirs by right of birth. And he doubts whether the remedy is not worse than the disease; whether they will not do better to submit to tyranny from their own Government than obtain justice from another. 'I see plainly,' he writes, 'where this remedy leads, and I feel the heart of the citizen die within me. Accordingly I propose nothing. There is no advice I can bring myself to give[3].'

If he felt thus of a temporary loss of Sovereignty, what would he have said to a surrender of which the first condition is to be permanent and unchanging? Is it not clear that he was bound to prefer a Confederation, in which the individual State surrenders few or none of its sovereign rights, to the Federal system, in which it yields some of the most important? Can we doubt that, in the choice which half a century later was to lie before the Swiss Cantons, he would have stood for the loose league of the eighteenth

---

[1] *Dialogue*, III.; *Œuvres*, T. IX. p. 287. 'Il avait travaillé pour sa patrie et pour les petits États constitués comme elle.'

[2] *i.e.* the mediation of Zürich, Berne and France, to which Geneva had already had recourse in 1737.

[3] *Lettres de la Montagne*, IX. See Vol. II. p. 291. We may further appeal to the opening pages of the *Extrait du projet de paix perpétuelle* (see below, p. 365); in particular, to the following paragraph: 'Quoique cette forme [de gouvernement confédérative] paraisse nouvelle à certains égards, et qu'elle n'ait en effet été bien entendue que par les modernes, les anciens ne l'ont pas ignorée. Les Grecs eurent leurs amphictyons...et les derniers soupirs de la Grèce devinrent encore illustres dans la ligue achéenne. Mais nulles de ces Confédérations n'approchèrent, pour la sagesse, de celle du Corps germanique, de la Ligue helvétique, et des États généraux.' All of these—it will be remembered that he is speaking of the Empire, as it was before Austerlitz—were of the confederative, rather than the federal, type.

century rather than for the close Federation of the nineteenth? that, in the alternative which confronted America ten years after his death, he would have been found on the side of Jefferson and the champions of State rights rather than on that of Hamilton and *The Federalist*? That either form of association implies some surrender of State rights and the establishment of some form of central Government, he would doubtless have admitted. But, on the evidence before us, it is hard to believe that he would not have wished to make that surrender as small, and the powers of the central Government as limited, as the needs of the case allowed. So much we are entitled to say. To define more closely is to travel beyond the record.

From all this it is manifest that the doctrine of Federation, so far from being a mere offshoot, springs from the very root of Rousseau's political ideal; that the international Contract is necessary to complete the demands of that which gives birth to each nation taken singly; that it is still more necessary for the protection of the small State, which is also the 'free' State, against the aggressions of the large. His dream was to 'unite the external strength of a great nation with the free discipline, the healthy order, of a small one[1].' Well might he say that 'the subject was wholly untouched, and the first principles of it still to ascertain[2].'

Rousseau was the apostle of the small State. And since his death, the cause of the small State, so far from advancing, seems to have hopelessly fallen back. The United Provinces, the Germanic Body, the Helvetic Confederation, have all vanished from the map of Europe. The first has become a hereditary Monarchy, under the descendants of the old Stadtholders of Holland. The second, the loose structure of which went far to fulfil Rousseau's ideal, has given way to a Federal Empire, cemented by 'blood and iron.' The third—it lay nearer to Rousseau's heart than any other—has been replaced by a Federal State, which has largely 'trenched upon the Sovereignty' of the component units. And with those

[1] Compare his advice to the Poles: 'Appliquez-vous à étendre et perfectionner le système des gouvernements fédératifs, le seul qui réunisse les avantages des grands et des petits États, et par là le seul qui puisse vous convenir.' *Gouvernement de Pologne*, v. Vol. II. p. 443. It should be remarked that here it is rather Federation than a Confederacy which he has in view: to speak more strictly, provincial home-rule.

[2] 'Je ferai voir ci-après comment on peut réunir la puissance extérieure d'un grand peuple avec la police aisée et le bon ordre d'un petit État....Matière toute neuve, et où les principes sont encore à établir.' *C. S.* III. 15.

units Geneva, once a sovereign city with Rousseau for member of the sovereign body, has fallen into line.

The same movement has made itself felt upon a wider scale. A cluster of small States—a mere 'geographical expression,' as it was scornfully described—has been welded into a great nation. Nations, already too large to satisfy Rousseau's requirements, have swollen into Empires. And it has been seriously argued that this is the only goal worth striving for, the only consummation in which a generous spirit can take pride. The author of the *Contrat social* thought little of Kingdoms. What would he have said to the 'imperialist' ideal?

For this change, or series of changes, two main causes may be assigned. The first is the industrial revolution which, with its call for rapid transit, has done much to break down the barriers between one State and another. The second cuts even deeper. It is the sudden growth of the nationalist spirit, which is one of the strangest and least foreseen consequences of the French Revolution and the Napoleonic tyranny that followed. It was this, more than anything else, that secured the reversion of Italy for the House of Savoy rather than for that Federation of Republics to which many enlightened patriots had looked forward. It was this that gave Bismarck and Prussia their lever against the 'particularists' of the Free Cities and the South. For good or for evil—perhaps for good and for evil—the strongest force in Europe during the first three quarters of the nineteenth century was the spirit of nationality. To some minds, this will seem the strongest condemnation of Rousseau's ideal. The verdict of history, they will say, has gone against him beyond all hope of appeal. One thing, however, must be borne in mind. The verdict of history is to be gathered not from years, but from ages. It is valid only for its own time; there are few cases in which it is not liable to reversal, or to modification so great as to be hardly distinguishable from reversal. Who shall say, for instance, that the spirit of nationality is as great a force now as it was half a century ago? or that this is solely because its claims have, in large measure, been already satisfied? It played a decisive, and in the main a salutary, part for two generations. But what are they in the whole history of mankind?

At the moment when Rousseau wrote, neither the industrial, nor the nationalist, movement could have been readily foreseen. Industry was still, for the most part, a matter of the home or the small workshop. The application of steam to industrial processes—

much more, to transit—was still in the future. The nationalist movement was even less likely to be forecast. On the contrary, a vague form of cosmopolitanism, a thing hateful to Rousseau, was, at least in France, the sentiment generally in fashion[1]. In its earlier phases, even the Revolution was cosmopolitan, rather than nationalist, in tendency. It was only foreign invasion that drove France back upon the aggressive policy of Richelieu and Louis XIV. Indeed, there were moments in the history of the Revolution when it seemed not unlikely that the old centralised kingdom would break up into a loose Federation of Republics. It was the belief of Burke that this must inevitably follow from its division by Departments[2]. And it is a fact that the instructions of some of the *Cahiers* pointed straight in that direction[3]; that the charge of 'Federalism' was one of the most deadly weapons forged by Jacobin against Girondin.

Not that Rousseau himself was under any illusions on the subject. He was keenly aware that the tide of events, still more the tide of opinion, ran strong against the small State. He had little, or no, hope of converting the large States to his view. All he strove for was to strengthen the smaller communities in the maintenance of their own ideal against the force or treachery of their more powerful neighbours. He had seen that the one chance of doing so lay in some form of Federation. And from that moment, Federation took its place as an integral part of his whole system. Without it, his theory would have been incomplete; his practical ideal beyond hope of attainment.

[1] 'Il semble que le sentiment de l'humanité s'évapore et s'affaiblisse en s'étendant sur toute la terre....Il faut en quelque manière borner et comprimer l'intérêt et la commisération pour lui donner de l'activité.' *Éc. pol.* pp. 250—1. Compare: 'Par où l'on voit ce qu'il faut penser de ces prétendus cosmopolites qui, justifiant leur amour pour la patrie par leur amour pour le genre humain, se vantent d'aimer tout le monde pour avoir droit de n'aimer personne.' Geneva MS. I. ii.; below, p. 453.

[2] See *Reflections on the French Revolution*; Burke's *Works* (ed. 1842, 2 vols.), Vol. I. p. 450. 'You cannot but perceive in this scheme that it has a direct and immediate tendency to sever France into a variety of republics, and to render them totally independent of each other.' He speaks of it, a few paragraphs later, as 'the resolution to break their country into separate republics.' *Ib.* p. 451.

[3] *i.e.* the *Cahiers* of Provence: and their claim was taken up by the deputies of Navarre. See Brette, *Les limites et les divisions territoriales de la France en 1789*, pp. 33, 35, 71—2. I owe the reference to Mr Clapham's *Abbé Sieyès*, pp. 45, 46 (London, 1912).

(c) *Punishment and Property.*

Punishment and Property are two test questions. There are few which more promptly call out the difference between the individualist and the collectivist ideal.

The former may be swiftly despatched. Rousseau is in no doubt whatever as to the answer. The very connection in which he puts the question shews what his solution is to be. The right of the State to punish the criminal stands to him on the same footing as her right to demand that he shall risk life and limb in her defence. In both cases this is part of the 'surrender' which he made on entering the civil state. It is part of the price he pays for the untold benefits of civil life. From that moment his very existence is in her power. It 'ceases to be the pure boon of nature; it becomes a gift bestowed on him conditionally by the State.' If he risks his life in war, it is because the State, for whom he risks it, has hitherto guarded him and those dear to him from the dangers of ravage and massacre. If he ends his life in prison or on the gallows, it is because from the first he has accepted these penalties as the only possible safeguard against robbery or murder. It is quite true that, in the latter instance, he presumably did not foresee that he himself would be among those to suffer from the punishments he set up. But this is one of the cases in which, thanks to the very nature of the civil state and the Law which upholds it, a man is bound by his own past; in which 'his will is chained by his own permission, his past consent set off against his present refusal, and compulsion laid on him to punish himself for having acted against his own deliberate intention[1].'

The appeal to the consent of the criminal is, no doubt, an act of homage to the individualist assumptions which underlie the whole conception of the state of nature and the Contract that brings it to a close. But, taken as a whole, the argument is one that no individualist could possibly have used. It differs in words only from Burke's vindication of punishment, as the subjection of 'the occasional will of man to his permanent reason.'

This, however, is not all. Rousseau is clear-sighted enough to see that he has not covered the case of the deliberate and habitual criminal. And in order to do so, he adds a supplementary argument which is still less individualist in character than the first. 'Every criminal,' he writes, 'is a rebel and a public enemy. It is as such, rather than as citizen, that he suffers....For a public enemy

[1] *C. S.* II. v.; *Éc. pol.* p. 245; Geneva MS. I. vii.; below, p. 475.

is not a moral person, but a mere human being[1]. And in this case it is the right of war to kill the vanquished.' Once again, no doubt, he reverts to the fact that, by mere residence if by nothing else, the criminal is a consenting party to the State and to its laws. But the sting of the plea is now manifestly drawn; the second argument is still more unreservedly collectivist than the first[2].

As to the nature and origin of Property, the mind of Rousseau went through more than one change. When he wrote the second *Discourse* (1755), Property was to him the corner-stone of Society; it was presupposed in the very existence of the State. It was, in fact, the hope of turning an usurpation into a right, of converting a precarious into a fixed tenure, that brought the individual from liberty into servitude, from the natural to the civil state. But the right thus created is the greatest of all wrongs. And when Proudhon declared that 'Property is theft,' he was in reality saying no more than Rousseau, in yet more memorable words, had said a century before[3].

In the *Économie politique*, published (it will be remembered) less than six months later, we find a very different account of the matter. Property is still the foundation of Society; the preservation of it is still the main object for which Society was established. But, Rousseau's view of the value of Society having changed in the interval, the value of Property has of necessity changed to correspond. It is no longer a curse, but a blessing; no longer a wrong, but the most fundamental of all rights[4].

It is not until the *Contrat social* that we come to Rousseau's final judgment on the matter: the judgment to which, in substance, he remained faithful to the end. Before the foundation of the civil state, he now holds, the individual could claim no more than possession—a possession founded upon the 'right of the first occupant.' But, on entry into the civil state, he surrenders such possession, together with all his other powers, into the hands of the community. And the community, respecting the 'right' of

---

[1] *i.e.* he has renounced all moral responsibilities himself, and therefore the State has no moral responsibilities towards him. They are to each other as in the state of nature.

[2] *C. S.* II. v. (*Du droit de vie et de mort*). Compare above, p. 51 (note).

[3] See the opening paragraph of the *Discours sur l'inégalité* (Part II.); below, p. 169.

[4] 'Il est certain que le droit de propriété est le plus sacré de tous les droits des citoyens...parce que la propriété est le vrai fondement de la société et le vrai garant des engagements des citoyens.' *Éc. pol.* pp. 259, 260, 265, 273.

the existing occupant, who is assumed to be the first occupant, converts the imperfect right into a complete right, mere possession into legitimate ownership. It is, therefore, only from and through the community that the right of property takes its rise. In this case, as in all others, 'the social order'—or, as it is put elsewhere, the Social Contract—'is a sacred right, which serves as base for all the rest[1].'

At this point we are confronted with a difficulty which Rousseau makes little or no effort to disguise. The right of the community is itself based upon that of the individuals who compose it[2]. And, in this instance, that primary right is based—to say the least, there is no presumption that it is not based—upon a wrong: upon the 'right of the stronger,' which, on Rousseau's own principles, is no right at all[3]. So far as the claims of other communities go, he admits this at once, and without reserve. And that can only mean that, in case of war, the conqueror is entitled to confiscate all the land—and why not all the other private possessions?— of his enemies, and distribute it among the members of his own body. It is true that Rousseau himself does not draw this consequence. But, on his premises, how can it be denied? And how is it to be reconciled with the brand justly inflicted on such practices in his early Fragment, *L'état de guerre*? No man had denounced this and other iniquities of war in more burning language than the author of that Fragment. No man had brought a more irresistible armoury of reasoning to bear against them. It is disquieting to find that, in an unguarded moment, he should now make an admission which surrenders his whole case.

But what about the relation of the community to its own members in this matter, and the rights of property which each party in turn confers upon the other? It must be owned that Rousseau is not as outspoken in this, as in the previous case. He admits, no doubt, that the 'right of the first occupant' is a 'feeble' right. He does not admit that, in practice, it is commonly only another name for the 'right of the stronger': in other words, for brute force. On the contrary, in order to ward off this suspicion,

[1] *C. S.* I. i., I. ix. (*Du domaine réel*); Geneva MS. I. iii., I. v. The very title of the chapter foreshadows the doctrine of State ownership. It should be noted that Rousseau also contemplates the possibility of cases in which private 'possession' did not exist before the foundation of the State (paragraph beginning 'Il peut arriver aussi,' *C. S.* I. ix.).

[2] This, of course, does not apply to the cases mentioned in the last note.

[3] *C. S.* I. iii.—iv.; Geneva MS. I. v.; MS. Neuchâtel, 7856. See below, pp. 466—473 and pp. 302—4.

he surrounds the 'right of the first occupant' with a hedge of safeguards, the only fault of which is that not one of them could be enforced. The existing occupant must be, in fact as well as in name, the first occupant; he must have occupied 'what he needs for subsistence, and no more'; and 'he must have taken possession not by a vain ceremony, but by his own labour and the tillage of the soil[1].' Imagine the primitive State appointing a Commission to overhaul the 'feeble' and imperfect title-deeds of its members; and we see at once the hornet's nest of impossibilities which Rousseau has brought about his ears.

On the principles of the *Contrat social*, it is, in truth, impossible that the 'right' of property should ever be other than a wrong. The distinction between the 'right of the first occupant' and the 'right of the stronger' can never be maintained. In spite of all he can do to conceal it, the author is driven back upon brute force as the ultimate basis of 'possession.' And on his principles, brute force can never yield anything but wrong.

The strange thing is that, in his account of Property, he comes nearer than in any other part of his work to recognising the place of force in the first beginnings of Society. And had he but followed out the line of thought which he here opens, it would seem hardly possible that he should not have ended by acknowledging the fact plainly and without reserve. This, no doubt, would have compelled him to recast all the opening stages of his theory. But that, as we have seen, would have been nothing but a gain. The state of nature and the Contract, which accord so ill with the general tenor of his argument, would have been swept away. So would the miraculous intervention of the Lawgiver. And the idea of progress—of the gradual moralisation of barbarous and unjust customs, the gradual refinement of brute force into Right, of the antisocial into the social temper—would have taken their place. Unfortunately, the idea of progress was wholly alien to his mind. The nearest approach he made to it was the corresponding, but wofully different, idea of retrogression and decay. Of all the defects in his theory, this was the most deep-reaching and the most fatal.

It may be objected that to admit force as the original title to possession, and consequently (in the sense just indicated) to Property, though well enough in regard to the members of the State itself, affords no protection whatever against other States and their members; that it still leaves another State free, in case

[1] *C. S.* I. ix.

of a victorious war, to confiscate the goods of the conquered for the benefit of the conquerors. The latter, it may be said, are, on Rousseau's own shewing, in regard to the citizens of other communities still in the state of nature. They stand therefore on a footing the very opposite of that which finds place between any one member of the community and his fellows. They are untouched by the moralising process which goes on within the bounds of the community itself. They are entitled to transfer to themselves the property of their enemies by the same force which originally created it.

Now, if one community were really, as Rousseau commonly argues, in the state of nature with regard to others, this consequence would undoubtedly follow. In fact, however, the same process which slowly converts force into Right within the bounds of the State is also, but still more slowly, at work between one State and another. The 'rights' of States, like the 'rights' of individuals, are being gradually curtailed. What was permitted at the time of the Thirty Years' War, or even the wars of the Revolution, is no longer possible or conceivable. Public opinion —the opinion of Europe at any rate—would put on the pillory any nation that attempted it. And this is admitted by Rousseau himself in a passage of the first draft of the *Contrat social*— a passage which, in the final version, was unfortunately suppressed. 'Everything which visibly contributes to the greater good of the community, but which the laws have not specifically prescribed, constitutes acts of "civility" and beneficence; and the habit which disposes us to perform such acts, even to our own prejudice, is what we call force or virtue. Extend this maxim to the "general society," the first idea of which is derived from the State. Protected by the society of which we are members, or by that in which we live[1], we find that our natural repugnance to do harm is no longer checked by our fear of suffering it. Accordingly we are inclined at once by nature, habit and reason to deal with other men almost as with our fellow-citizens; and from this disposition, reduced to act, spring the rules of natural, or rational, Right. This differs from "natural right," in the strict sense, which is founded on nothing stronger than sentiment—true in itself, but extremely vague and often stifled by selfishness[2].' If this does not mean that there is such a thing—or rather, that there has come to

[1] Rousseau himself, when he wrote this, was living in a society of which he was not a member, *i.e.* France. I wrote the above before the present war.
[2] Geneva MS. II. iv.; below, p. 494.

be such a thing—as international Right, it means nothing. And if there is, it is clear that the States which recognise such a Right are no longer in the state of nature to one another.

So much for Rousseau's doctrine of Property, as it affects the central ideas of the *Contrat social*. It remains to add a few words on its narrower aspects. He brushes aside all individualist foundations of Property; in particular, the argument from Formation, so carefully elaborated by the Roman Jurists. He recognises from the first—and recognises more unequivocally than Kant was to do a generation later—that Property is only possible in and through the State. To him, as we have seen, Property is the creation of the State; and it rests with the State to make any regulations for its tenure that the 'general will' may approve; subject, of course, to the limitation that all such provisions must be general in their scope, that none of them shall be directed either to the advantage, or the prejudice, of particular classes or particular individuals. It follows from this that any arguments against Socialism, which may rest upon the supposed rights of the individual, are thrown to the winds; that, so far as principle goes, Rousseau is ready to accept it, the moment it may be proved to be for the interest of the community at large.

There is a passage of *Émile* which states this in so many words. After reverting once more—but this time as a mere hypothesis—to the doctrine that the 'State itself is founded on the right of Property,' 'This right,' he adds, 'is inviolable and sacred for the State, so long as it remains private and individual. But directly it is considered as a right common to all the citizens, it is subordinated to the general will, and the general will can annul it. The sovereign has no right to touch the possessions either of one individual, or of several. But it has every right to appropriate the possessions of all. It did so at Sparta in the time of Lycurgus. On the other hand, the abolition of debts by Solon'—seeing that it was in the nature of class legislation—'was an act of wrong[1].'

A yet franker avowal of socialist principles is to be found in the *Projet de Constitution pour la Corse*: 'Far from desiring the State to be poor, I should wish, on the contrary, to see all property in its hands, and no individual admitted to any share of the common stock, save in proportion to his services....My desire is not absolutely to destroy private property—for that is impossible—but to

[1] *Émile*, Liv. v., Vol. II. p. 152. The language of the first two sentences is, I cannot but think, extremely incorrect. It has to be interpreted in the light of the corresponding passage of the *Contrat social* (I. ix.).

keep it within the narrowest bounds: to give it a standard, a rule, a curb to restrain it, direct it, subdue it and keep it always subordinate to the public good. In a word, I desire that the property of the State should be as large, as strong, and that of the individual as small, as weak, as possible[1].'

A fuller acceptance of Socialism, as a principle, it would be difficult to find. And if, in the face of this declaration, Rousseau still refuses to range himself with the socialists, that is on grounds not of principle, but convenience; of expediency, not of right. 'To destroy private property root and branch is,' in his view, 'impossible.' The love of it is too deeply rooted in human nature; too closely bound up with the industry which lies at the core of all social energy and the more active of the qualities which go to make up individual worth. That, if he had been pressed on the point, is the ground on which he would have based his refusal. And it is the same treatise, that on Corsica, which entitles us to draw this conclusion. 'Every Government which desires to throw the seeds of activity among its people must have taken pains to put within their reach objects capable of tempting them. Let labour offer great advantages to your citizens,...and you will not fail to make them laborious[2].' The love of esteem is doubtless the first of these advantages, in his eyes. But the love of honourable gain is by no means excluded.

From the passage above quoted one further inference may be drawn. If, in spite of strong leanings in that direction, Rousseau is no socialist, still less is he a communist. If his dream—a dream by his own avowal impossible of attainment—is to see all property vested in the State, that is because he would wish to see it allotted, from time to time, 'in proportion to services' rendered to the State. And that is a principle as different from Communism as it is possible to conceive.

But, if it is neither expedient nor possible absolutely to destroy private property, must we conclude that nothing can be done to correct and regulate its inequalities? It is clear that Rousseau

---

[1] *Projet de Constitution pour la Corse*; Vol. II. p. 337. How far Rousseau's views of Property may have been affected by Morelly (whose *Code de la nature*, one of the boldest writings of the century, was published in 1755) it is impossible to say. The principles of Morelly are those of pure Communism: see *Code* (ed. 1841), pp. 152—6. The same, though in a qualified sense, is true of Mably: see *Droits et devoirs du citoyen* (1758), *Œuvres*, XI. pp. 379—386 (ed. 1794—5).

[2] *Projet de Constitution pour la Corse*, Vol. II. p. 345; also *ib.* pp. 344–7.

did not think so. On the contrary, he explicitly recognises this as one of the main duties of any Government. Having asserted that 'the two chief ends of government are liberty and equality,' 'as for equality,' he continues, 'we must not understand by this term that the amounts of power and wealth are to be absolutely the same, but that...in regard to wealth no citizen shall be rich enough to buy another, and none poor enough to be forced to sell himself....It is just because the force of circumstances is always tending to destroy equality, that the force of legislation ought always to tend towards maintaining it[1].'

He had already laid down the same principle in the *Économie politique*. And, if asked by what means this end is to be accomplished, he is ready with his answer. It is to be done not directly, but indirectly: 'not by robbing the owner of his possessions, but by depriving him of the means of amassing them; not by building alms-houses for the poor, but by saving the citizen from becoming so[2].' And if pressed to define more closely, he has two practical proposals to bring forward. The first is to set aside a large domain land, which shall serve the double purpose of saving the tax-payer and of reducing the amount of landed property open to the avarice of the rich[3]. And the second is to throw the brunt of taxation on the rich rather than on the poor; it being very certain that, however heavily they may be taxed, the rich will always gain more from the benefits, and lose less by the burdens, of civil society than the poor[4]. Translated into the language of current politics, these proposals mean, on the one hand, a progressive Income Tax; and on the other, a large, though not complete, nationalisation of the land, and perhaps also of the means of industry. Rousseau, it must again be said, was no socialist. But the germs, and something more than the germs, of Socialism are clearly visible in his writings.

[1] *C. S.* II. xi. Compare: 'Il faut prévenir l'augmentation continuelle de l'inégalité des fortunes'; 'un ordre économique qui...rapprocherait insensiblement toutes les fortunes de cette médiocrité qui fait la véritable force d'un État.' *Éc. pol.* pp. 271—2.

[2] *Éc. pol.* pp. 266—7.

[3] *Éc. pol.* p. 261. See also the passage quoted above from the *Projet de Constitution pour la Corse*.

[4] *Éc. pol.* pp. 267—8. The paragraph beginning 'Un troisième rapport qu'on ne compte jamais,' with the two following paragraphs, is among the most characteristic that Rousseau ever wrote. He is, however, fully alive to the dangers of fraud attending the Income Tax. *Éc. pol.* pp. 268—9.

VII

CONCLUSION

This brings us back to the point from which we started. Socialist, in the strict sense, Rousseau was not; but he was collectivist, heart and soul. So far from being the charter of individualism, the *Contrat social* is a defiant statement of the collectivist ideal. The state of nature and the Contract may be taken over from the individualists and, in particular, from Locke. But they are altered out of all knowledge in the taking. The former is reduced to a condition of pure animalism, from which it is man's first interest to escape. The latter, so far from being an instrument of liberty for the individual, is one by which he makes total surrender of all the powers he has hitherto enjoyed. It is true that, whatever turn may be given to them, these conceptions still betray the source from which they are drawn. A taint of individualism still hangs about them, in whatever setting they are placed. Even this, however, disappears directly Rousseau gets fairly under way. It is only the first few chapters that are affected. Throughout the rest of the treatise, the only complaint to make is that he gives not too much, but too little, power to the individual; that, with the zeal of the new convert, he ruthlessly burns the idol he had once inconsiderately adored. It is on this side, not on the other, that his theory is open to attack. And the task that lay before subsequent thinkers was not to overthrow his 'individualism,' but to bring his collectivism within bounds.

That, then, is the first, the signal service that Rousseau rendered to political philosophy. Other writers, Vico and Montesquieu, had assailed the individualist theory indirectly, and from the side of history[1]. It was reserved for Rousseau to attack and vanquish it in its stronghold, as a speculative theory of Right. With unerring aim, he flies straight at the central idea of his antagonists, and proves it to be an assumption which there is nothing to support. The 'individual,' he argues, has no existence save in the imagination

---

[1] 'Je n'ai jamais ouï parler du droit public, qu'on n'ait commencé par rechercher soigneusement quelle est l'origine des sociétés ; ce qui me paraît ridicule. Si les hommes n'en formaient point, s'ils se quittaient et se fuyaient les uns les autres, il faudrait en demander la raison, et chercher pourquoi ils se tiennent séparés. Mais ils naissent tous liés les uns aux autres ; un fils est né auprès de son père, et il s'y tient : voilà la société, et la cause de la société.' Montesquieu, *Lettres Persanes*, XCIV.

of the individualist. In himself, he is nothing but a 'stupid and limited animal'; it is only in and through the State that he becomes 'a reasoning being and a man.' It is to the State that he owes his moral and intellectual being, his self and all that constitutes his individuality. It is to the State therefore—as, under God, the author of all which makes his life of more value than the beast's—that he owes reverence and love.

But if Rousseau exalts the State, and exalts it unduly, at the expense of the individual, it must not be forgotten of what nature is the State that he has in mind. It is of the essence of his theory that the State is no power which imposes itself from without; that, on the contrary, it is more truly part of the individual than the individual himself. The change he wrought in the conception of the individual involves a corresponding change in the conception of the State. The bureaucratic machinery, which had slowly fastened itself on Europe, is thrown to the winds. Its place is taken by the idea of a free community, each member of which has as large a share in determining the 'general will' as any of his fellows; in which, so far as human frailty allows, the general will takes up into itself the will of all. It is the ideal of Rousseau— an ideal never, perhaps, wholly attainable—that the individual will, in the old and bad sense of the term, should lose itself in the general will; that, purged of all selfish interests, all should now have the right—a right hitherto reserved for one only—of saying, *L'État, c'est moi*. In other words, the only State he recognises as legitimate is the State of which the sovereign is the people. On this side he is no less original than in the assault on individualism with which the *Contrat social* opens. To his mind, indeed, the two things are inseparable. The one without the other would have seemed tyrannical and absurd.

It is to the latter side of his theory that he would have appealed, if charged with inconsistency; if challenged to prove that his collectivist autocracy leaves room for the individual freedom of which, in his earlier writings, he was the champion and apostle. On the score of consistency, he is hardly to be acquitted. When all allowance has been made for the successive checks which he sets upon its powers, it remains true that the State of the *Contrat social* is virtually absolute; that the individual is but too likely to find himself helpless in its grasp. Yet, whatever the practical outcome of his later doctrine, his intention never varied. In the *Contrat social* it may be overlaid and obscured. But it is there, all the same. And his bitterest enemies must admit that, of all those who have pleaded the cause of individual freedom, he is the most passionate and inspired. Here, if anywhere, we must look for the root and secret of his influence. And the most precious gift he left the world was the 'inextinguishable hatred of oppression' which fired his own soul[1].

A free citizen in a free State—that, on the sum of the whole matter, is the ideal of Rousseau. But, on each side of the count, he gives to the term a meaning different from that which it has ordinarily borne. As regards the citizen, the freedom in question is not freedom from restraint. Rather, it is the release from bondage to his baser self; the willing acceptance of burdens for the sake of others, of that service to a larger whole in which alone his true self, his real freedom, is to be found. In other words, it is essentially a moral freedom; a freedom which brings with it at least as much of self-sacrifice as of ease. And this amounts to nothing short of a revolution in political theory; a reversion from the cramped and narrowing view of Locke and the individualists to the wider and more inspiring outlook of the Greek world and, above all, of its master spirit, Plato. Generations come and go; the deepest truths become faint in men's minds, and we think at times that they are irrevocably forgotten. But it is idle to lose faith. No truth that men have once beaten out can ever, except by their own fault, be utterly torn from them. And few more signal instances of this are to be found than in the courage of the man who challenged the individualist creed at the moment of its triumph, and forced the world to reverse the verdict which seemed to have gone against him beyond all hope of appeal.

No less distinctive is the meaning which Rousseau gives to the freedom of the State. The two terms of the relation are manifestly in close correspondence with each other; a change in the one necessarily carries with it a change also in the other. To Rousseau, no doubt, as to other men, the freedom of the State means, in the first instance, its freedom from outward interference; its right to live its own life, to shape its destinies according to its own will. And in his hands, as we have seen, this leads straight to the doctrine of Federation; to the necessity of banding the small States together in defence of themselves against the large. But to him the freedom of the State means something more, and something higher, than this. It means not only the outward independence of the State, but also an ideal of citizenship which

---

[1] See *Confessions*, Liv. IV.; *Œuvres*, VIII. p. 116.

can be drawn only from within. It means an intensity of civic life, a consuming zeal for the welfare of the community and all its members, such as the modern world has seldom known. Of all the energies possible to man this, in his view, is the highest. And he reserves for it, with deliberate intention, the Roman name of 'virtue[1].' It is the power which lifts a man out of himself, which makes him capable of a heroism such as nothing else can inspire. Even in the humbler sense, virtue—the recognition of duty, the recognition also of a specific code of moral duties—is the creation of the State; and without this no State can hold together. But the virtue of which Rousseau is here speaking is a thing yet rarer and more exalted. It is to be found—or, if that be too strong, it is to be found as the ruling spirit—only in the fewest States: only in those which the world has recognised as the purest and the best. Yet it is the noblest gift which the State has to offer. And no State which is not, in some measure, leavened by this spirit, deserves the name of 'free.' Here again, to the State no less than to the individual, it is certain that freedom brings not ease but strife, not peace but the sword. The consequence is accepted by Rousseau. 'The citizen must arm himself with courage and constancy. Every day of his life he must say in his inmost heart what the Polish Palatine exclaimed at the Diet: *Malo periculosam libertatem quam quietum servitium*—Rather the perils of freedom than slavery and peace[2].' Few utterances bring us nearer to the heart of Rousseau's theory, of his civic ideal, than this.

The argument of the *Contrat social* is cast in an abstract mould which has too often blinded readers to its practical bearing and effect. A comparatively slight change would have done away with this objection. But it is a change which Rousseau could

---

[1] 'Il est certain que les plus grands prodiges de vertu ont été produits par l'amour de la patrie.' *Éc. pol.*; below, p. 248. See the whole passage, pp. 246—251. Hence Rousseau describes the Law as 'la plus sublime de toutes les institutions humaines'; and the act of the Lawgiver as 'le plus sublime effort de la sagesse et de la prévoyance humaine.' Geneva MS. I. vii.; below, p. 476.

[2] *C. S.* III. iv. Compare 'Fière et sainte liberté! si ces pauvres gens pouvaient te connaître, s'ils savaient à quel prix on t'acquiert et te conserve, s'ils sentaient combien les lois sont plus austères que n'est dur le joug des tyrans, leurs faibles âmes, esclaves de passions qu'il faudrait étouffer, te craindraient plus cent fois que la servitude; ils te fuiraient avec effroi, comme un fardeau prêt à les écraser.' *Gouvernement de Pologne*, VI.; Vol. II. p. 445.

never have brought himself to make. Strike out the state of nature and the Contract from the opening pages of the treatise. Replace them by the idea of a gradual growth from barbarism to what may fairly be called the 'civil state.' Admit that the discipline which slowly brought men to that state was, in its earlier stages, largely a discipline of force; that the history of man is the unfolding of a long drama in which this initial conquest is for ever repeating itself upon a higher, and yet a higher, plane; the element of force gradually diminishing, that of Right and of willing obedience gradually increasing; until the ideal, dimly present from the first, at length works itself into clear consciousness; and one community after another is brought to recognise that it is the essence of Right not to stand still, but to advance; to be not a fixed standard, but an ideal for ever unrealised, because subject to endless development and growth. Make these changes in Rousseau's argument, and its inconsistencies, its other inherent blemishes, will have largely disappeared. He would no longer have been hampered by the necessity of basing a collectivist structure upon a foundation of individualism. He would have been freed from the embarrassment of torturing the abstract man of his opening chapters into the creature of circumstances—the being determined by outward conditions, by national character, by historical accident—whom he brings before us at the close. But to have recast his argument in this fashion would have been to accept the idea of progress. And, as we have seen, the idea of progress was wholly alien to his way of thought.

'A free citizen in a free State.' Did Rousseau ever look forward into the future? did he ever dream of a time when Europe should at length cast off the spell of her enchantment, and his ideal be made good? It is difficult to say. He tells us himself, at the sad close of his life, that, except for the smaller States, he saw no hope on the horizon; that he 'toiled solely for his own country and for the small States ordered, more or less closely, on her model[1].' This, doubtless, was the prevailing temper of his mind; this was the hope that supported him through long years of labour and apparent defeat. But he would have been more than human if there had not been moments when his heart beat higher, and a wider prospect was flashed, if but for an instant, upon his view. Might not the large States also come at last to see the misery of their delusion? might not France herself one day throw off the fetters she had forged for her own ruin? A cancelled sentence in one of his

[1] *Dialogues*, III. (1776); *Œuvres*, IX. p. 287.

letters to Mirabeau would seem to shew that this was the case[1]. But if it were so, the hope was no sooner lit than it was quenched. And had he lived to see France 'standing on the top of golden hours,' there is no assurance that he would not have reckoned her freedom, like her long bondage, to be born under a curse. Bold even to recklessness in speculation, he was cautious, not to say timid, when it came to action. And he had a reasoned 'horror of revolutions[2]' which was but too likely to damp the fire of his zeal and, behind the golden dawn of brotherhood, to raise visions of the hatred and violence which might follow.

But if the moments of hope were few and brief, so also, one would fain trust, were those of utter discouragement and despair. The evidence is double-edged. In the same letter to Mirabeau, one of the very few passages which throw light upon the subject, he writes as follows: 'According to my old ideas, the great problem of Politics, which I compare to the squaring of the circle in geometry,...is to find a form of Government which puts the Law above the individual....If such a form is unhappily beyond our power to find—and I frankly admit that in my belief it is—then my conviction is that we must fly to the opposite extreme, set the individual at one bound as high as possible above the Law, and establish arbitrary despotism—the most arbitrary that can be devised. I should wish the despot to be God. In a word, I see no possible mean between the austerest democracy and the most complete Hobbism. For of all conditions, the conflict between the individual and the Law, which plunges the State into ceaseless civil war, is the very worst.—But Caligula, Nero, Tiberius! Good God! I roll myself in the dust and groan to think I am a man[3].'

The greater part of this passage is a bitter cry of disillusionment. The closing sentence, though gloomy enough, brings back some faint glimmering of light. And that, it is probable, was, at least in his closing years, the prevailing mood of Rousseau: a mood neither of settled doubt, nor yet of faith, in his own cause. One would have wished it had been otherwise; that his own life

---

[1] 'Aussi je suis fâché de vous dire que, *tant que la monarchie durera en France*, il n'y sera jamais adopté,' *i.e.* the system advocated by Mirabeau and the Physiocrats. The Mirabeau in question is, of course, not the hero of the Revolution, but his father, 'l'ami des hommes.' For the whole letter, in its original form, see Vol. II. pp. 159—161.

[2] *Dialogues*, III.: same passage as above.

[3] Letter to Mirabeau of July 26, 1767. See Vol. II. pp. 160—1.

had been cheered by the hope with which he fired the heart of others. His theory was marred both by inconsistencies and extravagances. No attempt has been made in these pages either to hide them or make light of them. But there are two things which can never be forgotten. He gave men faith in their power to redress the wrongs of ages. And he held forth an ideal of civic life which has changed the face of Europe. Thanks to the *Contrat social,* the leaden rule of bureaucracy, hard though it be to break, is weakened and discredited. The ideal of a free people, united in one 'corporate self' and working out one 'general will,' is coming, slowly but none the less surely, to take its place. That is the debt which the world owes to Rousseau. That is the glory which nothing can take from him.

DISCOURS SUR L'INÉGALITÉ

THE *Discours sur l'inégalité* was published in June, 1755[1], and more than confirmed the fame which the writer had won by the first *Discourse* and the polemic that followed. Like the first *Discourse*, it was written for a prize offered by the Academy of Dijon (1754). But this time the prize was given to another, the Abbé Talbert[2]. It was only what Rousseau had expected. 'I knew,' he tells us, 'that Academies do not found prizes for pieces of this stuff[3].'

It is dedicated, in terms of sincere but perhaps extravagant praise, to the Republic of Geneva, which Rousseau had revisited in the summer of 1754 and to the citizenship of which he was then formally admitted[4]. The whole piece, indeed, is written in a glow of 'republican enthusiasm' which may be hard to reconcile with the anti-social framework of the argument but which, in spite of persecution and misusage of all kinds, remained with Rousseau to the end. And it is this which forms the connecting link between the earlier writings and the later: in particular, between this *Discourse* and the *Économie politique,* composed immediately after it, or the *Contrat social,* the earlier portions of which must go back to this period or, as some have thought, to one slightly earlier yet.

A review of the *Discourse,* written directly after its appearance, will be found in the *Correspondance littéraire* of Grimm[5]. It

---

[1] See above, Introduction, p. 14.

[2] For Talbert's Essay, see Migne, *Orateurs sacrés,* t. LXVI. pp. 546—556. It is commonplace enough; the work of a docile theological student, with a turn for pulpit eloquence. D'Argenson was also a candidate.

[3] *Confessions,* Liv. VIII.; *Œuvres,* VIII. p. 277.

[4] *ib.* p. 280. The 'Republic' means the whole body of citizens; *i.e.* all those who were members of the sovereign body—the *Conseil Géneral.* The executive body, the *Petit Conseil,* took offence at this; and in this resentment Rousseau traced the seeds of the ill will which the *Petit Conseil* subsequently shewed against him. *ib.* pp. 279—282. Comp. *ib.* Liv. XI.; *Œuvres,* IX. p. 28.

[5] *Corr. litt.* I. pp. 394—403 (ed. Paris, 1813). The article is dated July 15, 1755. It would seem more probable that it was written by Raynal than by Grimm

contains some perfectly fair criticism, most of which amounts to a not unnatural charge of exaggeration and 'love of system.' But the tone is throughout respectful. The author is described as a 'deep and luminous philosopher.' His views are recognised as being 'large, subtle and original.' His style is praised as 'at once simple and elevated; full of light, warmth and energy'; and a tribute is paid to its 'masculine and moving eloquence.' And this, we may suppose, was the general verdict of the time. It is probably not very different at the present day.

The *Discourse on Inequality*, however, is not merely a masterpiece of 'manly eloquence.' Nor is it enough to say that its thought is original, and that it sheds a large and bright light upon the themes of which it treats. If the first *Discourse*, in the words of the same critic, made 'a kind of revolution in Paris,' the second did no less for the whole of western Europe[1]. And it did so in two quite distinct ways.

It was, and still remains, the most complete expression of the revolt against human law and human convention—of the craving for a return to simpler and freer conditions, for a renewal of man's communion with God and nature—which was to breathe a new life into the thought, the imagination, the social ideals of the civilised world. In this sense, it stands at the fountain head of the influences which largely went to remould the philosophy, the literature, the practical energies of Europe during the next two generations, and which, even now, have not wholly spent their force.

But that is not all. When we turn to the special field of political philosophy, the second *Discourse* is once more a landmark of the first importance. And that, perhaps, still more from its practical consequences than from the intrinsic novelty of its speculative ideas. It suggested, no doubt, if it did not explicitly proclaim, a more extreme form of individualism than any previous writer had ventured to set forth. The very exaggerations of Rousseau have, on this ground, a value which the more cautious plea of Locke can hardly claim to possess. Yet, but for the flame it lighted in the hearts of men, this service would have been comparatively slight. When all is said and done, the chief significance of the *Discourse*, politically speaking, is to be found in the vast influence which it wielded upon the French Revolution; upon the efforts to secure juster laws and a freer outlet for the energies of the individual, of which the Revolution in France was

[1] *Corr. litt.* I. pp. 122—8 (article of Feb. 15, 1754).

the most startling but, from its very violence, the most questionable, and by no means the most effective in its ultimate results.

It remains only to notice the materials of which Rousseau availed himself in the building of his argument; the hints which he gleaned from various writers who had been before him in the field. We are apt to think of him as the sworn foe of study, and bent on drawing solely from himself. In fact, few things are more remarkable than the care he took, here as always, to make himself acquainted with the best things already written on the themes of which he treated. In this instance he is careful to tell us of two authors, both of them his personal friends, to whom he was indebted. And it is with these, Diderot and Condillac, that it is well to begin.

Apart from certain touches of satire, which in after years he came to regard as treacherously meant[1], it is possible, though by no means certain[2], that Rousseau may have owed to Diderot[3] the part he attributes to the motive power of passion[4]; his belief in the evolution of man from the lower animals, as at least a tenable hypothesis[5]; and finally, though this surely is far less likely, his assault on Property as at once the cause and the seal of the injustice which lies at the root of man's social existence[6]. It must be remembered that, at the time when the *Discourse* was written, he was in daily intercourse with Diderot, closely associated with him in the workshop of the *Encyclopédie*. And this

[1] See above, General Introduction, p. 19.
[2] The whole subject is discussed in an article by M. Morel, *Sources du Discours sur l'inégalité*, to be found in *Annales de la Société J.-J. Rousseau*, t. v. (1909). What follows in the text is, in the main, a summary of this.
[3] The works of Diderot here in question are his translation of Shaftesbury, *Essai sur le mérite et la vertu, avec réflexions* (1745); *Pensées philosophiques* (1746); *Lettres sur les sourds et muëts* (1751); *Pensées sur l'interprétation de la nature* (1754); and various articles in the first four volumes of the *Encyclopédie* (1751—4). Diderot must have discussed with Rousseau the subjects of the writings published in 1754, even if they appeared in print after the *Discourse* was completed.
[4] *Discours*, pp. 150—1; 163—5. Compare *Pensées philosophiques*, I.—v.
[5] *Discours*, p. 142. Compare *Interprétation de la nature*, XII. xlix.—li.
[6] *Discours*, p. 169. Compare article *Bacchionites* in the *Encyclopédie*. This, however, is nothing more than a schoolboy outbreak about 'les distinctions funestes du tien et du mien.' To the possible sources mentioned in the text should be added *La Basiliade*, the prose poem of Morelly, which appeared in 1753. See the passages quoted from it in *Code de la nature* (ed. 1841), pp. 184—8. And see above, p. 109.

fact, as we shall see when we come to consider the article on *Droit naturel*, makes it extremely difficult, indeed impossible, to ascertain which of the two is to be regarded as the first author of ideas found in the published works of either. The two men had thrown their minds into common stock: the one quick as lightning, a born *improvisatore*; the other slow, brooding and tenacious[1]. It is hard therefore to say which of them is likely to have contributed the more to results a great part of which, at any rate, must have been beaten out in common. And this applies to the publications of Diderot no less than to those of Rousseau.

With Condillac we are likely to be on surer ground, though here, too, the possibility of private intercourse is by no means to be excluded. Rousseau himself tells us that his enquiry into the origin of speech was, or may have been, suggested to him by the researches of Condillac[2]. And he is sharp-sighted enough to lay his finger on the weak spot of his friend's position: the assumption, namely—for it is no more than an assumption—that, before speech came into being, society was already formed. Other points might be mentioned. But we need only pause on the idea of development, which plays so large a part in the *Discourse* and which has certain obvious analogies with Condillac's brilliant image of the living statue. Yet here again the author of the *Discourse* is careful to avoid the rather gross materialism into which his friend is not seldom betrayed by the very brilliance of the mechanical image which forms the groundwork of his argument. Moreover, while the argument of Condillac is, in the main, based on analysis, that of Rousseau is a masterpiece of synthesis.

Apart from Lucretius[3], who supplied several touches to Rousseau's description of the state of nature, the only other writers it is necessary to refer to are the political philosophers; Grotius, Hobbes, Pufendorf and Locke. The two former—the first,

[1] See *Confessions*, Liv. III.; *Œuvres*, VIII. pp. 79—81.
[2] *Discours*, p. 153. The reference is to the earliest work of Condillac, *Essai sur l'origine des connaissances* (1746). The other works in question are *Traité des Systèmes* (1749) and *Traité des Sensations* (1754). The last did not appear until the *Discourse* was virtually completed. But it is probable that Rousseau was acquainted with at least the plan of its argument, which indeed had been dimly anticipated by Diderot in the *Lettre sur les sourds et muëts*. For Rousseau's relations with Condillac, to whom he had one time been tutor, see in particular *Confessions*, Liv. VII.; *Œuvres*, VIII. p. 246, and *Dialogues*; *Œuvres*, IX. pp. 319—320. Condillac is not named in the latter passage, but it is clear that he is meant.
[3] Lucretius, v. ll. 925—1135. Quoted by Pufendorf (II. ii.), whence I suspect that Rousseau drew his knowledge of it. See also Horace, *Sat.* I. iii. 99 etc.

however, is only once mentioned by name[1]—are raked by a running fire of criticism, which, in the case of Hobbes at any rate, is not incompatible with the keenest admiration[2]. And the same, though in a less degree, is true of Pufendorf. Even Locke, though Rousseau is far more in sympathy with his principles, is combated at several points[3]. And our general conclusion must be that, if Rousseau carefully studied the works of his predecessors, it was in no slavish spirit; that he treats them not as masters, but as equals; and that here, as elsewhere, no opinion is so well established that he is not willing to reconsider and, if necessary, to reject it.

There was, indeed, one influence to which, now as always, he surrendered without a struggle. That is the influence of Montaigne[4]. But this was because in Montaigne he found a spirit akin to his own; because, of all French writers, Montaigne had most in common with his hatred of convention, his love of what he conceived to be the primitive, and therefore the essential, elements of man's nature. And nowhere is the print of Montaigne so apparent as it is in this *Discourse* and in *Émile*[5].

There are now left only the natural historians and the travellers. Of the former, Buffon is the only one there is need to mention; Rousseau profited largely by the study of his great work, and always regarded the author with deep respect. On the latter he would seem to have spent considerable pains; his references to the travels of Corréal, Chardin, Kempfer and others are hardly less frequent than those of Montesquieu. And from his lament over the looseness of 'travellers' tales,' as well as from other indications, we may fairly conclude that he had read not only widely, but with discrimination. We are apt to forget that, side by side with the philosopher and the moralist, there was also in Rousseau no small vein of the man of science. Witness the keen interest he took in Physics and the theory of Music. Witness,

[1] *Discours*, p. 178. He is mentioned again, but for a quite different purpose, in the Dedication, p. 131.

[2] 'Un des plus beaux génies qui aient existé,' *L'état de guerre*, p. 305.

[3] *Discours*, Note L. Pufendorf is named, where Grotius might have been expected, p. 187.

[4] See, in particular, *Discours*, pp. 147—9; and Note I.

[5] 'Tout ce que j'ai pu retenir de ces foules de grandes vérités a été bien faiblement épars dans les trois principaux de mes écrits : savoir, ce premier *Discours*, celui de l'*Inégalité* et le *Traité de l'Éducation* ; lesquels trois ouvrages sont inséparables et forment ensemble un même tout.' Letter to Malesherbes of Jan. 12, 1762 ; *Œuvres*, x. p. 302.

above all, the zeal with which, during the last years of his life, he threw himself into the study of Botany. A medical reviewer of the time may have gone too far when he mentioned the *Discourse* among the books 'likely to be most useful to students of Medicine.' But, in the sense just indicated, there is a grain of truth in his tribute. In this manner was Saul also enrolled among the prophets[1].

This brings us to the last point which calls for notice. Among the memorable things in the *Discourse* is the author's marked acceptance of evolutionary methods and ideas. This appears not only in the opening remarks on the possibility of the animal descent of man; but also—and this is still more notable—in the whole tenor of the argument. From the first page to the last, the *Discourse* is a brilliant, if somewhat erratic, example of the evolutionary method. And that, at a time when, except for stray hints from Condillac and Diderot, there was no model later than Aristotle's *Politics* for the author to work upon. The *Scienza nuova*, the earliest modern example of the method, had indeed been before the world for a generation. But outside of Italy it was still utterly unknown[2]. And it is to the last degree unlikely that Rousseau had ever seen, or even heard of it. In this sense therefore, as in so many others, he may fairly be counted a pioneer. From the nature of the subjects on which he wrote, he had not often occasion to return to the method in question. But he did so, and with most fruitful results, when, at the height of his powers, he set himself to trace the growth of the child's mind in *Émile*.

[1] The collection of Travels which Rousseau would seem to have worked most diligently is the *Histoire Générale des Voyages*, published by the Abbé Prévost and others, 1746—70 (19 volumes, 4°). As the references to Corréal appear only in the Edition of 1782, I conclude that he cannot have read that traveller's record until after he had written the *Discourse* and the Notes; though a French translation was published at Amsterdam in 1738, and several references to it are to be found in Prévost's Collection (Vols. XII. and XIV., published respectively in 1754 and 1757). Nor do I think that he can have read Mandelslo (French translation, 1718, Leyden) at the time when he wrote the *Discourse* and Notes; though a Fragment, presumably later, shews that he did so eventually. All the references to Kolben seem to be drawn from Prévost's Collection (Vol. V., 1746).

[2] It has been thought by some that the *Scienza nuova* was known to Montesquieu. If so, he was careful to keep it dark. Goethe, who had clearly never heard the name of Vico before, tells us of the almost religious awe with which Filangieri shewed him a volume of the 'Sibylline oracles.' But that was in Vico's native city, Naples. And it may be doubted whether his fame had, even then, spread much further. *Italienische Reise*, March 5, 1787; *Werke* (ed. Weimar), XXXI. p. 27.

AVERTISSEMENT SUR LES NOTES.

J'ai ajouté quelques notes à cet ouvrage, selon ma coutume paresseuse de travailler à bâton rompu. Ces notes s'écartent quelquefois assez du sujet pour n'être pas bonnes à lire avec le texte. Je les ai donc rejetées à la fin du Discours, dans lequel j'ai tâché de suivre de mon mieux le plus droit chemin. Ceux qui auront le courage de recommencer pourront s'amuser la[1] seconde fois à battre les buissons, et tenter de parcourir les notes : il y aura peu de mal que les autres ne les lisent point du tout.

[1] Hachette, against all the authorities, has *une seconde fois*.

DISCOURS

SUR L'ORIGINE ET LES FONDEMENTS DE L'INÉGALITÉ PARMI LES HOMMES[1] :

PAR JEAN JAQUES ROUSSEAU, CITOYEN DE GENÈVE[2].

Non in depravatis, sed in his quæ bene secundum naturam se habent, considerandum est quid sit naturale.
Aristotle, Politic. lib. I. cap. ii.

À LA RÉPUBLIQUE DE GENÈVE.

MAGNIFIQUES, TRÈS HONORÉS ET SOUVERAINS SEIGNEURS,

Convaincu qu'il n'appartient qu'au citoyen vertueux de rendre à sa patrie des honneurs qu'elle puisse avouer, il y a trente ans que je travaille à mériter de vous offrir un hommage public ; et cette heureuse occasion suppléant en partie à ce que mes efforts n'ont pu faire, j'ai cru qu'il me serait permis de consulter ici le zèle qui m'anime, plus que le droit qui devrait m'autoriser. Ayant eu le bonheur de naître parmi vous, comment pourrais-je méditer sur l'égalité que la nature a mise entre les hommes, et sur l'inégalité qu'ils ont instituée, sans penser à la profonde sagesse avec laquelle l'une et l'autre, heureusement combinées dans cet État, concourent, de la manière la plus approchante de la loi naturelle et la plus favorable à la société, au maintien de l'ordre public et au bonheur des particuliers ? En recherchant les meilleures maximes que le

---

[1] The title of the Question proposed by the Academy of Dijon was: *Quelle est l'origine de l'inégalité parmi les hommes, et si elle est autorisée par la loi naturelle?*

[2] First Ed., Rey, Amsterdam, 1755. Several changes, mostly by way of addition, were made in the Ed. of 1782. These are indicated in the Notes. The Ed. of 1801 (Bozerian-Didot ; with Naigeon and others for editors) claims to be based upon Romilly's copy, corrected by Rousseau himself. Its variants, given in the Notes, have therefore some authority.

bon sens puisse dicter sur la constitution d'un Gouvernement, j'ai été si frappé de les voir toutes en exécution dans le vôtre, que, même sans être né dans vos murs, j'aurais cru ne pouvoir me dispenser d'offrir ce tableau de la société humaine à celui de tous les peuples qui me paraît en posséder les plus grands avantages, et en avoir le mieux prévenu les abus.

Si j'avais eu à choisir le lieu de ma naissance, j'aurais choisi une société d'une grandeur bornée par l'étendue des facultés humaines, c'est-à-dire par la possibilité d'être bien gouvernée, et où, chacun suffisant à son emploi, nul n'eût été contraint de commettre à d'autres les fonctions dont il était chargé : un État où, tous les particuliers se connaissant entre eux, les manœuvres obscures du vice, ni la modestie de la vertu, n'eussent pu se dérober aux regards et au jugement du public, et où cette douce habitude de se voir et de se connaître fît de l'amour de la patrie l'amour des citoyens plutôt que celui de la terre.

J'aurais voulu naître dans un pays où le souverain et le peuple ne pussent avoir qu'un seul et même intérêt, afin que tous les mouvements de la machine ne tendissent jamais qu'au bonheur commun; ce qui ne pouvant se faire à moins que le peuple et le souverain ne soient une même personne, il s'ensuit que j'aurais voulu naître sous un Gouvernement démocratique, sagement tempéré.

J'aurais voulu vivre et mourir libre, c'est-à-dire tellement soumis aux lois, que ni moi ni personne n'en pût secouer l'honorable joug: ce joug salutaire et doux, que les têtes les plus fières portent d'autant plus docilement qu'elles sont faites pour n'en porter aucun autre.

J'aurais donc voulu que personne dans l'État n'eût pu se dire au-dessus de la Loi, et que personne au dehors n'en pût imposer que l'État fût obligé de reconnaître. Car, quelle que puisse être la constitution d'un Gouvernement, s'il s'y trouve un seul homme qui ne soit pas soumis à la Loi, tous les autres sont nécessairement à la discrétion de celui-là (a); et s'il y a un chef national et un autre chef étranger, quelque partage d'autorité qu'ils puissent faire, il est impossible que l'un et l'autre soient bien obéis, et que l'État soit bien gouverné.

Je n'aurais point voulu habiter une République de nouvelle institution, quelques bonnes lois qu'elle pût avoir, de peur que le Gouvernement, autrement constitué peut-être qu'il ne faudrait pour le moment, ne convenant pas aux nouveaux citoyens, ou les

(a) The references to Rousseau's Notes are indicated by (a), (b), etc.

citoyens au nouveau Gouvernement, l'État ne fût sujet à être ébranlé et détruit presque dès sa naissance. Car il en est de la liberté comme de ces aliments solides et succulents, ou de ces vins généreux, propres à nourrir et fortifier les tempéraments robustes qui en ont l'habitude, mais qui accablent, ruinent et enivrent les faibles et délicats qui n'y sont point faits. Les peuples une fois accoutumés à des maîtres ne sont plus en état de s'en passer. S'ils tentent de secouer le joug, ils s'éloignent d'autant plus de la liberté, que, prenant pour elle une licence effrénée qui lui est opposée, leurs révolutions les livrent presque toujours à des séducteurs qui ne font qu'aggraver leurs chaînes. Le peuple romain lui-même, ce modèle de tous les peuples libres, ne fut point en état de se gouverner en sortant de l'oppression des Tarquins. Avili par l'esclavage et les travaux ignominieux qu'ils lui avaient imposés, ce n'était d'abord qu'une stupide populace qu'il fallut ménager et gouverner avec la plus grande sagesse, afin que, s'accoutumant peu à peu à respirer l'air salutaire de la liberté, ces âmes énervées, ou plutôt abruties, sous la tyrannie acquissent par degrés cette sévérité de mœurs et cette fierté de courage qui en firent enfin le plus respectable de tous les peuples. J'aurais donc cherché, pour ma patrie, une heureuse et tranquille République, dont l'ancienneté se perdît en quelque sorte dans la nuit des temps, qui n'eût éprouvé que des atteintes propres à manifester et affermir dans ses habitants le courage et l'amour de la patrie, et où les citoyens, accoutumés de longue main à une sage indépendance, fussent non seulement libres, mais dignes de l'être.

J'aurais voulu me choisir une patrie détournée, par une heureuse impuissance, du féroce amour des conquêtes, et garantie, par une position encore plus heureuse, de la crainte de devenir elle-même la conquête d'un autre État ; une ville libre, placée entre plusieurs peuples dont aucun n'eût intérêt à l'envahir, et dont chacun eût intérêt d'empêcher les autres de l'envahir eux-mêmes ; une République, en un mot, qui ne tentât point l'ambition de ses voisins, et qui pût raisonnablement compter sur leur secours au besoin. Il s'ensuit que, dans une position si heureuse, elle n'aurait eu rien à craindre que d'elle-même ; et que, si ses citoyens s'étaient exercés aux armes, c'eût été plutôt pour entretenir chez eux cette ardeur guerrière et cette fierté de courage qui sied si bien à la liberté et qui en nourrit le goût, que par la nécessité de pourvoir à leur propre défense.

J'aurais cherché un pays où le droit de législation fût commun à tous les citoyens ; car qui peut mieux savoir qu'eux sous quelles conditions il leur convient de vivre ensemble dans une même société ? Mais je n'aurais pas approuvé des plébiscites semblables à ceux des Romains, où les chefs de l'État, et les plus intéressés à sa conservation, étaient exclus des délibérations dont souvent dépendait son salut ; et où, par une absurde inconséquence, les magistrats étaient privés des droits dont jouissaient les simples citoyens.

Au contraire, j'aurais désiré que, pour arrêter les projets intéressés et mal conçus et les innovations dangereuses qui perdirent enfin les Athéniens, chacun n'eût pas le pouvoir de proposer de nouvelles lois à sa fantaisie ; que ce droit appartînt aux seuls magistrats ; qu'ils en usassent même avec tant de circonspection, que le peuple, de son côté, fût si réservé à donner son consentement à ces lois, et que la promulgation ne pût s'en faire qu'avec tant de solennité, qu'avant que la constitution fût ébranlée on eût le temps de se convaincre que c'est surtout la grande antiquité des lois qui les rend saintes et vénérables ; que le peuple méprise bientôt celles qu'il voit changer tous les jours ; et qu'en s'accoutumant à négliger les anciens usages, sous prétexte de faire mieux, on introduit souvent de grands maux pour en corriger de moindres.

J'aurais fui surtout, comme nécessairement mal gouvernée, une République où le peuple, croyant pouvoir se passer de ses magistrats, ou ne leur laisser qu'une autorité précaire, aurait imprudemment gardé l'administration des affaires civiles et l'exécution de ses propres lois : telle dut être la grossière constitution des premiers Gouvernements sortant immédiatement de l'état de nature ; et telle fut encore un des vices qui perdirent la République d'Athènes.

Mais j'aurais choisi celle où les particuliers, se contentant de donner la sanction aux lois, et de décider en corps, et sur le rapport des chefs, les plus importantes affaires publiques, établiraient des tribunaux respectés, en distingueraient avec soin les divers départements, éliraient d'année en année les plus capables et les plus intègres de leurs concitoyens pour administrer la justice et gouverner l'État ; et où, la vertu des magistrats portant ainsi témoignage de la sagesse du peuple, les uns et les autres s'honoreraient mutuellement. De sorte que, si jamais de funestes malentendus venaient à troubler la concorde publique, ces temps même[1] d'aveuglement et d'erreurs fussent marqués par des témoignages de modération, d'estime réciproque, et d'un commun respect pour

[1] Ed. 1755 has *mêmes*. Eds. 1782 and 1801, as in the text.

les lois : présages et garants d'une réconciliation sincère et perpétuelle.

Tels sont, magnifiques, très honorés et souverains Seigneurs, les avantages que j'aurais recherchés dans la patrie que je me serais choisie. Que si la Providence y avait ajouté de plus une situation charmante, un climat tempéré, un pays fertile, et l'aspect le plus délicieux qui soit sous le ciel, je n'aurais désiré, pour combler mon bonheur, que de jouir de tous ces biens dans le sein de cette heureuse patrie, vivant paisiblement dans une douce société avec mes concitoyens, exerçant envers eux, et à leur exemple, l'humanité, l'amitié et toutes les vertus, et laissant après moi l'honorable mémoire d'un homme de bien et d'un honnête et vertueux patriote.

Si, moins heureux ou trop tard sage, je m'étais vu réduit à finir en d'autres climats une infirme et languissante carrière, regrettant inutilement le repos et la paix dont une jeunesse imprudente m'aurait privé, j'aurais du moins nourri dans mon âme ces mêmes sentiments dont je n'aurais pu faire usage dans mon pays ; et, pénétré d'une affection tendre et désintéressée pour mes concitoyens éloignés, je leur aurais adressé du fond de mon cœur à peu près le discours suivant :

'Mes chers concitoyens, ou plutôt mes frères, puisque les liens du sang ainsi que les lois nous unissent presque tous, il m'est doux de ne pouvoir penser à vous, sans penser en même temps à tous les biens dont vous jouissez, et dont nul de vous peut-être ne sent mieux le prix que moi, qui les ai perdus. Plus je réfléchis sur votre situation politique et civile, et moins je puis imaginer que la nature des choses humaines puisse en comporter une meilleure. Dans tous les autres Gouvernements, quand il est question d'assurer le plus grand bien de l'État, tout se borne toujours à des projets en idées, et tout au plus à de simples possibilités. Pour vous, votre bonheur est tout fait, il ne faut qu'en jouir ; et vous n'avez plus besoin, pour devenir parfaitement heureux, que de savoir vous contenter de l'être. Votre souveraineté, acquise ou recouvrée à la pointe de l'épée, et conservée durant deux siècles à force de valeur et de sagesse, est enfin pleinement et universellement reconnue. Des traités honorables fixent vos limites, assurent vos droits et affermissent votre repos. Votre constitution est excellente, dictée par la plus sublime raison, et garantie par des Puissances amies et respectables ; votre État est tranquille ; vous n'avez ni guerres ni conquérants à craindre ; vous n'avez point d'autres maîtres que de sages lois que vous avez faites, administrées par des magistrats intègres qui sont de votre choix. Vous n'êtes ni assez riches pour vous énerver par la mollesse et perdre dans de vaines délices le goût du vrai bonheur et des solides vertus, ni assez pauvres pour avoir besoin de plus de secours étrangers que ne vous en procure votre industrie. Et cette liberté précieuse, qu'on ne maintient chez les grandes nations qu'avec des impôts exorbitants, ne vous coûte presque rien à conserver.

'Puisse durer toujours, pour le bonheur de ses citoyens et l'exemple des peuples, une République si sagement et si heureusement constituée! Voilà le seul vœu qui vous reste à faire, et le seul soin qui vous reste à prendre. C'est à vous seuls désormais, non à faire votre bonheur, vos ancêtres vous en ont évité la peine, mais à le rendre durable par la sagesse d'en bien user. C'est de votre union perpétuelle, de votre obéissance aux lois, de votre respect pour leurs ministres, que dépend votre conservation. S'il reste parmi vous le moindre germe d'aigreur ou de défiance, hâtez-vous de le détruire, comme un levain funeste d'où résulteraient tôt ou tard vos malheurs et la ruine de l'État. Je vous conjure de rentrer tous au fond de votre cœur, et de consulter la voix secrète de votre conscience. Quelqu'un parmi vous connaît-il dans l'univers un corps plus intègre, plus éclairé, plus respectable que celui de votre magistrature? Tous ses membres ne vous donnent-ils pas l'exemple de la modération, de la simplicité de mœurs, du respect pour les lois, et de la plus sincère réconciliation? Rendez donc sans reserve à de si sages chefs cette salutaire confiance que la raison doit à la vertu; songez qu'ils sont de votre choix, qu'ils le justifient, et que les honneurs, dus à ceux que vous avez constitués en dignité, retombent nécessairement sur vous-mêmes. Nul de vous n'est assez peu éclairé pour ignorer qu'où cesse la vigueur[1] des lois et l'autorité de leurs défenseurs, il ne peut y avoir ni sûreté ni liberté pour personne. De quoi s'agit-il donc entre vous, que de faire de bon cœur et avec une juste confiance ce que vous seriez toujours obligés de faire par un véritable intérêt, par devoir et pour la raison[2]? Qu'une coupable et funeste indifférence pour le maintien de la constitution ne vous fasse jamais négliger au besoin les sages avis des plus éclairés et des plus zélés d'entre vous; mais que l'équité, la modération, la plus respectueuse fermeté, continuent de régler toutes vos

---

[1] Ed. 1782 has *rigueur*, probably by a slip. Eds. 1755 and 1801 read as in the text.

[2] Ed. 1801 reads *par la raison*. Eds. 1755 and 1782, as in the text.

démarches, et de montrer en vous, à tout l'univers, l'exemple d'un peuple fier et modeste, aussi jaloux de sa gloire que de sa liberté. Gardez-vous surtout, et ce sera mon dernier conseil, d'écouter jamais des interprétations sinistres et des discours envenimés, dont les motifs secrets sont souvent plus dangereux que les actions qui en sont l'objet. Toute une maison s'éveille et se tient en alarmes aux premiers cris d'un bon et fidèle gardien, qui n'aboie jamais qu'à l'approche des voleurs ; mais on hait l'importunité de ces animaux bruyants qui troublent sans cesse le repos public, et dont les avertissements continuels et déplacés ne se font pas même écouter au moment qu'ils sont nécessaires.'

Et vous, magnifiques et très honorés Seigneurs, vous, dignes et respectables magistrats d'un peuple libre, permettez-moi de vous offrir en particulier mes hommages et mes devoirs. S'il y a dans le monde un rang propre à illustrer ceux qui l'occupent, c'est sans doute celui que donnent les talents et la vertu, celui dont vous vous êtes rendus dignes, et auxquels vos concitoyens vous ont élevés. Leur propre mérite ajoute encore au vôtre un nouvel éclat ; et, choisis par des hommes, capables d'en gouverner d'autres, pour les gouverner eux-mêmes, je vous trouve autant au-dessus des autres magistrats, qu'un peuple libre, et surtout celui que vous avez l'honneur de conduire, est, par ses lumières et par sa raison, au-dessus de la populace des autres États.

Qu'il me soit permis de citer un exemple, dont il devrait rester de meilleures traces, et qui sera toujours présent à mon cœur. Je ne me rappelle point sans la plus douce émotion la mémoire du vertueux citoyen de qui j'ai reçu le jour, et qui souvent entretint mon enfance du respect qui vous était dû. Je le vois encore, vivant du travail de ses mains, et nourrissant son âme des vérités les plus sublimes. Je vois Tacite, Plutarque et Grotius, mêlés devant lui avec les instruments de son métier. Je vois à ses côtés un fils chéri, recevant avec trop peu de fruit les tendres instructions du meilleur des pères. Mais si les égarements d'une folle jeunesse me firent oublier durant un temps de si sages leçons, j'ai le bonheur d'éprouver enfin que, quelque penchant qu'on ait vers le vice, il est difficile qu'une éducation, dont le cœur se mêle, reste perdue pour toujours.

Tels sont, magnifiques et très honorés Seigneurs, les Citoyens et même les simples habitants nés dans l'État que vous gouvernez ; tels sont ces hommes instruits et sensés dont, sous le nom d'ouvriers et de peuple, on a chez les autres nations des idées si basses et si fausses. Mon père, je l'avoue avec joie, n'était point distingué parmi ses concitoyens : il n'était que ce qu'ils sont tous ; et, tel qu'il était, il n'y a point de pays où sa société n'eût été recherchée, cultivée, et même avec fruit, par les plus honnêtes gens. Il ne m'appartient pas, et, grâce au ciel, il n'est pas nécessaire de vous parler des égards que peuvent attendre de vous des hommes de cette trempe, vos égaux par l'éducation, ainsi que par les droits de la nature et de la naissance ; vos inférieurs par leur volonté, par la préférence qu'ils doivent à votre mérite, qu'ils lui ont accordée, et pour laquelle vous leur devez à votre tour une sorte de reconnaissance. J'apprends avec une vive satisfaction de combien de douceur et de condescendance vous tempérez avec eux la gravité convenable aux ministres des lois, combien vous leur rendez en estime et en attentions[1] ce qu'ils vous doivent d'obéissance et de respects[2] : conduite pleine de justice et de sagesse, propre à éloigner de plus en plus la mémoire des événements malheureux qu'il faut oublier pour ne les revoir jamais ; conduite d'autant plus judicieuse, que ce peuple équitable et généreux se fait un plaisir de son devoir, qu'il aime naturellement à vous honorer, et que les plus ardents à soutenir leurs droits sont les plus portés à respecter les vôtres.

Il ne doit pas être étonnant que les chefs d'une société civile en aiment la gloire et le bonheur ; mais il l'est trop, pour le repos des hommes, que ceux qui se regardent comme les magistrats, ou plutôt comme les maîtres d'une patrie plus sainte et plus sublime, témoignent quelque amour pour la patrie terrestre qui les nourrit. Qu'il m'est doux de pouvoir faire en notre faveur une exception si rare, et placer au rang de nos meilleurs citoyens ces zélés dépositaires des dogmes sacrés, autorisés par les lois, ces vénérables pasteurs des âmes, dont la vive et douce éloquence porte d'autant mieux dans les cœurs les maximes de l'Évangile, qu'ils commencent toujours par les pratiquer eux-mêmes ! Tout le monde sait avec quel succès le grand art de la chaire est cultivé à Genève. Mais, trop accoutumés à voir dire d'une manière et faire d'une autre, peu de gens savent jusqu'à quel point l'esprit du christianisme, la sainteté des mœurs, la sévérité pour soi-même et la douceur pour autrui, règnent dans le corps de nos ministres. Peut-être appartient-il à la seule ville de Genève de montrer l'exemple édifiant d'une aussi parfaite union entre une société de théologiens et de gens de lettres ; c'est en grande partie sur leur sagesse et

---

[1] Hachette has *attention*, without any authority. Eds. 1755, 1782 and 1801, as in the text.

[2] Ed. 1801 has *respect*. Eds. 1755 and 1782, as in the text.

leur modération reconnues, c'est sur leur zèle pour la prospérité de l'État, que je fonde l'espoir de son éternelle tranquillité; et je remarque, avec un plaisir mêlé d'étonnement et de respect, combien ils ont d'horreur pour les affreuses maximes de ces hommes sacrés et barbares dont l'histoire fournit plus d'un exemple, et qui, pour soutenir les prétendus droits de Dieu, c'est-à-dire leurs intérêts, étaient d'autant moins avares du sang humain, qu'ils se flattaient que le leur serait toujours respecté.

Pourrais-je oublier cette précieuse moitié de la République qui fait le bonheur de l'autre, et dont la douceur et la sagesse y maintiennent la paix et les bonnes mœurs ? Aimables et vertueuses citoyennes, le sort de votre sexe sera toujours de gouverner le nôtre. Heureux, quand votre chaste pouvoir, exercé seulement dans l'union conjugale, ne se fait sentir que pour la gloire de l'État et le bonheur public ! C'est ainsi que les femmes commandaient à Sparte, et c'est ainsi que vous méritez de commander à Genève. Quel homme barbare pourrait résister à la voix de l'honneur et de la raison dans la bouche d'une tendre épouse ? et qui ne mépriserait un vain luxe, en voyant votre simple et modeste parure, qui, par l'éclat qu'elle tient de vous, semble être la plus favorable à la beauté ? C'est à vous[1] de maintenir toujours, par votre aimable et innocent empire, et par votre esprit insinuant, l'amour des lois dans l'État et la concorde parmi les Citoyens ; de réunir, par d'heureux mariages, les familles divisées, et surtout de corriger, par la persuasive douceur de vos leçons, et par les grâces modestes de votre entretien, les travers que nos jeunes gens vont prendre en d'autres pays ; d'où, au lieu de tant de choses utiles dont ils pourraient profiter, ils ne rapportent, avec un ton puéril et des airs ridicules pris parmi des femmes perdues, que l'admiration de je ne sais quelles prétendues grandeurs, frivoles dédommagements de la servitude, qui ne vaudront jamais l'auguste liberté. Soyez donc toujours ce que vous êtes, les chastes gardiennes des mœurs et les doux liens de la paix ; et continuez de faire valoir, en toute occasion, les droits du cœur et de la nature au profit du devoir et de la vertu.

Je me flatte de n'être point démenti par l'événement, en fondant sur de tels garants l'espoir du bonheur commun des citoyens et de la gloire de la République. J'avoue qu'avec tous ces avantages elle ne brillera pas de cet éclat dont la plupart des yeux sont éblouis, et dont le puéril et funeste goût est le plus mortel ennemi

---

[1] Rousseau had originally written, *C'est donc à vous.* The correction is made in the *Errata* to Ed. 1755. See Bosscha, p. 12.

du bonheur et de la liberté. Qu'une jeunesse dissolue aille chercher ailleurs des plaisirs faciles et de longs repentirs; que les prétendus gens de goût admirent en d'autres lieux la grandeur des palais, la beauté des équipages, les superbes ameublements, la pompe des spectacles, et tous les raffinements de la mollesse et du luxe. À Genève on ne trouvera que des hommes; mais pourtant un tel spectacle a bien son prix, et ceux qui le rechercheront vaudront bien les admirateurs du reste.

Daignez, magnifiques, très honorés et souverains Seigneurs, recevoir tous avec la même bonté les respectueux témoignages de l'intérêt que je prends à votre prospérité commune. Si j'étais assez malheureux pour être coupable de quelque transport indiscret dans cette vive effusion de mon cœur, je vous supplie de le pardonner à la tendre affection d'un vrai patriote, et au zèle ardent et légitime d'un homme qui n'envisage point de plus grand bonheur pour lui-même que celui de vous voir tous heureux.

Je suis avec le plus profond respect,

    Magnifiques, très honorés et souverains Seigneurs,
    Votre très humble et très obéissant serviteur et concitoyen,

                      JEAN JAQUES ROUSSEAU.

À Chambéri, le 12 juin 1754.

PRÉFACE.

La plus utile et la moins avancée de toutes les connaissances humaines me paraît être celle de l'homme (*b*); et j'ose dire que la seule inscription du temple de Delphes contenait un précepte plus important et plus difficile que tous les gros livres des moralistes[1]. Aussi je regarde le sujet de ce Discours comme une des questions les plus intéressantes que la philosophie puisse proposer, et, malheureusement pour nous, comme une des plus épineuses que les philosophes puissent résoudre: car comment connaître la source de l'inégalité parmi les hommes, si l'on ne commence par les connaître eux-mêmes? et comment l'homme viendra-t-il à bout

---

[1] The original form of this sentence is found on a loose slip of paper in the Neuchâtel Library (MS. 7854): 'S'il est vrai que l'inscription du temple de Delphes fut une des plus utiles leçons de la sagesse humaine, s'il est vrai qu'il importe tant à l'homme de se connaître, on ne peut nier que le sujet de ce Discours ne soit une des questions les plus importantes que la philosophie puisse....'

de se voir tel que l'a formé la nature, à travers tous les changements que la succession des temps et des choses a dû produire dans sa constitution originelle, et de démêler ce qu'il tient de son propre fonds d'avec ce que les circonstances et ses progrès ont ajouté ou changé à son état primitif? Semblable à la statue de Glaucus, que le temps, la mer et les orages avaient tellement défigurée qu'elle ressemblait moins à un dieu qu'à une bête féroce, l'âme humaine, altérée au sein de la société par mille causes sans cesse renaissantes, par l'acquisition d'une multitude de connaissances et d'erreurs, par les changements arrivés à la constitution des corps, et par le choc continuel des passions, a pour ainsi dire changé d'apparence au point d'être presque méconnaissable; et l'on n'y trouve[1] plus, au lieu d'un être agissant toujours par des principes certains et invariables, au lieu de cette céleste et majestueuse simplicité dont son auteur l'avait empreinte, que le difforme contraste de la passion qui croit raisonner, et de l'entendement en délire.

Ce qu'il y a de plus cruel encore, c'est que, tous les progrès de l'espèce humaine l'éloignant sans cesse de son état primitif, plus nous accumulons de nouvelles connaissances, et plus nous nous ôtons les moyens d'acquérir la plus importante de toutes; et que c'est, en un sens, à force d'étudier l'homme que nous nous sommes mis hors d'état de le connaître.

Il est aisé de voir que c'est dans ces changements successifs de la constitution humaine qu'il faut chercher la première origine des différences qui distinguent les hommes; lesquels, d'un commun aveu, sont naturellement aussi égaux entre eux que l'étaient les animaux de chaque espèce avant que diverses causes physiques eussent introduit dans quelques-unes les variétés que nous y remarquons. En effet, il n'est pas concevable que ces premiers changements, par quelque moyen qu'ils soient arrivés, aient altéré, tout à la fois et de la même manière, tous les individus de l'espèce; mais les uns s'étant perfectionnés ou détériorés, et ayant acquis diverses qualités, bonnes ou mauvaises, qui n'étaient point inhérentes à leur nature, les autres restèrent plus longtemps dans leur état originel. Et telle fut parmi les hommes la première source de l'inégalité, qu'il est plus aisé de démontrer ainsi en général que d'en assigner avec précision les véritables causes.

Que mes lecteurs ne s'imaginent donc pas que j'ose me flatter d'avoir vu ce qui me paraît si difficile à voir. J'ai commencé quelques raisonnements, j'ai hasardé quelques conjectures, moins

---

[1] Eds. 1755 and 1801 read *l'on n'y retrouve plus*. Ed. 1782, as in the text.

dans l'espoir de résoudre la question, que dans l'intention de l'éclaircir et de la réduire à son véritable état. D'autres pourront aisément aller plus loin dans la même route, sans qu'il soit facile à personne d'arriver au terme ; car ce n'est pas une légère entreprise de démêler ce qu'il y a d'originaire et d'artificiel dans la nature actuelle de l'homme, et de bien connaître un état qui n'existe plus, qui n'a peut-être point existé, qui probablement n'existera jamais, et dont il est pourtant nécessaire d'avoir des notions justes, pour bien juger de notre état présent. Il faudrait même plus de philosophie qu'on ne pense à celui qui entreprendrait de déterminer exactement les précautions à prendre, pour faire sur ce sujet de solides observations ; et une bonne solution du problème suivant ne me paraîtrait pas indigne des Aristotes et des Plines de notre siècle : *Quelles expériences seraient nécessaires pour parvenir à connaître l'homme naturel ? et quels sont les moyens de faire ces expériences au sein de la société ?* Loin d'entreprendre de résoudre ce problème, je crois en avoir assez médité le sujet pour oser répondre d'avance que les plus grands philosophes ne seront pas trop bons pour diriger ces expériences, ni les plus puissants souverains pour les faire : concours auquel il n'est guère raisonnable de s'attendre, surtout avec la persévérance ou plutôt la succession de lumières et de bonne volonté, nécessaire, de part et d'autre, pour arriver au succès.

Ces recherches si difficiles à faire, et auxquelles on a si peu songé jusqu'ici, sont pourtant les seuls moyens qui nous restent de lever une multitude de difficultés qui nous dérobent la connaissance des fondements réels de la société humaine. C'est cette ignorance de la nature de l'homme qui jette tant d'incertitude et d'obscurité sur la véritable définition du droit naturel : car l'idée du droit, dit M. Burlamaqui, et plus encore celle du droit naturel, sont manifestement des idées relatives à la nature de l'homme. C'est donc de cette nature même de l'homme, continue-t-il, de sa constitution et de son état, qu'il faut déduire les principes de cette science.

Ce n'est point sans surprise et sans scandale qu'on remarque le peu d'accord qui règne sur cette importante matière entre les divers auteurs qui en ont traité. Parmi les plus graves écrivains, à peine en trouve-t-on deux qui soient du même avis sur ce point. Sans parler des anciens philosophes, qui semblent avoir pris à tâche de se contredire entre eux sur les principes les plus fondamentaux, les jurisconsultes romains assujettissent indifféremment l'homme et tous les autres animaux à la même loi naturelle, parce qu'ils considèrent plutôt sous ce nom la loi que la nature s'impose à elle-même que celle qu'elle prescrit; ou plutôt à cause de l'acception particulière selon laquelle ces jurisconsultes entendent le mot de *loi*, qu'ils semblent n'avoir pris en cette occasion que pour l'expression des rapports généraux établis par la nature entre tous les êtres animés, pour leur commune conservation. Les modernes ne reconnaissant, sous le nom de *loi*, qu'une règle prescrite à un être moral, c'est-à-dire intelligent, libre, et considéré dans ses rapports avec d'autres êtres, bornent conséquemment au seul animal doué de raison, c'est-à-dire à l'homme, la compétence de la loi naturelle; mais, définissant cette loi chacun à sa mode, ils l'établissent tous sur des principes si métaphysiques, qu'il y a, même parmi nous, bien peu de gens en état de comprendre ces principes, loin de pouvoir les trouver d'eux-mêmes. De sorte que toutes les définitions de ces savants hommes, d'ailleurs en perpétuelle contradiction entre elles, s'accordent seulement en ceci, qu'il est impossible d'entendre la loi de nature, et par conséquent d'y obéir, sans être un très grand raisonneur et un profond métaphysicien: ce qui signifie précisément que les hommes ont dû employer, pour l'établissement de la société, des lumières qui ne se développent qu'avec beaucoup de peine, et pour fort peu de gens, dans le sein de la société même.

Connaissant si peu la nature, et s'accordant si mal sur le sens du mot *loi*, il serait bien difficile de convenir d'une bonne définition de la loi naturelle. Aussi toutes celles qu'on trouve dans les livres, outre le défaut de n'être point uniformes, ont-elles encore celui d'être tirées de plusieurs connaissances que les hommes n'ont point naturellement, et des avantages dont ils ne peuvent concevoir l'idée qu'après être sortis de l'état de nature. On commence par rechercher les règles dont, pour l'utilité commune, il serait à propos que les hommes convinssent entre eux; et puis on donne le nom de *loi naturelle* à la collection de ces règles, sans autre preuve que le bien qu'on trouve qui résulterait de leur pratique universelle. Voilà assurément une manière très commode de composer des définitions, et d'expliquer la nature des choses par des convenances presque arbitraires.

Mais, tant que nous ne connaîtrons point l'homme naturel, c'est en vain que nous voudrons déterminer la loi qu'il a reçue, ou celle qui convient le mieux à sa constitution. Tout ce que nous pouvons voir très clairement au sujet de cette loi, c'est que non seulement, pour qu'elle soit loi, il faut que la volonté de celui qu'elle oblige puisse s'y soumettre avec connaissance; mais qu'il faut encore, pour qu'elle soit naturelle, qu'elle parle immédiatement par la voix de la nature.

Laissant donc tous les livres scientifiques, qui ne nous apprennent qu'à voir les hommes tels qu'ils se sont faits, et méditant sur les premières et plus simples opérations de l'âme humaine, j'y crois apercevoir deux principes antérieurs à la raison, dont l'un nous intéresse ardemment à notre bien-être et à la conservation de nous-mêmes, et l'autre nous inspire une répugnance naturelle à voir périr ou souffrir tout être sensible, et principalement nos semblables. C'est du concours et de la combinaison que notre esprit est en état de faire de ces deux principes, sans qu'il soit nécessaire d'y faire entrer celui de la sociabilité, que me paraissent découler toutes les règles du droit naturel : règles que la raison est ensuite forcée de rétablir sur d'autres fondements, quand, par ses développements successifs, elle est venue à bout d'étouffer la nature.

De cette manière, on n'est point obligé de faire de l'homme un philosophe avant que d'en faire un homme. Ses devoirs envers autrui ne lui sont pas uniquement dictés par les tardives leçons de la sagesse ; et, tant qu'il ne résistera point à l'impulsion intérieure de la commisération, il ne fera jamais du mal à un autre homme, ni même à aucun être sensible, excepté dans le cas légitime où, sa conservation se trouvant intéressée, il est obligé de se donner la préférence à lui-même. Par ce moyen, on termine aussi les anciennes disputes sur la participation des animaux à la loi naturelle ; car il est clair que, dépourvus de lumières et de liberté, ils ne peuvent reconnaître cette loi. Mais, tenant en quelque chose à notre nature par la sensibilité dont ils sont doués, on jugera qu'ils doivent aussi participer au droit naturel, et que l'homme est assujetti envers eux à quelque espèce de devoirs. Il semble, en effet, que, si je suis obligé de ne faire aucun mal à mon semblable, c'est moins parce qu'il est un être raisonnable que parce qu'il est un être sensible : qualité qui, étant commune à la bête et à l'homme, doit au moins donner à l'une le droit de n'être point maltraitée inutilement par l'autre.

Cette même étude de l'homme originel, de ses vrais besoins et des principes fondamentaux de ses devoirs, est encore le seul bon moyen qu'on puisse employer pour lever ces foules de difficultés qui se présentent sur l'origine de l'inégalité morale, sur les vrais fondements du Corps politique, sur les droits réciproques de ses membres, et sur mille autres questions semblables, aussi importantes que mal éclaircies.

En considérant la société humaine d'un regard tranquille et désintéressé, elle ne semble montrer d'abord que la violence des hommes puissants et l'oppression des faibles: l'esprit se révolte contre la dureté des uns; on est porté[1] à déplorer l'aveuglement des autres. Et comme rien n'est moins stable parmi les hommes que ces relations extérieures que le hasard produit plus souvent que la sagesse, et que l'on appelle faiblesse ou puissance, richesse ou pauvreté, les établissements humains paraissent, au premier coup d'œil, fondés sur des monceaux de sable mouvant. Ce n'est qu'en les examinant de près, ce n'est qu'après avoir écarté la poussière et le sable qui environnent l'édifice, qu'on aperçoit la base inébranlable sur laquelle il est élevé, et qu'on apprend à en respecter les fondements. Or, sans l'étude sérieuse de l'homme, de ses facultés naturelles et de leurs développements successifs, on ne viendra jamais à bout de faire ces distinctions, et de séparer, dans l'actuelle constitution des choses, ce qu'a fait la volonté divine d'avec ce que l'art humain a prétendu faire. Les recherches politiques et morales, auxquelles donne lieu l'importante question que j'examine, sont donc utiles de toutes manières; et l'histoire hypothétique des Gouvernements est pour l'homme une leçon instructive à tous égards. En considérant ce que nous serions devenus abandonnés à nous-mêmes, nous devons apprendre à bénir celui dont la main bienfaisante, corrigeant nos institutions et leur donnant une assiette inébranlable, a prévenu les désordres qui devraient en résulter, et fait naître notre bonheur des moyens qui semblaient devoir combler notre misère.

                        Quem te Deus esse
Jussit, et humana qua parte locatus es in re,
Disce[2].

DISCOURS.

C'est de l'homme que j'ai à parler; et la question que j'examine m'apprend que je vais parler à des hommes; car on n'en propose point de semblables quand on craint d'honorer la vérité[3]. Je

---

[1] Ed. 1801 reads *ou est porté*. Eds. 1755 and 1782, as in the text. Rousseau insists on the reading of the text in his letter to Rey of Jan. 24, 1755 (Bosscha, p. 11).

[2] Persius, III. 71.

[3] Bosscha gives a facsimile of the first paragraph, as sent in a letter to Rey (Nov. 8, 1754):—' Page première du Discours, premier Alinea. Ôtez l'alinea en entier, et substituez-le de cette manière : C'est de l'homme que j'ai à parler, et la Question que j'examine m'apprend encore que [j'aurai à parler devant les hommes; et que c'est à des hommes que je vais parler] je

défendrai donc avec confiance la cause de l'humanité devant les sages qui m'y invitent, et je ne serai pas mécontent de moi-même si je me rends digne de mon sujet et de mes juges.

Je conçois dans l'espèce humaine deux sortes d'inégalité[1]: l'une, que j'appelle naturelle ou physique, parce qu'elle est établie par la nature, et qui consiste dans la différence des âges, de la santé, des forces du corps et des qualités de l'esprit ou de l'âme; l'autre, qu'on peut appeler inégalité morale ou politique, parce qu'elle dépend d'une sorte de convention, et qu'elle est établie, ou du moins autorisée, par le consentement des hommes. Celle-ci consiste dans les différents priviléges dont quelques-uns jouissent au préjudice des autres; comme d'être plus riches, plus honorés, plus puissants qu'eux, ou même de s'en faire obéir.

On ne peut pas demander quelle est la source de l'inégalité naturelle, parce que la réponse se trouverait énoncée dans la simple définition du mot. On peut encore moins chercher s'il n'y aurait point quelque liaison essentielle entre les deux inégalités. Car ce serait demander, en d'autres termes, si ceux qui commandent valent nécessairement mieux que ceux qui obéissent, et si la force du corps ou de l'esprit, la sagesse ou la vertu, se trouvent toujours dans les mêmes individus en proportion de la puissance ou de la richesse: question bonne peut-être[2] à agiter entre des esclaves entendus de leurs maîtres, mais qui ne convient pas à des hommes raisonnables et libres, qui cherchent la vérité.

De quoi s'agit-il donc précisément dans ce Discours? De marquer dans le progrès des choses le moment où, le droit succédant à la violence, la nature fut soumise à la Loi; d'expliquer par quel enchaînement de prodiges le fort put se résoudre à servir le faible, et le peuple à acheter un repos en idée au prix d'une félicité réelle.

Les philosophes qui ont examiné les fondements de la société ont tous senti la nécessité de remonter jusqu'à l'état de nature, mais aucun d'eux n'y est arrivé. Les uns n'ont point balancé à supposer à l'homme, dans cet état, la notion du juste et de l'injuste, sans se soucier de montrer qu'il dût avoir cette notion, ni

vais parler des hommes. [Car il n'y a en pas moins de courage à la proposer qu'à la résoudre; et ceux qui font connaître la vérité sur de pareilles matières ne s'honorent] pas moins que ceux qui l'osent soutenir. Je défendrai donc,' etc. (Bosscha, p. 4).

[1] Ed. 1801 and Hachette read *inégalités*. Eds. 1755 and 1782, as in the text.

[2] Hachette reads *peut-être bonne*, without any authority. Eds. 1755, 1782 and 1801 read as in the text.

même qu'elle lui fût utile. D'autres ont parlé du droit naturel que chacun a de conserver ce qui lui appartient, sans expliquer ce qu'ils entendaient par *appartenir*. D'autres, donnant d'abord au plus fort l'autorité sur le plus faible, ont aussitôt fait naître le Gouvernement, sans songer au temps qui dut s'écouler, avant que le sens des mots d'autorité et de Gouvernement pût exister parmi les hommes. Enfin tous, parlant sans cesse de besoin, d'avidité, d'oppression, de désirs et d'orgueil, ont transporté à l'état de nature des idées qu'ils avaient prises dans la société : ils parlaient de l'homme sauvage, et ils peignaient l'homme civil. Il n'est pas même venu dans l'esprit de la plupart des nôtres de douter que l'état de nature eût existé, tandis qu'il est évident, par la lecture des livres sacrés, que le premier homme, ayant reçu immédiatement de Dieu des lumières et des préceptes, n'était point lui-même dans cet état ; et qu'en ajoutant aux écrits de Moïse la foi que leur doit tout philosophe chrétien, il faut nier que, même avant le déluge, les hommes se soient jamais trouvés dans le pur état de nature, à moins qu'ils n'y soient retombés par quelque événement extraordinaire : paradoxe fort embarrassant à défendre, et tout à fait impossible à prouver.

Commençons donc par écarter tous les faits ; car ils ne touchent point à la question. Il ne faut pas prendre les recherches, dans lesquelles on peut entrer sur ce sujet, pour des vérités historiques ; mais seulement pour des raisonnements hypothétiques et conditionnels, plus propres à éclaircir la nature des choses qu'à en[1] montrer la véritable origine, et semblables à ceux que font tous les jours nos physiciens sur la formation du monde. La religion nous ordonne de croire que, Dieu lui-même ayant tiré les hommes de l'état de nature immédiatement après la création[2], ils sont inégaux parce qu'il a voulu qu'ils le fussent ; mais elle ne nous défend pas de former des conjectures tirées de la seule nature de l'homme et des êtres qui l'environnent, sur ce qu'aurait pu devenir le genre humain, s'il fût resté abandonné à lui-même. Voilà ce qu'on me demande, et ce que je me propose d'examiner dans ce Discours. Mon sujet intéressant l'homme en général, je tâcherai de prendre un langage qui convienne à toutes les nations ; ou plutôt, oubliant les temps et les lieux pour ne songer qu'aux hommes à qui je parle, je me supposerai dans le Lycée d'Athènes,

---

[1] Ed. 1755 omits *en*, by an oversight. Eds. 1782 and 1801, as in the text.
[2] *immédiatement après la création*, wanting in Ed. 1755. Eds. 1782 and 1801 read as in the text.

répétant les leçons de mes maîtres, ayant les Platons et les Xénocrates[1] pour juges, et le genre humain pour auditeur.

O homme, de quelque contrée que tu sois, quelles que soient tes opinions, écoute : voici ton histoire, telle que j'ai cru la lire, non dans les livres de tes semblables, qui sont menteurs, mais dans la nature, qui ne ment jamais. Tout ce qui sera d'elle sera vrai ; il n'y aura de faux que ce que j'y aurai mêlé du mien, sans le vouloir. Les temps dont je vais parler sont bien éloignés : combien tu as changé de ce que tu étais ! C'est, pour ainsi dire, la vie de ton espèce que je te vais décrire d'après les qualités que tu as reçues, que ton éducation et tes habitudes ont pu dépraver, mais qu'elles n'ont pu détruire. Il y a, je le sens, un âge auquel l'homme individuel voudrait s'arrêter : tu chercheras l'âge auquel tu désirerais que ton espèce se fût arrêtée. Mécontent de ton état présent, par des raisons qui annoncent à ta postérité malheureuse de plus grands mécontentements encore, peut-être voudrais-tu pouvoir rétrograder ; et ce sentiment doit faire l'éloge de tes premiers aïeux, la critique de tes contemporains, et l'effroi de ceux qui auront le malheur de vivre après toi.

PREMIÈRE PARTIE.

Quelque important qu'il soit, pour bien juger de l'état naturel de l'homme, de le considérer dès son origine et de l'examiner, pour ainsi dire, dans le premier embryon de l'espèce, je ne suivrai point son organisation à travers ses développements successifs : je ne m'arrêterai pas à rechercher dans le système animal ce qu'il put être au commencement, pour devenir enfin ce qu'il est. Je n'examinerai pas si, comme le pense Aristote, ses ongles allongés ne furent point d'abord des griffes crochues ; s'il n'était point velu comme un ours ; et si, marchant à quatre pieds (c), ses regards dirigés vers la terre et bornés à un horizon de quelques pas, ne marquaient point à la fois le caractère et les limites de ses idées. Je ne pourrais former sur ce sujet que des conjectures vagues et presque imaginaires. L'anatomie comparée a fait encore trop peu de progrès, les observations des naturalistes sont encore trop incertaines, pour qu'on puisse établir sur de pareils fondements la base d'un raisonnement solide. Ainsi, sans avoir recours aux connaissances surnaturelles que nous avons sur ce point, et sans avoir égard aux changements qui ont dû survenir dans la conformation,

---

[1] Ed. 1801, *les Platon et les Xénocrate*. Eds. 1755, 1782, as in the text.

tant intérieure qu'extérieure, de l'homme, à mesure qu'il appliquait ses membres à de nouveaux usages et qu'il se nourrissait de nouveaux aliments, je le supposerai conformé de tout[1] temps, comme je le vois aujourd'hui : marchant à deux pieds, se servant de ses mains comme nous faisons des nôtres, portant ses regards sur toute la nature, et mesurant des yeux la vaste étendue du ciel.

En dépouillant cet être ainsi constitué de tous les dons surnaturels qu'il a pu recevoir, et de toutes les facultés artificielles qu'il n'a pu acquérir que par de longs progrès ; en le considérant, en un mot, tel qu'il a dû sortir des mains de la nature, je vois un animal moins fort que les uns, moins agile que les autres, mais, à tout prendre, organisé le plus avantageusement de tous. Je le vois se rassasiant sous un chêne, se désaltérant au premier ruisseau, trouvant son lit au pied du même arbre qui lui a fourni son repas ; et voilà ses besoins satisfaits.

La terre, abandonnée à sa fertilité naturelle (d), et couverte de forêts immenses que la cognée ne mutila jamais, offre à chaque pas des magasins et des retraites aux animaux de toute espèce. Les hommes, dispersés parmi eux, observent, imitent leur industrie, et s'élèvent ainsi jusqu'à l'instinct des bêtes : avec cet avantage que chaque espèce n'a que le sien propre, et que l'homme, n'en ayant peut-être aucun qui lui appartienne, se les approprie tous ; se nourrit également de la plupart des aliments divers (e) que les autres animaux se partagent ; et trouve par conséquent sa subsistance plus aisément que ne peut faire aucun d'eux.

Accoutumés dès l'enfance aux intempéries de l'air et à la rigueur des saisons, exercés à la fatigue, et forcés de défendre nus et sans armes leur vie et leur proie contre les autres bêtes féroces, ou de leur échapper à la course, les hommes se forment un tempérament robuste et presque inaltérable. Les enfants, apportant au monde l'excellente constitution de leurs pères, et la fortifiant par les mêmes exercices qui l'ont produite, acquièrent ainsi toute la vigueur dont l'espèce humaine est capable. La nature en use précisément avec eux comme la loi de Sparte avec les enfants des citoyens ; elle rend forts et robustes ceux qui sont bien constitués, et fait périr tous les autres : [2]différente en cela de nos sociétés, où l'État, en rendant les enfants onéreux aux pères, les tue indistinctement avant leur naissance [2].

Le corps de l'homme sauvage étant le seul instrument qu'il connaisse, il l'emploie à divers usages, dont, par le défaut d'exercice, les nôtres sont incapables ; et c'est notre industrie qui nous ôte la

---

[1] Ed. 1755, *tous*.   [2] For the rough draft of this sentence, see p. 350.

force et l'agilité, que la nécessité l'oblige d'acquérir. S'il avait eu une hache, son poignet romprait-il de si fortes branches ? s'il avait eu une fronde, lancerait-il de la main une pierre avec tant de raideur ? S'il avait eu une échelle, grimperait-il si légèrement sur un arbre ? s'il avait eu un cheval, serait-il si vite à la course ? Laissez à l'homme civilisé le temps de rassembler toutes ses machines autour de lui; on ne peut douter qu'il ne surmonte facilement l'homme sauvage. Mais, si vous voulez voir un combat plus inégal encore, mettez-les nus et désarmés vis-à-vis l'un de l'autre ; et vous reconnaîtrez bientôt quel est l'avantage d'avoir sans cesse toutes ses forces à sa disposition, d'être toujours prêt à tout événement, et de se porter, pour ainsi dire, toujours tout entier avec soi (*f*).

Hobbes prétend que l'homme est naturellement intrépide, et ne cherche qu'à attaquer et combattre. Un philosophe illustre[1] pense, au contraire, et Cumberland et Pufendorf l'assurent aussi, que rien n'est si timide que l'homme dans l'état de nature, et qu'il est toujours tremblant et prêt à fuir au moindre bruit qui le frappe, au moindre mouvement qu'il aperçoit. Cela peut être ainsi pour les objets qu'il ne connaît pas ; et je ne doute point qu'il ne soit effrayé par tous les nouveaux spectacles qui s'offrent à lui, toutes les fois qu'il ne peut distinguer le bien et le mal physiques qu'il en doit attendre, ni comparer ses forces avec les dangers qu'il a à courir : circonstances rares dans l'état de nature, où toutes choses marchent d'une manière si uniforme, et où la face de la terre n'est point sujette à ces changements brusques et continuels qu'y causent les passions et l'inconstance des peuples réunis. Mais, l'homme sauvage vivant dispersé parmi les animaux et se trouvant de bonne heure dans le cas de se mesurer avec eux, il en fait bientôt la comparaison ; et, sentant qu'il les surpasse plus en adresse qu'ils ne le surpassent en force, il apprend à ne les plus craindre. Mettez un ours ou un loup aux prises avec un sauvage robuste, agile, courageux, comme ils sont tous, armé de pierres et d'un bon bâton ; et vous verrez que le péril sera tout au moins réciproque, et qu'après plusieurs expériences pareilles, les bêtes féroces, qui n'aiment point à s'attaquer l'une à l'autre, s'attaqueront peu volontiers à l'homme, qu'elles auront trouvé tout aussi féroce qu'elles. À l'égard des animaux qui ont réellement plus de force qu'il n'a d'adresse, il est vis-à-vis d'eux dans le cas des autres espèces plus faibles, qui ne laissent pas de subsister ; avec cet avantage pour l'homme que, non moins dispos qu'eux à la course,

---

[1] Montesquieu, *Esprit des lois*, I. ii.

et trouvant sur les arbres un refuge presque assuré, il a partout le prendre et le laisser dans la rencontre, et le choix de la fuite ou du combat. Ajoutons qu'il ne paraît pas qu'aucun animal fasse naturellement la guerre à l'homme hors le cas de sa propre défense ou d'une extrême faim, ni témoigne contre lui de ces violentes antipathies, qui semblent annoncer qu'une espèce est destinée par la nature à servir de pâture à l'autre.

Voilà[1] sans doute les raisons pourquoi les nègres et les sauvages se mettent si peu en peine des bêtes féroces qu'ils peuvent rencontrer dans les bois. Les Caraïbes de Venezuela vivent entre autres, à cet égard, dans la plus profonde sécurité et sans le moindre inconvénient. Quoiqu'ils soient presque nus, dit François Corréal, ils ne laissent pas de s'exposer hardiment dans les bois, armés seulement de la flèche et de l'arc ; mais on n'a jamais ouï dire qu'aucun d'eux ait été dévoré des bêtes.

D'autres ennemis plus redoutables, et dont l'homme n'a pas les mêmes moyens de se défendre, sont les infirmités naturelles, l'enfance, la vieillesse, et les maladies de toute espèce : tristes signes de notre faiblesse, dont les deux premiers sont communs à tous les animaux, et dont le dernier appartient principalement à l'homme vivant en société. J'observe même, au sujet de l'enfance, que la mère, portant partout son enfant avec elle, a beaucoup plus de facilité à le nourrir que n'ont les femelles de plusieurs animaux, qui sont forcées d'aller et venir sans cesse avec beaucoup de fatigue, d'un côté pour chercher leur pâture, et de l'autre, pour allaiter ou nourrir leurs petits. Il est vrai que, si la femme vient à périr, l'enfant risque fort de périr avec elle ; mais ce danger est commun à cent autres espèces, dont les petits ne sont de longtemps en état d'aller chercher eux-mêmes leur nourriture ; et si l'enfance est plus longue parmi nous, la vie étant plus longue aussi, tout est encore à peu près égal en ce point (g), quoiqu'il y ait sur la durée du premier âge, et sur le nombre des petits (h), d'autres règles qui ne sont pas de mon sujet. Chez les vieillards qui agissent et transpirent peu, le besoin d'aliments diminue avec la faculté d'y pourvoir ; et comme la vie sauvage éloigne d'eux la goutte et les rhumatismes, et que la vieillesse est de tous les maux celui que les secours humains peuvent le moins soulager, ils s'éteignent enfin, sans qu'on s'aperçoive qu'ils cessent d'être, et presque sans s'en apercevoir eux-mêmes.

À l'égard des maladies, je ne répéterai point les vaines et

---

[1] This paragraph appeared for the first time in the Ed. of 1782.

fausses déclamations que font contre la médecine la plupart des gens en santé; mais je demanderai s'il y a quelque observation solide de laquelle on puisse conclure que, dans les pays où cet art est le plus négligé, la vie moyenne de l'homme soit plus courte que dans ceux où il est cultivé avec le plus de soin. Et comment cela pourrait-il être, si nous nous donnons plus de maux que la médecine ne peut nous fournir de remèdes ? L'extrême inégalité dans la manière de vivre, l'excès d'oisiveté dans les uns, l'excès de travail dans les autres, la facilité d'irriter et de satisfaire nos appétits et notre sensualité, les aliments trop recherchés des riches, qui les nourrissent de sucs échauffants et les accablent d'indigestions, la mauvaise nourriture des pauvres, dont ils manquent même le plus souvent, et dont le défaut les porte à surcharger avidement leur estomac dans l'occasion; les veilles, les excès de toute espèce, les transports immodérés de toutes les passions, les fatigues et l'épuisement d'esprit, les chagrins et les peines sans nombre qu'on éprouve dans tous les états et dont les âmes sont perpétuellement rongées : voilà les funestes garants que la plupart de nos maux sont notre propre ouvrage, et que nous les aurions presque tous évités, en conservant la manière de vivre simple, uniforme et solitaire qui nous était prescrite par la nature. Si elle nous a destinés à être sains, j'ose presque assurer que l'état de réflexion est un état contre nature, et que l'homme qui médite est un animal dépravé. Quand on songe à la bonne constitution des sauvages, au moins de ceux que nous n'avons pas perdus avec nos liqueurs fortes; quand on sait qu'ils ne connaissent presque d'autres maladies que les blessures et la vieillesse, on est très porté à croire qu'on ferait aisément l'histoire des maladies humaines en suivant celle des sociétés civiles. C'est au moins l'avis de Platon, qui juge, sur certains remèdes employés ou approuvés par Podalyre et Macaon au siége de Troie, que diverses maladies que ces remèdes devaient exciter n'étaient point encore alors connues parmi les hommes[1]; [2]et Celse rapporte que la diète, aujourd'hui si nécessaire, ne fut inventée que par Hippocrate[2].

Avec si peu de sources de maux, l'homme dans l'état de nature n'a donc guère besoin de remèdes, moins encore de médecins; l'espèce humaine n'est point non plus à cet égard de pire condition que toutes les autres; et il est aisé de savoir des chasseurs si dans leurs courses ils trouvent beaucoup d'animaux infirmes.

---

[1] Plato, *Republic*, III. 14. The reference is to *Iliad*, XI. 639.
[2] This sentence appeared for the first time in Ed. 1782.

Plusieurs en trouvent-ils[1] qui ont reçu des blessures considérables très bien cicatrisées, qui ont eu des os et même des membres rompus, et repris sans autre chirurgien que le temps, sans autre régime que leur vie ordinaire, et qui n'en sont pas moins parfaitement guéris pour n'avoir point été tourmentés d'incisions, empoisonnés de drogues, ni exténués de jeûnes. Enfin, quelque utile que puisse être parmi nous la médecine bien administrée, il est toujours certain que, si le sauvage malade, abandonné à lui-même, n'a rien à espérer que de la nature, en revanche il n'a rien à craindre que de son mal : ce qui rend souvent sa situation préférable à la nôtre.

Gardons-nous donc de confondre l'homme sauvage avec les hommes que nous avons sous les yeux. La nature traite tous les animaux abandonnés à ses soins avec une prédilection qui semble montrer combien elle est jalouse de ce droit. Le cheval, le chat, le taureau, l'âne même, ont la plupart une taille plus haute, tous une constitution plus robuste, plus de vigueur, de force et de courage dans les forêts que dans nos maisons : ils perdent la moitié de ces avantages en devenant domestiques, et l'on dirait que tous nos soins à bien traiter et nourrir ces animaux n'aboutissent qu'à les abâtardir. Il en est ainsi de l'homme même : en devenant sociable et esclave il devient faible, craintif, rampant ; et sa manière de vivre molle et efféminée achève d'énerver à la fois sa force et son courage. Ajoutons qu'entre les conditions sauvage et domestique la différence d'homme à homme doit être plus grande encore que celle de bête à bête : car, l'animal et l'homme ayant été traités également par la nature, toutes les commodités, que l'homme se donne de plus qu'aux animaux qu'il apprivoise, sont autant de causes particulières qui le font dégénérer plus sensiblement.

Ce n'est donc pas un si grand malheur à ces premiers hommes, ni surtout un si grand obstacle à leur conservation, que la nudité, le défaut d'habitation, et la privation de toutes ces inutilités que nous croyons si nécessaires. S'ils n'ont pas la peau velue, ils n'en ont aucun besoin dans les pays chauds ; et ils savent bientôt, dans les pays froids, s'approprier celles des bêtes qu'ils ont vaincues.

---

[1] Ed. 1755 reads *Plusieurs en trouvent qui*. But the reading is corrected in the *Errata*. In his letter to Rey of Feb. 20, 1755, Rousseau writes : ' Il faut lire : *plusieurs en trouvent-ils qui*. Quoique cette façon de parler soit un peu sauvage, comme elle fait un sens tout différent, j'ai eu mes raisons pour l'employer' (Bosscha, p. 14). Ed. 1782 reads as in the text. Ed. 1801 adopts the reading which Rousseau rejected ; so does Hachette.

S'ils n'ont que deux pieds pour courir, ils ont deux bras pour pourvoir à leur défense et à leurs besoins. Leurs enfants marchent peut-être tard et avec peine, mais les mères les portent avec facilité : avantage qui manque aux autres espèces, où la mère, étant poursuivie, se voit contrainte d'abandonner ses petits ou de régler son pas sur le leur[1]. Enfin, à moins de supposer ces concours singuliers et fortuits de circonstances dont je parlerai dans la suite, et qui pouvaient fort bien ne jamais arriver, il est clair, en tout état de cause, que le premier qui se fit des habits ou un logement se donna en cela des choses peu nécessaires, puisqu'il s'en était passé jusqu'alors, et qu'on ne voit pas pourquoi il n'eût pu supporter, homme fait, un genre de vie qu'il supportait dès son enfance.

Seul, oisif, et toujours voisin du danger, l'homme sauvage doit aimer à dormir, et avoir le sommeil léger, comme les animaux, qui, pensant peu, dorment, pour ainsi dire, tout le temps qu'ils ne pensent point. Sa propre conservation faisant presque son unique soin, ses facultés les plus exercées doivent être celles qui ont pour objet principal l'attaque et la défense, soit pour subjuguer sa proie, soit pour se garantir d'être celle d'un autre animal. Au contraire, les organes qui ne se perfectionnent que par la mollesse et la sensualité doivent rester dans un état de grossièreté qui exclut en lui toute espèce de délicatesse : et ses sens se trouvant partagés sur ce point, il aura le toucher et le goût d'une rudesse extrême ; la vue, l'ouïe et l'odorat, de la plus grande subtilité. Tel est l'état animal en général ; et c'est aussi, selon le rapport des voyageurs, celui de la plupart des peuples sauvages. Ainsi il ne faut point s'étonner que les Hottentots du Cap de Bonne-Espérance découvrent à la simple vue des vaisseaux en haute mer d'aussi loin que les Hollandais avec des lunettes ; ni que les sauvages de l'Amérique sentissent les Espagnols à la piste comme auraient pu faire les meilleurs chiens ; ni que toutes ces nations barbares supportent sans peine leur nudité, aiguisent leur goût à force de piment, et boivent les liqueurs européennes comme de l'eau.

---

[1] 'Il peut y avoir à ceci quelques exceptions : celle, par exemple, de cet animal de la Province de Nicaragua, qui ressemble à un renard, qui a les pieds comme les mains d'un homme, et qui, selon Corréal, a sous le ventre un sac où la mère met ses petits, lorsqu'elle est obligée de fuir. C'est, sans doute, le même animal qu'on appelle *tlaquatzin* au Mexique, et à la femelle duquel Laët donne un semblable sac pour le même usage.' [This note appeared for the first time in the Ed. of 1782. It is carelessly omitted by Hachette.]

rare ou touffu, clair ou foncé; et s'il dépendait de vous de n'y voir que ce qui se trouve en tout arbre, cette image ne ressemblerait plus à un arbre. Les êtres purement abstraits se voient de même, ou ne se conçoivent que par le discours. La définition seule du triangle vous en donne la véritable idée : sitôt que vous en figurez un dans votre esprit, c'est un tel triangle et non pas un autre, et vous ne pouvez éviter d'en rendre les lignes sensibles ou le plan coloré. Il faut donc énoncer des propositions, il faut donc parler, pour avoir des idées générales : car, sitôt que l'imagination s'arrête, l'esprit ne marche plus qu'à l'aide du discours. Si donc les premiers inventeurs n'ont pu donner des noms qu'aux idées qu'ils avaient déjà, il s'ensuit que les premiers substantifs n'ont jamais pu être que des noms propres.

Mais lorsque, par des moyens que je ne conçois pas, nos nouveaux grammairiens commencèrent à étendre leurs idées et à généraliser leurs mots, l'ignorance des inventeurs dut assujettir cette méthode à des bornes fort étroites; et, comme ils avaient d'abord trop multiplié les noms des individus faute de connaître les genres et les espèces, ils firent ensuite trop peu d'espèces et de genres, faute d'avoir considéré les êtres par toutes leurs différences. Pour pousser les divisions assez loin, il eût fallu plus d'expérience et de lumière[1] qu'ils n'en pouvaient avoir, et plus de recherches et de travail qu'ils n'y en voulaient employer. Or, si, même aujourd'hui, l'on découvre chaque jour de nouvelles espèces qui avaient échappé jusqu'ici à toutes nos observations, qu'on pense combien il dut s'en dérober à des hommes qui ne jugeaient des choses que sur le premier aspect. Quant aux classes primitives et aux notions les plus générales, il est superflu d'ajouter qu'elles durent leur échapper encore. Comment, par exemple, auraient-ils imaginé ou entendu les mots de matière, d'esprit, de substance, de mode, de figure, de mouvement, puisque nos philosophes, qui s'en servent depuis si longtemps, ont bien de la peine à les entendre eux-mêmes, et que, les idées qu'on attache à ces mots étant purement métaphysiques, ils n'en trouvaient aucun modèle dans la nature ?

Je m'arrête à ces premiers pas, et je supplie mes juges de suspendre ici leur lecture pour considérer, sur l'invention des seuls substantifs physiques, c'est-à-dire sur la partie de la langue la plus facile à trouver, le chemin qui lui reste à faire pour exprimer toutes les pensées des hommes, pour prendre une forme constante,

---

[1] Ed. 1801 and Hachette read *lumières*. Eds. 1755 and 1782, as in the text.

pouvoir[1] être parlée en public, et influer sur la société. Je les supplie de réfléchir à ce qu'il a fallu de temps et de connaissances pour trouver les nombres (*n*), les mots abstraits, les aoristes, et tous les temps des verbes, les particules, la syntaxe, lier les propositions, les raisonnements, et former toute la logique du discours. Quant à moi, effrayé des difficultés qui se multiplient, et convaincu de l'impossibilité presque démontrée que les langues aient pu naître et s'établir par des moyens purement humains, je laisse à qui voudra l'entreprendre la discussion de ce difficile problème : lequel a été le plus nécessaire, de la société déjà liée à l'institution des langues, ou des langues déjà inventées à l'établissement de la société ?

Quoi qu'il en soit de ces origines, on voit du moins, au peu de soin qu'a pris la nature de rapprocher les hommes par des besoins mutuels et de leur faciliter l'usage de la parole, combien elle a peu préparé leur sociabilité, et combien elle a peu mis du sien dans tout ce qu'ils ont fait pour en établir les liens. En effet, il est impossible d'imaginer pourquoi, dans cet état primitif, un homme aurait plutôt besoin d'un autre homme, qu'un singe ou un loup de son semblable ; ni, ce besoin supposé, quel motif pourrait engager l'autre à y pourvoir, ni même, en ce dernier cas, comment ils pourraient convenir entre eux des conditions. Je sais qu'on nous répète sans cesse que rien n'eût été si misérable que l'homme dans cet état ; et s'il est vrai, comme je crois l'avoir prouvé, qu'il n'eût pu qu'après bien des siècles avoir le désir et l'occasion d'en sortir, ce serait un procès à faire à la nature, et non à celui qu'elle aurait ainsi constitué. Mais si j'entends bien ce terme de *misérable*, c'est un mot qui n'a aucun sens, ou qui ne signifie qu'une privation douloureuse, et la souffrance du corps ou de l'âme : or, je voudrais bien qu'on m'expliquât quel peut être le genre de misère d'un être libre dont le cœur est en paix et le corps en santé. Je demande laquelle, de la vie civile ou naturelle, est la plus sujette à devenir insupportable à ceux qui en jouissent. Nous ne voyons presque autour de nous que des gens qui se plaignent de leur existence, plusieurs mêmes qui s'en privent autant qu'il est en eux ; et la réunion des lois divines et humaine suffit à peine pour arrêter ce désordre. Je demande si jamais on a ouï dire qu'un sauvage en liberté ait seulement songé à se plaindre de la vie et à se donner la mort. Qu'on juge donc, avec moins d'orgueil, de quel côté est la véritable misère. Rien au contraire n'eût été si misérable que l'homme sauvage ébloui par des lumières, tourmenté

---

[1] Ed. 1801 and Hachette, *pour pouvoir*. Eds. 1755, 1782, as above.

par des passions, et raisonnant sur un état différent du sien. Ce fut par une providence très sage que les facultés qu'il avait en puissance ne devaient se développer qu'avec les occasions de les exercer, afin qu'elles ne lui fussent ni superflues et à charge avant le temps, ni tardives et inutiles au besoin. Il avait dans le seul instinct tout ce qu'il lui fallait pour vivre dans l'état de nature ; il n'a dans une raison cultivée que ce qu'il lui faut pour vivre en société.

Il paraît d'abord que les hommes dans cet état, n'ayant entre eux aucune sorte de relation morale ni de devoirs connus, ne pouvaient être ni bons ni méchants, et n'avaient ni vices ni vertus ; à moins que, prenant ces mots dans un sens physique, on n'appelle vices dans l'individu les qualités qui peuvent nuire à sa propre conservation, et vertus celles qui peuvent y contribuer : auquel cas, il faudrait appeler le plus vertueux celui qui résisterait le moins aux simples impulsions de la nature. Mais, sans nous écarter du sens ordinaire, il est à propos de suspendre le jugement que nous pourrions porter sur une telle situation, et de nous défier de nos préjugés jusqu'à ce que, la balance à la main, on ait examiné s'il y a plus de vertus que de vices parmi les hommes civilisés ; ou si leurs vertus sont plus avantageuses que leurs vices ne sont funestes ; ou si le progrès de leurs connaissances est un dédommagement suffisant des maux qu'ils se font mutuellement, à mesure qu'ils s'instruisent du bien qu'ils devraient se faire ; ou s'ils ne seraient pas, à tout prendre, dans une situation plus heureuse de n'avoir ni mal à craindre ni bien à espérer de personne, que de s'être soumis à une dépendance universelle, et de s'obliger à tout recevoir de ceux qui ne s'obligent à leur rien donner.

N'allons pas surtout conclure avec Hobbes que, pour n'avoir aucune idée de la bonté, l'homme soit naturellement méchant ; qu'il soit vicieux, parce qu'il ne connaît pas la vertu ; qu'il refuse toujours à ses semblables des services qu'il ne croit pas leur devoir ; ni qu'en vertu du droit qu'il s'attribue avec raison aux choses dont il a besoin il s'imagine follement être le seul propriétaire de tout l'univers. Hobbes a très bien vu le défaut de toutes les définitions modernes du droit naturel ; mais les conséquences qu'il tire de la sienne montrent qu'il la prend dans un sens qui n'est pas moins faux. En raisonnant sur les principes qu'il établit, cet auteur devait dire que, l'état de nature étant celui où le soin de notre conservation est le moins préjudiciable à celle d'autrui, cet état était par conséquent le plus propre à la paix et le plus convenable au genre humain. Il dit précisément le contraire, pour avoir fait entrer mal à propos dans le soin de la conservation de l'homme sauvage le besoin de satisfaire une multitude de passions qui sont l'ouvrage de la société, et qui ont rendu les lois nécessaires. Le méchant, dit-il, est un enfant robuste. Il reste à savoir si l'homme sauvage est un enfant robuste. Quand on le lui accorderait, qu'en conclurait-il? Que si, quand il est robuste, cet homme était aussi dépendant des autres que quand il est faible, il n'y a sorte d'excès auxquels il ne se portât : qu'il ne battît sa mère, lorsqu'elle tarderait trop à lui donner la mamelle ; qu'il n'étranglât un de ses jeunes frères, lorsqu'il en serait incommodé ; qu'il ne mordît la jambe à l'autre, lorsqu'il en serait heurté ou troublé. Mais ce sont deux suppositions contradictoires dans l'état de nature, qu'être robuste et dépendant : l'homme est faible quand il est dépendant, et il est émancipé avant que d'être robuste. Hobbes n'a pas vu que la même cause qui empêche les sauvages d'user de leur raison, comme le prétendent nos jurisconsultes, les empêche en même temps d'abuser de leurs facultés, comme il le prétend lui-même. De sorte qu'on pourrait dire que les sauvages ne sont pas méchants, précisément parce qu'ils ne savent pas ce que c'est qu'être bons ; car ce n'est ni le développement des lumières, ni le frein de la Loi, mais le calme des passions et l'ignorance du vice, qui les empêchent de mal faire : *Tanto plus in illis proficit vitiorum ignoratio quam in his cognitio virtutis*[1]. Il y a d'ailleurs un autre principe que Hobbes n'a point aperçu, et qui, ayant été donné à l'homme pour adoucir en certaines circonstances la férocité de son amour-propre ou le désir de se conserver, avant la naissance de cet amour (*o*), tempère l'ardeur qu'il a pour son bien-être par une répugnance innée à voir souffrir son semblable. Je ne crois pas avoir aucune contradiction à craindre, en accordant à l'homme la seule vertu naturelle qu'ait été forcé de reconnaître le détracteur le plus outré des vertus humaines[2]. Je parle de la pitié, disposition convenable à des êtres aussi faibles et sujets à autant de maux que nous le sommes : vertu d'autant plus universelle et d'autant plus utile à l'homme, qu'elle précède en lui l'usage de toute réflexion ; et si naturelle, que les bêtes mêmes en donnent quelquefois des signes sensibles. Sans parler de la tendresse des mères pour leurs petits, et des périls qu'elles bravent pour les en garantir, on observe tous les jours la répugnance qu'ont les chevaux à fouler aux pieds un corps vivant. Un animal ne passe point sans

---

[1] Justin. *Histor.* lib. II, cap. ii.
[2] *i.e.* Mandeville, as appears from what follows.

.nquiétude auprès d'un animal mort de son espèce : il y en a même qui leur donnent une sorte de sépulture ; et les tristes mugissements du bétail entrant dans une boucherie annoncent l'impression qu'il reçoit de l'horrible spectacle qui le frappe. On voit avec plaisir l'auteur de la *Fable des Abeilles*, forcé de reconnaître l'homme pour[1] un être compatissant et sensible, sortir, dans l'exemple qu'il en donne, de son style froid et subtil, pour nous offrir la pathétique image d'un homme enfermé qui aperçoit au dehors une bête féroce arrachant un enfant du sein de sa mère, brisant sous sa dent meurtrière [2]les faibles membres, et déchirant de ses ongles les entrailles palpitantes, de cet enfant. Quelle affreuse agitation n'éprouve point ce témoin d'un événement auquel il ne prend aucun intérêt personnel ! quelles angoisses ne souffre-t-il pas à cette vue, de ne pouvoir porter aucun secours à la mère évanouie, ni à l'enfant expirant !

Tel est le pur mouvement de la nature, antérieur à toute réflexion ; telle est la force de la pitié naturelle, que les mœurs les plus dépravées ont encore peine à détruire, puisqu'on voit tous les jours dans nos spectacles s'attendrir et pleurer, aux malheurs d'un infortuné, tel qui, s'il était à la place du tyran, aggraverait encore les tourments de son ennemi ; [3]semblable au sanguinaire Sylla, si sensible aux maux qu'il n'avait pas causés, ou à cet Alexandre de Phère qui n'osait assister à la représentation d'aucune tragédie, de peur qu'on ne le vît gémir avec Andromaque et Priam, tandis qu'il écoutait sans émotion les cris de tant de citoyens qu'on égorgeait tous les jours par ses ordres.

> Mollissima corda
> Humano generi dare se natura fatetur,
> Quæ lacrimas dedit[3].

Mandeville a bien senti qu'avec toute leur morale les hommes n'eussent jamais été que des monstres, si la nature ne leur eût donné la pitié à l'appui de la raison ; mais il n'a pas vu que de cette seule qualité découlent toutes les vertus sociales qu'il veut disputer aux hommes. En effet, qu'est-ce que la générosité, la clémence, l'humanité, sinon la pitié appliquée aux faibles, aux coupables, ou à l'espèce humaine en général ? La bienveillance

---

[1] Originally *comme un être* ; corrected to *pour* in *Errata* to Ed. 1755.
[2] For *les faibles membres* (Ed. 1755), Eds. 1782 and 1801 read *ses faibles membres*.
[3] This passage appeared for the first time in the Ed. of 1782. The quotation is from Juvenal (xv. ll. 131—3).

et l'amitié même sont, à le bien prendre, des productions d'une pitié constante, fixée sur un objet particulier; car désirer que quelqu'un ne souffre point, qu'est-ce autre chose que désirer qu'il soit heureux ? Quand il serait vrai que la commisération ne serait qu'un sentiment qui nous met à la place de celui qui souffre, sentiment obscur et vif dans l'homme sauvage, développé mais faible dans l'homme civil, qu'importerait cette idée à la vérité de ce que je dis, sinon de lui donner plus de force ? En effet, la commisération sera d'autant plus énergique, que l'animal spectateur s'identifiera plus intimement avec l'animal souffrant. Or, il est évident que cette identification a dû être infiniment plus étroite dans l'état de nature que dans l'état de raisonnement. C'est la raison qui engendre l'amour-propre, et c'est la réflexion qui le fortifie; c'est elle qui replie l'homme sur lui-même; c'est elle qui le sépare de tout ce qui le gêne et l'afflige. C'est la philosophie qui l'isole; c'est par elle qu'il dit en secret, à l'aspect d'un homme souffrant: 'Péris, si tu veux; je suis en sûreté.' Il n'y a plus que les dangers de la société entière qui troublent le sommeil tranquille du philosophe et qui l'arrachent de son lit. On peut impunément égorger son semblable sous sa fenêtre; il n'a qu'à mettre ses mains sur ses oreilles, et s'argumenter un peu, pour empêcher la nature qui se révolte en lui de l'identifier avec celui qu'on assassine[1]. L'homme sauvage n'a point cet admirable talent; et, faute de sagesse et de raison, on le voit toujours se livrer étourdiment au premier sentiment de l'humanité. Dans les émeutes, dans les querelles des rues, la populace s'assemble, l'homme prudent s'éloigne; c'est la canaille, ce sont les femmes des halles qui séparent les combattants, et qui empêchent les honnêtes gens de s'entr'égorger.

Il est donc bien certain que la pitié est un sentiment naturel, qui, modérant dans chaque individu l'activité de l'amour de soi-même, concourt à la conservation mutuelle de toute l'espèce. C'est elle qui nous porte sans réflexion au secours de ceux que nous voyons souffrir; c'est elle qui, dans l'état de nature, tient lieu de lois, de mœurs et de vertu, avec cet avantage que nul

[1] Rousseau tells us (*Confessions*, Liv. VIII.) that this passage, together with other like outbreaks, was suggested to him, and even written, by Diderot. He attributes this to Diderot's malice. But there is no reason for supposing that, at this time (1753—4), Diderot was other than friendly to him. The truth is that Diderot was a born declaimer, and never so happy as when mounted on one of his thousand hobbies. The mistake the critics have made is to take him too seriously.

n'est tenté de désobéir à sa douce voix ; c'est elle qui détournera tout sauvage robuste d'enlever à un faible enfant ou à un vieillard infirme sa subsistance acquise avec peine, si lui-même espère pouvoir trouver la sienne ailleurs ; c'est elle qui, au lieu de cette maxime sublime de justice raisonnée, *Fais à autrui comme tu veux qu'on te fasse*, inspire à tous les hommes cette autre maxime de bonté naturelle, bien moins parfaite, mais plus utile peut-être, que la précédente : *Fais ton bien avec le moindre mal d'autrui qu'il est possible*. C'est, en un mot, dans ce sentiment naturel, plutôt que dans des arguments subtils, qu'il faut chercher la cause de la répugnance que tout homme éprouverait à mal faire, même indépendamment des maximes de l'éducation. Quoiqu'il puisse appartenir à Socrate et aux esprits de sa trempe d'acquérir de la vertu par raison, il y a longtemps que le genre humain ne serait plus, si sa conservation n'eût dépendu que des raisonnements de ceux qui le composent.

Avec des passions si peu actives, et un frein si salutaire, les hommes, plutôt farouches que méchants, et plus attentifs à se garantir du mal qu'ils pouvaient recevoir, que tentés d'en faire à autrui, n'étaient pas sujets à des démêlés fort dangereux. Comme ils n'avaient entre eux aucune espèce de commerce, qu'ils ne connaissaient par conséquent ni la vanité, ni la considération, ni l'estime, ni le mépris ; qu'ils n'avaient pas la moindre notion du tien et du mien, ni aucune véritable idée de la justice ; qu'ils regardaient les violences qu'ils pouvaient essuyer comme un mal facile à réparer, et non comme une injure qu'il faut punir, et qu'ils ne songeaient pas même à la vengeance, si ce n'est peut-être machinalement et sur-le-champ, comme le chien qui mord la pierre qu'on lui jette ; leurs disputes eussent eu rarement des suites sanglantes, si elles n'eussent point eu de sujet plus sensible que la pâture. Mais j'en vois un plus dangereux dont il me reste à parler.

Parmi les passions qui agitent le cœur de l'homme, il en est une ardente, impétueuse, qui rend un sexe nécessaire à l'autre : passion terrible qui brave tous les dangers, renverse tous les obstacles, et qui, dans ses fureurs, semble propre à détruire le genre humain, qu'elle est destinée à conserver. Que deviendront les hommes en proie à cette rage effrénée et brutale, sans pudeur, sans retenue, et se disputant chaque jour leurs amours au prix de leur sang ?

Il faut convenir d'abord que plus les passions sont violentes, plus les lois sont nécessaires pour les contenir. Mais, outre que les désordres et les crimes que ces passions causent tous les jours parmi nous montrent assez l'insuffisance des lois à cet égard, il serait encore bon d'examiner si ces désordres ne sont point nés avec les lois mêmes; car alors, quand elles seraient capables de les réprimer, ce serait bien le moins qu'on en dût exiger que d'arrêter un mal qui n'existerait point sans elles.

Commençons par distinguer le moral du physique dans le sentiment de l'amour. Le physique est ce désir général qui porte un sexe à s'unir à l'autre. Le moral est ce qui détermine ce désir et le fixe sur un seul objet exclusivement, ou qui du moins lui donne pour cet objet préféré un plus grand degré d'énergie. Or, il est facile de voir que le moral de l'amour est un sentiment factice né de l'usage de la société, et célébré par les femmes avec beaucoup d'habileté et de soin pour établir leur empire, et rendre dominant le sexe qui devrait obéir. Ce sentiment, étant fondé sur certaines notions du mérite ou de la beauté qu'un sauvage n'est point en état d'avoir, et sur des comparaisons qu'il n'est point en état de faire, doit être presque nul pour lui. Car comme son esprit n'a pu se former des idées abstraites de régularité et de proportion, son cœur n'est point non plus susceptible des sentiments d'admiration et d'amour, qui, même sans qu'on s'en aperçoive, naissent de l'application de ces idées. Il écoute uniquement le tempérament qu'il a reçu de la nature, et non le goût qu'il n'a pu acquérir; et toute femme est bonne pour lui.

Bornés au seul physique de l'amour, et assez heureux pour ignorer ces préférences qui en irritent le sentiment et en augmentent les difficultés, les hommes doivent sentir moins fréquemment et moins vivement les ardeurs du tempérament, et par conséquent avoir entre eux des disputes plus rares et moins cruelles. L'imagination, qui fait tant de ravages parmi nous, ne parle point à des cœurs sauvages; chacun attend paisiblement l'impulsion de la nature, s'y livre sans choix, avec plus de plaisir que de fureur; et, le besoin satisfait, tout le désir est éteint.

C'est donc une chose incontestable que l'amour même, ainsi que toutes les autres passions, n'a acquis que dans la société cette ardeur impétueuse qui le rend si souvent funeste aux hommes; et il est d'autant plus ridicule de représenter les sauvages comme s'entr'égorgeant sans cesse pour assouvir leur brutalité, que cette opinion est directement contraire à l'expérience, et que les Caraïbes, celui de tous les peuples existants qui jusqu'ici s'est écarté le moins de l'état de nature, sont précisément les plus paisibles dans leurs amours, et les moins sujets à la jalousie, quoique vivant sous un climat brûlant, qui semble toujours donner à ces passions une plus grande activité.

À l'égard des inductions qu'on pourrait tirer, dans plusieurs espèces d'animaux, des combats des mâles qui ensanglantent en tout temps nos basses-cours, ou qui font retentir au printemps nos forêts de leurs cris en se disputant la femelle, il faut commencer par exclure toutes les espèces où la nature a manifestement établi dans la puissance relative des sexes d'autres rapports que parmi nous : ainsi les combats des coqs ne forment point une induction pour l'espèce humaine. Dans les espèces où la proportion est mieux observée, ces combats ne peuvent avoir pour causes que la rareté des femelles, eu égard au nombre des mâles, ou les intervalles exclusifs durant lesquels la femelle refuse constamment l'approche du mâle, ce qui revient à la première cause; car, si chaque femelle ne souffre le mâle que durant deux mois de l'année, c'est à cet égard comme si le nombre des femelles était moindre des cinq sixièmes. Or, aucun de ces deux cas n'est applicable à l'espèce humaine, où le nombre des femelles surpasse généralement celui des mâles, et où l'on n'a jamais observé que, même parmi les sauvages, les femelles aient, comme celles des autres espèces, des temps de chaleur et d'exclusion. De plus, parmi plusieurs de ces animaux, toute l'espèce entrant à la fois en effervescence, il vient un moment terrible d'ardeur commune, de tumulte, de désordre et de combat : moment qui n'a point lieu parmi l'espèce humaine, où l'amour n'est jamais périodique. On ne peut donc pas conclure des combats de certains animaux pour la possession des femelles, que la même chose arriverait à l'homme dans l'état de nature ; et quand même on pourrait tirer cette conclusion, comme ces dissensions ne détruisent point les autres espèces, on doit penser au moins qu'elles ne seraient pas plus funestes à la nôtre ; et il est très apparent qu'elles y causeraient encore moins de ravages[1] qu'elles ne font dans la société, surtout dans les pays où, les mœurs étant encore comptées pour quelque chose, la jalousie des amants et la vengeance des époux causent chaque jour des duels, des meurtres, et pis encore ; où le devoir d'une éternelle fidélité ne sert qu'à faire des adultères ; et où les lois mêmes de la continence et de l'honneur étendent nécessairement la débauche et multiplient les avortements.

Concluons qu'errant dans les forêts, sans industrie, sans parole, sans domicile, sans guerre et sans liaison[1], sans nul besoin de ses

---

[1] Ed. 1755 reads *ravage, liaisons.* Eds. 1782 and 1801, as in the text.

semblables, comme sans nul désir de leur nuire, peut-être même sans jamais en reconnaître aucun individuellement, l'homme sauvage, sujet à peu de passions, et se suffisant à lui-même, n'avait que les sentiments et les lumières propres à cet état ; qu'il ne sentait que ses vrais besoins, ne regardait que ce qu'il croyait avoir intérêt de voir, et que son intelligence ne faisait pas plus de progrès que sa vanité. Si par hasard il faisait quelque découverte, il pouvait d'autant moins la communiquer qu'il ne reconnaissait pas même ses enfants. L'art périssait avec l'inventeur. Il n'y avait ni éducation, ni progrès ; les générations se multipliaient inutilement ; et chacune partant toujours du même point, les siècles s'écoulaient dans toute la grossièreté des premiers âges ; l'espèce était déjà vieille, et l'homme restait toujours enfant.

Si je me suis étendu si longtemps sur la supposition de cette condition primitive, c'est qu'ayant d'anciennes erreurs et des préjugés invétérés à détruire j'ai cru devoir creuser jusqu'à la racine, et montrer, dans le tableau du véritable état de nature, combien l'inégalité, même naturelle, est loin d'avoir dans cet état autant de réalité et d'influence que le prétendent nos écrivains.

En effet, il est aisé de voir qu'entre les différences qui distinguent les hommes plusieurs passent pour naturelles, qui sont uniquement l'ouvrage de l'habitude et des divers genres de vie que les hommes adoptent dans la société. Ainsi un tempérament robuste ou délicat, la force ou la faiblesse qui en dépendent, viennent souvent plus de la manière dure ou efféminée dont on a été élevé, que de la constitution primitive des corps. Il en est de même des forces de l'esprit ; et non seulement l'éducation met de la différence entre les esprits cultivés et ceux qui ne le sont pas, mais elle augmente celle qui se trouve entre les premiers, à proportion de la culture ; car, qu'un géant et un nain marchent sur la même route, chaque pas qu'ils feront l'un et l'autre donnera un nouvel avantage au géant[1]. Or, si l'on compare la diversité prodigieuse d'éducations et de genres de vie qui règne dans les différents ordres de l'état civil avec la simplicité et l'uniformité de la vie animale et sauvage, où tous se nourrissent des mêmes aliments, vivent de la même manière, et font exactement les mêmes choses, on comprendra combien la différence d'homme à homme

---

[1] In MS. Neuchâtel, 7854, there is what appears to be a rough draft of this sentence : 'et commencant leur carrière avec des forces si disproportionnées, leur différence augmentera encore de tout le chemin que l'un aura fait de plus que l'autre.' For other fragments, see below, pp. 349–50.

doit être moindre dans l'état de nature que dans celui de société, et combien l'inégalité naturelle doit augmenter dans l'espèce humaine par l'inégalité d'institution.

Mais, quand la nature affecterait dans la distribution de ses dons autant de préférences qu'on le prétend, quel avantage les plus favorisés en tireraient-ils au préjudice des autres, dans un état de choses qui n'admettrait presque aucune sorte de relation entre eux ? Là où il n'y a point d'amour, de quoi servira la beauté ? Que sert[1] l'esprit à des gens qui ne parlent point, et la ruse à ceux qui n'ont point d'affaires ? J'entends toujours répéter que les plus forts opprimeront les faibles. Mais qu'on m'explique ce qu'on veut dire par ce mot d'oppression. Les uns domineront avec violence, les autres gémiront asservis à tous leurs caprices. Voilà précisément ce que j'observe parmi nous ; mais je ne vois pas comment cela pourrait se dire des hommes sauvages, à qui l'on aurait même bien de la peine à faire entendre ce que c'est que servitude et domination. Un homme pourra bien s'emparer des fruits qu'un autre a cueillis, du gibier qu'il a tué, de l'antre qui lui servait d'asile ; mais comment viendra-t-il jamais à bout de s'en faire obéir ? et quelles pourront être les chaînes de la dépendance parmi des hommes qui ne possèdent rien ? Si l'on me chasse d'un arbre, j'en suis quitte pour aller à un autre : si l'on me tourmente dans un lieu, qui m'empêchera de passer ailleurs ? Se trouve-t-il un homme d'une force assez supérieure à la mienne, et, de plus, assez dépravé, assez paresseux et assez féroce, pour me contraindre à pourvoir à sa subsistance pendant qu'il demeure oisif ? il faut qu'il se résolve à ne pas me perdre de vue un seul instant, à me tenir lié avec un très grand soin durant son sommeil, de peur que je ne m'échappe ou que je ne le tue : c'est-à-dire qu'il est obligé de s'exposer volontairement à une peine beaucoup plus grande que celle qu'il veut éviter, et que celle qu'il me donne à moi-même. Après tout cela, sa vigilance se relâche-t-elle un moment ? un bruit imprévu lui fait-il détourner la tête ? je fais vingt pas dans la forêt, mes fers sont brisés, et il ne me revoit de sa vie.

Sans prolonger inutilement ces détails, chacun doit voir que, les liens de la servitude n'étant formés que de la dépendance mutuelle des hommes et des besoins réciproques qui les unissent, il est impossible d'asservir un homme sans l'avoir mis auparavant dans le cas de ne pouvoir se passer d'un autre : situation qui,

---

[1] Ed. 1755 reads *sera*, probably by a misprint. Ed. 1782 has *sert*.

n'existant pas dans l'état de nature, y laisse chacun libre du joug, et rend vaine la loi du plus fort.

Après avoir prouvé que l'inégalité est à peine sensible dans l'état de nature, et que son influence y est presque nulle, il me reste à montrer son origine et ses progrès dans les développements successifs de l'esprit humain. Après avoir montré que la *perfectibilité*, les vertus sociales, et les autres facultés que l'homme naturel avait reçues en puissance, ne pouvaient jamais se développer d'elles-mêmes, qu'elles avaient besoin pour cela du concours fortuit de plusieurs causes étrangères, qui pouvaient ne jamais naître, et sans lesquelles il fût demeuré éternellement dans sa condition primitive, il me reste à considérer et à rapprocher les différents hasards qui ont pu perfectionner la raison humaine en détériorant l'espèce, rendre un être méchant en le rendant sociable, et d'un terme si éloigné amener enfin l'homme et le monde au point où nous les voyons.

J'avoue que, les événements que j'ai à décrire ayant pu arriver de plusieurs manières, je ne puis me déterminer sur le choix que par des conjectures. Mais, outre que ces conjectures deviennent des raisons quand elles sont les plus probables qu'on puisse tirer de la nature des choses, et les seuls moyens qu'on puisse avoir de découvrir la vérité, les conséquences que je veux déduire des miennes ne seront point pour cela conjecturales, puisque, sur les principes que je viens d'établir, on ne saurait former aucun autre système qui ne me fournisse les mêmes résultats, et dont je ne puisse tirer les mêmes conclusions.

Ceci me dispensera d'étendre mes réflexions sur la manière dont le laps de temps compense le peu de vraisemblance des événements; sur la puissance surprenante des causes très légères, lorsqu'elles agissent sans relâche; sur l'impossibilité où l'on est d'un côté de détruire certaines hypothèses, si de l'autre on se trouve hors d'état de leur donner le degré de certitude des faits; sur ce que, deux faits étant donnés comme réels à lier par une suite de faits intermédiaires, inconnus ou regardés comme tels, c'est à l'histoire, quand on l'a, de donner les faits qui les lient; c'est à la philosophie, à son défaut, de déterminer les faits semblables qui peuvent les lier; enfin, sur ce qu'en matière d'événements la similitude réduit les faits à un beaucoup plus petit nombre de classes différentes qu'on ne se l'imagine. Il me suffit d'offrir ces objets à la considération de mes juges; il me suffit d'avoir fait en sorte que les lecteurs vulgaires n'eussent pas besoin de les considérer.

SECONDE PARTIE.

Le premier qui ayant enclos un terrain s'avisa de dire, *Ceci est à moi*, et trouva des gens assez simples pour le croire, fut le vrai fondateur de la société civile[1]. Que de crimes, de guerres, de meurtres, que de misères et d'horreurs n'eût point épargnés au genre humain celui qui, arrachant les pieux ou comblant le fossé, eût crié à ses semblables : 'Gardez-vous d'écouter cet imposteur ; vous êtes perdus si vous oubliez que les fruits sont à tous, et que la terre n'est à personne!' Mais il y a grande apparence qu'alors les choses en étaient déjà venues au point de ne pouvoir plus durer comme elles étaient. Car cette idée de propriété, dépendant de beaucoup d'idées antérieures qui n'ont pu naître que successivement, ne se forma pas tout d'un coup dans l'esprit humain. Il fallut faire bien des progrès, acquérir bien de l'industrie et des lumières, les transmettre et les augmenter d'âge en âge, avant que d'arriver à ce dernier terme de l'état de nature. Reprenons donc les choses de plus haut, et tâchons de rassembler sous un seul point de vue cette lente succession d'événements et de connaissances dans leur ordre le plus naturel.

Le premier sentiment de l'homme fut celui de son existence ; son premier soin celui de sa conservation. Les productions de la terre lui fournissaient tous les secours nécessaires ; l'instinct le porta à en faire usage. La faim, d'autres appétits, lui faisant éprouver tour à tour diverses manières d'exister, il y en eut une qui l'invita à perpétuer son espèce ; et ce penchant aveugle, dépourvu de tout sentiment du cœur, ne produisait qu'un acte purement animal. Le besoin satisfait, les deux sexes ne se reconnaissaient plus, et l'enfant même n'était plus rien à la mère sitôt qu'il pouvait se passer d'elle.

Telle fut la condition de l'homme naissant ; telle fut la vie d'un animal borné d'abord aux pures sensations, et profitant à peine des dons que lui offrait la nature, loin de songer à lui rien arracher. Mais il se présenta bientôt des difficultés ; il fallut apprendre à les vaincre. La hauteur des arbres qui l'empêchait d'atteindre à leurs fruits, la concurrence des animaux qui cherchaient à s'en nourrir, la férocité de ceux qui en voulaient à sa

---

[1] 'Ce chien est à moi, disaient ces pauvres enfants ; c'est là ma place au soleil : voilà le commencement et l'image de l'usurpation de toute la terre.' Pascal, *Pensées*, I. ix. § 53. This reference was added by Petitain, or one of the other modern editors. It does not appear in the Eds. of 1755, 1782, or 1801.

propre vie, tout l'obligea de s'appliquer aux exercices du corps; il fallut se rendre agile, vite à la course, vigoureux au combat. Les armes naturelles, qui sont les branches d'arbres et les pierres, se trouvèrent bientôt sous sa main. Il apprit à surmonter les obstacles de la nature, à combattre au besoin les autres animaux, à disputer sa subsistance aux hommes mêmes, ou à se dédommager de ce qu'il fallait céder au plus fort.

À mesure que le genre humain s'étendit, les peines se multiplièrent avec les hommes. La différence des terrains, des climats, des saisons, put les forcer à en mettre dans leurs manières de vivre. Des années stériles, des hivers longs et rudes, des étés brûlants, qui consument tout, exigèrent d'eux une nouvelle industrie. Le long de la mer et des rivières, ils inventèrent la ligne et l'hameçon, et devinrent pêcheurs et ichthyophages. Dans les forêts, ils se firent des arcs et des flèches, et devinrent chasseurs et guerriers. Dans les pays froids, ils se couvrirent des peaux des bêtes qu'ils avaient tuées. Le tonnerre, un volcan, ou quelque heureux hasard, leur fit connaître le feu, nouvelle ressource contre la rigueur de l'hiver : ils apprirent à conserver cet élément, puis à le reproduire, et enfin à en préparer les viandes qu'auparavant ils dévoraient crues.

Cette application reitérée des êtres divers à lui-même, et des[1] uns aux autres, dut naturellement engendrer dans l'esprit de l'homme les perceptions de certains rapports. Ces relations que nous exprimons par les mots de grand, de petit, de fort, de faible, de vite, de lent, de peureux, de hardi, et d'autres idées pareilles, comparées au besoin, et presque sans y songer, produisirent enfin chez lui quelque sorte de réflexion ; ou plutôt, une prudence machinale qui lui indiquait les précautions les plus nécessaires à sa sûreté.

Les nouvelles lumières qui résultèrent de ce développement augmentèrent sa supériorité sur les autres animaux, en la lui faisant connaître. Il s'exerça à leur dresser des piéges, il leur donna le change en mille manières ; et quoique plusieurs le surpassassent en force au combat, ou en vitesse à la course, de ceux qui pouvaient lui servir ou lui nuire, il devint avec le temps le maître des uns et le fléau des autres. C'est ainsi que le premier regard qu'il porta sur lui-même y produisit le premier mouvement d'orgueil ; c'est ainsi que, sachant encore à peine distinguer les rangs, et se contemplant au premier par son espèce, il se préparait de loin à y prétendre par son individu.

---

[1] Eds. 1755 and 1801 read *les*. Ed. 1782, as in the text.

Quoique ses semblables ne fussent pas pour lui ce qu'ils sont pour nous, et qu'il n'eût guère plus de commerce avec eux qu'avec les autres animaux, ils ne furent pas oubliés dans ses observations. Les conformités que le temps put lui faire apercevoir entre eux, sa femelle et lui-même, le[1] firent juger de celles qu'il n'apercevait pas; et, voyant qu'ils se conduisaient tous comme il aurait fait en pareilles circonstances, il conclut que leur manière de penser et de sentir était entièrement conforme à la sienne; et cette importante vérité, bien établie dans son esprit, lui fit suivre, par un pressentiment aussi sûr et plus prompt que la dialectique, les meilleures règles de conduite que, pour son avantage et sa sûreté, il lui convînt de garder avec eux.

Instruit par l'expérience que l'amour du bien-être est le seul mobile des actions humaines, il se trouva en état de distinguer les occasions rares où l'intérêt commun devait le faire compter sur l'assistance de ses semblables, et celles plus rares encore où la concurrence devait le faire défier d'eux. Dans le premier cas, il s'unissait avec eux en troupeau; ou, tout au plus, par quelque sorte d'association libre qui n'obligeait personne, et qui ne durait qu'autant que le besoin passager qui l'avait formée. Dans le second, chacun cherchait à prendre ses avantages, soit à force ouverte, s'il croyait le pouvoir, soit par adresse et subtilité, s'il se sentait le plus faible.

Voilà comment les hommes purent insensiblement acquérir quelque idée grossière des engagements mutuels, et de l'avantage de les remplir; mais seulement, autant que pouvait l'exiger l'intérêt présent et sensible: car la prévoyance n'était rien pour eux; et, loin de s'occuper d'un avenir éloigné, ils ne songeaient pas même au lendemain. S'agissait-il de prendre un cerf, chacun sentait bien qu'il devait pour cela garder fidèlement son poste; mais, si un lièvre venait à passer à la portée de l'un d'eux, il ne faut pas douter qu'il ne le poursuivît sans scrupule, et qu'ayant atteint sa proie il ne se souciât fort peu de faire manquer la leur à ses compagnons.

Il est aisé de comprendre qu'un pareil commerce n'exigeait pas un langage beaucoup plus raffiné que celui des corneilles ou des singes qui s'attroupent à peu près de même. Des cris inarticulés, beaucoup de gestes, et quelques bruits imitatifs, durent composer pendant longtemps la langue universelle; à quoi joignant dans chaque contrée quelques sons articulés et conventionnels, dont,

---

[1] Eds. 1755, 1782, 1801 read as in the text. Hachette reads *lui*.

comme je l'ai déjà dit, il n'est pas trop facile d'expliquer l'institution, on eut des langues particulières, mais grossières, imparfaites, et telles à peu près qu'en ont encore aujourd'hui diverses nations sauvages.

Je parcours comme un trait des multitudes de siècles, forcé par le temps qui s'écoule, par l'abondance des choses que j'ai à dire, et par le progrès presque insensible des commencements ; car, plus les événements étaient lents à se succéder, plus ils sont prompts à décrire.

Ces premiers progrès mirent enfin l'homme à portée d'en faire de plus rapides. Plus l'esprit s'éclairait, et plus l'industrie se perfectionna. Bientôt, cessant de s'endormir sous le premier arbre, ou de se retirer dans des cavernes, on trouva quelques sortes de haches de pierres dures et tranchantes qui servirent à couper du bois, creuser la terre, et faire des huttes de branchages qu'on s'avisa ensuite d'enduire d'argile et de boue. Ce fut là l'époque d'une première révolution qui forma l'établissement et la distinction des familles, et qui introduisit une sorte de propriété ; d'où peut-être naquirent déjà bien des querelles et des combats. Cependant, comme les plus forts furent vraisemblablement les premiers à se faire des logements qu'ils se sentaient capables de défendre, il est à croire que les faibles trouvèrent plus court et plus sûr de les imiter que de tenter de les déloger ; et quant à ceux qui avaient déjà des cabanes, chacun dut peu[1] chercher à s'approprier celle de son voisin ; moins parce qu'elle ne lui appartenait pas, que parce qu'elle lui était inutile, et qu'il ne pouvait s'en emparer sans s'exposer à un combat très vif avec la famille qui l'occupait.

Les premiers développements du cœur furent l'effet d'une situation nouvelle qui réunissait dans une habitation commune les maris et les femmes, les pères et les enfants. L'habitude de vivre ensemble fit naître les plus doux sentiments qui soient connus des hommes, l'amour conjugal et l'amour paternel. Chaque famille devint une petite société d'autant mieux unie, que l'attachement réciproque et la liberté en étaient les seuls liens ; et ce fut alors que s'établit la première différence dans la manière de vivre des deux sexes, qui jusqu'ici n'en avaient eu qu'une. Les femmes devinrent plus sédentaires, et s'accoutumèrent à garder la cabane et les enfants, tandis que l'homme allait chercher la subsistance commune. Les deux sexes commencèrent aussi, par une vie un

---

[1] Eds. of 1755 and 1782 read as in the text. Ed. 1801 and Hachette read *aucun d'eux ne dut chercher*.

peu plus molle, à perdre quelque chose de leur férocité et de leur vigueur. Mais, si chacun séparément devint moins propre à combattre les bêtes sauvages, en revanche il fut plus aisé de s'assembler pour leur résister en commun.

Dans ce nouvel état, avec une vie simple et solitaire, des besoins très bornés, et les instruments qu'ils avaient inventés pour y pourvoir, les hommes, jouissant d'un fort grand loisir, l'employèrent à se procurer plusieurs sortes de commodités inconnues à leurs pères; et ce fut là le premier joug qu'ils s'imposèrent, sans y songer, et la première source de maux qu'ils préparèrent à leur descendants. Car, outre qu'ils continuèrent ainsi à s'amollir le corps et l'esprit, ces commodités ayant par l'habitude perdu presque tout leur agrément, et étant en même temps dégénérées en de vrais besoins, la privation en devint beaucoup plus cruelle que la possession n'en était douce; et l'on était malheureux de les perdre, sans être heureux de les posséder.

On entrevoit un peu mieux ici comment l'usage de la parole s'établit, ou se perfectionna, insensiblement dans le sein de chaque famille; et l'on peut conjecturer encore comment diverses causes particulières purent étendre le langage et en accélérer le progrès, en le rendant plus nécessaire. De grandes inondations ou des tremblements de terre environnèrent d'eaux ou de précipices des cantons habités; des révolutions du globe détachèrent et coupèrent en îles des portions du continent. On conçoit qu'entre des hommes ainsi rapprochés, et forcés de vivre ensemble, il dut se former un idiome commun, plutôt qu'entre ceux qui erraient librement dans les forêts de la terre ferme. Ainsi, il est très possible qu'après leurs premiers essais de navigation, des insulaires aient porté parmi nous l'usage de la parole; et il est au moins très vraisemblable que la société et les langues ont pris naissance dans les îles, et s'y sont perfectionnées avant que d'être connues dans le continent.

Tout commence à changer de face. Les hommes errant jusqu'ici dans les bois, ayant pris une assiette plus fixe, se rapprochent lentement, se réunissent en diverses troupes, et forment enfin dans chaque contrée une nation particulière, unie de mœurs et de caractères, non par des règlements et des lois, mais par le même genre de vie et d'aliments, et par l'influence commune du climat. Un voisinage permanent ne peut manquer d'engendrer enfin quelque liaison entre diverses familles. De jeunes gens de différents sexes habitent des cabanes voisines; le commerce passager que demande la nature en amène bientôt un autre non moins doux et plus permanent par la fréquentation mutuelle. On s'accoutume à considérer différents objets et à faire des comparaisons ; on acquiert insensiblement des idées de mérite et de beauté qui produisent des sentiments de préférence. À force de se voir, on ne peut plus se passer de se voir encore. Un sentiment tendre et doux s'insinue dans l'âme, et par la moindre opposition devient une fureur impétueuse. La jalousie s'éveille avec l'amour ; la discorde triomphe, et la plus douce des passions reçoit des sacrifices de sang humain.

À mesure que les idées et les sentiments se succèdent, que l'esprit et le cœur s'exercent, le genre humain continue à s'apprivoiser ; les liaisons s'étendent, et les liens se resserrent. On s'accoutuma à s'assembler devant les cabanes ou autour d'un grand arbre ; le chant et la danse, vrais enfants de l'amour et du loisir, devinrent l'amusement ou plutôt l'occupation des hommes et des femmes oisifs et attroupés. Chacun commença à regarder les autres et à vouloir être regardé soi-même, et l'estime publique eut un prix. Celui qui chantait ou dansait le mieux, le plus beau, le plus fort, le plus adroit, ou le plus éloquent, devint le plus considéré ; et ce fut là le **premier pas vers l'inégalité**, et vers le vice en même temps. De ces premières préférences naquirent d'un côté la vanité et le mépris, de l'autre la honte et l'envie ; et la fermentation causée par ces nouveaux levains produisit enfin des composés funestes au bonheur et à l'innocence.

Sitôt que les hommes eurent commencé à s'apprécier mutuellement, et que l'idée de la considération fut formée dans leur esprit, chacun prétendit y avoir droit, et il ne fut plus possible d'en manquer impunément pour personne. De là sortirent les premiers devoirs de la civilité, même parmi les sauvages ; et de là, tout tort volontaire devint un outrage, parce qu'avec le mal qui résultait de l'injure l'offensé y voyait le mépris de sa personne, souvent plus insupportable que le mal même. C'est ainsi que, chacun punissant le mépris qu'on lui avait témoigné d'une manière proportionnée au cas qu'il faisait de lui-même, les vengeances devinrent terribles, et les hommes sanguinaires et cruels. Voilà précisément le degré où étaient parvenus la plupart des peuples sauvages qui nous sont connus ; et c'est faute d'avoir suffisamment distingué les idées, et remarqué combien ces peuples étaient déjà loin du premier état de nature, que plusieurs se sont hâtés de conclure que l'homme est naturellement cruel, et qu'il a besoin de police pour l'adoucir ; tandis que rien n'est si doux que lui dans son état primitif, lorsque, placé par la nature à des distances égales de la stupidité des brutes et des lumières funestes de l'homme civil, et borné également par l'instinct et par la raison à se garantir du mal qui le menace, il est retenu par la pitié naturelle de faire lui-même du mal à personne, sans y être porté par rien, même après en avoir reçu. Car, selon l'axiome du sage Locke, *il ne saurait y avoir d'injure, où il n'y a point de propriété.*

Mais il faut remarquer que la société commencée et les relations déjà établies entre les hommes exigeaient en eux des qualités différentes de celles qu'ils tenaient de leur constitution primitive ; que la moralité commençant à s'introduire dans les actions humaines, et chacun, avant les lois, étant seul juge et vengeur des offenses qu'il avait reçues, la bonté convenable au pur état de nature n'était plus celle qui convenait à la société naissante ; qu'il fallait que les punitions devinssent plus sévères, à mesure que les occasions d'offenser devenaient plus fréquentes ; et que c'était à la terreur des vengeances de tenir lieu du frein des lois. Ainsi, quoique les hommes fussent devenus moins endurants, et que la pitié naturelle eût déjà souffert quelque altération, ce période du développement des facultés humaines, tenant un juste milieu entre l'indolence de l'état primitif et la pétulante activité de notre amour-propre, dut être l'époque la plus heureuse et la plus durable. Plus on y réfléchit, plus on trouve que cet état était le moins sujet aux révolutions, le meilleur à l'homme (*p*), et qu'il n'en a dû sortir que par quelque funeste hasard, qui, pour l'utilité commune, eût dû ne jamais arriver. L'exemple des sauvages, qu'on a presque tous trouvés à ce point, semble confirmer que le genre humain était fait pour y rester toujours ; que cet état est la véritable jeunesse du monde ; et que tous les progrès ultérieurs ont été, en apparence, autant de pas vers la perfection de l'individu, et, en effet, vers la décrépitude de l'espèce.

Tant que les hommes se contentèrent de leurs cabanes rustiques, tant qu'ils se bornèrent à coudre leurs habits de peaux avec des épines ou des arêtes, à se parer de plumes et de coquillages, à se peindre le corps de diverses couleurs, à perfectionner ou embellir leurs arcs et leurs flèches, à tailler avec des pierres tranchantes quelques canots de pêcheurs ou quelques grossiers instruments de musique ; en un mot, tant qu'ils ne s'appliquèrent qu'à des ouvrages qu'un seul pouvait faire, et qu'à des arts qui n'avaient pas besoin du concours de plusieurs mains, ils vécurent libres, sains, bons et heureux autant qu'ils pouvaient l'être par leur nature, et continuèrent à jouir entre eux des douceurs d'un commerce indépendant. Mais, dès l'instant qu'un homme eut besoin du secours d'un autre, dès qu'on s'aperçut qu'il était utile à un seul d'avoir des provisions pour deux, l'égalité disparut, la propriété s'introduisit, le travail devint nécessaire ; et les vastes forêts se changèrent en des campagnes riantes qu'il fallut arroser de la sueur des hommes, et dans lesquelles on vit bientôt l'esclavage et la misère germer et croître avec les moissons.

La métallurgie et l'agriculture furent les deux arts dont l'invention produisit cette grande révolution. Pour le poëte, c'est l'or et l'argent ; mais pour le philosophe, ce sont le fer et le blé qui ont civilisé les hommes et perdu le genre humain. Aussi l'un et l'autre étaient-ils inconnus aux sauvages de l'Amérique, qui pour cela sont toujours demeurés tels ; les autres peuples semblent même être restés barbares tant qu'ils ont pratiqué l'un de ces arts sans l'autre. Et l'une des meilleures raisons peut-être pourquoi l'Europe a été, sinon plus tôt, du moins plus constamment et mieux policée que les autres parties du monde, c'est qu'elle est à la fois la plus abondante en fer et la plus fertile en blé.

Il est très[1] difficile de conjecturer comment les hommes sont parvenus à connaître et employer le fer ; car il n'est pas croyable qu'ils aient imaginé d'eux-mêmes de tirer la matière de la mine, et de lui donner les préparations nécessaires pour la mettre en fusion, avant que de savoir ce qui en résulterait. D'un autre côté, on peut d'autant moins attribuer cette découverte à quelque incendie accidentel, que les mines ne se forment que dans les lieux arides et dénués d'arbres et de plantes ; de sorte qu'on dirait que la nature avait pris des précautions pour nous dérober ce fatal secret. Il ne reste donc que la circonstance extraordinaire de quelque volcan qui, vomissant des matières métalliques en fusion, aura donné aux observateurs l'idée d'imiter cette opération de la nature. Encore faut-il leur supposer bien du courage et de la prévoyance pour entreprendre un travail aussi pénible, et envisager d'aussi loin les avantages qu'ils en pouvaient retirer : ce qui ne convient guère qu'à des esprits déjà plus exercés que ceux-ci ne le devaient être.

Quant à l'agriculture, le principe en fut connu longtemps avant que la pratique en fût établie, et il n'est guère possible que les hommes, sans cesse occupés à tirer leur subsistance des arbres et des plantes, n'eussent assez promptement l'idée des voies que la nature emploie pour la génération des végétaux. Mais leur industrie ne se tourna probablement que fort tard de ce côté-là ;

---

[1] Eds. 1755, 1782 and 1801 read as in the text. Hachette omits *très*.

soit parce que les arbres qui, avec la chasse et la pêche, fournissaient à leur nourriture, n'avaient pas besoin de leurs soins, soit faute de connaître l'usage du blé, soit faute d'instruments pour le cultiver, soit faute de prévoyance pour le besoin à venir, soit enfin faute de moyens pour empêcher les autres de s'approprier le fruit de leur travail. Devenus plus industrieux, on peut croire qu'avec des pierres aiguës et des bâtons pointus ils commencèrent par cultiver quelques légumes ou racines autour de leurs cabanes, longtemps avant de savoir[1] préparer le blé et d'avoir les instruments nécessaires pour la culture en grand ; sans compter que, pour se livrer à cette occupation et ensemencer des terres, il faut se résoudre à perdre d'abord quelque chose pour gagner beaucoup dans la suite : précaution fort éloignée du tour d'esprit de l'homme sauvage, qui, comme je l'ai dit, a bien de la peine à songer le matin à ses besoins du soir.

L'invention des autres arts fut donc nécessaire pour forcer le genre humain de s'appliquer à celui de l'agriculture. Dès qu'il fallut des hommes pour fondre et forger le fer, il fallut d'autres hommes pour nourrir ceux-là. Plus le nombre des ouvriers vint à se multiplier, moins il y eut de mains employées à fournir à la subsistance commune, sans qu'il y eût moins de bouches pour la consommer ; et, comme il fallut aux uns des denrées en échange de leur fer, les autres trouvèrent enfin le secret d'employer le fer à la multiplication des denrées. De là naquirent d'un côté le labourage et l'agriculture, et de l'autre l'art de travailler les métaux et d'en multiplier les usages.

De la culture des terres s'ensuivit nécessairement leur partage ; et de la propriété, une fois reconnue, les premières règles de justice. Car, pour rendre à chacun le sien, il faut que chacun puisse avoir quelque chose ; de plus, les hommes commençant à porter leurs vues dans l'avenir, et se voyant tous quelques biens à perdre, il n'y en avait aucun qui n'eût à craindre pour soi la représaille des torts qu'il pouvait faire à autrui. Cette origine est d'autant plus naturelle, qu'il est impossible de concevoir l'idée de la propriété naissante d'ailleurs que de la main-d'œuvre ; car on ne voit pas ce que, pour s'approprier les choses qu'il n'a point faites, l'homme y peut mettre de plus que son travail. C'est le seul travail qui, donnant droit au cultivateur sur le produit de la terre qu'il a labourée, lui en donne par conséquent sur le fonds, au moins jusqu'à la récolte, et ainsi d'année en année : ce qui, faisant une possession continue, se transforme aisément en propriété. Lorsque

[1] Eds. 1755, 1782, as in the text. Ed. 1801 and Hachette, *avant que de savoir*.

les anciens, dit Grotius, ont donné à Cérès l'épithète de législatrice, et à une fête célébrée en son honneur le nom de Thesmophories[1], ils ont fait entendre par là que le partage des terres a produit une nouvelle sorte de droit : c'est-à-dire, le droit de propriété, différent de celui qui résulte de la loi naturelle.

Les choses en cet état eussent pu demeurer égales, si les talents eussent été égaux, et que, par exemple, l'emploi du fer et la consommation des denrées eussent toujours fait une balance exacte. Mais la proportion, que rien ne maintenait, fut bientôt rompue ; le plus fort faisait plus d'ouvrage ; le plus adroit tirait meilleur parti du sien ; le plus ingénieux trouvait des moyens d'abréger le travail ; le laboureur avait plus besoin de fer, ou le forgeron plus besoin de blé ; et en travaillant également, l'un gagnait beaucoup, tandis que l'autre avait peine à vivre. C'est ainsi que l'inégalité naturelle se déploie insensiblement avec celle de combinaison ; et que les différences des hommes, développées par celles des circonstances, se rendent plus sensibles, plus permanentes dans leurs effets, et commencent à influer dans la même proportion sur le sort des particuliers.

Les choses étant parvenues à ce point, il est facile d'imaginer le reste. Je ne m'arrêterai pas à décrire l'invention successive des autres arts, le progrès des langues, l'épreuve et l'emploi des talents, l'inégalité des fortunes, l'usage ou l'abus des richesses, ni tous les détails qui suivent ceux-ci, et que chacun peut aisément suppléer. Je me bornerai seulement à jeter un coup d'œil sur le genre humain, placé dans ce nouvel ordre de choses.

Voilà donc toutes nos facultés développées, la mémoire et l'imagination en jeu, l'amour-propre intéressé, la raison rendue active, et l'esprit arrivé presque au terme de la perfection dont il est susceptible. Voilà toutes les qualités naturelles mises en action, le rang et le sort de chaque homme établi[2], non seulement sur la quantité des biens et le pouvoir de servir ou de nuire, mais sur l'esprit, la beauté, la force ou l'adresse, sur le mérite ou les talents ; et ces qualités étant les seules qui pouvaient attirer de la considération, il fallut bientôt les avoir ou les affecter ; il fallut, pour son avantage, se montrer autre que ce qu'on était en effet. Être et paraître devinrent deux choses tout à fait différentes ; et de cette distinction sortirent le faste imposant, la ruse trompeuse, et tous les vices qui en sont le cortége. D'un autre côté, de libre

---

[1] Ed. 1801 and Hachette read *Thesmophorie*. Eds. 1755 and 1782, as in the text.

[2] Eds. 1755 and 1782 have *établi*. Ed. 1801 and Hachette read *établis*.

et indépendant qu'était auparavant l'homme, le voilà, par une multitude de nouveaux besoins, assujetti pour ainsi dire à toute la nature, et surtout à ses semblables, dont il devient l'esclave en un sens, même en devenant leur maître : riche, il a besoin de leurs services ; pauvre, il a besoin de leurs secours ; et la médiocrité ne le met point en état de se passer d'eux. Il faut donc qu'il cherche sans cesse à les intéresser à son sort, et à leur faire trouver, en effet ou en apparence, leur profit à travailler pour le sien : ce qui le rend fourbe et artificieux avec les uns, impérieux et dur avec les autres, et le met dans la nécessité d'abuser tous ceux dont il a besoin, quand il ne peut s'en faire craindre, et qu'il ne trouve pas son intérêt à les servir utilement. Enfin, l'ambition dévorante, l'ardeur d'élever sa fortune relative, moins par un véritable besoin que pour se mettre au-dessus des autres, inspire à tous les hommes un noir penchant à se nuire mutuellement, une jalousie secrète d'autant plus dangereuse, que, pour faire son coup plus en sûreté, elle prend souvent le masque de la bienveillance : en un mot, concurrence et rivalité d'une part, de l'autre opposition d'intérêts[1], et toujours le désir caché de faire son profit aux dépens d'autrui. Tous ces maux sont le premier effet de la propriété et le cortège inséparable de l'inégalité naissante.

Avant qu'on eût inventé les signes représentatifs des richesses, elles ne pouvaient guère consister qu'en terres et en bestiaux, les seuls biens réels que les hommes puissent posséder. Or, quand les héritages se furent accrus en nombre et en étendue au point de couvrir le sol entier et de se toucher tous, les uns ne purent plus s'agrandir qu'aux dépens des autres; et les surnuméraires que la faiblesse ou l'indolence avaient empêchés d'en acquérir à leur tour, devenus pauvres sans avoir rien perdu, parce que, tout changeant autour d'eux, eux seuls n'avaient point changé, furent obligés de recevoir ou de ravir leur subsistance de la main des riches ; et de là commencèrent à naître, selon les divers caractères des uns et des autres, la domination et la servitude, ou la violence et les rapines. Les riches, de leur côté, connurent à peine le plaisir de dominer, qu'ils dédaignèrent bientôt tous les autres, et, se servant de leurs anciens esclaves pour en soumettre de nouveaux, ils ne songèrent qu'à subjuguer et asservir leurs voisins : semblables à ces loups affamés qui, ayant une fois goûté de la chair humaine, rebutent toute autre nourriture, et ne veulent plus que dévorer des hommes.

C'est ainsi que, les plus puissants ou les plus misérables se

[1] Ed. 1755 has *opposition d'intérêt*; Eds. 1782 and 1801, as in the text.

faisant de leurs forces ou de leurs besoins une sorte de droit au bien d'autrui, équivalent, selon eux, à celui de propriété, l'égalité rompue fut suivie du plus affreux désordre ; c'est ainsi que les usurpations des riches, les brigandages des pauvres, les passions effrénées de tous, étouffant la pitié naturelle et la voix encore faible de la justice, rendirent les hommes avares, ambitieux et méchants. Il s'élevait entre le droit du plus fort et le droit du premier occupant un conflit perpétuel qui ne se terminait que par des combats et des meurtres (*q*). La société naissante fit place au plus horrible état de guerre : le genre humain, avili et désolé, ne pouvant plus retourner sur ses pas, ni renoncer aux acquisitions malheureuses qu'il avait faites, et ne travaillant qu'à sa honte par l'abus des facultés qui l'honorent, se mit lui-même à la veille de sa ruine.

> Attonitus novitate mali, divesque, miserque,
> Effugere optat opes, et quæ modo voverat odit[1].

Il n'est pas possible que les hommes n'aient fait enfin des réflexions sur une situation aussi misérable et sur les calamités dont ils étaient accablés. Les riches surtout durent bientôt sentir combien leur était désavantageuse une guerre perpétuelle dont ils faisaient seuls tous les frais, et dans laquelle le risque de la vie était commun, et celui des biens particulier. D'ailleurs, quelque couleur qu'ils pussent donner à leurs usurpations, ils sentaient assez qu'elles n'étaient établies que sur un droit précaire et abusif ; et que, n'ayant été acquises que par la force, la force pouvait les leur ôter sans qu'ils eussent raison de s'en plaindre. Ceux même que la seule industrie avait enrichis ne pouvaient guère fonder leur propriété sur de meilleurs titres. Ils avaient beau dire : 'C'est moi qui ai bâti ce mur ; j'ai gagné ce terrain par mon travail.'—'Qui vous a donné les alignements, leur pouvait-on répondre, et en vertu de quoi prétendez-vous être payés à nos dépens d'un travail que nous ne vous avons point imposé ? Ignorez-vous qu'une multitude de vos frères périt ou souffre du besoin de ce que vous avez de trop, et qu'il vous fallait un consentement exprès et unanime du genre humain pour vous approprier sur la subsistance commune tout ce qui allait au delà de la vôtre ?' Destitué de raisons valables pour se justifier et de forces suffisantes pour se défendre ; écrasant facilement un particulier, mais écrasé lui-même par des troupes de bandits ; seul contre tous, et ne pouvant, à cause des jalousies mutuelles, s'unir avec ses égaux contre des ennemis unis par l'espoir commun du pillage, le riche,

---

[1] Ovid, *Metamorphoses*, XI. 127—8.

pressé par la nécessité, conçut enfin le projet le plus réfléchi qui soit jamais entré dans l'esprit humain : ce fut d'employer en sa faveur les forces mêmes de ceux qui l'attaquaient, de faire ses défenseurs de ses adversaires, de leur inspirer d'autres maximes, et de leur donner d'autres institutions qui lui fussent aussi favorables que le droit naturel lui était contraire.

Dans cette vue, après avoir exposé à ses voisins l'horreur d'une situation qui les armait tous les uns contre les autres, qui leur rendait leurs possessions aussi onéreuses que leurs besoins, et où nul ne trouvait sa sûreté ni dans la pauvreté ni dans la richesse, il inventa aisément des raisons spécieuses pour les amener à son but. ' Unissons-nous, leur dit-il, pour garantir de l'oppression les faibles, contenir les ambitieux, et assurer à chacun la possession de ce qui lui appartient : instituons des règlements de justice et de paix auxquels tous soient obligés de se conformer, qui ne fassent acception de personne, et qui réparent en quelque sorte les caprices de la fortune, en soumettant également le puissant et le faible à des devoirs mutuels. En un mot, au lieu de tourner nos forces contre nous-mêmes, rassemblons-les en un pouvoir suprême qui nous gouverne selon de sages lois, qui protége et défende tous les membres de l'association, repousse les ennemis communs, et nous maintienne dans une concorde éternelle.'

Il en fallut beaucoup moins que l'équivalent de ce discours pour entraîner des hommes grossiers, faciles à séduire, qui d'ailleurs avaient trop d'affaires à démêler entre eux pour pouvoir se passer d'arbitres, et trop d'avarice et d'ambition pour pouvoir longtemps se passer de maîtres. Tous coururent au-devant de leurs fers, croyant assurer leur liberté ; car, avec assez de raison pour sentir les avantages d'un établissement politique, ils n'avaient pas assez d'expérience pour en prévoir les dangers. Les plus capables de pressentir les abus étaient précisément ceux qui comptaient d'en profiter ; et les sages même[1] virent qu'il fallait se résoudre à sacrifier une partie de leur liberté à la conservation de l'autre, comme un blessé se fait couper le bras pour sauver le reste du corps.

Telle fut, ou dut être, l'origine de la société et des lois, qui donnèrent de nouvelles entraves au faible et de nouvelles forces au riche (*r*), détruisirent sans retour la liberté naturelle, fixèrent pour jamais la loi de la propriété et de l'inégalité, d'une adroite usurpation firent un droit irrévocable, et, pour le profit de quelques ambitieux, assujettirent désormais tout le genre humain au travail, à la servitude et à la misère. On voit aisément comment

[1] Ed. 1801 and Hachette, *mêmes*. Eds. 1755, 1782, *même*.

l'établissement d'une seule société rendit indispensable celui de toutes les autres, et comment, pour faire tête à des forces unies, il fallut s'unir à son tour[1]. Les sociétés, se multipliant ou s'étendant rapidement, couvrirent bientôt toute la surface de la terre ; et il ne fut plus possible de trouver un seul coin dans l'univers où l'on pût s'affranchir du joug, et soustraire sa tête au glaive, souvent mal conduit, que chaque homme vit perpétuellement suspendu sur la sienne. Le droit civil étant ainsi devenu la règle commune des citoyens, la loi de nature n'eut plus lieu qu'entre les diverses sociétés, où, sous le nom de droit des gens, elle fut tempérée par quelques conventions tacites, pour rendre le commerce possible et suppléer à la commisération naturelle, qui, perdant de société à société presque toute la force qu'elle avait d'homme à homme, ne réside plus que dans quelques grandes âmes cosmopolites, qui franchissent les barrières imaginaires qui séparent les peuples, et qui, à l'exemple de l'Être souverain qui les a créés[2], embrassent tout le genre humain dans leur bienveillance.

Les Corps politiques, restant ainsi entre eux dans l'état de nature, se ressentirent bientôt des inconvénients qui avaient forcé les particuliers d'en sortir ; et cet état devint encore plus funeste entre ces grands Corps qu'il ne l'avait été auparavant entre les individus dont ils étaient composés. De là sortirent les guerres nationales, les batailles, les meurtres, les représailles, qui font frémir la nature et choquent la raison, et tous ces préjugés horribles qui placent au rang des vertus l'honneur de répandre le sang humain. Les plus honnêtes gens apprirent à compter parmi leurs devoirs celui d'égorger leurs semblables ; on vit enfin les hommes se massacrer par milliers, sans savoir pourquoi ; et il se commettait plus de meurtres en un seul jour de combat, et plus d'horreurs à la prise d'une seule ville, qu'il ne s'en était commis dans l'état de nature durant des siècles entiers, sur toute la face de la terre. Tels sont les premiers effets qu'on entrevoit de la division du genre humain en différentes sociétés. Revenons à leur institution[3].

Je sais que plusieurs ont donné d'autres origines aux sociétés politiques, comme les conquêtes du plus puissant, ou l'union des

[1] Compare: 'De la première société formée s'ensuit nécessairement la formation de toutes les autres. Il faut en faire partie, ou s'unir pour lui résister.' *L'état de guerre*, p. [122]. This limitation on the freedom of the Contract has been commonly overlooked by the critics.

[2] Ed. 1801 and Hachette read *créées*. Eds. 1755, 1782, *créés*.

[3] Hachette reads *institutions*, by a blunder. Eds. 1755, 1782 and 1801, as in the text.

faibles; et le choix entre ces causes est indifférent à ce que je veux établir. Cependant, celle que je viens d'exposer me paraît la plus naturelle, par les raisons suivantes : 1° Que, dans le premier cas, le droit de conquête, n'étant point un droit, n'en a pu fonder aucun autre, le conquérant et les peuples conquis restant toujours entre eux dans l'état de guerre, à moins que la nation, remise en pleine liberté, ne choisisse volontairement son vainqueur pour son chef. Jusque-là, quelques capitulations qu'on ait faites, comme elles n'ont été fondées que sur la violence, et que par conséquent elles sont nulles par le fait même, il ne peut y avoir, dans cette hypothèse, ni véritable société, ni Corps politique, ni d'autre loi que celle du plus fort. 2° Que ces mots de *fort* et de *faible* sont équivoques dans le second cas ; que, dans l'intervalle qui se trouve entre l'établissement du droit de propriété ou de premier occupant et celui des Gouvernements politiques, le sens de ces termes est mieux rendu par ceux de *pauvre* et de *riche*, parce qu'en effet un homme n'avait point, avant les lois, d'autre moyen d'assujettir ses égaux qu'en attaquant leur bien, ou leur faisant quelque part du sien. 3° Que, les pauvres n'ayant rien à perdre que leur liberté, c'eût été une grande folie à eux de s'ôter volontairement le seul bien qui leur restait, pour ne rien gagner en échange ; qu'au contraire les riches étant, pour ainsi dire, sensibles dans toutes les parties de leurs biens, il était beaucoup plus aisé de leur faire du mal ; qu'ils avaient par conséquent plus de précautions à prendre pour s'en garantir ; et qu'enfin il est raisonnable de croire qu'une chose a été inventée par ceux à qui elle est utile, plutôt que par ceux à qui elle fait du tort.

Le Gouvernement naissant n'eut point une forme constante et régulière. Le défaut de philosophie et d'expérience ne laissait apercevoir que les inconvénients présents ; et l'on ne songeait à remédier aux autres qu'à mesure qu'ils se présentaient. Malgré tous les travaux des plus sages Législateurs, l'état politique demeura toujours imparfait, parce qu'il était presque l'ouvrage du hasard, et que, mal commencé, le temps, en découvrant les défauts et suggérant des remèdes, ne put jamais réparer les vices de la constitution : on raccommodait sans cesse, au lieu qu'il eût fallu commencer par nettoyer l'aire et écarter tous les vieux matériaux, comme fit Lycurgue à Sparte, pour élever ensuite un bon édifice. La société ne consista d'abord qu'en quelques conventions générales que tous les particuliers s'engageaient à observer, et dont la communauté se rendait garante envers chacun d'eux. Il fallut que l'expérience montrât combien une pareille constitution était faible, et combien il était facile aux infracteurs d'éviter la conviction ou le châtiment des fautes dont le public seul devait être le témoin et le juge ; il fallut que la loi fût éludée de mille manières ; il fallut que les inconvénients et les désordres se multipliassent continuellement, pour qu'on songeât enfin à confier à des particuliers le dangereux dépôt de l'autorité publique, et qu'on commît à des magistrats le soin de faire observer les délibérations du peuple. Car de dire que les chefs furent choisis avant que la confédération fût faite, et que les ministres des lois existèrent avant les lois mêmes, c'est une supposition qu'il n'est pas permis de combattre sérieusement.

Il ne serait pas plus raisonnable de croire que les peuples se sont d'abord jetés entre les bras d'un maître absolu, sans conditions et sans retour, et que le premier moyen de pourvoir à la sûreté commune, qu'aient imaginé des hommes fiers et indomptés, a été de se précipiter dans l'esclavage. En effet, pourquoi se sont-ils donné des supérieurs, si ce n'est pour les défendre contre l'oppression, et protéger leurs biens, leurs libertés et leurs vies, qui sont, pour ainsi dire, les éléments constitutifs de leur être ? Or, dans les relations d'homme à homme, le pis qui puisse arriver à l'un étant de se voir à la discrétion de l'autre, n'eût-il pas été contre le bon sens de commencer par se dépouiller entre les mains d'un chef des seules choses, pour la conservation desquelles ils avaient besoin de son secours ? Quel équivalent eût-il pu leur offrir pour la concession d'un si beau droit ? et s'il eût osé l'exiger sous le prétexte de les défendre, n'eût-il pas aussitôt reçu la réponse de l'apologue : 'Que nous fera de plus l'ennemi ?' Il est donc incontestable, et c'est la maxime fondamentale de tout le droit politique, que les peuples se sont donné des chefs pour défendre leur liberté, et non pour les asservir. *Si nous avons un prince*, disait Pline à Trajan, *c'est afin qu'il nous préserve d'avoir un maître*[1].

[2]Nos politiques font sur l'amour de la liberté les mêmes sophismes que nos philosophes[2] ont faits sur l'état de nature. Par les choses qu'ils voient ils jugent des choses très différentes qu'ils n'ont pas vues ; et ils attribuent aux hommes un penchant naturel à la servitude, par la patience avec laquelle ceux qu'ils ont sous les yeux supportent la leur ; sans songer qu'il en est de la liberté

---

[1] 'Illi enim (Bruti, Camilli) regem hostemque victorem manibus depulerunt. Hic (Trajanus) regnum ipsum, quæque alia captivitas gignit, arcet et summovet ; sedemque obtinet principis, ne sit domino locus.' *Panegyricus*, chap. 55.

[2] Eds. 1755 and 1801 read *Les politiques, les philosophes*. Ed. 1782, as in the text.

comme de l'innocence et de la vertu, dont on ne sent le prix qu'autant qu'on en jouit soi-même, et dont le goût se perd sitôt qu'on les a perdues. 'Je connais les délices de ton pays, disait Brasidas à un satrape qui comparait la vie de Sparte à celle de Persépolis; mais tu ne peux connaître les plaisirs du mien.'

Comme un coursier indompté hérisse ses crins, frappe la terre du pied et se débat impétueusement à la seule approche du mors, tandis qu'un cheval dressé souffre patiemment la verge et l'éperon, l'homme barbare ne plie point sa tête au joug que l'homme civilisé porte sans murmure, et il préfère la plus orageuse liberté à un assujettissement tranquille. Ce n'est donc pas par l'avilissement des peuples asservis qu'il faut juger des dispositions naturelles de l'homme pour ou contre la servitude, mais par les prodiges qu'ont faits tous les peuples libres pour se garantir de l'oppression. Je sais que les premiers ne font que vanter sans cesse la paix et le repos dont ils jouissent dans leurs fers, et que *miserrimam servitutem pacem appellant*[1]. Mais quand je vois les autres sacrifier les plaisirs, le repos, la richesse, la puissance, et la vie même, à la conservation de ce seul bien si dédaigné de ceux qui l'ont perdu; quand je vois des animaux nés libres, et abhorrant la captivité, se briser la tête contre les barreaux de leur prison; quand je vois des multitudes de sauvages tout nus mépriser les voluptés européennes, et braver la faim, le feu, le fer et la mort, pour ne conserver que leur indépendance, je sens que ce n'est pas à des esclaves qu'il appartient de raisonner de liberté.

Quant à l'autorité paternelle, dont plusieurs ont fait dériver le gouvernement absolu et toute la société, sans recourir aux preuves contraires de Locke et de Sidney, il suffit de remarquer que rien au monde n'est plus éloigné de l'esprit féroce du despotisme que la douceur de cette autorité, qui regarde plus à l'avantage de celui qui obéit qu'à l'utilité de celui qui commande; que, par la loi de nature, le père n'est le maître de l'enfant qu'aussi longtemps que son secours lui est nécessaire; qu'au delà de ce terme ils deviennent égaux, et qu'alors le fils, parfaitement indépendant du père, ne lui doit que du respect et non de l'obéissance : car la reconnaissance est bien un devoir qu'il faut rendre, mais non pas un droit qu'on puisse exiger. Au lieu de dire que la société civile dérive du pouvoir paternel, il fallait dire, au contraire, que c'est d'elle que ce pouvoir tire sa principale force. Un individu ne fut reconnu pour le père de plusieurs que quand ils restèrent assemblés

[1] Tacit. *Hist.* Lib. IV. cap. XVII.

autour de lui. Les biens du père, dont il est véritablement le maître, sont les liens qui retiennent ses enfants dans sa dépendance ; et il peut ne leur donner part à sa succession qu'à proportion qu'ils auront bien mérité de lui par une continuelle déférence à ses volontés. Or, loin que les sujets aient quelque faveur semblable à attendre de leur despote, comme ils lui appartiennent en propre, eux et tout ce qu'ils possèdent, ou du moins qu'il le prétend ainsi ; ils sont réduits à recevoir comme une faveur ce qu'il leur laisse de leur propre bien. Il fait justice, quand il les dépouille ; il fait grâce, quand il les laisse vivre.

En continuant d'examiner ainsi les faits par le droit, on ne trouverait pas plus de solidité que de vérité dans l'établissement volontaire de la tyrannie ; et il serait difficile de montrer la validité d'un contrat qui n'obligerait qu'une des parties, où l'on mettrait tout d'un côté et rien de l'autre, et qui ne tournerait qu'au préjudice de celui qui s'engage. Ce système odieux est bien éloigné d'être, même aujourd'hui, celui des sages et bons monarques, et surtout des rois de France ; comme on peut le voir en divers endroits de leurs édits, et en particulier dans le passage suivant d'un écrit célèbre, publié en 1667, au nom et par les ordres de Louis XIV : 'Qu'on ne dise donc point que le souverain ne soit pas sujet aux lois de son État, puisque la proposition contraire est une vérité du droit des gens, que la flatterie a quelquefois attaquée, mais que les bons princes ont toujours défendue comme une divinité tutélaire de leurs États. Combien est-il plus légitime de dire, avec le sage Platon, que la parfaite félicité d'un royaume est qu'un prince soit obéi de ses sujets, que le prince obéisse à la Loi, et que la Loi soit droite et toujours dirigée au bien public[1] !' Je ne m'arrêterai point à rechercher si, la liberté étant la plus noble des facultés de l'homme, ce n'est pas dégrader sa nature, se mettre au niveau des bêtes esclaves de l'instinct, offenser même l'auteur de son être, que de renoncer sans réserve au plus précieux de tous ses dons, que de se soumettre à commettre tous les crimes qu'il nous défend, pour complaire à un maître féroce ou insensé ; et si cet ouvrier sublime doit être plus irrité de voir détruire que déshonorer son plus bel ouvrage. Je négligerai, si l'on veut, l'autorité de Barbeyrac, qui déclare nettement, d'après Locke, que nul ne peut vendre sa liberté jusqu'à se soumettre à une puissance arbitraire qui le traite à sa fantaisie : *Car*, ajoute-t-il, *ce serait*

---

[1] *Traité des Droits de la reine très chrétienne sur divers États de la monarchie d'Espagne*, 1667, in 4°. [Quoted from Hachette.]

vendre sa propre vie, dont on n'est pas le maître[1]. Je demanderai seulement de quel droit ceux, qui n'ont pas craint de s'avilir eux-mêmes jusqu'à ce point, ont pu soumettre leur postérité à la même ignominie, et renoncer pour elle à des biens qu'elle ne tient point de leur libéralité, et sans lesquels la vie même est onéreuse à tous ceux qui en sont dignes.

Pufendorf dit que, tout de même qu'on transfère son bien à autrui par des conventions et des contrats, on peut aussi se dépouiller de sa liberté en faveur de quelqu'un[2]. C'est là, ce me semble, un fort mauvais raisonnement. Car, premièrement, le bien que j'aliène me devient une chose tout à fait étrangère, et dont l'abus m'est indifférent ; mais il m'importe qu'on n'abuse point de ma liberté, et je ne puis, sans me rendre coupable du mal qu'on me forcera de faire, m'exposer à devenir l'instrument du crime. De plus, le droit de propriété n'étant que de convention et d'institution humaine, tout homme peut à son gré disposer de ce qu'il possède. Mais il n'en est pas de même des dons essentiels de la nature, tels que la vie et la liberté, dont il est permis à chacun de jouir, et dont il est au moins douteux qu'on ait droit de se dépouiller : en s'ôtant l'une on dégrade son être, en s'ôtant l'autre on l'anéantit autant qu'il est en soi ; et, comme nul bien temporel ne peut dédommager de l'une et de l'autre, ce serait offenser à la fois la nature et la raison que d'y renoncer, à quelque prix que ce fût. Mais quand on pourrait aliéner sa liberté comme ses biens, la différence serait très grande pour les enfants, qui ne jouissent des biens du père que par la transmission de son droit ; au lieu que, la liberté étant un don qu'ils tiennent de la nature en qualité d'hommes, leurs parents n'ont eu aucun droit de les en dépouiller. De sorte que, comme pour établir l'esclavage il a fallu faire violence à la nature, il a fallu la changer pour perpétuer ce droit ; et les jurisconsultes, qui ont gravement prononcé que l'enfant d'une esclave naîtrait esclave, ont décidé en d'autres termes qu'un homme ne naîtrait pas homme.

Il me paraît donc certain que non seulement les Gouvernements n'ont point commencé par le pouvoir arbitraire, qui n'en est que la corruption, le terme extrême, et qui les ramène enfin à la seule loi du plus fort, dont ils furent d'abord le remède ; mais encore que, quand même ils auraient ainsi commencé, ce pouvoir, étant par sa nature illégitime, n'a pu servir de

---

[1] The sentence from *Je négligerai* to *on n'est pas le maître* appeared for the first time in the Ed. of 1782.
[2] Pufendorf, *De jure naturæ et gentium*, VII. §§ v., vi.

fondement aux droits[1] de la société, ni par conséquent à l'inégalité d'institution.

Sans entrer aujourd'hui dans les recherches qui sont encore à faire sur la nature du pacte fondamental de tout Gouvernement, je me borne, en suivant l'opinion commune, à considérer ici l'établissement du Corps politique comme un vrai contrat entre le peuple et les chefs qu'il se choisit : contrat par lequel les deux parties s'obligent à l'observation des lois qui y sont stipulées et qui forment les liens de leur union. Le peuple ayant, au sujet des relations sociales, réuni toutes ses volontés en une seule, tous les articles sur lesquels cette volonté s'explique deviennent autant de lois fondamentales qui obligent tous les membres de l'État sans exception, et l'une desquelles règle le choix et le pouvoir des magistrats chargés de veiller à l'exécution des autres. Ce pouvoir s'étend à tout ce qui peut maintenir la constitution, sans aller jusqu'à la changer. On y joint des honneurs qui rendent respectables les lois et leurs ministres, et pour ceux-ci personnellement des prérogatives qui les dédommagent des pénibles travaux que coûte une bonne administration. Le magistrat, de son côté, s'oblige à n'user du pouvoir qui lui est confié que selon l'intention des commettants, à maintenir chacun dans la paisible jouissance de ce qui lui appartient, et à préférer en toute occasion l'utilité publique à son propre intérêt.

Avant que l'expérience eût montré, ou que la connaissance du cœur humain eût fait prévoir, les abus inévitables d'une telle constitution, elle dut paraître d'autant meilleure, que ceux qui étaient chargés de veiller à sa conservation y étaient eux-mêmes les plus intéressés. Car, la magistrature et ses droits n'étant établis que sur les lois fondamentales, aussitôt qu'elles seraient détruites, les magistrats cesseraient d'être légitimes, le peuple ne serait plus tenu de leur obéir ; et comme ce n'aurait pas été le magistrat, mais la Loi, qui aurait constitué l'essence de l'État, chacun rentrerait de droit dans sa liberté naturelle.

Pour peu qu'on y réfléchit attentivement, ceci se confirmerait par de nouvelles raisons ; et par la nature du contrat on verrait qu'il ne saurait être irrévocable. Car, s'il n'y avait point de pouvoir supérieur qui pût être garant de la fidélité des contractants, ni les forcer à remplir leurs engagements réciproques, les parties demeureraient seules juges dans leur propre cause, et chacune d'elles aurait toujours le droit de renoncer au contrat, sitôt qu'elle

---

[1] Eds. of 1755, 1782 and 1801 read as in the text. Hachette reads *lois*, which is as much against the sense as against authority.

trouverait que l'autre en[1] enfreint les conditions, ou qu'elles cesseraient de lui convenir. C'est sur ce principe qu'il semble que le droit d'abdiquer peut être fondé. Or, à ne considérer, comme nous faisons, que l'institution humaine, si le magistrat, qui a tout le pouvoir en main et qui s'approprie tous les avantages du contrat, avait pourtant le droit de renoncer à l'autorité, à plus forte raison le peuple, qui paye toutes les fautes des chefs, devrait avoir le droit de renoncer à la dépendance. Mais les dissensions affreuses, les désordres infinis qu'entraînerait nécessairement ce dangereux pouvoir, montrent, plus que toute autre chose, combien les Gouvernements humains avaient besoin d'une base plus solide que la seule raison, et combien il était nécessaire au repos public que la volonté divine intervînt pour donner à l'autorité souveraine un caractère sacré et inviolable qui ôtât aux sujets le funeste droit d'en disposer. Quand la religion n'aurait fait que ce bien aux hommes, c'en serait assez pour qu'ils dussent tous la chérir et l'adopter, même avec ses abus, puisqu'elle épargne encore plus de sang que le fanatisme n'en fait couler. Mais suivons le fil de notre hypothèse.

Les diverses formes des[2] Gouvernements tirent leur origine des différences plus ou moins grandes qui se trouvèrent entre les particuliers au moment de l'institution. Un homme était-il éminent en pouvoir, en vertu, en richesse ou en crédit, il fut seul élu magistrat, et l'État devint monarchique. Si plusieurs, à peu près égaux entre eux, l'emportaient sur tous les autres, ils furent élus conjointement, et l'on eut une aristocratie. Ceux dont la fortune ou les talents étaient moins disproportionnés, et qui s'étaient le moins éloignés de l'état de nature, gardèrent en commun l'administration suprême, et formèrent une démocratie. Le temps vérifia laquelle de ces formes était la plus avantageuse aux hommes. Les uns restèrent uniquement soumis aux lois, les autres obéirent bientôt à des maîtres. Les citoyens voulurent garder leur liberté; les sujets ne songèrent qu'à l'ôter à leurs voisins, ne pouvant souffrir que d'autres jouissent d'un bien dont ils ne jouissaient plus eux-mêmes. En un mot, d'un côté furent les richesses et les conquêtes, et de l'autre le bonheur et la vertu.

Dans ces divers Gouvernements, toutes les magistratures furent d'abord électives; et quand la richesse ne l'emportait pas, la préférence était accordée au mérite, qui donne un ascendant

[1] Eds. 1755, 1782 and 1801, as in the text. Hachette omits *en*.
[2] Hachette has *de*. Eds. 1755, 1782, 1801, as in the text.

naturel, et à l'âge, qui donne l'expérience dans les affaires et le sang-froid dans les délibérations. Les anciens des Hébreux, les gérontes de Sparte, le sénat de Rome, et l'étymologie même de notre mot *seigneur*, montrent combien autrefois la vieillesse était respectée. Plus les élections tombaient sur des hommes avancés en âge, plus elles devenaient fréquentes, et plus leurs embarras se faisaient sentir ; les brigues s'introduisirent, les factions se formèrent, les partis s'aigrirent, les guerres civiles s'allumèrent ; enfin le sang des citoyens fut sacrifié au prétendu bonheur de l'État, et l'on fut à la veille de retomber dans l'anarchie des temps antérieurs. L'ambition des principaux profita de ces circonstances pour perpétuer leurs charges dans leurs familles ; le peuple, déjà accoutumé à la dépendance, au repos et aux commodités de la vie, et déjà hors d'état de briser ses fers, consentit à laisser augmenter sa servitude pour affermir sa tranquillité. Et c'est ainsi que les chefs, devenus héréditaires, s'accoutumèrent à regarder leur magistrature comme un bien de famille, à se regarder eux-mêmes comme les propriétaires de l'État, dont ils n'étaient d'abord que les officiers ; à appeler leurs concitoyens leurs esclaves ; à les compter, comme du bétail, au nombre des choses qui leur appartenaient ; et à s'appeler eux-mêmes égaux aux dieux, et rois des rois.

Si nous suivons le progrès de l'inégalité dans ces différentes révolutions, nous trouverons que l'établissement de la Loi et du droit de propriété fut son premier terme ; l'institution de la magistrature le second ; que le troisième et dernier fut le changement du pouvoir légitime en pouvoir arbitraire. En sorte que l'état de riche et de pauvre fut autorisé par la première époque, celui de puissant et de faible par la seconde, et par la troisième celui de maître et d'esclave, qui est le dernier degré de l'inégalité, et le terme auquel aboutissent enfin tous les autres ; jusqu'à ce que de nouvelles révolutions dissolvent tout à fait le Gouvernement, ou le rapprochent de l'institution légitime.

Pour comprendre la nécessité de ce progrès, il faut moins considérer les motifs de l'établissement du Corps politique, que la forme qu'il prend dans son exécution et les inconvénients qu'il entraîne après lui. Car les vices qui rendent nécessaires les institutions sociales sont les mêmes qui en rendent l'abus inévitable. Et comme, excepté la seule Sparte, où la Loi veillait principalement à l'éducation des enfants, et où Lycurgue établit des mœurs qui le dispensaient presque d'y ajouter des lois, les lois, en général moins fortes que les passions, contiennent les hommes sans les changer, il serait aisé de prouver que tout Gouvernement qui, sans se corrompre ni s'altérer, marcherait toujours exactement selon la fin de son institution, aurait été institué sans nécessité ; et qu'un pays, où personne n'éluderait les lois et n'abuserait de la magistrature, n'aurait besoin ni de magistrats ni de lois.

Les distinctions politiques amènent nécessairement les[1] distinctions civiles. L'inégalité croissant entre le peuple et ses chefs se fait bientôt sentir parmi les particuliers, et s'y modifie en mille manières selon les passions, les talents et les occurrences. Le magistrat ne saurait usurper un pouvoir illégitime sans se faire des créatures auxquelles il est forcé d'en céder quelque partie. D'ailleurs, les citoyens ne se laissent opprimer qu'autant qu'entraînés par une aveugle ambition, et regardant plus au-dessous qu'au-dessus d'eux, la domination leur devient plus chère que l'indépendance, et qu'ils consentent à porter des fers pour en pouvoir donner à leur tour. Il est très difficile de réduire à l'obéissance celui qui ne cherche point à commander ; et le politique le plus adroit ne viendrait pas à bout d'assujettir des hommes qui ne voudraient qu'être libres. Mais l'inégalité s'étend sans peine parmi des[2] âmes ambitieuses et lâches, toujours prêtes à courir les risques de la fortune, et à dominer ou servir presque indifféremment, selon qu'elle leur devient favorable ou contraire. C'est ainsi qu'il dut venir un temps où les yeux du peuple furent fascinés à tel point que ses conducteurs n'avaient qu'à dire au plus petit des hommes : 'Sois grand, toi et toute ta race' ; aussitôt il paraissait grand à tout le monde ainsi qu'à ses propres yeux, et ses descendants s'élevaient encore à mesure qu'ils s'éloignaient de lui. Plus la cause était reculée et incertaine, plus l'effet augmentait ; plus on pouvait compter de fainéants dans une famille, et plus elle devenait illustre.

Si c'était ici le lieu d'entrer en des détails, j'expliquerais facilement comment, [3] sans même que le Gouvernement s'en mêle[3], l'inégalité de crédit et d'autorité devient inévitable entre les particuliers (s), sitôt que, réunis en une même société, ils sont forcés de se comparer entre eux, et de tenir compte des différences qu'ils trouvent dans l'usage continuel qu'ils ont à faire les uns des autres. Ces différences sont de plusieurs espèces. Mais, en général, la richesse, la noblesse ou le rang, la puissance et le

---

[1] Eds. 1755, 1782 and 1801, read as in the text. Hachette reads *des*.
[2] Eds. 1755, 1782 and 1801, as in the text. Hachette reads *les*.
[3] This clause appeared for the first time in the Ed. of 1782.

mérite personnel, étant les distinctions principales par lesquelles on se mesure dans la société, je prouverais que l'accord ou le conflit de ces forces diverses est l'indication la plus sûre d'un État bien ou mal constitué. Je ferais voir qu'entre ces quatre sortes d'inégalité, les qualités personnelles étant l'origine de toutes les autres, la richesse est la dernière à laquelle elles se réduisent à la fin, parce qu'étant la plus immédiatement utile au bien-être et la plus facile à communiquer on s'en sert aisément pour acheter tout le reste : observation qui peut faire juger assez exactement de la mesure dont chaque peuple s'est éloigné de son institution primitive, et du chemin qu'il a fait vers le terme extrême de la corruption. Je remarquerais combien ce désir universel de réputation, d'honneurs et de préférences, qui nous dévore tous, exerce et compare les talents et les forces ; combien il excite et multiplie les passions ; et combien, rendant tous les hommes concurrents, rivaux, ou plutôt ennemis, il cause tous les jours de revers, de succès et de catastrophes de toute espèce, en faisant courir la même lice à tant de prétendants. Je montrerais que c'est à cette ardeur de faire parler de soi, à cette fureur de se distinguer qui nous tient presque toujours hors de nous-mêmes, que nous devons ce qu'il y a de meilleur et de pire parmi les hommes : nos vertus et nos vices, nos sciences et nos erreurs, nos conquérants et nos philosophes : c'est-à-dire, une multitude de mauvaises choses sur un petit nombre de bonnes. Je prouverais enfin que si l'on voit une poignée de puissants et de riches au faîte des grandeurs et de la fortune, tandis que la foule rampe dans l'obscurité et dans la misère, c'est que les premiers n'estiment les choses dont ils jouissent qu'autant que les autres en sont privés, et que, sans changer d'état, ils cesseraient d'être heureux, si le peuple cessait d'être misérable.

Mais ces détails seraient seuls la matière d'un ouvrage considérable, dans lequel on pèserait les avantages et les inconvénients de tout Gouvernement, relativement aux droits de l'état de nature, et où l'on dévoilerait toutes les faces différentes sous lesquelles l'inégalité s'est montrée jusqu'à ce jour, et pourra se montrer dans les siècles futurs[1], selon la nature de ces Gouvernements et les révolutions que le temps y amènera nécessairement. On verrait la multitude opprimée au dedans par une suite des précautions mêmes qu'elle avait prises contre ce qui la menaçait au dehors ; on verrait l'oppression s'accroître continuellement, sans que les

---

[1] The word *futurs* appeared for the first time in Ed. 1782.

Le despotisme

opprimés pussent jamais savoir quel terme elle aurait, ni quels moyens légitimes[1] il leur resterait pour l'arrêter; on verrait les droits des citoyens et les libertés nationales s'éteindre peu à peu, et les réclamations des faibles traitées de murmures séditieux; on verrait la politique restreindre à une portion mercenaire du peuple l'honneur de défendre la cause commune; on verrait de là sortir la nécessité des impôts, le cultivateur découragé quitter son champ, même durant la paix, et laisser la charrue pour ceindre l'épée; on verrait naître les règles funestes et bizarres du point d'honneur; on verrait les défenseurs de la patrie en devenir tôt ou tard les ennemis, tenir sans cesse le poignard levé sur leurs concitoyens; et il viendrait un temps où on[2] les entendrait dire à l'oppresseur de leur pays :

> Pectore si fratris gladium juguloque parentis
> Condere me jubeas, gravidæque in viscera partu
> Conjugis, invita peragam tamen omnia dextra[3].

De l'extrême inégalité des conditions et des fortunes, de la diversité des passions et des talents, des arts inutiles, des arts pernicieux, des sciences frivoles, sortiraient des foules de préjugés également contraires à la raison, au bonheur et à la vertu. On verrait fomenter par les chefs tout ce qui peut affaiblir des hommes rassemblés, en les désunissant; tout ce qui peut donner à la société un air de concorde apparente et y semer un germe de division réelle; tout ce qui peut inspirer aux différents ordres une défiance et une haine mutuelle par l'opposition de leurs droits et de leurs intérêts, et fortifier par conséquent le pouvoir qui les contient tous.

C'est du sein de ce désordre[4] et de ces révolutions que le despotisme, élevant par degrés sa tête hideuse et dévorant tout ce qu'il aurait aperçu de bon et de sain dans toutes les parties de l'État, parviendrait enfin à fouler aux pieds les lois et le peuple, et à s'établir sur les ruines de la République. Les temps qui précéderaient ce dernier changement seraient des temps de troubles et de calamités; mais à la fin tout serait englouti par le monstre; et les peuples n'auraient plus de chefs ni de lois, mais seulement des tyrans. Dès cet instant aussi il cesserait d'être question de mœurs et de vertu. Car partout où règne le despotisme, *cui ex*

---

[1] So Eds. 1755, 1782 and 1801. Hachette, *quel moyen légitime*.
[2] Ed. 1755, *l'on*. Eds. 1782, 1801, *on*.
[3] Lucan, *Phars.* I. ll. 376—8. For *gravidæ*, the true reading is *plenæ*.
[4] Eds. 1755, 1782 and 1801, as in the text. Hachette reads *ces désordres*.

honesto nulla est spes[1], il ne souffre aucun autre maître; sitôt qu'il parle, il n'y a ni probité ni devoir à consulter; et la plus aveugle obéissance est la seule vertu qui reste aux esclaves.

C'est ici le dernier terme de l'inégalité, et le point extrême qui ferme le cercle et touche au point d'où nous sommes partis; c'est ici que tous les particuliers redeviennent égaux, parce qu'ils ne sont rien, et que les sujets n'ayant plus d'autre loi que la volonté du maître, ni le maître d'autre règle que ses passions, les notions du bien et les principes de la justice s'évanouissent derechef; c'est ici que tout se ramène à la seule loi du plus fort, et par conséquent à un nouvel état de nature différent de celui par lequel nous avons commencé, en ce que l'un était l'état de nature dans sa pureté, et que ce dernier est le fruit d'un excès de corruption. Il y a si peu de différence d'ailleurs entre ces deux états, et le contrat de Gouvernement est tellement dissous par le despotisme, que le despote n'est le maître qu'aussi longtemps qu'il est le plus fort; et que, sitôt qu'on peut l'expulser, il n'a point à réclamer contre la violence. L'émeute qui finit par étrangler ou détrôner un sultan est un acte aussi juridique que ceux par lesquels il disposait la veille des vies et des biens de ses sujets. La seule force le maintenait, la seule force le renverse. Toutes choses se passent ainsi selon l'ordre naturel; et, quel que puisse être l'événement de ces courtes et fréquentes révolutions, nul ne peut se plaindre de l'injustice d'autrui, mais seulement de sa propre imprudence ou de son malheur.

En découvrant et suivant ainsi les routes oubliées et perdues, qui de l'état naturel ont dû mener l'homme à l'état civil; en rétablissant, avec les positions intermédiaires que je viens de marquer, celles que le temps qui me presse m'a fait supprimer, ou que l'imagination ne m'a point suggérées; tout lecteur attentif ne pourra qu'être frappé de l'espace immense qui sépare ces deux états. C'est dans cette lente succession des choses qu'il verra la solution d'une infinité de problèmes de morale et de politique que les philosophes ne peuvent résoudre. Il sentira que, le genre humain d'un âge n'étant pas le genre humain d'un autre âge, la raison pourquoi Diogène ne trouvait point d'homme, c'est qu'il cherchait parmi ses contemporains l'homme d'un temps qui n'était plus. Caton, dira-t-il, périt avec Rome et la liberté, parce qu'il fut déplacé dans son siècle; et le plus grand des hommes ne fit qu'étonner le monde, qu'il eût gouverné cinq cents ans plus tôt. En un mot, il expliquera comment l'âme et les passions humaines,

[1] Perhaps a variant on *cui compositis rebus nulla spes* (Tac. *His.* I. 21).

s'altérant insensiblement, changent pour ainsi dire de nature; pourquoi nos besoins et nos plaisirs changent d'objets à la longue; pourquoi, l'homme originel s'évanouissant par degrés, la société n'offre plus aux yeux du sage qu'un assemblage d'hommes artificiels et de passions factices, qui sont l'ouvrage de toutes ces nouvelles relations et n'ont aucun vrai fondement dans la nature. Ce que la réflexion nous apprend là-dessus, l'observation le confirme parfaitement: l'homme sauvage et l'homme policé diffèrent tellement par le fond du cœur et des inclinations, que ce qui fait le bonheur suprême de l'un réduirait l'autre au désespoir. Le premier ne respire que le repos et la liberté; il ne veut que vivre et rester oisif; et l'ataraxie même du stoïcien n'approche pas de sa profonde indifférence pour tout autre objet. Au contraire, le citoyen, toujours actif, sue, s'agite, se tourmente sans cesse pour chercher des occupations encore plus laborieuses; il travaille jusqu'à la mort, il y court même pour se mettre en état de vivre, ou renonce à la vie pour acquérir l'immortalité. Il fait sa cour aux grands qu'il hait, et aux riches qu'il méprise; il n'épargne rien pour obtenir l'honneur de les servir; il se vante orgueilleusement de sa bassesse et de leur protection; et, fier de son esclavage, il parle avec dédain de ceux qui n'ont pas l'honneur de le partager. Quel spectacle pour un Caraïbe que les travaux pénibles et enviés d'un ministre européen! Combien de morts cruelles ne préférerait pas cet indolent sauvage à l'horreur d'une pareille vie, qui souvent n'est pas même adoucie par le plaisir de bien faire! Mais, pour voir le but de tant de soins, il faudrait que ces mots, *puissance* et *réputation,* eussent un sens dans son esprit; qu'il apprît qu'il y a une sorte d'hommes qui comptent pour quelque chose les regards du reste de l'univers, qui savent être heureux et contents d'eux-mêmes sur le témoignage d'autrui plutôt que sur le leur propre. Telle est, en effet, la véritable cause de toutes ces différences: le sauvage vit en lui-même; l'homme sociable, toujours hors de lui, ne sait vivre que[1] dans l'opinion des autres; et c'est, pour ainsi dire, de leur seul jugement qu'il tire le sentiment de sa propre existence. Il n'est pas de mon sujet de montrer comment d'une telle disposition naît tant d'indifférence pour le bien et le mal, avec de si beaux discours de morale; comment, tout se réduisant aux apparences, tout devient factice et joué: honneur, amitié, vertu, et souvent jusqu'aux vices mêmes, dont on trouve enfin le secret de se glorifier; comment, en un mot, demandant toujours aux autres ce que nous sommes, et n'osant jamais nous

[1] So Eds. 1755, 1782 and 1801. Hachette reads *ne sait que vivre.*

interroger là-dessus nous-mêmes, au milieu de tant de philosophie, d'humanité, de politesse et de maximes sublimes, nous n'avons qu'un extérieur trompeur et frivole : de l'honneur sans vertu, de la raison sans sagesse, et du plaisir sans bonheur. Il me suffit d'avoir prouvé que ce n'est point là l'état originel de l'homme ; et que c'est le seul esprit de la société, et l'inégalité qu'elle engendre, qui changent et altèrent ainsi toutes nos inclinations naturelles.

J'ai tâché d'exposer l'origine et le progrès de l'inégalité, l'établissement et l'abus des sociétés politiques, autant que ces choses peuvent se déduire de la nature de l'homme par les seules lumières de la raison, et indépendamment des dogmes sacrés qui donnent à l'autorité souveraine la sanction du droit divin. Il suit de cet exposé que l'inégalité, étant presque nulle dans l'état de nature, tire sa force et son accroissement du développement de nos facultés et des progrès de l'esprit humain, et devient enfin stable et légitime par l'établissement de la propriété et des lois. Il suit encore que l'inégalité morale, autorisée par le seul droit positif, est contraire au droit naturel toutes les fois qu'elle ne concourt pas en même proportion avec l'inégalité physique : distinction qui détermine suffisamment ce qu'on doit penser à cet égard de la sorte d'inégalité qui règne parmi tous les peuples policés ; puisqu'il est manifestement contre la loi de nature, de quelque manière qu'on la définisse, qu'un enfant commande à un vieillard, qu'un imbécile conduise un homme sage, et qu'une poignée de gens regorge de superfluités, tandis que la multitude affamée manque du nécessaire.

NOTES

Page 126. (*a*) Hérodote raconte qu'après le meurtre du faux Smerdis, les sept libérateurs de la Perse s'étant assemblés pour délibérer sur la forme du gouvernement qu'ils donneraient à l'État, Otanès opina fortement pour la République : avis d'autant plus extraordinaire dans la bouche d'un satrape, qu'outre la prétention qu'il pouvait avoir à l'empire les grands craignent plus que la mort une sorte de Gouvernement qui les force à respecter les hommes. Otanès, comme on peut bien croire, ne fut point écouté ; et voyant qu'on allait procéder à l'élection d'un monarque, lui, qui ne voulait ni obéir ni commander, céda volontairement aux autres concurrents son droit à la couronne, demandant pour tout dédommagement d'être libre et indépendant, lui et sa postérité : ce qui lui fut accordé. Quand Hérodote ne nous apprendrait pas la restriction qui fut mise à ce privilége, il faudrait nécessairement la supposer ; autrement Otanès, ne reconnaissant aucune sorte de loi, et n'ayant de compte à rendre à personne, aurait été tout-puissant dans l'État et plus puissant que le roi même. Mais il n'y avait guère d'apparence qu'un homme capable de se contenter, en pareil cas, d'un tel privilége fût capable d'en abuser. En effet, on ne voit pas que ce droit ait jamais causé le moindre trouble dans le royaume, ni par le sage Otanès, ni par aucun de ses descendants. [See Bosscha, p. 17.]

Page 134. (*b*) Dès mon premier pas je m'appuie avec confiance sur une de ces autorités respectables pour les philosophes, parce qu'elles viennent d'une raison solide et sublime, qu'eux seuls savent trouver et sentir.

'Quelque intérêt que nous ayons à nous connaître nous-mêmes, je ne sais si nous ne connaissons pas mieux tout ce qui n'est pas nous. Pourvus par la nature d'organes uniquement destinés à notre conservation, nous ne les employons qu'à recevoir les impressions étrangères : nous ne cherchons qu'à nous répandre au dehors, et à exister hors de nous. Trop occupés à multiplier les fonctions de nos sens et à augmenter l'étendue extérieure de notre être, rarement faisons-nous usage de ce sens intérieur qui nous réduit à nos vraies dimensions, et qui sépare de nous tout ce qui n'en est pas. C'est cependant de ce sens dont il faut nous servir, si nous voulons nous connaître ; c'est le seul par lequel nous puissions nous juger. Mais comment donner à ce sens son activité et toute son étendue ? comment dégager notre âme, dans laquelle il réside, de toutes les illusions de notre esprit ? Nous avons perdu l'habitude de l'employer, elle est demeurée sans exercice au milieu du tumulte de nos sensations corporelles, elle s'est desséchée par le feu de nos passions ; le cœur, l'esprit, les sens[1], tout a travaillé contre elle.' (HIST. NAT., IV. p. 151, *De la nature de l'homme* ; t. II. p. 430, Ed. 1749, 4°.)

Page 142. (*c*) Les changements qu'un long usage de marcher sur deux pieds a pu produire dans la conformation de l'homme, les rapports qu'on observe encore entre ses bras et les jambes antérieures des quadrupèdes, et l'induction tirée de leur manière de marcher, ont pu faire naître des doutes sur celle qui devait nous être la plus naturelle. Tous les enfants commencent par marcher à quatre pieds, et ont besoin de notre exemple et de nos leçons pour apprendre à se tenir debout. Il y a même des nations sauvages, telles que les Hottentots, qui, négligeant beaucoup les enfants, les laissent marcher sur les mains

[1] Eds. 1755 and 1782 read *le sens*, by a slip. Buffon and 1801, as in the text.

si longtemps qu'ils ont ensuite bien de la peine à les redresser ; autant en font les enfants des Caraïbes des Antilles. Il y a divers exemples d'hommes quadrupèdes ; et je pourrais entre autres citer celui de cet enfant qui fut trouvé, en 1344, auprès de Hesse, où il avait été nourri par des loups, et qui disait depuis, à la cour du prince Henri, que, s'il n'eût tenu qu'à lui, il eût mieux aimé retourner avec eux que de vivre parmi les hommes. Il avait tellement pris l'habitude de marcher comme ces animaux, qu'il fallut lui attacher des pièces de bois qui le forçaient à se tenir debout et en équilibre sur ses deux pieds. Il en était de même de l'enfant qu'on trouva, en 1694, dans les forêts de Lithuanie, et qui vivait parmi les ours. Il ne donnait, dit M. de Condillac, aucune marque de raison, marchait sur ses pieds et sur ses mains, n'avait aucun langage, et formait des sons qui ne ressemblaient en rien à ceux d'un homme. Le petit sauvage d'Hanovre, qu'on mena, il y a plusieurs années, à la cour d'Angleterre, avait toutes les peines du monde à s'assujettir à marcher sur deux pieds ; et l'on trouva, en 1719, deux autres sauvages dans les Pyrénées, qui couraient par les montagnes à la manière des quadrupèdes. Quant à ce qu'on pourrait objecter que c'est se priver de l'usage des mains, dont nous tirons tant d'avantages ; outre que l'exemple des singes montre que la main peut fort bien être employée des deux manières ; cela prouverait seulement que l'homme peut donner à ses membres une destination plus commode que celle de la nature, et non que la nature a destiné l'homme à marcher autrement qu'elle ne lui enseigne.

Mais il y a, ce me semble, de beaucoup meilleures raisons à dire, pour soutenir que l'homme est un bipède. Premièrement, quand on ferait voir qu'il a pu d'abord être conformé autrement que nous ne le voyons, et cependant devenir enfin ce qu'il est, ce n'en serait pas assez pour conclure que cela se soit fait ainsi ; car, après avoir montré la possibilité de ces changements, il faudrait encore, avant que de les admettre, en montrer au moins la vraisemblance. De plus, si les bras de l'homme paraissent avoir pu lui servir de jambes au besoin, c'est la seule observation favorable à ce système, sur un grand nombre d'autres qui lui sont contraires. Les principales sont, que la manière dont la tête de l'homme est attachée à son corps, au lieu de diriger sa vue horizontalement, comme l'ont tous les autres animaux, et comme il l'a lui-même en marchant debout, lui eût tenu, marchant à quatre pieds, les yeux directement fichés[1] vers la terre, situation très peu favorable à la conservation de l'individu ; que la queue qui lui manque, et dont il n'a que faire marchant à deux pieds, est utile aux quadrupèdes, et qu'aucun d'eux n'en est privé ; que le sein de la femme, très-bien situé pour un bipède, qui tient son enfant dans ses bras, l'est si mal pour un quadrupède, que nul ne l'a placé de cette manière ; que le train de derrière étant d'une excessive hauteur à proportion des jambes de devant, ce qui fait que marchant à quatre nous nous traînons sur les genoux, le tout eût fait un animal mal proportionné et marchant peu commodément ; que s'il eût posé le pied à plat ainsi que la main, il aurait eu dans la jambe postérieure une articulation de moins que les autres animaux, savoir celle qui joint le canon au tibia ; et qu'en ne posant que la pointe du pied, comme il aurait sans doute été contraint de faire[2], le tarse, sans parler de la pluralité des os qui le composent, paraît trop gros pour tenir lieu de canon, et ses articulations avec le métatarse et le tibia trop rapprochées pour

---
[1] Hachette, *fixés*, without authority. Eds. 1755, 1782 and 1801, *fichés*.
[2] Ed. 1801 and Hachette, *de le faire*. Eds. 1755, 1782, *de faire*.

donner à la jambe humaine, dans cette situation, la même flexibilité qu'ont celles des quadrupèdes. L'exemple des enfants, étant pris dans un âge où les forces naturelles ne sont point encore développées ni les membres raffermis, ne conclut rien du tout ; et j'aimerais autant dire que les chiens ne sont pas destinés à marcher, parce qu'ils ne font que ramper quelques semaines après leur naissance. Les faits particuliers ont encore peu de force contre la pratique universelle de tous les hommes, même des nations qui, n'ayant eu aucune communication avec les autres, n'avaient pu rien imiter d'elles. Un enfant abandonné dans une forêt avant que de pouvoir marcher, et nourri par quelque bête, aura suivi l'exemple de sa nourrice, en s'exerçant à marcher comme elle ; l'habitude lui aura pu donner des facilités qu'il ne tenait point de la nature ; et comme des manchots parviennent, à force d'exercice, à faire avec leurs pieds tout ce que nous faisons de nos mains, il sera parvenu enfin à employer ses mains à l'usage des pieds.

Page 143. (d) S'il se trouvait parmi mes lecteurs quelque assez mauvais physicien pour me faire des difficultés sur la supposition de cette fertilité naturelle de la terre, je vais lui répondre par le passage suivant :

'Comme les végétaux tirent pour leur nourriture beaucoup plus de substance de l'air et de l'eau qu'ils n'en tirent de la terre, il arrive qu'en pourrissant ils rendent à la terre plus qu'ils n'en ont tiré ; d'ailleurs une forêt détermine les eaux de la pluie, en arrêtant les vapeurs. Ainsi, dans un bois que l'on conserverait bien longtemps sans y toucher, la couche de terre qui sert à la végétation augmenterait considérablement ; mais les animaux rendant moins à la terre qu'ils n'en tirent, et les hommes faisant des consommations énormes de bois et de plantes pour le feu et pour d'autres usages, il s'ensuit que la couche de terre végétale d'un pays habité doit toujours diminuer et devenir enfin comme le terrain de l'Arabie Pétrée, et comme celui de tant d'autres provinces de l'Orient, qui est en effet le climat le plus anciennement habité, où l'on ne trouve que du sel et des sables. Car le sel fixe des plantes et des animaux reste, tandis que toutes les autres parties se volatilisent.' (HIST. NAT., *Preuves de la théorie de la terre*, art. 7.)

On peut ajouter à cela la preuve de fait par la quantité d'arbres et de plantes de toute espèce dont étaient remplies presque toutes les îles désertes qui ont été découvertes dans ces derniers siècles, et par ce que l'histoire nous apprend des forêts immenses qu'il a fallu abattre par toute la terre à mesure qu'elle s'est peuplée ou policée. Sur quoi je ferai encore les trois remarques suivantes : l'une, que, s'il y a une sorte de végétaux qui puissent compenser la déperdition de matière végétale qui se fait par les animaux selon le raisonnement de M. de Buffon, ce sont surtout les bois, dont les têtes et les feuilles rassemblent et s'approprient plus d'eaux et de vapeurs que ne font les autres plantes ; la seconde, que la destruction du sol, c'est-à-dire la perte de la substance propre à la végétation, doit s'accélérer à proportion que la terre est plus cultivée, et que les habitants plus industrieux consomment en plus grande abondance ses productions de toute espèce. Ma troisième et plus importante remarque est que les fruits des arbres fournissent à l'animal une nourriture plus abondante que ne peuvent faire les autres végétaux : expérience que j'ai faite moi-même, en comparant les produits de deux terrains égaux en grandeur et en qualité, l'un couvert de châtaigniers, et l'autre semé de blé. [See p. 512.]

Page 143. (e) Parmi les quadrupèdes, les deux distinctions les plus universelles des espèces voraces se tirent, l'une de la figure des dents, et l'autre de la conformation des intestins. Les animaux qui ne vivent que de végétaux ont tous les dents plates, comme le cheval, le bœuf, le mouton, le lièvre ; mais les voraces les ont pointues, comme le chat, le chien, le loup, le renard. Et quant aux intestins, les frugivores en ont quelques-uns, tels que le colon, qui ne se trouvent pas dans les animaux voraces. Il semble donc que l'homme, ayant les dents et les intestins comme les ont les animaux frugivores, devrait naturellement être rangé dans cette classe ; et non seulement les observations anatomiques confirment cette opinion, mais les monuments de l'antiquité y sont encore très favorables. 'Dicéarque, dit saint Jérôme, rapporte dans ses livres des Antiquités grecques que, sous le règne de Saturne, où la terre était encore fertile par elle-même, nul homme ne mangeait de chair, mais que tous vivaient des fruits et des légumes qui croissaient naturellement.' (Lib. II. adv. Jovinian.) [1] Cette opinion se peut encore appuyer sur les relations de plusieurs voyageurs modernes. François Corréal témoigne, entre autres, que la plupart des habitants des Lucayes que les Espagnols transportèrent aux îles de Cuba, de Saint-Domingue et ailleurs, moururent pour avoir mangé de la chair[1]. On peut voir par là que je néglige bien des avantages que je pourrais faire valoir. Car la proie étant presque l'unique sujet de combat entre les animaux carnassiers, et les frugivores vivant entre eux dans une paix continuelle, si l'espèce humaine était de ce dernier genre, il est clair qu'elle aurait eu beaucoup plus de facilité à subsister dans l'état de nature, beaucoup moins de besoin et d'occasions[2] d'en sortir.

Page 144. (f) Toutes les connaissances qui demandent de la réflexion, toutes celles qui ne s'acquièrent que par l'enchaînement des idées et ne se perfectionnent que successivement, semblent être tout à fait hors de la portée de l'homme sauvage, faute de communication avec ses semblables: c'est-à-dire, faute de l'instrument qui sert à cette communication et des besoins qui la rendent nécessaire. Son savoir et son industrie se bornent à sauter, courir, se battre, lancer une pierre, escalader un arbre. Mais s'il ne sait que ces choses, en revanche il les sait beaucoup mieux que nous, qui n'en avons pas le même besoin que lui ; et comme elles dépendent uniquement de l'exercice du corps, et ne sont susceptibles d'aucune communication ni d'aucun progrès d'un individu à l'autre, le premier homme a pu y être tout aussi habile que ses derniers descendants.

Les relations des voyageurs sont pleines d'exemples de la force et de la vigueur des hommes chez les nations barbares et sauvages ; elles ne vantent guère moins leur adresse et leur légèreté : et comme il ne faut que des yeux pour observer ces choses, rien n'empêche qu'on n'ajoute foi à ce que certifient là-dessus des témoins oculaires. J'en tire au hasard quelques exemples des premiers livres qui me tombent sous la main.

'Les Hottentots, dit Kolben, entendent mieux la pêche que les Européens du Cap. Leur habileté est égale au filet, à l'hameçon et au dard, dans les anses comme dans les rivières. Ils ne prennent pas moins habilement le poisson avec la main. Ils sont d'une adresse incomparable à la nage. Leur manière de nager a quelque chose de surprenant, et qui leur est tout à fait propre. Ils nagent le corps droit et les mains étendues hors de l'eau, de sorte qu'ils paraissent marcher sur la terre. Dans la plus grande agitation de la mer et lorsque les flots forment autant de montagnes, ils dansent en

[1] This passage appeared for the first time in Ed. 1782.
[2] Hachette reads *occasion*. Eds. 1755, 1782 and 1801, as in the text.

quelque sort sur le dos des vagues, montant et descendant comme un morceau de liége.

'Les Hottentots, dit encore le même auteur, sont d'une adresse surprenante à la chasse, et la légèreté de leur course passe l'imagination.' Il s'étonne qu'ils ne fassent pas plus souvent un mauvais usage de leur agilité : ce qui leur arrive pourtant quelquefois, comme on peut juger par l'exemple qu'il en donne. 'Un matelot hollandais, en débarquant au Cap, chargea, dit-il, un Hottentot de le suivre à la ville avec un rouleau de tabac d'environ vingt livres. Lorsqu'ils furent tous deux à quelque distance de la troupe, le Hottentot demanda au matelot s'il savait courir. "Courir ? répond le Hollandais ; oui, fort bien.—Voyons," reprit l'Africain ; et, fuyant avec le tabac, il disparut presque aussitôt. Le matelot, confondu de cette merveilleuse vitesse, ne pensa point à le poursuivre, et ne revit jamais ni son tabac ni son porteur.

'Ils ont la vue si prompte et la main si certaine, que les Européens n'en approchent point. À cent pas ils toucheront d'un coup de pierre une marque de la grandeur d'un demi-sou ; et ce qu'il y a de plus étonnant, c'est qu'au lieu de fixer comme nous les yeux sur le but, ils font des mouvements et des contorsions continuelles. Il semble que leur pierre soit portée par une main invisible.'

Le père du Tertre dit à peu près, sur les sauvages des Antilles, les mêmes choses qu'on vient de lire sur les Hottentots du Cap de Bonne-Espérance. Il vante surtout leur justesse à tirer avec leurs flèches les oiseaux au vol et les poissons à la nage, qu'ils prennent ensuite en plongeant. Les sauvages de l'Amérique septentrionale ne sont pas moins célèbres par leur force et par leur adresse ; et voici un exemple qui pourra faire juger de celle des Indiens de l'Amérique méridionale.

En l'année 1746, un Indien de Buénos-Ayres, ayant été condamné aux galères à Cadix, proposa au gouverneur de racheter sa liberté en exposant sa vie dans une fête publique. Il promit qu'il attaquerait seul le plus furieux taureau sans autre arme en main qu'une corde ; qu'il le terrasserait, qu'il le saisirait avec sa corde par telle partie qu'on indiquerait, qu'il le sellerait, le briderait, le monterait, et combattrait, ainsi monté, deux autres taureaux des plus furieux qu'on ferait sortir du Torillo, et qu'il les mettrait tous à mort, l'un après l'autre, dans l'instant qu'on le lui commanderait, et sans le secours de personne : ce qui lui fut accordé. L'Indien tint parole, et réussit dans tout ce qu'il avait promis. Sur la manière dont il s'y prit, et sur tout le détail du combat, on peut consulter le premier tome in-12 des *Observations sur l'histoire naturelle*, de M. Gautier, d'où ce fait est tiré, page 262.

Page 145. (g) 'La durée de la vie des chevaux, dit M. de Buffon, est, comme dans toutes les autres espèces d'animaux, proportionnée à la durée du temps de leur accroissement. L'homme, qui est quatorze ans à croître, peut vivre six ou sept fois autant de temps, c'est-à-dire quatre-vingt-dix ou cent ans ; le cheval, dont l'accroissement se fait en quatre ans, peut vivre six ou sept fois autant, c'est-à-dire vingt-cinq ou trente ans. Les exemples qui pourraient être contraires à cette règle sont si rares, qu'on ne doit pas même les regarder comme une exception dont on puisse tirer des conséquences ; et comme les gros chevaux prennent leur accroissement en moins de temps que les chevaux fins, ils vivent aussi moins de temps, et sont vieux dès l'âge de quinze ans.' (*Histoire naturelle du cheval.*)

Page 145. (*h*) Je crois voir entre les animaux carnassiers et les frugivores une autre différence encore plus générale que celle que j'ai remarquée dans la note (*e*), puisque celle-ci s'étend jusqu'aux oiseaux. Cette différence consiste dans le nombre des petits, qui n'excède jamais deux à chaque portée pour les espèces qui ne vivent que de végétaux, et qui va ordinairement au delà de ce nombre pour les animaux voraces. Il est aisé de connaître, à cet égard, la destination de la nature par le nombre des mamelles, qui n'est que de deux dans chaque femelle de la première espèce, comme la jument, la vache, la chèvre, la biche, la brebis, etc., et qui est toujours de six ou de huit dans les autres femelles, comme la chienne, la chatte, la louve, la tigresse, etc. La poule, l'oie, la cane, qui sont toutes des oiseaux voraces, ainsi que l'aigle, l'épervier, la chouette, pondent aussi et couvent un grand nombre d'œufs, ce qui n'arrive jamais à la colombe, à la tourterelle, ni aux oiseaux qui ne mangent absolument que du grain, lesquels ne pondent et ne couvent guère que deux œufs à la fois. La raison qu'on peut donner de cette différence est que les animaux qui ne vivent que d'herbes et de plantes, demeurant presque tout le jour à la pâture, et étant forcés d'employer beaucoup de temps à se nourrir, ne pourraient suffire à allaiter plusieurs petits : au lieu que les voraces, faisant leur[1] repas presque en un instant, peuvent plus aisément et plus souvent retourner à leurs petits et à leur chasse, et réparer la dissipation d'une si grande quantité de lait. Il y aurait à tout ceci bien des observations particulières et des réflexions à faire ; mais ce n'en est pas ici le lieu, et il me suffit d'avoir montré dans cette partie le système le plus général de la nature : système qui fournit une nouvelle raison de tirer l'homme de la classe des animaux carnassiers, et de le ranger parmi les espèces frugivores. [See pp. 512–3.]

Page 150. (*i*) Un auteur célèbre, calculant les biens et les maux de la vie humaine, et comparant les deux sommes, a trouvé que la dernière surpassait l'autre de beaucoup, et qu'à tout prendre la vie était pour l'homme un assez mauvais présent[2]. Je ne suis point surpris de sa conclusion ; il a tiré tous ses raisonnements de la constitution de l'homme civil. S'il fût remonté jusqu'à l'homme naturel, on peut juger qu'il eût trouvé des résultats très différents ; qu'il eût aperçu que l'homme n'a guère de maux que ceux qu'il s'est donnés lui-même ; et que la nature eût été justifiée. Ce n'est pas sans peine que nous sommes parvenus à nous rendre si malheureux. Quand, d'un côté, l'on considère les immenses travaux des hommes, tant de sciences approfondies, tant d'arts inventés, tant de forces employées, des abîmes comblés, des montagnes rasées, des rochers brisés, des fleuves rendus navigables, des terres défrichées, des lacs creusés, des marais desséchés, des bâtiments énormes élevés sur la terre, la mer couverte de vaisseaux et de matelots ; et que, de l'autre, on recherche avec un peu de méditation les vrais avantages qui ont résulté de tout cela pour le bonheur de l'espèce humaine ; on ne peut qu'être frappé de l'étonnante disproportion qui règne entre ces choses, et déplorer l'aveuglement de l'homme, qui, pour nourrir son fol orgueil et je ne sais quelle vaine admiration de lui-même, le fait courir avec ardeur après toutes les misères dont il est susceptible, et que la bienfaisante nature avait pris soin d'écarter de lui.

Les hommes sont méchants ; une triste et continuelle expérience dispense de la preuve. Cependant, l'homme est naturellement bon, je crois l'avoir

---

[1] Ed. 1801 and Hachette, *leurs*. Eds. 1755, 1782, *leur*.
[2] I am unable to suggest the name of the author referred to.

démontré. Qu'est-ce donc qui peut l'avoir dépravé à ce point, sinon les changements survenus dans sa constitution, les progrès qu'il a faits, et les connaissances qu'il a acquises ? Qu'on admire tant qu'on voudra la société humaine ; il n'en sera pas moins vrai qu'elle porte nécessairement les hommes à s'entre-haïr à proportion que leurs intérêts se croisent, à se rendre mutuellement des services apparents, et à se faire en effet tous les maux imaginables. Que peut-on penser d'un commerce, où la raison de chaque particulier lui dicte des maximes directement contraires à celles que la raison publique prêche au corps de la société, et où chacun trouve son compte dans le malheur d'autrui ? Il n'y a peut-être pas un homme aisé à qui des héritiers avides, et souvent ses propres enfants, ne souhaitent la mort en secret ; pas un vaisseau en mer dont le naufrage ne fût une bonne nouvelle pour quelque négociant ; pas une maison qu'un débiteur de mauvaise foi ne voulût voir brûler avec tous les papiers qu'elle contient ; pas un peuple qui ne se réjouisse des désastres de ses voisins. C'est ainsi que nous trouvons notre avantage dans le préjudice de nos semblables, et que la perte de l'un fait presque toujours la prospérité de l'autre. Mais ce qu'il y a de plus dangereux encore, c'est que les calamités publiques font l'attente et l'espoir d'une multitude de particuliers : les uns veulent des maladies, d'autres la mortalité, d'autres la guerre, d'autres la famine. J'ai vu des hommes affreux pleurer de douleur aux apparences d'une année fertile ; et le grand et funeste incendie de Londres, qui coûta la vie ou les biens à tant de malheureux, fit peut-être la fortune à plus de dix mille personnes. Je sais que Montaigne blâme l'Athénien Démadès d'avoir fait punir un ouvrier qui, vendant fort cher des cercueils, gagnait beaucoup à la mort des citoyens : mais, la raison que Montaigne allègue étant qu'il faudrait punir tout le monde, il est évident qu'elle confirme les miennes. Qu'on pénètre donc, au travers de nos frivoles démonstrations de bienveillance, ce qui se passe au fond des cœurs, et qu'on réfléchisse à ce que doit être un état de choses où tous les hommes sont forcés de se caresser et de se détruire mutuellement, et où ils naissent ennemis par devoir et fourbes par intérêt. Si l'on me répond que la société est tellement constituée que chaque homme gagne à servir les autres, je répliquerai que cela serait fort bien, s'il ne gagnait encore plus à leur nuire. Il n'y a point de profit si légitime qui ne soit surpassé par celui qu'on peut faire illégitimement, et le tort fait au prochain est toujours plus lucratif que les services. Il ne s'agit donc plus que de trouver les moyens de s'assurer l'impunité ; et c'est à quoi les puissants emploient toutes leurs forces, et les faibles toutes leurs ruses.

L'homme sauvage, quand il a dîné, est en paix avec toute la nature, et l'ami de tous ses semblables. S'agit-il quelquefois de disputer son repas, il n'en vient jamais aux coups sans avoir auparavant comparé la difficulté de vaincre avec celle de trouver ailleurs sa subsistance ; et, comme l'orgueil ne se mêle pas du combat, il se termine par quelques coups de poing ; le vainqueur mange, le vaincu va chercher fortune, et tout est pacifié. Mais, chez l'homme en société, ce sont bien d'autres affaires : il s'agit premièrement de pourvoir au nécessaire, et puis au superflu : ensuite viennent les délices, et puis les immenses richesses, et puis des sujets, et puis des esclaves : il n'a pas un moment de relâche. Ce qu'il y a de plus singulier, c'est que moins les besoins sont naturels et pressants, plus les passions augmentent, et, qui pis est, le pouvoir de les satisfaire ; de sorte qu'après de longues prospérités, après avoir englouti bien des trésors et désolé bien des hommes, mon héros finira par tout égorger jusqu'à ce qu'il soit l'unique maître de l'univers. Tel est en abrégé le tableau moral, sinon de la vie humaine, au moins des prétentions secrètes du cœur de tout homme civilisé.

Comparez sans préjugés l'état de l'homme civil avec celui de l'homme sauvage, et recherchez, si vous le pouvez, combien, outre sa méchanceté, ses besoins et ses misères, le premier a ouvert de nouvelles portes à la douleur et à la mort. Si vous considérez les peines d'esprit qui nous consument, les passions violentes qui nous épuisent et nous désolent, les travaux excessifs dont les pauvres sont surchargés, la mollesse encore plus dangereuse à laquelle les riches s'abandonnent, et qui font mourir les uns de leurs besoins, et les autres de leurs excès ; si vous songez aux monstrueux mélanges des aliments, à leurs pernicieux assaisonnements, aux denrées corrompues, aux drogues falsifiées, aux friponneries de ceux qui les vendent, aux erreurs de ceux qui les administrent, au poison des vaisseaux dans lesquels on les prépare ; si vous faites attention aux maladies épidémiques engendrées par le mauvais air parmi des multitudes d'hommes rassemblés, à celles qu'occasionnent la délicatesse de notre manière de vivre, les passages alternatifs de l'intérieur de nos maisons au grand air, l'usage des habillements pris ou quittés avec trop peu de précaution, et tous les soins que notre sensualité excessive a tournés en habitudes nécessaires, et dont la négligence ou la privation nous coûte ensuite la vie ou la santé ; si vous mettez en ligne de compte les incendies et les tremblements de terre qui, consumant ou renversant des villes entières, en font périr les habitants par milliers ; en un mot, si vous réunissez les dangers que toutes ces causes assemblent continuellement sur nos têtes, vous sentirez combien la nature nous fait payer cher le mépris que nous avons fait de ses leçons.

Je ne répéterai point ici sur la guerre ce que j'en ai dit ailleurs ; mais je voudrais que les gens instruits voulussent ou osassent donner une fois au public le détail des horreurs qui se commettent dans les armées par les entrepreneurs des vivres et des hôpitaux : on verrait que leurs manœuvres, non trop secrètes, par lesquelles les plus brillantes armées se fondent en moins de rien, font plus périr de soldats que n'en moissonne le fer ennemi. C'est encore un calcul non moins étonnant que celui des hommes que la mer engloutit tous les ans, soit par la faim, soit par le scorbut, soit par les pirates, soit par le feu, soit par les naufrages. Il est clair qu'il faut mettre aussi sur le compte de la propriété établie, et par conséquent de la société, les assassinats, les empoisonnements, les vols de grands chemins, et les punitions mêmes de ces crimes : punitions nécessaires pour prévenir de plus grands maux, mais qui, pour le meurtre d'un homme, coûtant la vie à deux ou davantage, ne laissent pas de doubler réellement la perte de l'espèce humaine. Combien de moyens honteux d'empêcher la naissance des hommes, et de tromper la nature ; soit par ces goûts brutaux et dépravés qui insultent son plus charmant ouvrage, goûts que les sauvages ni les animaux ne connurent jamais, et qui ne sont nés dans les pays policés que d'une imagination corrompue ; soit par ces avortements secrets, dignes fruits de la débauche et de l'honneur vicieux ; soit par l'exposition ou le meurtre d'une multitude d'enfants, victimes de la misère de leurs parents, ou de la honte barbare de leurs mères ; soit enfin par la mutilation de ces malheureux dont une partie de l'existence et toute la postérité sont sacrifiées à de vaines chansons, ou, ce qui est pis encore, à la brutale jalousie de quelques hommes : mutilation qui, dans ce dernier cas, outrage doublement la nature, et par le traitement que reçoivent ceux qui la souffrent, et par l'usage auquel ils sont destinés !

[1]Mais n'est-il pas mille cas plus fréquents et plus dangereux encore, où les droits paternels offensent ouvertement l'humanité ? Combien de talents enfouis et d'inclinations forcées par l'imprudente contrainte des pères ! Combien d'hommes se seraient distingués dans un état sortable, qui meurent malheureux et déshonorés dans un autre état pour lequel ils n'avaient aucun goût ! Combien de mariages heureux, mais inégaux, ont été rompus ou troublés, et combien de chastes épouses déshonorées, par cet ordre des conditions toujours en contradiction avec celui de la nature ! Combien d'autres unions bizarres formées par l'intérêt et désavouées par l'amour et par la raison ! Combien même d'époux honnêtes et vertueux font mutuellement leur supplice pour avoir été mal assortis ! Combien de jeunes et malheureuses victimes de l'avarice de leurs parents se plongent dans le vice, ou passent leurs tristes jours dans les larmes, et gémissent dans des liens indissolubles que le cœur repousse et que l'or seul a formés ! Heureuses quelquefois celles que leur courage et leur vertu même arrachent à la vie avant qu'une violence barbare les force à la passer dans le crime ou dans le désespoir ! Pardonnez-le-moi, père et mère à jamais déplorables : j'aigris à regret vos douleurs ; mais puissent-elles servir d'exemple éternel et terrible à quiconque ose, au nom même de la nature, violer le plus sacré de ses droits !

Si je n'ai parlé que de ces nœuds mal formés qui sont l'ouvrage de notre police, pense-t-on que ceux où l'amour et la sympathie ont présidé soient eux-mêmes exempts d'inconvénients ?[1] Que serait-ce si j'entreprenais de montrer l'espèce humaine attaquée dans sa source même, et jusque dans le plus saint de tous les liens, où l'on n'ose plus écouter la nature qu'après avoir consulté la fortune, et où, le désordre civil confondant les vertus et les vices, la continence devient une précaution criminelle, et le refus de donner la vie à son semblable un acte d'humanité ! Mais, sans déchirer le voile qui couvre tant d'horreurs, contentons-nous d'indiquer le mal auquel d'autres doivent apporter le remède.

Qu'on ajoute à tout cela cette quantité de métiers malsains qui abrègent les jours ou détruisent le tempérament, tels que sont les travaux des mines, les diverses préparations des métaux, des minéraux, surtout du plomb, du cuivre, du mercure, du cobalt, de l'arsenic, du réalgar ; ces autres métiers périlleux qui coûtent tous les jours la vie à quantité d'ouvriers, les uns couvreurs, d'autres charpentiers, d'autres maçons, d'autres travaillant aux carrières ; qu'on réunisse, dis-je, tous ces objets, et l'on pourra voir dans l'établissement et la perfection des sociétés les raisons de la diminution de l'espèce, observée par plus d'un philosophe.

Le luxe, impossible à prévenir chez des hommes avides de leurs propres commodités et de la considération des autres, achève bientôt le mal que les sociétés ont commencé ; et, sous prétexte de faire vivre les pauvres, qu'il n'eût pas fallu faire, il appauvrit tout le reste, et dépeuple l'État tôt ou tard.

Le luxe est un remède beaucoup pire que le mal qu'il prétend guérir ; ou plutôt il est lui-même le pire de tous les maux, dans quelque État, grand ou

---

[1] This paragraph and the first sentence of the next (*Mais n'est-il pas... exempts d'inconvénients*) appeared for the first time in the Ed. of 1782. *Que serait-ce...apporter le remède* was added, while the book was in the Press (Bosscha, p. 17).

petit, que ce puisse être, et qui, pour nourrir des foules de valets et de misérables qu'il a faits, accable et ruine le laboureur et le citoyen : semblable à ces vents brûlants du midi qui, couvrant l'herbe et la verdure d'insectes dévorants, ôtent la subsistance aux animaux utiles, et portent la disette et la mort dans tous les lieux où ils se font sentir.

De la société et du luxe qu'elle engendre naissent les arts libéraux et mécaniques, le commerce, les lettres, et toutes ces inutilités qui font fleurir l'industrie, enrichissent et perdent les États. La raison de ce dépérissement est très simple. Il est aisé de voir que, par sa nature, l'agriculture doit être le moins lucratif de tous les arts, parce que, son produit étant de l'usage le plus indispensable pour tous les hommes, le prix en doit être proportionné aux facultés des plus pauvres. Du même principe on peut tirer cette règle, qu'en général les arts sont lucratifs en raison inverse de leur utilité, et que les plus nécessaires doivent enfin devenir les plus négligés. Par où l'on voit ce qu'il faut penser des vrais avantages de l'industrie, et de l'effet réel qui résulte de ses progrès.

Telles sont les causes sensibles de toutes les misères où l'opulence précipite enfin les nations les plus admirées. À mesure que l'industrie et les arts s'étendent et fleurissent, le cultivateur méprisé, chargé d'impôts nécessaires à l'entretien du luxe, et condamné à passer sa vie entre le travail et la faim, abandonne ses champs pour aller chercher dans les villes le pain qu'il y devrait porter. Plus les capitales frappent d'admiration les yeux stupides du peuple, plus il faudrait gémir de voir les campagnes abandonnées, les terres en friche, et les grands chemins inondés de malheureux citoyens devenus mendiants ou voleurs, et destinés à finir un jour leur misère sur la roue ou sur un fumier. C'est ainsi que l'État s'enrichissant d'un côté s'affaiblit et se dépeuple de l'autre, et que les plus puissantes monarchies, après bien des travaux pour se rendre opulentes et désertes, finissent par devenir la proie des nations pauvres qui succombent à la funeste tentation de les envahir, et qui s'enrichissent et s'affaiblissent à leur tour, jusqu'à ce qu'elles soient elles-mêmes envahies et détruites par d'autres.

Qu'on daigne nous expliquer une fois ce qui avait pu produire ces nuées de barbares qui, durant tant de siècles, ont inondé l'Europe, l'Asie et l'Afrique. Était-ce à l'industrie de leurs arts, à la sagesse de leurs lois, à l'excellence de leur police, qu'ils devaient cette prodigieuse population ? Que nos savants veuillent bien nous dire pourquoi, loin de multiplier à ce point, ces hommes féroces et brutaux, sans lumières, sans frein, sans éducation, ne s'entr'égorgeaient pas tous à chaque instant pour se disputer leur pâture ou leur chasse ; qu'ils nous expliquent comment ces misérables ont eu seulement la hardiesse de regarder en face de si habiles gens que nous étions, avec une si belle discipline militaire, de si beaux codes et de si sages lois ; enfin pourquoi, depuis que la société s'est perfectionnée dans les pays du nord, et qu'on y a tant pris de peine pour apprendre aux hommes leurs devoirs mutuels et l'art de vivre agréablement et paisiblement ensemble, on n'en voit plus rien sortir de semblable à ces multitudes d'hommes qu'il produisait autrefois. J'ai bien peur que quelqu'un ne s'avise à la fin de me répondre que toutes ces grandes choses, savoir, les arts, les sciences et les lois, ont été très sagement inventées par les hommes comme une peste salutaire pour prévenir l'excessive multiplication de l'espèce, de peur que ce monde, qui nous est destiné, ne devînt à la fin trop petit pour ses habitants.

[1] Quoi donc ! faut-il détruire les sociétés, anéantir le tien et le mien, et retourner vivre dans les forêts avec les ours ? conséquence à la manière de mes adversaires, que j'aime autant prévenir que de leur laisser la honte de la tirer. O vous à qui la voix céleste ne s'est point fait entendre, et qui ne reconnaissez pour votre espèce d'autre destination que d'achever en paix cette courte vie ; vous qui pouvez laisser au milieu des villes vos funestes acquisitions, vos esprits inquiets, vos cœurs corrompus et vos désirs effrénés ; reprenez, puisqu'il dépend de vous, votre antique et première innocence ; allez dans les bois perdre la vue et la mémoire des crimes de vos contemporains, et ne craignez point d'avilir votre espèce, en renonçant à ses lumières pour renoncer à ses vices. Quant aux hommes semblables à moi, dont les passions ont détruit pour toujours l'originelle simplicité, qui ne peuvent plus se nourrir d'herbe et de gland[2], ni se passer de lois et de chefs ; ceux qui furent honorés dans leur premier père de leçons surnaturelles ; ceux qui verront, dans l'intention de donner d'abord aux actions humaines une moralité qu'elles n'eussent de longtemps acquise, la raison d'un précepte indifférent par lui-même et inexplicable dans tout autre système ; ceux, en un mot, qui sont convaincus que la voix divine appela tout le genre humain aux lumières et au bonheur des célestes intelligences : tous ceux-là tâcheront, par l'exercice des vertus qu'ils s'obligent à pratiquer en apprenant à les connaître, de mériter le prix éternel qu'ils en doivent attendre ; ils respecteront les sacrés liens des sociétés dont ils sont les membres ; ils aimeront leurs semblables et les serviront de tout leur pouvoir ; ils obéiront scrupuleusement aux lois, et aux hommes qui en sont les auteurs et les ministres ; ils honoreront surtout les bons et sages princes qui sauront prévenir, guérir ou pallier cette foule d'abus et de maux toujours prêts à nous accabler ; ils animeront le zèle de ces dignes chefs, en leur montrant, sans crainte et sans flatterie, la grandeur de leur tâche et la rigueur de leur devoir : mais ils n'en mépriseront pas moins une constitution qui ne peut se maintenir qu'à l'aide de tant de gens respectables, qu'on désire plus souvent qu'on ne les obtient, et de laquelle, malgré tous leurs soins, naissent toujours plus de calamités réelles que d'avantages apparents[1].

Page 150. (*j*) Parmi les hommes que nous connaissons, ou par nous-mêmes, ou par les historiens, ou par les voyageurs, les uns sont noirs, les autres blancs, les autres rouges ; les uns portent de longs cheveux, les autres n'ont que de la laine frisée ; les uns sont presque tout velus, les autres n'ont pas même de barbe. Il y a eu, et il y a peut-être encore, des nations d'hommes d'une taille gigantesque ; et laissant à part la fable des Pygmées, qui peut bien n'être qu'une exagération, on sait que les Lapons, et surtout les Groënlandais, sont fort au-dessous de la taille moyenne de l'homme. On prétend même qu'il y a des peuples entiers qui ont des queues comme les quadrupèdes. Et, sans ajouter une foi aveugle aux relations d'Hérodote et de Ctésias, on en peut du moins tirer cette opinion très vraisemblable, que, si l'on avait pu faire de bonnes observations dans ces temps anciens où les peuples divers suivaient des manières de vivre plus différentes entre elles qu'ils ne font aujourd'hui, on y aurait aussi remarqué, dans la figure et l'habitude du corps, des variétés beaucoup plus frappantes. Tous ces faits, dont il est aisé de fournir des

---

[1] This paragraph was added, while the book was in the press (Bosscha, p. 18).
[2] So Ed. 1755. Ed. 1782 has *herbe, glands* ; Ed. 1801 and Hachette, *herbes, glands*.

preuves incontestables, ne peuvent surprendre que ceux qui sont accoutumés à ne regarder que les objets qui les environnent, et qui ignorent les puissants effets de la diversité des climats, de l'air, des aliments, de la manière de vivre, des habitudes en général, et surtout la force étonnante des mêmes causes, quand elles agissent continuellement sur de longues suites de générations. Aujourd'hui que le commerce, les voyages et les conquêtes réunissent davantage les peuples divers, et que leurs manières de vivre se rapprochent sans cesse par la fréquente communication, on s'aperçoit que certaines différences nationales ont diminué ; et, par exemple, chacun peut remarquer que les Français d'aujourd'hui ne sont plus ces grands corps blancs et blonds décrits par les historiens latins, quoique le temps, joint au mélange des Francs et des Normands, blancs et blonds eux-mêmes, eût dû rétablir ce que la fréquentation des Romains avait pu ôter à l'influence du climat, dans la constitution naturelle et le teint des habitants. Toutes ces observations sur les variétés que mille causes peuvent produire et ont produites[1] en effet dans l'espèce humaine, me font douter si divers animaux semblables aux hommes, pris par les voyageurs pour des bêtes sans beaucoup d'examen, ou à cause de quelques différences qu'ils remarquaient dans la conformation extérieure, ou seulement parce que ces animaux ne parlaient pas, ne seraient point en effet de véritables hommes sauvages, dont la race dispersée anciennement dans les bois n'avait eu occasion de développer aucune de ses facultés virtuelles, n'avait acquis aucun degré de perfection, et se trouvait encore dans l'état primitif de nature. Donnons un exemple de ce que je veux dire.

'On trouve, dit le traducteur de l'*Histoire des voyages*, dans le royaume de Congo, quantité de ces grands animaux qu'on nomme *orangs-outangs*[2] aux Indes orientales, qui tiennent comme le milieu entre l'espèce humaine et les babouins. Battel raconte que dans les forêts de Mayomba, au royaume de Loango, on voit deux sortes de monstres dont les plus grands se nomment *pongos* et les autres *enjocos*. Les premiers ont une ressemblance exacte avec l'homme, mais ils sont beaucoup plus gros et de fort haute taille. Avec un visage humain, ils ont les yeux fort enfoncés. Leurs mains, leurs joues, leurs oreilles, sont sans poil, à l'exception des sourcils qu'ils ont fort longs. Quoiqu'ils aient le reste du corps assez velu, le poil n'en est pas fort épais, et sa couleur est brune. Enfin, la seule partie qui les distingue des hommes est la jambe qu'ils ont sans mollet. Ils marchent droits, en se tenant de la main le poil du cou ; leur retraite est dans les bois ; ils dorment sur les arbres, et s'y font une espèce de toit qui les met à couvert de la pluie. Leurs aliments sont des fruits ou des noix sauvages. Jamais ils ne mangent de chair. L'usage des nègres qui traversent les forêts est d'y allumer des feux pendant la nuit : ils remarquent que le matin, à leur départ, les pongos prennent leur place autour du feu, et ne se retirent pas qu'il ne soit éteint ; car, avec beaucoup d'adresse, ils n'ont point assez de sens pour l'entretenir en y apportant du bois.

'Ils marchent quelquefois en troupes, et tuent les nègres qui traversent les forêts. Ils tombent même sur les éléphants qui viennent paître dans les lieux qu'ils habitent, et les incommodent si fort à coups de poing ou de bâtons[3], qu'ils les forcent à prendre la fuite en poussant des cris. On ne prend jamais de pongos en vie, parce qu'ils sont si robustes que dix hommes ne suffiraient

---

[1] Eds. 1755 and 1782 read *produit*, by a slip. Ed. 1801, *produites*.
[2] Ed. 1755 has *Orang-Outang* ; so also, p. 209.
[3] Eds. 1755, 1782 and 1801, as in the text. Hachette reads *bâton*.

pas pour les arrêter : mais les nègres en prennent quantité de jeunes après avoir tué la mère, au corps de laquelle le petit s'attache fortement. Lorsqu'un de ces animaux meurt, les autres couvrent son corps d'un amas de branches ou de feuillages. Purchass ajoute que, dans les conversations qu'il avait eues avec Battel, il avait appris de lui-même qu'un pongo lui enleva un petit nègre qui passa un mois entier dans la société de ces animaux ; car ils ne font aucun mal aux hommes qu'ils surprennent, du moins lorsque ceux-ci ne les regardent point, comme le petit nègre l'avait observé. Battel n'a point décrit la seconde espèce de monstre.

'Dapper confirme que le royaume de Congo est plein de ces animaux qui portent aux Indes le nom d'orangs-outangs, c'est-à-dire habitants des bois, et que les Africains nomment *quojas morros*. Cette bête, dit-il, est si semblable à l'homme, qu'il est tombé dans l'esprit à quelques voyageurs qu'elle pouvait être sortie d'une femme et d'un singe : chimère que les nègres mêmes rejettent. Un de ces animaux fut transporté du Congo en Hollande, et présenté au prince d'Orange, Frédéric-Henri. Il était de la hauteur d'un enfant de trois ans, et d'un embonpoint médiocre, mais carré et bien proportionné, fort agile et fort vif, les jambes charnues et robustes, tout le devant du corps nu, mais le derrière couvert de poils noirs. À la première vue, son visage ressemblait à celui d'un homme, mais il avait le nez plat et recourbé ; ses oreilles étaient aussi celles de l'espèce humaine ; son sein, car c'était une femelle, était potelé, son nombril enfoncé, ses épaules fort bien jointes, ses mains divisées en doigts et en pouces, ses mollets et ses talons gras et charnus. Il marchait souvent droit sur ses jambes, il était capable de lever et porter des fardeaux assez lourds. Lorsqu'il voulait boire, il prenait d'une main le couvercle du pot, et tenait le fond de l'autre, ensuite il s'essuyait gracieusement les lèvres. Il se couchait, pour dormir, la tête sur un coussin, se couvrant avec tant d'adresse qu'on l'aurait pris pour un homme au lit. Les nègres font d'étranges récits de cet animal : ils assurent non seulement qu'il force les femmes et les filles, mais qu'il ose attaquer des hommes armés. En un mot, il y a beaucoup d'apparence que c'est le satyre des anciens. Merolla ne parle peut-être que de ces animaux, lorsqu'il raconte que les nègres prennent quelquefois dans leurs chasses des hommes et des femmes sauvages.'

Il est encore parlé de ces espèces d'animaux anthropoformes dans le troisième tome de la même *Histoire des voyages*, sous le nom de *beggos* et de *mandrills* : mais, pour nous en tenir aux relations précédentes, on trouve dans la description de ces prétendus monstres des conformités frappantes avec l'espèce humaine, et des différences moindres que celles qu'on pourrait assigner d'homme à homme. On ne voit point dans ces passages les raisons sur lesquelles les auteurs se fondent pour refuser aux animaux en question le nom d'hommes sauvages ; mais il est aisé de conjecturer que c'est à cause de leur stupidité, et aussi parce qu'ils ne parlaient pas : raisons faibles pour ceux qui savent que, quoique l'organe de la parole soit naturel à l'homme, la parole elle-même ne lui est pourtant pas naturelle, et qui connaissent jusqu'à quel point sa perfectibilité peut avoir élevé l'homme civil au-dessus de son état originel. Le petit nombre de lignes que contiennent ces descriptions nous peut faire juger combien ces animaux ont été mal observés, et avec quels préjugés ils ont été vus. Par exemple, ils sont qualifiés de monstres, et cependant on convient qu'ils engendrent. Dans un endroit, Battel dit que les pongos tuent les nègres qui traversent les forêts ; dans un autre, Purchass ajoute qu'ils ne leur font aucun mal, même quand ils les surprennent, du moins lorsque les nègres ne s'attachent pas à les regarder. Les pongos s'assemblent autour des feux allumés par les nègres quand ceux-ci se retirent, et se retirent à leur tour quand le feu est éteint : voilà le fait. Voici maintenant le commentaire de l'observateur : *car, avec beaucoup d'adresse, ils n'ont point assez de sens pour l'entretenir en y apportant du bois.* Je voudrais deviner comment Battel, ou Purchass, son compilateur, a pu savoir que la retraite des pongos était un effet de leur bêtise plutôt que de leur volonté. Dans un climat tel que Loango, le feu n'est pas une chose fort nécessaire aux animaux ; et si les nègres en allument, c'est moins contre le froid que pour effrayer les bêtes féroces : il est donc très simple qu'après avoir été quelque temps réjouis par la flamme, ou s'être bien réchauffés, les pongos s'ennuient de rester toujours à la même place, et s'en aillent à leur pâture, qui demande plus de temps que s'ils mangeaient de la chair. D'ailleurs, on sait que la plupart des animaux, sans en excepter l'homme, sont naturellement paresseux, et qu'ils se refusent à toutes sortes de soins qui ne sont pas d'une absolue nécessité. Enfin il paraît fort étrange que les pongos, dont on vante l'adresse et la force, les pongos qui savent enterrer leurs morts et se faire des toits de branchages, ne sachent pas pousser des tisons dans le feu. Je me souviens d'avoir vu un singe faire cette même manœuvre qu'on ne veut pas que les pongos puissent faire : il est vrai que, mes idées n'étant pas alors tournées de ce côté, je fis moi-même la faute que je reproche à nos voyageurs, et je négligeai d'examiner si l'intention du singe était en effet d'entretenir le feu, ou simplement, comme je crois, d'imiter l'action d'un homme. Quoi qu'il en soit, il est bien démontré que le singe n'est pas une variété de l'homme, non seulement parce qu'il est privé de la faculté de parler, mais surtout parce qu'on est sûr que son espèce n'a point celle de se perfectionner, qui est le caractère spécifique de l'espèce humaine : expériences qui ne paraissent pas avoir été faites sur le pongo et l'orang-outang avec assez de soin pour en pouvoir tirer la même conclusion. Il y aurait pourtant un moyen par lequel, si l'orang-outang ou d'autres étaient de l'espèce humaine, les observateurs les plus grossiers pourraient s'en assurer même avec démonstration : mais, outre qu'une seule génération ne suffirait pas pour cette expérience, elle doit passer pour impraticable, parce qu'il faudrait que ce qui n'est qu'une supposition fût démontré vrai, avant que l'épreuve qui devrait constater le fait pût être tentée innocemment.

Les jugements précipités, qui ne sont point le fruit d'une raison éclairée, sont sujets à donner dans l'excès. Nos voyageurs font sans façon des bêtes, sous les noms de *pongos*, de *mandrills*, d'*orangs-outangs*, de ces mêmes êtres dont, sous les noms de *satyres*, de *faunes*, de *sylvains*, les anciens faisaient des divinités. Peut-être, après des recherches plus exactes, trouvera-t-on que ce ne sont ni des bêtes ni des dieux, mais des hommes[1]. En attendant, il me paraît qu'il y a bien autant de raison de s'en rapporter là-dessus à Merolla, religieux lettré, témoin oculaire, et qui, avec toute sa naïveté, ne laissait pas d'être homme d'esprit, qu'au marchand Battel, à Dapper, à Purchass, et aux autres compilateurs.

Quel jugement pense-t-on qu'eussent porté de pareils observateurs sur l'enfant trouvé en 1694, dont j'ai déjà parlé ci-devant, qui ne donnait aucune

---

[1] Ed. 1755 has *trouvera-t-on que ce sont des hommes.* Eds. 1782 and 1801, as in the text.

marque de raison, marchait sur ses pieds et sur ses mains, n'avait aucun langage, et formait des sons qui ne ressemblaient en rien à ceux d'un homme ? 'Il fut longtemps, continue le même philosophe qui me fournit ce fait, avant de pouvoir proférer quelques paroles, encore le fit-il d'une manière barbare. Aussitôt qu'il put parler, on l'interrogea sur son premier état ; mais il ne s'en souvint non plus que nous nous souvenons de ce qui nous est arrivé au berceau.' Si, malheureusement pour lui, cet enfant fût tombé dans les mains de nos voyageurs, on ne peut douter qu'après avoir remarqué son silence et sa stupidité, ils n'eussent pris le parti de le renvoyer dans les bois ou de l'enfermer dans une ménagerie ; après quoi, ils en auraient savamment parlé dans de belles relations, comme d'une bête fort curieuse qui ressemblait assez à l'homme.

Depuis trois ou quatre cents ans que les habitants de l'Europe inondent les autres parties du monde, et publient sans cesse de nouveaux recueils de voyages et de relations, je suis persuadé que nous ne connaissons d'hommes que les seuls Européens ; encore paraît-il, aux préjugés ridicules qui ne sont pas éteints même parmi les gens de lettres, que chacun ne fait guère, sous le nom pompeux d'étude de l'homme, que celle des hommes de son pays. Les particuliers ont beau aller et venir, il semble que la philosophie ne voyage point : aussi celle de chaque peuple est-elle peu propre pour un autre. La cause de ceci est manifeste, au moins pour les contrées éloignées : il n'y a guère que quatre sortes d'hommes qui fassent des voyages de long cours, les marins, les marchands, les soldats et les missionnaires. Or, on ne doit guère s'attendre que les trois premières classes fournissent de bons observateurs ; et quant à ceux de la quatrième, occupés de la vocation sublime qui les appelle, quand ils ne seraient pas sujets à des préjugés d'état comme tous les autres, on doit croire qu'ils ne se livreraient pas volontiers à des recherches qui paraissent de pure curiosité, et qui les détourneraient des travaux plus importants auxquels ils se destinent. D'ailleurs, pour prêcher utilement l'Évangile, il ne faut que du zèle, et Dieu donne le reste ; mais, pour étudier les hommes, il faut des talents que Dieu ne s'engage à donner à personne, et qui ne sont pas toujours le partage des saints. On n'ouvre pas un livre de voyages où l'on ne trouve des descriptions de caractères et de mœurs. Mais on est tout étonné d'y voir que ces gens qui ont tant décrit de choses n'ont dit que ce que chacun savait déjà, n'ont su apercevoir, à l'autre bout du monde, que ce qu'il n'eût tenu qu'à eux de remarquer sans sortir de leur rue ; et que ces traits vrais qui distinguent les nations, et qui frappent les yeux faits pour voir, ont presque toujours échappé aux leurs. De là est venu ce bel adage de morale, si rebattu par la tourbe philosophesque[1] : 'Que les hommes sont partout les mêmes' ; qu'ayant partout les mêmes passions et les mêmes vices, il est assez inutile de chercher à caractériser les différents peuples : ce qui est à peu près aussi bien raisonné que si l'on disait qu'on ne saurait distinguer Pierre d'avec Jacques, parce qu'ils ont tous deux un nez, une bouche et des yeux.

Ne verra-t-on jamais renaître ces temps heureux où les peuples ne se mêlaient point de philosopher, mais où les Platons[2], les Thalès et les Pythagores[2],

---

[1] Rousseau warns Rey against printing *troupe philosophesque* (Bosscha, p. 19).
[2] Eds. 1755 and 1782, as in text. Ed. 1801 and Hachette read *Platon, Pythagore*.

épris d'un ardent désir de savoir, entreprenaient les plus grands voyages uniquement pour s'instruire, et allaient au loin secouer le joug des préjugés nationaux, apprendre à connaître les hommes par leurs conformités et par leurs différences, et acquérir ces connaissances universelles qui ne sont point celles d'un siècle ou d'un pays exclusivement, mais qui, étant de tous les temps et de tous les lieux, sont pour ainsi dire la science commune des sages ?

On admire la magnificence de quelques curieux qui ont fait, ou fait faire, à grands frais des voyages en Orient avec des savants et des peintres, pour y dessiner des masures et déchiffrer ou copier des inscriptions. Mais j'ai peine à concevoir comment, dans un siècle où l'on se pique de belles connaissances, il ne se trouve pas deux hommes bien unis, riches, l'un en argent, l'autre en génie, tous deux aimant la gloire, et aspirant à l'immortalité, dont l'un sacrifie vingt mille écus de son bien et l'autre dix ans de sa vie, à un célèbre voyage autour du monde, pour y étudier, non toujours des pierres et des plantes, mais une fois les hommes et les mœurs, et qui, après tant de siècles employés à mesurer et considérer la maison, s'avisent enfin d'en vouloir connaître les habitants.

Les académiciens qui ont parcouru les parties septentrionales de l'Europe, et méridionales de l'Amérique, avaient plus pour objet de les visiter en géomètres qu'en philosophes. Cependant, comme ils étaient à la fois l'un et l'autre, on ne peut pas regarder comme tout à fait inconnues les régions qui ont été vues et décrites par les La Condamine et les Maupertuis. Le joaillier Chardin, qui a voyagé comme Platon, n'a rien laissé à dire sur la Perse. La Chine paraît avoir été bien observée par les jésuites. Kempfer donne une idée passable du peu qu'il a vu dans le Japon. À ces relations près, nous ne connaissons point les peuples des Indes orientales, fréquentées uniquement par des Européens plus curieux de remplir leurs bourses que leurs têtes. L'Afrique entière, et ses nombreux habitants, aussi singuliers par leur caractère que par leur couleur, sont encore à examiner ; toute la terre est couverte de nations dont nous ne connaissons que les noms : et nous nous mêlons de juger le genre humain ! Supposons un Montesquieu, un Buffon, un Diderot, un Duclos, un d'Alembert, un Condillac, ou des hommes de cette trempe, voyageant pour instruire leurs compatriotes, observant et décrivant, comme ils savent faire, la Turquie, l'Égypte, la Barbarie, l'empire de Maroc, la Guinée, le pays des Cafres, l'intérieur de l'Afrique et ses côtes orientales, les Malabares, le Mogol, les rives du Gange, les royaumes de Siam, de Pégu et d'Ava, la Chine, la Tartarie et surtout le Japon ; puis, dans l'autre hémisphère le Mexique, le Pérou, le Chili, les terres Magellaniques, sans oublier les Patagons vrais ou faux, le Tucuman, le Paraguai, s'il était possible, le Brésil, enfin les Caraïbes, la Floride, et toutes les contrées sauvages : voyage le plus important de tous, et celui qu'il faudrait faire avec le plus de soin. Supposons que ces nouveaux Hercules, de retour de ces courses mémorables, fissent ensuite à loisir l'histoire naturelle, morale et politique de ce qu'ils auraient vu, nous verrions nous-mêmes sortir un monde nouveau de dessous leur plume, et nous apprendrions ainsi à connaître le nôtre. Je dis que quand de pareils observateurs affirmeront d'un tel animal que c'est un homme, et d'un autre que c'est une bête, il faudra les en croire ; mais ce serait une grande simplicité de s'en rapporter là-dessus à des voyageurs grossiers, sur lesquels on serait quelquefois tenté de faire la même question qu'ils se mêlent de résoudre sur d'autres animaux.

Page 151. (*k*) Cela me paraît de la dernière évidence, et je ne saurais concevoir d'où nos philosophes peuvent faire naître toutes les passions qu'ils prêtent à l'homme naturel. Excepté le seul nécessaire physique, que la nature même demande, tous nos autres besoins ne sont tels que par l'habitude, avant laquelle ils n'étaient point des besoins, ou par nos désirs ; et l'on ne désire point ce qu'on n'est pas en état de connaître. D'où il suit que l'homme sauvage ne désirant que les choses qu'il connaît, et ne connaissant que celles dont la possession est en son pouvoir ou facile à acquérir, rien ne doit être si tranquille que son âme, et rien si borné que son esprit.

Page 154. (*l*) Je trouve dans le *Gouvernement civil* de Locke une objection qui me paraît trop spécieuse pour qu'il me soit permis de la dissimuler. 'La fin de la société entre le mâle et la femelle, dit ce philosophe, n'étant pas simplement de procréer, mais de continuer l'espèce, cette société doit durer, même après la procréation, du moins aussi longtemps qu'il est nécessaire pour la nourriture et la conservation des procréés : c'est-à-dire, jusqu'à ce qu'ils soient capables de pourvoir eux-mêmes à leurs besoins. Cette règle, que la sagesse infinie du Créateur a établie sur les œuvres de ses mains, nous voyons que les créatures inférieures à l'homme l'observent constamment et avec exactitude. Dans ces animaux qui vivent d'herbe, la société entre le mâle et la femelle ne dure pas plus longtemps que chaque acte de copulation, parce que, les mamelles de la mère étant suffisantes pour nourrir les petits jusqu'à ce qu'ils soient capables de paître l'herbe, le mâle se contente d'engendrer, et il ne se mêle plus après cela de la femelle ni des petits, à la subsistance desquels il ne peut rien contribuer. Mais, au regard des bêtes de proie, la société dure plus longtemps, à cause que, la mère ne pouvant pas bien pourvoir à sa subsistance propre et nourrir en même temps ses petits par sa seule proie, qui est une voie de se nourrir et plus laborieuse et plus dangereuse que n'est celle de se nourrir d'herbe, l'assistance du mâle est tout à fait nécessaire pour le maintien de leur commune famille, si l'on peut user de ce terme ; laquelle, jusqu'à ce qu'elle puisse aller chercher quelque proie, ne saurait subsister que par les soins du mâle et de la femelle. On remarque la même chose dans tous les oiseaux, si l'on excepte quelques oiseaux domestiques qui se trouvent dans des lieux où la continuelle abondance de nourriture exempte le mâle du soin de nourrir les petits ; on voit que, pendant que les petits dans leur nid ont besoin d'aliments, le mâle et la femelle y en portent, jusqu'à ce que ces petits-là puissent voler et pourvoir à leur subsistance.

'Et en cela, à mon avis, consiste la principale, si ce n'est la seule, raison pourquoi le mâle et la femelle dans le genre humain sont obligés à une société plus longue que n'entretiennent les autres créatures. Cette raison est que la femme est capable de concevoir, et est pour l'ordinaire derechef grosse et fait un nouvel enfant, longtemps avant que le précédent soit hors d'état de se passer du secours de ses parents, et puisse lui-même pourvoir à ses besoins. Ainsi, un père étant obligé de prendre soin de ceux qu'il a engendrés, et de prendre ce soin-là pendant longtemps, il est aussi dans l'obligation de continuer à vivre dans la société conjugale avec la même femme de qui il les a eus, et de demeurer dans cette société beaucoup plus longtemps que les autres créatures, dont les petits pouvant subsister d'eux-mêmes avant que le temps d'une nouvelle procréation vienne, le lien du mâle et de la femelle se rompt de lui-même, et l'un et l'autre se trouvent dans une pleine liberté, jusqu'à ce que cette saison, qui a coutume de solliciter les animaux à se joindre ensemble, les oblige à se choisir de nouvelles compagnes. Et ici l'on ne saurait admirer assez la sagesse du Créateur, qui, ayant donné à l'homme des qualités propres pour pourvoir à l'avenir aussi bien qu'au présent, a voulu et a fait en sorte que la société de l'homme durât beaucoup plus longtemps que celle du mâle et de la femelle parmi les autres créatures, afin que par là l'industrie de l'homme et de la femme fût plus excitée, et que leurs intérêts fussent mieux unis, dans la vue de faire des provisions pour leurs enfants et de leur laisser du bien; rien ne pouvant être plus préjudiciable à des enfants qu'une conjonction incertaine et vague, ou une dissolution facile et fréquente de la société conjugale.'

Le même amour de la vérité qui m'a fait exposer sincèrement cette objection m'excite à l'accompagner de quelques remarques, sinon pour la résoudre, au moins pour l'éclaircir.

1. J'observerai d'abord que les preuves morales n'ont pas une grande force en matière de physique, et qu'elles servent plutôt à rendre raison des faits existants qu'à constater l'existence réelle de ces faits. Or, tel est le genre de preuve que M. Locke emploie dans le passage que je viens de rapporter; car, quoiqu'il puisse être avantageux à l'espèce humaine que l'union de l'homme et de la femme soit permanente, il ne s'ensuit pas que cela ait été ainsi établi par la nature; autrement, il faudrait dire qu'elle a aussi institué la société civile, les arts, le commerce, et tout ce qu'on prétend être utile aux hommes.

2. J'ignore où M. Locke a trouvé qu'entre les animaux de proie la société du mâle et de la femelle dure plus longtemps que parmi ceux qui vivent d'herbe, et que l'un aide à l'autre à nourrir les petits : car on ne voit pas que le chien, le chat, l'ours, ni le loup, reconnaissent leur femelle mieux que le cheval, le bélier, le taureau, le cerf, ni tous les autres quadrupèdes[1], ne reconnaissent la leur. Il semble au contraire que, si le secours du mâle était nécessaire à la femelle pour conserver ses petits, ce serait surtout dans les espèces qui ne vivent que d'herbe, parce qu'il faut fort longtemps à la mère pour paître et que, durant tout cet intervalle, elle est forcée de négliger sa portée; au lieu que la proie d'une ourse ou d'une louve est dévorée en un instant, et qu'elle a, sans souffrir la faim, plus de temps pour allaiter ses petits. Ce raisonnement est confirmé par une observation sur le nombre relatif de mamelles et de petits qui distingue les espèces carnassières des frugivores, et dont j'ai parlé dans la note (h). Si cette observation est juste et générale, la femme n'ayant que deux mamelles et ne faisant guère qu'un enfant à la fois, voilà une forte raison de plus pour douter que l'espèce humaine soit naturellement carnassière ; de sorte qu'il semble que, pour tirer la conclusion de Locke, il faudrait retourner tout à fait son raisonnement. Il n'y a pas plus de solidité dans la même distinction appliquée aux oiseaux. Car qui pourra se persuader que l'union du mâle et de la femelle soit plus durable parmi les vautours et les corbeaux que parmi les tourterelles ? Nous avons deux espèces d'oiseaux domestiques, la cane et le pigeon, qui nous fournissent des exemples directement contraires au système de cet auteur. Le pigeon, qui ne vit que de grain, reste uni à sa femelle, et ils nourrissent leurs petits en commun. Le canard, dont la voracité est connue, ne reconnaît ni sa femelle ni ses petits et n'aide en rien à leur subsistance ; et parmi les

---

[1] Ed. 1782 (12mo) has *animaux quadrupèdes*. Eds. 1755, 1782 (4º) and 1801, as in the text.

poules, espèce qui n'est guère moins carnassière, on ne voit pas que le coq se mette aucunement en peine de la couvée. Que si dans d'autres espèces le mâle partage avec la femelle le soin de nourrir les petits, c'est que les oiseaux, qui d'abord ne peuvent voler et que la mère ne peut allaiter, sont beaucoup moins en état de se passer de l'assistance du père que les quadrupèdes, à qui suffit la mamelle de la mère, au moins durant quelque temps.

3. Il y a bien de l'incertitude sur le fait principal qui sert de base à tout le raisonnement de M. Locke : car pour savoir si, comme il prétend, dans le pur état de nature, la femme est pour l'ordinaire derechef grosse et fait un nouvel enfant longtemps avant que le précédent puisse pourvoir lui-même à ses besoins, il faudrait des expériences qu'assurément M. Locke n'avait pas faites et que personne n'est à portée de faire. La cohabitation continuelle du mari et de la femme est une occasion si prochaine de s'exposer à une nouvelle grossesse, qu'il est bien difficile de croire que la rencontre fortuite, ou la seule impulsion du tempérament, produisît des effets aussi fréquents dans le pur état de nature que dans celui de la société conjugale : lenteur qui contribuerait peut-être à rendre les enfants plus robustes, et qui d'ailleurs pourrait être compensée par la faculté de concevoir, prolongée dans un plus grand âge chez les femmes, qui en auraient moins abusé dans leur jeunesse. À l'égard des enfants, il y a bien des raisons de croire que leurs forces et leurs organes se développent plus tard parmi nous qu'ils ne faisaient dans l'état primitif dont je parle. La faiblesse originelle qu'ils tirent de la constitution des parents, les soins qu'on prend d'envelopper et gêner tous leurs membres, la mollesse dans laquelle ils sont élevés, peut-être l'usage d'un autre lait que celui de leur mère, tout contrarie et retarde en eux les premiers progrès de la nature. L'application qu'on les oblige de donner à mille choses sur lesquelles on fixe continuellement leur attention, tandis qu'on ne donne aucun exercice à leurs forces corporelles, peut encore faire une diversion considérable à leur accroissement ; de sorte que, si, au lieu de surcharger et fatiguer d'abord leurs esprits de mille manières, on laissait exercer leurs corps aux mouvements continuels que la nature semble leur demander, il est à croire qu'ils seraient beaucoup plus tôt en état de marcher, d'agir et de pourvoir eux-mêmes à leurs besoins.

4. Enfin, M. Locke prouve tout au plus qu'il pourrait bien y avoir dans l'homme un motif de demeurer attaché à la femme lorsqu'elle a un enfant ; mais il ne prouve nullement qu'il a dû s'y attacher avant l'accouchement et pendant les neuf mois de la grossesse. Si telle femme est indifférente à l'homme pendant ces neuf mois, si même elle lui devient inconnue, pourquoi la secourra-t-il après l'accouchement ? pourquoi lui aidera-t-il à élever un enfant qu'il ne sait pas seulement lui appartenir, et dont il n'a résolu ni prévu la naissance ? M. Locke suppose évidemment ce qui est en question ; car il ne s'agit pas de savoir pourquoi l'homme demeurera attaché à la femme après l'accouchement, mais pourquoi il s'attachera à elle après la conception. L'appétit satisfait, l'homme n'a plus besoin de telle femme, ni la femme de tel homme. Celui-ci n'a pas le moindre souci, ni peut-être la moindre idée, des suites de son action. L'un s'en va d'un côté, l'autre d'un autre[1], et il n'y a pas d'apparence qu'au bout de neuf mois ils aient la mémoire de s'être connus : car cette espèce de mémoire, par laquelle un individu donne la

---

[1] Hachette has *de l'autre*. Eds. 1755, 1782 and 1801, as in the text.

préférence à un individu pour l'acte de la génération, exige, comme je le prouve dans le texte, plus de progrès ou de corruption dans l'entendement humain, qu'on ne peut lui en supposer dans l'état d'animalité dont il s'agit ici. Une autre femme peut donc contenter les nouveaux désirs de l'homme aussi commodément que celle qu'il a déjà connue, et un autre homme contenter de même la femme, supposé qu'elle soit pressée du même appétit pendant l'état de grossesse, de quoi l'on peut raisonnablement douter. Que si, dans l'état de nature, la femme ne ressent plus la passion de l'amour après la conception de l'enfant, l'obstacle à sa société avec l'homme en devient encore beaucoup plus grand, puisque alors elle n'a plus besoin ni de l'homme qui l'a fécondée, ni d'aucun autre. Il n'y a donc dans l'homme aucune raison de rechercher la même femme, ni dans la femme aucune raison de rechercher le même homme. Le raisonnement de Locke tombe donc en ruine, et toute la dialectique de ce philosophe ne l'a pas garanti de la faute que Hobbes et d'autres ont commise. Ils avaient à expliquer un fait de l'état de nature, c'est-à-dire d'un état où les hommes vivaient isolés, et où tel homme n'avait aucun motif de demeurer à côté de tel homme, ni peut-être les hommes de demeurer à côté les uns des autres, ce qui est bien pis; et ils n'ont pas songé à se transporter au delà des siècles de société, c'est-à-dire de ces temps où les hommes ont toujours une raison de demeurer près les uns des autres, et où tel homme a souvent une raison de demeurer à côté de tel homme ou de telle femme. [See p. 513.]

Page 154. (*m*) Je me garderai bien de m'embarquer dans les réflexions philosophiques qu'il y aurait à faire sur les avantages et les inconvénients de cette institution des langues : ce n'est pas à moi qu'on permet d'attaquer les erreurs vulgaires, et le peuple lettré respecte trop ses préjugés pour supporter patiemment mes prétendus paradoxes. Laissons donc parler des gens à qui l'on n'a point fait un crime d'oser prendre quelquefois le parti de la raison contre l'avis de la multitude. 'Nec quidquam felicitati humani generis decederet, si, pulsa tot linguarum peste et confusione, unam artem callerent mortales, et signis, motibus, gestibusque licitum foret quidvis explicare. Nunc vero ita comparatum est, ut animalium quæ vulgo bruta creduntur melior longe quam nostra hac in parte videatur conditio, utpote quæ promptius, et forsan felicius, sensus et cogitationes suis sine interprete significent, quam ulli queant mortales, præsertim si peregrino utantur sermone.' (Is. Vossius, *de Poemat. cant. et viribus rhythmi*, p. 66.)

Page 158. (*n*) [1] Platon, montrant combien les idées de la quantité discrète et de ses rapports sont nécessaires dans les moindres arts, se moque avec raison des auteurs de son temps qui prétendaient que Palamède avait inventé les nombres au siége de Troie; comme si, dit ce philosophe, Agamemnon eût pu ignorer jusque-là combien il avait de jambes[1]. En effet, on sent l'impossibilité que la société et les arts fussent parvenus où ils étaient déjà du temps du siége de Troie, sans que les hommes eussent l'usage des nombres et du calcul : mais la nécessité de connaître les nombres, avant que d'acquérir d'autres connaissances, n'en rend pas l'invention plus aisée à imaginer. Les noms des nombres une fois connus, il est aisé d'en expliquer le sens et d'exciter les idées que ces noms représentent; mais, pour les inventer, il fallut,

---

[1] *De Rep.* Lib. VII. This sentence occurs on a loose slip, written in pencil (MSS. Neuchâtel, 7854) : one of the earliest fragments preserved.

avant que[1] de concevoir ces mêmes idées, s'être pour ainsi dire familiarisé avec les méditations philosophiques, s'être exercé à considérer les êtres par leur seule essence et indépendamment de toute autre perception : abstraction très pénible, très métaphysique, très peu naturelle, et sans laquelle cependant ces idées n'eussent jamais pu se transporter d'une espèce ou d'un genre à un autre, ni les nombres devenir universels. Un sauvage pouvait considérer séparément sa jambe droite et sa jambe gauche, ou les regarder ensemble sous l'idée indivisible d'une couple, sans jamais penser qu'il en avait deux ; car autre chose est l'idée représentative qui nous peint un objet, et autre chose l'idée numérique qui le détermine. Moins encore pouvait-il calculer jusqu'à cinq ; et quoique, appliquant ses mains l'une sur l'autre, il eût pu remarquer que les doigts se répondaient exactement, il était bien loin de songer à leur égalité numérique ; il ne savait pas plus le compte de ses doigts que de ses cheveux ; et si, après lui avoir fait entendre ce que c'est que nombres, quelqu'un lui eût dit qu'il avait autant de doigts aux pieds qu'aux mains, il eût peut-être été fort surpris, en les comparant, de trouver que cela était vrai.

Page 160. (o) Il ne faut pas confondre l'amour-propre et l'amour de soi-même, deux passions très différentes par leur nature et par leurs effets. L'amour de soi-même est un sentiment naturel qui porte tout animal à veiller à sa propre conservation, et qui, dirigé dans l'homme par la raison et modifié par la pitié, produit l'humanité et la vertu. L'amour-propre n'est qu'un sentiment relatif, factice, et né dans la société, qui porte chaque individu à faire plus de cas de soi que de tout autre, qui inspire aux hommes tous les maux qu'ils se font mutuellement, et qui est la véritable source de l'honneur[2].

Ceci bien entendu, je dis que, dans notre état primitif, dans le véritable état de nature, l'amour-propre n'existe pas ; car chaque homme en particulier se regardant lui-même comme le seul spectateur qui l'observe, comme le seul être dans l'univers qui prenne intérêt à lui, comme le seul juge de son propre mérite, il n'est pas possible qu'un sentiment, qui prend sa source dans des comparaisons qu'il n'est pas à portée de faire, puisse germer dans son âme. Par la même raison cet homme ne saurait avoir ni haine ni désir de vengeance, passions qui ne peuvent naître que de l'opinion de quelque offense reçue ; et comme c'est le mépris ou l'intention de nuire, et non le mal, qui constitue l'offense, des hommes qui ne savent ni s'apprécier ni se comparer peuvent se faire beaucoup de violences mutuelles, quand il leur en revient quelque avantage, sans jamais s'offenser réciproquement. En un mot, chaque homme, ne voyant guère ses semblables que comme il verrait des animaux d'une autre espèce, peut ravir la proie au plus faible ou céder la sienne au plus fort, sans envisager ces rapines que comme des événements naturels, sans le moindre mouvement d'insolence ou de dépit, et sans autre passion que la douleur ou la joie d'un bon ou mauvais succès.

Page 175. (p) C'est une chose extrêmement remarquable que, depuis tant d'années que les Européens se tourmentent pour amener les sauvages de diverses contrées du monde à leur manière de vivre, ils n'aient pas pu encore en gagner un seul, non pas même à la faveur du christianisme ; car nos missionnaires en font quelquefois des chrétiens, mais jamais des hommes civilisés. Rien

---

[1] Hachette, against all the authorities, omits *que*.
[2] For this contrast, compare *Dialogue* I. ; *Œuvres*, IX. pp. 107—110.

ne peut surmonter l'invincible répugnance qu'ils ont à prendre nos mœurs et vivre à notre manière. Si ces pauvres sauvages sont aussi malheureux qu'on le prétend, par quelle inconcevable dépravation de jugement refusent-ils constamment de se policer à notre imitation, ou d'apprendre à vivre heureux parmi nous; tandis qu'on lit en mille endroits que des Français et d'autres Européens se sont réfugiés volontairement parmi ces nations, y ont passé leur vie entière, sans pouvoir plus quitter une si étrange manière de vivre, et qu'on voit même des missionnaires sensés regretter avec attendrissement les jours calmes et innocents qu'ils ont passés chez ces peuples si méprisés ? Si l'on répond qu'ils n'ont pas assez de lumières pour juger sainement de leur état et du nôtre, je répliquerai que l'estimation du bonheur est moins l'affaire de la raison que du sentiment. D'ailleurs, cette réponse peut se rétorquer contre nous avec plus de force encore ; car il y a plus loin de nos idées à la disposition d'esprit où il faudrait être, pour concevoir le goût que trouvent les sauvages à leur manière de vivre, que des idées des sauvages à celles qui peuvent leur faire concevoir la nôtre. En effet, après quelques observations, il leur est aisé de voir que tous nos travaux se dirigent sur deux seuls objets : savoir, pour soi les commodités de la vie, et la considération parmi les autres. Mais le moyen pour nous d'imaginer la sorte de plaisir qu'un sauvage prend à passer sa vie seul au milieu des bois, ou à la pêche, ou à souffler dans une mauvaise flûte, sans jamais savoir en tirer un seul ton, et sans se soucier de l'apprendre ?

On a plusieurs fois amené des sauvages à Paris, à Londres, et dans d'autres villes ; on s'est empressé de leur étaler notre luxe, nos richesses, et tous nos arts les plus utiles et les plus curieux ; tout cela n'a jamais excité chez eux qu'une admiration stupide, sans le moindre mouvement de convoitise. Je me souviens entre autres de l'histoire d'un chef de quelques Américains septentrionaux qu'on mena à la cour d'Angleterre, il y a une trentaine d'années. On lui fit passer mille choses devant les yeux pour chercher à lui faire quelque présent qui pût lui plaire, sans qu'on trouvât rien dont il parût[1] se soucier. Nos armes lui semblaient lourdes et incommodes, nos souliers lui blessaient les pieds, nos habits le gênaient, il rebutait tout ; enfin on s'aperçut qu'ayant pris une couverture de laine il semblait prendre plaisir à s'en envelopper les épaules. 'Vous conviendrez au moins, lui dit-on aussitôt, de l'utilité de ce meuble ?'—'Oui, répondit-il, cela me paraît presque aussi bon qu'une peau de bête.' Encore n'eût-il pas dit cela, s'il eût porté l'une et l'autre à la pluie.

Peut-être me dira-t-on que c'est l'habitude qui, attachant chacun à sa manière de vivre, empêche les sauvages de sentir ce qu'il y a de bon dans la nôtre : et, sur ce pied-là, il doit paraître au moins fort extraordinaire que l'habitude ait plus de force pour maintenir les sauvages dans le goût de leur misère que les Européens dans la jouissance de leur félicité. Mais, pour faire à cette dernière objection une réponse à laquelle il n'y ait pas un mot à répliquer, sans alléguer tous les jeunes sauvages qu'on s'est vainement efforcé de civiliser, sans parler des Groënlandais et des habitants de l'Islande, qu'on a tenté d'élever et nourrir en Danemark, et que la tristesse et le désespoir ont tous fait périr, soit de langueur, soit dans la mer, où ils avaient tenté de regagner leur pays à la nage, je me contenterai de citer un seul exemple

---

[1] Ed. 1755 and Hachette read *parut*. Eds. 1782 and 1801, as in the text.

bien attesté, et que je donne à examiner aux admirateurs de la police européenne.

'Tous les efforts des missionnaires hollandais du cap de Bonne-Espérance n'ont jamais été capables de convertir un seul Hottentot. Van der Stel, gouverneur du Cap, en ayant pris un dès l'enfance, le fit élever dans les principes de la religion chrétienne, et dans la pratique des usages de l'Europe. On le vêtit richement, on lui fit apprendre plusieurs langues, et ses progrès répondirent fort bien aux soins qu'on prit pour son éducation. Le gouverneur, espérant beaucoup de son esprit, l'envoya aux Indes avec un commissaire général qui l'employa utilement aux affaires de la compagnie. Il revint au Cap après la mort du commissaire. Peu de jours après son retour, dans une visite qu'il rendit à quelques Hottentots de ses parents, il prit le parti de se dépouiller de sa parure européenne pour se revêtir d'une peau de brebis. Il retourna au fort dans ce nouvel ajustement, chargé d'un paquet qui contenait ses anciens habits; et, les présentant au gouverneur, il lui tint ce discours: *Ayez la bonté, monsieur, de faire attention que je renonce pour toujours à cet appareil; je renonce aussi pour toute ma vie à la religion chrétienne; ma résolution est de vivre et de mourir dans la religion, les manières et les usages de mes ancêtres. L'unique grâce que je vous demande est de me laisser le collier et le coutelas que je porte; je les garderai pour l'amour de vous.* Aussitôt, sans attendre la réponse de Van der Stel, il se déroba par la fuite, et jamais on ne le revit au Cap.' (*Histoire des voyages*, tome v. page 175.)

Page 180. (*q*) On pourrait m'objecter que, dans un pareil désordre, les hommes, au lieu de s'entr'égorger opiniâtrément, se seraient dispersés, s'il n'y avait point eu de bornes à leur dispersion. Mais, premièrement, ces bornes eussent au moins été celles du monde; et si l'on pense à l'excessive population qui résulte de l'état de nature, on jugera que la terre, dans cet état, n'eût pas tardé à être couverte d'hommes, ainsi forcés à se tenir rassemblés. D'ailleurs, ils se seraient dispersés, si le mal avait été rapide, et que c'eût été un changement fait du jour au lendemain. Mais ils naissaient sous le joug; ils avaient l'habitude de le porter quand ils en sentaient la pesanteur, et ils se contentaient d'attendre l'occasion de le secouer. Enfin, déjà accoutumés à mille commodités qui les forçaient à se tenir rassemblés, la dispersion n'était plus si facile que dans les premiers temps, où, nul n'ayant besoin que de soi-même, chacun prenait son parti sans attendre le consentement d'un autre.

Page 181. (*r*) Le maréchal de Villars[1] contait que, dans une de ses campagnes, les excessives friponneries d'un entrepreneur des vivres ayant fait souffrir et murmurer l'armée, il le tança vertement, et le menaça de le faire pendre. 'Cette menace ne me regarde pas, lui répondit[2] hardiment le fripon, et je suis bien aise de vous dire qu'on ne pend point un homme qui dispose de cent mille écus.'—'Je ne sais comment cela se fit, ajoutait naïvement le maréchal; mais en effet il ne fut point pendu, quoiqu'il eût cent fois mérité de l'être.'

Page 191. (*s*) La justice distributive s'opposerait même à cette égalité rigoureuse de l'état de nature, quand elle serait praticable dans la société civile; et, comme tous les membres de l'État lui doivent des services proportionnés à leurs talents et à leurs forces, les citoyens à leur tour doivent être distingués

---

[1] In Eds. 1755, 1782 and 1801, this appears as *Le maréchal de V****.
[2] Eds. 1755, 1782 and 1801, read as in the text. Hachette reads *répond*.

et favorisés à proportion de leurs services. C'est en ce sens qu'il faut entendre un passage d'Isocrate[1] dans lequel il loue les premiers Athéniens d'avoir bien su distinguer quelle était la plus avantageuse des deux sortes d'égalité, dont l'une consiste à faire part des mêmes avantages à tous les citoyens indifféremment, et l'autre à les distribuer selon le mérite de chacun. Ces habiles politiques, ajoute l'orateur, bannissant cette injuste égalité qui ne met aucune différence entre les méchants et les gens de bien, s'attachèrent inviolablement à celle qui récompense et punit chacun selon son mérite. Mais, premièrement, il n'a jamais existé de société, à quelque degré de corruption qu'elles aient pu parvenir, dans laquelle on ne fît aucune différence des méchants et des gens de bien ; et dans les matières de mœurs, où la Loi ne peut fixer de mesure assez exacte pour servir de règle au magistrat, c'est très sagement que, pour ne pas laisser le sort ou le rang des citoyens à sa discrétion, elle lui interdit le jugement des personnes, pour ne lui laisser que celui des actions. Il n'y a que des mœurs aussi pures que celles des anciens Romains qui puissent supporter des censeurs ; et de pareils tribunaux auraient bientôt tout bouleversé parmi nous. C'est à l'estime publique à mettre de la différence entre les méchants et les gens de bien. Le magistrat n'est juge que du droit rigoureux ; mais le peuple est le véritable juge des mœurs : juge intègre et même éclairé sur ce point, qu'on abuse quelquefois, mais qu'on ne corrompt jamais. Les rangs des citoyens doivent donc être réglés, non sur leur mérite personnel, ce qui serait laisser aux magistrats le moyen de faire une application presque arbitraire de la Loi, mais sur les services réels qu'ils rendent à l'État, et qui sont susceptibles d'une estimation plus exacte.

[1] *Areopagit.* § 8.

LETTRE DE J. J. ROUSSEAU A M. PHILOPOLIS[1]

[MS. Neuchâtel, 7836.]

Vous voulez, monsieur, que je vous réponde, puisque vous me faites des questions. Il s'agit, d'ailleurs, d'un ouvrage dédié à mes concitoyens : je dois, en le défendant, justifier l'honneur qu'ils m'ont fait de l'accepter. Je laisse à part dans votre lettre ce qui me regarde en bien et en mal, parce que l'un compense l'autre à peu près, que j'y prends peu d'intérêt, le public encore moins, et que tout cela ne fait rien à la recherche de la vérité. Je commence donc par le raisonnement que vous me proposez, comme essentiel à la question que j'ai tâché de résoudre.

L'état de société, me dites-vous, résulte immédiatement des facultés de l'homme, et par conséquent de sa nature. Vouloir que l'homme ne devînt point sociable, ce serait donc vouloir qu'il ne fût point homme; et c'est attaquer l'ouvrage de Dieu que de s'élever contre la société humaine. Permettez-moi, monsieur, de vous proposer à mon tour une difficulté, avant de résoudre la vôtre. Je vous épargnerais ce détour si je connaissais un chemin plus sûr pour aller au but.

Supposons que quelques savants trouvassent un jour le secret d'accélérer la vieillesse, et l'art d'engager les hommes à faire usage de cette rare découverte : persuasion qui ne serait peut-être pas si difficile à produire qu'elle paraît au premier aspect; car la raison, ce grand véhicule de toutes nos sottises, n'aurait garde de nous manquer à celle-ci. Les philosophes surtout, et les gens sensés[2], pour secouer le joug des passions et goûter le précieux repos de l'âme, gagneraient à grands pas l'âge de Nestor, et renonceraient volontiers aux désirs qu'on peut satisfaire, afin de se garantir de ceux qu'il faut étouffer. Il n'y aurait que quelques étourdis, qui, rougissant même de leur faiblesse, voudraient follement rester jeunes et heureux, au lieu de vieillir pour être sages.

Supposons qu'un esprit singulier, bizarre, et, pour tout dire,

[1] Charles Bonnet, of Geneva, the celebrated naturalist. His letter, signed *Philopolis*, appeared in the *Mercure de France*, October, 1755. Rousseau's answer followed immediately.

[2] The MS. and Ed. 1782 read as in the text. Ed. 1801 and Hachette read *les philosophes, et surtout les hommes sensés*; against both the authorities and the sense

un homme à paradoxes, s'avisât alors de reprocher aux autres l'absurdité de leurs maximes, de leur prouver qu'ils courent à la mort en cherchant la tranquillité, qu'ils ne font que radoter à force d'être raisonnables, et que, s'il faut qu'ils soient vieux un jour, ils devraient tâcher au moins de l'être le plus tard qu'il serait possible.

Il ne faut pas demander si nos sophistes, craignant le décri de leur arcane, se hâteraient d'interrompre ce discoureur importun[1]: 'Sages vieillards, diraient-ils à leurs sectateurs, remerciez le ciel des grâces qu'il vous accorde, et félicitez-vous sans cesse d'avoir si bien suivi ses volontés. Vous êtes décrépits, il est vrai, languissants, cacochymes, tel est le sort inévitable de l'homme ; mais votre entendement est sain. Vous êtes perclus de tous les membres, mais votre tête en est plus libre ; vous ne sauriez agir, mais vous parlez comme des oracles ; et si vos douleurs augmentent de jour en jour, votre philosophie augmente avec elles. Plaignez cette jeunesse impétueuse, que sa brutale santé prive des biens attachés à votre faiblesse. Heureuses infirmités, qui rassemblent autour de vous tant d'habiles pharmaciens fournis de plus de drogues que vous n'avez de maux, tant de savants médecins qui connaissent à fond votre pouls, qui savent en grec les noms de tous vos rhumatismes, tant de zélés consolateurs et d'héritiers fidèles qui vous conduisent agréablement à votre dernière heure ! Que de secours perdus pour vous, si vous n'aviez su vous donner les maux qui les ont rendus nécessaires !'

Ne pouvons-nous pas imaginer qu'apostrophant ensuite notre imprudent avertisseur ils lui parleraient à peu près ainsi ?

'Cessez, déclamateur téméraire, de tenir ces discours impies. Osez-vous blâmer ainsi la volonté de celui qui a fait le genre humain ? L'état de vieillesse ne découle-t-il pas de la constitution de l'homme ? n'est-il pas naturel à l'homme de vieillir ? Que faites-vous donc dans vos discours séditieux que d'attaquer une loi de la nature, et par conséquent la volonté de son créateur ? Puisque l'homme vieillit, Dieu veut qu'il vieillisse. Les faits sont-ils autre chose que l'expression de sa volonté ? Apprenez que l'homme jeune n'est point celui que Dieu a voulu faire, et que, pour s'empresser d'obéir à ses ordres, il faut se hâter de vieillir.'

Tout cela supposé, je vous demande, monsieur, si l'homme aux paradoxes doit se taire ou répondre ; et, dans ce dernier cas, de vouloir bien m'indiquer ce qu'il doit dire. Je tâcherai de résoudre alors votre objection.

---

[1] Rousseau had originally written *cet importun*.

Puisque vous prétendez m'attaquer par mon propre système, n'oubliez pas, je vous prie, que, selon moi, la société est naturelle à l'espèce humaine, comme la décrépitude à l'individu; et qu'il faut des arts, des lois, des Gouvernements aux peuples, comme il faut des béquilles aux vieillards. Toute la différence est que l'état de vieillesse découle de la seule nature de l'homme, et que celui de société découle de la nature du genre humain, non pas immédiatement comme vous le dites, mais seulement, comme je l'ai prouvé, à l'aide de certaines circonstances extérieures qui pouvaient être ou n'être pas, ou du moins arriver plus tôt ou plus tard, et par conséquent accélérer ou ralentir le progrès. Plusieurs même de ces circonstances dépendent de la volonté des hommes; j'ai été obligé, pour établir une parité parfaite, de supposer dans l'individu le pouvoir d'accélérer sa vieillesse, comme l'espèce a celui de retarder la sienne. L'état de société ayant donc un terme extrême, auquel les hommes sont les maîtres d'arriver plus tôt ou plus tard, il n'est pas inutile de leur montrer le danger d'aller si vite, et les misères d'une condition qu'ils prennent pour la perfection de l'espèce.

À l'énumération des maux dont les hommes sont accablés et que je soutiens être leur propre ouvrage, vous m'assurez, Leibnitz et vous, que tout est bien, et qu'ainsi la Providence est justifiée. J'étais éloigné de croire qu'elle eût besoin pour sa justification du secours de la philosophie leibnitzienne, ni d'aucune autre. Pensez-vous sérieusement, vous-même, qu'un système de philosophie, quel qu'il soit, puisse être plus irrépréhensible que l'univers, et que, pour disculper la Providence, les arguments d'un philosophe soient plus convaincants que les ouvrages de Dieu ? Au reste, nier que le mal existe est un moyen fort commode d'excuser l'auteur du mal. Les stoïciens se sont autrefois rendus ridicules à meilleur marché.

Selon Leibnitz et Pope, tout ce qui est est bien. S'il y a des sociétés, c'est que le bien général veut qu'il y en ait ; s'il n'y en a point, le bien général veut qu'il n'y en ait pas ; et si quelqu'un persuadait aux hommes de retourner vivre dans les forêts, il serait bon qu'ils y retournassent vivre. On ne doit pas appliquer à la nature des choses une idée de bien ou de mal qu'on ne tire que de leurs rapports ; car elles peuvent être bonnes relativement au tout, quoique mauvaises en elles-mêmes. Ce qui concourt au bien général peut être un mal particulier, dont il est permis de se délivrer, quand il est possible. Car si ce mal, tandis qu'on le supporte, est utile au tout, le bien contraire, qu'on s'efforce de lui substituer, ne lui sera pas moins utile, sitôt qu'il aura lieu. Par la même raison que tout est bien comme il est, si quelqu'un s'efforce de changer l'état de choses, il est bon qu'il s'efforce de le changer; et s'il est bien ou mal qu'il réussisse, c'est ce qu'on peut apprendre de l'événement seul, et non de la raison. Rien n'empêche en cela que le mal particulier ne soit un mal réel pour celui qui le souffre. Il était bon pour le tout que nous fussions civilisés, puisque nous le sommes; mais il eût certainement été mieux pour nous de ne pas l'être. Leibnitz n'eût jamais rien tiré de son système, qui pût combattre cette proposition; et il est clair que l'optimisme bien entendu ne fait rien ni pour, ni contre, moi.

Aussi n'est-ce ni à Leibnitz ni à Pope que j'ai à répondre, mais à vous seul, qui, sans distinguer le mal universel qu'ils nient du mal particulier qu'ils ne nient pas, prétendez que c'est assez qu'une chose existe, pour qu'il ne soit pas permis de désirer qu'elle existât autrement. [1]Mais, monsieur, si tout est bien comme il est, tout était bien comme il était, avant qu'il y eût des Gouvernements et des lois: il fut donc au moins superflu de les établir; et Jean-Jacques alors, avec votre système, eût eu beau jeu contre Philopolis. Si tout est bien comme il est, de la manière dont vous l'entendez, à quoi bon corriger nos vices, guérir nos maux, redresser nos erreurs? que servent nos chaires, nos tribunaux, nos académies? pourquoi faire appeler un médecin quand vous avez la fièvre? que savez-vous si le bien du plus grand tout, que vous ne connaissez pas, n'exige point que vous ayez le transport, et si la santé des habitants de Saturne ou de Sirius ne souffrirait point du rétablissement de la vôtre? Laissez aller tout comme il pourra, afin que tout aille toujours bien. Si tout est le mieux qu'il peut être, vous devez blâmer toute action quelconque; car toute action produit nécessairement quelque changement dans l'état où sont les choses au moment qu'elle se fait. On ne peut donc toucher à rien sans mal faire; et le quiétisme le plus parfait est la seule vertu qui reste à l'homme. Enfin, si tout est bien comme il est, il est bon qu'il y ait des Lapons, des Esquimaux, des Algonquins, des Chicacas, des Caraïbes, qui se passent de notre police, des Hottentots qui s'en moquent, et un Genevois qui les approuve[1]. Leibnitz lui-même conviendrait de ceci.

L'homme, dites-vous, est tel que l'exigeait la place qu'il devait occuper dans l'univers. Mais les hommes diffèrent tellement, selon les temps et les lieux, qu'avec une pareille logique on serait sujet

---

[1] For the rough draft of this passage see p. 308.

à tirer du particulier à l'universel des conséquences fort contradictoires et fort peu concluantes. Il ne faut qu'une erreur de géographie pour bouleverser toute cette prétendue doctrine qui déduit ce qui doit être de ce qu'on voit. 'C'est à faire aux castors, dira l'Indien, de s'enfouir dans des tanières; l'homme doit dormir à l'air dans un hamac suspendu à des arbres.— Non, non, dira le Tartare, l'homme est fait pour coucher dans un chariot.— Pauvres gens! s'écrieront nos Philopolis d'un air de pitié, ne voyez-vous pas que l'homme est fait pour bâtir des villes?' Quand il est question de raisonner sur la nature humaine, le vrai philosophe n'est ni Indien, ni Tartare, ni de Genève, ni de Paris, mais il est homme.

Que le singe soit une bête, je le crois, et j'en ai dit la raison. Que l'orang-outang en soit une aussi, voilà ce que vous avez la bonté de m'apprendre; et j'avoue qu'après les faits que j'ai cités la preuve de celui-là me semblait difficile. Vous philosophez trop bien pour prononcer là-dessus aussi légèrement que nos voyageurs, qui s'exposent quelquefois, sans beaucoup de façons, à mettre leurs semblables au rang des bêtes. Vous obligerez donc sûrement le public, et vous instruirez même les naturalistes, en nous apprenant les moyens que vous avez employés pour décider cette question.

Dans mon épître dédicatoire, j'ai félicité ma patrie d'avoir un des meilleurs Gouvernements qui pussent exister; j'ai trouvé[1] dans le Discours, qu'il devait y avoir très peu de bons Gouvernements: je ne vois pas où est la contradiction que vous remarquez en cela. Mais comment savez-vous, monsieur, que j'irais vivre dans les bois, si ma santé me le permettait, plutôt que parmi mes concitoyens, pour lesquels vous connaissez ma tendresse? Loin de rien dire de semblable dans mon ouvrage, vous y avez dû voir des raisons très fortes de ne point choisir ce genre de vie. Je sens trop en mon particulier combien peu je puis me passer de vivre avec des hommes aussi corrompus que moi; et le sage même, s'il en est, n'ira pas aujourd'hui chercher le bonheur au fond d'un désert. Il faut fixer, quand on le peut, son séjour dans sa patrie, pour l'aimer et la servir. Heureux celui qui, privé de cet avantage, peut au moins vivre au sein de l'amitié, dans la patrie commune du genre humain, dans cet asile immense ouvert à tous les hommes, où se plaisent également l'austère sagesse et la jeunesse folâtre; où règnent l'humanité, l'hospitalité, la douceur, et tous les charmes d'une société facile; où le pauvre trouve encore des amis, la vertu

---

[1] Ed. 1801 and Hachette read *prouvé*. MS. and Ed. 1782, as in the text.

des exemples qui l'animent, et la raison des guides qui l'éclairent ! C'est sur ce grand théâtre de la fortune, du vice, et quelquefois des vertus, qu'on peut observer avec fruit le spectacle de la vie ; mais c'est dans son pays que chacun devrait en paix achever la sienne.

Il me semble, monsieur, que vous me censurez bien gravement sur une réflexion qui me paraît très juste, et qui, juste ou non, n'a point dans mon écrit le sens qu'il vous plaît de lui donner par l'addition d'une seule lettre. *Si la nature nous a destinés à être saints*[1], me faites-vous dire, *j'ose presque assurer que l'état de réflexion est un état contre nature, et que l'homme qui médite est un animal dépravé.* Je vous avoue que si j'avais ainsi confondu la santé avec la sainteté, et que la proposition fût vrai, je me croirais très propre à devenir un grand saint moi-même dans l'autre monde, ou du moins à me porter toujours bien dans celui-ci.

Je finis, monsieur, en répondant à vos trois dernières questions. Je n'abuserai pas du temps que vous me donnez pour y réfléchir ; c'est un soin que j'avais pris d'avance.

Un homme, ou tout autre être sensible, qui n'aurait jamais connu la douleur, aurait-il de la pitié, et serait-il ému à la vue d'un enfant qu'on égorgerait ? Je réponds que non.

Pourquoi la populace, à qui M. Rousseau accorde une si grande dose de pitié, se repaît-elle avec tant d'avidité du spectacle d'un malheureux expirant sur la roue ? Par la même raison que vous allez pleurer au théâtre et voir Séide égorger son père, ou Thyeste boire le sang de son fils. La pitié est un sentiment si délicieux, qu'il n'est pas étonnant qu'on cherche à l'éprouver. D'ailleurs, chacun a une curiosité secrète d'étudier les mouvements de la nature aux approches de ce moment redoutable que nul ne peut éviter. Ajoutez à cela le plaisir d'être pendant deux mois l'orateur du quartier, et de raconter pathétiquement aux voisins la belle mort du dernier roué.

L'affection que les femelles des animaux témoignent pour leurs petits, a-t-elle ces petits pour objet, ou la mère ? D'abord la mère, pour son besoin ; puis les petits[2], par habitude. Je l'avais dit dans le Discours. *Si par hasard c'était celle-ci, le bien-être des petits n'en serait que plus assuré.* Je le croirais ainsi. Cependant, cette maxime demande moins à être étendue que resserrée ; car, lorsque les poussins sont éclos, on ne voit pas que la poule ait aucun

---

[1] In Bonnet's Letter, as published in the *Mercure, sains* had appeared as *saints*, by a misprint (*Merc.* Oct. 1755, p. 76). Rousseau, rather absurdly, takes advantage of the error.

[2] Hachette reads *ses petits*. MS. and Ed. 1782, as in the text.

besoin d'eux, et sa tendresse maternelle ne le cède pourtant à nulle autre.

Voilà, monsieur, mes réponses. Remarquez au reste que, dans cette affaire comme dans celle du premier Discours, je suis toujours le monstre qui soutient[1] que l'homme est naturellement bon; et que mes adversaires sont toujours les honnêtes gens qui, à l'édification publique, s'efforcent de prouver que la nature n'a fait que des scélérats.

Je suis, autant qu'on peut l'être de quelqu'un qu'on ne connaît point, monsieur, etc.

[1] Ed. 1801 and Hachette reads *qui soutiens*. MS. and Ed. 1782, as in the text.

[The *Lettre de Philopolis* is printed in *Œuvres de Rousseau* (Geneva, 1782, 12mo), T. xxviii. pp. 63—71. Rousseau's Reply was published not in the *Mercure*, but as a separate pamphlet, towards the end of 1755.]

ÉCONOMIE POLITIQUE

THE *Économie politique* was first published in the fifth volume of the *Encyclopédie*, which appeared in November, 1755[1]. It was republished for the first time, as a separate treatise, by Duvillard of Geneva in 1758, apparently without the consent of the author[2]. This edition, like all others published in the author's lifetime[3], is (with trifling exceptions) an exact reprint of the article, as it originally appeared in the *Encyclopédie*. And it is in the collected edition, published after Rousseau's death under the supervision of du Peyrou and Moultou (Geneva, 1782), that most of the author's corrections appear for the first time. As will be seen from the notes to the text, they do not amount to much.

Considerable portions of the rough draft of the treatise are preserved in a manuscript, now in the Bibliothèque de la Ville, Neuchâtel[4]. They amount to more than one third of the whole

[1] See General Introduction, p. 14.
[2] See letter to Vernes of Oct. 22, 1758; *Œuvres*, x. p. 196.
[3] *e.g.* that published by Duchesne (Paris, 1763—4) with the connivance, though not the formal approval, of the author. See *Œuvres*, xi. pp. 35, 47, 57, 69. Rousseau intended to include it in the authorised edition of his Works which was to have been published by Fauche or du Peyrou (and, failing them, by Rey) at the time when he was living at Motiers. But all these arrangements were abandoned. See letters to du Peyrou of Nov. 29 and Dec. 13, 1764, and Jan. 24, Feb. 14, 1765; *Œuvres*, xi. pp. 176, 182, 201, 219. See also letters to Rey of May 13, 1764, and March 18, 1765; Bosscha, pp. 205—9 and 250—5; and compare the letter of Rousseau to Rey (Oct. 18, 1765) quoted in Rey's collected edition (11 vols. 8vo) of 1772 (*Avertissement*). The *Économie politique* would have come between the *Discours sur l'inégalité* and the *Contrat social*, at the beginning of Vol. I. See Bosscha, p. 254.
[4] MS. Neuchâtel, 7840. For a description of this MS., the most important of the whole collection, see Appendix II. The rough draft of the *Économie politique* occupies pp. 85—73 of the MS. (the numbering of the pages being from the other end of the book). The two pages torn off are p. 86 (about one third of which is still left and to the lost part of which there is a reference on p. 85) and p. 80, the bottom corner of which still remains, written (like many other pages) on both sides. The writing throughout the draft is close; and there are many erasures, which greatly increase the difficulty of deciphering it.

work; and, if we reckon two pages (folio) which have been partially torn out, and a few paragraphs not included in the final version, the proportion would rise to much over a half. A large part of the rough draft is written in the shape of detached fragments, and in an order very different from that in which they were finally arranged[1]. It is a curious illustration of the way in which Rousseau worked, at any rate in the earlier part of his life as an author. To judge from the rough draft of the *Lettres de la Montagne*, preserved in the same manuscript, it was very different at the close[2]. But that, in his earlier years, he was apt to write each paragraph as it occurred to his mind and without much reference to its place in the final whole, is what we should have inferred from his own statements in the *Confessions*[3]. And, as he says himself with reference to the first *Discourse*, 'the art of writing is not learned in a day[4].'

It must further be noted that two passages of the *Économie politique* reappear almost word for word in the first draft of the *Contrat social*. The first of these is concerned with the relation between the State and the Family; it forms, allowance being made for one introductory paragraph, the opening of the *Économie politique*[5]. The second is the striking passage to be found a few pages further on, which describes the miracles wrought by the Law[6]. It is obvious that this repetition raises the question of priority. But that is better reserved until we come to discuss the date, or dates, of the Geneva Manuscript as a whole.

The only other point of this nature that calls for notice is a couple of references—explicit in one case, implicit in the

[1] Thus p. 85 opens with the paragraph, 'C'est ainsi qu'un gouvernement attentif' (below, p. 258—*i.e.* more than two thirds of the way through the treatise). And what were clearly intended for the opening paragraphs of the treatise do not occur until p. 74—*i.e.* the last page but one. The Fragments printed in this volume (pp. 274—280) bear witness to the same peculiarity.

[2] It must, of course, be remembered that the *Lettres de la Montagne* is a controversial writing, and that the order of the matter was therefore to a large extent determined by the nature of the case. But something of the same orderly arrangement appears in the MS. of the treatise on Corsica. This is certainly not controversial, and the MS. is no more than a rough draft. Yet it does not seem likely that Rousseau would have altered the order greatly, on revising it for publication.

[3] *Confessions*, Liv. III.; *Œuvres*, VIII. p. 80; and Liv. VIII.; *ib.* p. 249.

[4] *ib.* Liv. VIII. p. 250.

[5] *Éc. pol.* pp. 236—240 ('Quand il y aurait...peu de bons magistrats'); Geneva MS. f. 225, Liv. I. Chap. v.; below, pp. 463—5.

[6] Geneva MS. Liv. I. Chap. vii. See Note 2, p. 445.

other[1]—to an article by Diderot on *Droit naturel*, which appeared in the same volume of the *Encyclopédie* and which we shall find again referred to, and at greater length, in the first draft of the *Contrat social*[2]. But the various questions which arise out of these references will be most conveniently treated in the Introduction to that article, which will be found in this volume.

This completes what may be called the antiquities of the subject. We may now turn to more vital matters. As has already been said, the first thing to strike us in the *Économie politique* is the closeness of its relation to the *Contrat social*. The conception of the corporate self (*le moi commun*)[3], of the general will as its organ[4], and of the Law as its outward expression[5]—all the ideas, that is, which lie at the heart of the *Contrat social* and constitute its originality—may be here found summarily anticipated. The analogy between the social and the animal organism, which is implicit throughout the *Contrat social*, is here explicitly drawn out. Indeed, it would hardly be too much to say that the whole political theory of Rousseau, on its more abstract side, was already formed when he wrote the *Économie politique*.

To this statement there are, however, two important exceptions. The idea of the Contract, which lies at the threshold of the later treatise, is here hurriedly slurred over. The scheme of the article, which assumes the existence of the State, did not compel the author to dwell upon it; and it may be that, as appears to have been the case when he wrote the *Discours sur l'inégalité*, he had not yet completely worked it out[6]. Again, the conception of a 'general

---

[1] *Éc. pol.* p. 242 and p. 244. The sentence—'C'est ainsi que les brigands mêmes, qui sont les ennemis de la vertu dans la grande société, en adorent le simulacre dans leurs cavernes'—is a direct reference to the words of Diderot. See below, p. 244.

[2] Geneva MS. of *Contrat social*, Liv. I. Chap. ii. Below, pp. 450—4.

[3] Below, p. 241. The instructive contrast with 'le *moi humain* lequel a acquis cette méprisable activité qui absorbe toute vertu et fait la vie des petites âmes' is peculiar to the *Économie politique, ib.* p. 256.

[4] *ib.* pp. 241—7.   [5] *ib.* p. 245.

[6] The only passages in which the Contract is mentioned are on pp. 244, 252, 265. Of these p. 252 is the most definite: 'La sûreté particulière est tellement liée avec la confédération publique que cette convention serait détruite, s'il périssait dans l'État un seul citoyen qu'on eût pu secourir...; car, les conventions fondamentales étant enfreintes, on ne voit plus quel droit ni quel intérêt pourrait maintenir le peuple dans l'union sociale, à moins qu'il n'y fût retenu par la seule force, qui fait la dissolution de l'état civil.'

society of the human race' preceding the formation of particular States—a conception implicitly rejected in the final version of the *Contrat social* and expressly denounced in the earlier draft of that treatise—is here explicitly accepted[1]. It may be observed that this divergence carries with it a further difference in the conception of Property. In the *Contrat social*, as we have seen, Property is treated as the creation of the State. In the *Économie politique*, where the social bond is regarded as having existed in a rudimentary form before the State came into being, Property is again and again asserted to be prior to the State; more than that, to be the foundation upon which the State itself is subsequently built[2].

In the former case, that of the Contract, it is manifest that the *Économie politique* represents a more consistent conception than the *Contrat social*; and that Rousseau only embarrassed himself by the modifications which he subsequently introduced. In the latter case, it is equally clear that the advantage is on the other side; that the conceptions of 'natural society,' 'natural Law' and Property, as an institution existing, if only in a rudimentary form, before the foundation of the State, are all of them conceptions inconsistent with the fundamental ideas which are common to both treatises and which it is at once the essential service and the true originality of Rousseau to have proclaimed. They are, in fact, survivals of an alien theory, the theory of Locke and the individualists, which it was his mission to destroy. In these points, therefore, the later treatise represents a marked and decisive advance upon the earlier.

In the face of these exceptions, it remains true that the theory of the *Contrat social* is, broadly speaking, forestalled in the *Économie politique*. There are, of course, many points in each treatise which are not referred to in the other. Thus the *Économie politique* contains no mention of the civil religion; one only of the Lawgiver, or of the necessity for reckoning with conditions of soil, climate and national character, which plays so large a part in the *Contrat social*. The last is one of the many proofs that the teaching of Montesquieu was slow to sink into the mind of Rousseau. On the other hand, the earlier writing deals

---

[1] 'Cherchez les motifs qui ont porté les hommes, unis par leurs besoins dans la grande société, à s'unir plus étroitement par des sociétés civiles.' *ib.* p. 244. Contrast *C. S.* I. vi. and Geneva MS. I. ii.

[2] 'La propriété est le vrai fondement de la société civile, et le vrai garant des engagements des citoyens.' *ib.* p. 259. Compare pp. 238, 260, 265, 273; and contrast *C. S.* I. ix.

with several subjects which are left unnoticed in the later. Finance—a subject only once mentioned, and that merely by the way, in the *Contrat social*[1]—occupies no less than a third part of the *Économie politique*[2]. And the duty of the State to give a public education to its children[3]—a duty on which the *Contrat social* is entirely silent—is here pressed home with a force which the author never again approached until his last work, *Le Gouvernement de Pologne*[4].

On the former subject, the mind of Rousseau seems to have varied considerably at different periods of his life. In the present treatise, he is disposed to reject both the land-tax and a tax on corn and other products, as being both ruinous and oppressive[5]. In the treatise on Poland, on the other hand, he is willing to accept a proportional tax on the produce of the land, so long as it is paid in kind and the administration of the tax farmed out to men responsible to the State for its collection[6]. Again, a capitation tax on income is discussed with some favour in the *Économie politique*; on the express condition, it must be noted, that it shall be proportioned not only to the receipts, but also to the vital needs, of those who pay it[7]. In the treatise on Poland, however, the objections to such a tax, in any form, are apparently regarded as outweighing any advantages it may offer[8]. Lastly, taxes on luxuries, which the earlier treatise declares to be both the most just and the most expedient[9], seem to be hurriedly dismissed in

---

[1] 'Je crois les corvées moins contraires à la liberté que les taxes.' *C. S.* III. xv. Compare *Projet pour la Corse*, Vol. II. pp. 339, 355.

[2] pp. 258—273.

[3] 'Ne doutons pas qu'ils n'apprennent ainsi...à devenir un jour les défenseurs et les pères de la patrie, dont ils auront été si longtemps les enfants.' *Éc. pol.* p. 257. The passage on Education is from p. 255 to p. 258 of *Éc. pol.*

[4] *Gouvernement de Pologne*, Chap. iv.; Vol. II. pp. 437—441.

[5] *Éc. pol.* pp. 269—271. It may be observed that, in this passage, he admits the objections to the corn-tax to be less if it is paid in kind than in money.

[6] Vol. II. pp. 482—4.

[7] *Éc. pol.* pp. 266—9. 'L'imposition n'en doit pas être faite seulement en raison des biens des contribuables mais en raison composée de la différence de leurs conditions et du superflu de leurs biens.' What did Rousseau mean by *la différence de leurs conditions*? He expressly tells us (pp. 267—8) that he does *not* mean their rank. I suggest that he means their style of life, married or single, and the size of their families.

[8] Vol. II. p. 483.

[9] *Éc. pol.* pp. 271—3.

the later treatise, on the ground that they are certain to lead to fraud and smuggling[1].

Yet, in spite of these differences, the fundamental principles of both treatises are much the same. In both, as again in the *Projet pour la Corse*, the author pronounces in favour of raising revenue from domain-land rather than by taxation[2]. In both, he maintains that the State fulfils its duty better by reducing expenditure than by increasing revenue[3]. In both, he raises his voice against prodigality, whether in public or in private life, as a canker fatal to the true ends both of the individual and the State. And if in the *Économie politique* he does not suggest the substitution of personal service for payments in kind or money, he makes ample amends for the omission by a spirited defence of the *corvée* in the *Contrat social*[4]: a defence again and again repeated in the *Gouvernement de Pologne*[5].

As for the other point—the superiority of a public to a private education—there is little or no ground for supposing that Rousseau ever wavered in his conviction. He asserts it in the *Économie politique* (1755). He asserts it no less decisively in the *Gouvernement de Pologne* (1772)[6]. And if he refrains from doing so in the *Contrat social*, which belongs to the interval between these two writings (1762), that is probably because he is there avowedly concerned with the more abstract side of political theory, *Principes du droit politique*, and because Education would naturally have found its place among the practical applications of that theory: in the work on *Institutions politiques* which was either never

[1] Vol. II. p. 483.
[2] *Éc. pol.* pp. 261—2 ; Vol. II. p. 482.
[3] *Éc. pol.* p. 262 ; Vol. II. p. 479.
[4] *C. S.* III. xv. 'Dans un pays vraiment libre, les citoyens font tout avec leurs bras, et rien avec de l'argent....Je crois les corvées moins contraires à la liberté que les taxes.'
[5] Vol. II. pp. 481—2,. 486—9. The main reason for the absence of this recommendation in the *Éc. pol.* is probably the individualist conception of Property which runs through the whole treatise and which appears strongly in the plea for the taxation of luxuries : 'car alors, le particulier n'étant point absolument contraint à payer, sa contribution peut passer pour volontaire.' *Éc. pol.* p. 273. For some of the other differences the reason may be sought in the difference of circumstances, as between Poland and France. Rousseau clearly had the latter country in view when he wrote the *Éc. pol.*
[6] *Éc. pol.* pp. 291—3 ; *Pologne*, pp. 437—41 : 'C'est ici l'article important. C'est l'éducation qui doit donner aux âmes la forme nationale.... L'éducation nationale n'appartient qu'aux hommes libres ; il n'y a qu'eux qui aient une existence commune et qui soient vraiment liés par la Loi.'

written, or else deliberately destroyed[1]. The only argument to the contrary is to be found in the elaborate scheme of private education—the most drastic of that kind ever devised by man—which is set forth in *Émile*. This, however, when fairly considered, is seen to be the exception which proves the rule. In the opening pages of that treatise, the author makes no secret of his conviction that, wherever a public life worthy of the name exists to make it possible, a public education is without doubt to be preferred; and that, if under present conditions such an ideal is beyond the reach of Europe, that is because the civic spirit, the very idea of the fatherland and the citizen, has been swept away—and, with it, the last possibility of education by the State[2]. In the face of that avowal and of all else that we know of Rousseau, can we doubt that, to him, this was among the worst disasters which could happen to man? that his acceptance of private education in the volume that followed was, at bottom, a counsel of despair?

The question of origins played some little part in our discussion of the *Discours sur l'inégalité*. It is a matter of small moment in *Économie politique*. To the writers of his own time it is doubtful whether Rousseau owes anything worth mentioning. His doctrine of Property, to a less extent his views on Taxation, have, no doubt, something in common with the teaching of the Physiocrats. But for the former he had no need to look further than the *Civil Government* of Locke. And as, in discussing the right of the State to tax its members, he explicitly refers to Locke's treatise[3],

[1] See *C. S.*, *Avertissement* and IV. ix. Compare *Confessions*, Liv. x.; *Œuvres*, VIII. p. 370. Corancez tells us that, some time between the publication of *Émile* and his flight from England (1762—7), Rousseau composed a *Comparison between public and private Education*, and that he destroyed it in a panic before his flight to France (1767). See Introduction to *Émile* (II. p. 142).

[2] *Émile*, Liv. I.; Vol. II. p. 146. In this passage occurs the following significant remark on the *Republic*: 'Voulez-vous prendre une idée de l'éducation publique, lisez la *République* de Platon. Ce n'est point un ouvrage de politique; c'est le plus beau traité d'éducation qu'on ait jamais fait.'

[3] See *Éc. pol.* p. 265: the paragraph beginning 'Il faut se ressouvenir ici.' The reference to Locke will not be found in the final text, as published. But in the margin of the manuscript (Neuchâtel, 7840, p. 79) is written, *Voyez Locke*. The passage referred to is *Civil Government*, II. xi. §§ 138—140. I half suspect that the reference was suppressed on account of the amazing looseness of Locke's argument. Having started by insisting that 'no Body hath a right to take men's substance, or any part of it, from them without *their own* consent,' he ends with the gloss, 'with his own consent, *i.e.* the consent of the Majority, giving it either by themselves or their Representatives chosen by them.'

there is no reason to suppose that he had consulted—much less, been influenced by—more recent thinkers[1]. In matters of taxation, again, the possible alternatives are so limited that they must of themselves occur to every vigorous and open mind. And, as Rousseau is certainly no slave either to the physiocratic, or to any other, authority, it is impossible to say how far he was familiar with anything that had been said or written by such men as Gournai or Quesnai upon the subject[2]. The influence of Locke, on the contrary, is beyond dispute. And it works havoc with the argument. The central thought of the *Économie politique*—the doctrine of the general will and the corporate self—is strongly collectivist. The doctrine of Property and, in the main, the theory of taxation are pure relics of individualism. The contradiction is glaring. And an acute reader might have safely predicted that in his next work the author would eliminate—or, at the least, greatly reduce—either the one element, or the other: that he would either slide backwards to the full-blooded individualism of the *Discours sur l'inégalité*, or move forward to a more consistent collectivism than he had yet attained. The latter was the course which he actually took. And, so far as Property is concerned, the *Contrat social* gets rid of the individualist elements which had brought so much confusion into the *Économie politique*. It is to be wished that Rousseau had applied the same process with equal vigour to other matters also. Here, however, tradition was too strong for him. To the end, the state of nature and the Contract remain embedded in a theory with which no ingenuity can bring them into accord.

It is not to the moderns, but to the ancients, that the real debt of Rousseau, in the *Économie politique*, is due. The moderns had nothing to teach him in the new field of thought which he was

---

[1] The difficulty is increased by the fact that no Physiocrat had apparently published anything before 1758. That is the date of Quesnai's *Maximes générales de gouvernement économique d'un royaume agricole*. But their doctrines were probably matter of notoriety, before they had published anything. It must be remembered that Gournai, the founder of the school, published nothing original. He was known only as the leading spirit of the *Bureau du commerce*. See Martin, *Histoire de France*, XVI. pp. 163—7. He died in 1759.

[2] I should rather infer, from the letter to Mirabeau of July 26, 1767— it deals with the *Ordre naturel et essentiel des sociétés politiques* of Mercier de la Rivière, a physiocratic manifesto issued earlier in the year—that the doctrines of the Physiocrats were, till then, unknown to him. *Œuvres*, XII. p. 24. See Vol. II. pp. 159—162.

here striving to open out. If any advance was to be made, it was by going back to Aristotle and Plato. That he had studied the works of both writers, is very clear. It is equally clear that, of the two, he, like most other men, had found Plato the more fruitful and inspiring. And this was to be expected. His own mind was essentially poetic. And in the poetry of Plato his imagination found a spur which the cold severity of Aristotle was powerless to supply. Neither author receives more than a casual mention by name: Plato twice, Aristotle only once[1]. And in the latter case, the debt of Rousseau may not go much deeper than one mention would suggest. The spirit of Plato, on the other hand, may be traced through the whole tissue of the treatise. And from this moment it is the moulding influence upon Rousseau's political ideas. The disciple of Locke has transferred his allegiance to a greater master. And, with modifications due to the influence of Montesquieu, he remains essentially a Platonist to the end.

[1] For Aristotle, see *Éc. pol.* p. 280—the reference being to *Politics*, I. ii.; and (for a different account of the matter) III. xv. Plato is mentioned in *Éc. pol.* p. 246 and p. 269. The reference in the latter case is purely vague and general; and it is significant that Plato's name is here coupled with that of Montesquieu. In the former case, the reference is to *Laws*, IV. and V. pp. 720—735. It is strange that, in combating the view expressed in *Politics*, I. 2, Rousseau fails to mention that the same account is given by Plato in *Laws*, III. p. 680 D. It may be remarked, finally, that Rousseau expresses himself much more strongly against the derivation of the State from the Family in this passage and in the Geneva MS. (I. v.) than he does in the final version of the *Contrat social* (I. ii.).

DE L'ÉCONOMIE POLITIQUE

[Five Editions have been consulted for the text of this treatise : the original issue in the *Encyclopédie*, T. v. (1755); that of Duvillard (Geneva, 1758); that of 1765 (Geneva); that of Rey in 11 volumes (Amsterdam, 1772); and that of du Peyrou and Moultou in 17 volumes 4º (Geneva, 1782). The first of these differs slightly in different copies. I have consulted those in the British Museum, in the Rylands Library and in the Bibliothèque de la Ville, Neuchâtel. The Geneva Edition of 1782 is, after the first, the most authoritative. It is clear that du Peyrou had access to corrections made by Rousseau himself.]

[MS. Neuchâtel, 7840, contains the rough draft.]

Le mot d'ÉCONOMIE ou d'ŒCONOMIE vient de οἶκος, *maison*, et de νόμος, *loi*, et ne signifie originairement que le sage et légitime gouvernement de la maison pour le bien commun de toute la famille. Le sens de ce terme a été dans la suite étendu au gouvernement de la grande famille, qui est l'État. Pour distinguer ces deux acceptions, on l'appelle, dans ce dernier cas, *économie générale* ou *politique*; et dans l'autre, *économie domestique* ou *particulière*. Ce n'est que de la première qu'il est question dans cet article.

[1]Quand il y aurait entre l'État et la famille autant de rapport que plusieurs auteurs le prétendent, il ne s'ensuivrait pas pour cela que les règles de conduite propres à l'une de ces deux sociétés fussent convenables à l'autre. Elles diffèrent trop en grandeur pour pouvoir être administrées de la même manière; et il y aura toujours une extrême différence entre le gouvernement domestique, où le père peut tout voir par lui-même, et le gouvernement civil, où le chef ne voit presque rien que par les yeux d'autrui. Pour que les choses devinssent égales à cet égard, il faudrait que les talents, la force, et toutes les facultés du père augmentassent en raison de la grandeur de la famille, et que l'âme d'un puissant

---

[1] This, together with the four following paragraphs, reappears (with the modifications noticed below) in the first draft of the *Contrat social* (I. v., *Fausses notions du lien social*). With one exception, the merely verbal variations are not noticed.

monarque fût à celle d'un homme ordinaire, comme l'étendue de son empire est à l'héritage d'un particulier.

Mais comment le gouvernement de l'État pourrait-il être semblable à celui de la famille, dont le fondement est si différent? Le père étant physiquement plus fort que ses enfants, aussi longtemps que son secours leur est nécessaire le pouvoir paternel passe avec raison pour être établi par la nature. Dans la grande famille, dont tous les membres sont naturellement égaux, l'autorité politique, purement arbitraire quant à son institution, ne peut être fondée que sur des conventions, ni le magistrat commander aux autres qu'en vertu des lois. [1]Le pouvoir du père sur les enfants, fondé sur leur avantage particulier, ne peut, par sa nature, s'étendre jusqu'au droit de vie et de mort; mais le pouvoir souverain, qui n'a d'autre objet que le bien commun, n'a d'autres bornes que celles de l'utilité publique bien entendue: distinction que j'expliquerai dans son lieu[1]. Les devoirs du père lui sont dictés par des sentiments naturels, et d'un ton qui lui permet rarement de désobéir. Les chefs n'ont point de semblable règle, et ne sont réellement tenus envers le peuple qu'à ce qu'ils lui ont promis de faire, et dont il est en droit d'exiger l'exécution. Une autre différence plus importante encore, c'est que, les enfants n'ayant rien que ce qu'ils reçoivent du père, il est évident que tous les droits de propriété lui appartiennent, ou émanent de lui. C'est tout le contraire dans la grande famille, où l'administration générale n'est établie que pour assurer la propriété particulière, qui lui est antérieure. Le principal objet des travaux de toute la maison est de conserver et d'accroître le patrimoine du père, afin qu'il puisse un jour le partager entre ses enfants sans les appauvrir: au lieu que [2]la richesse du fisc n'est qu'un moyen, souvent fort mal entendu, pour maintenir les particuliers dans la paix et dans l'abondance[2]. En un mot, la petite famille est destinée à s'éteindre, et à se résoudre un jour en plusieurs autres familles semblables: mais, la grande étant faite pour durer toujours dans le même état, il faut que la première s'augmente pour se multiplier; et non seulement il suffit que l'autre se conserve, mais on peut prouver aisément que toute augmentation lui est plus préjudiciable qu'utile.

---

[1] This sentence is wanting in the *Encyclopédie*, in the Geneva MS., in Duvillard (1758), in Rey (1772). It appears for the first time in the Geneva Edition of 1782.

[2] The Geneva MS. reads: 'la richesse du prince, loin de rien ajouter au bien-être des particuliers, leur coûte presque toujours la paix et l'abondance.' This is probably what Rousseau originally wrote.

Par plusieurs raisons tirées de la nature de la chose, le père doit commander dans la famille. Premièrement, l'autorité ne doit pas être égale entre le père et la mère; mais il faut que le gouvernement soit un, et que, dans les partages d'avis, il y ait une voix prépondérante qui décide. 2° Quelque légères qu'on veuille supposer les incommodités particulières à la femme, comme elles sont toujours pour elle un intervalle d'inaction, c'est une raison suffisante pour l'exclure de cette primauté: car, quand la balance est parfaitement égale, une paille[1] suffit pour la faire pencher. De plus, le mari doit avoir inspection sur la conduite de sa femme, parce qu'il lui importe de s'assurer que les enfants, qu'il est forcé de reconnaître et de nourrir, n'appartiennent pas à d'autres qu'à lui. La femme, qui n'a rien de semblable à craindre, n'a pas le même droit sur le mari. 3° Les enfants doivent obéir au père, d'abord par nécessité, ensuite par reconnaissance; après avoir reçu de lui leurs besoins durant la moitié de leur vie, ils doivent consacrer l'autre à pourvoir aux siens. 4° À l'égard des domestiques, ils lui doivent aussi leurs services en échange de l'entretien qu'il leur donne, sauf à rompre le marché dès qu'il cesse de leur convenir. Je ne parle point de l'esclavage, parce qu'il est contraire à la nature, et qu'aucun droit ne peut l'autoriser.

Il n'y a rien de tout cela dans la société politique. Loin que le chef ait un intérêt naturel au bonheur des particuliers, il ne lui est pas rare de chercher le sien dans leur misère. La magistrature est-elle héréditaire, c'est souvent un enfant qui commande à des hommes : est-elle élective, mille inconvénients se font sentir dans les élections; et l'on perd, dans l'un et l'autre cas, tous les avantages de la paternité. Si vous n'avez qu'un seul chef, vous êtes à la discrétion d'un maître qui n'a nulle raison de vous aimer; si vous en avez plusieurs, il faut supporter à la fois leur tyrannie et leurs divisions. En un mot, les abus sont inévitables et leurs suites funestes, dans toute société où l'intérêt public et les lois n'ont aucune force naturelle et sont sans cesse attaqués par l'intérêt personnel et les passions du chef et des membres.

Quoique les fonctions du père de famille et du premier magistrat doivent tendre au même but, c'est par des voies si différentes, leur devoir et leurs droits sont tellement distingués, qu'on ne peut les confondre sans se former de fausses idées des lois fondamentales de la société, et sans tomber dans des erreurs fatales au genre humain. En effet, si la voix de la nature est le meilleur conseil

---

[1] Geneva MS. has *un rien*.

que doive écouter un bon père pour bien remplir ses devoirs, elle n'est, pour le magistrat, qu'un faux guide qui travaille sans cesse à l'écarter des siens, et qui l'entraîne tôt ou tard à sa perte ou à celle de l'État, s'il n'est retenu par la plus sublime vertu. La seule précaution nécessaire au père de famille est de se garantir de la dépravation, et d'empêcher que les inclinations naturelles ne se corrompent en lui; mais ce sont elles qui corrompent le magistrat. Pour bien faire, le premier n'a qu'à consulter son cœur; l'autre devient un traître au moment qu'il écoute le sien: sa raison même lui doit être suspecte, et il ne doit suivre d'autre règle que la raison publique, qui est la Loi. Aussi la nature a-t-elle fait une multitude de bons pères de famille; [1]mais, depuis l'existence du monde, la sagesse humaine a fait bien peu de bons magistrats[1].

De tout ce que je viens d'exposer, il s'ensuit que c'est avec raison qu'on a distingué l'*économie publique* de l'*économie particulière*, et que, la Cité n'ayant rien de commun avec la famille que l'obligation qu'ont les chefs de rendre heureux l'un et l'autre, [2]leurs droits ne sauraient dériver de la même source, ni[2] les mêmes règles de conduite convenir à tous les deux. J'ai cru qu'il suffirait de ce peu de lignes pour renverser l'odieux système que le chevalier Filmer a tâché d'établir dans un ouvrage intitulé *Patriarcha*, auquel deux hommes illustres ont fait trop d'honneur en écrivant des livres pour lui répondre[3]. Au reste, cette erreur est fort ancienne, puisque Aristote même, [4]qui l'adopte en certains lieux de ses *Politiques*, juge à propos de la combattre en d'autres[4].

[1] Duvillard (1758) reads: 'mais il est douteux que, depuis l'existence du monde, la sagesse humaine ait jamais fait dix hommes capables de gouverner leurs semblables.' So Rey (1772). Some copies of the *Encyclopédie* (*e.g.* that in the British Museum) read the same; others (*e.g.* that in the Neuchâtel Library) read 'ait jamais fait dix bons magistrats.' This must mean that Rousseau himself altered the sentence as the work went through the press. The reading of the text appears for the first time in the Geneva Edition (1782).

[2] This clause appears for the first time in Edition 1782: *ne sauraient*, in the earlier Editions, occurs between *conduite* and *convenir*. All the authoritative Editions, including that of 1782, read *heureux l'un et l'autre* and *tous les deux*. Hachette has *heureuses l'une et l'autre* and *toutes les deux*.

[3] Sidney, *Discourses concerning Government*; Locke, *Of Civil Government* (I.).

[4] The *Encyclopédie* reads: 'puisque Aristote même a jugé à propos de la combattre par des raisons qu'on peut voir au premier livre de ses *Politiques*.' So Duvillard (1758) and Rey (1772). The reading of the text appears first in Geneva Edition (1782). The subject is discussed in Aristotle's *Politics*, I. ii. ;

Je prie mes lecteurs de bien distinguer encore l'*économie publique*, dont j'ai à parler et que j'appelle *Gouvernement*, de l'autorité suprême que j'appelle *Souveraineté*: distinction qui consiste en ce que l'une a le droit législatif, et oblige, en certains cas, le Corps même de la nation, tandis que l'autre n'a que la puissance exécutrice, et ne peut obliger que les particuliers[1].

[2]Qu'on me permette d'employer pour un moment une comparaison commune et peu exacte à bien des égards, mais propre à me faire mieux entendre.

Le Corps politique, pris individuellement, peut être considéré comme un corps organisé, vivant, et semblable[3] à celui de l'homme. Le pouvoir souverain représente la tête; les lois et les coutumes sont le cerveau, principe des nerfs et siége de l'entendement, de la volonté et des sens, dont les juges et magistrats sont les organes; le commerce, l'industrie et l'agriculture sont la bouche et l'estomac, qui préparent la subsistance commune; les finances publiques sont le sang, qu'une sage *économie*, en faisant les fonctions du cœur, renvoie distribuer par tout le corps la nourriture et la vie; les citoyens sont le corps et les membres qui font mouvoir, vivre et travailler la machine, et qu'on ne saurait blesser en aucune partie qu'aussitôt l'impression douloureuse ne s'en porte au cerveau, si l'animal est dans un état de santé.

La vie de l'un et de l'autre est le *moi* commun au tout, la sensibilité réciproque et la correspondance interne de toutes les parties. Cette communication vient-elle à cesser, l'unité formelle à s'évanouir, et les parties contiguës à n'appartenir plus l'une à l'autre que par juxtaposition; l'homme est mort, ou l'État est dissous.

Le Corps politique est donc aussi un être moral qui a une volonté; et cette volonté générale, qui tend toujours à la conservation

and incidentally in III. xiv. and VII. ii. None of these passages affords any ground for Rousseau's charge of inconsistency. More colour for this may perhaps be drawn from the incidental remarks made in *Ethics*, x. ix.

[1] In *Encycl.* this is followed by *Voyez* POLITIQUE & SOUVERAINETÉ, which is retained in Ed. 1782.

[2] In the rough draft (MS. 7840) this is preceded by the following: 'Si je veux déterminer exactement en quoi consiste l'Économie politique, je trouverai que ses fonctions se réduisent à ces trois principales: administrer les lois, maintenir la liberté civile et pourvoir aux besoins de l'État. Mais pour apercevoir la liaison de ces trois objets il faut remonter au principe qui les unit. Pour entrer en matière, je demande qu'on me permette d'employer,' etc.

[3] Rough draft has 'tout à fait semblable.'

et au bien-être du tout et de chaque partie, et qui est la source des lois, est, pour tous les membres de l'État, par rapport à eux et à lui, la règle du juste et de l'injuste : vérité qui, pour le dire en passant, montre avec combien de sens tant d'écrivains ont traité de vol la subtilité prescrite aux enfants de Lacédémone pour gagner leur frugal repas[1]; comme si tout ce qu'ordonne la Loi pouvait ne pas être légitime. [2]Voyez au mot DROIT la source de ce grand et lumineux principe, dont cet article est le développement[2].

Il est important de remarquer que cette règle de justice, sûre par rapport à tous les citoyens, peut être fautive avec les étrangers; et la raison de ceci est évidente : c'est qu'alors la volonté de l'État, quoique générale par rapport à ses membres, ne l'est plus par rapport aux autres États et à leurs membres, mais devient pour eux une volonté particulière et individuelle, qui a sa règle de justice dans la loi de nature; ce qui rentre également dans le principe établi. Car alors la grande ville du monde devient le Corps politique dont la loi de nature est toujours la volonté générale, et dont les États et peuples divers ne sont que des membres individuels.

De ces mêmes distinctions, appliquées à chaque société politique et à ses membres, découlent les règles les plus universelles et les plus sûres sur lesquelles on puisse juger d'un bon ou d'un mauvais Gouvernement, et en général de la moralité de toutes les actions humaines.

Toute société politique est composée d'autres sociétés plus petites de différentes espèces, dont chacune a ses intérêts et ses maximes. Mais ces sociétés, que chacun aperçoit parce qu'elles ont une forme extérieure et autorisée, ne sont pas les seules qui existent réellement dans l'État; tous les particuliers qu'un intérêt commun réunit en composent autant d'autres, permanentes ou passagères, dont la force n'est pas moins réelle pour être moins apparente, et dont les divers rapports bien observés font la véritable connaissance des mœurs. Ce sont toutes ces associations tacites ou formelles qui modifient de tant de manières les apparences de la volonté publique par l'influence de la leur. La volonté

[1] Compare 'Vous ne parviendrez jamais à faire des sages, si vous ne faites d'abord des polissons : c'était l'éducation des Spartiates ; au lieu de les coller sur les livres, on commençait par leur apprendre à voler leur dîner.' *Émile*, Liv. II.

[2] This sentence is wanting in Editions of 1758 and 1772. In the rough draft it is replaced by 'Voyez *Droit*.' See below, pp. 425—7.

de ces sociétés particulières a toujours deux relations : pour les membres de l'association, c'est une volonté générale ; pour la grande société, c'est une volonté particulière, qui très souvent se trouve droite au premier égard, et vicieuse au second. Tel peut être prêtre dévot, ou brave soldat, ou patricien zélé, et mauvais citoyen. Telle délibération peut être avantageuse à la petite communauté et très pernicieuse [1]à la grande[1]. Il est vrai que, les sociétés particulières étant toujours subordonnées à celles qui les contiennent, on doit obéir à celle-ci préférablement aux autres ; que les devoirs du citoyen vont avant ceux du sénateur, et ceux de l'homme avant ceux du citoyen. Mais malheureusement l'intérêt personnel se trouve toujours en raison inverse du devoir, et augmente à mesure que l'association devient plus étroite et l'engagement moins sacré : preuve invincible que la volonté la plus générale est aussi toujours la plus juste, et que la voix du peuple est en effet la voix de Dieu.

Il ne s'ensuit pas pour cela que les délibérations publiques soient toujours équitables ; elles peuvent ne l'être pas lorsqu'il s'agit d'affaires étrangères ; j'en ai dit la raison. Ainsi il n'est pas impossible qu'une République bien gouvernée fasse une guerre injuste. Il ne l'est pas non plus que le Conseil d'une démocratie passe de mauvais décrets et condamne les innocents : mais cela n'arrivera jamais que le peuple ne soit séduit par des intérêts particuliers, qu'avec du crédit et de l'éloquence quelques hommes adroits sauront substituer aux siens. Alors autre chose sera la délibération publique, et autre chose la volonté générale. Qu'on ne m'oppose donc point la démocratie d'Athènes, parce qu'Athènes n'était point en effet une démocratie, mais une aristocratie très tyrannique, gouvernée par des savants et des orateurs. Examinez avec soin ce qui se passe dans une délibération quelconque, et vous verrez que la volonté générale est toujours pour le bien commun ; mais très souvent il se fait une scission secrète, une confédération tacite, qui, pour des vues particulières, sait éluder la disposition naturelle de l'assemblée. Alors le Corps social se divise réellement en d'autres dont les membres prennent une volonté générale, bonne et juste à l'égard de ces nouveaux corps, injuste et mauvaise à l'égard du tout dont chacun d'eux se démembre.

On voit avec quelle facilité l'on explique, à l'aide de ces principes, les contradictions apparentes qu'on remarque dans la conduite de tant d'hommes remplis de scrupule et d'honneur à certains égards, trompeurs et fripons à d'autres ; foulant aux pieds

[1] Some copies of *Encycl.* have *à l'État*. Others, and all the Eds., as above.

les plus sacrés devoirs, et fidèles jusqu'à la mort à des engagements souvent illégitimes. C'est ainsi que les hommes les plus corrompus rendent toujours quelque sorte d'hommage à la foi publique; c'est ainsi, [1]comme on l'a remarqué à l'article *Droit*[1], que les brigands mêmes, qui sont les ennemis de la vertu dans la grande société, en adorent le simulacre dans leurs cavernes[2].

En établissant la volonté générale pour premier principe de l'*économie* publique et règle fondamentale du Gouvernement, je n'ai pas cru nécessaire d'examiner sérieusement si les magistrats appartiennent au peuple ou le peuple aux magistrats, et si, dans les affaires publiques, on doit consulter le bien de l'État ou celui des chefs. Depuis longtemps cette question a été décidée d'une manière par la pratique, et d'une autre par la raison; et en général ce serait une grande folie d'espérer que ceux qui dans le fait sont les maîtres préféreront un autre intérêt au leur. Il serait donc à propos de diviser encore l'*économie* publique en populaire et tyrannique. La première est celle de tout État où règne entre le peuple et les chefs unité d'intérêt et de volonté : l'autre existera nécessairement partout où le Gouvernement et le peuple auront des intérêts différents, et par conséquent des volontés opposées. Les maximes de celle-ci sont inscrites au long dans les archives de l'histoire et dans les satires de Machiavel[3]. Les autres ne se trouvent que dans les écrits des philosophes qui osent réclamer les droits de l'humanité.

I. La première et plus importante maxime du Gouvernement légitime ou populaire, c'est-à-dire de celui qui a pour objet le bien du peuple, est donc, comme je l'ai dit, de suivre en tout la volonté générale. Mais pour la suivre il faut la connaître, et surtout la bien distinguer de la volonté particulière, en commençant par soi-même : distinction toujours fort difficile à faire, et pour laquelle il n'appartient qu'à la plus sublime vertu de donner de suffisantes lumières. Comme pour vouloir il faut être libre, une autre difficulté, qui n'est guère moindre, est d'assurer à la fois la liberté publique et l'autorité du Gouvernement. Cherchez les motifs qui ont porté les hommes, unis par leurs besoins mutuels dans la grande société, à s'unir plus étroitement par des sociétés civiles, vous n'en trouverez point d'autre que celui d'assurer les biens, la

---

[1] This clause is omitted in Ed. 1782 and all later Eds.
[2] This is a reference to Diderot's article, *Droit naturel*. See below, p. 433.
[3] The same view of Machiavelli is taken in the *Contrat social*, III. vi., 'Le *Prince* de Machiavel est le livre des républicains'; and 'Machiavel était un honnête homme et bon citoyen.'

vie et la liberté de chaque membre par la protection de tous. Or, comment forcer des hommes à défendre la liberté de l'un d'entre eux sans porter atteinte à celle des autres ? et comment pourvoir aux besoins publics sans altérer la propriété particulière de ceux qu'on force d'y contribuer ? De quelques sophismes qu'on puisse colorer tout cela, il est certain que, si l'on peut contraindre ma volonté, je ne suis plus libre ; et que je ne suis plus maître de mon bien, si quelque autre peut y toucher. [1]Cette difficulté, qui devait sembler insurmontable, a été levée, avec la première, par la plus sublime de toutes les institutions humaines, ou plutôt par une inspiration céleste, qui apprit à l'homme à imiter ici-bas les décrets immuables de la Divinité. Par quel art inconcevable a-t-on pu trouver le moyen d'assujettir les hommes pour les rendre libres ? d'employer au service de l'État les biens, les bras et la vie même de tous ses membres, sans les contraindre et sans les consulter ? d'enchaîner leur volonté de leur propre aveu ? de faire valoir leur consentement contre leur refus, et de les forcer à se punir eux-mêmes quand ils font ce qu'ils n'ont pas voulu ? Comment se peut-il faire qu'ils obéissent et que personne ne commande, qu'ils servent et n'aient point de maître ; d'autant plus libres en effet, que, sous une apparente sujétion, nul ne perd de sa liberté que ce qui peut nuire à celle d'un autre ? Ces prodiges sont l'ouvrage de la Loi. C'est à la Loi seule que les hommes doivent la justice et la liberté ; c'est cet organe salutaire de la volonté de tous qui rétablit dans le droit l'égalité naturelle entre les hommes ; c'est cette voix céleste qui dicte à chaque citoyen les préceptes de la raison publique, et lui apprend à agir selon les maximes de son propre jugement, et à n'être pas en contradiction avec lui-même[1]. C'est elle seule aussi que les chefs doivent faire parler quand ils commandent ; car, sitôt qu'indépendamment des lois un homme en prétend soumettre un autre à sa volonté privée, il sort à l'instant de l'état civil et se met vis-à-vis de lui dans le pur état de nature, où l'obéissance n'est jamais prescrite que par la nécessité.

Le plus pressant intérêt du chef, de même que son devoir le plus indispensable, est donc de veiller à l'observation des lois dont il est le ministre, et sur lesquelles est fondée toute son autorité. S'il doit les faire observer aux autres, à plus forte raison doit-il les observer lui-même, qui jouit de toute leur faveur : car son exemple est de telle force, que, quand même le peuple voudrait bien souffrir qu'il s'affranchît du joug de la Loi, il devrait se garder de profiter

---

[1] This passage reappears in the first draft of the *Contrat social*, I. vii. See below, p. 475. In the final clause, *C. S.* has *sans cesse* after *à n'être pas*.

d'une si dangereuse prérogative, que d'autres s'efforceraient bientôt d'usurper à leur tour, et souvent à son préjudice. Au fond, comme tous les engagements de la société sont réciproques par leur nature, il n'est pas possible de se mettre au-dessus de la Loi sans renoncer à ses avantages; et personne ne doit rien à quiconque prétend ne rien devoir à personne. Par la même raison nulle exemption de la Loi ne sera jamais accordée, à quelque titre que ce puisse être, dans un Gouvernement bien policé. Les citoyens mêmes qui ont bien mérité de la patrie doivent être récompensés par des honneurs, et jamais par des priviléges; car la République est à la veille de sa ruine, sitôt que quelqu'un peut penser qu'il est beau de ne pas obéir aux lois. Mais si jamais la noblesse, ou le militaire, ou quelque autre ordre de l'État, adoptait une pareille maxime, tout serait perdu sans ressource.

La puissance des lois dépend encore plus de leur propre sagesse que de la sévérité de leurs ministres, et la volonté publique tire son plus grand poids de la raison qui l'a dictée: c'est pour cela que Platon regarde comme une précaution très importante de mettre toujours à la tête des édits un préambule raisonné qui en montre la justice et l'utilité[1]. En effet, la première des lois est de respecter les lois: la rigueur des châtiments n'est qu'une vaine ressource imaginée par de petits esprits pour substituer la terreur à ce respect qu'ils ne peuvent obtenir. On a toujours remarqué que les pays où les supplices sont le plus terribles sont aussi ceux où ils sont le plus fréquents; de sorte que la cruauté des peines ne marque guère que la multitude des infracteurs, et qu'en punissant tout avec la même sévérité l'on force les coupables de commettre des crimes pour échapper à la punition de leurs fautes.

Mais quoique le Gouvernement ne soit pas le maître de la Loi, c'est beaucoup d'en être le garant et d'avoir mille moyens de la faire aimer. Ce n'est qu'en cela que consiste le talent de régner. Quand on a la force en main, il n'y a point d'art à faire trembler tout le monde, et il n'y en a pas même beaucoup à gagner les cœurs; car l'expérience a depuis longtemps appris au peuple à tenir grand compte à ses chefs de tout le mal qu'ils ne lui font pas, et à les adorer quand il n'en est pas haï. Un imbécile obéi peut, comme un autre, punir les forfaits: le véritable homme d'État sait les prévenir; c'est sur les volontés encore plus que sur les actions qu'il étend son respectable empire. S'il pouvait obtenir que tout le monde fît bien, il n'aurait lui-même plus rien à faire,

[1] *De Legibus*, Books IV. and V. pp. 720—735.

et le chef-d'œuvre de ses travaux serait de pouvoir rester oisif. Il est certain, du moins, que le plus grand talent des chefs est de déguiser leur pouvoir pour le rendre moins odieux, et de conduire l'État si paisiblement qu'il semble n'avoir pas besoin de conducteurs.

Je conclus donc que, comme le premier devoir du Législateur est de conformer les lois à la volonté générale, la première règle de l'*économie* publique est que l'administration soit conforme aux lois. C'en sera même assez pour que l'État ne soit pas mal gouverné, si le Législateur a pourvu, comme il le devait, à tout ce qu'exigeaient les lieux, le climat, le sol, les mœurs, le voisinage, et tous les rapports particuliers du peuple qu'il avait à instituer. Ce n'est pas qu'il ne reste encore une infinité de détails de police et d'*économie*, abandonnés à la sagesse du Gouvernement. Mais il a toujours deux règles infaillibles pour se bien conduire dans ces occasions : l'une est l'esprit de la Loi, qui doit servir à la décision des cas qu'elle n'a pu prévoir ; l'autre est la volonté générale, source et supplément de toutes les lois, et qui doit toujours être consultée à leur défaut. Comment, me dira-t-on, connaître la volonté générale dans les cas où elle ne s'est point expliquée ? faudra-t-il assembler toute la nation à chaque événement imprévu ? Il faudra d'autant moins l'assembler, qu'il n'est pas sûr que sa décision fût l'expression de la volonté générale ; que ce moyen est impraticable dans un grand peuple, et qu'il est rarement nécessaire quand le Gouvernement est bien intentionné. Car les chefs savent assez que la volonté générale est toujours pour le parti le plus favorable à l'intérêt public, c'est-à-dire le plus équitable ; de sorte qu'il ne faut qu'être juste pour s'assurer de suivre la volonté générale. Souvent, quand on la choque trop ouvertement, elle se laisse apercevoir malgré le frein terrible de l'autorité publique. Je cherche le plus près qu'il m'est possible[1] les exemples à suivre en pareil cas. À la Chine, le prince a pour maxime constante de donner le tort à ses officiers dans toutes les altercations qui s'élèvent entre eux et le peuple. Le pain est-il cher dans une province, l'intendant est mis en prison. Se fait-il dans une autre une émeute, le gouverneur est cassé, et chaque mandarin répond sur sa tête de tout le mal qui arrive dans son département. Ce n'est pas qu'on n'examine ensuite l'affaire dans un procès régulier ; mais une longue expérience en a fait prévenir ainsi le jugement. L'on a rarement en cela quelque injustice à

---

[1] A satiric stroke against the Governments of modern Europe.

réparer ; et l'empereur, persuadé que la clameur publique ne s'élève jamais sans sujet, démêle toujours, au travers des cris séditieux qu'il punit, de justes griefs qu'il redresse.

C'est beaucoup que d'avoir fait régner l'ordre et la paix dans toutes les parties de la République ; c'est beaucoup que l'État soit tranquille et la Loi respectée. Mais, si l'on ne fait rien de plus, il y aura dans tout cela plus d'apparence que de réalité, et le Gouvernement se fera difficilement obéir s'il se borne à l'obéissance. S'il est bon de savoir employer les hommes tels qu'ils sont, il vaut beaucoup mieux encore les rendre tels qu'on a besoin qu'ils soient : l'autorité la plus absolue est celle qui pénètre jusqu'à l'intérieur de l'homme, et ne s'exerce pas moins sur la volonté que sur les actions. Il est certain que les peuples sont à la longue ce que le Gouvernement les fait être : guerriers, citoyens, hommes, quand il le veut ; populace et canaille, quand il lui plaît : et tout prince qui méprise ses sujets se déshonore lui-même en montrant qu'il n'a pas su les rendre estimables. Formez donc des hommes, si vous voulez commander à des hommes ; si vous voulez qu'on obéisse aux lois, faites qu'on les aime, et que, pour faire ce qu'on doit, il suffise de songer qu'on le doit faire. C'était là le grand art des Gouvernements anciens, dans ces temps reculés où les philosophes donnaient des lois aux peuples, et n'employaient leur autorité qu'à les rendre sages et heureux. De là tant de lois somptuaires, tant de règlements sur les mœurs, tant de maximes publiques admises ou rejetées avec le plus grand soin. Les tyrans mêmes n'oubliaient pas cette importante partie de l'administration, et on les voyait attentifs à corrompre les mœurs de leurs esclaves avec autant de soin qu'en avaient les magistrats à corriger celles de leurs concitoyens. Mais nos Gouvernements modernes, qui croient avoir tout fait quand ils ont tiré de l'argent, n'imaginent pas même qu'il soit nécessaire ou possible d'aller jusque-là.

II. Seconde règle essentielle de l'*économie* publique, non moins importante que la première. Voulez-vous que la volonté générale soit accomplie ? faites que toutes les volontés particulières s'y rapportent ; et comme la vertu n'est que cette conformité de la volonté particulière à la générale, pour dire la même chose en un mot, faites régner la vertu.

Si les politiques étaient moins aveuglés par leur ambition, ils verraient combien il est impossible qu'aucun établissement, quel qu'il soit, puisse marcher selon l'esprit de son institution, s'il n'est dirigé selon la loi du devoir ; ils sentiraient que le plus grand ressort de l'autorité publique est dans le cœur des citoyens, et que rien ne peut suppléer aux mœurs pour le maintien du Gouvernement. Non seulement il n'y a que des gens de bien qui sachent administrer les lois, mais il n'y a dans le fond que d'honnêtes gens qui sachent leur obéir. Celui qui vient à bout de braver les remords ne tardera pas à braver les supplices : châtiment moins rigoureux, moins continuel, et auquel on a du moins l'espoir d'échapper ; et, quelques précautions qu'on prenne, ceux qui n'attendent que l'impunité pour mal faire ne manquent guère de moyens d'éluder la Loi ou d'échapper à la peine. Alors, comme tous les intérêts particuliers se réunissent contre l'intérêt général, qui n'est plus celui de personne, les vices publics ont plus de force pour énerver les lois que les lois n'en ont pour réprimer les vices ; et la corruption du peuple et des chefs s'étend enfin jusqu'au Gouvernement, quelque sage qu'il puisse être. Le pire de tous les abus est de n'obéir en apparence aux lois que pour les enfreindre en effet avec sûreté. Bientôt les meilleures lois deviennent les plus funestes : il vaudrait mieux cent fois qu'elles n'existassent pas ; ce serait une ressource qu'on aurait encore quand il n'en reste plus. Dans une pareille situation l'on ajoute vainement édits sur édits, règlements sur règlements : tout cela ne sert qu'à introduire d'autres abus sans corriger les premiers. Plus vous multipliez les lois, plus vous les rendez méprisables ; et tous les surveillants que vous instituez ne sont que de nouveaux infracteurs destinés à partager avec les anciens, ou à faire leur pillage à part. Bientôt le prix de la vertu devient celui du brigandage : les hommes les plus vils sont les plus accrédités ; plus ils sont grands, plus ils sont méprisables ; leur infamie éclate dans leurs dignités, et ils sont déshonorés par leurs honneurs. S'ils achètent les suffrages des chefs ou la protection des femmes, c'est pour vendre à leur tour la justice, le devoir et l'État ; et le peuple, qui ne voit pas que ses vices sont la première cause de ses malheurs, murmure et s'écrie en gémissant : ' Tout mes maux ne viennent que de ceux que je paye pour m'en garantir.'

C'est alors qu'à la voix du devoir, qui ne parle plus dans les cœurs, les chefs sont forcés de substituer le cri de la terreur ou le leurre d'un intérêt apparent dont ils trompent leurs créatures. C'est alors qu'il faut recourir à toutes les petites et méprisables ruses qu'ils appellent *maximes d'État* et *mystères du cabinet.* Tout ce qui reste de vigueur au Gouvernement est employé par ses membres à se perdre et supplanter l'un l'autre, tandis que les affaires demeurent abandonnées, ou ne se font qu'à mesure que l'intérêt personnel le demande et selon qu'il les dirige. Enfin, toute l'habileté de ces grands politiques est de fasciner tellement les yeux de ceux dont ils ont besoin, que chacun croie travailler pour son intérêt en travaillant pour le leur; je dis *le leur*, si tant est qu'en effet le véritable intérêt des chefs soit d'anéantir les peuples pour les soumettre, et de ruiner[1] leur propre bien pour s'en assurer la possession.

Mais quand les citoyens aiment leur devoir, et que les dépositaires de l'autorité publique s'appliquent sincèrement à nourrir cet amour par leur exemple et par leurs soins, toutes les difficultés s'évanouissent; l'administration prend une facilité qui la dispense de cet art ténébreux dont la noirceur fait tout le mystère. Ces esprits vastes, si dangereux et si admirés, tous ces grands ministres dont la gloire se confond avec les malheurs du peuple, ne sont plus regrettés; les mœurs publiques suppléent au génie des chefs; et plus la vertu règne, moins les talents sont nécessaires. L'ambition même est mieux servie par le devoir que par l'usurpation. Le peuple, convaincu que ses chefs ne travaillent qu'à faire son bonheur, les dispense par sa déférence de travailler à affermir leur pouvoir; et l'histoire nous montre en mille endroits que l'autorité qu'il accorde à ceux qu'il aime et dont il est aimé est cent fois plus absolue que toute la tyrannie des usurpateurs. Ceci ne signifie pas que le Gouvernement doive craindre d'user de son pouvoir, mais qu'il n'en doit user que d'une manière légitime. On trouvera dans l'histoire mille exemples de chefs ambitieux ou pusillanimes que la mollesse ou l'orgueil ont perdus; aucun qui se soit mal trouvé de n'être qu'équitable. Mais on ne doit pas confondre la négligence avec la modération, ni la douceur avec la faiblesse. Il faut être sévère pour être juste. Souffrir la méchanceté qu'on a le droit et le pouvoir de réprimer, c'est être méchant soi-même. *Sicuti enim est aliquando misericordia puniens, ita est crudelitas parcens*[2].

Ce n'est pas assez de dire aux citoyens: *Soyez bons*; il faut leur apprendre à l'être; et l'exemple même, qui est à cet égard la première leçon, n'est pas le seul moyen qu'il faille employer. L'amour de la patrie est le plus efficace; car, comme je l'ai déjà dit, tout homme est vertueux quand sa volonté particulière est conforme en tout à la volonté générale; et nous voulons volontiers ce que veulent les gens que nous aimons.

[1] Some copies of *Encyclopédie* have *retirer*, by a slip. Duvillard and all subsequent Editions have *ruiner*.
[2] This quotation appears for the first time in the Geneva Edition (1782). It is taken from Augustine, *Ep.* CLII. (ed. Migne).

Il semble que le sentiment de l'humanité s'évapore et s'affaiblisse en s'étendant sur toute la terre, et que nous ne saurions être touchés des calamités de la Tartarie ou du Japon, comme de celles d'un peuple européen. Il faut en quelque manière borner et comprimer l'intérêt et la commisération pour lui donner de l'activité. Or, comme ce penchant en nous ne peut être utile qu'à ceux avec qui nous avons à vivre, il est bon que l'humanité, concentrée entre les concitoyens, prenne en eux une nouvelle force par l'habitude de se voir et par l'intérêt commun qui les réunit. Il est certain que les plus grands prodiges de vertu ont été produits par l'amour de la patrie : ce sentiment doux et vif, qui joint la force de l'amour-propre à toute la beauté de la vertu, lui donne une énergie qui, sans la défigurer, en fait la plus héroïque de toutes les passions. C'est lui qui produisit tant d'actions immortelles dont l'éclat éblouit nos faibles yeux, et tant de grands hommes dont les antiques vertus passent pour des fables depuis que l'amour de la patrie est tourné en dérision. Ne nous en étonnons pas ; les transports des cœurs tendres paraissent autant de chimères à quiconque ne les a point sentis : et l'amour de la patrie, plus vif et plus délicieux cent fois que celui d'une maîtresse, ne se conçoit de même qu'en l'éprouvant : mais il est aisé de remarquer dans tous les cœurs qu'il échauffe, dans toutes les actions qu'il inspire, cette ardeur bouillante et sublime dont ne brille pas la plus pure vertu quand elle en est séparée. Osons opposer Socrate même à Caton : l'un était plus philosophe, et l'autre plus citoyen. Athènes était déjà perdue, et Socrate n'avait plus de patrie que le monde entier : Caton porta toujours la sienne au fond de son cœur ; il ne vivait que pour elle et ne put lui survivre. La vertu de Socrate est celle du plus sage des hommes ; mais entre César et Pompée, Caton semble un dieu parmi des[1] mortels. L'un instruit quelques particuliers, combat les sophistes, et meurt pour la vérité : l'autre défend l'État, la liberté, les lois, contre les conquérants du monde, et quitte enfin la terre quand il n'y voit plus de patrie à servir. Un digne élève de Socrate serait le plus vertueux de ses contemporains ; un digne émule de Caton en serait le plus grand. La vertu du premier ferait son bonheur ; le second chercherait son bonheur dans celui de tous. Nous serions instruits par l'un et conduits par l'autre : et cela seul déciderait de la préférence ; car on n'a jamais fait un peuple de sages, mais il n'est pas impossible de rendre un peuple heureux.

Voulons-nous que les peuples soient vertueux ? commençons

[1] Hachette has *les*. *Encycl.* and Ed. 1782, *des*. So Ed. 1801.

donc par leur faire aimer la patrie. Mais comment l'aimeront-ils, si la patrie n'est rien de plus pour eux que pour des étrangers, et qu'elle ne leur accorde que ce qu'elle ne peut refuser à personne ? Ce serait bien pis s'ils n'y jouissaient pas même de la sûreté civile, et que leurs biens, leur vie ou leur liberté, fussent à la discrétion des hommes puissants, sans qu'il leur fût possible ou permis d'oser réclamer les lois. Alors, soumis aux devoirs de l'état civil, sans jouir même des droits de l'état de nature et sans pouvoir employer leurs forces pour se défendre, ils seraient par conséquent dans la pire condition où se puissent trouver des hommes libres, et le mot de *patrie* ne pourrait avoir pour eux qu'un sens odieux ou ridicule. Il ne faut pas croire que l'on puisse offenser ou couper un bras, que la douleur ne s'en porte à la tête ; et il n'est pas plus croyable que la volonté générale consente qu'un membre de l'État, quel qu'il soit, en blesse ou détruise un autre[1], qu'il ne l'est que les doigts d'un homme usant de sa raison aillent lui crever les yeux. La sûreté particulière est tellement liée avec la confédération publique, que, sans les égards que l'on doit à la faiblesse humaine, cette convention serait dissoute par le droit, s'il périssait dans l'État un seul citoyen qu'on eût pu secourir, si l'on en retenait à tort un seul en prison, et s'il se perdait un seul procès avec une injustice évidente. Car, les conventions fondamentales étant enfreintes, on ne voit plus quel droit ni quel intérêt pourrait maintenir le peuple dans l'union sociale, à moins qu'il n'y fût retenu par la seule force, qui fait la dissolution de l'état civil.

En effet, l'engagement du Corps de la nation n'est-il pas de pourvoir à la conservation du dernier de ses membres avec autant de soin qu'à celle de tous les autres ? et le salut d'un citoyen est-il moins la cause commune que celui de tout l'État ? Qu'on nous dise qu'il est bon qu'un seul périsse pour tous ; j'admirerai cette sentence dans la bouche d'un digne et vertueux patriote qui se consacre volontairement et par devoir à la mort pour le salut de son pays. Mais si l'on entend qu'il soit permis au Gouvernement de sacrifier un innocent au salut de la multitude, je tiens cette maxime pour une des plus exécrables que jamais la tyrannie ait inventées[2], la plus fausse qu'on puisse avancer, la plus dangereuse qu'on puisse admettre, et la plus directement opposée aux lois fondamentales de la société. Loin qu'un seul doive périr pour

---

[1] The rough draft has the reservation 'hors le cas de la conservation publique ou particulière.'
[2] So Ed. 1772 (Rey, Amsterdam, 11 vols. 8vo). *Encycl.* and Ed. 1782 have *inventée*.

tous, tous ont engagé leurs biens et leurs vies à la défense de chacun d'eux, afin que la faiblesse particulière fût toujours protégée par la force publique, et chaque membre par tout l'État. Après avoir par supposition retranché du peuple un individu après l'autre, pressez les partisans de cette maxime à mieux expliquer ce qu'ils entendent par *le Corps de l'État*; et vous verrez qu'ils le réduiront, à la fin, à un petit nombre d'hommes qui ne sont pas le peuple, mais les officiers du peuple; et qui, s'étant obligés par un serment particulier à périr eux-mêmes pour son salut, prétendent prouver par là que c'est à lui de périr pour le leur.

Veut-on trouver des exemples de la protection que l'État doit à ses membres et du respect qu'il doit à leurs personnes? ce n'est que chez les plus illustres et les plus courageuses nations de la terre qu'il faut les chercher, et il n'y a guère que les peuples libres où l'on sache ce que vaut un homme. À Sparte, on sait en quelle perplexité se trouvait toute la République lorsqu'il était question de punir un citoyen coupable. En Macédoine, la vie d'un homme était une affaire si importante, que, dans toute la grandeur d'Alexandre, ce puissant monarque n'eût osé de sang-froid faire mourir un Macédonien criminel, que l'accusé n'eût comparu pour se défendre devant ses concitoyens, et n'eût été condamné par eux. Mais les Romains se distinguèrent au-dessus de tous les peuples de la terre par les égards du Gouvernement pour les particuliers, et par son attention scrupuleuse à respecter les droits inviolables de tous les membres de l'État. Il n'y avait rien de si sacré que la vie des simples citoyens; il ne fallait pas moins que l'assemblée de tout le peuple pour en condamner un. Le Sénat même ni les Consuls, dans toute leur majesté, n'en avaient pas le droit; et, chez le plus puissant peuple du monde, le crime et la peine d'un citoyen était[1] une désolation publique. Aussi parut-il si dur d'en verser le sang pour quelque crime que ce pût être, que, par la loi *Porcia*, la peine de mort fut commuée en celle de l'exil, pour tous ceux qui voudraient survivre à la perte d'une si douce patrie. [2]Tout respirait à Rome et dans les armées cet amour des concitoyens les uns pour les autres, et ce respect pour le nom romain qui élevait le courage et animait la vertu de quiconque avait l'honneur de le porter. Le chapeau d'un citoyen délivré d'esclavage, la couronne

[1] Ed. 1801 and Hachette read *étaient*, against all the early Eds.
[2] In the rough draft appears here the following sentence, eventually cancelled : ' Ce sage et vertueux peuple connaissait en quoi consistait les vrais trésors de l'État, et préférait dans la pompe des triomphes la délivrance d'un seul Romain à toutes les richesses des vaincus.'

civique de celui qui avait sauvé la vie à un autre, étaient ce qu'on regardait avec le plus de plaisir dans la pompe des triomphes ; et il est à remarquer que, des couronnes dont on honorait à la guerre les belles actions, il n'y avait que la civique et celle des triomphateurs qui fussent d'herbe et de feuilles : toutes les autres n'étaient que d'or. C'est ainsi que Rome fut vertueuse et devint la maîtresse du monde. Chefs ambitieux, un pâtre gouverne ses chiens et ses troupeaux, et n'est que le dernier des hommes ! S'il est beau de commander, c'est quand ceux qui nous obéissent peuvent nous honorer. Respectez donc vos concitoyens, et vous vous rendrez respectables ; respectez la liberté, et votre puissance augmentera tous les jours ; ne passez jamais vos droits, et bientôt ils seront sans bornes.

Que la patrie se montre donc[1] la mère commune des citoyens ; que les avantages dont ils jouissent dans leur pays le leur rendent cher ; que le Gouvernement leur laisse assez de part à l'administration publique pour sentir qu'ils sont chez eux, et que les lois ne soient à leurs yeux que les garants de la commune liberté. Ces droits, tout beaux qu'ils sont, appartiennent à tous les hommes : mais, sans paraître les attaquer directement, la mauvaise volonté des chefs en réduit aisément l'effet à rien. La Loi dont on abuse sert à la fois au puissant d'arme offensive et de bouclier contre le faible ; et le prétexte du bien public est toujours le plus dangereux fléau du peuple[2]. Ce qu'il y a de plus nécessaire et peut-être de plus difficile dans le Gouvernement, c'est une intégrité sévère à rendre justice à tous, et surtout à protéger le pauvre contre la tyrannie du riche. Le plus grand mal est déjà fait, quand on a des pauvres à défendre et des riches à contenir. C'est sur la médiocrité seule que s'exerce toute la force des lois ; elles sont également impuissantes contre les trésors du riche et contre la misère du pauvre ; le premier les élude, le second leur échappe ; l'un brise la toile, et l'autre passe au travers.

C'est donc une des plus importantes affaires du Gouvernement de prévenir l'extrême inégalité des fortunes, non en enlevant les trésors à leurs possesseurs, mais en ôtant à tous les moyens d'en

---

[1] *donc* wanting in some copies of *Encyclopédie* ; present in others, in Duvillard (1758) and all subsequent Editions.

[2] Compare '*Bien publique, bonheur des sujets* : mots à jamais proscrits du cabinet, et si lourdement employés dans les édits publics qu'ils n'annoncent jamais que des ordres funestes, et que le peuple gémit d'avance quand ses maîtres lui parlent de leurs soins paternels.' *Jugement sur la paix perpétuelle.* See below, p. 389.

accumuler; ni en bâtissant des hôpitaux pour les pauvres, mais en garantissant les citoyens de le devenir. Les hommes inégalement distribués sur le territoire, et entassés dans un lieu tandis que les autres se dépeuplent; les arts d'agrément et de pure industrie favorisés aux dépens des métiers utiles et pénibles; l'agriculture sacrifiée au commerce; le publicain rendu nécessaire par la mauvaise administration des deniers de l'État[1]; enfin, la vénalité poussée à tel excès, que la considération se compte avec les pistoles, et que les vertus mêmes se vendent à prix d'argent: telles sont les causes les plus sensibles de l'opulence et de la misère, de l'intérêt particulier substitué à l'intérêt public, de la haine mutuelle des citoyens, de leur indifférence pour la cause commune, de la corruption du peuple, et de l'affaiblissement de tous les ressorts du Gouvernement. Tels sont par conséquent les maux qu'on guérit difficilement quand ils se font sentir, mais qu'une sage administration doit prévenir, pour maintenir avec les bonnes mœurs le respect pour les lois, l'amour de la patrie, et la vigueur de la volonté générale.

Mais toutes ces précautions seront insuffisantes, si l'on ne s'y prend de plus loin encore. Je finis cette partie de l'*économie* publique par où j'aurais dû la commencer. La patrie ne peut subsister sans la liberté, ni la liberté sans la vertu, ni la vertu sans les citoyens. Vous aurez tout si vous formez des citoyens; sans cela vous n'aurez que de méchants esclaves, à commencer par les chefs de l'État. Or, former des citoyens n'est pas l'affaire d'un jour; et, pour les avoir hommes, il faut les instruire enfants. Qu'on me dise que quiconque a des hommes à gouverner ne doit pas chercher hors de leur nature une perfection dont ils ne sont pas susceptibles; qu'il ne doit pas vouloir détruire en eux les passions[2], et que l'exécution d'un pareil projet ne serait pas plus désirable que possible. Je conviendrai d'autant mieux de tout cela, qu'un homme qui n'aurait point de passions serait certainement un fort mauvais citoyen. Mais il faut convenir aussi que, si l'on n'apprend point aux hommes à n'aimer rien, il n'est pas impossible de leur apprendre à aimer un objet plutôt qu'un autre, et ce qui est véritablement beau, plutôt que ce qui est difforme. Si, par exemple, on les exerce assez tôt à ne jamais regarder leur individu que par ses relations avec le Corps de l'État, et à n'apercevoir, pour ainsi dire, leur

[1] Compare 'à nul prix que ce puisse être, il ne faut point de publicain dans l'État.' *Projet de Constitution pour la Corse*; Vol. II. p. 340.
[2] The rough draft adds 'quand même à la place des passions on pourrait substituer la sagesse.'

propre existence que comme une partie de la sienne, ils pourront parvenir enfin à s'identifier en quelque sorte avec ce plus grand tout, à se sentir membres de la patrie, à l'aimer de ce sentiment exquis que tout homme isolé n'a que pour soi-même, à élever perpétuellement leur âme à ce grand objet, et à transformer ainsi en une vertu sublime cette disposition dangereuse d'où naissent tous nos vices. Non seulement la philosophie démontre la possibilité de ces nouvelles directions, mais l'histoire en fournit mille exemples éclatants : s'ils sont si rares parmi nous, c'est que personne ne se soucie qu'il y ait des citoyens, et qu'on s'avise encore moins de s'y prendre assez tôt pour les former. Il n'est plus temps de changer nos inclinations naturelles quand elles ont pris leur cours et que l'habitude s'est jointe à l'amour-propre ; il n'est plus temps de nous tirer hors de nous-mêmes, quand une fois le *moi humain* concentré dans nos cœurs y a acquis cette méprisable activité qui absorbe toute vertu et fait la vie des petites âmes. Comment l'amour de la patrie pourrait-il germer au milieu de tant d'autres passions qui l'étouffent ? et que reste-t-il pour les concitoyens d'un cœur déjà partagé entre l'avarice, une maîtresse, et la vanité ?

C'est du premier moment de la vie qu'il faut apprendre à mériter de vivre ; et, comme on participe en naissant aux droits des citoyens, l'instant de notre naissance doit être le commencement de l'exercice de nos devoirs. S'il y a des lois pour l'âge mûr, il doit y en avoir pour l'enfance, qui enseignent à obéir aux autres ; et, comme on ne laisse pas la raison de chaque homme unique arbitre de ses devoirs, on doit d'autant moins abandonner aux lumières et aux préjugés des pères l'éducation de leurs enfants, qu'elle importe à l'État encore plus qu'aux pères. [1]Car, selon le cours de la nature, la mort du père lui dérobe souvent les derniers fruits de cette éducation, mais la patrie en sent tôt ou tard les effets ; l'État demeure, et la famille se dissout. Que si l'autorité publique, en prenant la place des pères et se chargeant de cette importante fonction, acquiert leurs droits en remplissant leurs devoirs, ils ont d'autant moins sujet de s'en plaindre, qu'à cet égard ils ne font proprement que changer de nom, et qu'ils auront en commun, sous le nom de *citoyens*, la même autorité sur leurs enfants qu'ils exerçaient séparément sous le nom de *pères*, et n'en seront pas moins obéis en parlant au nom de la Loi, qu'ils l'étaient en parlant au nom de la nature. L'éducation publique, sous des règles

---

[1] In the rough draft is the following clause, subsequently cancelled : 'Car ils pourraient en faire de très bons fils et de très mauvais citoyens.'

prescrites par le Gouvernement, et sous des magistrats établis par le souverain, est donc une des maximes fondamentales du Gouvernement populaire ou légitime[1]. Si les enfants sont élevés en commun dans le sein de l'égalité, s'ils sont imbus des lois de l'État et des maximes de la volonté générale, s'ils sont instruits à les respecter par-dessus toutes choses, s'ils sont environnés d'exemples et d'objets qui leur parlent sans cesse de la tendre mère qui les nourrit, de l'amour qu'elle a pour eux, des biens inestimables qu'ils reçoivent d'elle, et du retour qu'ils lui doivent, ne doutons pas qu'ils n'apprennent ainsi à se chérir mutuellement comme des frères, à ne vouloir jamais que ce que veut la société, à substituer des actions d'hommes et de citoyens au stérile et vain babil des sophistes, et à devenir un jour les défenseurs et les pères de la patrie, dont ils auront été si longtemps les enfants.

Je ne parlerai point des magistrats destinés à présider à cette éducation, qui certainement est la plus importante affaire de l'État. On sent que si de telles marques de la confiance publique étaient légèrement accordées, si cette fonction sublime n'était pour ceux qui auraient dignement rempli toutes les autres le prix de leurs travaux l'honorable et doux repos de leur vieillesse et le comble de tous les honneurs, toute l'entreprise serait inutile et l'éducation sans succès : car, partout où la leçon n'est pas soutenue par l'autorité, et le précepte par l'exemple, l'instruction demeure sans fruit ; et la vertu même perd son crédit dans la bouche de celui qui ne la pratique pas. Mais que des guerriers illustres, courbés sous le faix de leurs lauriers, prêchent le courage ; que des magistrats intègres, blanchis dans la pourpre et sur les tribunaux, enseignent la justice ; les uns et les autres se formeront ainsi de vertueux successeurs, et transmettront d'âge en âge aux générations suivantes l'expérience et les talents des chefs, le courage et la vertu des citoyens, et l'émulation commune à tous de vivre et mourir[2] pour la patrie.

Je ne sache que trois peuples qui aient autrefois pratiqué l'éducation publique : savoir, les Crétois, les Lacédémoniens et les anciens Perses ; chez tous les trois elle eut le plus grand succès, et fit des prodiges chez les deux derniers. Quand le monde s'est

---

[1] The rough draft adds ' Et c'est par elle qu'on formera de bonne heure les jeunes citoyens à réunir toutes leurs passions dans l'amour de la patrie, toutes leurs volontés dans la volonté générale ; et par conséquent à porter toutes les vertus jusqu'où les peut porter l'âme humaine élevée à de si grands objets.'

[2] Eds. 1765, 1772 read *et de mourir*. Encycl., MS. and Ed. 1782, *et mourir*.

trouvé divisé en nations trop grandes pour pouvoir être bien gouvernées, ce moyen n'a plus été praticable ; et d'autres raisons, que le lecteur peut voir aisément, ont encore empêché qu'il n'ait été tenté chez aucun peuple moderne. C'est une chose très remarquable que les Romains aient pu s'en passer ; mais Rome fut, durant cinq cents ans, un miracle continuel que le monde ne doit plus espérer de revoir. La vertu des Romains, engendrée par l'horreur de la tyrannie et des crimes des tyrans, et par l'amour inné de la patrie, fit de toutes leurs maisons autant d'écoles de citoyens ; et le pouvoir sans bornes des pères sur leurs enfants mit tant de sévérité dans la police particulière, que le père, plus craint que les magistrats, était, dans son tribunal domestique, le censeur des mœurs et le vengeur des lois.

[1]C'est ainsi qu'un Gouvernement attentif et bien intentionné, veillant sans cesse à maintenir ou rappeler chez le peuple l'amour de la patrie et les bonnes mœurs, prévient de loin les maux qui résultent tôt ou tard de l'indifférence des citoyens pour le sort de la République, et contient dans d'étroites bornes cet intérêt personnel qui isole tellement les particuliers, que l'État s'affaiblit par leur puissance et n'a rien à espérer de leur bonne volonté. Partout où le peuple aime son pays, respecte les lois et vit simplement, il reste peu de chose à faire pour le rendre heureux ; et dans l'administration publique, où la fortune a moins de part qu'au sort des particuliers, la sagesse est si près du bonheur, que ces deux objets se confondent.

III. Ce n'est pas assez d'avoir des citoyens et de les protéger, il faut encore songer à leur subsistance ; et pourvoir aux besoins publics est une suite évidente de la volonté générale, et le troisième devoir essentiel du Gouvernement. Ce devoir n'est pas, comme on doit le sentir, de remplir les greniers des particuliers et les dispenser du travail, mais de maintenir l'abondance tellement à leur portée, que, pour l'acquérir, le travail soit toujours nécessaire et ne soit jamais inutile. Il s'étend aussi à toutes les opérations qui regardent l'entretien du fisc et les dépenses de l'administration publique. [2]Ainsi, après avoir parlé de l'*économie* générale par rapport au gouvernement des personnes, il nous reste à la considérer par rapport à l'administration des biens.

Cette partie n'offre pas moins de difficultés à résoudre ni de

---

[1] This paragraph forms the beginning of the rough draft in MS. 7840, p. 85. At end of preceding par., *Encycl.* and Ed. 1782 have *Voyez Éducation*.

[2] In the rough draft this sentence is introduced by the passage reproduced in Fragment (*b*), see p. 274.

contradictions à lever que la précédente. Il est certain que le droit de propriété est le plus sacré de tous les droits des citoyens, et plus important, à certains égards, que la liberté même : soit parce qu'il tient de plus près à la conservation de la vie ; soit parce que, les biens étant plus faciles à usurper et plus pénibles à défendre que la personne, on doit plus respecter ce qui peut se ravir[1] plus aisément ; soit enfin parce que la propriété est le vrai fondement de la société civile, et le vrai garant des engagements des citoyens : car, si les biens ne répondaient pas des personnes, rien ne serait si facile que d'éluder ses devoirs et de se moquer des lois. D'un autre côté, il n'est pas moins sûr que le maintien de l'État et du Gouvernement exige des frais et de la dépense ; et, comme quiconque accorde la fin ne peut refuser les moyens, il s'ensuit que les membres de la société doivent contribuer de leurs biens à son entretien. De plus, il est difficile d'assurer d'un côté la propriété des particuliers sans l'attaquer d'un autre ; et il n'est pas possible que tous les règlements qui regardent l'ordre des successions, les testaments, les contrats, ne gênent les citoyens, à certains égards, sur la disposition de leur propre bien, et par conséquent sur leur droit de propriété.

Mais, outre ce que j'ai dit ci-devant de l'accord qui règne entre l'autorité de la Loi et la liberté du citoyen, il y a, par rapport à la disposition des biens, une remarque importante à faire, qui lève bien des difficultés : c'est, comme l'a montré Pufendorf[2], que, par la nature du droit de propriété, il ne s'étend point au delà de la vie du propriétaire, et qu'à l'instant qu'un homme est mort son bien ne lui appartient plus. Ainsi, lui prescrire les conditions sous lesquelles il en peut disposer, c'est au fond moins altérer son droit en apparence que l'étendre en effet.

En général, quoique l'institution des lois qui règlent le pouvoir des particuliers dans la disposition de leur propre bien n'appartienne qu'au souverain, l'esprit de ces lois, que le Gouvernement doit suivre dans leur application, est que, de père en fils et de proche en proche, les biens de la famille en sortent et s'aliènent le moins qu'il est possible. Il y a une raison sensible de ceci en faveur des enfants, à qui le droit de propriété serait fort inutile si le père ne leur laissait rien, et qui, de plus, ayant souvent contribué par leur travail à l'acquisition des biens du père, sont de leur chef associés à son droit. Mais une autre raison, plus éloignée et non moins

---

[1] *Encycl.*, MS. and Ed. 1772 have *se peut ravir*. Ed. 1782, as above.
[2] *De jure naturæ et gentium*, IV. x. §§ 4—6 (ed. 4º, Amsterdam, 1698).

importante, est que rien n'est plus funeste aux mœurs et à la République que les changements continuels d'état et de fortune entre les citoyens : changements qui sont la preuve et la source de mille désordres, qui bouleversent et confondent tout, et par lesquels, ceux qui sont élevés pour une chose se trouvant[1] destinés pour une autre, ni ceux qui montent, ni ceux qui descendent, ne peuvent prendre les maximes ni les lumières convenables à leur nouvel état, et beaucoup moins en remplir les devoirs[2]. Je passe à l'objet des finances publiques.

Si le peuple se gouvernait lui-même, et qu'il n'y eût rien d'intermédiaire entre l'administration de l'État et les citoyens, ils n'auraient qu'à se cotiser dans l'occasion, à proportion des besoins publics et des facultés des particuliers ; et, comme chacun ne perdrait jamais de vue le recouvrement ni l'emploi des deniers, il ne pourrait se glisser ni fraude ni abus dans leur maniement ; l'État ne serait jamais obéré de dettes, ni le peuple accablé d'impôts ; ou du moins la sûreté de l'emploi le consolerait de la dureté de la taxe. Mais les choses ne sauraient aller ainsi ; et, quelque borné que soit un État, la société civile y est toujours trop nombreuse pour pouvoir être gouvernée par tous ses membres. Il faut nécessairement que les deniers publics passent par les mains des chefs, lesquels, outre l'intérêt de l'État, ont tous le leur particulier, qui n'est pas le dernier écouté. Le peuple de son côté, qui s'aperçoit plutôt de l'avidité des chefs et de leurs folles dépenses que des besoins publics, murmure de se voir dépouiller du nécessaire pour fournir au superflu d'autrui ; et, quand une fois ces manœuvres l'ont aigri jusqu'à un certain point, la plus intègre administration ne viendrait pas à bout de rétablir la confiance. Alors, si les contributions sont volontaires, elles ne produisent rien ; si elles sont forcées, elles sont illégitimes ; et c'est dans cette cruelle alternative de laisser périr l'État ou d'attaquer le droit sacré de la propriété, qui en est le soutien, que consiste la difficulté d'une juste et sage *économie*.

[3]La première chose que doit faire, après l'établissement des lois,

---

[1] Some copies of *Encycl.* read *se trouvent*, probably by a printer's error. Others, and all the early Eds., as in the text. MS. is here illegible.

[2] MS. 7840 has here 'Grand sujet à méditer pour tout lecteur qui a l'âme honnête et l'esprit éclairé.' I think it refers to the preceding sentence.

[3] In the rough draft this paragraph was originally introduced by the following sentence, subsequently cancelled : 'Pour lever ces contradictions, reprenons les choses de plus haut, depuis l'institution du Gouvernement, et continuons d'examiner moins ce qui est que ce qui devrait être.'

l'instituteur d'une République, c'est de trouver un fonds suffisant pour l'entretien des magistrats et autres officiers, et pour toutes les dépenses publiques. Ce fonds s'appelle *œrarium* ou *fisc*, s'il est en argent; *domaine public*, s'il est en terres; et ce dernier est de beaucoup préférable à l'autre, par des raisons faciles à voir. Quiconque aura suffisamment réfléchi sur cette matière ne pourra guère être à cet égard d'un autre avis que Bodin[1], qui regarde le domaine public comme le plus honnête et le plus sûr de tous les moyens de pourvoir aux besoins de l'État; et il est à remarquer que le premier soin de Romulus, dans la division des terres, fut d'en destiner le tiers à cet usage. J'avoue qu'il n'est pas impossible que le produit du domaine mal administré se réduise à rien; mais il n'est pas de l'essence du domaine d'être mal administré.

Préalablement à tout emploi, ce fonds doit être assigné ou accepté par l'assemblée du peuple ou des États du pays, qui doit ensuite en déterminer l'usage. Après cette solennité, qui rend ces fonds inaliénables, ils changent pour ainsi dire de nature, et leurs revenus deviennent tellement sacrés que c'est non seulement le plus infâme de tous les vols, mais un crime de lèse-majesté, que d'en détourner la moindre chose au préjudice de leur destination. C'est un grand déshonneur pour Rome que l'intégrité du questeur Caton y ait été un sujet de remarque, et qu'un empereur, récompensant de quelques écus le talent d'un chanteur, ait eu besoin d'ajouter que cet argent venait du bien de sa famille, et non de celui de l'État. Mais s'il se trouve peu de Galba[2], où chercherons-nous des Catons? Et quand une fois le vice ne déshonorera plus, quels seront les chefs assez scrupuleux pour s'abstenir de toucher aux revenus publics abandonnés à leur discrétion, et pour ne pas s'en imposer bientôt à eux-mêmes, en affectant de confondre leurs vaines et scandaleuses dissipations avec la gloire de l'État, et les moyens d'étendre leur autorité avec ceux d'augmenter sa puissance? C'est surtout en cette délicate partie de l'administration que la vertu est le seul instrument efficace, et que l'intégrité du magistrat est le seul frein capable de contenir son avarice. Les livres et tous les comptes des régisseurs servent moins à déceler leurs infidélités qu'à les couvrir; et la prudence n'est jamais aussi prompte à

---

[1] Bodin, *Six livres de la République*, VI. ii. pp. 617—9 (ed. 1577). 'Il y a sept moyens en général de faire fonds aux finances.... Quant au premier, qui est le domaine, il semble être le plus honnête et le plus sûr de tous.' It may be remarked that the passage about Bodin is wanting in MS. 7840.

[2] Ed. 1801 and Hachette have *Galbas*. All the early Eds. *Galba*.

imaginer de nouvelles précautions, que la friponnerie à les éluder. Laissez donc les registres et papiers, et remettez les finances en des mains fidèles ; c'est le seul moyen qu'elles soient fidèlement régies.

Quand une fois les fonds publics sont établis, les chefs de l'État en sont de droit les administrateurs ; car cette administration fait une partie du Gouvernement, toujours essentielle, quoique non toujours également. Son influence augmente à mesure que celle des autres ressorts diminue ; et l'on peut dire qu'un Gouvernement est parvenu à son dernier degré de corruption, quand il n'a plus d'autre nerf que l'argent. Or, comme tout Gouvernement tend sans cesse au relâchement, cette seule raison montre pourquoi nul État ne peut subsister si ses revenus n'augmentent sans cesse.

Le premier sentiment de la nécessité de cette augmentation est aussi le premier signe du désordre intérieur de l'État ; et le sage administrateur, en songeant à trouver de l'argent pour pourvoir au besoin présent, ne néglige pas de rechercher la cause éloignée de ce nouveau besoin : comme un marin, voyant l'eau gagner son vaisseau, n'oublie pas, en faisant jouer les pompes, de faire aussi chercher et boucher la voie.

De cette règle découle la plus importante maxime de l'administration des finances, qui est de travailler avec beaucoup plus de soin à prévenir les besoins qu'à augmenter les revenus. De quelque diligence qu'on puisse user, le secours qui ne vient qu'après le mal, et plus lentement, laisse toujours l'État en souffrance : tandis qu'on songe à remédier à un mal, un autre se fait déjà sentir, et les ressources mêmes produisent de nouveaux inconvénients ; de sorte qu'à la fin la nation s'obère, le peuple est foulé, le Gouvernement perd toute sa vigueur, et ne fait plus que peu de chose avec beaucoup d'argent. Je crois que de cette grande maxime bien établie découlaient les prodiges des Gouvernements anciens, qui faisaient plus avec leur parcimonie que les nôtres avec tous leurs trésors ; et c'est peut-être de là qu'est dérivée l'acception vulgaire du mot d'*économie*, qui s'entend plutôt du sage ménagement de ce qu'on a que des moyens d'acquérir ce que l'on n'a pas.

Indépendamment du domaine public, qui rend à l'État à proportion de la probité de ceux qui le régissent, si l'on connaissait assez toute la force de l'administration générale, surtout quand elle se borne aux moyens légitimes, on serait étonné des ressources qu'ont les chefs pour prévenir tous les besoins publics sans toucher aux biens des particuliers. Comme ils sont les maîtres de tout le commerce de l'État, rien ne leur est si facile que de le diriger d'une manière qui pourvoie à tout, souvent sans qu'ils paraissent s'en mêler. La distribution des denrées, de l'argent et des marchandises, par de justes proportions selon les temps et les lieux, est le vrai secret des finances et la source de leurs richesses, pourvu que ceux qui les administrent sachent porter leurs vues assez loin, et faire dans l'occasion une perte apparente et prochaine, pour avoir réellement des profits immenses dans un temps éloigné. Quand on voit un Gouvernement payer des droits, loin d'en recevoir, pour la sortie des blés dans les années d'abondance, et pour leur introduction dans les années de disette, on a besoin d'avoir de tels faits sous les yeux pour les croire véritables; et on les mettrait au rang des romans, s'ils se fussent passés anciennement. Supposons que, pour prévenir la disette dans les mauvaises années, on proposât d'établir des magasins publics; dans combien de pays l'entretien d'un établissement si utile ne servirait-il pas de prétexte à de nouveaux impôts! À Genève, ces greniers, établis et entretenus par une sage administration, font la ressource publique dans les mauvaises années, et le principal revenu de l'État dans tous les temps: *Alit et ditat*, c'est la belle et juste inscription qu'on lit sur la façade de l'édifice. Pour exposer ici le système économique d'un bon Gouvernement, j'ai souvent tourné les yeux sur celui de cette République: heureux de trouver ainsi dans ma patrie l'exemple de la sagesse et du bonheur que je voudrais voir régner dans tous les pays!

Si l'on examine comment croissent les besoins d'un État, on trouvera que souvent cela arrive à peu près comme chez les particuliers, moins par une véritable nécessité que par un accroissement de désirs inutiles, et que souvent on n'augmente la dépense que pour avoir le prétexte d'augmenter la recette; de sorte que l'État gagnerait quelquefois à se passer d'être riche, et que cette richesse apparente lui est au fond plus onéreuse que ne serait la pauvreté même. On peut espérer, il est vrai, de tenir les peuples dans une dépendance plus étroite, en leur donnant d'une main ce qu'on leur a pris de l'autre; et ce fut la politique dont usa Joseph avec les Égyptiens. Mais ce vain sophisme est d'autant plus funeste à l'État, que l'argent ne rentre plus dans les mêmes mains dont il est sorti, et qu'avec de pareilles maximes on n'enrichit que des fainéants de la dépouille des hommes utiles.

Le goût des conquêtes est une des causes les plus sensibles et les plus dangereuses de cette augmentation. Ce goût, engendré souvent par une autre espèce d'ambition que celle qu'il semble annoncer, n'est pas toujours ce qu'il paraît être, et n'a pas tant pour véritable motif le désir apparent d'agrandir la nation que le désir caché d'augmenter au dedans l'autorité des chefs, à l'aide de l'augmentation des troupes et à la faveur de la diversion que font les objets de la guerre dans l'esprit des citoyens.

Ce qu'il y a du moins de très certain, c'est que rien n'est si foulé ni si misérable que les peuples conquérants, et que leurs succès mêmes ne font qu'augmenter leurs misères. Quand l'histoire ne nous l'apprendrait pas, la raison suffirait pour nous démontrer que plus un État est grand, et plus les dépenses y deviennent proportionnellement fortes et onéreuses; car il faut que toutes les provinces fournissent leur contingent aux frais de l'administration générale, et que chacune, outre cela, fasse pour la sienne particulière la même dépense que si elle était indépendante. Ajoutez que toutes les fortunes se font dans un lieu et se consomment dans un autre: ce qui rompt bientôt l'équilibre du produit et de la consommation, et appauvrit beaucoup de pays pour enrichir une seule ville.

Autre source de l'augmentation des besoins publics, qui tient à la précédente. Il peut venir un temps où les citoyens, ne se regardant plus comme intéressés à la cause commune, cesseraient d'être les défenseurs de la patrie, et où les magistrats aimeraient mieux commander à des mercenaires qu'à des hommes libres, ne fût-ce qu'afin d'employer en temps et lieu les premiers pour mieux assujettir les autres. Tel fut l'état de Rome sur la fin de la République et sous les empereurs; car toutes les victoires des premiers Romains, de même que celles d'Alexandre, avaient été remportées par de braves citoyens, qui savaient donner au besoin leur sang pour la patrie, mais qui ne le vendaient jamais. [1]Ce ne fut qu'au siége de Véies qu'on commença de payer l'infanterie romaine[1]; et Marius fut le premier qui, dans la guerre de Jugurtha, déshonora les légions, en y introduisant des affranchis, vagabonds et autres mercenaires. Devenus les ennemis des peuples qu'ils s'étaient chargés de rendre heureux, les tyrans établirent des troupes réglées, en apparence pour contenir l'étranger, et en effet pour opprimer l'habitant. Pour former ces troupes, il fallut enlever à la terre des cultivateurs dont le défaut diminua la quantité des denrées, et dont l'entretien introduisit des impôts qui en augmentèrent le prix. Ce premier désordre fit murmurer les peuples. Il fallut, pour les réprimer, multiplier les troupes, et par conséquent

---

[1] This sentence is wanting in *Encycl.* It appears in all the later Eds. from 1758 (Geneva) onwards. After *les légions* some copies of *Encycl.* have *romaines*, which is omitted in others and in all later Eds.

la misère; et plus le désespoir augmentait, plus on se voyait contraint de l'augmenter encore pour en prévenir les effets. D'un autre côté ces mercenaires, qu'on pouvait estimer sur le prix auquel ils se vendaient eux-mêmes, fiers de leur avilissement, méprisant les lois dont ils étaient protégés et leurs frères dont ils mangeaient le pain, se crurent plus honorés d'être les satellites de César que les défenseurs de Rome; et, dévoués à une obéissance aveugle, tenaient par état le poignard levé sur leurs concitoyens, prêts à tout égorger au premier signal. Il ne serait pas difficile de montrer que ce fut là une des principales causes de la ruine de l'empire romain.

L'invention de l'artillerie et des fortifications a forcé de nos jours les souverains de l'Europe à rétablir l'usage des troupes réglées pour garder leurs places; mais, avec des motifs plus légitimes, il est à craindre que l'effet n'en soit également funeste. Il n'en faudra pas moins dépeupler les campagnes pour former les armées et les garnisons; pour les entretenir, il n'en faudra pas moins fouler les peuples; et ces dangereux établissements s'accroissent depuis quelque temps avec une telle rapidité dans tous nos climats, qu'on n'en peut prévoir que la dépopulation prochaine de l'Europe, et tôt ou tard la ruine des peuples qui l'habitent.

Quoi qu'il en soit, on doit voir que de telles institutions renversent nécessairement le vrai système économique qui tire le principal revenu de l'État du domaine public, et ne laissent que la ressource fâcheuse des subsides et impôts, dont il me reste à parler.

Il faut se ressouvenir ici que le fondement du pacte social est la propriété; et sa première condition, que chacun soit maintenu dans la paisible jouissance de ce qui lui appartient. Il est vrai que, par le même traité, chacun s'oblige, au moins tacitement, à se cotiser dans les besoins publics. Mais, cet engagement ne pouvant nuire à la loi fondamentale et supposant l'évidence du besoin reconnue par les contribuables, on voit que, pour être légitime, cette cotisation doit être volontaire: non d'une volonté particulière, comme s'il était nécessaire d'avoir le consentement de chaque citoyen, et qu'il ne dût fournir que ce qu'il lui plaît[1], ce qui serait directement contre l'esprit de la confédération, mais d'une volonté générale, à la pluralité des voix, et sur un tarif proportionnel qui ne laisse rien d'arbitraire à l'imposition[1].

Cette vérité, que les impôts ne peuvent être établis légitimement

[1] In the rough draft *Voyez Locke* is here written in the margin. The reference is to *Civil Government* (II. xi.). See Introduction, p. 234.

que du consentement du peuple ou de ses[1] représentants, a été reconnue généralement de tous les philosophes et jurisconsultes qui se sont acquis quelque réputation dans les matières de droit politique, sans excepter Bodin même[2]. Si quelques-uns ont établi des maximes contraires en apparence, outre qu'il est aisé de voir les motifs particuliers qui les y ont portés, ils y mettent tant de conditions et de restrictions qu'au fond la chose revient exactement au même. Car que le peuple puisse refuser, ou que le souverain ne doive pas exiger, cela est indifférent quant au droit; et s'il n'est question que de la force, c'est la chose la plus inutile que d'examiner ce qui est légitime ou non.

Les contributions qui se lèvent sur le peuple sont de deux sortes : les unes réelles, qui se perçoivent sur les choses ; les autres personnelles, qui se payent par tête. On donne aux unes et aux autres les noms d'*impôts*, ou de *subsides* : quand le peuple fixe la somme qu'il accorde, elle s'appelle *subside* ; quand il accorde tout le produit d'une taxe, alors c'est un *impôt*. On trouve dans le livre de l'*Esprit des lois*[3] que l'imposition par tête est plus propre à la servitude, et la taxe réelle plus convenable à la liberté. Cela serait incontestable si les contingents par tête étaient égaux; car il n'y aurait rien de plus disproportionné qu'une pareille taxe; et c'est surtout dans les proportions exactement observées que consiste l'esprit de la liberté. Mais si la taxe par tête est exactement proportionnée aux moyens des particuliers, comme pourrait être celle qui porte en France le nom de *capitation*, et qui de cette manière est à la fois réelle et personnelle, elle est la plus équitable, et par conséquent la plus convenable à des hommes libres. Ces proportions paraissent d'abord très faciles à observer, parce que, étant relatives à l'état que chacun tient dans le monde, les indications sont toujours publiques. Mais, outre que l'avarice, le crédit et la fraude savent éluder jusqu'à l'évidence, il est rare qu'on tienne compte dans ces calculs de tous les éléments qui doivent y entrer. Premièrement, on doit considérer le rapport des quantités, selon lequel, toutes choses égales, celui qui a dix fois plus de bien qu'un autre doit payer dix fois plus que lui ; secondement, le rapport des

---

[1] It may be observed that Rousseau, still under the influence of Locke, does not here reject the representative system as he does in the *Contrat social* (III. xv.).

[2] *Six livres de la République*, I. ix. (p. 138, Ed. 1577). Eds. 1765 and 1772, *sans en excepter*. *Encycl.* and Ed. 1782, *sans excepter*. The phrase is wanting in the MS., which has 'Si quelques uns, tels que Bodin,' in the next sentence.   [3] Liv. XIII. Chap. xiv.

usages: c'est-à-dire, la distinction du nécessaire et du superflu. Celui qui n'a que le simple nécessaire ne doit rien payer du tout ; la taxe de celui qui a du superflu peut aller au besoin jusqu'à la concurrence de tout ce qui excède son nécessaire. À cela il dira qu'eu égard à son rang ce qui serait superflu pour un homme inférieur est nécessaire pour lui. Mais c'est un mensonge : car un Grand a deux jambes ainsi qu'un bouvier, et n'a qu'un ventre non plus que lui. De plus, ce prétendu nécessaire est si peu nécessaire à son rang, que, s'il savait y renoncer pour un sujet louable, il n'en serait que plus respecté. Le peuple se prosternerait devant un ministre qui irait au Conseil à pied, pour avoir vendu ses carrosses dans un pressant besoin de l'État. Enfin la Loi ne prescrit la magnificence à personne, et la bienséance n'est jamais une raison contre le droit.

Un troisième rapport qu'on ne compte jamais, et qu'on devrait toujours compter le premier, est celui des utilités que chacun retire de la confédération sociale, qui protége fortement les immenses possessions du riche, et laisse à peine un misérable jouir de la chaumière qu'il a construite de ses mains. Tous les avantages de la société ne sont-ils pas pour les puissants et les riches ? tous les emplois lucratifs ne sont-ils pas remplis par eux seuls ? toutes les grâces, toutes les exemptions, ne leur sont-elles pas réservées ? et l'autorité publique n'est-elle pas toute[1] en leur faveur ? Qu'un homme de considération vole ses créanciers ou fasse d'autres friponneries, n'est-il pas toujours sûr de l'impunité ? Les coups de bâton qu'il distribue, les violences qu'il commet, les meurtres mêmes et les assassinats dont il se rend coupable, ne sont-ce pas des affaires qu'on assoupit, et dont au bout de six mois il n'est plus question ? Que ce même homme soit volé, toute la police est aussitôt en mouvement ; et malheur aux innocents qu'il soupçonne ! Passe-t-il dans un lieu dangereux, voilà les escortes en campagne ; l'essieu de sa chaise vient-il à rompre, tout vole à son secours ; fait-on du bruit à sa porte, il dit un mot, et tout se tait ; la foule l'incommode-t-elle, il fait un signe, et tout se range ; [2]un charretier se trouve-t-il sur son passage[2], ses gens sont prêts à l'assommer ; et cinquante honnêtes piétons allant à leurs affaires seraient plutôt écrasés qu'un faquin oisif retardé dans son équipage. [3]Tous ces égards ne lui coûtent pas un sou ; ils sont le droit de l'homme riche, et non le prix de la richesse[3]. Que le tableau du pauvre est

---

[1] Hachette omits *toute* in defiance of all the early Eds. (*Encycl.* included).
[2] The rough draft has 'un malheureux chartier barre-t-il son passage.'
[3] The rough draft has 'Cependant il n'a pas besoin de débourser un sol

différent! plus l'humanité lui doit, plus la société lui refuse. Toutes les portes lui sont fermées, même quand il a le droit de les faire ouvrir; et si quelquefois il obtient justice, c'est avec plus de peine qu'un autre n'obtiendrait grâce. S'il y a des corvées à faire, une milice à tirer, c'est à lui qu'on donne la préférence; il porte toujours, outre sa charge, celle dont son voisin plus riche a le crédit de se faire exempter. Au moindre accident qui lui arrive, chacun s'éloigne de lui; si sa pauvre charrette renverse[1], loin d'être aidé par personne, je le tiens heureux s'il évite en passant [2]les avanies des gens lestes d'un jeune duc[2]. En un mot, toute assistance gratuite le fuit au besoin, précisément parce qu'il n'a pas de quoi la payer; [3]mais je le tiens pour un homme perdu[3], s'il a le malheur d'avoir l'âme honnête, une fille aimable, et un puissant voisin.

Une autre attention non moins importante à faire, c'est que les pertes des pauvres sont beaucoup moins réparables que celles du riche, et que la difficulté d'acquérir croît toujours en raison du besoin. On ne fait rien avec rien; cela est vrai dans les affaires comme en physique : l'argent est la semence de l'argent, et la première pistole est quelquefois plus difficile à gagner que le second million. Il y a plus encore : c'est que tout ce que le pauvre paye est à jamais perdu pour lui, et reste ou revient dans les mains du riche; et comme c'est aux seuls hommes qui ont part au Gouvernement, ou à ceux qui en approchent, que passe tôt ou tard le produit des impôts, ils ont, même en payant leur contingent, un intérêt sensible à les augmenter.

Résumons en quatre mots le pacte social des deux états. 'Vous avez besoin de moi, car je suis riche et vous êtes pauvre; faisons donc un accord entre nous : je permettrai que vous ayez l'honneur de me servir, à condition que vous me donnerez le peu qui vous reste pour la peine que je prendrai de vous commander.'

Si l'on combine avec soin toutes ces choses, on trouvera que, pour répartir les taxes d'une manière équitable et vraiment proportionnelle, l'imposition n'en doit pas être faite seulement en raison des biens des contribuables, mais en raison composée de la différence

---

pour jouir de tous ces avantages ; et quand tout vole audevant de ses désirs, ils ne sont point le prix de la richesse, mais seulement le droit de l'homme riche.'

[1] Hachette has *verse*. MS., *Encycl.* and all the early Eds. *renverse*.
[2] The rough draft has 'les avanies d'un jeune duc.'
[3] The rough draft has 'mais je le plains surtout des hontes qui le menacent, s'il a le malheur,' etc.

de leurs conditions et du superflu de leurs biens : [1]opération très importante et très difficile, que font tous les jours des multitudes de commis honnêtes gens et qui savent l'arithmétique, mais dont les Platons et les Montesquieux[2] n'eussent osé se charger qu'en tremblant, et en demandant au ciel des lumières et de l'intégrité[1].

Un autre inconvénient de la taxe personnelle, c'est de se faire trop sentir et d'être levée avec trop de dureté: ce qui n'empêche pas qu'elle ne soit sujette à beaucoup de non-valeurs, parce qu'il est plus aisé de dérober au rôle et aux poursuites sa tête que ses possessions.

De toutes les autres impositions, le cens sur les terres, ou la taille réelle, a toujours passé pour la plus avantageuse dans les pays où l'on a plus d'égard à la quantité du produit et à la sûreté du recouvrement qu'à la moindre incommodité du peuple. On a même osé dire qu'il fallait charger le paysan pour éveiller sa paresse, et qu'il ne ferait rien s'il n'avait rien à payer. Mais l'expérience dément chez tous les peuples du monde cette maxime ridicule : c'est en Hollande, en Angleterre, où le cultivateur paye très peu de chose, et surtout à la Chine, où il ne paye rien, que la terre est le mieux cultivée. Au contraire, partout où le laboureur se voit chargé à proportion du produit de son champ, il le laisse en friche, ou n'en retire exactement que ce qu'il lui faut pour vivre. Car pour qui perd le fruit de sa peine, c'est gagner que ne rien faire; et mettre le travail à l'amende est un moyen fort singulier de bannir la paresse.

De la taxe sur les terres ou sur le blé, surtout quand elle est excessive, résultent deux inconvénients si terribles, qu'ils doivent dépeupler et ruiner à la longue tous les pays où elle est établie.

Le premier vient du défaut de circulation des espèces : car le commerce et l'industrie attirent dans les capitales tout l'argent de la campagne; et l'impôt détruisant la proportion qui pouvait se trouver encore entre les besoins du laboureur et le prix de son blé, l'argent vient sans cesse et ne retourne jamais; plus la ville est riche, plus le pays est misérable. Le produit des tailles passe des mains du prince ou du financier dans celles des artistes et des marchands; et le cultivateur, qui n'en reçoit jamais que la moindre

---

[1] The rough draft originally had this version, subsequently cancelled : ' Telles sont les justes considérations dont un sage et vertueux administrateur doit pénétrer son âme au moment qu'il s'occupe de l'importante affaire de la répartition des taxes : [ouvrage dont on charge ordinairement les grimauds] ouvrage qu'on confie ordinairement à quelques vils commis, et dont les Platons,' etc.

[2] Ed. 1801 and Hachette read *les Platon, les Montesquieu*. MS., *Encycl.* and all the early Eds., as above. Hachette misreads *et l'intégrité*.

partie, s'épuise enfin en payant toujours également et en recevant toujours moins. Comment voudrait-on que pût vivre un homme qui n'aurait que des veines et point d'artères, ou dont les artères ne porteraient le sang qu'à quatre doigts du cœur ? Chardin dit qu'en Perse les droits du roi sur les denrées se payent aussi en denrées. Cet usage, qu'Hérodote témoigne avoir autrefois été pratiqué dans le même pays jusqu'à Darius, peut prévenir le mal dont je viens de parler. Mais, à moins qu'en Perse les intendants, directeurs, commis et gardes-magasin ne soient[1] une autre espèce de gens que partout ailleurs, j'ai peine à croire qu'il arrive jusqu'au roi la moindre chose de tous ces produits, que les blés ne se gâtent pas dans tous les greniers, et que le feu ne consume pas la plupart des magasins.

Le second inconvénient vient d'un avantage apparent, qui laisse aggraver les maux avant qu'on les aperçoive: c'est que le blé est une denrée que les impôts ne renchérissent point dans le pays qui la produit, et dont, malgré son absolue nécessité, la quantité diminue sans que le prix en augmente: ce qui fait que beaucoup de gens meurent de faim, quoique le blé continue d'être à bon marché, et que le laboureur reste seul chargé de l'impôt, qu'il n'a pu défalquer sur le prix de la vente. Il faut bien faire attention qu'on ne doit pas raisonner de la taille réelle comme des droits sur toutes les marchandises, qui en font hausser le prix, et sont ainsi payés moins par les marchands que par les acheteurs. Car ces droits, quelque forts qu'ils puissent être, sont pourtant volontaires et ne sont payés par le marchand qu'à proportion des marchandises qu'il achète; et comme il n'achète qu'à proportion de son débit, il fait la loi au particulier. Mais le laboureur, qui, soit qu'il vende ou non, est contraint de payer à des termes fixes pour le terrain qu'il cultive, n'est pas le maître d'attendre qu'on mette à sa denrée le prix qu'il lui plaît; et quand il ne la vendrait pas pour s'entretenir, il serait forcé de la vendre pour payer la taille; de sorte que c'est quelquefois l'énormité de l'imposition qui maintient la denrée à vil prix.

Remarquez encore que les ressources du commerce et de l'industrie, loin de rendre la taille plus supportable par l'abondance de l'argent, ne la rendent que plus onéreuse. Je n'insisterai point sur une chose très évidente: savoir, que, si la plus grande ou moindre quantité d'argent dans un État peut lui donner plus ou moins de crédit au dehors, elle ne change en aucune manière la

---

[1] Some copies of *Encycl.* read *soit*. Others, and all the early Eds., *soient*. Ed. 1801 and Hachette have *garde-magasins*. Eds. 1765 and 1772, *gardes-magasins*. *Encycl.* and Ed. 1782, *gardes-magasin*.

fortune réelle des citoyens, et ne les met ni plus ni moins à leur aise. Mais je ferai ces deux remarques importantes : l'une, qu'à moins que l'État n'ait des denrées superflues, et que l'abondance de l'argent ne vienne de leur débit chez l'étranger, les villes où se fait le commerce se sentent seules de cette abondance, et que le paysan ne fait qu'en devenir relativement plus pauvre ; l'autre, que, le prix de toutes choses haussant avec la multiplication de l'argent, il faut aussi que les impôts haussent à proportion ; de sorte que le laboureur se trouve plus chargé sans avoir plus de ressources.

On doit voir que la taille sur les terres est un véritable impôt sur leur produit. Cependant chacun convient que rien n'est si dangereux qu'un impôt sur le blé, payé par l'acheteur : comment ne voit-on pas que le mal est cent fois pire quand cet impôt est payé par le cultivateur même ? N'est-ce pas attaquer la substance de l'État jusque dans sa source ? n'est-ce pas travailler aussi directement qu'il est possible à dépeupler le pays, et par conséquent à le ruiner à la longue ? car il n'y a point pour une nation de pire disette que celle des hommes.

Il n'appartient qu'au véritable homme d'État d'élever ses vues dans l'assiette des impôts plus haut que l'objet des finances, de transformer des charges onéreuses en d'utiles règlements de police, et de faire douter au peuple si de tels établissements n'ont pas eu pour fin le bien de la nation plutôt que le produit des taxes.

Les droits sur l'importation des marchandises étrangères, dont les habitants sont avides sans que le pays en ait besoin, sur l'exportation de celles du crû du pays, dont il n'a pas de trop et dont les étrangers ne peuvent se passer, sur les productions des arts inutiles et trop lucratifs, sur les entrées dans les villes des choses de pur agrément, et en général sur tous les objets du luxe, rempliront tout ce double objet. C'est par de tels impôts, qui soulagent le pauvre et chargent la richesse, qu'il faut prévenir l'augmentation continuelle de l'inégalité des fortunes, l'asservissement aux riches d'une multitude d'ouvriers et de serviteurs inutiles, la multiplication des gens oisifs dans les villes, et la désertion des campagnes.

Il est important de mettre entre le prix des choses et les droits dont on les charge une telle proportion, que l'avidité des particuliers ne soit point trop portée à la fraude par la grandeur des profits. Il faut encore prévenir la facilité de la contrebande, en préférant les marchandises les moins faciles à cacher. Enfin il convient que l'impôt soit payé par celui qui emploie la chose taxée plutôt que par celui qui la vend, auquel la quantité des droits dont il se trouverait chargé donnerait plus de tentations et de moyens de les frauder. C'est l'usage constant de la Chine, le pays du monde où les impôts sont les plus forts et les mieux payés : le marchand ne paye rien ; l'acheteur seul acquitte le droit, sans qu'il en résulte ni murmures ni séditions, parce que, les denrées nécessaires à la vie, telles que le riz et le blé, étant absolument franches, le peuple n'est point foulé, et l'impôt ne tombe que sur les gens aisés. Au reste, toutes ces précautions ne doivent pas tant être dictées par la crainte de la contrebande que par l'attention que doit avoir le Gouvernement à garantir les particuliers de la séduction des profits illégitimes, qui, après en avoir fait de mauvais citoyens, ne tarderait pas d'en faire de malhonnêtes gens.

Qu'on établisse de fortes taxes sur la livrée, sur les équipages, sur les glaces, lustres et ameublements, sur les étoffes et la dorure, sur les cours et jardins des hôtels, sur les spectacles de toute espèce, sur les professions oiseuses, comme baladins, chanteurs, histrions, en un mot, sur cette foule d'objets de luxe, d'amusement et d'oisiveté, qui frappent tous les yeux, et qui peuvent d'autant moins se cacher que leur seul usage est de se montrer, et qu'ils seraient inutiles s'ils n'étaient vus. Qu'on ne craigne pas que de tels produits fussent arbitraires, pour n'être fondés que sur des choses qui ne sont pas d'une absolue nécessité. C'est bien mal connaître les hommes que de croire qu'après s'être une fois laissé séduire par le luxe ils y puissent jamais renoncer ; ils renonceraient cent fois plutôt au nécessaire, et aimeraient encore mieux mourir de faim que de honte. L'augmentation de la dépense ne sera qu'une nouvelle raison pour la soutenir, quand la vanité de se montrer opulent fera son profit du prix de la chose et des frais de la taxe. Tant qu'il y aura des riches, ils voudront se distinguer des pauvres ; et l'État ne saurait se former un revenu moins onéreux ni plus assuré que sur cette distinction.

Par la même raison, l'industrie n'aurait rien à souffrir d'un ordre économique qui enrichirait les finances, ranimerait l'agriculture en soulageant le laboureur, et rapprocherait insensiblement toutes les fortunes de cette médiocrité qui fait la véritable force d'un État. Il se pourrait, je l'avoue, que les impôts contribuassent à faire passer plus rapidement quelques modes : mais ce ne serait jamais que pour en substituer d'autres sur lesquelles l'ouvrier gagnerait sans que le fisc eût rien à perdre. En un mot, supposons que l'esprit du Gouvernement soit constamment d'asseoir toutes les taxes sur le superflu des richesses, il arrivera de deux choses l'une : ou les riches renonceront à leurs dépenses superflues pour n'en faire que d'utiles, qui retourneront au profit de l'État ; alors l'assiette des impôts aura produit l'effet des meilleures lois somptuaires, les dépenses de l'État auront nécessairement diminué avec celles des particuliers, et le fisc ne saurait moins recevoir de cette manière qu'il n'ait beaucoup moins encore à débourser : ou, si les riches ne diminuent rien de leurs profusions, le fisc aura dans le produit des impôts les ressources qu'il cherchait pour pourvoir aux besoins réels de l'État. Dans le premier cas, le fisc s'enrichit de toute la dépense qu'il a de moins à faire ; dans le second, il s'enrichit encore de la dépense inutile des particuliers.

Ajoutons à tout ceci une importante distinction en matière de droit politique, et à laquelle les Gouvernements, jaloux de faire tout par eux-mêmes, devraient donner une grande attention. J'ai dit que les taxes personnelles et les impôts sur les choses d'absolue nécessité, attaquant directement le droit de propriété, et par conséquent le vrai fondement de la société politique, sont toujours sujets à des conséquences dangereuses, s'ils ne sont établis avec l'exprès consentement du peuple ou de ses représentants. Il n'en est pas de même des droits sur les choses dont on peut s'interdire l'usage. Car alors, le particulier n'étant point absolument contraint à payer, sa contribution peut passer pour volontaire ; de sorte que le consentement particulier de chacun des contribuants supplée au consentement général, et le suppose même en quelque manière : car pourquoi le peuple s'opposerait-il à toute imposition qui ne tombe que sur quiconque veut bien la payer ? Il me paraît certain que tout ce qui n'est ni proscrit par les lois, ni contraire aux mœurs, et que le Gouvernement peut défendre, il peut le permettre moyennant un droit. Si, par exemple, le Gouvernement peut interdire l'usage des carrosses, il peut, à plus forte raison, imposer une taxe sur les carrosses : moyen sage et utile d'en blâmer l'usage sans le faire cesser. Alors on peut regarder la taxe comme une espèce d'amende dont le produit dédommage de l'abus qu'elle punit.

Quelqu'un m'objectera peut-être que ceux que Bodin appelle *imposteurs*[1], c'est-à-dire ceux qui imposent ou imaginent les taxes, étant dans la classe des riches, n'auront garde d'épargner les autres à leurs propres dépens, et de se charger eux-mêmes pour soulager les pauvres. Mais il faut rejeter de pareilles idées. Si, dans chaque nation, ceux à qui le souverain commet le gouvernement des peuples en étaient les ennemis par état, ce ne serait pas la peine de rechercher ce qu'ils doivent faire pour les rendre heureux[2].

[1] *Six livres de la République*, VI. ii. (p. 635, ed. 1577).
[2] For the original close of the Treatise, see the last of the Fragments following (*y*). The existing close is a finished piece of irony.

Fragments of the Rough Draft of *Économie politique*.

[MS. Neuchâtel, 7840 (pp. 86—73 v°).]

[Nearly one-half of the Treatise is to be found in the MS. If the lost pages and the six paragraphs which survive in the Geneva MS. of the *Contrat social* (I. v. and vii.) be reckoned, something like three-quarters of the Treatise can be accounted for. Only those passages which were not incorporated in the final Text are reproduced here. Any variants on the existing Text, which seem to be of special importance or interest, are given in the notes to the Treatise itself.]

(*a*) On est libre, quoique soumis aux lois, non quand[1] on obéit à un homme, parce qu'en ce dernier cas[2] j'obéis à la volonté d'autrui; mais en obéissant à la Loi je n'obéis qu'à la volonté publique, qui est autant la mienne que celle de qui que ce soit. D'ailleurs un maître[3] peut permettre à l'un ce qu'il défend à l'autre; au lieu que[4], la Loi ne faisant aucune acception, la condition de tous est égale et par conséquent il n'y a ni maître ni serviteur[5]. [This passage must have been intended to come about p. 245.] [D. B.]

*(*b*) Ayant à parler du Gouvernement et non de la souveraineté, ayant de plus à me borner aux règles générales qui peuvent s'appliquer à tout[6], j'ai commencé par supposer de bonnes lois: des lois[7] qui n'aient été dictées par aucun intérêt particulier et qui par conséquent soient l'ouvrage du Corps de la nation. J'ai demandé qu'elles fussent exactement observées et que les chefs, pour leur propre intérêt, n'y fussent pas moins soumis que le peuple. J'ai montré qu'on ne pouvait parvenir à cela qu'avec[8] des mœurs et l'amour de la patrie. J'ai parlé des moyens d'obtenir l'un et l'autre. Je crois maintenant pouvoir conclure[9] que, toutes ces règles étant praticables et suffisantes parce que l'amour de la patrie supplée à tout, il n'est pas impossible de gouverner heureusement et sagement par elles un peuple libre, sans qu'il soit

---

D. B. = the passages published by M. Dreyfus-Brisac; W., by M. Windenberger; *, those which, to the best of my knowledge, are now first printed.

[1] [et on n'est point libre quand.]   [2] [en obéissant à un homme.]
[3] [homme.]   [4] [mais.]
[5] [nul n'en peut tirer avantage contre un autre.] MS. p. 86.
[6] [gouvernement.]   [7] [c'est à dire des lois.]
[8] [l'aide de.]   [9] [Je conclus donc qu'il n'est pas....]

nécessaire d'imaginer pour cela une espèce d'hommes[1] plus parfaite que la nôtre, quand même on prétendrait que[2] les Romains et les Spartiates étaient[3] d'une autre nature que nous. Voilà tout ce que j'avais à dire de cette partie de l'Économie publique qui regarde l'administration[4] des personnes; il me reste à parler de celle des biens. [In the MS. (p. 85) this immediately follows the paragraph which closes § II. of *L'Économie politique*, and which begins 'C'est ainsi qu'un gouvernement attentif.' It forms the transition from § II. to § III. (p. 258).]

*(c) Les impôts sont une sorte de revenu[5] qui, par sa nature fondant en grande partie dans les mains qui le recueillent, appauvrit[6] le peuple sans enrichir[7] l'épargne, et qui par conséquent fait toujours plus de mal que de bien. [Intended to come about p. 266.]

*(d) Après avoir longtemps puisé dans les bourses des riches par des emprunts et dans celle des pauvres par des impôts, il faut nécessairement que l'Angleterre finisse par faire banqueroute, par cette unique raison qu'elle ne paye ses emprunts que par les impôts. [Written on cover of MS. opposite either p. 86 (the upper part of which is torn away) or p. 85. It must have been intended for about p. 266.]

*(e) Et selon la définition que j'ai donnée[8] de la vertu, l'amour de la patrie y conduit nécessairement, puisque nous voulons volontiers ce que veulent ceux que nous aimons. [This is a variant on the paragraph p. 250 (Ce n'est pas assez de dire...nous aimons). p. 85.]

*(f) Il est également dangereux que le Souverain empiète sur les fonctions de la magistrature ou[9] le Magistrat sur celle de la souveraineté. [Pencil, MS. p. 85. It must have been intended for *E. P.* pp. 241—5.]

*(g) Ce doit être une des premières lois de l'État qu'une même personne ne puisse occuper à la fois plusieurs charges, soit pour qu'un plus grand nombre de citoyens ait part au Gouvernement, soit pour ne laisser à aucun d'eux plus de pouvoir que n'a voulu le Législateur. [Pencil, MS. p. 85. Intended for *E. P.* about pp. 244—5.]

*(h) Le premier objet que se sont proposé les hommes dans la confédération civile a été leur sûreté mutuelle; c'est à dire la

---

[1] [des hommes.]   [2] [attendu que.]
[3] [n'étaient pas eux-mêmes.]   [4] [le gouvernement.]
[5] [ressource.]   [6] [nécessairement.]   [7] [plus qu'il n'enrichit.]
[8] Alternative reading, *l'idée que je me suis faite.*   [9] [et.]

garantie de la vie et de la liberté de chacun par toute la communauté. Le premier devoir du Gouvernement est donc de faire jouir paisiblement les citoyens de l'une et de l'autre ; et l'observation des lois mêmes[1] n'est si sévèrement exigée que parce que la Loi n'est qu'une déclaration de la volonté publique[2], et qu'on ne saurait l'enfreindre sans attaquer la liberté[3]. Comme le public n'est autre chose que la collection des particuliers, ses droits ne sont fondés que sur les leurs, et l'engagement du Corps de la nation est de pourvoir à la conservation du dernier de ses membres[4]. [MS. v° of p. 85. This is a variant on the passage at the end of the paragraph of *E. P.* which begins 'Voulons-nous que les peuples soient vertueux?' Indeed, the closing words of the Fragment in the MS. open the next paragraph in the existing Text, and the whole of that paragraph follows immediately in the MS. The following Fragment (*i*) is another variant of the same.]

(*i*) C'est tellement là l'esprit de la société que la confédération publique serait dissoute par le droit s'il périssait dans l'État un seul citoyen qu'on eût pu secourir et si l'on en retenait un seul injustement en prison ; car, excepté la force, on ne verrait plus après cela quel intérêt pourrait maintenir les membres ; car, les conventions fondamentales étant enfreintes, on ne voit plus quel droit ni quel intérêt pourrait maintenir les membres dans l'union sociale, à moins qu'ils n'y fussent retenus par la force[5]. Les Romains se distinguèrent par-dessus tous les peuples par le respect du Gouvernement pour les particuliers[6], et par son attention scrupuleuse à respecter les droits inviolables de tous les membres de l'État. Il n'y avait rien de si sacré que la vie des simples citoyens ; il ne fallait pas moins que l'assemblée de tout le peuple pour les condamner[7]. Le Sénat même, ni les Consuls, dans toute leur majesté n'en avaient pas le droit ; et chez le plus puissant peuple du monde, le crime et la peine[8] d'un seul citoyen était une désolation publique[9]. Ce sage et vertueux peuple connaissait

---

[1] [les lois mêmes ne sont si....]
[2] [n'était que la volonté publique, la liberté.]
[3] [Le premier devoir d'un bon gouvernement est donc....]
[4] [et il n'est pas moins du devoir du corps d' (*sic*) à la conservation du dernier—moindre... : et l'engagement du corps de la nation est de [veiller] pourvoir de toutes ses forces aux besoins de tout le peuple....]
[5] [Or la force qui ne....]
[6] [par l'attention scrupuleuse du gouvernement à respecter.]
[7] [juger à la mort.]   [8] [la mort.]
[9] [Toute l'histoire de ce vertueux peuple fourmille d'exemples de son attention.]

en quoi consistait (*sic*) les vrais trésors de l'État et préférait dans les pompes des triomphes la délivrance d'un seul Romain à toutes les richesses des vaincus. [MS. p. 84. It will be observed that this is a shortened form of two paragraphs which appear in the final Text of *Économie politique* (pp. 252—3).]

*(*j*) Tous les devoirs essentiels du Gouvernement sont contenus dans ce petit[1] nombre d'articles principaux : faire observer les lois, défendre la liberté, maintenir les mœurs et pourvoir aux besoins publics. Mais quelque importants que ces préceptes puissent paraître, ils se réduiront à[2] de vaines et stériles maximes, s'ils ne sont rendus efficaces par le principe actif et sublime qui doit les inspirer. C'est ce que je voudrais tâcher de rendre sensible. [M.S. p. 83 v°. It must have been intended, like the next Fragment, to come near the beginning of the Treatise.]

(*k*) Il est étonnant que parmi tant de différences sensibles Aristote n'en ait observé qu'une, qui même n'est pas universelle. C'est que la République est gouvernée par plusieurs chefs, au lieu que la Famille n'en a jamais qu'un[3]. [MS. p. 83 v°. Intended for one of the opening paragraphs of the Treatise (pp. 298—9).] Et c'est par elle [*i.e.* l'éducation publique] qu'on formera de bonne heure les jeunes citoyens à réunir toutes leurs passions dans l'amour de la patrie, toutes leurs volontés dans la volonté générale ; et par conséquent à porter toutes les vertus jusqu'où les peut porter l'âme humaine élevée à de si grands objets. [MS. p. 83 v°. Intended for p. 257, after 'populaire ou légitime.'] [W.]

*(*l*) Vous pourriez peut-être éviter ou prévenir certains maux qui peut-être aussi ne vous arriveront jamais ; mais vous ne le sauriez qu'en vous donnant des maux plus certains et non moins funestes. [Pencil, MS. p. 78 v°. Reference uncertain. Indeed, it would appear to have been intended for the early part of *Émile*, Liv. II.]

*(*m*) Jamais Jésus-Christ, dont le règne n'était pas de ce monde, n'a songé à demander pouce de terre à qui que ce soit, et n'en a point possédé lui-même ; mais son humble vicaire, après s'être approprié le territoire de César, distribua l'empire du monde aux serviteurs de Dieu. [Pencil, MS. p. 78 v°. Reference uncertain. It is more than doubtful whether it was intended for the *Économie politique*.]

*(*n*) Si les citoyens tirent d'elle tout ce qui peut leur donner

---

[1] [peuvent se réduire à un petit.]   [2] [ne seront que.]
[3] [le Père est toujours l'unique chef de la famille.]

du prix à[1] leur propre existence—de sages lois, des mœurs simples, le nécessaire, la paix, la liberté et l'estime des autres peuples[2]—leur zèle s'enflammera pour une si tendre mère[3]. Ils ne connaîtront de véritable vie que celle qu'ils tiendront d'elle[4], ni de vrai bonheur[5] que de l'employer à son service; et ils compteront au nombre de ses bienfaits l'honneur de verser au besoin tout leur sang pour sa défense. [Pencil, MS. p. 77. Intended to come about pp. 252—4.]

*(o) [6]En remontant à l'origine du droit politique, on trouve qu'avant qu'il y eut des chefs il y eut nécessairement des lois. Il en fallut au moins une, pour établir la confédération publique; il en fallut une seconde, pour établir la forme du Gouvernement. Et ces deux en supposent plusieurs intermédiaires, dont la plus solennelle[7] et la plus sacrée fut celle par laquelle on s'engagea à l'observation de toutes les autres. Si les lois existent avant le Gouvernement, ils sont donc indépendantes de lui. Le Gouvernement lui-même dépend des lois, puisque c'est d'elles seules qu'il tire son autorité[8]; et loin d'en être l'auteur ou le maître[9], il n'en est que le garant, l'administrateur et tout au plus l'interprète. [MS. p. 75 v°. Intended for the opening pages of the Treatise.]

(p) Comme on a dit que la beauté n'est que l'assemblage des traits les plus communs, on peut dire que la vertu n'est que la collection des volontés les plus générales. [MS. p. 75 v°. Intended for opening pages of the Treatise.] [W.]

*(q) La méchanceté n'est au fond qu'une opposition de la volonté[10] particulière à la volonté publique, et c'est pour cela qu'il ne saurait y avoir[11] de liberté parmi les méchants; parce que, si chacun fait sa volonté[12], elle contrariera[13] la volonté publique et celle de son voisin, et le plus souvent toutes les deux; et s'il est contraint d'obéir à la volonté publique, il ne fera jamais la sienne. [MS. p. 75 v°. Intended for pp. 242—3.]

(r) Dans les États où les mœurs valent mieux que les lois, comme était la République de Rome, l'autorité du père ne saurait

---

[1] [ce qui peut leur rendre sensible.]   [2] [personnes.]
[3] There is a reference here to the opposite page, which has been torn out.
[4] [qu'elle leur....]   [5] [de véritable gloire.]
[6] [J'ignore ce qu'on doit penser de tous les contes que nous font les historiens sur l'origine des nations.]
[7] [entre lesquelles il y en eut une plus solennelle.]
[8] [et toute l'autorité publique leur est soumise et n'en est que l'administration.]
[9] [il n'en est ni l'auteur....]   [10] [liberté.]   [11] [il n'y a jamais.]
[12] [si chacun d'eux en commet les actions.]   [13] [nécessairement.]

être trop absolue[1]; mais partout où, comme à Sparte, les lois sont la source des mœurs, il faut que l'autorité privée soit tellement[2] subordonnée à l'autorité publique que même dans la famille la République commande préférablement au père. Cette maxime me paraît incontestable, quoiqu'elle fournisse une conséquence[3] opposée à celle de l'*Esprit des Lois*. [MS. p. 75 v°. Intended for p. 258 or p. 240 of Treatise.] [D.B., W.]

*(s) Ceci bien entendu, l'on voit[4] que l'autorité publique[5], à laquelle je donne le nom de Gouvernement, ne s'étend que sur[6] les particuliers. Ces éclaircissements sont nécessaires pour distinguer l'économie publique, que j'appelle Gouvernement, de l'autorité suprême, que j'appelle souveraineté : distinction qui consiste en ce que l'une a le droit législatif[7] et oblige, en certains cas, le Corps même de la nation ; tandis que l'autre n'a que la puissance exécutrice[8] et ne peut obliger[9] que les particuliers. (Voyez *Politique, Souveraineté*.) [MS. p. 74. *E. P.* p. 241.]

*(t) [10]Si je veux déterminer exactement en quoi consiste l'Économie publique, je trouverai que ses fonctions se réduisent à ces trois principales[11] : administrer les lois, maintenir la liberté civile et pourvoir aux besoins de l'État. Mais pour apercevoir[12] la liaison de ces trois objets, il faut remonter au principe qui les unit. [MS. p. 74. Intended for opening pages of *E. P.* pp. 237—241.]

*(u) La volonté générale étant dans l'État la règle du juste et de l'injuste et toujours portée au bien public[13] et particulier, l'autorité publique ne doit être que l'exécutrice de cette volonté, d'où il suit que, de toutes les espèces de Gouvernement, le meilleur par sa nature est celui qui s'y rapporte le mieux : celui dont les membres ont le moins[14] d'intérêt personnel contraire à celui du peuple. Car cette duplicité d'intérêts ne peut manquer[15] de donner aux chefs une volonté particulière qui l'emporte souvent sur la générale dans leur administration. Si[16] l'embonpoint du corps porte[17] préjudice à la tête, elle aura grand soin d'empêcher le corps d'engraisser[18]. Si

---

[1] [et son pouvoir sur ses enfants.]   [2] D. B. reads 'nettement.'
[3] [directement.]   [4] [comprendra plus aisément.]   [5] [le gouvernement.]
[6] [est subordonné à l'autorité....]   [7] [prescrit les lois.]
[8] [l'autre est seulement le ministre des lois.]   [9] [n'oblige.]
[10] [Demandez à un politique [quelles sont] de déterminer exactement les fonctions du gouvernement, il me dira sans doute qu'elles consistent en ces trois choses.]
[11] [savoir.]   [12] [mieux voir.]   [13] [général.]
[14] [n'ont point.]   [15] [car cet intérêt ne manquerait pas.]
[16] [Comme si dans l'homme.]   [17] [portait.]
[18] [elle ne manquerait guère de le maintenir dans un état de maigresse.]

le bonheur du peuple est un obstacle à l'ambition des chefs, que le peuple ne se flatte pas d'être jamais heureux[1].

Mais si le Gouvernement est constitué comme il doit l'être et s'il suit les principes qu'il doit avoir, son premier soin dans l'économie ou administration publique sera donc de veiller sans cesse à l'exécution de la volonté générale, qui est à la fois le droit du Peuple et la source de son bonheur. Toute décision[2] publique[3] de cette volonté s'appelle loi, et par conséquent le premier devoir des chefs est de veiller à l'observation des lois. [MS. p. 73. Intended for *E. P.* pp. 242—3.]

(*v*) La vertu n'est que la conformité de la volonté particulière avec la volonté générale. [MS. p. 74 v°. *E. P.* p. 248.]

*(*w*) Il ne faut pas qu'on puisse couper un membre que la tête ne s'en aperçoive. [MS. p. 74 v°. *E. P.* p. 252.]

*(*x*) La grande société n'a pu s'établir sur le modèle de la famille parce qu'étant composée d'une multitude de familles, qui avant l'association n'avaient aucune[4] règle commune, leur exemple n'en pouvait pas fournir à l'État. Au contraire l'État, s'il est bien gouverné, doit donner dans toutes les familles des règles communes[5] et pourvoir[6] d'une manière uniforme à l'autorité du père, à l'obéissance des serviteurs et à l'éducation des enfants. [MS. p. 74 v°. *E. P.* pp. 238—240.]

*(*y*) Je n'ai plus qu'un mot à dire en finissant cet article. Toute l'Économie générale se rapporte à un dernier objet qui est l'effet et la preuve d'une bonne administration. Cet objet, relatif au bien général de l'espèce humaine, est la multiplication du peuple, suite infaillible de sa prospérité. Voulez-vous savoir si un État est bien ou mal gouverné? Examinez si le nombre de ses habitants augmente ou diminue. Toutes choses d'ailleurs égales, il est évident que le pays qui, proportion gardée, nourrit et conserve un plus grand nombre d'habitants est celui où ils se trouvent le mieux, et l'on juge avec raison des soins du berger par l'accroissement des troupeaux. [MS. p. 73. Intended for closing paragraph of *E. P.* Compare *Contrat social*, III. ix.]

---

[1] [ils sauront bien l'empêcher d'être heureux.]
[2] [Tous les points sur lesquels....]
[3] [générale.]
[4] [point de.]
[5] [une règle commune.]
[6] [pour fixer à....]

L'ÉTAT DE GUERRE

THE Fragment, *Que l'état de guerre naît de l'état social*[1], constitutes MS. 7856 in the Bibliothèque de la Ville, Neuchâtel. The MS. consists of three sheets of note-paper, *i.e.* three quarto pages folded in two. In its existing arrangement, these three sheets are folded inside each other, and therefore in the following order: 1 (*a*), 1 (*b*); 2 (*a*), 2 (*b*); 3 (*a*), 3 (*b*); 3 (*c*), 3 (*d*); 2 (*c*), 2 (*d*); 1 (*c*), 1 (*d*)[2]. This is the order in which they are printed both by M. Dreyfus-Brisac and M. Windenberger.

This arrangement, however, produces some extremely awkward breaks in the argument; especially as between pages 2 and 3, where the 'examples' mentioned—examples which, in fact, have not been given at all—cannot, to judge from what follows, have had any bearing upon the question which he has been discussing in the preceding paragraph. It seems clear to me that the first sheet was written from beginning to end before either of the other sheets was taken in hand: *i.e.* that Rousseau passed straight from the paragraph ending 'Mais cet exemple est unique dans l'histoire' to that beginning 'On peut demander encore.' Both paragraphs are concerned to enforce the principle that, in the civil state, war is not between individuals, but between communities; and the argument is unbroken. The inference, thus based on the continuity of the argument, is confirmed by the handwriting and the colour of the ink; both of which are the same throughout this sheet, but slightly different in the other two.

As for the two remaining sheets, there is more room for doubt. For careful consideration shews that, in any case, there are breaks in the argument; and, consequently, that we have to do, not with one Fragment, but with two or three. It is my belief that one of

---

[1] The title is retained, for convenience of reference. It was, however, cancelled on the MS. by the hand of Rousseau himself. In the following remarks I consider also the other, and shorter, Fragments (MS. Neuchâtel, 7840), which were manifestly written in connection with it.

[2] Here, and in note 4 on the following page, 1 (*a*), 1 (*b*), etc., indicate the first and second leaves of each sheet, each leaf containing two pages.

the two sheets in question was really, as Rousseau wrote them, folded inside the other—but in the reverse order from that which has hitherto been supposed. I consider, that is, that Rousseau meets the objection raised at the end of his fourth page[1]—*i.e.* that commerce is no necessity to nations—by the answer that, whether necessary or no in the physical sense, both commerce and all other international dealings have always been, and must always be, a vital part of the life of nations, considered as moral beings. It is, he argues, a matter not of material interest or necessity, but of instinct and of passion. And he continues this line of argument down to the end of the page following (p. 6 in both arrangements).

At the end of this page, however, there is a slight gap in the argument. Still dwelling on the principle that war is essentially a matter not of individuals but of states, he asks[2]: By what means can one state most effectively shew hostility against another? Unfortunately, he speaks as if he had given examples of various forms of hostility, although he has done nothing of the kind. But, when allowance has been made for this omission, it will be seen that the argument still continues its course. And there is no further gap till the end of p. 8.

At that point[3] he begins on an entirely new subject, *i.e.* an attack on the philosophers of his own time. And this leads him (pp. 11—12) to an assault upon Hobbes, in two variants, the first of which is cancelled; and that closes the whole treatise.

In a writing, which thus contains at least three separate fragments, it is obvious that absolute certainty of order is not to be attained. I have adopted that which seems to me the least open to objection[4].

The Fragment, as has already been said, has been twice published; first by M. Dreyfus-Brisac, as an Appendix to his edition of the *Contrat social* (Paris, 1896); again, by M. Windenberger in *La République Confédérative des petits États* (Paris, 1900). As the writing is often in the last degree difficult to decipher, it is small wonder that both editors should have sometimes failed to

[1] p. 12 of the existing arrangement.

[2] Beginning of p. 7 (new arrangement. So with p. 8, in this paragraph, and pp. 11—12 in the next).

[3] Beginning of p. 9 (n. a.).

[4] My order is as follows : 1 (*a*), 1 (*b*), 1 (*c*), 1 (*d*) ; 3 (*a*), 3 (*b*) ; 2 (*a*), 2 (*b*) ; 2 (*c*), 2 (*d*) ; 3 (*c*), 3 (*d*). Or in the numbering of the arrangement hitherto adopted : 1, 2, 11, 12, 5, 6, 3, 4, 9, 10, 7, 8. I assume a slight break between pp. 6 and 7 of the paging I have adopted ; and more serious breaks between pp. 8 and 9, and between pp. 10 and 11.

reproduce what Rousseau actually wrote. And there are one or two passages about which, after repeated efforts, I must confess myself still in doubt. These are indicated in the notes. As for the instances in which my reading of the text differs from that of either, or both, of the preceding editors, I have noticed only those which seriously affect the author's meaning. A facsimile of a characteristic page, containing one of these instances, is given below.

The question at once arises: Was the Fragment written with a view to publication? and if so, in which of Rousseau's works was it intended to find place? The answer to the former question hardly admits of doubt. If he did not design it for publication, it is incredible that Rousseau should have spent as much pains upon the style as he manifestly did. Nor again is it possible that he should not have been aware how original was the chain of reasoning that he had beaten out. On both grounds we are driven to the conclusion that it cannot have been written merely for his own satisfaction; that he must have meant to use it—and that, without much alteration—in one or other of his political writings. It has been suggested that the writing in question was that which, in a letter to Rey, Rousseau describes as *Principes du droit de la guerre*[1]. At the moment when that letter was written, it is certain that he intended to publish this, as a separate work. And if that intention had been carried out, it is more than likely that the Fragment before us would have appeared as a chapter, or section, of it. It is clear, however, that this was but a fleeting design. We hear nothing of it before the letter to Rey, and we hear nothing of it again[2]. It seems to me much more likely that the *Principes du droit de la guerre* was itself to be detached from the larger work, *Institutions politiques*, which Rousseau had long had on the stocks and which, at the time when the letter to Rey was written, must have been carried about as far as it ever was. He tells us that, by the following year (1759), he had definitely come to the conclusion that this larger work could never be finished. And it was at the same time that he determined to 'detach from it all that could be detached, and to burn the rest[3].'

[1] March 9, 1758; Bosscha, p. 32.
[2] Rousseau says nothing of it when he tells us of the plans he formed in the spring of 1756 (*Confessions*; *Œuvres*, x. p. 288); or again, early in 1759 (*ib.* p. 370). In each of these passages he speaks only of the *Institutions politiques*; and they are, so far as I know, the only passages bearing on the subject.
[3] *Œuvres*, x. p. 370.

The part detached is that which has come down to us as the *Contrat social*. But it is quite possible that in the preceding year (1758) he may have thought that another part, that relating to the rights of war, would better lend itself to separate treatment, and that he may have thrown out something to this effect in the course of conversation with Rey[1]. The subject is one which was bound to find place in the *Institutions politiques*. It is in fact handled, briefly and incidentally, in the opening chapters of the *Contrat social*, which give the results of the criticism of Hobbes and Grotius contained in the present Fragment. In view of all these facts, I can hardly think that the *Principes du droit de la guerre* was originally designed to form a separate and independent work. I believe it to have been nothing more than a part of the *Institutions politiques*. And if that be the case, it is as a part of the *Institutions politiques* that we must conceive the Fragment before us to have been originally composed.

The date of the Fragment cannot be exactly determined. The handwriting points to a time comparatively early. But whether that time should be placed before or after 1755—the year in which both the second *Discourse* and the *Économie politique* were published—it is impossible to decide. It is improbable that it should have been written much earlier than this date; and almost certain that it was not written much later. That is all we are entitled to say[2]. For myself, I am disposed to think that the earlier date (1753—5) is the more likely of the two. In no case, however, can it be put earlier than 1750 or 1751, the time at which Rousseau himself tells us that he began to work at the *Institutions politiques*[3].

In regard to matter, it is one of the most notable pieces that ever came from the hand of Rousseau. It is a reasoned statement of his convictions on two questions of crucial importance: the state of nature and the rights of war. It contains a brilliant criticism of the two writers, Hobbes and Grotius, to whose views on these subjects he was the most bitterly opposed. And, so far as the rights of war are concerned, it is based on principles

---

[1] Rey had visited him at the Hermitage in the last months of 1757; Bosscha, p. 29. The letter of March 9, 1758, manifestly implies some business negotiation with Rey, which was probably opened at that time.

[2] It deals, as we shall see, with many of the questions which lie at the bottom of the *Discours sur l'inégalité*, and it deals with them in much the same spirit. In style, moreover, it is more closely akin to the *Discours* than to any other of Rousseau's writings.

[3] *Confessions*, Liv. IX.; *Œuvres*, VIII. p. 289.

probably sounder, and certainly more humane, than any propounded before his day, or commonly accepted even in ours. It is therefore of no merely historic—still less, of antiquarian—interest. It is a contribution, and a contribution of the first moment, to what is still a burning question of the day. It must be added that the style, though unequal, is often of extraordinary power; that there are not a few passages which, in his more rhetorical vein, the writer never surpassed. In such passages, the noble indignation which inspired the whole Fragment, forces its way, in words of fire, to the surface.

Broadly speaking, we may say that the Fragment—including with it the shorter Fragments on the same subject found in MS. 7840—falls into two unequal halves: that dealing with the state of nature, and that dealing with the civil state. The former contains the refutation of Hobbes; the latter is one long assault upon the methods and principles of Grotius[1].

In the refutation of Hobbes, Rousseau takes up the theme which he had already treated, or was soon to treat, in other writings, and assails his opponent on the threefold ground of method, fact and logical inference. The method of Hobbes, in his view, is vicious because it is analytic[2]; and by this, as appears from the context, he means that, while the question before him is, 'What *was* the nature of man in his primitive state?' the question he actually answers is 'What *is* the nature of man in the civil state?' The term *analytic* is perhaps unhappily chosen. For the point is not so much that Hobbes put analysis in the place of synthesis as that he analysed one thing when, alike by the nature of the case and his own profession, he should have analysed another. Yet, when allowance has been made for this misleading use of terms, the criticism is perfectly just; it lays bare a fatal flaw both in the method and therefore in the logical validity of the whole argument of *Leviathan*[3]. It is, in fact, the same flaw that Rousseau exposes in one of the most striking

---

[1] Grotius, however, is nowhere mentioned by name. And it is possible that Rousseau was thinking rather of Pufendorf (*De jure naturæ et gentium*, VII. v., vi.). In favour of this suggestion is the fact that, when in the second *Discourse*, Rousseau assails the doctrine in question (above, p. 187), he attributes it to Pufendorf, with no mention of Grotius. On the other hand, in the Fragments which treat of the same subject, his blows are expressly directed against Grotius. See p. 310.

[2] See p. 307.

[3] It must be remembered that the only form of Hobbes' theory known to Rousseau was apparently the Latin version, *De Cive* (1642).

passages of the second *Discourse*: the same that he had in view when he wrote, 'All political philosophers have felt the need of going back to the state of nature; but none of them has ever got there[1].' Can we doubt that the brunt of this blow was intended to fall upon Hobbes?

The question of fact comes back, in the last resort, to much the same thing as the question of method. Once again, Rousseau's complaint is that the state of nature, as painted by Hobbes, is something utterly different from what it can ever have been in fact; and that this misrepresentation arises because, consciously or unconsciously, he has transferred to the state of nature the qualities—and, in particular, the vices—which came into being only with the civil state. 'The error of Hobbes and others is to confound the natural man with the man they have before their own eyes, and to transplant into one state of things a being who can exist only in another.' 'Man is by nature peaceful and timid; at the least whisper of danger, his first instinct is to fly; he acquires boldness only by experience and habit. Honour, self-interest, prejudice, vengeance—all the passions which nerve him to face death and peril—are far from him in the state of nature.' 'To eat and sleep are the sole needs he feels, and hunger alone has the power to tear him from his indolence. But of this sluggard the philosophers have made a madman, who is always burning to torment his fellows at the prompting of passions to which he is an utter stranger[2].'

It is no answer to this criticism to say that the 'state of nature' is a pure fiction; and that every writer is therefore entitled to make what assumptions he pleases about its character. For, in the first place, Hobbes was, or affected to be, firmly convinced of its reality. Unless he succeeds in convincing his readers of this, the whole of his subsequent argument falls in pieces. At every awkward bend of that argument, at each moment when its practical consequences become too outrageous, he turns round upon the reader with the triumphant question: Is not even this better than chaos come again? is not despotism, with all its admitted evils, a thing infinitely less terrible than the reign of force and

---

[1] *Discours sur l'inégalité*; above, p. 140.

[2] See pp. 306, 293, 298. Compare *Discours sur l'inégalité*, pp. 144, 147, 159, 160, 185; and Note I. Compare also Geneva MS. of *C. S.* I. ii.; below, pp. 447—9; and the note to the *Essai sur l'origine des langues*, beginning 'Il est inconcevable à quel point l'homme est naturellement paresseux'; *Œuvres*, I. p. 388.

fraud, of the wolf and the serpent, which made man's life intolerable in the state of nature ? Everything therefore, on Hobbes' own shewing, comes back to the question : Is the state of nature, as painted in *Leviathan*, true to the actual facts, or is it not ? And if it can be shewn that it is not—still more, if it can be shewn that, whatever the facts may have been, they cannot by any possibility have been what Hobbes assures us that they were—then the very foundation of his argument is shattered, and the whole fabric falls in ruins. This, in the latter and more convincing form, is precisely what Rousseau may fairly claim to have done. His proof that the vices which Hobbes attributes to the state of nature are such as can only have arisen in the close quarters and daily provocations of the civil state—that the aggressive vanity which prompts man to incessant deeds of force and fraud is, and can only be, the product of surroundings so artificial as to be inconceivable in the barbarism and unsettlement of the primitive state—is complete and deadly. It is as fatal to the hopeless truculence of Hobbes, as his corresponding assault on the idea of 'natural law' is to the easy-going optimism of Locke.

This, however, is not all. Even allowing that the initial assumptions of Hobbes are as true as they are manifestly false, the inferences which he draws from them are none the less absurd. Even granting that man is by his original nature the mass of spite, envy and cruelty that Hobbes imagines, considerations of mere self-interest would debar him from the war to the knife which Hobbes supposes inevitably to result. 'Even if it were true that this overmastering covetousness had gone to the lengths which our sophist supposes, it could never give rise to that war of all against all, of which Hobbes remorselessly draws so odious a picture[1].'

What are the grounds on which Rousseau comes to this conclusion ? And what are the plainest terms to which it can be reduced ? The object of war, as Hobbes himself insists, is the utter destruction of the enemy—*homo homini lupus*; and this can only mean that the one party will never rest until he has cleared the field of all his rivals and put himself in sole possession of the spoils. In so doing, however, he will find that he has simply defeated his own ends, that he has robbed himself of all the advantages which he had set himself to gain. Left alone upon the earth—or in that part of it which counts for all with him—

[1] See p. 293.

he will be reduced to misery, if not starvation; he will have to toil without remission, in order to keep himself alive. Even his vanity—and that is one of the chief springs of his villainy—will find no satisfaction in his triumph. For, without applause, vanity dies of starvation; and, by his own act, none is left to applaud his prowess, or offer incense to the 'cardinal virtues' which he has victoriously displayed. Thus, when put to the test, the theory of Hobbes is seen to involve a network of contradictions. Primitive man is incapable of the passions with which he is credited in *Leviathan*; and, even if capable, he could never have satisfied them without bringing himself to misery and death. 'This unbridled lust of drawing all things to himself is incompatible with the lust of destroying all his fellows; and the conqueror who, having slain all, should have the misfortune to be left alone upon the earth, would enjoy nothing, for the simple reason that he would be master of all. What good would he get from the possession of the whole universe, if he were its sole inhabitant? Who will gather for him the harvest of every climate? Who will carry the fame of his empire into the vast deserts which he will never reach? What will he do with his treasures? Who will consume the food that he has stored? In whose eyes will he make boast of his power? I see. Instead of slaying all, he will bind all in chains, so that at least he may have slaves. That changes the whole face of the argument at a single stroke. It is no longer a question of destruction. The state of war is done away[1].'

So ends the refutation of Hobbes. And at this point the fire is opened upon Grotius. Having demolished a false theory of the state of nature, Rousseau now passes to a theory, in his eyes no less false, concerning the origin of the civil state. The idea that men will barter their freedom to save their lives is the battle-horse of Grotius. Whether he acknowledges it or no, it forms the foundation of his whole argument about the rights of war[2]. And convinced as he was that the results of that argument were pernicious, Rousseau had no choice but to prove, if he could, that the 'rights' of Grotius were nothing better than a pretentious name for an intolerable wrong.

---

[1] See p. 293. Compare *Discours sur l'inégalité*, pp. 140—1, 159, 160, and Note I.
[2] See Grotius, *De Jure Belli et Pacis*, I. III. viii.; III. v. xviii.—xxix.; III. vii.—viii. And contrast the 'temperament' put forward, *ib.* III. xi. It is a mark of Rousseau's acuteness that he fastened on this as the corner-stone of Grotius' argument.

That men have, in fact, sold their freedom to save their lives, that history is full of such examples, Rousseau is much too cautious, much too clear-sighted, to deny. To trust himself to an argument with Grotius on the ground of fact, of historical evidence, would, he was well aware, be to court defeat. He is even willing to make the same admission with regard to nations. He allows it to be not inconceivable that, in the hope of avoiding destruction, one whole community should enslave itself to another. He does not formally dispute the assertion, for which Hobbes no less than Grotius is responsible, that a whole community may be found willing to enslave itself—virtually, if not actually and deliberately —to a single man. In the region of fact, he is ready to grant, if only for the sake of argument, all that the enemy in his wildest moments had taken upon him to demand. What he does is to counter it all by denying that it has any bearing upon the question of right. The true method, he urges, is 'to test the fact by the principles of Right.' 'The invariable practice of Grotius, on the contrary, is to infer the Right from the fact[1].'

The challenge could not have been more roughly thrown down. A mere denial, however, is not sufficient for Rousseau. And in the Fragment, as well as in other passages of his writings, it is justified in detail[2]. What is it, he asks, that makes it impossible to accept the fact as the last word upon the matter ? It is, in the first place, that the fact, varying as it does from place to place and from time to time, yields a standard so shifting as to be no standard at all. It is, in the second place, that the 'fact' universally tends to mean, and in the hands of Grotius does actually mean, the most barbarous and irrational fact: the fact which, if accepted as the standard or even tamely submitted to in one particular instance, would be most fatal to the liberty and happiness of mankind. This is notoriously the case with the matter at issue. Assume that slavery is the basis of civil society, and what is the result ? By his own act, man has robbed himself of that which makes him what he is; he has degraded his own being; he has put it in the power of others to degrade him still further by compelling him to acts against all right and justice. But more remains behind. The degradation of those immediately concerned would be of no avail, if it were not perpetuated in their offspring. It is the whole object of Grotius to prove that the liberty sacrificed

[1] See *Discours sur l'inégalité*, p. 186 ; and *C. S.* I. ii. (with Note) and iv.
[2] See below, pp. 309—311 ; *C. S.* I. ii.—iv.; Geneva MS. I. ii. and v. (p. 267) ; *Discours sur l'inégalité*, pp. 186—7.

by these men is for ever lost to their descendants; that their posterity for all time is condemned to the slavery which they have courted. Unless this consequence can be proved to follow, the whole argument misses fire.

At neither point will the theory stand examination. There are some possessions so essential to man, so much part and parcel of his being, that he has no right to surrender them. And of these —it would be more true to say, first of these—is the liberty without which his moral responsibility, and with it his whole moral life, is cut up by the roots. To surrender it is to inflict moral death upon himself. More than that. It is, if we examine the matter closely, to perpetuate the very state of war from which it is supposed to offer an escape. For to call a state of slavery a state of peace is a contradiction in terms. The master, just because he is the master, is at standing war—a war none the less bitter because it is masked under a false name—with those he treats as his chattels and his tools. And they in their turn have the right of reprisal whenever they are strong enough to enforce it. War is maintained in fact upon the one side; and that fact begets a right of resistance upon the other. 'The state of war necessarily subsists between them for the simple reason that the one are masters, and the others their slaves[1].'

And if this be true of those who in the first instance were enslaved by the conqueror, still more is it true of their children and descendants. The latter were, on no shewing, parties to the covenant which, by a cruel sophistry, is imputed to the former. As against the children, therefore, the conqueror has not even the false semblance of right he might claim against the fathers. And as he is just as much in a state of war against them, it follows that their right of resistance is yet clearer. There is, however, a further and yet more fatal consequence behind. If the argument breaks down in the case of the children, it breaks down altogether. It was framed for no other purpose than to provide a permanent basis for the tyranny of the conqueror. And if that tyranny necessarily ceases with the first generation, it might just as well have never been set up. The whole theory of Grotius is built upon a rotten foundation. At the first touch it crumbles in pieces.

So far the argument, whether against Hobbes or against Grotius, has gone on the assumption that there can be such a thing as a 'state of war' between one man, or one loose

[1] See p. 302 (*L'état de guerre*). It is said with reference to the Spartiates and the Helots.

assemblage of men, and another. Yet even this is a point to be disputed. In the state of nature it may conceivably have been so. But then each man lived isolated from the rest. The occasions of strife were therefore rare, and when they did arise, the quarrel was over almost as soon as it began. To call a struggle of this kind, however often it might be repeated, a 'state of war' is an abuse of terms. It is not a state, but a passing incident; not a war, but an affray. And an affray, even when it ends in murder, does not constitute a war.

This forms the transition to the final section of the Fragment: that in which Rousseau, once more in vehement protest against Grotius, attempts to determine the nature and the 'rights' of war. To him, war is essentially a relation not of man to man, nor even of band to band, but of one organised community to another: that is, of State to State. The relation is, of course, a hostile relation. But it is by no means necessary that the hostility should lead to bloodshed. Signs of a settled ill-will, on one side or both, are enough to constitute the state of war. And, apart from bloodshed or indeed any form of physical violence, there are a hundred ways in which this ill-will may be displayed.

It follows from this argument that war is not waged for the purpose of destroying life, of winning slaves, of annexing territory, of amassing spoil. Its sole end is, or ought to be, to assert the equality of one State with another, to vindicate the national rights of one community as against another. This is the key with which Rousseau unlocks all the intricacies of the problem. In the light of this principle he condemns all territorial aggression, as manifestly against right; all the barbarities of war, as not only morally odious but practically futile; all the attempts of philosophers to defend such things, as not only personally degrading but intellectually absurd. In support of these conclusions he appeals not only to conscience but to reason. And that remains true, although, here as always, he is content rather to set forth his convictions than to argue them in detail. But once grant his conception of the State as a self-contained unit, with rights which nothing can take from it, and the consequences which he here draws follow of themselves. No war which is not waged to maintain these rights is to be distinguished from brigandage. No measures, beyond such as are absolutely necessary to guard them, are other than robbery and murder. The State which launches a war with the object of stealing territory from its neighbour is assailing a right which is the foundation of its own being. The State which adopts methods of barbarism in warfare stands convicted, quite apart from its moral guilt, of confounding the distinction between the body politic, which alone is the legitimate object of hostility, and the individuals who compose it. In either case, there is a flagrant violation of the first principles on which the State is founded: a violation of its autonomy in the former instance, of its corporate unity in the latter.

Rousseau would have been the first to admit that this is, and will long continue to be, no more than an ideal: a principle which may have done something to mitigate the wrongs of war, but which is still very far from being universally recognised as a right. Indeed, the one serious flaw in his statement of the argument is his despair of its acceptance. In his hatred of the iniquities of the present, he forgets to acknowledge that they are as nothing in comparison with those of the past. Had he looked back to the *Iliad* or the Old Testament, to the Peloponnesian or Punic Wars, to the Thirty Years' War or the wars of Louis XIV, he would have seen that, both in respect for right and in reduction of cruelty, the record was one of slow, but continuous, improvement[1]. More than that. He would have seen that the improvement had exactly followed the lines which he himself laid down; that the constant tendency had been to make war less and less a conflict between individuals, more and more a condition of hostility between States. But, here as always, his eye was closed to the signs, to the very idea, of progress. And the argument from history, which might have lent effective support to his plea, is almost entirely neglected.

The omission is significant. It points not only to the weakness of Rousseau, but also to his strength: not only to his feeble grasp of history and outward conditions, but also to his overmastering faith in speculative ideas. And for the task before him, that was the one thing needful. An evil tradition—a tradition as irrational as it was cruel—had come down from the past. It was not by an appeal to the past, but by a return to the first principles of reason and conscience, that the wrong was to be redressed. Here, as always, it is not the fact, but the Right, which is in question. Here, as always, it is not 'the Right which has to be established from the facts, but the facts which have to be judged by the Right.' Few men have grasped this fundamental truth so firmly as Rousseau. And that is why, in this as in other matters, his work forms so memorable a landmark in the history of mankind.

[1] Unhappily, this can no longer be said with truth (Dec. 1914).

FRAGMENTS

I. L'ÉTAT DE GUERRE[1].

[MS. Neuchâtel, 7856.]

Mais, quand il serait vrai que cette convoitise illimitée et indomptable serait développée dans tous les hommes au point que le suppose notre sophiste, encore ne produirait-elle pas cet état de guerre universelle de chacun contre tous, dont Hobbes ose tracer l'odieux tableau. Ce désir[2] effréné de s'approprier toutes choses[3] est incompatible avec celui de détruire tous ses semblables; et le vainqueur[4], qui ayant tout tué aurait le malheur de rester seul au monde, n'y jouirait de rien par cela même qu'il aurait tout. Les richesses elles-mêmes, à quoi sont-elles bonnes si ce n'est à être communiquées? que lui servirait la possession de tout l'univers, s'il en était l'unique habitant[5]? Quoi! Son estomac dévorera-t-il tous les fruits[6] de la terre? Qui lui rassemblera[7] les productions de tous les climats? qui portera le témoignage de son empire dans les vastes solitudes qu'il n'habitera point? Que fera-t-il de ses trésors? qui consommera ses denrées? à quels yeux étalera-t-il son pouvoir? J'entends[8]. Au lieu de tout massacrer, il mettra tout dans les fers pour avoir au moins des esclaves. Cela change à l'instant tout l'état de la question[9]; et puisqu'il n'est plus question de détruire, l'état de guerre est anéanti. Que le lecteur suspende ici son jugement. Je n'oublierai pas de traiter ce point.

L'homme est naturellement pacifique et craintif; au moindre danger, son premier mouvement est de fuir; il ne s'aguerrit qu'à force d'habitude et d'expérience. L'honneur, l'intérêt, les préjugés,

---

[1] The original title of these Fragments, *Que l'état de guerre naît de l'état social*, was cancelled by Rousseau himself. The title above is kept for convenience of reference. New paging of MS. in Arabic, old in Roman, figures.

[2] or *dessin*.   [3] [de tout posséder.]
[4] [le malheureux, celui qui.]   [5] [s'il était seul à en jouir.]
[6] [productions.]   [7] [pour lui seul.]
[8] 'J'entends' is an afterthought.
[9] After *question*, originally 'et la guerre est anéantie. Je n'oublierai,' etc. D. B. reads *Cela a changé*.

la vengeance, toutes les passions qui peuvent lui faire braver les périls et la mort, sont loin de lui dans l'état de nature. Ce n'est qu'après avoir fait société avec quelque homme qu'il se détermine à en attaquer un autre ; et il ne devient soldat qu'après avoir été citoyen[1]. On ne voit pas là de grandes dispositions[2] à faire la guerre à tous ses semblables. Mais c'est trop m'arrêter sur un système aussi révoltant qu'absurde, qui a déjà cent fois[3] été réfuté.

Il n'y a donc point de guerre générale d'homme à homme[4] ; et l'espèce humaine n'a pas été formée uniquement pour s'entre-détruire. Reste à considérer la guerre accidentelle et particulière, qui peut naître entre deux ou plusieurs individus.

Si la loi naturelle n'était écrite que dans la raison humaine, elle serait peu capable de diriger la plupart de nos actions. Mais elle est encore gravée dans le cœur de l'homme en caractères ineffaçables ; et c'est là qu'elle lui parle plus fortement que tous les préceptes des philosophes[5] ; c'est là qu'elle lui crie[6] qu'il ne lui est permis de sacrifier la vie de son semblable qu'à la conservation de la sienne, et qu'elle lui fait horreur de verser le sang humain[7] sans colère, même quand il s'y voit obligé.

Je conçois[8] que, dans les querelles sans arbitres qui peuvent s'élever dans l'état de nature, un homme irrité pourra quelquefois en tuer un autre, soit à force ouverte, soit par surprise[9]. Mais, s'il s'agit d'une guerre véritable, qu'on imagine dans quelle étrange position doit être ce même homme, pour ne pouvoir conserver sa vie qu'aux dépens de celle d'un autre, et que par un rapport établi entre eux il faille que l'un meure pour que l'autre vive[10]. La guerre est un état permanent qui suppose des relations constantes ; et ces relations ont très rarement lieu d'homme à homme, où tout est entre les individus dans un flux continuel qui change incessamment les rapports et les intérêts[11]. De sorte qu'un sujet de dispute s'élève et cesse presqu'au même instant ; qu'une querelle commence et finit en un jour ; et qu'il peut y avoir des combats et des meurtres, mais jamais ou très rarement de longues inimitiés et des guerres.

---

[1] [Voilà le vrai progrès de la nature.]   [2] [naturelles.]
[3] D. B. reads *une fois*.
[4] End of p. 1 (i).   [5] [de son semblable.]
[6] or *dira*.   [7] D. B. and W., *de l'humanité*.   [8] [donc.]
[9] [ou qu'ému d'un puissant désir de vengeance il veut l'attendre et le tuer par surprise.]
[10] [soit conservé.]
[11] [les intérêts et les rapports.]

Dans l'état civil, où la vie de tous les citoyens est au pouvoir du souverain et où nul n'a droit de disposer de la sienne ou de celle d'autrui, l'état de guerre ne peut avoir lieu non plus entre les particuliers ; et quant[1] aux duels, défis, cartels, appels en combat singulier, outre que c'était un abus illégitime et barbare d'une constitution toute militaire, il n'en résultait pas un véritable état de guerre, mais une affaire particulière qui se vidait en temps et lieu limités, tellement que pour un second combat il fallait un nouvel appel[2]. On en doit[3] excepter les guerres privées[4] qu'on suspendait par des trèves journalières, appelées la paix de Dieu, et qui reçurent la sanction par les Établissements de Saint Louis. Mais[5] cet exemple est unique dans l'histoire[6].

On peut demander encore si les rois, qui dans le fait sont indépendants de[7] puissance humaine, pourraient établir entre eux des guerres personnelles et particulières, indépendantes de celles de l'État. C'est là certainement une question oiseuse ; car ce n'est pas, comme on sait, la coutume des princes d'épargner autrui[8] pour s'exposer personnellement. De plus, cette question dépend d'une autre qu'il ne m'appartient pas de décider : savoir, si le prince est soumis lui-même aux lois de l'État, ou non ; car, s'il y est soumis, sa personne est liée et sa vie appartient à l'État, comme celle du dernier citoyen. Mais si le prince est au-dessus[9] des lois, il vit dans le pur état de nature, et ne doit compte ni à ses sujets ni à personne d'aucune de ses actions.

DE L'ÉTAT SOCIAL.

Nous entrons maintenant dans un nouvel ordre de choses. Nous allons voir les hommes, unis par une concorde artificielle, se rassembler pour s'entr'égorger, et toutes les horreurs de la guerre naître des soins qu'on avait pris pour la[10] prévenir. Mais il importe premièrement[11] de se former sur l'essence du Corps politique des notions plus exactes que l'on n'a fait jusqu'ici. Que le lecteur songe seulement qu'il s'agit moins ici d'histoire et de faits que de

---

[1] Here, as always in the phrase 'quant à,' Rousseau writes *quand*.
[2] [dans un temps et dans un lieu limité : et cela est si vrai que, quand il était question d'un second combat, on faisait un nouvel appel.]
[3] [Il en faut.]   [4] [querelles particulières.]
[5] [je crois.]   [6] End of p. 2 (ii).
[7] [toute] puissance humaine.   [8] [les autres.]
[9] [exempt des lois] [exempt de l'observation des lois.]
[10] [les.]   [11] [Mais avant d'entrer en matière, il est bon.]

droit et de justice[1], et que je veux examiner[2] les choses par leur nature plutôt que par nos préjugés[3].

De la première société formée s'ensuit nécessairement la formation de toutes les autres. Il faut en faire partie, ou s'unir pour lui résister. Il faut l'imiter, ou se laisser engloutir par elle[4].

Ainsi, toute la face de la terre est changée ; partout la nature a disparu ; partout l'art humain a pris sa place[5] ; l'indépendance et la liberté naturelle ont fait place aux lois et à l'esclavage ; il n'existe plus d'être libre ; le philosophe cherche un homme et n'en trouve plus. Mais c'est en vain qu'on pense anéantir la nature ; elle renaît et se montre où l'on l'attendait le moins. L'indépendance, qu'on ôte aux hommes, se réfugie dans les sociétés ; et ces grands corps, livrés à leurs propres impulsions, produisent des chocs plus terribles à proportion que[6] leurs masses l'emportent sur celles des individus.

Mais, dira-t-on, chacun de ces corps ayant une assiette aussi solide, comment est-il[7] possible qu'ils viennent jamais à s'entreheurter ? Leur propre constitution ne devrait-elle pas les maintenir entre eux dans une paix éternelle ? Sont-ils obligés, comme les hommes, d'aller chercher au dehors de quoi pourvoir à leurs besoins ? N'ont-ils pas en eux-mêmes tout ce qui est nécessaire à leur conservation ? La concurrence et les échanges[8] sont-ils une source de discorde inévitable ? et dans tous les pays du monde les habitants n'ont-ils pas existé avant le commerce, preuve invincible qu'ils y pouvaient subsister sans lui ?

[Fin du chapitre : il n'y a point de guerre entre les hommes : il n'y en a qu'entre les États[9].]

À cela je pourrais me contenter de répondre par les faits, et[10] je

---

[1] [qu'il n'est pas] [qu'il ne s'agit pas ici d'histoire et de faits, mais de droit et de justice.] D. B. and W. read *des faits*.

[2] or *j'examine*. It is not clear whether *veux* is cancelled.

[3] [et que je n'entreprends point de dire [d'expliquer] ce que] [et que j'entreprends d'examiner ce que sont les choses par leur nature, et non par ce qu'elles sont par nos [erreurs] préjugés.] End of p. 3 (xi).

[4] [Il ne reste d'autre parti que de l'imiter, pour éviter d'être englouti par elle.] D. B. omits *Il faut* before *l'imiter*. Compare above, pp. 181-2.

[5] [Le philosophe cherche l'homme et ne le trouve plus.]

[6] [des chocs d'autant plus terribles que.]

[7] [comment chacun de ces corps, ayant une assiette aussi solide, peuvent-ils.]   [8] [mêmes.]

[9] End of p. 4 (xii). In the MS. the sentence in brackets is separated, by a line drawn across the page, from the preceding paragraph.

[10] D. B. reads *ici*.

n'aurais point de réplique à craindre. Mais je n'ai pas oublié que je raisonne ici sur la nature des choses et non sur les[1] événements, qui peuvent avoir mille causes particulières, indépendantes du principe commun[2]. Mais considérons attentivement la constitution des Corps politiques; et[3], quoiqu'à la rigueur chacun suffise à sa propre conservation, nous trouverons que leurs mutuelles relations ne laissent pas d'être beaucoup plus intimes que celles des individus. Car l'homme, au fond, n'a nul rapport nécessaire avec ses semblables; il peut subsister sans leur concours dans toute la vigueur possible[4]; il n'a pas tant besoin des soins de l'homme que des fruits[5] de la terre; et la terre produit plus qu'il ne faut pour nourrir[6] tous ses habitants. Ajoutez que l'homme a un terme de force et de grandeur fixé par la nature, et qu'il ne saurait passer. De quelque sens qu'il s'envisage, il trouve toutes ses facultés limitées. Sa vie est courte, ses ans sont comptés. Son estomac ne s'agrandit pas avec ses richesses; ses passions ont beau s'accroître, ses plaisirs ont leur mesure; son cœur est borné comme tout le reste; sa capacité de jouir est toujours la même. Il a beau s'élever[7] en idée, il demeure[8] toujours petit.

L'État, au contraire, étant un corps artificiel, n'a nulle mesure déterminée; la grandeur qui lui est propre est indéfinie; il peut toujours l'augmenter; il se sent faible tant qu'il en est[9] de plus forts que lui. Sa sûreté, sa conservation, demandent qu'il se rende[10] plus puissant que tous ses voisins. Il ne peut augmenter, nourrir, exercer ses forces qu'à leurs dépens; et, s'il n'a pas besoin de chercher sa subsistance hors de lui-même, il[11] y cherche sans cesse de nouveaux membres qui lui donnent[12] une consistance plus inébranlable. Car l'inégalité des hommes a des bornes posées par les mains de la nature; mais celle des sociétés peut croître incessamment, jusqu'à ce qu'une seule absorbe toutes les autres.

Ainsi, la grandeur du Corps politique étant purement relative, il est forcé de se comparer[13] pour se connaître; il[14] dépend de tout

---

[1] or *des*.
[2] [que mille causes particulières peuvent [rendre directement contraires aux effets les plus naturels] changer.] In the next sentence, D. B. reads *considérant*.
[3] [nous trouverons que, bien qu'à la rigueur.]
[4] D. B. reads *dans toute la rigueur possible*.
[5] [productions.]
[6] [la nourriture de.]
[7] [vouloir s'agrandir.]
[8] [reste.]
[9] [existe.]
[10] [soit.] W. reads *qu'il semble.*
[11] [faut qu'.]
[12] [le fortifient] [le renforcent.]
[13] [sans cesse.]
[14] [est forcé de.]

ce qui l'environne, et doit[1] prendre intérêt à tout ce qui s'y passe. Car il aurait beau vouloir se tenir au dedans de lui, sans rien gagner ni perdre; il devient petit ou grand, faible ou fort[2], selon que son voisin s'étend ou se resserre, se renforce ou s'affaiblit. Enfin sa solidité même, en rendant ses rapports plus constants[3], donne un effet plus sûr à toutes ses actions et rend toutes ses querelles plus dangereuses[4].

Il semble qu'on ait pris à tâche de renverser toutes les vraies idées des choses. Tout porte l'homme naturel au repos; manger et dormir sont les seuls besoins qu'il connaisse, et la faim seule l'arrache à la paresse. On en a fait un furieux, toujours prompt à tourmenter ses semblables par[5] des passions qu'il ne connaît point. Au contraire, ces passions, exaltées au sein de la société par tout ce qui peut les enflammer, passent pour n'y pas exister. Mille écrivains[6] ont osé dire que [7]le Corps politique[7] est sans passions, et qu'il n'y a point d'autre[8] raison d'État que la raison même. Comme si l'on ne voyait pas, au contraire, que l'essence de la société consiste dans l'activité de ses membres, et qu'un État sans mouvement ne serait qu'un corps mort. Comme si toutes les histoires du monde ne nous montraient pas les sociétés les mieux constituées être aussi les plus actives et, soit au dedans soit au dehors, l'action ou[9] réaction continuelle de tous leurs membres porter témoignage de la vigueur du corps entier[10].

La différence de l'art[11] humain à l'ouvrage de la nature se fait sentir dans ses effets. Les citoyens ont beau[12] s'appeler membres de l'État, ils ne sauraient[13] s'unir à lui comme de vrais membres le sont au corps; il est impossible de faire que chacun d'eux n'ait pas une existence individuelle et séparée, par laquelle il peut seul suffire à sa propre conservation; les nerfs sont moins sensibles, les muscles ont moins de vigueur, tous les liens sont plus lâches, le moindre accident peut tout désunir.

Que l'on considère combien, dans l'agrégation du Corps politique, la force publique est inférieure à la somme des forces particulières, combien il y a, pour ainsi dire, de frottement dans

---

[1] [ne peut se dispenser de.]

[2] [il augmente ou diminue et se ...(illegible).] Both M. Dreyfus-Brisac and M. Windenberger have gone wrong over this sentence.

[3] MS. *constant*.

[4] [difficiles à terminer.]   End of p. 5 (v).   [5] [pour contenter.]

[6] [Et les passions politiques.]   [7] [l'État.]   [8] D. B. omits *autre*.

[9] or *et*.   [10] du [corps] [tout.]

[11] [ouvrage.]   [12] [on a beau.]

[13] [il leur est impossible de.]

le jeu de toute la machine ; et l'on trouvera que, toute proportion gardée, l'homme le plus débile a plus de force pour sa propre conservation que l'État le plus robuste n'en a pour la sienne.

Il faut donc, pour que l'État[1] subsiste, que la vivacité de ses passions[2] supplée à celle de ses mouvements, et que sa volonté s'anime autant que son pouvoir[3] se relâche. C'est la loi conservatrice que la nature elle-même établit entre les espèces et qui les maintient toutes, malgré leur inégalité. C'est aussi, pour le dire en passant, la raison pourquoi les petits États ont à[4] proportion plus de vigueur que les grands. Car la sensibilité publique n'augmente pas[5] avec le territoire ; plus il s'étend, plus la volonté s'attiédit, plus les mouvements s'affaiblissent ; et ce grand corps, surchargé[6] de son propre poids, s'affaisse, tombe en langueur et dépérit[7].

Ces exemples suffisent[8] pour donner une idée des divers moyens dont on peut affaiblir[9] un État, et de ceux dont la guerre semble autoriser[10] l'usage pour nuire à son ennemi. À l'égard[11] des traités dont quelques-uns[12] de ces moyens sont les conditions, que sont au fond que de pareilles paix[13], si non une guerre continuée avec d'autant plus de cruauté que l'ennemi n'a plus le droit de se défendre ? J'en parlerai dans un autre lieu.

Joignez à tout cela[14] les témoignages sensibles de mauvaise volonté, qui annoncent l'intention de nuire : comme de refuser à une Puissance les titres qui lui sont dus, de méconnaître ses droits, rejeter[15] ses prétentions, d'ôter à ses sujets la liberté du commerce, de lui susciter des ennemis ; enfin, d'enfreindre à son égard le droit des gens, sous quelque prétexte que ce puisse être.

Ces diverses manières d'offenser un Corps politique ne sont toutes ni également praticables, ni également[16] utiles à celui qui les emploie ; et celles dont résulte à la fois notre propre avantage et le préjudice de l'ennemi sont naturellement préférées. La

---

[1] or *cet État*.   [2] [facultés sensibles.]
[3] [sa force.]   D. B. and W. read *l'anime*.   [4] D. B. and W. read *en*.
[5] [ne croît point.]   [6] [accablé.]
[7] [dépérit et tombe en langueur.]   End of page 6 (vi).
[8] [De ces exemples on peut tirer] [Voilà une légère idée de tous les divers moyens.]
[9] [nuire à.]   [10] [autorise et permet de mettre en usage.]
[11] [en effet.]   [12] MS. has *quelqu'un*.
[13] [mais à l'égard de toute paix dont ces moyens sont les conditions, qu'est-ce au fond qu'une pareille paix.]
[14] [À tout cela je joignerai.]   [15] [de lui disputer.]
[16] D. B. omits *également*.

terre, l'argent, les hommes, toutes les dépouilles qu'on peut s'approprier, deviennent ainsi les principaux objets des hostilités réciproques[1]. Cette basse avidité changeant insensiblement les idées des choses, la guerre[2] enfin dégénère en brigandage, et d'ennemis et guerriers[3] on devient peu à peu tyrans et voleurs.

De peur d'adopter sans y songer ces changements d'idées, fixons d'abord les nôtres par une définition, et tâchons de la rendre si simple qu'il soit impossible d'en abuser.

J'appelle donc guerre de Puissance à Puissance l'effet d'une disposition[4] mutuelle, constante et manifestée de détruire l'État ennemi, ou de l'affaiblir au moins par tous les moyens qu'on le peut[5]. Cette disposition réduite en acte est la guerre[6] proprement dite ; tant qu'elle reste sans effet, elle n'est que l'état de guerre.

Je prévois une objection : puisque selon moi l'état de guerre[7] est naturel entre les Puissances, pourquoi[8] la disposition dont elle résulte a-t-elle besoin d'être manifestée ? À cela je réponds[9] que j'ai parlé ci-devant de l'état naturel, que je parle ici de l'état légitime, et que je ferai voir ci-après comment, pour le rendre tel[10], la guerre a besoin d'une déclaration[11].

DISTINCTIONS FONDAMENTALES.

Je prie les lecteurs de ne point oublier[12] que je ne cherche pas ce qui rend la guerre avantageuse[13] à celui qui la fait, mais ce qui la rend légitime. Il en coûte presque toujours pour être juste. Est-on pour cela dispensé de l'être ?

S'il n'y eut jamais[14], et qu'il ne puisse y avoir, de véritable guerre

---

[1] [La terre, l'argent, les h. [qu'on peut s'approprier] sont ordinairement les principaux objets de la guerre et les dépouilles qu'on recherche pour se les approprier.]

[2] [c'est ainsi que la guerre.]

[3] [qu'on était.]

[4] Originally 'une disposition' immediately followed 'puissance.' [le rapport qui résulte entre elles d'une disposition.]

[5] After *au moins* [de tout autant qu'il est possible en [lui ôtant] attaquant ses sujets, ses biens et son territoire. Je n'ajoute pas sa liberté, parce que la lui ôter [sa] c'est le détruire, [et que cela a déjà été dit] comme je le ferai voir en son lieu.] *possibles* variant for *qu'on le peut.*

[6] D. B. reads *la guerre possible proprement dite.* But this is a confusion with *possibles* of the preceding line (see note 5).

[7] [puisque la guerre.]   [8] [qu'est-il besoin.]
[9] [répondrai.]   [10] D. B. reads *pour la rendre telle.*
[11] End of p. 7 (iii).   [12] [se bien souvenir] [penser toujours.]
[13] [commode et facile.]   [14] D. B. reads *S'il n'y a jamais eu.*

entre les particuliers, qui¹ sont donc ceux entre lesquels elle a lieu et qui peuvent s'appeler² réellement ennemis ? Je réponds que ce sont les personnes publiques. Et qu'est-ce qu'une personne publique ? Je réponds que c'est cet être moral qu'on appelle souverain, à qui le pacte social a donné l'existence, et dont toutes les volontés portent le nom de lois. Appliquons ici les distinctions précédentes³ ; on peut dire, dans les effets de la guerre, que c'est le souverain qui fait le dommage et⁴ l'État qui le reçoit.

Si la guerre n'a lieu qu'entre des êtres moraux, on n'en veut⁵ point aux hommes, et l'on peut la faire sans ôter la vie à personne. Mais ceci demande explication.

À n'envisager les choses que selon la rigueur du pacte social, la terre, l'argent, les hommes, et⁶ tout ce qui est compris dans l'enceinte de l'État, lui appartient sans réserve. Mais les⁶ droits de la société, fondés sur ceux de la nature, ne pouvant les anéantir, tous ces objets doivent être considérés sous un double rapport : savoir, le sol comme territoire public et comme patrimoine⁷ des particuliers ; les biens comme appartenant dans un sens au souverain et dans un autre aux propriétaires ; les habitants comme citoyens et comme hommes. Au fond, le Corps politique, n'étant qu'une personne morale, n'est qu'un être de raison. Ôtez la convention publique, à l'instant⁸ l'État est détruit, sans la moindre altération dans tout ce qui le compose ; et jamais toutes les conventions des hommes ne sauraient changer rien dans le physique des choses⁹. Qu'est-ce donc que faire la guerre à un souverain ? c'est attaquer la convention publique et tout ce qui en résulte ; car l'essence de l'État ne consiste qu'en cela. Si le pacte social pouvait être tranché d'un seul coup, à l'instant il n'y aurait plus de guerre ; et de ce seul coup l'État serait tué, sans qu'il mourût un seul homme. Aristote dit que pour autoriser les cruels traitements¹⁰ qu'on faisait souffrir à Sparte aux Ilotes, les Éphores, en entrant en charge, leur déclaraient solennellement la guerre¹¹. Cette déclaration était

---

¹ [quels.]
² [s'appliquer.]
³ [Si on se souvient des distinctions.]
⁴ [que c'est.]
⁵ D. B. reads *elle ne nuit point*.
⁶ 'et' may be cancelled. D. B. reads *mais ces droits*.
⁷ [possession.]
⁸ D. B. omits *à l'instant*.
⁹ [et l'on sait bien que jamais toutes les conventions des h. ne peuvent rien changer dans la nature des hommes.]
¹⁰ [les traitements inhumains.]
¹¹ The paragraph originally ended thus : 'C'était une excuse aussi vaine qu'inhumaine, et un étrange renversement d'idées. Si la guerre ne peut avoir lieu contre des hommes libres et indépendants, combien moins contre de

aussi superflue que barbare. L'état de guerre subsistait nécessairement entre eux par cela seul que les uns étaient les maîtres, et les autres les esclaves. Il n'est pas douteux que, puisque les Lacédémoniens tuaient les Ilotes, les Ilotes ne fussent en droit de tuer les Lacédémoniens[1].

J'ouvre les livres de droit et de morale; j'écoute les savants et les jurisconsultes; et pénétré de leurs discours insinuants, je déplore les misères de la nature, j'admire la paix et la justice établies par l'ordre civil, je bénis la sagesse[2] des institutions publiques[3] et me console d'être homme en me voyant citoyen[4]. Bien instruit de mes devoirs et de mon bonheur[5], je ferme le livre, sors de la classe[6], et regarde autour de moi; je vois des peuples infortunés gémissant sous un joug de fer, le genre humain écrasé par une poignée[7] d'oppresseurs, une foule affamée, accablée de peine et de faim[8], dont le riche boit en paix le sang et les larmes[9], et partout le fort armé contre le faible du redoutable pouvoir des lois.

[10]Tout cela se fait paisiblement et sans résistance[11]. C'est la tranquillité des compagnons d'Ulysse enfermés dans la caverne du Cyclope, en attendant qu'ils soient dévorés[12]. Il faut gémir et se taire. Tirons un voile éternel sur ces objets d'horreur. J'élève

malheureux esclaves!' M. Windenberger incorporates the latter sentence in the text, omitting the former. Both are cancelled in the MS.

[1] End of p. 8 (iv).
[2] [et la bonté.] [3] [humaines.]
[4] [et me félicite d'être homme au milieu.]
[5] Originally the sentence began with *Je ferme.*
[6] Both M. Dreyfus-Brisac and M. Windenberger read 'sous...de la classe.' The former states that there are 'one or two illegible words' between *sous* and *de*; the latter that there is an 'interval.' Neither statement is in accordance with the facts. There is no interval, and there are no words between. *Sors* is badly written, and, but for the sense, might well have been *sous*. But, owing to Rousseau's peculiar way of forming *r*, the difference between it and *u* is but slight. See the Facsimile opposite.
[7] [sous une foule.]
[8] 'Gémissante de faim—accablée de peine,' written above as afterthought. But the MS. is here almost indecipherable.
[9] [pleurs.]
[10] Originally paragraph began [Ah...couvrez d'un voile éternel ces objets d'horreur].
[11] After *résistance* [Il est vrai. Mais la tranquillité qu'on m'a vantée est celle des compagnons, etc.].
[12] [qu'il les dévore.] The same comparison is used in *Contrat social*, I. iv. W. reads *tous dévorés*.

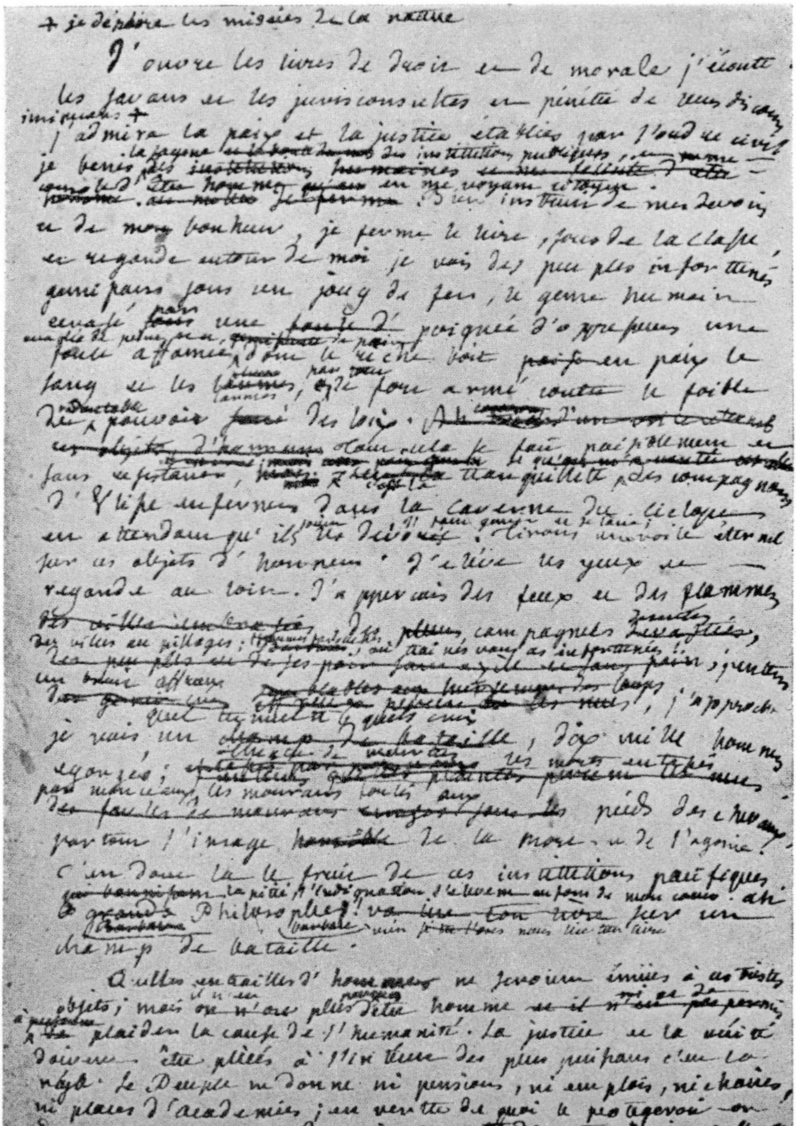

+ je déplore les misères de la nature

J'ouvre les livres de droit et de morale j'écoute les savans et les jurisconsultes et pénétré de leurs discours insinuans + j'admire la paix et la justice établies par l'ordre civil je bénis la sagesse des institutions publiques, et me console d'être homme en me voyant citoyen. Bien instruit de mes devoirs et de mon bonheur, je ferme le livre, sors de la classe et regarde autour de moi je vois des peuples infortunés gémissans sous un joug de fer, le genre humain écrasé par une poignée d'oppresseurs une foule affamée, accablée de peine et de faim, dont le riche boit en paix le sang et les larmes, et partout le fort armé contre le foible du redoutable pouvoir des loix. Tout cela se fait paisiblement et sans résistance, c'est la tranquillité des compagnons d'Ulysse enfermés dans la caverne du Cyclope en attendant qu'ils soient dévorés. Il faut gémir et se taire. Tirons un voile éternel sur ces objets d'horreur. J'élève les yeux et regarde au loin. J'apperçois des feux et des flammes, des campagnes désertes, des villes au pillage; Hommes farouches, où traînez-vous ces infortunés! j'entends un bruit affreux; quel tumulte! quels cris! j'approche je vois un théâtre de meurtres, dix mille hommes égorgés, les morts entassés par monceaux, les mourans foulés aux pieds des chevaux, partout l'image de la mort et de l'agonie! C'est donc là le fruit de ces institutions pacifiques. La pitié, l'indignation s'élèvent au fond de mon cœur. Ah barbare Philosophe! viens nous lire ton livre sur un champ de bataille.

Quelles entrailles d'homme ne seroient émues à ces tristes objets; mais il n'est plus permis d'être homme et de plaider la cause de l'humanité. La justice et la vérité doivent être pliées à l'intérêt des plus puissans c'est la règle. Le peuple ne donne ni pensions, ni emplois, ni chaires, ni places d'académies; en vertu de quoi le protégeroit-on? Princes magnanimes de qui nous attendons tout, je parle au

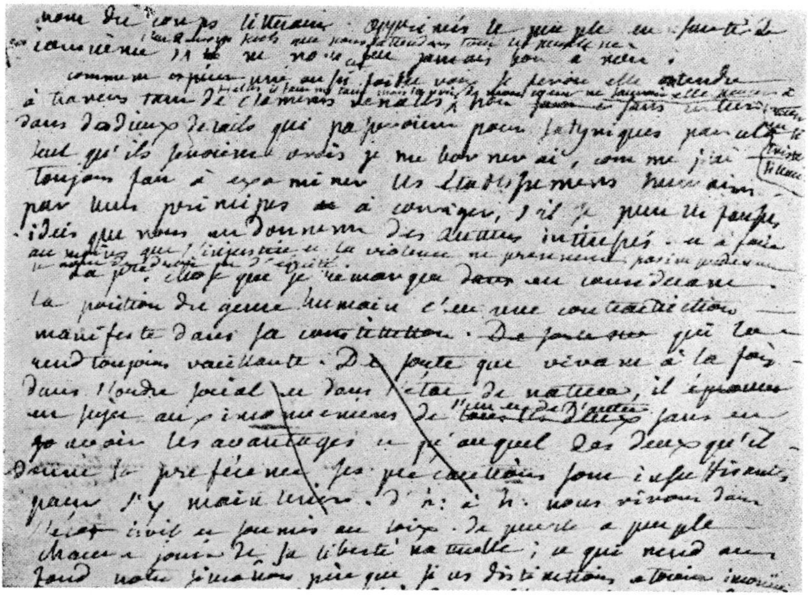

les yeux et regarde au loin. J'aperçois des feux et des flammes[1], des campagnes désertes[2], des villes au pillage. Hommes farouches, où trainez-vous ces infortunés ? J'entends un bruit affreux; quel tumulte ! quels cris ! J'approche ; je vois un théâtre de meurtres, dix mille hommes égorgés, les morts entassés par monceaux, les mourants foulés aux pieds des chevaux, partout l'image de la mort et de l'agonie. C'est donc là le fruit de ces institutions pacifiques. La pitié, l'indignation s'élèvent au fond de mon cœur. Ah ! philosophe barbare, viens nous lire ton livre sur un champ de bataille !

Quelles entrailles d'hommes ne seraient émues à ces tristes objets ? mais il n'est plus permis d'être homme et[3] de plaider la cause de l'humanité. La justice et la vérité doivent être pliées à l'intérêt des plus puissants : c'est la règle. Le peuple ne donne ni pensions, ni emplois, ni chaires, ni places d'Académies ; en vertu de quoi le protégerait-on ? Princes magnanimes, je parle au[4] nom du corps littéraire ; opprimez le peuple en sûreté de conscience ; c'est de vous seuls que nous attendons tout[5] ; le peuple ne nous est[6] bon à rien.

Comment[7] une aussi faible voix se ferait-elle entendre à travers tant de clameurs vénales ? Hélas ! il faut me taire ; mais la voix de mon cœur ne saurait-elle percer à travers un si triste silence[8] ? Non ; sans entrer dans d'odieux détails, qui passeraient

[1] [des villes embrasées.]
[2] [dévastées, des peuples au désespoir sans asile et sans pain. J'entends des gémissements ; quel tumulte et quels cris affreux, semblables aux hurlements des loups, percent les nues ! j'approche, je vois un champ de bataille, dix mille hommes égorgés ; j'entends ; quelles plaintes percent les nues ! des foules de mourants écrasés sous les pieds des chevaux, partout l'image [horrible] de la mort, de l'agonie. C'est donc là le fruit de ces institutions pacifiques, qui banissent la pitié. Ah ! grand Philosophe, va lire ton livre sur un champ de bataille !] My reading of the text, which is here very intricate, differs slightly from that both of D. B. and W.
[3] [mais on n'ose plus être homme, et il n'est plus permis à personne de plaider.]
[4] End of p. 9 (ix).
[5] In the MS. *Princes magnanimes* is followed by *de qui nous attendons tout*, which has not been cancelled. But as the phrase is repeated in the last clause but one (where it is written in over the line) it is clear that it should have been cancelled in the earlier clause. It will be observed that Rousseau had turned over a page in the interval. Both M. Dreyfus-Brisac and M. Windenberger have gone wrong over this sentence.
[6] [ne nous sera jamais.]   [7] Comment [espérer].
[8] MM. Dreyfus-Brisac and Windenberger read *penser à tracer un si triste sillon*. It is possible that they may be right ; but I doubt it. The

pour satiriques par cela seul qu'ils seraient vrais, je me bornerai, comme j'ai toujours fait, à examiner les établissements humains par leurs principes ; à corriger, s'il se peut, les fausses idées que nous en donnent des auteurs intéressés ; et à faire au moins que l'injustice et la violence ne prennent pas impudemment le nom de droit et d'équité.

La première chose que je remarque, en considérant la position du genre humain, c'est une contradiction manifeste dans sa constitution, qui la rend toujours vacillante[1]. D'homme à homme, nous vivons dans l'état civil et soumis aux lois; de peuple à peuple, chacun jouit de la liberté naturelle: ce qui rend au fond notre situation pire que si ces distinctions étaient inconnues[2]. Car vivant à la fois dans l'ordre social et dans l'état de nature, nous sommes assujettis aux inconvénients de l'un et de l'autre, sans trouver la sûreté dans aucun des deux[3]. La perfection de l'ordre social consiste, il est vrai, dans le concours de la force et de la Loi. Mais il faut pour cela que la Loi dirige la force ; au lieu que, dans les idées de l'indépendance absolue des princes, la seule force, parlant aux citoyens sous le nom de Loi et aux étrangers sous le nom de raison d'État, ôte à ceux-ci le pouvoir, et aux autres la volonté, de résister ; en sorte que le vain nom de justice ne sert partout que de sauvegarde à la violence[4].

Quant à ce qu'on appelle communément le droit des gens[5], il est certain que, faute de sanction, ses lois ne sont que des chimères plus faibles encore que la loi de nature. Celle-ci parle au moins au cœur des particuliers ; au lieu que, le droit des gens n'ayant

writing, so far as I can judge, might be taken either way ; but the phrase, as they read it, is hardly, I think, in the style of Rousseau.

[1] [De sorte que, vivant à la fois dans l'ordre social et dans l'état de nature, il est sujet aux inconvénients de l'un et de l'autre sans en avoir les avantages, et qu'auquel des deux qu'il donne la préférence, ses précautions sont insuffisantes pour s'y maintenir.] See *Paix perpétuelle*, p. 365, and *Émile*, Vol. II. pp. 157—8
[2] or *inouïes*.
[3] [Sans en avoir les avantages.]
[4] There is much confusion in the arrangement of this and the following paragraph. After *la violence*, Rousseau had left a gap and, about three-fifths of an inch lower, had drawn a line across the page. Beneath this line he wrote the paragraph beginning *Quant à ce qu'on appelle*. But, for some reason, he completed the paragraph above the line from the words *auquel des deux systèmes* to the end. Hence, at least in part, the difference between my version and those of MM. Dreyfus-Brisac and Windenberger. There are also great difficulties in the punctuation. I believe that my version is that warranted by the MS., and it certainly makes better sense.
[5] [Quant à ce beau nom de droit des gens, dont on fait tant de bruit.]

d'autre garant que l'utilité de celui qui s'y soumet, ses décisions ne sont respectées qu'autant que l'intérêt les confirme. [1]Dans la condition mixte où nous nous trouvons, auquel des deux systèmes qu'on donne la préférence, en faisant trop ou trop peu, nous n'avons rien fait, et nous sommes mis dans le pire état où nous puissions nous trouver. Voilà, ce me semble, la véritable origine des calamités publiques.

Mettons un moment ces idées en opposition avec l'horrible système de Hobbes; et nous trouverons, tout au rebours[2] de son absurde doctrine, que, bien loin que l'état de guerre soit naturel à l'homme, la guerre est née de la paix, ou du moins des précautions que les hommes ont prises pour s'assurer une paix durable. Mais, avant que d'entrer dans cette discussion, tâchons [d'expliquer ce qu'il...][3].

[[4]Qui peut avoir imaginé sans frémir le système insensé[5] de la guerre naturelle de chacun contre tous? Quel étrange animal que celui qui croirait son bien attaché à la destruction de toute son espèce! et comment concevoir que cette espèce, aussi monstrueuse et aussi détestable, pût durer seulement deux générations? Voilà pourtant jusqu'où le désir ou plutôt la fureur d'établir le despotisme et l'obéissance passive ont conduit un des plus beaux génies[6] qui aient existé. Un principe[7] aussi féroce était digne de son objet.

L'état de société qui contraint toutes nos inclinations naturelles ne les saurait pourtant anéantir; malgré nos préjugés et malgré nous-mêmes, elles parlent encore au fond de nos cœurs et nous ramènent souvent au vrai que nous quittons pour des chimères. Si cette inimitié mutuelle et destructive était attachée à notre constitution, elle se ferait donc sentir encore et nous repousserait, malgré nous, à travers toutes les chaînes sociales. L'affreuse haine de l'humanité serait souverain reconnu de l'homme[8]. Il s'affligerait[9] à la naissance de ses propres enfants[10]; il se réjouirait à la mort de

---

[1] [Ainsi.]   [2] [contraire.] D. B. reads *trouverons tous, au rebours.*

[3] These words cancelled and the sentence left unfinished. End of p. 10 (x).

[4] From here to end of next paragraph but three [qu'il en fait naître] cancelled in MS.

[5] [Imagine-t-on jamais de système plus absurde que celui de la guerre.] D. B. and W. embody this in the text, with *justice* for *système*.

[6] [un des plus grands philosophes et des plus beaux génies.]

[7] [système.]

[8] [se ferait sentir à l'homme.] Both M. Dreyfus-Brisac and M. Windenberger have gone wrong here.   [9] [nous nous affligerions.]

[10] [des enfants.]

ses frères[1] ; et lorsqu'il trouverait quelqu'un endormi, son premier mouvement serait de le tuer[2].

La bienveillance qui nous fait prendre part au bonheur de nos semblables, la compassion qui nous identifie avec celui qui souffre et nous afflige de sa douleur[3], seraient des sentiments inconnus et directement contraires à la nature. Ce serait un monstre qu'un homme sensible et pitoyable ; et nous serions naturellement ce que nous avons bien de la peine à devenir au milieu de la dépravation qui nous poursuit.

Le sophiste dirait en vain que cette mutuelle inimitié n'est pas innée et immédiate, mais fondée sur la concurrence inévitable du droit de chacun pour[4] toutes choses. Car le sentiment de ce prétendu droit n'est pas plus naturel à l'homme que la guerre qu'il en fait naître[5].]

Je l'ai déjà dit et ne puis trop le répéter, l'erreur de Hobbes et des philosophes[6] est de confondre l'homme naturel avec les hommes qu'ils ont sous les yeux, et de transporter dans un système un être qui ne peut subsister que dans un autre. L'homme veut son bien-être et tout ce qui peut y contribuer : cela est incontestable. Mais naturellement ce bien-être de l'homme se borne au nécessaire physique ; car, quand il a l'âme saine et que son corps ne souffre pas, que lui manque-t-il pour être heureux selon sa constitution ? Celui qui n'a rien désire peu de chose ; celui qui ne commande à personne a peu d'ambition. Mais le superflu éveille la convoitise[7] ; plus on obtient, plus on désire. Celui qui a beaucoup veut tout avoir ; et la folie de la monarchie universelle n'a jamais tourmenté que le cœur d'un grand roi. Voilà la marche de la nature, voilà le développement des passions. Un philosophe superficiel observe[8] des âmes cent fois[9] repétries et fermentées dans le levain de la société, et croit avoir observé l'homme. Mais, pour le bien connaître[10], il faut savoir démêler la gradation naturelle de ses

---

[1] [des frères.]

[2] [le premier mouvement de la nature serait d'être tenté de le tuer.]

[3] [et porte au fond de notre âme la peur de celui qui souffre] [et nous afflige de l'affligeante image du sentiment de sa douleur.]

[4] *or sur.* The two following words are not absolutely certain.

[5] End of p. 11 (vii), the whole of which is cancelled in MS. The next page—the two paragraphs beginning 'Je l'ai déjà dit' and 'Ainsi cette méthode analytique'—is intended for a variant of it.

[6] [de la plupart des phil.]

[7] [c'est ce qu'on a de trop qui rend les désirs si immodérés.]   [8] [voit.]

[9] M. Windenberger reads *une fois* ; M. Dreyfus-Brisac omits both words.

[10] [Mais quand on veut étudier le cœur de l'homme.]

sentiments; et ce n'est point chez les habitants d'une grande ville[1] qu'il faut chercher[2] le premier trait de la nature dans l'empreinte du cœur humain.

[3]Ainsi, cette méthode analytique n'offre-t-elle qu'abîmes et mystères, où le plus sage comprend le moins. Qu'on demande pourquoi les mœurs se corrompent à mesure que les esprits s'éclairent; n'en pouvant trouver la cause[4], ils auront le front de nier le fait. Qu'on demande pourquoi les sauvages transportés parmi nous ne partagent ni nos passions ni nos plaisirs[5], et ne se soucient point de tout ce que nous désirons avec tant d'ardeur. Ils ne l'expliqueront jamais, ou ne l'expliqueront que par mes principes[6]. Ils ne connaissent que ce qu'ils voient, et n'ont jamais vu la nature. Ils savent fort bien ce que c'est qu'un bourgeois de Londres ou de Paris; mais ils ne sauront jamais ce que c'est qu'un homme[7].

II. Two Fragments relating to the *Discourses*[8].

*[MS. Neuchâtel, 7854. Intended for the *Réponse au Roi de Pologne*. As that was published in 1751, this is the earliest of the dateable Fragments. It is written in pencil.] Je prévois qu'un jour le ton de ce petit ouvrage excitera la curiosité des lecteurs. 'Quel est,' dira-t-on, 'cet adversaire auquel on parle avec tant de respect et de fermeté, auquel on témoigne une si grande estime et si peu de crainte de lui déplaire?' Après la réponse, on ajoutera sans doute: 'Le citoyen de Genève osa lui dire la vérité.' Et malheureusement pour les peuples, ce n'est pas à moi que ce Discours fera le plus d'honneur[9].

[1] [dans une grande ville.]   [2] [qu'on voit] [qu'on distingue.]
[3] To the sentence 'Ainsi...le moins'—or possibly to the whole paragraph —the words *en note* are appended by Rousseau.
[4] [raison.]
[5] [ni notre avidité.]
[6] [Cela s'explique aisément par mes principes.] D. B. reads *s'expliqueront* (*bis*).   [7] End of p. 12 (viii).
[8] Throughout the remainder of the Fragments, I have marked (at the end of each Fragment) if, and by whom, it has been published before. D. B. =Dreyfus-Brisac; W.=Windenberger; S. M.=Streckeisen-Moultou. If, to the best of my knowledge, any Fragment has not been previously published, I have placed * at the beginning of it. I must express the sincere hope that I have not overlooked any of the work of my predecessors.
[9] The King of Poland's criticism of the first *Discourse* (published in the *Mercure*, Sept. 1751) will be found in his collected Works (*Œuvres du Philosophe bienfaisant*), T. IV. pp. 317—346 (ed. Marin, Paris, 1763). Rousseau quotes from his *Observations sur Pologne* more than once; see Vol. II. pp. 274, 426.

*[Written in pencil, MS. Neuchâtel, 7840, p. 70. This is the rough draft of a paragraph to be found in Rousseau's *Lettre à Philopolis* (Charles Bonnet) who had attacked the second *Discourse*. Both attack and rejoinder appeared in the late autumn of 1755. The rough draft is shorter than the printed text; and, in the closing sentence of the latter, there is one alteration worth noting: 'des Caraïbes qui se passent de notre police, des Hottentots qui s'en moquent, et un Genevois qui les approuve.'] Si tout est bien comme il est, tout était bien comme il était avant qu'il y eût des Gouvernements et des lois. Il fut donc superflu de les établir[1]. Si tout est aussi bien qu'il peut être, on ne peut toucher[2] à rien sans mal faire, et le quiétisme le plus parfait est la seule vertu qui reste à l'homme. Si tout est bien comme il est, il ne faut ni corriger nos vices, ni guérir nos maux, ni redresser nos erreurs. De quoi servent donc nos chaires, nos tribunaux, nos académies? Laissons[3] tout aller comme il pourra[4]; tout ira[5] toujours bien. Si tout est bien comme il est, il est bon qu'il y ait des Esquimaux, des Algonquins, des Chicacas, des Caraïbes, des Hottentots, qui rejettent[6] notre merveilleuse police, et un Jean-Jacques Rousseau qui s'en moque.

See also the first draft of a few passages in the *Discours sur l'inégalité*, recorded in their respective places in the text. These also are found in MS. Neuchâtel, 7854 (below, pp. 349—350).

III. Fragments relating to the earlier chapters of Le Contrat social.

[MS. Neuchâtel, 7840.]

[MS. p. 73 v°.] Il n'y a que des peuples tranquillement établis depuis très longtemps qui puissent imaginer de faire de la guerre un véritable métier à part[7], et des gens qui l'exercent une classe particulière. Chez un nouveau peuple, où l'intérêt commun est encore en toute sa vigueur, tous les citoyens sont soldats en temps de guerre, et il n'y a plus de soldats[8] en temps de paix. C'est un des meilleurs signes de la jeunesse et de la vigueur d'une nation[9]. Il faut nécessairement que des hommes toujours armés soient par

---

[1] [il ne les fallait donc pas établir.]
[2] [on ne peut donc rien changer.]   [3] [Que ne laissons-nous.]
[4] [comme il va.]   [5] [tout n'ira-t-il pas.]   [6] [méprisent.]
[7] [des gens de guerre une classe à part des autres citoyens.] D. B. and W. omit *véritable*.
[8] [tous les soldats redeviennent....]   [9] [de l'État.]

état les ennemis de tous les autres. On n'emploie jamais ces forces artificielles que comme une ressource contre l'affaiblissement intérieur[1] ; et les premières troupes réglées sont en quelque sorte les premières rides qui annoncent la prochaine décrépitude du Gouvernement. [D. B.; W.]

*[MS. p. 73 v°.] Le temps des plus honteux dérèglements et des plus grandes misères de l'homme fut[2] celui où, de nouvelles passions ayant étouffé les sentiments naturels, l'entendement humain n'avait[3] pas fait encore assez de progrès pour suppléer par[4] les maximes de la sagesse aux mouvements de la nature. Une autre époque, moins affreuse au premier aspect mais plus funeste encore dans la réalité, c'est celle où les hommes, à force de subtiliser et renchérir sur l'art de raisonner, sont parvenus à[5] renverser et confondre toute la doctrine de la société et des mœurs, et à ne regarder un système de morale que comme un leurre[6] entre les mains des gens d'esprit, pour tirer parti de la crédulité des simples.

[MS. pp. 72 v°, and 71 r°. Probably written as an early draft of *C. S.* I. chaps. iii., iv.] Grâce à Dieu, on ne voit plus rien[7] de pareil parmi les Européens. On aurait horreur d'un prince qui ferait massacrer ses prisonniers. On s'indigne même contre ceux qui les traitent mal. Et ces maximes abominables, qui révoltent la raison et font frémir l'humanité[8], ne sont plus connues que des jurisconsultes, qui en font tranquillement la base de leurs systèmes politiques, et qui, au lieu de nous montrer l'autorité souveraine[9] comme la source du bonheur des hommes, osent nous la montrer comme le supplice des vaincus[10].

Pour peu qu'on marche[11] de conséquence en conséquence, l'erreur du principe se fait sentir à chaque pas ; et l'on voit[12] partout que dans une aussi téméraire décision l'on n'a pas plus consulté la

---

[1] [de sorte que les troupes... : que l'État s'affaiblissant à tous égards par l'entretien de ce qu'on appelle ses forces....] D. B. omits from *On n'emploie jamais* to *intérieur*. W. reads *ou n'emploient*.

[2] [est.]   [3] [n'a pas.]   [4] [substituer.]   [5] [tout.]

[6] [à regarder toutes les préceptes de la morale comme des instruments.]

[7] MS. has *plus de rien*, by a slip.

[8] [qui dégradent [effrayent] l'humanité.] D. B. reads *les maximes*.

[9] [les gouvernements.]

[10] [le supplice dans lequel on a commencé pour eux la peine de mort.] Between the two paragraphs the MS. has the following cancelled line : ' Les jurisconsultes ont laissé cette matière dans un embrouillement....'

[11] [avance.]   [12] [aboutit.]

raison que la nature[1]. Si je voulais approfondir la notion de l'état de guerre, je démontrerais aisément qu'il ne peut résulter que du libre consentement des parties belligérantes; que, si l'une veut attaquer et l'autre ne veuille pas se défendre, il n'y a point d'état de guerre, mais seulement violence et agression; que[2], l'état de guerre étant établi par le libre consentement des parties, ce libre et mutuel consentement est aussi nécessaire pour rétablir[3] la paix; et qu'à moins que l'un des adversaires[4] ne soit anéanti la guerre ne peut finir entre eux qu'à l'instant[5] que tous deux en liberté déclarent qu'ils y renoncent; de sorte[6] qu'en vertu de la relation du maître à l'esclave ils continuent, même malgré eux[7], d'être toujours dans l'état de guerre. Je pourrais mettre en question[8] si les promesses arrachées par la force, et pour éviter la mort, sont obligatoires dans l'état de liberté[9]; et si toutes celles que le prisonnier fait à son maître dans cet état peuvent signifier autre chose que celle-ci[10]: Je m'engage à vous obéir aussi longtemps qu'étant le plus fort[11] vous n'attenterez pas à ma vie.

Il y a plus. Qu'on me dise lesquels doivent l'emporter, des engagements[12] solennels et irrévocables pris avec la patrie en pleine liberté, ou de ceux que l'effroi de la mort nous fera contracter avec l'ennemi vainqueur[13]. Le prétendu[14] droit d'esclavage, auquel sont asservis[15] les prisonniers de[16] guerre, est sans bornes. Les jurisconsultes le décident formellement. Il n'y a rien, dit Grotius, qu'on ne puisse impunément faire souffrir à de tels esclaves. Il n'est point d'action qu'on ne puisse leur commander, ou à laquelle on ne puisse les contraindre, de quelque manière que ce soit. Mais si, leur faisant grâce de mille tourments, on se contente d'exiger qu'ils portent les armes contre leur pays[17], je demande

[1] [Je ne m'arrêterai—je ne chercherai point à concilier l'obligation....]
[2] [mais que sitôt.]   [3] [terminer....]
[4] [des parties.]   [5] [au moment.]   [6] D. B. reads *j'ajoute*.
[7] [que le maître continuent (*sic*) malgré d'être.]   [8] [examiner.]
[9] [Si les consentements forcés par la violence et sous peine de la vie sont obligatoires pour celui qui les a contractés.] D. B. has strangely altered this sentence.
[10] [je pourrais—ferais voir que l'accomplissement des promesses arrachées par la force ne peut être exigé dans l'état de liberté,—et si les engagements d'un prisonnier avec son maître peuvent jamais avoir une autre force— : peut y avoir dans ces promesses du prisonnier à son maître pour sauver sa vie... ;]
[11] [que vous serez le plus fort et que vous.]
[12] [ne serait-il pas de la dernière absurdité que les engagements.]
[13] [que l'ennemi vainqueur peut nous extorquer par la crainte de la mort.]
[14] [Me voilà entre deux promesses. Quel est.]   [15] D. B. reads *assujettis*.
[16] *de* missing in MS.   [17] [et aident à massacrer leurs concitoyens.]

lequel ils doivent remplir : du serment qu'ils ont fait librement à leur patrie, ou de celui que l'ennemi vient d'arracher à leur faiblesse. Désobéiront-ils à leurs maîtres, ou massacreront-ils leurs concitoyens ?

Peut-être osera-t-on[1] me dire que, l'état d'esclavage assujettissant les prisonniers à leur maître, ils changent d'État à l'instant[2] ; et que, devenant sujets de leur nouveau[3] souverain, ils renoncent à leur ancienne patrie. [D. B. ; W.]

[MS. p. 71 r°. This Fragment, though written after a long blank space, really forms part of the preceding one.] Quand mille peuples féroces[4] auraient massacré leurs prisonniers, quand mille docteurs vendus à la tyrannie auraient excusé[5] ces crimes, qu'importe à la vérité[6] l'erreur des hommes, et leur barbarie à la justice ? Ne cherchons point ce qu'on a fait, mais ce qu'on doit faire ; et rejetons[7] de viles et mercenaires autorités, qui ne tendent qu'à rendre les hommes esclaves, méchants[8] et malheureux. [D. B. ; W.]

*[MS. p. 61. This and the remaining Fragments are written as from the other end of the volume, and therefore follow the right order of the pages.] Sur quoi, l'on doit se garder de confondre l'essence de la société civile avec celle de la souveraineté. Car le Corps[9] social résulte d'un seul acte de volonté ; et toute sa durée n'est que la suite et l'effet d'un engagement antérieur, dont la force ne cesse d'agir que quand le corps est dissous. Mais la souveraineté, qui n'est que l'exercice de la volonté générale, est libre comme elle et n'est soumise à aucune espèce d'engagement. Chaque acte de souveraineté, ainsi que chaque instant de sa durée, est absolu, indépendant de celui qui[10] précède ; et jamais le souverain n'agit parce qu'il a voulu, mais parce qu'il veut.

[MS. p. 61. Written in pencil.] Plusieurs sans doute aimeraient mieux n'être pas que d'être esclaves ; mais comme l'acte de mourir est rude, ils aiment mieux être esclaves que d'être tués ; et chargés[11] de fer, ils existent malgré eux. [D. B. ; W.]

*[MS. p. 62 v°.] Il paraît par divers traits de l'histoire romaine, et entre d'autres par celui d'Attilius Régulus, que les Romains qui tombaient entre les mains de l'ennemi se regardaient comme déchus du droit de citoyens et naturalisés, pour ainsi dire, parmi ceux

---

[1] [Je suis sûr qu'il y aura des gens qui— : qu'on ose.]
[2] [qu'ils changent à l'instant de patrie.]
[3] D. B. omits *nouveau*.
[4] D. B. omits *féroces*.
[5] [justifié.]
[6] [justice.]
[7] [ni les autorités....]
[8] [méchants, esclaves.]
[9] [l'union.]
[10] [tout ce qui.]
[11] [de honte et.]

qui les tenaient prisonniers. Mais cette absurde maxime n'était que dans leur opinion, et l'on n'aperçoit rien qui s'y rapporte dans la conduite de ces hommes vertueux[1]. Régulus lui-même, qui se traitait de Carthaginois et qui refusait de prendre sa place dans le Sénat de Rome, y parla tellement contre les intérêts[2] de sa nouvelle patrie et contre les institutions de ses maîtres que, s'il était vrai qu'il fut obligé de leur être fidèle et d'obéir à leurs ordres, la plus sublime des actions humaines ne serait plus que le crime d'un traître, et l'on devrait équitablement approuver le supplice affreux que lui imposèrent les féroces Carthaginois en punition de sa désobéissance.

[MS. v° of p. 3.] Si Carthage eût été dans l'Italie, et Athènes dans le Péloponèse, Rome et Sparte subsisteraient peut-être encore. [W.]

*[MS. p. 62 v°. Written in pencil. It must refer to the legislation of Lycurgus.] Car, que des hommes effrénés et dissolus se soient soumis tout d'un coup et volontairement à la plus dure et sévère police qui fut jamais, c'est un miracle qui n'a pu se faire que par un subit enthousiasme de mœurs et de vertu répandu chez tout un peuple.

[MS. p. 63. Probably an early version of *Contrat social*, I. iii.—iv. Written in pencil.] Pour connaître exactement quels sont les droits de la guerre, examinons avec soin la nature de la chose, et n'admettons pour vrai que ce qui s'en déduit nécessairement. Que deux hommes se battent dans l'état de nature, voilà la guerre allumée entre eux. Mais pourquoi se battent-ils? Est-ce pour se manger l'un l'autre? Cela n'arrive parmi les animaux qu'entre[3] différentes espèces. Entre les hommes, de même qu'entre les loups, le sujet de la querelle est toujours entièrement étranger à la vie des combattants. [4]Il peut très bien arriver que l'un des deux périsse dans le combat, mais alors sa mort est le moyen et non l'objet de la victoire. Car, sitôt que le vaincu cède, le vainqueur s'empare de la chose contestée, le combat cesse et la guerre est finie[4]. Il faut remarquer que, l'état social rassemblant autour de nous une multitude de choses qui tiennent[5] plus à nos fantaisies qu'à nos besoins et qui nous étaient naturellement indifférentes,

---

[1] [l'on ne voit pas que la conduite de ces hommes vertueux confirmait....]
[2] [y soutint fort mal le parti.]
[3] D. B. reads *qu'à différentes espèces*, against MS. and sense.
[4] D. B. and W. reverse the order of these two sentences and transfer *Car* to before *Il faut remarquer*, against the MS.   [5] [nous intéressent.]

la plupart des sujets de guerre deviennent encore plus étrangers à la vie des hommes que dans l'état de nature, et que cela va souvent au point que les particuliers se soucient fort peu des événements de la guerre publique. On prend les armes pour disputer de puissance, de richesses, de considération; et le sujet de la querelle se trouve enfin si éloigné de la personne des citoyens qu'ils n'en sont[1] ni mieux, ni plus mal, d'être vainqueurs ou vaincus. Il serait bien étrange qu'une guerre ainsi constituée eût quelque rapport à leur vie, et qu'on se crût en droit d'égorger[2] des hommes, seulement pour montrer qu'on est plus fort qu'eux[3]. On tue pour vaincre; mais il n'y a point d'homme si féroce qu'il cherche à vaincre pour tuer. [D. B.; W.]

[MS. p. 63 v°. Same reference as preceding Fragment. Written in pencil.] Maintenant que l'état de nature est aboli parmi nous, la guerre n'existe plus entre particuliers; et les hommes qui de leur chef en attaquent d'autres, même après avoir reçu d'eux[4] quelque injure, ne sont point regardés comme leurs ennemis, mais comme de véritables brigands. Cela est si vrai qu'un sujet qui, prenant à la lettre les termes d'une déclaration de guerre, voudra sans brevet ni lettres de marque courre sus aux ennemis de son Prince, serait puni ou devrait l'être. [D. B.; W.]

[MS. p. 63 v° and p. 64 r°. It is clearly a continuation of the earlier Fragment [p. 72]—'Grâce à Dieu, on ne voit plus.' Written in pencil.] Premièrement, le vainqueur n'étant pas plus en droit[5] de faire cette menace[6] que de l'exécuter, l'effet n'en saurait être légitime[7]. En second lieu, si jamais serment extorqué par force fut nul[8], c'est surtout celui qui nous soumet à l'engagement le plus étendu que des hommes puissent prendre, et qui par conséquent suppose la plus parfaite liberté dans ceux qui le contractent. Le serment antérieur qui nous lie à la patrie annulle d'autant mieux[9] en pareil cas celui qui nous soumet à un autre souverain, que le premier a été contracté en pleine liberté, et le second[10] dans les fers. Pour juger si l'on peut contraindre un homme à se faire[11] naturaliser dans un État étranger, il faut toujours remonter à l'objet essentiel et primordial des sociétés politiques, qui est le

---

[1] D. B. reads *qu'il ne vaut.*
[2] [tuer.]
[3] D. B. and W. omit *et qu'on se crût...plus fort qu'eux.*
[4] D. B. omits *d'eux.*
[5] [n'ayant pas plus de droit.]
[6] [à ses captifs.]
[7] [l'effet n'en peut être qu'illégitime.]
[8] [fut nul pour être extorqué.]
[9] [plus évidemment.]
[10] [l'autre.]
[11] D. B. omits *faire.*

bonheur des peuples. Or, il répugne à la loi de raison de dire à autrui: Je veux que vous soyez heureux autrement que vous ne voulez vous-même.

Si l'on ne peut pas... [D. B.; W.]

FRAGMENTS DIVERS

A.
[MS. Neuchâtel, 7840.]
I. A comparison between Rome and Sparta.
[MS. pp. 1—3.]

Je laisse aux admirateurs de l'histoire moderne à chercher[1], décider quel est celui de ces deux tableaux qui doit le mieux lui convenir. Quant à moi, qui n'aime à considérer[2] que les exemples dont l'humanité s'instruise et s'honore[3]: moi qui ne sais voir parmi mes contemporains que des maîtres insensibles et des peuples gémissants, des guerres qui n'intéressent personne et désolent tout le monde[4], des armées immenses[5] en temps de paix et sans effet en temps de guerre, des ministres toujours occupés pour ne rien faire, des traités mystérieux sans objet, des alliances longtemps négociées et rompues le lendemain, enfin des sujets[6] d'autant plus méprisés que le prince est plus puissant: je tire le rideau[7] sur ces objets de douleur et de désolation; et ne pouvant soulager[8] nos maux, j'évite au moins de les contempler.

Mais je me plais[9] à tourner les yeux sur ces vénérables images[10] de l'antiquité, où je vois les hommes[11] élevés par de sublimes institutions[12] au plus haut degré de grandeur et de vertus où puisse atteindre la sagesse humaine. L'âme[13] s'élève à son tour et le courage s'inflamme, en parcourant[14] ces respectables monuments. On participe en quelque sorte aux actions héroïques de ces grands

---

[1] [dans les annales. 'Chercher' is not cancelled; but it is possible that 'décider' is intended to replace it.]
[2] [qui ne sais voir parmi... ; ne contemple avec plaisir.]
[3] [qui élèvent et honorent l'humanité capable....] W. reads *s'instruit*.
[4] [guerres indifférentes aux peuples; guerres qui n'intéressent ni les peuples qu'elles désolent [qui les ignorent] ni les troupes qui se massacrent.]
[5] [immenses pour ne rien....] [6] [et les peuples sujets.]
[7] [je cherche à m'ôter.] [8] [secourir.]
[9] [J'aime.] [10] [majestueux monuments; simulacres.]
[11] [l'humanité.] [12] [par des Lois.]
[13] [Il semble à la manière.] [14] [en lisant.]

hommes; il semble que la méditation de leur grandeur nous en communique une partie; et l'on pourrait dire de leur personne et de leurs discours ce que Pythagore disait des simulacres des Dieux, qu'ils donnent[1] une âme nouvelle à ceux qui s'en approchent pour recueillir leurs oracles.

Ce que les poètes peuvent trouver dans l'invention de leurs fables de plus propre à nous plaire, et même à nous instruire, est l'union du mérite et de la fortune[2]. Le cœur ne peut se défendre d'un tendre intérêt pour les gens de bien; et quand on les voit prospérer, les bons aiment leur bonheur à cause de leur vertu, et les autres aiment leurs vertus à cause de leur bonheur. Si l'histoire a rarement le même avantage, elle en tire en revanche[3] un plus grand effet; et, quand à l'image de la sagesse heureuse se joint le sacré caractère[4] de la vérité, elle apprend aux hommes[5] à respecter les décrets de la Providence et donne[6] aux cœurs droits et sensibles un nouveau courage[7] à bien faire[8]. L'histoire peut suppléer encore à ce qui manque à ses récits pour l'instruction des lecteurs, en réunissant sous un même aspect les faits et les héros propres[9] à s'éclairer mutuellement. L'on démêle mieux dans ces comparaisons l'ouvrage de la fortune et celui de la prudence. Quand on met les hommes ou les peuples[10] en opposition, tout ce qui les distingue, les fautes que l'un commet font remarquer[11] la sagesse de l'autre à les éviter, et l'on tire une égale instruction de leurs défauts et de leurs vertus[12].

Si l'on peut imaginer un parallèle qui rassemble tous ces avantages, c'est, ce me semble, celui des deux Républiques que je voudrais comparer[13]. Rome et Sparte portèrent la gloire humaine aussi haut qu'elle puisse atteindre; toutes deux brillèrent à la fois par les vertus et par la valeur; toutes deux eurent de grands revers, de plus grands succès, secondèrent ou vainquirent la fortune à force de sagesse, et démentirent, par une constitution ferme et durable, les préjugés vulgaires contre l'instabilité des peuples libres. Si les objets[14]

---

[1] [de leurs discours sentencieux ce que Pythagore disait des hommes consultant les oracles des Dieux, qu'ils inspirent.]
[2] [du bonheur et de la vertu.]   [3] [en revanche elle lui donne.]
[4] [l'impre....]   [5] [fait dans les cœurs.]
[6] [porte.]
[7] [une confiance.]   [8] [une impression qui ne s'efface jamais.]
[9] [qui peuvent.]   [10] [nations.]   [11] [mieux.]
[12] [sert à les faire mieux connaître, et par les qualités des uns fait mieux sortir les vices des autres.]
[13] [Je ne suis plus dans ma vie... ; J'ai cru voir tous ces avantages réunis dans l'étude des deux Peuples.]   [14] End of p. 1.

sont grands, les rapports sont sensibles : l'une et l'autre République eut d'abord des rois, devint ensuite un État libre et s'éteignit sous des tyrans[1]. Chacune eut à combattre une rivale redoutable qui la mit souvent à la veille de sa ruine, qu'elle surmonta pourtant, mais dont la défaite devint fatale aux vainqueurs ; [2] l'agrandissement de toutes deux, quoiqu'à des termes fort inégaux, fut également la cause de leur ruine. Enfin[3], la même fierté, les mêmes mœurs, les mêmes maximes[4], surtout le même enthousiasme pour la patrie, se remarquent dans l'une et dans l'autre. À l'égard des différences[5], il ne s'en trouvera toujours que trop pour me justifier du parallèle ; et j'aurai tant d'occasions d'en parler dans la suite qu'il serait inutile de les observer[6] ici.

[Two inches space in MS.]

L'institution de la République de Sparte eut des causes non moins singulières que ses lois, et son établissement fut amené d'une manière toute opposée à ceux des autres Gouvernements. La liberté civile est, dans les divers états de l'homme sociable, une des extrémités dont l'autre est la liberté naturelle. Les différentes[7] institutions politiques forment, entre ces deux termes, autant de degrés intermédiaires qui commencent par les excès de la licence et finissent par ceux de la tyrannie[8]. Sparte, au contraire, après avoir commencé par le despotisme dégénéra bientôt en anarchie : progrès rétrograde à l'ordre naturel, qui fut une suite de la conquête du Péloponèse par les Héraclides[9]. [10] D'abord, Eurysthène et Proclès ayant eu l'imbécile avidité[11] de s'emparer de toutes les

[1] [La même fierté, les mêmes vertus et les mêmes exploits [maximes] se remarquent dans l'une et dans l'autre.]
[2] [et enfin.]   [3] [au surplus.]   [4] [innombrables.]
[5] [c'est si rarement par leur défaut que péchent les comparaisons.]
[6] [m'y arrêter.]   W. retains this reading.   [7] [Toutes les.]
[8] [du despotisme.]
[9] What follows stood originally thus : [Elle reçut tout à coup avec un nouvel être, une nouvelle vie et de nouvelles forces qu'elle conserva durant six cents ans.] [L'immortalité dans la mémoire des hommes, une gloire qu'elle conservera toujours. La conquête du Péloponèse par les Héraclides, la Royauté commune aux deux branches des enfants de...et l'affaiblissement de leur pouvoir par l'abus qu'ils en avaient fait furent les premières causes de l'illustration de Sparte, en y rendant indispensable une nouvelle institution, un autre Gouvernement] [l'abus qu'ils firent d'abord de leur pouvoir et qui leur coûta dans la suite la meilleure partie, enfin la mésintelligence qui ne cessa de régner entre les deux Rois.] W. omits *progrès...naturel.*
[10] W. omits *D'abord...pays de conquête.*
[11] [assez peu de lumières pour s'emparer comme propriétaires du pays dont ils n'étaient que les conquérants, firent déserter à leur patrie les habitants, etc.]

possessions des particuliers, sous prétexte que la Laconie était un pays de conquête[1], les habitants, que rien n'attachait plus à leur patrie, désertèrent dans les pays voisins ; et les deux tyrans, maîtres d'une vaste solitude, apprirent à leur dépens que la souveraineté et la propriété sont incompatibles, que les droits du Prince ne sont fondés que sur ceux des sujets, et qu'il est impossible de commander longtemps gratuitement à des gens qui[2] n'ont plus rien à perdre.

Pour remplacer les habitants qu'on n'avait pas voulu retenir en leur cédant une partie de leur propre bien, on attira des étrangers auxquels il fallait donner plus qu'on n'avait pris à leurs prédécesseurs. De sorte qu'il arriva, comme il arrivera toujours, que les rois s'appauvrirent, pour avoir tout usurpé. Mais, à donner sans cesse et ne rien recevoir, il était impossible au Gouvernement de durer longtemps[3]. Il fallut donc enfin revenir aux impôts dont on aurait dû d'abord se contenter. Ils furent exigés par Agis avec la dureté[4] d'un prince, qui se croit tout permis et que l'expérience ne corrigera point. Le peuple passa du murmure à la révolte. On prit les armes ; Agis fut le plus fort ; et les habitants d'Hélos, vaincus et asservis à jamais, donnèrent dans Sparte[5] le vain et funeste exemple du plus cruel esclavage au sein de la plus parfaite liberté.

Loin d'affermir leur pouvoir par ces violences, les rois, en négligeant de couvrir d'une administration légitime une injuste usurpation, s'ôtaient des ressources pour ces inévitables moments de faiblesse, où le droit seul supplée à la force et où le plus vigoureux Gouvernement se trouve, quoiqu'il fasse, à la discrétion du peuple. Ainsi fallut-il bientôt changer de méthode ; et ces princes que la raison ne conduisait jamais, aussi peu mesurés dans leur complaisance que dans leurs rigueurs, laissèrent trop voir[6] qu'ils n'étaient justes que par crainte, et qu'il fallait sans cesse[7] attaquer leur autorité[8] pour en prévenir l'abus. Mais ce qui contribua le plus à ruiner le pouvoir souverain, ce fut son partage entre les deux rois. Car, pour avoir travaillé[9] sans cesse à

---

[1] W. omits *D'abord...pays de conquête.*

[2] [qui ne gagnent rien et.]

[3] End of p. 2.

[4] [ordinaire qui ne révolta pas moins les nouveaux venus, le Peuple ; on eut recours aux armes ; le Prince fut le plus fort.]

[5] [offrirent dans le sein de Sparte.]

[6] [au peuple.]   [7] [toujours.]

[8] [non pour la détruire mais.]   [9] [cherchant.]

l'usurper l'un sur l'autre, ils se l'ôtèrent à tous les deux. Ne sachant se faire aimer par la clémence ni respecter par la justice, ils se virent forcés à l'envi de flatter bassement la multitude, et s'attirèrent[1] plus d'ennemis que de créatures par une aveugle partialité, qui les fit haïr, et par une impunité des crimes, qui les rendit méprisables[2].

Toutes ces causes réunies anéantirent entièrement la monarchie au bout de quelques générations; et il ne restait plus du Gouvernement qu'une vaine forme sans réalité, qui ne servait que d'obstacle à l'établissement d'une meilleure police. L'État tomba dans une anarchie pire que l'indépendance naturelle, parce qu'il n'y avait aucun moyen d'en sortir et que, le peuple ne pouvant se donner des lois ni des magistrats tant qu'il avait des rois[3], la royauté sans pouvoir ne servait plus que de sauvegarde à la licence et au brigandage. C'est dans ces circonstances[4], où le Corps politique était prêt à se dissoudre, que parut le Législateur.

Pour bien juger ce qu'exécuta Lycurgue, imaginons un instant qu'il s'en tînt au simple projet…[5].

Mais il ne voyait pas que le goût[6] des conquêtes était un vice dans son institution plus puissant que la loi qui le réprimait. Car la vie civile[7] des Lacédémoniens avait tant d'austérité qu'ils vivaient à l'armée avec[8] plus de douceur que dans leurs maisons, et les fatigues de la guerre étaient[9] la mollesse de Sparte : mollesse qui, pour être d'une nouvelle espèce, n'en resserra pas moins l'ancienne grandeur de la République dans les limites de son territoire, en rabaissant ses citoyens[10] jusqu'à n'être plus qu'égaux aux autres hommes[11].

[The four following Fragments are written on v° of p. 52 of the same MS. But, to judge from the handwriting, they were clearly written about the same time as the preceding Fragments and refer to the same subject.]

[1] MS. reads *s'attirent* [se firent]. [2] MS. reads *méprisable*.
[3] [Il n'y avait des Rois que pour empêcher qu'il n'y eût des magistrats. Tant qu'il y avait des hommes qui n'avaient plus que…. Le nom des Rois ne servait qu'à empêcher l'établissement des lois et des magistrats.]
[4] [ainsi.]
[5] End of p. 3. This paragraph—Pour bien juger—is written in pencil.
[6] [l'esprit.] This paragraph is written on v° of p. 3.
[7] [les mœurs—la vie particulière.]
[8] [beaucoup.]   [9] [tellement.]   [10] [soldats.]
[11] [qui corrompit à la fin et les Lacédémoniens, ses habitants….Je crois que ce fut enfin par là que dégénérèrent les mœurs et par conséquence la valeur de ses citoyens : mollesse d'un genre nouveau.]

Ils établirent tous deux beaucoup de spectacles, d'assemblées et de cérémonies ; beaucoup de colléges et de sociétés particulières, pour engendrer et fomenter entre les citoyens ces douces habitudes et ce commerce innocent et désintéressé, qui forment et nourrissent l'amour de la patrie[1]. Ils employèrent ainsi des moyens semblables pour aller aux mêmes fins par des routes opposées. Car l'un, inspirant à ses peuples la crainte des Dieux, le goût de leur culte et celui d'une société paisible, éclaira leur courage et tempéra leur férocité[2]. L'autre, par les mêmes exercices de la paix, sut donner aux siens les inclinations et les talents militaires. Et tous deux, ennemis de la violence et des conquêtes, ne songèrent qu'à rendre l'État indépendant et tranquille.

Quant à la grandeur de l'État, il n'y a nulle comparaison à faire entre ces deux Républiques. Sparte, presque bornée à ses murs, ne put même venir à bout d'assujettir la Grèce, qui ne faisait pour ainsi dire qu'un point dans l'Empire romain. Et Rome, dont tant de rois étaient les sujets, étendit si loin sa domination qu'elle fut enfin contrainte de se borner elle-même. Sparte n'eut pas même sur Rome l'avantage, propre aux petits États, de soutenir avec fermeté les attaques des plus grands peuples, les revers de la fortune et les approches d'une ruine entière. Car leurs commencements furent aussi faibles à l'une qu'à l'autre ; et si l'une eut en tête les Rois de Perse, Épaminondas et Antipater, l'autre eut à soutenir les Gaulois, Pyrrhus, Annibal. Montrant une constance encore plus grande à résister à l'adversité, ses défaites ne la rendaient que plus inflexible ; et cette fierté, que Sparte n'eut pas au même point, fit enfin triompher Rome de tous ses ennemis. C'était des deux côtés la même vertu, guidée par différentes maximes. Toujours prêt à mourir pour son pays, un Spartiate aimait si tendrement la patrie qu'il eût sacrifié la liberté même pour la sauver. Mais jamais les Romains imaginèrent que la patrie put survivre à la liberté, ni même à la gloire.

Dans ces temps réculés, où le droit de propriété naissant et mal affermi n'était point encore établi par les lois, les richesses ne passaient que pour des usurpations ; et quand on en pouvait dépouiller les possesseurs, à peine regardait-on comme un vol de leur ôter ce qui

---

[1] Compare this sentence which occurs in the same MS. : 'Et quant à moi, je regarde les jeux Olympiques comme un des moyens qui ont le plus longtemps conservé dans la Grèce l'amour de la liberté.'

[2] [et régla et tempéra leur excessive férocité.]

leur¹ n'appartenait pas. Hercule et Thésée, ces héros de l'antiquité, n'étaient au fond que des brigands qui en pillaient d'autres.

Mais ce qu'il y a de plus heureux dans cette association, c'est que, bien qu'aucune de ces deux² Républiques n'ait atteint la perfection dont elle était susceptible, leurs défauts³ ne furent point les mêmes; et que, l'une ayant eu les vertus qui manquaient à l'autre⁴, le mal, en les comparant⁵, ne se montre qu'avec le remède. De sorte qu'un tel⁶ parallèle offre d'après les faits l'image du Gouvernement le plus excellent, et du peuple le plus vaillant et le plus sage, qui puisse exister. [W.]

*[p. 62.] On aurait beau dire que ces faits ne sont pas vrais; car, en les supposant faux, il fallait au moins qu'ils eussent dans ces temps-là quelque degré de probabilité, qui les fît adopter par les historiens. Si l'on nous racontait aujourd'hui un trait semblable de quelqu'un de nos contemporains, nous n'en ferions que rire, et personne ne daignerait en parler.

II. Further Fragments relating to the *Contrat social*.

[MS. 7840. Written, like the two following Fragments, in opening cover.] Qu'est-ce qui rend les lois si sacrées, même indépendamment de leur autorité, et si préférables à des simples actes de volonté? C'est premièrement qu'elles émanent d'une volonté générale et toujours droite à l'égard des particuliers; c'est encore qu'elles sont permanentes et que leur durée annonce⁷ à tous la sagesse qui les a⁷ dictées. [W.]

[Written in pencil.] De cette maxime, si elle est vraie, se déduit conséquemment celle-ci que, dans tout ce qui dépend de l'industrie humaine, on doit proscrire avec soin toute machine et toute invention qui peut⁸ abréger le travail, épargner la main d'œuvre et produire⁹ le même effet avec moins de peine. [W.]

Le Peuple ne peut contracter qu'avec lui-même. Car, s'il contractait avec ses officiers, comme il les rend dépositaires de toute sa puissance et qu'il n'y aurait aucun garant du contrat, ce ne serait pas contracter avec eux: ce serait réellement se mettre à leur discrétion. [W.]

---

¹ *ne* wanting in MS. ² [des deux.]
³ [les défauts de l'une....]
⁴ [contraires aux vices de....] ⁵ [unissant.] ⁶ [que ce.]
⁷ MS. has *annoncent, ont* by a slip. ⁸ [tend à.] ⁹ [faire.]

[Written in pencil on v° of p. 4.] Quand toutes les parties de l'État concourent à sa solidité, que toutes ses forces sont prêtes à se réunir pour sa défense au besoin, et que les particuliers ne songent à leur conservation qu'autant qu'elle est utile à la sienne, alors le corps[1] en est aussi assuré qu'il peut l'être, et résiste de toute sa masse[2] aux impulsions étrangères. Mais quand la chose publique est mal assise, que tout son poids ne porte pas sur la ligne de direction et que ses forces, divisées et s'opposant l'une à l'autre[3], se détruisent mutuellement, le moindre effort suffit pour renverser tout cet équilibre, et l'État est détruit aussitôt qu'attaqué. [W.]

*[Written in pencil on r° of p. 6.] Concluons que le cœur des citoyens est la meilleure garde de l'État, qu'il sera toujours bien défendu s'il est d'ailleurs bien gouverné, que cette partie de l'administration est tellement liée à toutes les autres qu'un bon Gouvernement n'a besoin ni de troupes ni d'alliés, et qu'un mauvais devient pire, appuyé sur de tels soutiens.

[Written on v° of p. 6 in pencil.] Ils sacrifient[4] leur liberté à la conservation de leur vie, comme un voyageur cède sa bourse à un voleur pour n'être pas égorgé ; est-ce donc à dire que la bourse soit bien acquise au voleur, et que le propriétaire n'ait pas le droit de la lui reprendre sitôt qu'il en a le pouvoir ? [W.]

[Written on v° of p. 10, as are the two following Fragments also.] En examinant la constitution des États qui composent l'Europe, j'ai vu que les uns étaient trop grands pour pouvoir être bien gouvernés, les autres trop petits pour pouvoir se maintenir dans l'indépendance. Les abus infinis qui règnent dans tous m'ont paru difficiles à prévenir, mais impossibles à corriger[5] ; parce que la plupart de ces abus sont fondés sur l'intérêt même des seuls qui les pourraient détruire[6]. [7]J'ai trouvé que les liaisons qui subsistent entre toutes les Puissances ne laisseraient jamais à aucune d'elles le temps et la sûreté nécessaire pour refondre sa constitution. Enfin, les préjugés sont tellement contraires à toute espèce de changement qu'à moins d'avoir la force en main il faut être[8]

---
[1] W. reads *souverain*.   [2] [de tout son poids.]
[3] [sont tellement compliquées, balancées, entravées (?), qu'il n'en reste rien pour résister aux moindres impulsions externes, alors l'État n'est rien.]
[4] [renoncent à : abandonnent.]
[5] [qu'il régnait tant d'abus dans tous que tous ces Gouvernements sont infiniment plus difficiles [impossibles] à corriger : de sorte qu'il serait....]
[6] [abolir.]   [7] [Enfin.]
[8] [tellement contraires [à tout changement] aux nouveaux plans de gouvernement que, quand tout concourrait à les favoriser, quiconque s'avise d'en proposer passera toujours pour un visionnaire, qu'il faudrait être.]

aussi simple que l'Abbé de Saint-Pierre pour proposer la moindre innovation dans quelque Gouvernement que ce soit. [W.][1]

La Loi n'agit qu'en dehors et ne règle que les actions ; les mœurs seuls pénètrent intérieurement et dirigent les volontés. [W.]

*Ce grand ressort de l'opinion publique, si habilement mis en œuvre par les anciens Législateurs et absolument ignoré des gouvernements modernes; car comme ils la bravent eux-mêmes, comment apprendraient-ils aux citoyens à la respecter?

*The only other entry on the v° of p. 10 is the following:

Paris 1758.

Morts 19202.
Baptêmes 19148.
Mariages 4342.
Enfants trouvés 5082.

[This entry has a personal interest, owing to the fate of Rousseau's own children.]

*[p. 61 v°.] Dans le sein de la superstition, où la raison n'a nulle force, il faut nécessairement que la philosophie prenne un air mystérieux, pour en imposer; sans quoi, toutes les vérités, qui ne sont que démontrées, ne trouveraient point de sectateurs.

*[ib.] Sans doute, il fallait dire de bonnes choses; mais, pour les dire utilement, il fallait commencer par se faire écouter.

*[ib.] Il n'y a guère que des fous qui puissent se donner pour des professeurs de sagesse: aussi, les temps de la foule des philosophes sont-ils toujours ceux où l'on voit le moins de sages.

*[ib.] C'est le défaut de fer qui fit négliger, puis oublier, la navigation aux Américains.

*[MS. Neuchâtel, 7854. The opening words of the original *Contrat social*]:—

CHAP. I.

Du Droit naturel et de la Société générale.

Commençons par lever une équivoque qui est la source de bien des sophismes. Il y a deux manières d'envisager le Droit naturel. [Only the upper part of the last three words remains, the paper having been torn across. By the *équivoque* Rousseau probably

[1] This Fragment may have been intended either for *La Paix perpétuelle*, or *La Polysynodie*. In the MS., it immediately follows a list of Saint-Pierre's Works, printed and manuscript. See below, p. 359.

means the double sense of 'Natural Right'—moral and unmoral. The title shews clearly that he had Diderot's article, *Droit naturel*, in mind. See Geneva MS. of *Contrat social*, I. ii.]

*[Written in pencil on v° of p. 5.] L'homme isolé est un être si faible, ou du moins dont la force est tellement mesurée à ses besoins[1] et à son état primitifs, que, pour peu que cet état change et que ces besoins augmentent, il ne peut plus se passer de ses semblables; et quand à force de progrès ses désirs embrassent toute la nature, le concours de tout le genre humain suffit à peine pour les assouvir. C'est ainsi que les mêmes causes qui nous rendent méchants nous rendent encore esclaves, et que[2] notre faiblesse naît de notre cupidité; nos besoins nous rapprochent à mesure que nos passions nous divisent; et plus nous devenons ennemis, moins nous pouvons nous passer les uns des autres[3].

*[Written, partly in pencil, on r° of p. 6.] Mais quoiqu'il n'y ait point de société naturelle et générale entre les hommes[4], quoiqu'ils deviennent méchants et malheureux en devenant sociables, quoique les lois de la justice et de l'égalité ne soient rien pour ceux qui vivent à la fois dans l'indépendance de l'état de nature et soumis aux besoins de l'état social; loin[5] de penser qu'il n'y ait plus ni vertu ni bonheur pour nous et que le ciel nous ait abandonné sans ressource à la dépravation de l'espèce; efforçons nous de tirer du mal même le remède qui doit le guérir; par de nouvelles associations réparons le vice interne de l'association générale. Que notre violent interlocuteur soit lui-même le juge[6] de nos travaux; montrons lui dans l'art perfectionné la réparation des maux que l'art commencé fit à la nature[7]. Montrons lui[8] toute la misère de l'état qu'il croyait heureux; faisons lui voir dans une constitution de choses mieux entendue[9] le prix des bonnes actions, le châtiment des mauvaises et l'accord aimable de la justice et du bonheur; éclairons sa raison de nouvelles lumières[10]; échauffons son cœur de nouveaux sentiments; et qu'il apprenne à sentir le plaisir

[1] [naturels.]
[2] [notre faiblesse augmente avec nos besoins; plus nos passions nous divisent plus....]
[3] This reappears, with a few variants, in Geneva MS. of *Contrat social*, I. ii. (p. 447). The same is the case with the two following paragraphs.
[4] [en général.]
[5] [gardons nous.]   [6] [Prenons pour juge.]   [7] [humaine.]
[8] [Faisons lui voir en leur personne.]
[9] MS. has *entendues*, probably by a slip. After *actions* [et].
[10] [portons insensiblement au fond de son âme ces sentiments.]

de multiplier[1] son être, en l'unissant à celui de ses semblables. Qu'il devienne pour son propre intérêt mieux entendu[2], juste, bienfaisant, modéré[3], vertueux, ami des hommes et le plus digne de nos citoyens[4].

[A variant on the last sentence of the foregoing is written on v° of p. 5.] Pour peu que nous lui sachions expliquer la véritable constitution d'un Gouvernement[5] sain et légitime, si mon zèle ne m'aveugle point[6] dans cette grande entreprise, ne doutons pas qu'avec une âme forte et un sens droit cet ennemi du genre humain[7] n'abjure enfin sa haine avec ses erreurs et que, d'un brigand féroce qu'il voulait être, il ne devienne, pour son propre intérêt mieux entendu, juste, bienfaisant, modéré, vertueux, ami des hommes et le plus digne de nos citoyens. [D. B.]

*[MS. Neuchâtel, 7830. Written in pencil.] Celui qui se croit capable de former[8] un peuple doit se sentir en état de changer, pour ainsi dire, la nature des hommes. Il faut qu'il transforme chaque individu, qui est par lui-même un tout parfait et solitaire, en partie d'un plus grand tout, dont cet individu reçoive en quelque sorte[9] sa vie et son être; qu'il mutile, pour ainsi dire, la constitution de l'homme, pour.... [See Geneva MS. of *C. S.* II. ii.; and final version of *C. S.* II. vii.]

*[MS. Neuchâtel, 7858. Written in pencil on the back of one of the notes which Rousseau had collected for his estimate of Saint-Pierre. The paper is cut aslant.] Comment compter sur des engagements qu'on ne peut forcer les contractants à tenir, et que l'intérêt qui les fait...venant à changer... ? The sense of the final clause must have been: 'and which, when the interest that makes them acceptable changes, they will inevitably desire to break.' [Compare *Discours sur l'inégalité*; above, pp. 188—9.]

[For other Fragments, bearing on like matters, see above, *Économie politique*, pp. 274—280.]

[1] [pour ainsi dire.]
[2] [Qu'il fasse enfin pour sa propre félicité tout ce qu'il refusait de faire pour sa raison : Tâchons de lui faire si bien connaître en quoi les vrais moyens d'être heureux.]
[3] [l'ami des hommes, bien modéré.]
[4] From *nos citoyens* D. B. infers—hazardously—that this was written at Geneva.
[5] [d'une société.]   [6] [si mes talents ne sont pas....]
[7] [cet homme.]   [8] [changer.]   [9] [son existence; il faut.]

B. Other Fragments.

I. Du bonheur public.

[MS. Neuchâtel, 7843, p. 12.]

[This Fragment can be dated precisely. It is quite certainly to be identified with Rousseau's projected Answer to certain Questions put to him by the *Société économique de Berne* in April, 1762: *i.e.* just at the moment when the *Contrat social* and *Émile* were about to appear. See his letter to the members of the Society above mentioned (April 29, 1762), *Œuvres*, x. pp. 321—3. In this letter Rousseau gives no hint that he intends to write a formal Answer. But the Questions propounded to him are mentioned in the letter; and the first—'Quel peuple a jamais été le plus heureux?'—corresponds word for word with the Question mentioned in the first line of the Fragment. M. Streckeisen-Moultou was, therefore, quite mistaken in supposing the Fragment to be part of the *Institutions politiques*.

It is probable, though not certain, that Fragments II and VI (MSS. Neuchâtel, 7849 and 7854) were written on the same occasion.]

Vous demandez, Messieurs[1], quel peuple a été jamais le plus heureux. Je ne suis pas assez savant pour résoudre cette question dans le fait, mais je tenterai d'établir des principes certains pour la résoudre; si je réussis, je pourrais croire être entré dans vos vues et ne m'être pas écarté du bon.

Où est l'homme heureux? S'il existe, qui le sait[2]? [3]Le bonheur n'est pas le plaisir; il ne consiste pas dans une modification passagère de l'âme, mais dans un sentiment permanent et tout intérieur, dont[3] nul ne peut juger que celui qui l'éprouve. [4]Nul ne peut donc décider avec certitude[4] qu'un autre est heureux, ni par conséquent établir des signes certains du bonheur des individus. Mais il n'en est pas de même des sociétés politiques; leurs biens, leurs maux sont tous apparents et visibles; leur sentiment intérieur est un sentiment public. Le vulgaire s'y trompe, sans doute; mais à quoi ne se trompe-t-il pas? mais pour tout

---

[1] For the opening words S. M. substitutes, quite without authority, 'Si l'on demande.'

[2] S. M. reads *qui le fait?*

[3] [Le bonheur de l'homme étant tout intérieur.]

[4] [C'est donc toujours une décision téméraire de prononcer.]

œil qui sait voir, elles sont ce qu'elles paraissent, et l'on peut sans témérité juger de leur être moral[1].

Ce qui fait la misère humaine est la contradiction qui se trouve entre notre état et nos désirs, entre nos devoirs et nos penchants, entre la nature et les institutions sociales, entre l'homme et le citoyen. Rendez l'homme un, et vous le rendrez aussi heureux qu'il peut l'être. Donnez-le tout entier à l'État, ou laissez-le tout entier à lui-même. Mais si vous partagez son cœur, vous le déchirez; [2]et n'allez pas vous imaginer que l'État puisse être heureux, quand tous ses membres pâtissent. Cet état moral[3] que vous appelez bonheur public est en lui-même une chimère: si ce sentiment du bien-être n'est chez personne, il n'est rien; et la famille n'est point florissante, quand les enfants ne prospèrent pas.

Rendez les hommes conséquents à eux-mêmes, étant ce qu'ils veulent paraître et paraissant ce qu'ils sont; vous aurez mis la loi sociale au fond des cœurs: hommes civils[4] par leur nature et citoyens par leurs inclinations, ils seront uns, ils seront bons, ils seront heureux, et leur félicité sera celle de la République. Car n'étant rien que par elle, ils ne seront rien que pour elle; elle aura tout ce qu'ils ont et sera tout ce qu'ils sont. [5]À la force de la contrainte vous avez ajouté celle de la volonté; au trésor public vous avez joint les biens des particuliers. Elle sera tout ce qu'elle peut être, quand elle embrassera tout. La famille, en montrant ses enfants, dira: c'est par là que je suis florissante[5]. Dans un autre système, il y aura toujours dans l'État[6] quelque chose qui n'appartiendra pas à l'État, ne fût-ce que la volonté de ses membres; et qui est-ce qui peut ignorer l'influence de cette volonté dans les affaires? Quand nul ne veut être heureux que pour lui, il n'y a point de bonheur pour la patrie. [S. M.]

*[ib. p. 13 and v° of p. 12.] Pour concevoir nettement comment un peuple peut être heureux, commençons par considérer l'état de ceux qui ne le sont pas. En cherchant ce qui leur manque pour l'être, nous pourrions trouver ce que doit avoir celui qui l'est: et

---

[1] [Voilà la question justifiée, et voilà l'écrivain condamné s'il la résout....]
[2] [Il est également malheureux quelque parti que...; et ne vous imaginez pas que, le citoyen vivant heureux, l'État puisse être en souffrance.]
[3] S. M. reads *cet être moral*.
[4] [sociaux.]
[5] Written, as an afterthought, in the margin of the MS., and omitted by S. M.
[6] *dans l'État*, omitted by S. M.

surtout, n'oublions pas que le bien public doit être le bien de tous en quelque chose, ou que c'est un mot vide de sens.

L'état moral d'un peuple résulte moins de l'état absolu de ses membres que de leurs rapports entre eux.

*[MS. Neuchâtel, 7854.] ...bonheur public, il ne suffirait pas même de compter les voix; et le bien-être des nations, qui dépend de tant de choses, ne s'estime pas aussi facilement que celui des particuliers. Il s'agit donc de discerner parmi beaucoup d'apparences, qui peuvent en imposer sur la félicité d'un peuple, les vrais signes qui la caractérisent. [The missing words at the beginning must be 'Pour déterminer le,' or their equivalents.]

II.

[MS. Neuchâtel, 7849.]

Si, pour commencer par bien établir la proposition disputée, je pouvais déterminer exactement en quoi consiste dans un Gouvernement quelconque la véritable supériorité de l'État, et quelles sont les marques les plus infaillibles sur lesquelles on puisse affirmer d'une nation qu'elle est heureuse et florissante, la question serait presque résolue par la définition même. Mais comme cette définition dépend d'une multitude de maximes particulières qu'on ne peut établir qu'à force de discussion[1] et à mesure qu'on avance en matière, je serai contraint, quant à présent, de me borner à une idée très générale, mais à laquelle je ne crois pas qu'aucun homme raisonnable puisse refuser son approbation. Je dis donc que la nation la plus heureuse est celle qui peut le plus aisément se passer de toutes les autres, et que la plus florissante est celle dont les autres peuvent le moins se passer[2].

Si j'avais tiré collectivement l'idée du bonheur de l'État de celle du bonheur particulier de chaque citoyen qui le compose, j'aurais pu dire une chose plus sensible à beaucoup de lecteurs. Mais, outre qu'on n'aurait jamais rien pu conclure de ces notions métaphysiques qui dépendent de la manière de penser et de l'humeur et du caractère de chaque individu, j'aurais donné une définition très peu juste. Un État pourrait être fort bien constitué et d'une

[1] S. M. reads *discussions*.
[2] Contrast *C. S.* II. x.: 'Quel peuple est donc propre à la législation ?... Celui qui peut se passer des autres peuples, et dont tout autre peuple peut se passer' (and the note). It is a pity that in the above Fragment, which seems to have been written later than the *C. S.*, Rousseau should have repudiated so wise a doctrine.

manière propre à le faire fleurir et prospérer à jamais, [1]que les citoyens[1], occupés chacun de ses vues particulières[2], n'en fussent guère contents. Quand Lycurgue établit ses lois, il eut à subir mille murmures, et même de mauvais traitements, de la part[3] des Lacédémoniens; il fut même contraint d'user de ruse et d'aller finir ses jours hors de sa patrie, pour obliger ses concitoyens à conserver une institution qui les a rendus le peuple le plus illustre et le plus respecté qui ait existé sur la terre. Les Romains ne se sont-ils pas plaints sans cesse d'un Gouvernement avec lequel ils sont devenus les maîtres du monde? et même actuellement, la nation la mieux gouvernée n'est-elle pas précisément celle qui murmure le plus?

Il n'y a aucun Gouvernement qui puisse forcer les citoyens à vivre heureux. Le meilleur est celui qui les met en état de l'être, s'ils sont raisonnables; et ce bonheur n'appartiendra jamais à la multitude. Ce n'est pas sur la situation la plus convenable aux inclinations ou aux fantaisies de chaque particulier que l'administration publique doit être modifiée; il faut, pour être bonne, qu'elle s'établisse sur des règles plus générales.

Dans quelque Gouvernement que ce soit, une sage administration peut former les mœurs publiques par l'éducation et par la coutume, et diriger tellement les inclinations des particuliers, qu'en général ils se trouvent plus contents du Gouvernement sous lequel ils vivent qu'ils ne le seraient sous tout autre, meilleur ou pire, indifféremment. Car, quoique les hommes se plaignent toujours, peut-être, dans quelque autre situation qu'on les mît, se plaindraient-ils encore davantage. Ce n'est donc pas par le sentiment que les citoyens ont de leur bonheur, ni par conséquent par leur bonheur même, qu'il faut juger de la prospérité de l'État.

[4]D'ailleurs, on peut dire que l'état de la nation le plus favorable au bonheur des particuliers est de n'avoir besoin, pour vivre heureux, du concours d'aucun autre peuple; car il ne leur reste plus, pour jouir de toute la félicité possible, que de pourvoir par de sages lois à tous leurs avantages mutuels: ce qui ne dépendrait pas si bien d'eux, s'il fallait nécessairement recourir aux étrangers. Que si, avec cela, d'autres peuples ont besoin de celui qui n'a besoin de personne, on ne saurait imaginer une position plus

---

[1] MS. has *et que*. So S. M. The emendation seems necessary.
[2] *occupés chacun de ses vues particulières*, omitted by S. M.
[3] *et même des mauvais traitements de la part*, omitted by S. M.
[4] By transposing two pages—which begin *Si j'avais tiré* and *D'ailleurs* respectively—S. M. has confused the argument.

propre à rendre heureux les membres d'une telle société, autant que des hommes peuvent l'être.

J'aurais pu dire aussi que la nation la plus heureuse est celle qui a le plus d'argent, ou celle qui fait le plus grand commerce, ou la plus ingénieuse dans les Arts ; et ceci aurait été le sentiment le plus unanime. Mais si ces définitions sont justes, celle que j'ai donnée en doit être une conséquence nécessaire : car, si l'argent rend les riches heureux, c'est moins par sa possession immédiate que parce qu'il les met à portée premièrement de pourvoir à leurs besoins et d'accomplir leurs volontés en toutes choses, sans jamais dépendre de personne ; puis de commander aux autres et de les tenir dans leur dépendance. Or, voilà précisément les idées dont j'ai composé celle d'une nation heureuse et florissante.

[1]À l'égard du Commerce et des Arts, leur objet principal étant de faire abonder et circuler l'argent, avec lequel on obtient tant qu'on veut l'un et l'autre, et supposant toujours la définition juste, il se trouve qu'elle rentre encore dans la mienne[1].

Après avoir montré que ma définition renferme toutes les autres et qu'elle est par conséquent la plus générale, il me reste à faire voir qu'elle est aussi la plus juste, et celle qui s'accorde le mieux avec les idées que nous avons du bonheur et de la prospérité.

Nos besoins sont de deux espèces : savoir, les besoins physiques nécessaires à notre conservation, et ceux qui regardent les commodités, le plaisir, la magnificence, et dont les objets portent en général le nom de luxe. Ces derniers deviennent à la lettre de véritables besoins, lorsqu'un long usage nous a fait contracter l'habitude d'en jouir, et que notre constitution s'est pour ainsi dire formée à cette habitude. Ainsi une femme de la ville, exposée pendant deux heures, dans les grandes ardeurs de l'été, en pleine campagne, sans parasol, y gagnerait presque infailliblement un coup de soleil et peut-être une maladie mortelle, tandis qu'une paysanne ne s'en trouverait point incommodée ; un bourgeois ne peut se passer d'un cheval pour aller à sa campagne, dont son fermier fait tous les jours le trajet à pied. Et tel courtisan, accoutumé aux aises d'une chaise de poste, ne pourrait, sans en être incommodé[2], faire le même voyage à cheval. Ainsi tout, jusqu'aux poisons mêmes, peut devenir besoin physique par l'habitude, comme l'opium chez les Turcs et le réalgar chez les Chinois. [S. M.]

[1] This paragraph is omitted by S. M.
[2] MS. has *incommodité*.

III. Des lois.

[MS. Neuchâtel, 7867.]

(a)

La seule étude qui convienne à un bon peuple est celle de ses lois. Il faut qu'il les médite sans cesse pour les aimer, pour les observer, pour les corriger même, avec les précautions que demande un sujet de cette importance, quand le besoin en est bien pressant et bien avéré. Tout État où il y a plus de lois que la mémoire de chaque citoyen n'en peut contenir est un État mal constitué; et tout homme qui ne sait pas par cœur les lois de son pays est un mauvais citoyen; aussi Lycurgue ne voulut-il écrire les siennes que dans les cœurs des Spartiates.

[1]Si l'on me demandait quel est le plus vicieux de tous les peuples, je répondrais sans hésiter que c'est celui qui a le plus de lois. La volonté de bien faire supplée à tout, et celui qui sait écouter la loi de sa conscience n'en a guère besoin d'autre; mais la multitude des lois annonce deux choses également dangereuses et qui marchent presque toujours ensemble: savoir, que les lois sont mauvaises et qu'elles sont sans vigueur. Si la Loi était assez claire, elle n'aurait pas besoin sans cesse de nouvelles interprétations, ou de nouvelles modifications; si elle était assez sage et si elle était aimée et respectée, on ne verrait pas ces funestes et odieuses contestations entre les citoyens, pour les éluder, et le souverain, pour les maintenir. Ces multitudes effroyables d'édits et de déclarations qu'on voit émaner journellement de certaines Cours ne font qu'apprendre à tous que le peuple méprise avec raison la volonté de son souverain, et[2] l'exciter à la mépriser encore davantage, en voyant qu'il ne sait lui-même ce qu'il veut. Le premier précepte de la Loi doit être de faire aimer tous les autres. Mais ce n'est ni le fer, ni le feu, ni le fouet des pédants de cour, qui font observer celui-là; et pourtant, sans celui-là, tous les autres servent de peu; car on prêche inutilement celui qui n'a nul désir de bien faire. Appliquons ces principes à toutes nos[3] lois: il nous serait facile d'assigner le degré d'estime qu'on doit à ceux qui les ont rédigées, et à ceux pour qui elles ont été faites. Par exemple,

---

[1] This paragraph is also to be found (written in pencil) in MS. 7872.
[2] S. M. reads *que l'exciter*, against the MS.
[3] S. M. reads *appliquant ces notions à toutes les lois*.

la première réflexion qui se présente en considérant le gros recueil de Justinien, c'est que cet ouvrage immense a été fait pour un grand peuple : c'est-à-dire, pour des hommes incapables d'aimer leurs lois, par conséquent de les observer et même de les connaître ; en sorte qu'en voulant tout prévoir Justinien a fait un ouvrage inutile.

[1]Soit qu'on fasse attention à la multitude énorme de ces lois, ou aux perpétuelles discussions d'intérêt sur lesquelles elles roulent presque uniquement, ou aux diverses interprétations dont on semble avoir eu soin de les rendre susceptibles, on y reconnaît aisément l'avarice qui les a dictées. Que Tribonien et Théodora les aient vendues au plus offrant, je n'ai pas besoin que Procope me l'apprenne. Procope a pu être un calomniateur. Mais un témoignage plus fort que le sien est celui de ces lois mêmes, et des mœurs de la Cour où elles ont été compilées[1].

Un Lacédémonien, interrogé par un étranger sur la peine infligée par Lycurgue aux parricides, lui répondit qu'on les obligeait de paître un bœuf qui du sommet du mont Tégète pût boire dans l'Eurotas : ' Comment, s'écria l'étranger, serait-il possible de trouver un tel bœuf ? — Plus aisément, reprit le Lacédémonien, qu'un parricide à Sparte.' La terreur peut contenir les scélérats ; mais ce n'est jamais par les grands crimes que commence la corruption d'un peuple ; et c'est à prévenir ces commencements qu'il faut employer toute la force des lois. Voilà le principe sur lequel il faut juger de ce que peuvent les lois, non seulement pour épouvanter le vice, mais aussi pour encourager la vertu. Je sais que le premier prix des bonnes actions est le plaisir de les avoir faites ; mais les hommes ne connaissent ce plaisir qu'après l'avoir goûté, et il leur faut des motifs plus sensibles pour leur donner la première habitude de bien faire. Ces motifs sont les récompenses bien choisies et encore mieux distribuées ; sans quoi, loin d'honorer la vertu, elles ne feraient qu'exciter l'hypocrisie et nourrir l'avarice. Ce choix et cette distribution sont le chef-d'œuvre du Législateur. Un mauvais précepteur ne sait que donner le fouet ; un mauvais ministre ne sait que faire pendre ou mettre en prison. Ainsi nos politiques, qui ne croient faisables que les petites choses qu'ils font, n'auront garde d'adopter ces maximes ; et c'est tant mieux pour nous. Car, s'ils admettaient l'utilité des récompenses, ils n'imagineraient qu'argent, pensions, gratifications ; ils établiraient vite[2] de nouveaux impôts dont ils distribueraient quelques petites portions à cette

---

[1] This paragraph is not printed by S. M. See below, p. 479.
[2] S. M. omits *vite* (spelt *viste*).

troupe d'esclaves et de coquins qui les environne, et mettraient le reste dans leur bourse. Voilà ce que le peuple gagnerait à cela[1].

Un auteur moderne qui sait instruire par les choses qu'il dit et par celles qu'il fait penser, nous apprend que *tout ce que la Loi propose pour récompense en devient une en effet*[2]. Il n'était donc pas plus difficile aux Législateurs d'exciter aux bonnes actions que d'empêcher les mauvaises. Cependant ils se sont presque tous bornés à assurer la vindicte publique et à régler entre les particuliers les discussions d'intérêt: deux objets qui devraient être les moindres de la législation dans un État bien constitué.

Les lois qui parlent sans cesse de punir, et jamais de récompenser, sont plus propres à contenir les scélérats qu'à former d'honnêtes gens. Tant que les lois s'arrêteront aux actions et qu'elles ne diront rien à la volonté, elles seront toujours mal observées; parce que, avec quelque sagesse qu'elles soient conçues, la mauvaise intention donne toujours des lumières suffisantes pour apprendre à les éluder.

[3]C'est une chose qu'on ne peut assez admirer chez les premiers Romains; l'unique punition portée par les lois des Douze Tables contre les plus grands criminels était d'être en horreur à tous: *Sacer estod*. On ne peut mieux concevoir combien ce peuple était vertueux, qu'en songeant que la haine ou l'estime publique y était une peine ou une récompense dispensée par la Loi[3].

De sorte que, dans un État sagement policé, la Loi pourrait dire comme la prêtresse Théano: 'Je ne suis point ministre des Dieux pour détester et maudire, mais pour louer et bénir[4].'

L'histoire ancienne est pleine de preuves de l'attention du peuple aux mœurs des particuliers; et cette attention même en était la peine ou la récompense la plus sensible.

Les Législateurs sanguinaires qui, à l'exemple de Dracon, ne savent que menacer et punir, ressemblent à ces mauvais précepteurs qui n'élèvent les enfants que le fouet à la main[5]. [S. M.]

---

[1] This paragraph is in the hand, and spelling, of Thérèse Levasseur. I have followed the transcription of S. M. He prints the original *literatim* in a note.

[2] The only reference I can suggest here is to *Esprit des lois*, VI. ix.: 'Tout ce que la loi appelle une peine est effectivement une peine.' But, as what is true of penalties would not necessarily be so of rewards, it is not satisfactory.

[3] This paragraph is very incorrectly printed by S. M.

[4] Plutarch (trans. Amyot), *Œuvres Morales*, II. 277; and *Vie d'Alcibiadès*, II. 733 (Paris, 1574 and 1567, respectively). Rousseau quotes from the latter.

[5] Bêtise des supplices cruels au Japon, où la honte a tant de force. Voyez

[Same MS.]

(b)

Dans tout pays où le luxe et la corruption ne règnent pas, le témoignage public de la vertu d'un homme est le plus doux prix qu'il en puisse recevoir ; et toute bonne action n'a besoin, pour sa récompense, que d'être dénoncée publiquement comme telle. Voilà une source d'intérêt plus sûre et moins dangereuse que les trésors ; car la gloire d'avoir bien fait n'est pas sujette aux mêmes inconvénients que celle d'être riche, et donne une satisfaction beaucoup plus vive à ceux qui ont appris à la goûter. De quoi s'agit-il donc pour exciter les hommes à la vertu ? de leur apprendre à la trouver belle et à estimer ceux qui la pratiquent. Un avantage très considérable pour un État ainsi constitué, c'est que les malintentionnés[1] n'y ont aucun pouvoir pour exécuter leurs mauvais desseins, et que le vice n'y peut faire aucune espèce de fortune. Je ne désespère pas d'entendre quelque philosophe moderne en dire un jour autant de ces brillantes nations, où l'on voit régner, avec les richesses, l'insatiable ardeur de les augmenter.

Je sens qu'il faut expliquer un peu ma pensée ; autrement peu de lecteurs seraient de mon avis. Car il s'agit de convaincre tous ceux qui ne jurent que par Mammon[2].

C'est une des singularités du cœur humain, que, malgré le penchant qu'ont tous les hommes à juger favorablement d'eux-mêmes, il y a des points sur lesquels ils s'estiment encore plus méprisables qu'ils ne le[3] sont en effet. Tel est l'intérêt, qu'ils regardent comme leur passion dominante, quoiqu'ils en aient une autre plus forte, plus générale et plus facile à rectifier, qui ne se sert de l'intérêt que comme d'un moyen pour se satisfaire : c'est l'amour des distinctions. On fait tout pour s'enrichir, mais c'est pour être considéré qu'on veut être riche. Cela se prouve en ce

Mandelslo, p. 424. [Note de J.-J. R. The reference is to Mandelslo's travels in the East (1638—40). He was attached to the Embassy sent by the Duke of Holstein to the Great Duke of Muscovy and the King of Persia, and continued his journey, from Persia onwards, on his own account. His Travels were published in German by Olearius, Secretary to the Embassy (Schleswig, 1658). There is an English translation, by J. Davies of Kidwelly (1662); and a French translation, by Wicquefort (Paris, 1666; Amsterdam, 1727). It is said that a good deal of the book, including the part about Japan, is not by Mandelslo himself. Compare *Esprit des lois*, VI. xiii. (*Impuissance des lois japonaises*).]

[1] MS. has *malintention*.
[2] This paragraph is omitted by S. M.   [3] MS. omits *le* by a slip.

que, au lieu de se borner à cette médiocrité qui constitue le bien-être, chacun veut parvenir à ce degré de richesse qui fixe tous les yeux, mais qui augmente les soins et les peines et devient presque aussi à charge que la pauvreté même. Cela se prouve encore par l'usage ridicule que les riches font de leurs biens. Ce ne sont point eux qui jouissent de leurs profusions, et elles ne sont faites que pour attirer les regards et l'admiration des autres. Il est assez évident que le désir de se distinguer est la seule source du luxe, des magnificences : car, quant à celui de mollesse, il n'y a qu'un bien petit nombre de voluptueux qui sachent le goûter et lui laisser la douceur et toute la simplicité dont il est susceptible. C'est donc ainsi qu'on voit, par le même principe, toutes les familles travailler sans cesse à s'enrichir et à se ruiner alternativement; c'est Sisyphe qui sue sang et eau pour porter au sommet d'une montagne le rocher qu'il en va faire rouler le moment d'après.

Il s'agirait d'exciter le désir et de faciliter les moyens de s'attirer par la vertu la même considération qu'on ne sait s'attirer aujourd'hui par la richesse[1]. Cette vérité découle des principes que je viens d'établir; et, pour l'honneur de l'humanité, l'expérience même la confirme. Quel était le mobile de la vertu des Lacédémoniens, si ce n'était d'être estimés vertueux? Qu'est-ce qui, après avoir conduit les triomphateurs au Capitole, les ramenait à leur charrue[2]?

Car quand on a épuisé toutes les recherches agréables, il faut bien, pour eviter le désœuvrement que l'habitude de penser ne laisse plus supporter, retomber enfin dans les recherches utiles. D'ailleurs les beaux arts les plus frivoles en apparence.... [S. M.]

IV. HISTOIRE DES MŒURS.
[MS. Neuchâtel, 7868.]

(a)

Que si, dans chaque action, on laisse à part les moyens pour ne considérer que la fin, on trouve incomparablement plus de bonnes actions que de mauvaises. Toutes ont pour objet immédiat ou éloigné le bien-être de leur auteur : motif très bon et très innocent en soi, si l'on n'employait pas des voies criminelles pour y parvenir.

[1] S. M. reads *que par la richesse*. MS., as in the text. The emendation is not necessary.

[2] This paragraph and the next are omitted, save for a mangled version of the opening sentence, by S. M. The final paragraph is quite disconnected.

Plusieurs font le bien par pure vertu, et sans autre objet que le bien même; mais il est très difficile de croire que jamais l'homme ait fait le mal pour le seul plaisir de mal faire. D'où je conclus qu'il y a dans toute notre conduite plus d'aveuglement que de malice, et qu'un seul homme de bien honore plus l'humanité que tous les méchants ne la dégradent. Je ne me sens point avili par les crimes de Caligula, de Néron ni d'Héliogabale; mais mon âme s'anoblit et s'élève au récit des vertus d'Antonin[1].

Plusieurs ont honoré la probité et récompensé la vertu; mais autre chose est le caractère du monarque, et autre chose l'esprit de la monarchie. Entendez sourdre et murmurer le parterre au dénoûment du *Tartufe*; ce murmure terrible, qui devrait faire frémir les rois, vous expliquera trop ce que je veux dire.

Chaque état, chaque profession, a son dictionnaire particulier pour exprimer en termes décents les vices qui leur sont propres. On ne dira pas d'un ministre qu'il vexe le peuple, mais qu'il trouve des expédients; ni d'un financier qu'il vole le prince, mais qu'il fait une bonne affaire; un filou dira qu'il a *gagné* une bourse, et une courtisane qu'elle s'est mise dans le monde. L'honnêteté n'est plus que dans les mots; et plus il y a de corruption dans les âmes, plus on affecte de choix et de pureté dans les discours. J'aimerais cent fois mieux qu'un homme vienne me dire[2] intrépidement qu'il en a trahi son bienfaiteur et son ami.

[Un ministre qui invente des expédients, un traitant qui fait une bonne affaire, un filou qui gagne une bourse, font tous à peu près la même chose; mais chacun d'eux tâche d'en adoucir l'idée par des termes du métier. Qu'un impudent me déclare sans détour qu'il vient de faire une insigne[3] friponnerie, je trouverai dans son discours un peu plus d'arrogance peut-être, mais à coup sûr beaucoup moins de lâcheté[4].]

Soit qu'un penchant naturel ait porté les hommes à s'unir en société, soit qu'ils y aient été forcés par leurs besoins mutuels, il est certain que c'est de ce commerce que sont nés leurs vertus et leurs vices, et, en quelque manière, leur être moral. Là où il n'y a point de société, il ne peut y avoir ni justice, ni clémence, ni humanité, ni générosité, ni modestie, ni surtout le mérite de toutes ces vertus:

---

[1] Underlined in MS. Originally 'de Socrate.'
[2] MS. has variant, *me dise*. S. M. omits this sentence.
[3] S. M. reads *indigne*; and, in the preceding sentence, *de métier*.
[4] This paragraph, which is manifestly a variant on the preceding one, occurs later in the MS. (p. 12).

je veux dire ce qu'il en coûte à les pratiquer parmi des êtres remplis de tous les vices contraires. À parler moralement, la société est-elle donc en soi un bien, ou un mal ? La réponse dépend de la comparaison du bon et du mauvais qui en résultent, et la balance des vices et des vertus qu'elle a engendrés chez ceux qui la composent : et de ce côté-là la question n'est que trop facile à résoudre[1]; et il vaudrait mieux tirer pour jamais le rideau sur toutes les actions humaines, que de dévoiler à nos regards un[2] odieux et dangereux spectacle qu'elles nous présentent. Mais en y regardant de plus près, on y voit bientôt qu'il entre dans la solution de ce problème d'autres éléments dont le philosophe doit tenir compte, et qui modifient beaucoup une si triste conclusion. Et la vertu d'un seul homme de bien anoblit plus la race humaine que tous les crimes des méchants ne peuvent la dégrader.

Je suis surpris que, parmi tant de découvertes singulières qui se sont faites de nos jours, personne ne se soit encore avisé de remarquer que c'est à la cour des rois que la philosophie a pris naissance ; il me semble que ce paradoxe en vaut bien un autre. Dans les premiers temps du monde, les hommes, encore grossiers, pensaient que, pour avoir droit de commander à d'autres, il fallait les surpasser en sagesse ; et, se réglant sur cette idée, les princes n'étaient pas seulement les juges de l'équitable et du bon, mais aussi du beau et du vrai.

[3]Premièrement, dans la constitution du bien et du mal les choses ne sont point égales. Une action, pour être juste et bonne, doit être telle non seulement dans sa fin, mais encore selon toutes les relations[4] qu'elle peut avoir. Au contraire, toute action vicieuse à un seul égard, quelque louable qu'elle pût être d'ailleurs, devient mauvaise en soi ; de sorte que, toutes choses égales, le mal doit nécessairement surpasser[5] le bien à proportion de la multitude des objets auxquels la moralité de chaque action peut se rapporter. De plus—

La nature sème toujours également, mais nous ne recueillons pas de même.

---

[1] [la négative n'est que trop évidente.]
[2] S. M. misreads *l'odieux*. He also prints the passage *Et il vaudrait...si triste conclusion*, as a note, instead of in the text.
[3] This paragraph takes up the argument of that next but one before it; the intervening paragraph is an interruption. S. M. omits *Premièrement*.
[4] S. M. misreads *solutions* ; and, earlier, *bonne et juste*.
[5] S. M. reads *compenser*.

Il sera toujours grand et difficile de soumettre les plus chères affections de la nature à la patrie et à la vertu.

Après avoir absous ou refusé de condamner son fils, comment Brutus eût-il jamais osé condamner un autre citoyen ? 'O consul! lui eût dit ce criminel, ai-je fait pis que de vendre ma patrie ? et ne suis-je pas aussi votre fils[1] ? '

Qu'on me montre aujourd'hui un seul juge capable de sacrifier à la patrie et aux lois la vie de ses enfants ! Quelques femmes mourront pour cet honneur apparent qui consiste dans l'opinion d'autrui ; mais qu'on m'en montre une seule capable de mourir pour ce véritable honneur qui consiste dans la pureté des actions !

Un seul homme de probité est capable de tenir en respect toute la rue où il demeure ; le vice est toujours honteux de se démasquer aux yeux de la vertu.

L'âme s'échauffe, l'esprit s'élève, en parlant de la vertu. Les plus pervers même en sentent parfois les divins transports ; et il n'y a point de si méchant homme qui n'ait senti dans son cœur quelques étincelles de ce feu céleste, et qui n'ait été capable de sentiments et d'actions héroïques, du moins une fois en[2] sa vie.

Quant à cette raison vulgaire, qu'il ne faut pas cesser d'occuper les gens[3] du peuple afin de distraire son imagination des choses du gouvernement, si l'on veut qu'il soit sage et tranquille, elle est démentie par l'expérience ; car jamais l'Angleterre n'a été si tranquille qu'elle l'est aujourd'hui, et jamais les particuliers ne se sont tant occupés, tant entretenus, des affaires de la nation. Au contraire, voyez la fréquence des révolutions en Orient, où les affaires du gouvernement sont toujours pour le peuple des mystères impénétrables. Il est fort apparent que toutes ces maximes barbares et sophistiques ont été introduites par des ministres infidèles et corrompus qui avaient grand intérêt que leurs prévarications ne fussent pas exposées au—

*S'il y a quelque souverain qui se conduise sur des maximes contraires, c'est un tyran. Et s'il y a quelque sujet capable d'inspirer de telles maximes à son souverain, c'est un traître[4].

---

[1] Between the two paragraphs comes : 'Je suis fâché pour St Augustin des plaisanteries qu'il a osé faire sur ce grand et bel acte de vertu. Les Pères de l'Église n'ont pas su voir le mal qu'ils faisaient à leur cause, en flétrissant ainsi tout ce que le courage et l'honneur avaient produit de plus grand. À force de vouloir élever la sublimité du Christianisme, ils ont appris aux chrétiens à devenir des hommes lâches et sans....' The pen is drawn through the paragraph, which is altogether omitted by S. M. See below, p. 341.

[2] S. M. reads *dans*.   [3] S. M. reads *les sens*.

[4] This paragraph and the three following are omitted by S. M.

*Mais quand on a lui-même un peuple à rendre heureux, faut-il écrire[1] des livres pour apprendre aux souverains à faire le bonheur des peuples ? Rois, instruisez d'exemple.

*S'ils se donnaient un peu moins de peine pour nous dire qu'il faut bien faire, et un peu plus pour bien faire eux-mêmes, croyez-vous que leurs exemples fussent moins utiles que leurs instructions ? Pourquoi faut-il qu'ils perdent, à nous avertir de notre devoir, le temps qu'ils devraient employer à faire le leur ?

*Faites les mêmes choses avec des motifs plus justes. Vous devez veiller à la sûreté de vos sujets, les défendre, eux et leurs biens, contre la violence et l'oppression. Mais ce n'est encore que la moitié de votre tâche : vous devez même les rendre heureux. Et voilà la perfection des devoirs du souverain....

Quand on considère d'un œil de philosophe le jeu de toutes les parties de ce vaste univers, on s'aperçoit bientôt que la plus grande beauté de chacune des pièces qui le composent ne consiste pas en elle-même ; et qu'elle n'a pas été formée pour demeurer seule et indépendante, mais pour concourir avec toutes les autres à la perfection de la machine entière.

Il en est de même dans l'ordre moral. Les vices et les vertus de chaque homme ne sont pas relatifs à lui seul. Leur plus grand rapport est avec la société, et c'est ce qu'ils sont à l'égard de l'ordre en général qui constitue leur essence et leur caractère. [S. M.]

(b)

L'histoire moderne n'est pas dépourvue de traits admirables ; mais ce ne sont que des traits ; j'y vois quelques grandes actions, mais je n'y vois de grands hommes.

Si l'on trouvait quelque moyen de rendre le labourage plus facile et d'épargner le nombre de bœufs qu'on y emploie, il résulterait nécessairement de cette invention une diminution de prix pour le blé et une augmentation pour la viande. Il reste à voir si cette industrie serait aussi utile aux pauvres qu'elle serait préjudiciable aux malades, qui ont plus besoin de bouillon que de pain.

En général, il faut observer que, si la main d'œuvre multipliée dans les arts fait subsister un grand nombre d'hommes, elle rend en même temps plus difficile la subsistance de tout le peuple, par le renchérissement des denrées qui en résulte nécessairement.

---

[1] [faire.] It looks as though in this and the two next paragraphs, Rousseau had Frederick's *Anti-Machiavel* in view.

*(c)

...qu'il y a cent fois plus de mérite et de vertu à porter honnêtement et patiemment la pauvreté qu'à répandre avec profusion ses bienfaits sur les pauvres.

*(d)

In MS. Neuchâtel, 7868, is the following scheme for a projected *Histoire des Mœurs*:

Liv. I. chap. I. Des mœurs en général; chap. II. Des peuples sauvages; chap. III. Des peuples barbares; chap. IV. Des peuples policés; chap. V. Des peuples lettrés; chap. VI. Des peuples ouvriers; chap. VII. Des peuples vertueux; chap. VIII. De la religion.

Liv. II. chap. I. Des Égyptiens; chap. II. Des Perses; chap. III. Des Scythes; chap. IV. Des Grecs; chap. V. Des Carthaginois; chap. VI. Des Gaulois; chap. VII. Des Germains; chap. VIII. Des Romains.

(e)

In MS. f. Genève, 228, is the following list of chapters for another treatise; possibly, a section of the *Institutions politiques*:

Grandeur des nations; Gouvernement; des Lois; de la Religion; de l'Honneur; des F... (Français); du Commerce; des Voyages; des Aliments; Abus de la société; Culture des sciences; Examen de la République de Platon. [S. M.]

It will be observed that several of these subjects are treated in one or other of this Collection of Fragments.

[MS. Neuchâtel, 7871 (bis).]

*(a) Voilà pourquoi l'autorité des magistrats, qui ne s'étendait d'abord que sur les hommes, fut bientôt un droit établi sur les possessions; et voilà comment le titre de chef de la nation se changea enfin en celui de souverain du territoire. [See *Contrat social*, I. ix.]

*(b) Dans tout serment qu'un ministre, ou autre officier quelconque, prête à son prince, on doit sousentendre toujours cette clause: Sauf les lois de l'État et le salut du peuple. [See *Contrat social*, III. xviii.; and below (e).]

(c) Les lois et l'exercice de la justice ne sont parmi nous que l'art de mettre le grand et le riche à l'abri des justes représailles du pauvre[1]. [See *Émile*, Liv. IV.; *Œuvres*, II. p. 206.] [S. M.]

[1] Compare the following Fragment (MS. Neuchâtel, 7854): *Ils font valoir toute la rigueur des lois, pour venger les torts qu'ils reçoivent, et les éludent facilement dans tous ceux qu'ils font aux autres.

*(d) Mais les démêlés étaient si rares et les secours mutuels si fréquents qu'il dut résulter de ce commerce libre beaucoup plus de bienveillance que de haine : disposition qui, jointe au sentiment de commisération que la nature a gravé dans tous les cœurs, dut faire vivre les hommes assez paisiblement en troupeau. [See *Discours sur l'inégalité* ; above, p. 175.]

*(e) Quoique les associations dont je viens de parler ne fussent guère que tacites, qu'elles n'eussent qu'un objet déterminé et ne durassent qu'autant que le besoin qui les avait formés, ils ne laissèrent pas de lui inspirer quelque idée grossière.... [See *Discours sur l'inégalité* ; above, p. 171.]

*(f) Ce sont ces capitulations qui font le droit et la sûreté des souverains, et nul n'est obligé d'obéir aux magistrats qu'en vertu des lois fondamentales de l'État : lois auxquelles les magistrats sont obligés d'obéir eux-mêmes. [See above (b).]

(g) Le moral a une grande réaction sur le physique, et change quelquefois jusqu'aux traits du visage. Il y a plus de sentiment et de beauté dans les visages des anciens Grecs qu'il n'y en a dans ceux d'aujourd'hui ; il y a plus d'astuce et moins de grandeur sur les physionomies des Romains modernes que sur celles des anciens. [S. M.]

(h) Toutes les fois qu'il est question d'un véritable acte de souveraineté, qui n'est qu'une déclaration de la volonté générale, le peuple ne peut avoir des représentants, parce qu'il lui est impossible de s'assurer qu'ils ne substitueront point leurs volontés aux siennes, et qu'ils ne forceront point les particuliers d'obéir en son nom à des ordres qu'il n'a ni donnés[1], ni voulu donner : crime de lèse-majesté dont peu de Gouvernements sont exempts. [See *Contrat social*, III. xv.] [S. M. ; W.]

(i) Cession qui ne peut jamais être légitime parce qu'elle est fondée sur un pouvoir, qui n'est avantageux ni au maître ni à l'esclave, et par conséquent contraire au droit naturel. Car l'avantage de commander n'est, au delà du service de la personne, qu'un bien imaginaire et purement d'opinion ; et il est très égal pour la commodité personnelle du prince qu'il ait cent mille sujets de plus, ou de moins. C'est encore moins un bien d'être contraint à l'obéissance, quand on n'a point de garant qu'on sera sagement commandé. Mais qu'on puisse à son gré faire passer les peuples de maître en maître, comme des troupeaux[2] de bétail, sans consulter

---

[1] MS. *donné*, by a slip. [2] MS. *des troupeau*, by a slip.

ni leur intérêt ni leur avis, c'est se moquer des gens de le dire sérieusement. [See *Contrat social*, I. iii. and iv.; II. ii.] [W.]

(*j*) Vous m'aviez soumis par force; et tant que vous avez été le plus fort, je vous ai fidèlement obéi. Maintenant, la raison qui m'assujettissait à vous ayant cessé, mon assujettissement cesse; et vous ne sauriez dire pourquoi je vous obéissais, sans dire au même temps pourquoi je ne vous obéis plus. [See *Contrat social*, I. iii. and iv.] [S. M.; W.]

V.

[MS. Neuchâtel, 7871.] Les Pères de l'Église ont affecté beaucoup de mépris pour les vertus des anciens païens, qui, selon eux, n'avaient d'autre principe que la vaine gloire. Je crois cependant qu'ils auraient pu être fort embarrassés de prouver solidement une assertion aussi téméraire; car, qu'auraient-ils trouvé dans la conduite de Socrate, de Phocion, d'Anaxagore, d'Aristide, de Caton, de Fabricius, ou dans les écrits de Platon, de Sénèque et de Marc-Antonin qui donnât la moindre prise à cette accusation? Probablement ils se seraient gardés de calomnier alors les païens avec tant d'amertume, s'ils eussent prévu qu'on serait un jour à portée de rétorquer avec justice, contre les chrétiens mêmes, tous les reproches qu'ils faisaient à la sagesse du paganisme. [See above, p. 337.] [S. M.]

VI. Sur le luxe, le commerce et les arts.

[MS. Neuchâtel, 7854.]

Si les hommes pouvaient connaître combien il leur est plus dangereux de se tromper qu'il ne leur est utile de savoir, ils recevraient avec moins d'avidité les leçons des philosophes; et les philosophes seraient plus circonspects à les donner, s'ils sentaient qu'un seul mauvais raisonnement leur ôte plus de réputation que cent vérités découvertes ne leur en peuvent acquérir. Le meilleur usage qu'on puisse faire de la philosophie, c'est de l'employer à détruire les maux qu'elle a causés, dût-on en même temps détruire le bien, s'il y en a. Car, dans ce qui est ajouté aux simples lumières de la raison et aux purs sentiments de la nature, il vaut encore mieux ôter le bon que de laisser le mauvais. Il faudrait, pour l'avantage de la société, que les philosophes distribuassent leurs travaux de telle sorte qu'après bien des livres et des disputes ils se trouvassent réfutés réciproquement, et que le tout fût comme non avenu. Il est vrai qu'alors nous ne saurions rien ; mais nous en conviendrions de bonne foi, et nous aurions réellement gagné, pour la recherche de la vérité, tout le chemin qu'il faut faire en rétrogradant de l'erreur jusqu'à l'ignorance.

Pour concourir à ce but salutaire, je vais tâcher d'examiner quelques questions de politique et de morale, agitées et résolues par plusieurs écrivains modernes et relatives aux matières sur lesquelles j'ai été obligé de méditer. J'espère aussi, par ce moyen, développer certains théorèmes que la crainte des digressions m'a fait avancer sans preuves dans d'autres écrits. Mais comme, dans tout ceci, je me propose plutôt d'attaquer des erreurs que d'établir de nouvelles vérités, j'avoue de bonne foi que, quand les ouvrages de mes adversaires ne subsisteront plus, les miens seront parfaitement inutiles. Sans vouloir être le guide de mes contemporains, je me contente de les avertir quand j'en observe un qui les égare ; et je n'aurais pas besoin de les fatiguer de mes avis, si personne ne se mêlait de les conduire.

La question que je me propose d'examiner ici regarde le luxe, le commerce et les arts : non précisément par rapport aux mœurs, comme je l'ai envisagée ci-devant[1], mais sous un nouveau point de vue, et par rapport à la prospérité de l'État.

Tous les anciens ont regardé le luxe comme un signe de corruption dans les mœurs et de faiblesse dans le Gouvernement. Les lois somptuaires sont presque aussi anciennes que les sociétés politiques. Il y en avait chez les Égyptiens ; les Hébreux en reçurent de leur Législateur ; on en trouve même chez les Perses ; et quant aux Grecs, leur profond mépris pour le faste asiatique était la meilleure loi somptuaire qu'ils pussent avoir.

Ce mépris était encore plus sensible chez les Romains. Le luxe et la magnificence des autres nations étaient pour eux de vrais objets de risée ; et l'usage qu'ils en faisaient dans leurs triomphes était beaucoup plus propre à tourner en ridicule toute cette vaine pompe des peuples vaincus qu'à donner aux vainqueurs le désir de l'imiter[2].

Il était naturel que le commerce se sentît du mépris qu'on avait pour le luxe. Les Romains le dédaignaient, les Grecs le laissaient faire chez eux par des étrangers ; les arts mécaniques n'étaient presque exercés que par des esclaves ; et les arts libéraux mêmes exigeaient une grande supériorité de talent dans ceux qui

---

[1] *i.e.* in the *Discours sur les Sciences et les Arts.*
[2] See *Gouvernement de Pologne*, Chap. iii. and *Éc. pol.* p. 254.

les exerçaient, pour leur donner quelque considération ; encore n'en purent-ils jamais obtenir à Rome durant tout le temps de la République. En un mot, dans des pays où l'argent était méprisé, il ne se pouvait guère que tous les moyens d'en gagner n'eussent quelque chose d'ignominieux.

Quand ces peuples commencèrent à dégénérer, que la vanité et l'amour du plaisir eurent succédé à celui de la patrie et de la vertu, alors le vice et la mollesse pénétrèrent de toutes parts ; et il ne fut plus question que de luxe et d'argent pour y satisfaire. Les particuliers s'enrichirent, le commerce et les arts fleurirent, et l'État ne tarda pas à périr.

Cependant, durant la plus grande dépravation, les philosophes et les politiques ne cessèrent de crier contre tous ces désordres, dont ils prévoyaient les suites. Personne ne les contredit et personne ne se corrigea. On convint que leurs raisons étaient bonnes, et l'on se conduisit de manière à les rendre encore meilleures. Ces déclamateurs eux-mêmes ne semblèrent relever les fautes du peuple que pour rendre les leurs plus inexcusables. Ils blâmaient publiquement les vices dont ils auraient donné l'exemple, s'ils n'avaient été prévenus.

C'est ainsi qu'en se livrant à une conduite opposée à leurs propres maximes ces hommes ne laissaient pas de rendre hommage à la vérité. C'est ainsi que toutes les nations se sont accordées, dans tous les temps, à condamner le luxe, même en s'y abandonnant ; sans que, durant une si longue suite de siècles, aucun philosophe se soit avisé de contredire là-dessus l'opinion publique.

Je ne prétends pas tirer avantage de ce consentement universel pour le parti que j'ai à soutenir. Je sais que la philosophie[1], en adoptant les preuves des philosophes, se passe bien de leur témoignage, et que la raison n'a que faire d'autorités. Mais, instruit par l'expérience du tort que peut faire le nom de paradoxe à des propositions démontrées[2], je suis bien aise d'ôter d'avance cette ressource à ceux qui n'en auront point d'autre pour combattre ce que j'ai à prouver. Je les avertis donc que c'est l'opinion que j'attaque, qu'on doit appeler un paradoxe aussi inouï jusqu'à ce jour qu'il est ridicule et pernicieux ; et qu'en réfutant cette philosophie molle et efféminée, dont les commodes maximes lui ont acquis tant de sectateurs parmi nous, je ne fais que joindre ma voix aux cris de toutes les nations et plaider la cause du sens commun ainsi que celle de la société.

[1] [se passe bien du témoignage des philosophes.]
[2] S. M. has *vérités démontrées*, without authority.

[3]Enfin, après tant de siècles, deux hommes[1], cherchant à se rendre célèbres par des opinions singulières qui pussent flatter le goût du leur, se sont avisés, de nos jours, de renverser toutes les maximes économiques des anciens politiques et de leur substituer un système de gouvernement tout nouveau, et si brillant qu'il était très difficile de ne pas s'en laisser séduire; sans compter que, l'intérêt particulier y trouvant[2] très bien son compte, c'était un autre moyen de succès dans un siècle où personne ne se soucie plus du bien public, et où ce mot, ridiculement profané, ne sert plus que d'excuse aux tyrans et de prétexte aux fripons[3].

Pour raisonner solidement sur la question dont il s'agit, je voudrais premièrement poser quelque principe clair et certain[4], que personne ne pût nier raisonnablement, et qui servît de base à toutes mes recherches; sans quoi, n'ayant, au lieu de définition, que des idées vagues que chacun se forme à sa fantaisie et selon ses inclinations particulières, jamais nous ne saurons bien ce qu'on doit entendre, à l'égard d'un peuple, par ces mots de bonheur et de prospérité.

Avant que de parler des moyens de rendre un peuple heureux et florissant, tâchons donc de déterminer en quoi consiste précisément la gloire et la félicité d'un peuple, ou à quelles marques certaines on pourra reconnaître qu'un peuple se trouve dans cet état[5].

Je sens bien que cette question paraîtra fort peu embarrassante à la plupart des politiques modernes. Car l'un me dira sans hésiter que la nation la plus heureuse est celle où tous les arts sont le mieux cultivés; un autre, celle où le commerce fleurit davantage; un autre, celle où il y a le plus d'argent; et le plus grand nombre sera pour celle qui réunit tous ces avantages à un plus haut degré. Examinons d'abord si ces définitions sont justes.

1° Quant au commerce et aux arts, il est de la dernière évidence, même dans le système que j'attaque, que ces choses sont plutôt les moyens que l'on emploie pour travailler à faire prospérer

---

[1] Helvétius (*De l'esprit*, 1758) and Diderot (art. *Luxe* in *Encycl.* T. IX. 1765) are probably meant. The second writer might, however, be Hume whose Essays on *Commerce* and *Luxury* (*Refinement in the Arts*) had appeared in 1752 and been translated into French in 1753. The doubt leaves the date of this Fragment uncertain. Possibly, it is part of the Fragment *Le bonheur public*.

[2] S. M. reads *trouvait*.

[3] S. M. omits this paragraph here, and inserts it at the end of the treatise.

[4] S. M. misreads *quelques principes clairs et certains...et qui servissent*.

[5] [de prospérité.]

l'État qu'ils ne sont l'essence de sa prospérité[1]. Car je ne crois pas que, pour montrer le bonheur d'une nation, aucun homme se soit jamais avisé d'avancer en preuve qu'elle est composée d'ouvriers et de marchands. Et, quand même je conviendrais que les ouvriers et les marchands y sont nécessaires pour fournir aux besoins publics, il ne s'ensuivra jamais de là que la nation soit heureuse; puisqu'on peut démontrer, comme je le ferai dans la suite, que le commerce et les arts, en pourvoyant à quelques besoins imaginaires, en introduisent un beaucoup plus grand[2] nombre de réels[3].

On me dira peut-être que les arts, les manufactures et le commerce n'ont pas tant pour objet les commodités particulières des citoyens que d'enrichir l'État, soit par l'introduction de l'argent étranger, soit par la circulation de celui qui s'y trouve: d'où il faut conclure que tout le bonheur d'un peuple consiste à être riche en espèces : ce qui me reste à examiner.

L'or et l'argent, n'étant que les signes représentatifs des matières contre lesquelles ils sont échangés, n'ont proprement aucune valeur absolue, et il ne dépend pas même du souverain de leur en donner une. Car, lorsque le prince ordonne par exemple qu'une pièce d'argent de tel poids, et marquée à tel coin, vaudra tant de livres ou de sols, il fixe une dénomination dans le commerce, et ne fait[4] rien de plus. L'écu vaut alors tant de livres, ou le florin tant de sols, très exactement; mais il est clair que le prix du sol ou de la livre, et par conséquent celui du florin ou de l'écu, restera tout aussi variable qu'il l'était auparavant, et qu'il continuera de hausser ou de baisser dans le commerce, non selon la volonté du prince, mais par de tout autres causes. Toutes les opérations qui se font sur les monnaies, pour en fixer la valeur, ne sont donc qu'imaginaires; ou, si elles produisent quelque effet réel, c'est seulement sur les appointements annuels, sur les pensions et sur tous les payements qui ne sont fixés que par des dénominations idéales de livres, florins[5], ou autres semblables. Ainsi, quand le Prince hausse le prix des monnaies, c'est une fraude par laquelle il trompe ses créanciers; et, quand il le rabaisse, c'est une autre fraude par laquelle il trompe ses débiteurs. Mais, le prix de toutes les marchandises haussant ou baissant à proportion de l'altération faite sur les monnaies, le même rapport demeure toujours dans le commerce entre le signe et la

---

[1] S. M. reads *qu'ils ne font pas l'essence de sa prospérité*.
[2] *grand* wanting in MS.
[3] [L'avantage le plus solide qu'une nation retire de son industrie, c'est attirer l'argent de l'étranger.]
[4] S. M. omits *ne fait*. [5] S. M. reads *de florins*.

chose représentée. Ce que je dis ici de l'argent monnayé se doit entendre également du prix du marc d'or ou d'argent, fixé par édit public. Ce prix n'est que ce que le cours du commerce le fait être ; et, malgré tous les édits, les mêmes variations s'y font sentir, selon que les affaires vont bien ou mal.

Quoique l'argent n'ait par lui-même aucune valeur réelle, il en prend une, par convention tacite, dans chaque pays où il est en usage ; et cette valeur varie selon le concours des causes qui servent à la déterminer. Ces causes peuvent se réduire à trois principales : savoir, 1° l'abondance ou la rareté de l'espèce ; 2° l'abondance ou la rareté des denrées et autres marchandises ; 3° le degré de circulation qui dépend de la quantité des échanges, c'est-à-dire de la vigueur du commerce. Selon la manière dont ces trois choses se trouvent combinées dans un pays, l'argent y peut monter à un prix exorbitant, ou retomber presqu'à rien : d'où il suit qu'un État peut se trouver dans une telle situation, qu'avec une fort grande quantité d'argent il ne laisserait pas d'être réellement très pauvre et de manquer du nécessaire ; et qu'au contraire il peut être dépourvu d'argent, et cependant se trouver fort riche par l'abondance de toutes les choses à l'acquisition desquelles les autres peuples sont contraints d'employer leurs especes.

À cette première observation il en faut ajouter une seconde qui n'est pas moins importante, et qui en découle par une conséquence éloignée : c'est qu'il y a bien des distinctions à faire entre les richesses exclusives de quelques particuliers et celles qui sont communes à toute une nation. Comme ces mots *pauvre* et *riche* sont relatifs, il n'y a des pauvres que parce qu'il y a des riches ; et cela se peut dire en plus d'un sens ; mais, quant à présent, je me borne à celui du rapport des deux idées.

On donne le nom de *riche* à un homme qui a plus de bien que le plus grand nombre n'est accoutumé[1] d'en avoir ; et l'on appelle *pauvre*, non seulement celui qui n'a pas assez de bien pour vivre, mais celui qui en a moins que les autres. Il peut survenir de telles révolutions dans la société, que le même homme se trouverait riche et pauvre alternativement, sans avoir augmenté ni diminué sa fortune[2]. On en peut dire autant des nations prises individuellement et comparées l'une à l'autre. Aussi chaque peuple n'emploie-t-il guère moins de soins, quoiqu'un peu plus couvertement, à nuire aux avantages de ses voisins qu'à travailler aux siens propres.

---

[1] MS. has *n'a accoutumé*, by a slip.
[2] S. M. reads *les mêmes hommes se trouveraient riches et pauvres...leurs fortunes*.

L'humanité est alors sacrifiée par le Corps politique à l'intérêt national, comme elle l'est tous les jours par les particuliers à l'esprit de propriété. Cependant on ne conçoit pas sans peine comment la pauvreté d'un pays peut contribuer au bien-être des habitants d'un autre.

Supposons qu'après de longs et pénibles efforts un peuple soit venu à bout de ses projets à cet égard, qu'il ait ruiné tous ses voisins et accumulé à lui seul autant d'or et d'argent qu'il y en a dans tout le reste du monde; et voyons ce qui résultera de cette prospérité publique pour la félicité particulière des citoyens:

1° Si ces richesses sont également distribuées, il est certain qu'elles ne sauraient demeurer dans cet état d'égalité, ou qu'elles seront comme non existantes pour ceux qui les possèdent; parce que, dans tout ce qui est au delà du nécessaire immédiat, ce n'est qu'en raison des différences que les avantages de la fortune se font sentir.

De sorte que si, dans cette supposition, tous ces trésors se trouvaient anéantis en une seule nuit, sans que les denrées et autres marchandises eussent souffert aucune altération, cette perte ne serait sensible à personne, et à peine s'en apercevrait-on le lendemain.

Mais ce serait trop abuser du temps que de s'arrêter sur une supposition aussi chimérique que celle de l'égale distribution des richesses. Cette égalité ne peut s'admettre même hypothétiquement, parce qu'elle n'est pas dans la nature des choses; et je crois qu'il n'y a point de lecteur sensé qui n'ait en lui-même prévenu cette réflexion.

2° Dès l'instant que l'usage de l'or a été connu des hommes, ils se sont tous efforcés d'en amasser beaucoup, et les succès ont dû naturellement répondre aux divers degrés d'industrie et d'avidité des concurrents: c'est-à-dire, être fort inégaux. Cette première inégalité, jointe à l'avarice et aux talents qui l'avaient produite, a dû encore augmenter par sa propre force. Car [1]ce qui montre une des extravagances[1] des sociétés établies, c'est que la difficulté d'acquérir y croît toujours en raison des besoins; et que c'est le superflu même des riches qui les met en état de dépouiller le pauvre de son nécessaire.

C'est un axiome dans les affaires, ainsi qu'en physique, qu'on ne fait rien avec rien. L'argent est la véritable semence de l'argent; et le premier écu est infiniment plus difficile à gagner que le second million[2].

[1] v.l. 'un des vices.'   [2] See *Éc. pol.* pp. 268, and 254.

D'ailleurs, les friponneries ne sont jamais punies[1] que quand la nécessité les rend pardonnables. Elles coûtent l'honneur et la vie à l'indigent, et font[2] la gloire et la fortune du riche. Un misérable qui, pour avoir du pain, prend un écu à un homme dur qui regorge d'or, est un coquin qu'on mène au gibet; tandis que des citoyens honorés s'abreuvent paisiblement du sang de l'artisan et du laboureur; tandis que les monopoles du commerçant et les concussions du publicain portent le nom de talents utiles, et assurent à ceux qui les exercent la faveur du Prince et la considération du public[3]. C'est ainsi que la richesse de toute une nation fait[4] l'opulence de quelques particuliers au préjudice du public, et que les trésors des millionnaires augmentent la misère des citoyens. Car, dans cette inégalité monstrueuse et forcée, il arrive nécessairement que la sensualité des riches dévore en délices la substance[5] du peuple, et ne lui vend[6] qu'à peine un pain sec et noir, au poids de la sueur et au prix de la servitude.

Que si l'on joint à ceci l'augmentation infaillible du prix de toutes choses, par l'abondance de l'espèce et surtout la rareté des denrées qui doit résulter nécessairement d'une pareille situation, comme je le prouverai dans la suite, on sentira combien il est aisé de démontrer que, plus un État est riche en argent, et[7] plus il doit y avoir de pauvres, et plus les pauvres y doivent souffrir.

Or, puisque le commerce et les arts ne sont dans une nation qu'une preuve de besoins, et que l'argent n'est point une preuve de véritable richesse, il s'ensuit que la réunion de toutes ces choses n'est point non plus une preuve de bonheur.

Pour écarter d'autres dénombrements inutiles, il faut distinguer les moyens que les particuliers emploient à tâcher de se rendre heureux, chacun selon son caractère et ses inclinations, de ceux que le Corps de la société peut mettre en usage pour le même but. Car, comme la société ne peut prévoir ni satisfaire les différents désirs de ceux qui la composent, elle ne se charge point de ce soin; mais seulement de pourvoir à la défense et à la sûreté commune, et, à l'égard de la subsistance, de mettre les particuliers à portée de pourvoir par eux-mêmes à leurs besoins. De sorte que tous[8]

---

[1] S. M. reads *ne sont jamais permises*, against the MS. and the sense.
[2] or *sont*.
[3] *tandis que les monopoles* etc. may be intended for a variant on the preceding clause.
[4] S. M. reads *C'est ainsi que les richesses...font*, against the MS.
[5] S. M. reads *subsistance*, without authority.   [6] MS. has *vent*.
[7] S. M. omits *et*.   [8] S. M. omits *tous*.

les engagements que la confédération peut prendre envers les confédérés se réduisent à ces deux points: la paix et l'abondance. Pourvu que sous ce mot de paix on entende non seulement la sûreté[1], qui fait la paix au dedans, mais aussi la liberté, sans laquelle il n'y a aucune paix véritable. Car la tyrannie et l'esclavage sont manifestement un état de guerre; et il est aisé de démontrer qu'un esclave qui tue son maître ne pèche en cela ni contre la loi naturelle, ni même contre le droit des gens.

À l'égard de l'abondance, je n'entends pas par ce mot une situation où quelques particuliers regorgent de toutes choses, tandis que tout le reste du peuple est contraint de recourir à eux pour en recevoir sa subsistance au prix qu'il leur plaît d'y mettre; ni cet autre état hypothétique et impossible, au moins pour sa durée, où tout le monde trouverait sous sa main, sans travail et sans peine, de quoi satisfaire à tous ses besoins; mais celui où toutes les choses nécessaires à la vie se trouvent rassemblées dans le pays en telle quantité que chacun peut, avec son travail, amasser aisément tout ce qu'il lui en faut pour son entretien. [S. M.]

VII. Fragments relating to the *Discours sur l'inégalité*.

[MS. Neuchâtel, 7854.]

La voix de la nature et celle de la raison ne se trouveraient jamais en contradiction, si l'homme ne s'était lui-même imposé des devoirs qu'il est ensuite forcé de préférer toujours à l'impulsion naturelle.

*De cette expérience, qu'il meurt plus d'hommes dans les grandes villes et qu'il en naît plus dans les campagnes, il faut conclure de deux choses l'une: ou que les habitants de la campagne multiplient continuellement tant[2] que, malgré tous ceux que la ville absorbe sans cesse, les terres restent toujours également peuplées; ou que le séjour de la campagne, où il y a plus de naissances, est plus favorable à la population que celui de la ville, où il y a plus de morts[3].

Si le nombre des naissances est égal à celui des morts dans les campagnes, et que celui des morts dépasse communément celui des naissances dans les villes, la dépopulation successive est manifeste.

---

[1] S. M. reads *santé*, against the MS. and the sense.
[2] MS. appears to have *plus*.   [3] This Fragment is omitted by S. M.

Car les riches et tous ceux qui sont contents de leur état ont grand intérêt que les choses restent comme elles sont, au lieu que les misérables ne peuvent que gagner aux révolutions.

Mais les devoirs de l'homme, dans l'état de nature, sont toujours subordonnés au soin de sa propre conservation, qui est le premier[1] et le plus fort de tous.

La puissance d'un peuple sert plutôt à montrer qu'il est en état de s'étendre, ou de se maintenir comme il est, qu'à prouver qu'en effet il est bien.

*Et qu'importe à la société qu'il en périsse moins par des meurtres, si l'État les tue avant leur naissance en rendant les enfants onéreux aux pères?

*D'où il suit qu'enfreindre la loi naturelle n'est autre chose que par une manière d'agir extraordinaire, et contraire à l'ordre de la nature, faire une exception particulière à quelqu'un de ces rapports généraux[2]. [S. M.]

VIII.

[MS. f. Geneva, 228.]

[Two quarto pages, written in right-hand column: on one side of sheet only, left-hand side blank. It is headed *Préface*, and may have been intended for the Fragment *Du bonheur public* (above, p. 325), or possibly for the *Institutions politiques*.]

Je vais dire la vérité, et je la dirai du ton qui lui convient. Lecteurs pusillanimes, que sa simplicité dégoûte et que sa franchise révolte, fermez mon livre; ce n'est point pour vous qu'il est écrit. Lecteurs satiriques, qui n'aimez de la vérité que ce qui peut nourrir la malignité de votre âme, fermez et jetez mon livre; vous n'y trouveriez point ce que vous cherchez et vous ne tarderiez pas d'y voir toute l'horreur que l'auteur a pour vous.

Si cet écrit tombe entre les mains d'un honnête homme qui chérisse la vertu, qui aime ses frères, qui plaigne leurs erreurs et déteste leurs vices, qui sache s'attendrir quelquefois sur les maux de l'humanité et surtout qui travaille à se rendre meilleur, il peut le lire en toute sûreté. Mon cœur va parler au sien.

J'aime à me flatter qu'un jour quelque homme d'État sera citoyen, qu'il ne changera point les choses uniquement pour faire

---

[1] S. M. reads *le plus saint et le plus fort*, without authority.
[2] The two concluding Fragments are omitted by S. M.

autrement que son prédécesseur, mais pour faire en sorte qu'elles aillent mieux; [1]qu'il n'aura point sans cesse le bonheur public à la bouche, mais qu'il l'aura un peu dans le cœur; qu'il ne rendra point les peuples malheureux pour affermir son autorité, mais qu'il fera servir son autorité à établir le bonheur des peuples; que par un heureux hasard il jettera les yeux sur ce livre; que mes idées informes lui en feront naître de plus utiles; qu'il travaillera à rendre les hommes meilleurs ou plus heureux; et que[2] j'y aurai peut-être contribué en quelque chose. Cette chimère m'a mis la plume à la main[3]....... [S. M.]

IX. Considérations sur l'influence des climats relativement à la civilisation.

[The following is printed by M. Streckeisen-Moultou, *Œuvres et Correspondance inédites de J. J. Rousseau*. I have been unable to find the MS. from which he took them.]

Pour suivre avec fruit l'histoire du genre humain, pour bien juger de la formation des peuples et de leurs révolutions, il faut remonter aux principes des passions des hommes, aux causes générales qui les font agir. Alors, en appliquant ces principes et ces causes aux diverses circonstances où ces peuples se sont trouvés, on saura la raison de ce qu'ils ont fait, et l'on saura même ce qu'ils ont dû faire dans les occasions où les événements nous sont moins connus que les situations qui les ont précédés. Sans ces recherches, l'histoire n'est d'aucune utilité pour nous; et la connaissance des faits, dépourvue de celle de leurs causes, ne sert qu'à surcharger la mémoire, sans instruction pour l'expérience et sans plaisir pour la raison.

L'homme ne peut se suffire à lui-même; ses besoins toujours renaissants le mettent dans la nécessité de chercher hors de lui les moyens d'y pourvoir. Il dépend toujours des choses et souvent de ses semblables. Nous sentons plus ou moins cette dépendance selon l'étendue et la nature de nos besoins; et c'est dans ces mêmes besoins, plus ou moins grands, plus ou moins sentis, qu'il faut chercher le principe de toutes les actions humaines.

---

[1] [parlera peut-être un peu moins du bonheur public et l'aimera davantage.]
[2] [que j'en aurai été la cause.]
[3] [et les hommes sont tellement fait (*sic*) pour l'illusion qu'en connaissant toute la grandeur de celle-ci je ne laisse pas de lui sacrifier....]

Nos besoins sont de plusieurs sortes ; les premiers sont ceux qui tiennent à la subsistance, et d'où dépend notre conservation. Ils sont tels, que tout homme périrait, s'il cessait d'y pouvoir satisfaire : ceux-ci s'appellent besoins physiques, parce qu'ils nous sont donnés par la nature et que rien ne peut nous en délivrer. Il n'y en a que deux de cette espèce : savoir, la nourriture et le sommeil.

D'autres besoins tendent moins à notre conservation qu'à notre bien-être, et ne sont proprement que des appétits, mais quelquefois si violents, qu'ils tourmentent plus que les vrais besoins ; cependant il n'est jamais d'une absolue nécessité d'y pourvoir, et chacun ne sait que trop que vivre n'est pas vivre dans le bien-être.

Les besoins de cette seconde classe ont pour objet le luxe de sensualité, de mollesse[1], l'union des sexes et tout ce qui flatte nos sens.

Un troisième ordre de besoins, qui, nés après les autres, ne laissent pas de primer enfin sur tous, sont ceux qui viennent de l'opinion. Tels sont les honneurs, la réputation, le rang, la noblesse, et tout ce qui n'a d'existence que dans l'estime des hommes, mais qui mène par cette estime aux biens réels qu'on n'obtiendrait point sans elle.

Tous ces divers besoins sont enchaînés les uns aux autres ; mais les premiers et les seconds ne se font sentir aux hommes que quand les premiers sont satisfaits. Tant qu'on n'est occupé qu'à chercher à vivre, on ne songe guère à la mollesse, encore moins à la vanité : l'amour de la gloire tourmente peu des gens affamés.

Ainsi tout se réduit d'abord à la subsistance ; et par là l'homme tient à tout ce qui l'environne. Il dépend de tout, et il devient ce que tout ce dont il dépend le force d'être. Le climat, le sol, l'air, l'eau, les productions de la terre et de la mer, forment son tempérament, son caractère, déterminent ses goûts, ses passions, ses travaux, ses actions de toute espèce. Si cela n'est pas exactement vrai des individus, il l'est incontestablement des peuples ; et, s'il sortait de la terre des hommes tout formés, en quelque lieu que ce pût être, qui connaîtrait bien l'état de tout ce qui les entoure pourrait déterminer à coup sûr ce qu'ils deviendront.

Avant donc que d'entamer l'histoire de notre espèce, il faudrait commencer par examiner son séjour et toutes les variétés qui s'y

---

[1] The phrase *le luxe de mollesse* occurs also in the Fragment on *Taste* (MS. Neuchâtel, 7840, p. 69) ; see Vol. II. Appendix I.

trouvent ; car de là vient la première cause de toutes les révolutions du genre humain. Au défaut du temps et des connaissances nécessaires pour entrer dans un si grand détail, je me bornerai ici aux observations indispensables pour entendre ce que j'ai à dire dans la suite.

Quoique, dans un circuit de trois mille lieues, la terre ne soit pas une sphère immense, elle l'étend, pour ainsi dire, par la variété de ses climats, qui, propres à diverses qualités de plantes et d'animaux, la divisent, pour ainsi dire, en autant de mondes dont les habitants, circonscrits chacun dans le sien, ne peuvent passer de l'un à l'autre. L'homme seul et quelques animaux domestiques subsistent naturellement partout, et peuvent prendre autant de manières de vivre que la diversité des climats et de leurs productions en exige d'eux. Une autre diversité qui multiplie et combine la précédente est celle des saisons. Leur succession, portant alternativement plusieurs climats en un seul, accoutume les hommes qui l'habitent à leurs impressions diverses, et les rend capables de passer et de vivre dans tous les pays dont la température se fait sentir dans le leur. Si l'écliptique se fût confondu avec l'équateur, peut-être n'y eût-il jamais eu d'émigration de peuple ; et chacun, faute de pouvoir supporter un autre climat que celui où il était né, n'en serait jamais sorti. Incliner du doigt l'axe du monde ou dire à l'homme: Couvre la terre et sois sociable, ce fut la même chose pour celui qui n'a besoin ni de main pour agir, ni de voix pour parler.

Sous l'équateur, dont le soleil s'éloigne peu, et où les jours sont toujours égaux et aux nuits et entre eux, l'hiver et l'été, marqués seulement par des alternatives de soleil et de pluie, font sentir à peine quelque différence de température. Mais, plus on s'éloigne de la ligne, plus la différence et des jours et des saisons augmente. Les nuits deviennent plus grandes et plus froides, les hivers plus longs et plus rudes, à mesure qu'on approche des pôles. La chaleur ne diminue pas en même proportion; sans quoi, la terre n'en aurait bientôt plus pour produire. Les étés sont courts mais ardents dans les pays septentrionaux ; le blé s'y sème et s'y coupe dans l'espace de deux mois ; encore, dans ce court espace, les nuits sont si froides, qu'on n'y doit compter pour été que le temps où le soleil est sur l'horizon ; toutes les vingt-quatre heures on passe alternativement de l'hiver à l'été.

De ces observations, il s'ensuivrait que les peuples des climats chauds, dont la température est peu variée, seraient moins propres aux émigrations que les peuples des climats froids, qui, jusqu'à certain point, ont chez eux deux excès. Je sais que l'opinion commune est, au contraire, que les habitants du Nord supportent moins le séjour des pays chauds que ces derniers le séjour des pays froids. On voit déjà lequel de ces deux principes est le mieux fondé en raison : on verra dans la suite lequel est le plus conforme à l'histoire et aux faits.

Les qualités de la terre et les espèces de ses productions ne se ressentent pas moins que les tempéraments des hommes des divers aspects du soleil; et le sol change autant d'un climat à l'autre que le naturel de ses habitants. La terre, plus raréfiée et plus poreuse dans les pays chauds, demande moins de travail et s'imprègne plus aisément des sels qui la fertilisent. Les plantes qu'elle produit sont plus nourrissantes, les arbres donnent en abondance de meilleurs fruits. Une seule espèce y peut fournir à l'homme tous ses besoins; presque sans travail et sans peine, sa fécondité naturelle suffit pour nourrir ses habitants.

Dans les pays froids, la terre, paresseuse et demi-morte, n'a pas assez de force pour élaborer dans les végétaux des sucs propres à la nourriture de l'homme. Si elle végète, elle ne produit que des herbes sans saveur et des arbres sans fruit qui ne peuvent nous fournir des aliments que par des voies intermédiaires, en nourrissant des animaux qui nous servent de nourriture.

Mille variétés sur la terre, dans la terre, déterminent les manières d'être de ses habitants et les assujettissent à certaines conditions. Généralement les montagnards sont pasteurs par état, les habitants des bois chasseurs par état, ceux des plaines laboureurs par état.

L'eau, l'air même peuvent fournir des aliments à ceux à qui la terre en refuse. Les habitants des côtes stériles sont tous pêcheurs et ichthyophages. Il y a, dit-on, dans les rochers du Caucase, des hommes dont les faucons et les aigles sont les pourvoyeurs; et le ciel, en de certains lieux, donne des sucs condensés durant la nuit qui peuvent servir de nourriture.

Enfin, souvent la terre aride et stérile, sans rien produire à sa surface, ne laisse pas de fournir médiatement la subsistance à ses habitants : soit par l'exploitation des mines qu'on trouve dans ses entrailles, soit par la commodité des transports, qui donne à ceux qui l'habitent le moyen d'aller partout faire échange de leurs travaux et de leurs personnes contre les choses dont ils ont besoin.

Si toute la terre était également fertile, peut-être les hommes ne se fussent-ils jamais rapprochés. Mais la nécessité, mère de l'industrie, les a forcés de se rendre utiles les uns aux autres, pour l'être à eux-mêmes. C'est par ces communications, d'abord forcées, puis volontaires, que leurs esprits se sont développés, qu'ils ont acquis des talents, des passions, des vices, des vertus, des lumières, et qu'ils sont devenus tout ce qu'ils peuvent être en bien et en mal. L'homme isolé demeure toujours le même ; il ne fait de progrès qu'en société.

D'autres causes, plus fortuites en apparence, ont concouru à disperser les hommes inégalement dans des lieux, à les rassembler par pelotons dans d'autres, et à resserrer ou à relâcher les liens des peuples, selon les accidents qui les ont réunis ou séparés. Des tremblements de terre, des volcans, des embrasements, des inondations, des déluges, changeant tout à coup, avec la face de la terre, le cours que prenaient les sociétés humaines, les ont combinées d'une manière nouvelle ; et ces combinaisons, dont les premières causes étaient physiques et naturelles, sont devenues, par fruit du temps, les causes morales qui, changeant[1] l'état des choses, ont produit des guerres, des émigrations, des conquêtes, enfin des révolutions qui remplissent l'histoire et dont on a fait l'ouvrage des hommes, sans remonter à ce qui les a fait agir ainsi. Il ne faut pas douter que ces grands accidents de la nature ne fussent plus fréquents dans les premiers temps, avant qu'une population plus égale eût mis la face de la terre dans l'état fixe où l'art et la main des hommes la maintiennent de nos jours ; et qu'ils ne le soient même encore aujourd'hui dans les contrées désertes, où rien ne rétablit l'équilibre que les accidents de la nature ont une fois rompu. [S. M.]

X.

[MS. Neuchâtel, 7843.]

(a) Des Juifs (pp. 8—9).

* Soit que dans les anciens temps les hommes, plus près de leur origine, n'eussent rien à voir au delà, soit qu'alors les traditions, moins répandues, périssent dans un prompt oubli, l'on ne voit plus, comme autrefois, des peuples se vanter d'être autochthones, aborigènes, enfants de la terre ou de la contrée où ils sont établis. Les fréquentes révolutions du genre humain ont tellement transplanté et confondu les nations qu'excepté peut-être en Afrique il n'en reste pas une sur la terre qui se puisse vanter d'être originaire du pays dont elle est en possession. Dans cette confusion de l'espèce humaine[2], tant de races diverses ont successivement habité les mêmes lieux, et s'y sont succédées ou mêlées,

---

[1] S.M. reads *changent*.   [2] [il ne reste de moyen.]

que ces races ne se distinguent plus, et que les divers noms des peuples ne sont plus que ceux des lieux qu'ils habitent. Que s'il reste en quelques uns des traces de filiation, comme chez les Parsis et Guèbres, ni on ne les trouve plus dans leur ancien territoire, ni l'on ne peut plus dire qu'ils fassent un corps de nation.

Mais un spectacle étonnant et vraiment unique est de voir un peuple expatrié, n'ayant plus ni lieu ni terre depuis près de deux mille ans; un peuple altéré, chargé d'étrangers depuis plus de temps encore, n'ayant plus peut-être un[1] seul rejeton des premières races; un peuple épars, dispersé sur la terre, asservi, persécuté, méprisé de toutes les nations, conserver pourtant ses coutumes, ses lois, ses mœurs, son amour patriotique et sa première union sociale, quand tous les liens en paraissent rompus.

Les Juifs nous donnent cet étonnant spectacle. Les lois de Solon, de Numa, de Lycurgue sont mortes. Celles de Moïse, bien plus antiques, vivent toujours. Athènes, Sparte, Rome ont péri, et n'ont plus laissé d'enfants sur la terre. Sion détruite n'a point perdu les siens. Ils se conservent, se multiplient, s'étendent par tout le monde. Ils se mêlent chez[2] tous les peuples, et ne s'y confondent jamais. Ils n'ont plus de chefs, et sont toujours peuple; ils n'ont plus de patrie, et sont toujours citoyens.

Quelle doit être la force d'une législation capable d'opérer de pareils prodiges; capable de braver les conquêtes, les dispersions, les révolutions, les siècles; capable de survivre aux coutumes, aux lois, à l'empire, de toutes les nations; qui promet enfin, par les épreuves qu'elle a soutenues, de les soutenir toutes, de vaincre les vicissitudes des choses humaines et de durer autant que le monde!

De tous les systèmes de législation qui nous sont connus, les uns sont des êtres de raison, dont la possibilité même est disputée; d'autres n'ont duré que quelques siècles; d'autres n'ont jamais fait un État bien constitué. Nul, excepté celui-là, n'a subi toutes les épreuves et n'y a toujours résisté. Le Juif et le Chrétien s'accordent à reconnaître en ceci le doigt de Dieu, qui selon l'un maintient sa nation, et selon l'autre qui la châtie. Mais tout homme, quel qu'il soit, y doit reconnaître une merveille unique, dont les causes divines ou humaines méritent certainement l'étude et l'admiration des sages, préférablement à tout ce que la Grèce et Rome nous offrent d'admirable en fait d'institutions politiques et d'établissements humains.

---

[1] [cent.]   [2] *les*, by a slip, *before tous*, as well as after.

(b)

[MS. Neuchâtel, 7843.] (p. 21.)

*'Que faites-tu parmi nous, O Hébreu[1]? Je t'y vois avec plaisir. Mais comment peux-tu t'y plaire?......Pourquoi n'es-tu pas resté avec les tiens?'

'Tu te trompes; je viens parmi les miens. J'ai vécu seul sur la terre. Lycurgue, Solon, Numa sont mes frères. Je viens rejoindre ma famille. Je viens goûter enfin la douceur de converser avec mes semblables...parler et entendre. C'est parmi vous, O amis illustres, que je viens enfin jouir de moi.'

[2]'Tu as bien changé de ton, de sentiments et d'idées....'
[3]'J'ai fait un peuple, et n'ai pu faire des hommes.'

(c) Du Royaume français (*ib.* pp. 138—9).

Vous me demandez, Monsieur, mon sentiment sur cette question que vous avez agitée : si l'abaissement des grands seigneurs en France a été avantageux, ou nuisible, au Royaume.

Royaume: car il est fort équivoque dans la bouche d'un Français, ce qui signifie pour vous ce mot, *Royaume.* Si par le Royaume vous entendez le Roi, la question n'est pas douteuse, et la solution saute aux yeux. Mais si vous entendez le Corps de la nation, c'est autre chose, et il y a matière à discussion.

Toute la différence est qu'alors le mal trouvait quelquefois de la résistance, et qu'il n'en trouve plus aujourd'hui.

Leur luxe d'alors augmentait leur puissance, et celui d'aujourd'hui la détruit. Il les tient dans la plus étroite dépendance de la Cour et des ministres, en les mettant hors d'état de subsister autrement que par des grâces continuelles, qui sont le fruit de la servitude du peuple, et le prix de la leur.

Il est vrai qu'ils vivaient dans la servitude. Mais qu'est-ce qu'un corps de noblesse, si ce n'est un corps de valets? La noblesse est faite essentiellement pour servir; elle n'existe que par là et que pour cela. La servitude est toujours la même; il n'y a que le maître de différent. [W.]

[From the dates of the surrounding entries it would appear that these three Fragments must belong to some time between 1761 and 1765.]

---

[1] [Moïse.]
[2] [Tu parlais bien différemment pendant ta vie.]
[3] Written opposite on v° of p. 20. W. gives it, but without context.

XI.

[The two following Fragments, which are connected in thought, are written on the back of the slip which contains the rough draft of the character of the Legislator. See above, p. 324.]

[MS. Neuchâtel, 7830.]

Extirpation des Corsaires.

*(*a*) Mais il n'y a point d'homme d'État parmi nous qui ne pense qu'en bonne politique il est plus important de faire du mal aux autres que de bien à lui-même.

*(*b*) L'Italie et l'Espagne étant situées plus favorablement que le reste de l'Europe pour le commerce des échelles du Levant et des côtes d'Afrique, il importe aux autres peuples de laisser subsister une barrière insurmontable qui empêche ces deux nations d'établir un pareil commerce, d'où ils profitent eux-mêmes de temps en temps ; de sorte qu'ils gagnent plus peut-être par intervalles à ce commerce exclusif qu'ils ne perdent par les prises que font sur eux les Corsaires durant la guerre, et par les prisons qu'ils exigent durant la paix. C'est du moins ce qu'il fallait examiner.

XII.

[MS. Neuchâtel, 7872.]

*À l'égard des peuples une fois corrompus, il est bien difficile de voir ce qu'il y aurait à faire pour les rendre meilleurs. J'ignore quelles lois pourraient faire ce miracle. Mais ce que je sais très bien, c'est que tout est perdu sans ressource, quand une fois il faut avoir recours à la potence et à l'échafaud.

[This must have formed part of the Fragment *Des lois* (MS. 7849). See above, pp. 330—4.]

LA PAIX PERPETUELLE ET LA POLYSYNODIE: EXTRAITS ET JUGEMENTS

1756.

THESE two pieces explain themselves. Both have a direct bearing upon Rousseau's doctrine of Federation, which has been already discussed in the General Introduction. Both throw a vivid light upon his faith in the small State, and his ingrained distrust of the large State and the monarchical form of government, which, in his view, it inevitably entailed. *La Paix perpétuelle* is a stirring indictment of that War which he denounced as 'one of the two worst scourges of mankind.' All this, however, is apparent at the first glance. And it is only necessary to add a few words as to the historical reference of each treatise, and the circumstances under which both were composed by Rousseau.

The original writings, of which Rousseau here offers an Abstract and a Criticism, are from the hand of the Abbé de Saint-Pierre (1658—1743), whom, as an old man, he had slightly known. The *Paix perpétuelle* was published, appropriately enough, in the year of the Peace of Utrecht (1712—3[1]); the *Polysynodie*, during the Regency which followed the death of Louis XIV (1719). Both were inspired by a sturdy distrust of autocracy and a deep-rooted disapproval of the monarch whom the author steadily refused to call 'the great[2].' But, with all his zeal for humanity, Saint-Pierre was totally without the power of expression. His writings—seventeen volumes of printed matter, and six 'cartons' of manuscript[3]—had been smothered by their own bulk[4]. And his family were naturally anxious to see them recast in a less tedious and more attractive form. Accordingly, when, at the prompting of Mably and Mme Dupin[5], Rousseau applied to the

---

[1] In two volumes; a third was added in 1717.

[2] He was deprived of his seat in the Academy on this account.

[3] A detailed list of them is given in MS. Neuchâtel, 7840, pp. 7 v°, 8 and 8 v°. The number exactly tallies with that mentioned in *Confessions*, Liv. IX.: 'vingt-trois volumes.' *Œuvres*, VIII. p. 291.

[4] 'Morts-nés' is Rousseau's description. *Œuvres*, VIII. p. 291.

[5] *Confessions*, IX.; *Œuvres*, VIII. p. 291. Saint-Lambert acted as intermediary. *Ib.*

Comte de Saint-Pierre for permission to re-edit his uncle's works, the request was readily granted. The necessary books and papers were handed over to him in the latter part of 1754[1]. And the task was completed—so far, that is, as it was ever completed—in the early days of his life at the Hermitage; some time during the summer or autumn of 1756[2].

The methods adopted in the two *Extraits* differ widely from each other. In the *Projet de Paix perpétuelle* Rousseau has treated his materials with the freest hand. The long introduction (pp. 365—374), itself a brilliant historical essay, is all his own; even in the Articles of Confederation, and the number of States to be admitted, he has made considerable changes (see Saint-Pierre, Vol. I. pp. 313—5, 323—342); and throughout he has translated the barren details and endless repetitions of Saint-Pierre into broad principles of political prudence. In a word, except as regards the mere kernel of the Project, there is much more of Rousseau than of Saint-Pierre in the whole statement. In the *Extrait de la Polysynodie*, on the other hand, he has kept with marked fidelity to his original; which, as he says himself, was a far better and more workmanlike performance. After the introductory chapter, he does little more than state the specific proposals of Saint-Pierre, with the specific arguments by which they were supported. He reserves his own views, whether of agreement or disagreement, for the *Jugement* to follow[3].

Rousseau had in the first instance intended to take a comprehensive survey of the Abbé's 'visions,' and to supplement them, in each case, by separate commentaries, or 'judgments,' of his own[4]. There was to be one volume of *Abstracts*, and one of *Judgments*. But, after carrying out this design with the *Paix perpétuelle* and

[1] 'Depuis mon retour de Genève.' *Confessions*, IX.; *Œuvres*, VIII. p. 291.
[2] *Ib.* p. 303. D'Argenson (Jan. 28, 1756) writes: 'Rousseau travaille actuellement à l'analyse des ouvrages politiques de Saint-Pierre' (*Journal*, IX. p. 182).
[3] Saint-Pierre's *Paix perpétuelle* was published in 1712 (2 vols. 8vo, containing 728 pages). The British Museum copy is without title-page; but the date is given in Saint-Pierre's autograph. His *Discours sur la Polysynodie* was published in 1719 (16mo, Amsterdam, pp. 249).
[4] *Œuvres*, VIII. pp. 302—3. He had also intended to prefix a Life of Saint-Pierre, 'pour laquelle j'avais amassé d'assez bons matériaux, que je me flattais de ne pas gâter en les employant.' *Ib.* Some fragments of this remain in MS. Neuchâtel, 7829 and 7858, *e.g.* 'C'était un homme très sage, s'il n'eût eu la folie de la raison. Il semblait ignorer que les princes, comme les autres hommes, ne se mènent que par leurs passions, et ne raisonnent que pour justifier les sottises qu'elles leur font faire.'

the *Polysynodie*, which have generally been reckoned the best of Saint-Pierre's writings, he came to a halt; partly from weariness, still more from motives of prudence and honour. He recognised that, as a foreigner, it was an awkward matter for him to criticise the Government of the country from which he accepted hospitality. 'I laid myself open,' he writes, 'to be asked roughly, but quite justly, what I had to do in the matter[1].'

He therefore put aside what he had already written, and resolved to attempt no more. So things remained until the end of 1760, when de Bastide, who was about to launch a periodical journal, *Le Monde comme il est*, applied to him, through Duclos, for a contribution[2]. *Émile* was at first suggested. But for this Rousseau had already made other arrangements; he therefore offered the Abstract of *la Paix perpétuelle* instead. And this was accepted, not without hopes that more would eventually be forthcoming[3]. Even the *Extrait*, however, proved too much for the patience, or courage, of the Censor[4]. And de Bastide, bowing before the storm, issued the first number of his journal without it. He discharged his debt to Rousseau by printing it a few weeks later safely across the frontier, at Amsterdam[5].

[1] Compare Introduction, p. 75. *Confessions*, *Œuvres*, VIII. p. 303.

[2] See letter to de Bastide, *Œuvres*, x. p. 220. In Hachette's Edition, this letter is dated Dec. 5, 1759. It is clear, however, that this is a mistake; for the original of the letter in which de Bastide acknowledges the receipt of the MS. is dated Dec. 9, 1760 (MSS. Neuchâtel). Compare the two letters of Duclos to Rousseau, S.M., *Rousseau, ses Amis et ses Ennemis*, I. pp. 293—4. Both these are dated 1760; the latter of them, Dec. 8, 1760, which tallies with the date actually given to the letter in question in the Ed. of 1782. And this date accords both with the '*six* years' (from 1754) mentioned in Rousseau's letter to de Bastide, and with the hope of approaching peace between France and England, expressed in the same letter. Compare Chatham's *Correspondence*, II. pp. 74–107. If this be so, we must also redate the letter to de Bastide of 'June 16, 1760.' It should probably be Jan. 16, 1761.

[3] Duclos, if not de Bastide himself, was anxious that the three remaining pieces relating to Saint-Pierre should follow. But the difficulties which arose over the *Extrait* would have obviously made this impossible; and it is doubtful whether Rousseau himself would have ever consented. See letter to de Bastide, *Œuvres*, x. p. 227; and from Duclos, March 12, 1761, S.M. I. p. 297.

[4] S.M. I. p. 296. There was some talk also of *La reine Fantasque*; but Duclos warned Rousseau that, as a satire upon monarchy, it was likely to bring him into trouble, S.M. I. p. 294.

[5] End of February, or beginning of March, 1761. See letter from Duclos (March 12, 1761) and from Deleyre (March 13, 1761), S.M. pp. 297, 207.

The three remaining pieces were laid by, and must have been handed to du Peyrou, together with all the other manuscripts then in existence, at the time when he was made the 'universal depositary' of Rousseau's papers[1]. What Rousseau wrote a few years later of the *Jugement sur la Paix perpétuelle* is equally true of the two other pieces—*la Polysynodie, Extrait* and *Jugement*: 'It has never been printed; and I do not know if it ever will be.' All three were published for the first time in the posthumous Edition of his Works, prepared by du Peyrou and Moultou (Geneva, 1782).

In all these pieces, Rousseau was working upon lines laid down by another. He was also working upon proposals which had reference to historical conditions, not of his own day: the scheme of Henry IV for curbing the power of the House of Austria, in the *Paix perpétuelle*; the scheme of Saint-Pierre for decentralising the power of the Monarchy, in the *Polysynodie*. He was, therefore, working in fetters. And it was hardly to be expected that his genius should take so free a flight as in the *Contrat social*, or the second *Discourse*. Yet he refers to the *Extrait* of the *Paix perpétuelle* more than once with satisfaction[2]. And the wonder is that he should have put as much of himself into this and the other pieces, as he did. The reason is that he was writing on themes which, once stripped of their antiquarian reference, lay very close to his heart: the wrong and misery of war; the defects of the large State and the virtues of Federation; the waste and slavery caused by the centralisation of power in the hands of an

[1] See letter to de Peyrou of Jan. 24, 1765, *Œuvres*, XI. p. 202. The MSS. of all three are in the Bibliothèque de la Ville, Neuchâtel. They were bequeathed to it, like all the rest, by du Peyrou.

[2] The chief references are *Confessions*, Liv. XII. ('Je crois qu'il—Mably—ne m'a pardonné ni le *Contrat social*, trop au-dessus de ses forces, ni la *Paix perpétuelle*; et qu'il n'avait paru désirer que je fisse un Extrait de l'abbé de Saint-Pierre, qu'en supposant que je ne m'en tirerais si bien'); *Œuvres*, IX. p. 56; *Dialogue* II. ('*Héloïse, Émile, le Contrat social, l'Essai sur la Paix perpétuelle*, et d'autres écrits non moins estimables qui n'ont point paru' [i.e. the three remaining pieces, and perhaps the treatises on Corsica and Poland], 'sont des fruits de la retraite de Jean-Jacques'); *ib.* p. 186; and *Dialogue* III.; *ib.* p. 279. It may be observed that, in the last reference, he appears to speak of the *Extrait de la Paix perpétuelle* as 'both written and published in 1760.' He is, however, speaking only of a note (that on the approaching decline of England) which was clearly added when he prepared the *Extrait* for the press (end of 1760). The date of publication is a trifling slip of the memory; seeing that the work was not actually published until the early weeks of 1761.

autocrat; and the inconceivable follies of monarchs. They also contain the first germ of that scheme for graduating the service of the State, which was afterwards more fully developed in the treatises upon Corsica and Poland. So it is that these writings throw a significant light upon the theories of the *Contrat social* and the *Économie politique*. They also prepare the way for the practical treatises which followed.

Partly from the accident of its early publication, still more from the inherent interest of the subject, the *Paix perpétuelle* has attracted far more attention than the *Polysynodie*. It is impossible not to believe that Kant had it before him when, a generation later, he wrote his pregnant appeal, *Zum ewigen Frieden* (1795). None of his works is written with so much passion. None of them bears so clearly the stamp of Rousseau[1].

Another example of Rousseau's influence in this field—though, here likewise, it is unacknowledged—is to be found in Saint-Simon's *La Réorganisation de la société européenne* (1814). It contains an interesting criticism of Saint-Pierre's scheme for a Confederation of Europe, and a rival scheme devised by the author. His proposals are open to all the objections which he urges against those of Saint-Pierre, and a good many more besides. He makes no mention either of Rousseau or of Kant[2].

Yet again: in 1851 Victor Hugo scandalised the Legislative Assembly by speaking of 'that vast edifice, which will one day be called the United States of Europe[3].' It was the phrase of the poet; but, once more, it is the voice of Saint-Pierre and Rousseau.

And now 'the star of hope is again in the sky.' Will the statesmen of Europe have the wisdom and courage to carry out the ideal for which Saint-Pierre laboured, and which won the praise of Rousseau and Kant?

---

[1] See, in particular, his acceptance of the sovereignty of the people, and his sarcasms on Monarchy, which do not spare even Frederick the Great; *Werke* (ed. Rosenkranz), VII. pp. 241—6; also, p. 233, note. Neither Saint-Pierre, nor Rousseau, is mentioned in *Zum ewigen Frieden*. Both are mentioned, as champions of Peace and Federation, in another remarkable work, *Idee zu einer allgemeinen Geschichte* (1784), *ib.* p. 327. The English reader will not readily believe that the method of Kant, in both writings, is far more abstract than that of Rousseau. But it is the case.

[2] *Œuvres de Saint-Simon*, Vol. I. pp. 155—248.

[3] *Actes et paroles*, I. p. 335.

EXTRAIT DU PROJET DE PAIX PERPÉTUELLE DE M. L'ABBÉ DE SAINT-PIERRE

[Written 1756 ; published 1761. Fragments of the Rough Copy are preserved in MS. Neuchâtel, 7829.]

> Tunc genus humanum positis sibi consulat armis,
> Inque vicem gens omnis amet.
> LUCAN, lib. I. 60.

Comme jamais projet plus grand, plus beau, ni plus utile n'occupa l'esprit humain, que celui d'une paix perpétuelle et universelle entre tous les peuples de l'Europe, jamais auteur ne mérita mieux l'attention du public que celui qui propose des moyens pour mettre ce projet en exécution. Il est même bien difficile qu'une pareille matière laisse un homme sensible et vertueux exempt d'un peu d'enthousiasme ; et je ne sais si l'illusion d'un cœur véritablement humain, à qui son zèle rend tout facile, n'est pas en cela préférable à cette âpre et repoussante raison, qui trouve toujours dans son indifférence pour le bien public le premier obstacle à tout ce qui peut le favoriser.

Je ne doute pas que beaucoup de lecteurs ne s'arment d'avance d'incrédulité pour résister au plaisir de la persuasion, et je les plains de prendre si tristement l'entêtement pour la sagesse. Mais j'espère que quelque âme honnête partagera l'émotion délicieuse avec laquelle je prends la plume sur un sujet si intéressant pour l'humanité. Je vais voir, du moins en idée, les hommes s'unir et s'aimer ; je vais penser à une douce et paisible société de frères, vivant dans une concorde éternelle, tous conduits par les mêmes maximes, tous heureux du bonheur commun : et, réalisant en moi-même un tableau si touchant, l'image d'une félicité qui n'est point m'en fera goûter quelques instants une véritable.

Je n'ai pu refuser ces premières lignes au sentiment dont j'étais plein. Tâchons maintenant de raisonner de sang-froid. Bien résolu de ne rien avancer que je ne le prouve, je crois pouvoir prier le lecteur à son tour de ne rien nier qu'il ne le réfute ; car ce ne sont pas tant les raisonneurs que je crains que ceux qui, sans se rendre aux preuves, n'y veulent rien objecter.

[1]Il ne faut pas avoir longtemps médité sur les moyens de perfectionner un Gouvernement quelconque, pour apercevoir des embarras et des obstacles, qui naissent moins de sa constitution que de ses relations externes ; de sorte que la plupart des soins qu'il faudrait consacrer à sa police, on est contraint de les donner à sa sûreté, et de songer plus à le mettre en état de résister aux autres qu'à le rendre parfait en lui-même. Si l'ordre social était, comme on le prétend, l'ouvrage de la raison plutôt que des passions, eût-on tardé si longtemps à voir qu'on en a fait trop ou trop peu pour notre bonheur[2]? que chacun de nous étant dans l'état civil avec ses concitoyens, et dans l'état de nature avec tout le reste du monde, nous n'avons prévenu les guerres particulières que pour en allumer de générales, qui sont mille fois plus terribles ? et qu'en nous unissant à quelques hommes nous devenons réellement les ennemis du genre humain ?

S'il y a quelque moyen de lever ces dangereuses contradictions, ce ne peut être que par une forme de Gouvernement confédérative, qui, unissant les peuples par des liens semblables à ceux qui unissent les individus, soumette également les uns et les autres à l'autorité des lois. Ce Gouvernement paraît d'ailleurs préférable à tout autre, en ce qu'il comprend à la fois les avantages des grands et des petits États, qu'il est redoutable au dehors par sa puissance, que les lois y sont en vigueur, et qu'il est le seul propre à contenir également les sujets, les chefs, et les étrangers.

Quoique cette forme paraisse nouvelle à certains égards, et qu'elle n'ait en effet été bien entendue que par les modernes, les anciens ne l'ont pas ignorée. Les Grecs eurent leurs amphictyons, les Étrusques leurs lucumonies, les Latins leurs féries, les Gaules leurs cités ; et les derniers soupirs de la Grèce devinrent encore illustres dans la Ligue achéenne. Mais nulles de ces confédérations n'approchèrent, pour la sagesse, de celle du Corps germanique, de la Ligue helvétique, et des États Généraux. Que si ces Corps politiques sont encore en si petit nombre et si loin de la perfection dont on sent qu'ils seraient susceptibles, c'est que le mieux ne s'exécute pas comme il s'imagine, et qu'en politique ainsi qu'en morale l'étendue de nos connaissances ne prouve guère que la grandeur de nos maux.

[1] The rough draft of this paragraph, and of the next as far as 'en ce qu'il comprend,' is to be found in MS. Neuchâtel, 7829.
[2] See *L'état de guerre* (above, p. 305) and *Émile*, Liv. v. (Vol. II. p. 157).

Outre ces confédérations publiques, il s'en peut former tacitement d'autres moins apparentes et non moins réelles, par l'union des intérêts, par le rapport des maximes, par la conformité des coutumes, ou par d'autres circonstances qui laissent subsister des relations communes entre des peuples divisés. C'est ainsi que toutes les Puissances de l'Europe forment entre elles une sorte de système qui les unit par une même religion, par un même droit des gens, par les mœurs, par les lettres, par le commerce, et par une sorte d'équilibre qui est l'effet nécessaire de tout cela, et qui, sans que personne songe en effet à le conserver, ne serait pourtant pas si facile à rompre que le pensent beaucoup de gens.

Cette société des peuples de l'Europe n'a pas toujours existé, et les causes particulières qui l'ont fait naître servent encore à la maintenir. En effet, avant les conquêtes des Romains, tous les peuples de cette partie du monde, barbares et inconnus les uns aux autres, n'avaient rien de commun que leur qualité d'hommes: qualité qui, ravalée alors par l'esclavage, ne différait guère dans leur esprit de celle de brute. Aussi les Grecs, raisonneurs et vains, distinguaient-ils, pour ainsi dire, deux espèces dans l'humanité : dont l'une, savoir la leur, était faite pour commander ; et l'autre, qui comprenait tout le reste du monde, uniquement pour servir. De ce principe il résultait qu'un Gaulois ou un Ibère n'était rien de plus pour un Grec que n'eût été un Cafre ou un Américain; et les barbares eux-mêmes n'avaient pas plus d'affinité entre eux que n'en avaient les Grecs avec les uns et les autres.

Mais quand ce peuple, souverain par nature, eut été soumis aux Romains ses esclaves, et qu'une partie de l'hémisphère connu eut subi le même joug, il se forma une union politique et civile entre tous les membres d'un même empire. Cette union fut beaucoup resserrée par la maxime, ou très sage ou très insensée, de communiquer aux vaincus tous les droits des vainqueurs, et surtout par le fameux décret de Claude, qui incorporait tous les sujets de Rome au nombre de ses citoyens.

À la chaîne politique, qui réunissait ainsi tous les membres en un corps, se joignirent les institutions civiles et les lois, qui donnèrent une nouvelle force à ces liens, en déterminant d'une manière équitable, claire et précise, du moins autant qu'on le pouvait dans un si vaste empire, les devoirs et les droits réciproques du prince et des sujets, et ceux des citoyens entre eux. Le Code de Théodose, et ensuite les livres de Justinien, furent une nouvelle chaîne de justice et de raison, substituée à propos à celle du pouvoir souverain, qui se relâchait très sensiblement. Ce supplément retarda beaucoup la dissolution de l'Empire, et lui conserva longtemps une sorte de juridiction sur les barbares mêmes qui le désolaient.

Un troisième lien, plus fort que les précédents, fut celui de la religion ; et l'on ne peut nier que ce ne soit surtout au christianisme que l'Europe doit encore aujourd'hui l'espèce de société qui s'est perpétuée entre ses membres : tellement que celui des membres qui n'a point adopté sur ce point le sentiment des autres est toujours demeuré comme étranger parmi eux. Le Christianisme, si méprisé à sa naissance, servit enfin d'asile à ses détracteurs. Après l'avoir si cruellement et si vainement persécuté, l'empire romain y trouva les ressources qu'il n'avait plus dans ses forces ; ses missions lui valaient mieux que des victoires ; il envoyait des évêques réparer les fautes de ses généraux, et triomphait par ses prêtres quand ses soldats étaient battus. C'est ainsi que les Francs, les Goths, les Bourguignons, les Lombards, les Avares, et mille autres, reconnurent enfin l'autorité de l'Empire après l'avoir subjugué, et reçurent du moins en apparence, avec la loi de l'Évangile, celle du prince qui la leur faisait annoncer.

Tel était le respect qu'on portait encore à ce grand corps expirant, que jusqu'au dernier instant ses destructeurs s'honoraient de ses titres : on voyait devenir officiers de l'empire les mêmes conquérants qui l'avaient avili ; les plus grands rois accepter, briguer même, les honneurs patriciaux, la préfecture, le consulat ; et, comme un lion qui flatte l'homme qu'il pourrait dévorer, on voyait ces vainqueurs terribles rendre hommage au trône impérial, qu'ils étaient maîtres de renverser.

Voilà comment le sacerdoce et l'Empire ont formé le lien social de divers peuples qui, sans avoir aucune communauté réelle d'intérêts, de droits[1] ou de dépendance, en avaient une de maximes et d'opinions, dont l'influence est encore demeurée quand le principe a été détruit. Le simulacre antique de l'Empire romain a continué de former une sorte de liaison entre les membres qui l'avaient composé ; et Rome ayant dominé d'une autre manière après la destruction de l'Empire, il est resté de ce double lien[2] une société

---

[1] Ed. 1772 reads *droit* ; Ed. 1782, *droits*.

[2] Le respect pour l'Empire romain a tellement survécu à sa puissance, que bien des jurisconsultes ont mis en question si l'empereur d'Allemagne n'était pas le souverain naturel du monde ; et Barthole a poussé les choses jusqu'à traiter d'hérétique quiconque osait* en douter. Les livres des canonistes sont pleins de décisions semblables sur l'autorité temporelle de l'Église

* Hachette has *oserait*. Eds. 1772, 1782, as above.

plus étroite entre les nations de l'Europe, où était le centre des deux Puissances, que dans les autres parties du monde, dont les divers peuples, trop épars pour se correspondre, n'ont de plus aucun point de réunion.

Joignez à cela la situation particulière de l'Europe, plus également peuplée, plus également fertile, mieux réunie en toutes ses parties ; le mélange continuel des intérêts que les liens du sang et les affaires du commerce, des arts, des colonies, ont mis entre les souverains ; la multitude des rivières, et la variété de leurs cours, qui rend toutes les communications faciles ; l'humeur inconstante des habitants, qui les porte à voyager sans cesse, et à se transporter fréquemment les uns chez les autres ; l'invention de l'imprimerie, et le goût général des lettres, qui a mis entre eux une communauté d'études et de connaissances ; enfin la multitude et la petitesse des États, qui, jointe aux besoins du luxe et à la diversité des climats, rend les uns toujours nécessaires aux autres. Toutes ces causes réunies forment de l'Europe, non seulement, comme l'Asie ou l'Afrique, une idéale collection de peuples qui n'ont de commun qu'un nom, mais une société réelle qui a sa religion, ses mœurs, ses coutumes et même ses lois, dont aucun des peuples qui la composent ne peut s'écarter sans causer aussitôt des troubles.

À voir, d'un autre côté, les dissensions perpétuelles, les brigandages, les usurpations, les révoltes, les guerres, les meurtres, qui désolent journellement ce respectable séjour des sages, ce brillant asile des sciences et des arts ; à considérer nos beaux discours et nos procédés horribles, tant d'humanité dans les maximes et de cruauté dans les actions, une religion si douce et une si sanguinaire intolérance, une politique si sage dans les livres et si dure dans la pratique, des chefs si bienfaisants et des peuples si misérables, des Gouvernements si modérés et des guerres si cruelles : on sait à peine comment concilier ces étranges contrariétés ; et cette fraternité prétendue des peuples de l'Europe ne semble être qu'un nom de dérision pour exprimer avec ironie leur mutuelle animosité.

Cependant les choses ne font que suivre en cela leur cours naturel. Toute société sans lois ou sans chefs, toute union formée ou maintenue par le hasard, doit nécessairement dégénérer en

romaine. [Note de J.-J. R.] The last sentence is wanting in Ed. 1772. I cannot find it among Rousseau's *addenda* for 'la grande édition' (MS. Neuchâtel, 7842). It must have been entered by Rousseau in some copy accessible to du Peyrou.

querelle et dissension à la première circonstance qui vient à changer. L'antique union des peuples de l'Europe a compliqué leurs intérêts et leurs droits de mille manières ; ils se touchent par tant de points, que le moindre mouvement des uns ne peut manquer de choquer les autres ; leurs divisions sont d'autant plus funestes que leurs liaisons sont plus intimes, et leurs fréquentes querelles ont presque la cruauté des guerres civiles.

Convenons donc que l'état relatif des Puissances de l'Europe est proprement un état de guerre, et que tous les traités partiels entre quelques-unes de ces Puissances sont plutôt des trêves passagères que de véritables paix : soit parce que ces traités n'ont point communément d'autres garants que les parties contractantes ; soit parce que les droits des unes et des autres n'y sont jamais décidés radicalement, et que ces droits mal éteints, ou les prétentions qui en tiennent lieu entre des Puissances qui ne reconnaissent aucun supérieur, seront infailliblement des sources de nouvelles guerres, sitôt que d'autres circonstances auront donné de nouvelles forces aux prétendants.

D'ailleurs, le droit public de l'Europe n'étant point établi ou autorisé de concert, n'ayant aucuns principes généraux, et variant incessamment selon les temps et les lieux, il est plein de règles contradictoires, qui ne se peuvent concilier que par le droit du plus fort : de sorte que, la raison, sans guide assuré, se pliant toujours vers l'intérêt personnel dans les choses douteuses, la guerre serait encore inévitable, quand même chacun voudrait être juste. Tout ce qu'on peut faire avec de bonnes intentions, c'est de décider ces sortes d'affaires par la voie des armes, ou de les assoupir par des traités passagers. Mais bientôt, aux occasions qui raniment les mêmes querelles, il s'en joint d'autres qui les modifient : tout s'embrouille, tout se complique ; on ne voit plus rien au fond des choses ; l'usurpation passe pour droit, la faiblesse pour injustice ; et, parmi ce désordre continuel, chacun se trouve insensiblement si fort déplacé, que, si l'on pouvait remonter au droit solide et primitif, il y aurait peu de souverains en Europe qui ne dussent rendre tout ce qu'ils ont.

Une autre semence de guerre, plus cachée et non moins réelle, c'est que les choses ne changent point de forme en changeant de nature ; que des États héréditaires en effet restent électifs en apparence ; qu'il y ait des Parlements ou États nationaux dans des Monarchies, des chefs héréditaires dans des Républiques ; qu'une Puissance dépendante d'une autre conserve encore une apparence de liberté ; que tous les peuples soumis au même pouvoir ne soient pas gouvernés par les mêmes lois ; que l'ordre de succession soit différent dans les divers États d'un même souverain ; enfin, que chaque Gouvernement tende toujours à s'altérer, sans qu'il soit possible d'empêcher ce progrès. Voilà les causes générales et particulières qui nous unissent pour nous détruire, et nous font écrire une si belle doctrine sociale avec des mains toujours teintes de sang humain.

Les causes du mal étant une fois connues, le remède, s'il existe, est suffisamment indiqué par elles. Chacun voit que toute société se forme par les intérêts communs ; que toute division naît des intérêts opposés ; que, mille événements fortuits pouvant changer et modifier les uns et les autres, dès qu'il y a société il faut nécessairement une force coactive qui ordonne et concerte les mouvements de ses membres, afin de donner aux communs intérêts et aux engagements réciproques la solidité qu'ils ne sauraient avoir par eux-mêmes.

Ce serait d'ailleurs une grande erreur d'espérer que cet état violent pût jamais changer par la seule force des choses et sans le secours de l'art. Le système de l'Europe a précisément le degré de solidité qui peut la maintenir dans une agitation perpétuelle, sans la renverser tout à fait ; et si nos maux ne peuvent augmenter, ils peuvent encore moins finir, parce que toute grande révolution est désormais impossible.

[1]Pour donner à ceci l'évidence nécessaire, commençons par jeter un coup d'œil général sur l'état présent de l'Europe. La situation des montagnes, des mers et des fleuves qui servent de bornes aux nations qui l'habitent, semble avoir décidé du nombre et de la grandeur de ces nations ; et l'on peut dire que l'ordre politique de cette partie du monde est, à certains égards, l'ouvrage de la nature.

En effet, ne pensons pas que cet équilibre si vanté ait été établi par personne, et que personne ait rien fait à dessein de le conserver. On trouve qu'il existe ; et ceux qui ne sentent pas en eux-mêmes assez de poids pour le rompre, couvrent leurs vues particulières du prétexte de le soutenir. Mais, qu'on y songe ou non, cet équilibre subsiste, et n'a besoin que de lui-même pour se conserver, sans que personne s'en mêle ; et quand il se romprait un moment d'un côté, il se rétablirait bientôt d'un autre : de sorte que, si les princes qu'on accusait d'aspirer à la monarchie

---

[1] The rough draft of this paragraph and the six following (...'les bornes du traité général') is to be found in MS. Neuchâtel, 7829.

universelle y ont réellement aspiré, ils montraient en cela plus d'ambition que de génie. Car comment envisager un moment ce projet, sans en voir aussitôt le ridicule? comment ne pas sentir qu'il n'y a point de potentat en Europe assez supérieur aux autres pour pouvoir jamais en devenir le maître? Tous les conquérants qui ont fait des révolutions se présentaient toujours avec des forces inattendues, ou avec des troupes étrangères et différemment aguerries, à des peuples ou désarmés, ou divisés, ou sans discipline. Mais où prendrait un prince européen des forces inattendues pour accabler tous les autres, tandis que le plus puissant d'entre eux est une si petite partie du tout, et qu'ils ont de concert une si grande vigilance? Aura-t-il plus de troupes qu'eux tous? Il ne le peut; ou n'en sera que plus tôt ruiné; ou ses troupes seront plus mauvaises, en raison de leur plus grand nombre. En aura-t-il de mieux aguerries? Il en aura moins à proportion. D'ailleurs la discipline est partout à peu près la même, ou le deviendra dans peu. Aura-t-il plus d'argent? Les sources en sont communes, et jamais l'argent ne fit de grandes conquêtes. Fera-t-il une invasion subite? La famine ou des places fortes l'arrêteront à chaque pas. Voudra-t-il s'agrandir pied à pied? Il donne aux ennemis le moyen de s'unir pour résister; le temps, l'argent et les hommes ne tarderont pas à lui manquer. Divisera-t-il les autres Puissances pour les vaincre l'une par l'autre? Les maximes de l'Europe rendent cette politique vaine; et le prince le plus borné ne donnerait pas dans ce piége. Enfin, aucun d'eux ne pouvant avoir de ressources exclusives, la résistance est, à la longue, égale à l'effort, et le temps rétablit bientôt les brusques accidents de la fortune, sinon pour chaque prince en particulier, au moins pour la constitution générale.

Veut-on maintenant supposer à plaisir l'accord de deux ou trois potentats pour subjuguer tout le reste? Ces trois potentats, quels qu'ils soient, ne feront pas ensemble la moitié de l'Europe. Alors l'autre moitié s'unira certainement contre eux : ils auront donc à vaincre plus fort qu'eux-mêmes. J'ajoute que les vues des uns sont trop opposées à celles des autres, et qu'il règne une trop grande jalousie entre eux, pour qu'ils puissent même former un semblable projet. J'ajoute encore que, quand ils l'auraient formé, qu'ils le mettraient en exécution, et qu'il aurait quelques succès, ces succès mêmes seraient, pour les conquérants alliés, des semences de discorde; parce qu'il ne serait pas possible que les avantages fussent tellement partagés que chacun se trouvât également satisfait des siens, et que le moins heureux s'opposerait bientôt aux progrès des autres, qui, par une semblable raison, ne tarderaient pas à se diviser eux-mêmes. Je doute que, depuis que le monde existe, on ait jamais vu trois ni même deux grandes Puissances bien unies en subjuguer d'autres sans se brouiller sur les contingents ou sur les partages, et sans donner bientôt, par leur mésintelligence, de nouvelles ressources aux faibles. Ainsi, quelque supposition qu'on fasse, il n'est pas vraisemblable que ni prince, ni ligue, puisse désormais changer considérablement et à demeure l'état des choses parmi nous.

Ce n'est pas à dire que les Alpes, le Rhin, la mer, les Pyrénées, soient des obstacles insurmontables à l'ambition ; mais ces obstacles sont soutenus par d'autres qui les fortifient, ou ramènent les États aux mêmes limites, quand des efforts passagers les en ont écartés. Ce qui fait le vrai soutien du système de l'Europe, c'est bien en partie le jeu des négociations, qui presque toujours se balancent mutuellement. Mais ce système a un autre appui plus solide encore ; et cet appui c'est le Corps germanique, placé presque au centre de l'Europe, lequel en tient toutes les autres parties en respect, et sert peut-être encore plus au maintien de ses voisins qu'à celui de ses propres membres : Corps redoutable aux étrangers par son étendue, par le nombre et la valeur de ses peuples ; mais utile à tous par sa constitution, qui, lui ôtant les moyens et la volonté de rien conquérir, en fait l'écueil des conquérants. Malgré les défauts de cette constitution de l'Empire, il est certain que, tant qu'elle subsistera, jamais l'équilibre de l'Europe ne sera rompu, qu'aucun potentat n'aura à craindre d'être détrôné par un autre, et que le traité de Westphalie sera peut-être à jamais parmi nous la base du système politique. Ainsi le droit public, que les Allemands étudient avec tant de soin, est encore plus important qu'ils ne pensent, et n'est pas seulement le droit public germanique, mais, à certains égards, celui de toute l'Europe.

Mais si le présent système est inébranlable, c'est en cela même qu'il est plus orageux ; car il y a entre les Puissances européennes une action et une réaction qui, sans les déplacer tout à fait, les tient dans une agitation continuelle ; et leurs efforts sont toujours vains et toujours renaissants, comme les flots de la mer, qui sans cesse agitent sa surface sans jamais en changer le niveau ; de sorte que les peuples sont incessamment désolés sans aucun profit sensible pour les souverains.

Il me serait aisé de déduire la même vérité des intérêts particuliers de toutes les cours de l'Europe ; car je ferais voir aisément que ces intérêts se croisent de manière à tenir toutes leurs forces mutuellement en respect. Mais les idées de commerce et d'argent, ayant produit une espèce de fanatisme politique, font si promptement changer les intérêts apparents de tous les princes, qu'on ne peut établir aucune maxime stable sur leurs vrais intérêts, parce que tout dépend maintenant des systèmes économiques, la plupart fort bizarres, qui passent par la tête des ministres. Quoi qu'il en soit, le commerce, qui tend journellement à se mettre en équilibre, ôtant à certaines Puissances l'avantage exclusif qu'elles en tiraient, leur ôte en même temps un des grands moyens qu'elles avaient de faire la loi aux autres[1].

Si j'ai insisté sur l'égale distribution de force qui résulte en Europe de la constitution[2] actuelle, c'était pour en déduire une conséquence importante à l'établissement d'une association générale. Car, pour former une confédération solide et durable, il faut en mettre tous les membres dans une dépendance tellement mutuelle, qu'aucun ne soit seul en état de résister à tous les autres, et que les associations particulières, qui pourraient nuire à la grande, y rencontrent des obstacles suffisants pour empêcher leur exécution; sans quoi la confédération serait vaine, et chacun serait réellement indépendant, sous une apparente sujétion. Or, si ces obstacles sont tels que j'ai dit ci-devant, maintenant que toutes les Puissances sont dans une entière liberté de former entre elles des ligues et des traités offensifs, qu'on juge de ce qu'ils seraient quand il y aurait une grande ligue armée, toujours prête à prévenir ceux qui voudraient entreprendre de la détruire ou de lui résister. Ceci suffit pour montrer qu'une telle association ne consisterait pas en délibérations vaines, auxquelles chacun pût résister impunément; mais qu'il en naîtrait une puissance effective, capable de forcer les ambitieux à se tenir dans les bornes du traité général.

[1] Les choses ont changé depuis que j'écrivais ceci; mais mon principe sera toujours vrai. Il est, par exemple, très aisé de prévoir que, dans vingt ans d'ici, l'Angleterre, avec toute sa gloire, sera ruinée, et, de plus, aura perdu le reste de sa liberté. Tout le monde assure que l'agriculture fleurit dans cette île; et moi je parie qu'elle y dépérit. Londres s'agrandit tous les jours; donc le royaume se dépeuple. Les Anglais veulent être conquérants; donc ils ne tarderont pas d'être esclaves. [Note de J.-J. R., 1761.] We learn from a letter of Rousseau to de Bastide (dated by Hachette June 16, 1760: really, I think, Jan. 16, 1761) that he had originally written *aura perdu sa liberté*. 'Je crois,' he writes, 'qu'il faut mettre *le reste de leur liberté*; car il y en a d'assez sots pour croire qu'ils l'ont encore.' *Œuvres*, x. p. 227.

[2] Hachette reads *de sa constitution*, against Ed. 1782. The reading of 1782 is justified by *dans la présente constitution*, p. 382.

Il résulte de cet exposé trois vérités incontestables : l'une, qu'excepté le Turc il règne entre tous les peuples de l'Europe une liaison sociale imparfaite, mais plus étroite que les nœuds généraux et lâches de l'humanité ; la seconde, que l'imperfection de cette société rend la condition de ceux qui la composent pire que la privation de toute société entre eux ; la troisième, que ces premiers liens, qui rendent cette société nuisible, la rendent en même temps facile à perfectionner ; en sorte que tous ses membres pourraient tirer leur bonheur de ce qui fait actuellement leur misère, et changer en une paix éternelle l'état de guerre qui règne entre eux.

Voyons maintenant de quelle manière ce grand ouvrage, commencé par la fortune, peut être achevé par la raison ; et comment la société libre et volontaire qui unit tous les États européens, prenant la force et la solidité d'un vrai Corps politique, peut se changer en une Confédération réelle. Il est indubitable qu'un pareil établissement, donnant à cette association la perfection qui lui manquait, en détruira l'abus, en étendra les avantages, et forcera toutes les parties à concourir au bien commun. Mais il faut pour cela que cette Confédération soit tellement générale, que nulle Puissance considérable ne s'y refuse ; qu'elle ait un tribunal judiciaire qui puisse établir les lois et les règlements qui doivent obliger tous les membres ; qu'elle ait une force coactive et coercitive pour contraindre chaque État de se soumettre aux délibérations communes, soit pour agir, soit pour s'abstenir ; enfin, qu'elle soit ferme et durable, pour empêcher que les membres ne s'en détachent à leur volonté, sitôt qu'ils croiront voir leur intérêt particulier contraire à l'intérêt général. Voilà les signes certains auxquels on reconnaîtra que l'institution est sage, utile et inébranlable. Il s'agit maintenant d'étendre cette supposition, pour chercher par analyse quels effets doivent en résulter, quels moyens sont propres à l'établir, et quel espoir raisonnable on peut avoir de la mettre en exécution.

Il se forme de temps en temps parmi nous des espèces de Diètes générales sous le nom de Congrès, où l'on se rend solennellement de tous les États de l'Europe pour s'en retourner de même ; où l'on s'assemble pour ne rien dire ; où toutes les affaires publiques se traitent en particulier ; où l'on délibère en commun si la table sera ronde ou carrée, si la salle aura plus ou moins de portes, si un tel plénipotentiaire aura le visage ou le dos tourné vers la fenêtre, si tel autre fera deux pouces de chemin de plus ou de moins dans une visite, et sur mille questions de pareille importance, inutilement agitées depuis trois siècles, et très dignes assurément d'occuper les politiques du nôtre.

[1]Il se peut faire que les membres d'une de ces assemblées soient une fois doués du sens commun ; il n'est pas même impossible qu'ils veuillent sincèrement le bien public ; et, par les raisons qui seront ci-après déduites, on peut concevoir encore qu'après avoir aplani bien des difficultés ils auront ordre de leurs souverains respectifs de signer la Confédération générale que je suppose sommairement contenue dans les cinq Articles suivants.

Par le premier, les souverains contractants établiront entre eux une alliance perpétuelle et irrévocable, et nommeront des plénipotentiaires pour tenir, dans un lieu déterminé, une Diète ou un Congrès permanent, dans lequel tous les différends des parties contractantes seront réglés et terminés par voies d'arbitrage ou de jugement.

Par le second, on spécifiera le nombre des souverains dont les plénipotentiaires auront voix à la Diète ; ceux qui seront invités d'accéder au traité ; l'ordre, le temps et la manière dont la présidence passera de l'un à l'autre par intervalles égaux ; enfin la quotité relative des contributions, et la manière de les lever pour fournir aux dépenses communes.

Par le troisième, la Confédération garantira à chacun de ses membres la possession et le gouvernement de tous les États qu'il possède actuellement, de même que la succession élective ou héréditaire, selon que le tout est établi par les lois fondamentales de chaque pays ; et, pour supprimer tout d'un coup la source des démêlés qui renaissent incessamment, on conviendra de prendre la possession actuelle et les derniers traités pour base de tous les droits mutuels des Puissances contractantes : renonçant pour jamais et réciproquement à toute autre prétention antérieure ; sauf les successions futures contentieuses, et autres droits à échoir, qui seront tous réglés à l'arbitrage de la Diète, sans qu'il soit permis de s'en faire raison par voies de fait, ni de prendre jamais les armes l'un contre l'autre, sous quelque prétexte que ce puisse être.

Par le quatrième, on spécifiera les cas où tout Allié, infracteur du traité, serait mis au ban de l'Europe, et proscrit comme ennemi public : savoir, s'il refusait d'exécuter les jugements de la grande Alliance, qu'il fît des préparatifs de guerre, qu'il négociât des traités contraires à la Confédération, qu'il prît les armes pour lui résister, ou pour attaquer quelqu'un des Alliés.

[1] The rough draft of this paragraph occurs in MS. Neuchâtel, 7829.

Il sera encore convenu par le même Article qu'on armera et agira offensivement, conjointement, et à frais communs, contre tout État au ban de l'Europe, jusqu'à ce qu'il ait mis bas les armes, exécuté les jugements et règlements de la Diète, réparé les torts, remboursé les frais, et fait raison même des préparatifs de guerre contraires au traité.

Enfin, par le cinquième, les plénipotentiaires du Corps européen auront toujours le pouvoir de former dans la Diète, à la pluralité des voix pour la provision, et aux trois quarts des voix cinq ans après pour la définitive, sur les instructions de leurs cours, les règlements qu'ils jugeront importants pour procurer à la République européenne et à chacun de ses membres tous les avantages possibles. Mais on ne pourra jamais rien changer à ces cinq Articles fondamentaux que du consentement unanime des Confédérés.

Ces cinq Articles, ainsi abrégés et couchés en règles générales, sont, je ne l'ignore pas, sujets à mille petites difficultés, dont plusieurs demanderaient de longs éclaircissements. Mais les petites difficultés se lèvent aisément au besoin ; et ce n'est pas d'elles qu'il s'agit dans une entreprise de l'importance de celle-ci. Quand il sera question du détail de la police du Congrès, on trouvera mille obstacles et dix mille moyens de les lever. Ici il est question d'examiner, par la nature des choses, si l'entreprise est possible ou non. On se perdrait dans des volumes de riens, s'il fallait tout prévoir et répondre à tout. En se tenant aux principes incontestables, on ne doit pas vouloir contenter tous les esprits, ni résoudre toutes les objections, ni dire comment tout se fera ; il suffit de montrer que tout se peut faire.

Que faut-il donc examiner pour bien juger de ce système ? Deux questions seulement ; car c'est une insulte que je ne veux pas faire au lecteur, de lui prouver qu'en général l'état de paix est préférable à l'état de guerre.

La première question est, si la Confédération proposée irait sûrement à son but et serait suffisante pour donner à l'Europe une paix solide et perpétuelle.

La seconde, s'il est de l'intérêt des souverains d'établir cette Confédération et d'acheter une paix constante à ce prix.

Quand l'utilité générale et particulière sera ainsi démontrée, on ne voit plus, dans la raison des choses, quelle cause pourrait empêcher l'effet d'un établissement qui ne dépend que de la volonté des intéressés.

Pour discuter d'abord le premier Article, appliquons ici ce que j'ai dit ci-devant du système général de l'Europe, et de l'effort commun qui circonscrit chaque Puissance à peu près dans ses bornes, et ne lui permet pas d'en écraser entièrement d'autres. Pour rendre sur ce point mes raisonnements plus sensibles, je joins ici la liste des dix-neuf Puissances qu'on suppose composer la République européenne ; en sorte que, chacune ayant voix égale, il y aurait dix-neuf voix dans la Diète ; savoir

    L'empereur des Romains,
    L'empereur de Russie,
    Le roi de France,
    Le roi d'Espagne,
    Le roi d'Angleterre,
    Les États Généraux,
    Le roi de Dannemarck,
    La Suède,
    La Pologne,
    Le roi de Portugal,
    Le souverain de Rome,
    Le roi de Prusse,
    L'électeur de Bavière et ses coassociés,
    L'électeur palatin et ses coassociés,
    Les Suisses et leurs coassociés,
    Les électeurs ecclésiastiques et leurs associés,
    La République de Venise et ses coassociés,
    Le roi de Naples,
    Le roi de Sardaigne.

Plusieurs souverains moins considérables, tels que la République de Gênes, les ducs de Modène et de Parme, et d'autres, étant omis dans cette liste, seront joints aux moins puissants, par forme d'association, et auront avec eux un droit de suffrage, semblable au *votum curiatum* des comtes de l'Empire. Il est inutile de rendre ici cette énumération plus précise, parce que, jusqu'à l'exécution du projet, il peut survenir d'un moment à l'autre des accidents sur lesquels il la faudrait réformer, mais qui ne changeraient rien au fond du système.

Il ne faut que jeter les yeux sur cette liste, pour voir avec la dernière évidence qu'il n'est pas possible ni qu'aucune des Puissances qui la composent soit en état de résister à toutes les autres unies en corps, ni qu'il s'y forme aucune ligue partielle capable de faire tête à la grande Confédération.

Car comment se ferait cette ligue ? serait-ce entre les plus puissants ? Nous avons montré qu'elle ne saurait être durable ; et il est bien aisé maintenant de voir encore qu'elle est incompatible avec le système particulier de chaque grande Puissance, et avec les intérêts inséparables de sa constitution. Serait-ce entre un grand État et plusieurs petits ? Mais les autres grands États, unis à la Confédération, auront bientôt écrasé la ligue : et l'on doit sentir que, la grande Alliance étant toujours unie et armée, il lui sera facile, en vertu du quatrième Article, de prévenir et d'étouffer d'abord toute alliance partielle et séditieuse qui tendrait à troubler la paix et l'ordre public. Qu'on voie ce qui se passe dans le Corps germanique, malgré les abus de sa police et l'extrême inégalité de ses membres. Y en a-t-il un seul, même parmi les plus puissants, qui osât s'exposer au ban de l'Empire en blessant ouvertement sa constitution, à moins qu'il ne crût avoir de bonnes raisons de ne point craindre que l'Empire voulût agir contre lui tout de bon ?

Ainsi je tiens pour démontré que la Diète européenne une fois établie n'aura jamais de rébellion à craindre, et que, bien qu'il s'y puisse introduire quelques abus, ils ne peuvent jamais aller jusqu'à éluder l'objet de l'institution. Reste à voir si cet objet sera bien rempli par l'institution même.

[1]Pour cela, considérons les motifs qui mettent aux princes les armes à la main. Ces motifs sont : ou de faire des conquêtes, ou de se défendre d'un conquérant, ou d'affaiblir un trop puissant voisin, ou de soutenir ses droits attaqués, ou de vider un différend qu'on n'a pu terminer à l'amiable, ou enfin de remplir les engagements d'un traité. Il n'y a ni cause ni prétexte de guerre qu'on ne puisse ranger sous quelqu'un de ces six chefs : or, il est évident qu'aucun des six ne peut exister dans ce nouvel état de choses.

Premièrement, il faut renoncer aux conquêtes par l'impossibilité d'en faire, attendu qu'on est sûr d'être arrêté dans son chemin par de plus grandes forces que celles qu'on peut avoir ; de sorte qu'en risquant de tout perdre on est dans l'impuissance de rien gagner. Un prince ambitieux, qui veut s'agrandir en Europe, fait deux choses : il commence par se fortifier de bonnes alliances, puis il tâche de prendre son ennemi au dépourvu. Mais les alliances particulières ne serviraient de rien contre une alliance plus forte, et toujours subsistante ; et nul prince n'ayant plus aucun prétexte d'armer, il ne saurait le faire sans être aperçu, prévenu et puni par la Confédération toujours armée.

La même raison, qui ôte à chaque prince tout espoir de conquêtes[2], lui ôte en même temps toute crainte d'être attaqué ; et

---

[1] The rough draft of this paragraph occurs in MS. Neuchâtel, 7829.
[2] Ed. 1772 (Rey, 11 vols. 8vo) has *conquête*.

non seulement ses États, garantis par toute l'Europe, lui sont aussi assurés qu'aux citoyens leurs possessions dans un pays bien policé, mais plus que s'il était leur unique et propre défenseur, dans le même rapport que l'Europe entière est plus forte que lui seul.

On n'a plus de raison de vouloir affaiblir un voisin dont on n'a plus rien à craindre; et l'on n'en est pas même tenté, quand on n'a nul espoir de réussir.

À l'égard du soutien de ses droits, il faut d'abord remarquer qu'une infinité de chicanes et de prétentions obscures et embrouillées seront toutes anéanties par le troisième Article de la Confédération, qui règle définitivement tous les droits réciproques des souverains alliés sur leur actuelle possession : ainsi toutes les demandes et prétentions possibles deviendront claires à l'avenir, et seront jugées dans la Diète, à mesure qu'elles pourront naître. Ajoutez que, si l'on attaque mes droits, je dois les soutenir par la même voie : or, on ne peut les attaquer par les armes, sans encourir le ban de la Diète ; ce n'est donc pas non plus par les armes que j'ai besoin de les défendre. On doit dire la même chose des injures, des torts, des réparations, et de tous les différends imprévus qui peuvent s'élever entre deux souverains ; et le même pouvoir qui doit défendre leurs droits doit aussi redresser leurs griefs.

Quant au dernier Article, la solution saute aux yeux. On voit d'abord que, n'ayant plus d'agresseur à craindre, on n'a plus besoin de traité défensif, et que, comme on n'en saurait faire de plus solide et de plus sûr que celui de la grande Confédération, tout autre serait inutile, illégitime, et par conséquent nul.

Il n'est donc pas possible que la Confédération, une fois établie, puisse laisser aucune semence de guerre entre les Confédérés, et que l'objet de la paix perpétuelle ne soit exactement rempli par l'exécution du système proposé.

Il nous reste maintenant à examiner l'autre question, qui regarde l'avantage des parties contractantes ; car on sent bien que vainement ferait-on parler l'intérêt public au préjudice de l'intérêt particulier. Prouver que la paix est en général préférable à la guerre, c'est ne rien dire à celui qui croit avoir des raisons de préférer la guerre à la paix ; et lui montrer les moyens d'établir une paix durable, ce n'est que l'exciter à s'y opposer.

En effet, dira-t-on, vous ôtez aux souverains le droit de se faire justice à eux-mêmes, c'est-à-dire le précieux droit d'être injustes quand il leur plaît ; vous leur ôtez le pouvoir de s'agrandir [1]aux dépens de leurs voisins[1]; vous les faites renoncer à ces antiques

[1] Wanting in Ed. 1772.

prétentions qui tirent leur prix de leur obscurité, parce qu'on les étend avec sa fortune, à cet appareil de puissance et de terreur dont ils aiment à effrayer le monde, à cette gloire des conquêtes dont ils tirent leur honneur ; [1]et, pour tout dire[1] enfin, vous les forcez d'être équitables et pacifiques. Quels seront les dédommagements de tant de cruelles[2] privations ?

Je n'oserais répondre, avec l'abbé de Saint-Pierre, que la véritable gloire des princes consiste à procurer l'utilité publique et le bonheur de leurs sujets ; que tous leurs intérêts sont subordonnés à leur réputation, et que la réputation qu'on acquiert auprès des sages se mesure sur le bien que l'on fait aux hommes ; que l'entreprise d'une paix perpétuelle, étant la plus grande qui ait jamais été faite, est la plus capable de couvrir son auteur d'une gloire immortelle ; que cette même entreprise, étant aussi la plus utile aux peuples, est encore la plus honorable aux souverains, la seule surtout qui ne soit pas souillée de sang, de rapines, de pleurs, de malédictions ; et qu'enfin le plus sûr moyen de se distinguer dans la foule des rois est de travailler au bonheur public. [3]Laissons aux harangueurs ces discours qui[3], dans les cabinets des ministres, ont couvert de ridicule l'auteur et ses projets. Mais ne méprisons pas comme eux ses raisons ; et, quoi qu'il en soit des vertus des princes, parlons de leurs intérêts.

Toutes les Puissances de l'Europe ont des droits ou des prétentions les unes contre les autres ; ces droits ne sont pas de nature à pouvoir jamais être parfaitement éclaircis, parce qu'il n'y a point, pour en juger, de règle commune et constante, et qu'ils sont souvent fondés sur des faits équivoques ou incertains. Les différends qu'ils causent ne sauraient non plus être jamais terminés sans retour : tant faute d'arbitre compétent, que parce que chaque prince revient dans l'occasion sans scrupule sur les cessions qui lui ont été arrachées par force dans des traités par les plus puissants, ou après des guerres malheureuses. C'est donc une erreur de ne songer qu'à ses prétentions sur les autres, et d'oublier celles des autres sur nous, lorsqu'il n'y a d'aucun côté ni plus de justice, ni plus d'avantage dans les moyens de faire valoir ces prétentions réciproques. Sitôt que tout dépend de la fortune, la possession actuelle est d'un prix que la sagesse ne permet pas de risquer contre le profit à venir, même à chance égale ; et tout le monde blâme un homme à son aise qui, dans l'espoir de doubler son bien, l'ose risquer en un coup de dé. Mais nous avons fait voir que, dans les

---

[1] Wanting in Ed. 1772.   [2] *cruelles*, wanting in Ed. 1772.
[3] *Laissons aux harangueurs* and *qui*, wanting in Ed. 1772.

projets d'agrandissement, chacun, même dans le système actuel, doit trouver une résistance supérieure à son effort ; d'où il suit que, les plus puissants n'ayant aucune raison de jouer, ni les plus faibles aucun espoir de profit, c'est un bien pour tous de renoncer à ce qu'ils désirent, pour s'assurer ce qu'ils possèdent.

Considérons la consommation d'hommes, d'argent, de forces de toute espèce, l'épuisement où la plus heureuse guerre jette un État quelconque ; et comparons ce préjudice aux avantages qu'il en retire : nous trouverons qu'il perd souvent quand il croit gagner, et que le vainqueur, toujours plus faible qu'avant la guerre, n'a de consolation que de voir le vaincu plus affaibli que lui. Encore cet avantage est-il moins réel qu'apparent, parce que la supériorité qu'on peut avoir acquise sur son adversaire, on l'a perdue en même temps contre les Puissances neutres, qui, sans changer d'état, se fortifient, par rapport à nous, de tout notre affaiblissement.

Si tous les rois ne sont pas revenus encore de la folie des conquêtes, il semble au moins que les plus sages commencent à entrevoir qu'elles coûtent quelquefois plus qu'elles ne valent. Sans entrer à cet égard dans mille distinctions qui nous mèneraient trop loin, on peut dire en général qu'un prince qui, pour reculer ses frontières, perd autant de ses anciens sujets qu'il en acquiert de nouveaux, s'affaiblit en s'agrandissant, parce que, avec un plus grand espace à défendre, il n'a pas plus de défenseurs. Or, on ne peut ignorer que, par la manière dont la guerre se fait aujourd'hui, la moindre dépopulation qu'elle produit est celle qui se fait dans les armées. C'est bien là la perte apparente et sensible ; mais il s'en fait en même temps dans tout l'État une plus grave et plus irréparable que celle des hommes qui meurent : par ceux qui ne naissent pas, par l'augmentation des impôts, par l'interruption du commerce, par la désertion des campagnes, par l'abandon de l'agriculture. Ce mal, qu'on n'aperçoit point d'abord, se fait sentir cruellement dans la suite ; et c'est alors qu'on est étonné d'être si faible, pour s'être rendu si puissant.

Ce qui rend encore les conquêtes moins intéressantes, c'est qu'on sait maintenant par quels moyens on peut doubler et tripler sa puissance, non seulement sans étendre son territoire, mais quelquefois en le resserrant, comme fit très sagement l'empereur Adrien. On sait que ce sont les hommes seuls qui font la force des rois ; et c'est une proposition qui découle de ce que je viens de dire, que de deux États qui nourrissent le même nombre d'habitants, celui qui occupe une moindre étendue de terre est réellement le plus puissant. C'est donc par de bonnes lois, par une sage police, par de grandes vues économiques, qu'un souverain judicieux est sûr d'augmenter ses forces sans rien donner au hasard. Les véritables conquêtes qu'il fait sur ses voisins sont les établissements plus utiles qu'il forme dans ses États ; et tous les sujets de plus qui lui naissent sont autant d'ennemis qu'il tue.

Il ne faut point m'objecter ici que je prouve trop, en ce que, si les choses étaient comme je les représente, chacun ayant un véritable intérêt de ne pas entrer en guerre et les intérêts particuliers s'unissant à l'intérêt commun pour maintenir la paix, cette paix devrait s'établir d'elle-même et durer toujours sans aucune confédération. Ce serait faire un fort mauvais raisonnement dans la présente constitution ; car, quoiqu'il fût beaucoup meilleur pour tous d'être toujours en paix, le défaut commun de sûreté à cet égard fait que chacun, ne pouvant s'assurer d'éviter la guerre, tâche au moins de la commencer à son avantage quand l'occasion le favorise, et de prévenir un voisin qui ne manquerait pas de le prévenir à son tour dans l'occasion contraire ; de sorte que beaucoup de guerres, même offensives, sont d'injustes précautions pour mettre en sûreté son propre bien, plutôt que des moyens d'usurper celui des autres. Quelque salutaires que puissent être généralement les maximes du bien public, il est certain qu'à ne considérer que l'objet qu'on regarde en politique, et souvent même en morale, elles deviennent pernicieuses à celui qui s'obstine à les pratiquer avec tout le monde, quand personne ne les pratique avec lui.

Je n'ai rien à dire sur l'appareil des armes, parce que, destitué de fondements solides, soit de crainte, soit d'espérance, cet appareil est un jeu d'enfants, et que les rois ne doivent point avoir de poupées. Je ne dis rien non plus de la gloire des conquérants, parce que s'il y avait quelques monstres qui s'affligeassent uniquement pour n'avoir personne à massacrer, il ne faudrait point leur parler raison, mais leur ôter les moyens d'exercer leur rage meurtrière. La garantie de l'Article troisième ayant prévenu toutes solides raisons de guerre, on ne saurait avoir de motif de l'allumer contre autrui, qui ne puisse en fournir autant à autrui contre nous-mêmes ; et c'est gagner beaucoup que de s'affranchir d'un risque où chacun est seul contre tous.

Quant à la dépendance où chacun sera du Tribunal commun, il est très clair qu'elle ne diminuera rien des droits de la souveraineté, mais les affermira, au contraire, et les rendra plus assurés par l'Article troisième : en garantissant à chacun, non seulement ses États contre toute invasion étrangère, mais encore son autorité contre toute rébellion de ses sujets. Ainsi les princes n'en seront pas moins absolus, et leur couronne en sera plus assurée ; de sorte qu'en se soumettant au jugement de la Diète dans leurs démêlés d'égal à égal, et s'ôtant le dangereux pouvoir de s'emparer du bien d'autrui, ils ne font que s'assurer de leurs véritables droits, et renoncer à ceux qu'ils n'ont pas. D'ailleurs, il y a bien de la différence entre dépendre d'autrui, ou seulement d'un Corps dont on est membre et dont chacun est chef à son tour. Car, en ce dernier cas, on ne fait qu'assurer sa liberté par les garants qu'on lui donne ; elle s'aliénerait dans les mains d'un maître, mais elle s'affermit dans celles des associés. Ceci se confirme par l'exemple du Corps germanique ; car, bien que la souveraineté de ses membres soit altérée à bien des égards par sa constitution, et qu'ils soient par conséquent dans un cas moins favorable que ne seraient ceux du Corps européen, il n'y en a pourtant pas un seul, quelque jaloux qu'il soit de son autorité, qui voulût, quand il le pourrait, s'assurer une indépendance absolue en se détachant de l'Empire.

Remarquez de plus que, le Corps germanique ayant un chef permanent, l'autorité de ce chef doit nécessairement tendre sans cesse à l'usurpation : ce qui ne peut arriver de même dans la Diète européenne, où la présidence doit être alternative et sans égard à l'inégalité de puissance.

À toutes ces considérations il s'en joint une autre bien plus importante encore pour des gens aussi avides d'argent que le sont toujours les princes : c'est une grande facilité de plus d'en avoir beaucoup par tous les avantages qui résulteront pour leurs peuples et pour eux d'une paix continuelle, et par l'excessive dépense qu'épargne la réforme de l'état militaire, de ces multitudes de forteresses, et de cette énorme quantité de troupes qui absorbe leurs revenus et devient chaque jour plus à charge à leurs peuples et à eux-mêmes. Je sais qu'il ne convient pas à tous les souverains de supprimer toutes leurs troupes, et de n'avoir aucune force publique en main pour étouffer une émeute inopinée, ou repousser une invasion subite[1]. Je sais encore qu'il y aura un contingent à fournir à la Confédération, tant pour la garde des frontières de l'Europe que pour l'entretien de l'armée confédérative, destinée à soutenir au besoin les décrets de la Diète. Mais toutes ces dépenses faites, et l'extraordinaire des guerres à jamais supprimé, il resterait encore plus de la moitié de la dépense militaire ordinaire

[1] Il se présente encore ici d'autres objections ; mais, comme l'auteur du *Projet* ne se les est pas faites, je les ai rejetées dans l'examen. [Note de J.-J. R. It is in Eds. 1772 and 1782 ; I conjecture, in Ed. 1761 also.]

à répartir entre le soulagement des sujets et les coffres du prince. De sorte que le peuple payerait beaucoup moins ; que le princé, beaucoup plus riche, serait en état d'exciter le commerce, l'agriculture, les arts, de faire des établissements utiles qui augmenteraient encore la richesse du peuple et la sienne ; et que l'État serait avec cela dans une sûreté beaucoup plus parfaite que celle qu'il peut tirer de ses armées et de tout cet appareil de guerre qui ne cesse de l'épuiser au sein de la paix.

On dira peut-être que les pays frontières de l'Europe seraient alors dans une position plus désavantageuse, et pourraient avoir également des guerres à soutenir, ou avec le Turc, ou avec les corsaires d'Afrique, ou avec les Tartares.

À cela je réponds : 1° que ces pays sont dans le même cas aujourd'hui, et que par conséquent ce ne serait pas pour eux un désavantage positif à citer, mais seulement un avantage de moins, et un inconvénient inévitable auquel leur situation les expose ; 2° que délivrés de toute inquiétude du côté de l'Europe, ils seraient beaucoup plus en état de résister au dehors ; 3° que la suppression de toutes les forteresses de l'intérieur de l'Europe et des frais nécessaires à leur entretien mettrait la Confédération en état d'en établir un grand nombre sur les frontières sans être à charge aux confédérés ; 4° que ces forteresses, construites, entretenues et gardées à frais communs, seraient autant de sûretés et de moyens d'épargne pour les Puissances frontières dont elles garantiraient les États ; 5° que les troupes de la Confédération, distribuées sur les confins de l'Europe, seraient toujours prêtes à repousser l'agresseur ; 6° qu'enfin[1] un Corps aussi redoutable que la République européenne ôterait aux étrangers l'envie d'attaquer aucun de ses membres : comme le Corps germanique, infiniment moins puissant, ne laisse pas de l'être assez pour se faire respecter de ses voisins et protéger utilement tous les princes qui le composent.

On pourra dire encore que, les Européens n'ayant plus de guerres entre eux, l'art militaire tomberait insensiblement dans l'oubli ; que les troupes perdraient leur courage et leur discipline ; qu'il n'y aurait plus ni généraux, ni soldats, et que l'Europe resterait à la merci du premier venu.

Je réponds qu'il arrivera de deux choses l'une : ou les voisins de l'Europe l'attaqueront et lui feront la guerre ; ou ils redouteront la Confédération et la laisseront en paix.

Dans le premier cas, voilà les occasions de cultiver le génie et les talents militaires, d'aguerrir et former des troupes ; les armées

[1] Hachette omits *enfin*, against Eds. 1772, 1782.

de la Confédération seront à cet égard l'école de l'Europe ; on ira sur la frontière apprendre la guerre ; dans le sein de l'Europe on jouira de la paix, et l'on réunira par ce moyen les avantages de l'une et de l'autre. Croit-on qu'il soit toujours nécessaire de se battre chez soi pour devenir guerrier ? et les Français sont-ils moins braves, parce que les provinces de Touraine et d'Anjou ne sont pas en guerre l'une contre l'autre ?

Dans le second cas, on ne pourra plus s'aguerrir, il est vrai ; mais on n'en aura plus besoin ; car à quoi bon s'exercer à la guerre pour ne la faire à personne ? Lequel vaut mieux de cultiver un art funeste, ou de le rendre inutile ? S'il y avait un secret pour jouir d'une santé inaltérable, y aurait-il du bon sens à le rejeter pour ne pas ôter aux médecins l'occasion d'acquérir de l'expérience ? Il reste à voir dans ce parallèle, lequel des deux arts est plus salutaire en soi, et mérite mieux d'être conservé.

Qu'on ne nous menace pas d'une invasion subite ; on sait bien que l'Europe n'en a point à craindre, et que ce premier venu ne viendra jamais. Ce n'est plus le temps de ces éruptions[1] de barbares qui semblaient tomber[1] des nues. Depuis que nous parcourons d'un œil curieux toute la surface de la terre, il ne peut plus rien venir jusqu'à nous qui ne soit prévu de très loin. Il n'y a nulle Puissance au monde qui soit maintenant en état de menacer l'Europe entière ; et si jamais il en vient une, ou l'on aura le temps de se préparer, ou l'on sera du moins plus en état de lui résister, étant unis en un corps, que quand il faudra terminer tout d'un coup de longs différends et se réunir à la hâte.

Nous venons de voir que tous les prétendus inconvénients de l'état de confédération, bien pesés, se réduisent à rien. Nous demandons maintenant si quelqu'un dans le monde en oserait dire autant de ceux qui résultent de la manière actuelle de vider les différends entre prince et prince par le droit du plus fort : c'est-à-dire, de l'état d'impolice et de guerre qu'engendre nécessairement l'indépendance absolue et mutuelle de tous les souverains dans la société imparfaite qui règne entre eux dans l'Europe. Pour qu'on soit mieux en état de peser ces inconvénients, j'en vais résumer en peu de mots le sommaire que je laisse examiner au lecteur.

1. Nul droit assuré que celui du plus fort. 2. Changements continuels et inévitables de relations entre les peuples, qui empêchent aucun d'eux de pouvoir fixer en ses mains la force dont il jouit. 3. Point de sûreté parfaite, aussi longtemps que les voisins ne sont pas soumis ou anéantis. 4. Impossibilité générale

[1] Hachette has *irruptions, tombés*, against all the Eds.

de les anéantir, attendu qu'en subjuguant les premiers on en trouve d'autres. 5. Précautions et frais immenses pour se tenir sur ses gardes. 6. Défaut de force et de défense dans les minorités et dans les révoltes; car, quand l'État se partage, qui peut soutenir un des partis contre l'autre? 7. Défaut de sûreté dans les engagements mutuels. 8. Jamais de justice à espérer d'autrui sans des frais et des pertes immenses, qui ne l'obtiennent pas toujours, et dont l'objet disputé ne dédommage que rarement. 9. Risque inévitable de ses États et quelquefois de sa vie dans la poursuite de ses droits. 10. Nécessité de prendre part malgré soi aux querelles de ses voisins, et d'avoir la guerre quand on la voudrait le moins. 11. Interruption du commerce et des ressources publiques au moment qu'elles sont le plus nécessaires. 12. Danger continuel de la part d'un voisin puissant, si l'on est faible; et d'une ligue, si l'on est fort. 13. Enfin, inutilité de la sagesse, où préside la fortune; désolation continuelle des peuples; affaiblissement de l'État dans les succès et dans les revers; impossibilité totale d'établir jamais un bon Gouvernement, de compter sur son propre bien, et de rendre heureux ni soi ni les autres.

Récapitulons de même les avantages de l'arbitrage européen pour les princes confédérés.

1. Sûreté entière que leurs différends présents et futurs seront toujours terminés sans aucune guerre; sûreté incomparablement plus utile pour eux que ne serait, pour les particuliers, celle de n'avoir jamais de procès.

2. Sujets de contestations[1] ôtés ou réduits à très peu de chose par l'anéantissement de toutes prétentions antérieures, qui compensera les renonciations et affermira les possessions.

3. Sûreté entière et perpétuelle, et de la personne du prince, et de sa famille, et de ses États, et de l'ordre de succession fixé par les lois de chaque pays, tant contre l'ambition des prétendants injustes et ambitieux, que contre les révoltes des sujets rebelles.

4. Sûreté parfaite de l'exécution de tous les engagements réciproques entre prince et prince, par la garantie de la République européenne.

5. Liberté et sûreté parfaite et perpétuelle à l'égard du commerce, tant d'État à État, que de chaque État dans les régions éloignées.

6. Suppression totale et perpétuelle de leur dépense militaire extraordinaire par terre et par mer en temps de guerre, et considérable diminution de leur dépense ordinaire en temps de paix.

[1] Ed. 1772 has *contestation*.

7. Progrès sensible[1] de l'agriculture et de la population, des richesses de l'État, et des revenus du prince.

8. Facilité de tous les établissements qui peuvent augmenter la gloire et l'autorité du souverain, les ressources publiques, et le bonheur des peuples.

Je laisse, comme je l'ai déjà dit, au jugement des lecteurs l'examen de tous ces articles, et la comparaison de l'état de paix qui résulte de la Confédération avec l'état de guerre qui résulte de l'impolice européenne.

Si nous avons bien raisonné dans l'exposition de ce projet, il est démontré : premièrement, que l'établissement de la paix perpétuelle dépend uniquement du consentement des souverains, et n'offre point à lever d'autre difficulté que leur résistance ; secondement, que cet établissement leur serait utile de toute manière, et qu'il n'y a nulle comparaison à faire, même pour eux, entre les inconvénients et les avantages ; en troisième lieu, qu'il est raisonnable de supposer que leur volonté s'accorde avec leur intérêt ; enfin que cet établissement, une fois formé sur le plan proposé, serait solide et durable, et remplirait parfaitement son objet. Sans doute, ce n'est pas à dire que les souverains adopteront ce projet (qui peut répondre de la raison d'autrui ?) mais seulement qu'ils l'adopteraient, s'ils consultaient leurs vrais intérêts. Car on doit bien remarquer que nous n'avons point supposé les hommes tels qu'ils devraient être, bons, généreux, désintéressés, et aimant le bien public par humanité ; mais tels qu'ils sont, injustes, avides, et préférant leur intérêt à tout. La seule chose qu'on leur suppose, c'est assez de raison pour voir ce qui leur est utile, et assez de courage pour faire leur propre bonheur. Si, malgré tout cela, ce projet demeure sans exécution, ce n'est donc pas qu'il soit chimérique ; c'est que les hommes sont insensés, et que c'est une sorte de folie d'être sage au milieu des fous.

[1] Hachette reads *sensibles*, against Eds. 1772, 1782.

JUGEMENT SUR LA PAIX PERPÉTUELLE

[Written 1756; published 1782. MS. Neuchâtel, 7859[1].]

Le Projet de la Paix perpétuelle, étant par son objet le plus digne d'occuper un homme de bien, fut aussi de tous ceux de l'abbé de Saint-Pierre celui qu'il médita le plus longtemps et qu'il suivit avec le plus d'opiniâtreté ; car on a peine à nommer autrement ce zèle de missionnaire qui ne l'abandonna jamais sur ce point, malgré l'évidente impossibilité du succès, le ridicule qu'il se donnait de jour en jour, et les dégoûts qu'il eut sans cesse à essuyer. Il semble que cette âme saine[2], uniquement attentive au bien public, mesurait les soins qu'elle donnait aux choses uniquement sur le degré de leur utilité, sans jamais se laisser rebuter par les obstacles ni songer à l'intérêt personnel.

Si jamais vérité morale fut démontrée, il me semble que c'est l'utilité générale et particulière de ce projet. Les avantages qui résulteraient de son exécution, et pour chaque prince, et pour chaque peuple, et pour toute l'Europe, sont immenses, clairs, incontestables ; on ne peut rien de plus solide et de plus exact que les raisonnements par lesquels l'auteur les établit. Réalisez sa République européenne durant un seul jour, c'en est assez pour la faire durer éternellement : tant chacun trouverait par l'expérience son profit particulier dans le bien commun. Cependant ces mêmes princes, qui la défendraient de toutes leurs forces si elle existait, s'opposeraient maintenant de même à son exécution, et l'empêcheront[3] infailliblement de s'établir comme ils l'empêcheraient de s'éteindre. Ainsi, l'ouvrage de l'abbé de Saint-Pierre sur la Paix perpétuelle paraît d'abord inutile pour la produire et superflu pour la conserver. C'est donc une vaine spéculation, dira quelque lecteur impatient. Non, c'est un livre solide et sensé, et il est très important qu'il existe.

Commençons par examiner les difficultés de ceux qui ne jugent pas des raisons par la raison, mais seulement par l'événement, et qui n'ont rien à objecter contre ce projet, sinon qu'il n'a pas été exécuté. En effet, diront-ils sans doute, si ses avantages sont si réels, pourquoi donc les souverains de l'Europe ne l'ont-ils pas

---

[1] On the MS. is written, in Rousseau's hand : 'N.B. Prenez garde de ne faire mettre au net ceci que par quelqu'un qui soit bien intelligent, bien exact, mais qui ne se mêle pas de deviner.' As will be seen from the following page, this counsel was not scrupulously followed.

[2] Rousseau had originally written, *Il semble que ce grand homme.*

[3] Hachette reads *l'empêcheraient*. MS. and Ed. 1782, as in the text.

adopté ? pourquoi négligent-ils leur propre intérêt, si cet intérêt leur est si bien démontré ? Voit-on qu'ils rejettent d'ailleurs les moyens d'augmenter leurs revenus et leur puissance ? Si celui-ci était aussi bon pour cela qu'on le prétend, est-il croyable qu'ils en fussent moins empressés que de tous ceux qui les égarent depuis si longtemps, et qu'ils préférassent mille ressources trompeuses à un profit évident ?

Sans doute, cela est croyable ; à moins qu'on ne suppose que leur sagesse est égale à leur ambition, et qu'ils voient d'autant mieux leurs avantages qu'ils les désirent plus fortement ; au lieu que c'est la grande punition des excès de l'amour-propre de recourir toujours à des moyens qui l'abusent, et que l'ardeur même des passions est presque toujours ce qui les détourne de leur but. Distinguons donc, en politique ainsi qu'en morale, l'intérêt réel de l'intérêt apparent. Le premier se trouverait dans la paix perpétuelle ; cela est démontré dans le *Projet*. Le second se trouve dans l'état d'indépendance absolue qui soustrait les souverains à l'empire de la Loi pour les soumettre à celui de la fortune ; semblables à un pilote insensé, qui, pour faire montre d'un vain savoir et commander à ses matelots, aimerait mieux flotter entre des rochers durant la tempête que d'assujettir son vaisseau par des ancres.

Toute l'occupation des rois, ou de ceux qu'ils chargent de leurs fonctions, se rapporte à deux seuls objets : étendre leur domination au dehors, et la rendre plus absolue au dedans. Toute autre vue, ou se rapporte à l'une de ces deux, ou ne leur sert que de prétexte. Telles sont celles du *bien public*, du *bonheur des sujets*, de la *gloire de la nation* : mots à jamais proscrits du cabinet, et si lourdement employés dans les édits publics, qu'ils n'annoncent jamais que des ordres funestes, et que le peuple gémit d'avance quand ses maîtres lui parlent de leurs soins paternels.

Qu'on juge, sur ces deux maximes fondamentales, comment les princes peuvent recevoir une proposition qui choque directement l'une, et qui n'est guère plus favorable à l'autre. Car on sent bien que par la Diète européenne le Gouvernement de chaque État n'est pas moins fixé que ses limites[1] ; qu'on ne peut garantir

[1] The Edition of 1782 (du Peyrou), which is the *Editio princeps* for this treatise, reads 'que *par* ses limites.' And, so far as I have observed, all the other editions follow suit. But this reading makes nonsense; and the original Manuscript (Neuchâtel, 7859) is clear against it. It is true that Rousseau, in that MS., had originally written *par* before *ses limites* ; but it is cancelled. The explanation of the cancelled word is that, as the rough copy (also in the Neuchâtel Library) shews, he had first written the sentence as follows : 'car on sent bien que par la diète européenne chaque État n'est

les princes de la révolte des sujets sans garantir en même temps les sujets de la tyrannie des princes ; et qu'autrement l'institution ne saurait subsister. Or, je demande s'il y a dans le monde un seul souverain qui, borné ainsi pour jamais dans ses projets les plus chéris, supportât sans indignation la seule idée de se voir forcé d'être juste, non seulement avec les étrangers, mais même avec ses propres sujets.

Il est facile encore de comprendre que d'un côté la guerre et les conquêtes, et de l'autre le[1] progrès du despotisme, s'entr'aident mutuellement ; qu'on prend à discrétion, dans un peuple d'esclaves, de l'argent et des hommes pour en subjuguer d'autres ; que réciproquement la guerre fournit un prétexte aux exactions pécuniaires, et un autre non moins spécieux d'avoir toujours de grandes armées pour tenir le peuple en respect. Enfin, chacun voit assez que les princes conquérants font pour le moins autant la guerre à leurs sujets qu'à leurs ennemis, et que la condition des vainqueurs n'est pas meilleure que celle des vaincus. [2]*J'ai battu les Romains*, écrivait Annibal aux Carthaginois ; *envoyez-moi des troupes : j'ai mis l'Italie à contribution ; envoyez-moi de l'argent*. Voilà ce que signifient[2] les *Te Deum*, les feux de joie, et l'allégresse du peuple aux triomphes de ses maîtres.

Quant aux différends entre prince et prince, peut-on espérer de soumettre à un tribunal supérieur des hommes qui s'osent vanter de ne tenir leur pouvoir que de leur épée, et qui ne font mention de Dieu même que parce qu'il est au ciel ? Les souverains se soumettront-ils dans leurs querelles à des voies juridiques, que toute la rigueur des lois n'a jamais pu forcer les particuliers d'admettre dans les leurs ? Un simple gentilhomme offensé dédaigne de porter ses plaintes au tribunal des Maréchaux de France[3] ; et vous voulez qu'un roi porte les siennes à la Diète européenne ? Encore y a-t-il cette différence, que l'un pèche contre les lois et expose doublement sa vie, au lieu que l'autre n'expose guère que ses sujets ; qu'il use, en prenant les armes, d'un droit avoué de tout le genre humain, et dont il prétend n'être comptable qu'à Dieu seul.

Un prince qui met sa cause au hasard de la guerre n'ignore pas qu'il court des risques ; mais il en est moins frappé que des avantages qu'il se promet, parce qu'il craint bien moins la fortune

---

point moins fixé quant à son Gouvernement que par ses limites.' When he altered the form of the sentence, he at first mechanically retained *par*.

[1] Ed. 1782 and Hachette read *les progrès*, against the MS.

[2] Instead of this quotation, Rousseau had originally written, 'De sorte qu'on ne peut guère imaginer de joie plus imbécile que celle qu'inspirent....'

[3] For Rousseau's opinion of duelling, see his *Lettre à d'Alembert*.

qu'il n'espère de sa propre sagesse. S'il est puissant, il compte sur ses forces ; s'il est faible, il compte sur ses alliances ; quelquefois il lui est utile au dedans de purger de mauvaises humeurs, d'affaiblir des sujets indociles, d'essuyer même des revers ; et le politique habile sait tirer avantage de ses propres défaites. J'espère qu'on se souviendra que ce n'est pas moi qui raisonne ainsi, mais le sophiste de cour, qui préfère un grand territoire et peu de sujets, pauvres et soumis, à l'empire inébranlable que donnent au prince la justice et les lois sur un peuple heureux et florissant.

C'est encore par le même principe qu'il réfute en lui-même l'argument tiré de la suspension du commerce, de la dépopulation, du dérangement des finances, et des pertes réelles que cause une vaine conquête. C'est un calcul très fautif que d'évaluer toujours en argent les gains ou les pertes des souverains ; le degré de puissance qu'ils ont en vue ne se compte point par les millions qu'on possède. Le prince fait toujours circuler ses projets ; il veut commander pour s'enrichir, et s'enrichir pour commander. Il sacrifiera tour à tour l'un et l'autre pour acquérir celui des deux qui lui manque : mais ce n'est qu'afin de parvenir à les posséder enfin tous les deux ensemble qu'il les poursuit séparément ; car, pour être le maître des hommes et des choses, il faut qu'il ait à la fois l'empire et l'argent.

Ajoutons enfin, sur les grands avantages qui doivent résulter, pour le commerce, d'une paix générale et perpétuelle, qu'ils sont bien en eux-mêmes certains et incontestables, mais qu'étant communs à tous ils ne seront réels pour personne ; attendu que de tels avantages ne se sentent que par leurs différences, et que, pour augmenter sa puissance relative, on ne doit chercher que des biens exclusifs.

Sans cesse abusés par l'apparence des choses, les princes rejetteraient donc cette paix, quand ils pèseraient leurs intérêts eux-mêmes ; que sera-ce quand ils les feront peser par leurs ministres, dont les intérêts sont toujours opposés à ceux du peuple et presque toujours à ceux du prince ? Les ministres ont besoin de la guerre pour se rendre nécessaires, pour jeter le prince dans des embarras dont il ne se puisse tirer sans eux, et pour perdre l'État, s'il le faut, plutôt que leur place ; ils en ont besoin pour vexer le peuple sous prétexte des nécessités publiques ; ils en ont besoin pour placer leurs créatures, gagner sur les marchés, et faire en secret mille odieux monopoles ; ils en ont besoin pour satisfaire leurs passions, et s'expulser mutuellement ; ils en ont besoin pour s'emparer du prince, en le tirant de la cour quand il s'y forme contre eux des intrigues dangereuses. Ils perdraient toutes ces ressources par la paix perpétuelle. Et le public ne laisse pas de demander pourquoi, si ce projet est possible, ils ne l'ont pas adopté ! Il ne voit pas qu'il n'y a rien d'impossible dans ce projet, sinon qu'il soit adopté par eux. Que feront-ils donc pour s'y opposer ? Ce qu'ils ont toujours fait : ils le tourneront en ridicule.

Il ne faut pas non plus croire avec l'abbé de Saint-Pierre que, même avec la bonne volonté que les princes ni leurs ministres n'auront jamais, il fût aisé de trouver un moment favorable à l'exécution de ce système ; car il faudrait pour cela que la somme des intérêts particuliers ne l'emportât pas sur l'intérêt commun, et que chacun crût voir dans le bien de tous le plus grand bien qu'il peut espérer pour lui-même. Or, ceci demande un concours de sagesse dans tant de têtes, et un concours de rapports dans tant d'intérêts, qu'on ne doit guère espérer du hasard l'accord fortuit de toutes les circonstances nécessaires. Cependant, si cet accord n'a pas lieu, il n'y a que la force qui puisse y suppléer : et alors il n'est plus question de persuader, mais de contraindre ; et il ne faut pas[1] écrire des livres, mais lever des troupes.

Ainsi, quoique le projet fût très sage, les moyens de l'exécuter se sentaient de la simplicité de l'auteur. Il s'imaginait bonnement qu'il ne fallait qu'assembler un Congrès, y proposer ses Articles, qu'on les allait signer, et que tout serait fait. Convenons que, dans tous les projets de cet honnête homme, il voyait assez bien l'effet des choses quand elles seraient établies, mais il jugeait comme un enfant des moyens de les établir[2].

Je ne voudrais, pour prouver que le projet de la République chrétienne n'est pas chimérique, que nommer son premier auteur : car assurément Henri IV n'était pas fou, ni Sully visionnaire. L'abbé de Saint-Pierre s'autorisait de ces grands noms pour renouveler leur système. Mais quelle différence dans le temps, dans les circonstances, dans la proposition, dans la manière de la faire, et dans son auteur !

Pour en juger, jetons un coup d'œil sur la situation générale des choses au moment choisi par Henri IV pour l'exécution de son projet.

[1] Ed. 1782 and Hachette read *plus*, against the MS.
[2] One of the loose scraps of paper, which Rousseau had written about Saint-Pierre, contains the following note : C'était un homme très sage [à cela], s'il n'avait eu la folie de la raison. Il semblait ignorer que les princes, comme les autres hommes, ne se mènent que par leurs passions, et ne raisonnent que pour justifier les sottises qu'elles leur font faire (MS. Neuchâtel, 7858). Another entry is as follows: Au lieu de résoudre une objection tirée de la résistance des particuliers, il se contente souvent de montrer l'utilité publique de la chose: comme si [l'intérêt du prince et celui de l'État] le prince même pouvait suivre son intérêt contre celui des gens qui l'environnent (MS. Neuchâtel, 7830).

La grandeur de Charles-Quint, qui régnait sur une partie du monde et faisait trembler l'autre, l'avait fait aspirer à la monarchie universelle avec de grands moyens de succès et de grands talents pour les employer. Son fils, plus riche et moins puissant, suivant sans relâche un projet qu'il n'était pas capable d'exécuter, ne laissa pas de donner à l'Europe des inquiétudes continuelles; et la maison d'Autriche avait pris un tel ascendant sur les autres Puissances, que nul prince ne régnait en sûreté s'il n'était bien avec elle. Philippe III, moins habile encore que son père, hérita de toutes ses prétentions. L'effroi de la puissance espagnole tenait encore l'Europe en respect, et l'Espagne continuait à dominer plutôt par l'habitude de commander que par le pouvoir de se faire obéir. En effet, la révolte des Pays-Bas, les armements contre l'Angleterre, les guerres civiles de France, avaient épuisé les forces d'Espagne et les trésors des Indes; la maison d'Autriche, partagée en deux branches, n'agissait plus avec le même concert; et, quoique l'empereur s'efforçât de maintenir ou recouvrer en Allemagne l'autorité de Charles-Quint, il ne faisait qu'aliéner les princes et fomenter des ligues qui ne tardèrent pas d'éclore et faillirent à le détrôner. Ainsi se préparait de loin la décadence de la maison d'Autriche et le rétablissement de la liberté commune. Cependant nul n'osait le premier hasarder de secouer le joug, et s'exposer seul à la guerre; l'exemple de Henri IV même, qui s'en était tiré si mal, ôtait le courage à tous les autres. D'ailleurs, si l'on excepte le duc de Savoie, trop faible et trop subjugué pour rien entreprendre, il n'y avait pas parmi tant de souverains un seul homme de tête en état de former et soutenir une entreprise; chacun attendait du temps et des circonstances le moment de briser ses fers. Voilà quel était en gros l'état des choses, quand Henri forma le plan de la République chrétienne, et se prépara à l'exécuter. Projet bien grand, bien admirable en lui-même, et dont je ne veux pas ternir l'honneur; mais qui, ayant pour raison secrète l'espoir d'abaisser un ennemi redoutable, recevait de ce pressant motif une activité qu'il eût difficilement tirée de la seule utilité commune.

Voyons maintenant quels moyens ce grand homme avait employés à préparer une si haute entreprise. Je compterais volontiers pour le premier d'en avoir bien vu toutes les difficultés; de telle sorte qu'ayant formé ce projet dès son enfance il le médita toute sa vie, et réserva l'exécution pour sa vieillesse: conduite qui prouve premièrement ce désir ardent et soutenu qui seul, dans les choses difficiles, peut vaincre les grands obstacles; et, de plus, cette sagesse patiente et réfléchie qui s'aplanit les routes de longue main à force de prévoyance et de préparation. Car il y a bien de la différence entre les entreprises nécessaires, dans lesquelles la prudence même veut qu'on donne quelque chose au hasard, et celles que le succès seul peut justifier, parce qu'ayant pu se passer de les faire on n'a dû les tenter qu'à coup sûr. Le profond secret qu'il garda toute sa vie, jusqu'au moment de l'exécution, était encore aussi essentiel que difficile dans une si grande affaire, où le concours de tant de gens était nécessaire, et que tant de gens avaient intérêt de traverser. Il paraît que, quoiqu'il eût mis la plus grande partie de l'Europe dans son parti, et qu'il fût ligué avec les plus puissants potentats, il n'eut jamais qu'un seul confident qui connut toute l'étendue de son plan; et, par un bonheur que le ciel n'accorda qu'au meilleur des rois, ce confident fut un ministre intègre. Mais sans que rien transpirât de ces[1] grands desseins, tout marchait en silence vers leur exécution. Deux fois Sully était allé à Londres : la partie était liée avec le roi Jacques, et le roi de Suède était engagé de son côté ; la ligue était conclue avec les protestants d'Allemagne; on était même sûr des princes d'Italie ; et tous concouraient au grand but sans pouvoir dire quel il était, comme les ouvriers qui travaillent séparément aux pièces d'une nouvelle machine dont ils ignorent la forme et l'usage. Qu'est-ce donc qui favorisait ce mouvement général? Était-ce la paix perpétuelle, que nul ne prévoyait et dont peu se seraient souciés? Était-ce l'intérêt public, qui n'est jamais celui de personne? L'abbé de Saint-Pierre eût pu l'espérer. Mais réellement chacun ne travaillait que dans la vue de son intérêt particulier, que Henri avait eu le secret de leur montrer à tous sous une face très attrayante. Le roi d'Angleterre avait à se délivrer des continuelles conspirations des catholiques de son royaume, toutes fomentées par l'Espagne. Il trouvait de plus un grand avantage à l'affranchissement des Provinces Unies, qui lui coûtaient beaucoup à soutenir, et le mettaient chaque jour à la veille d'une guerre qu'il redoutait, ou à laquelle il aimait mieux contribuer une fois avec tous les autres, afin de s'en délivrer pour toujours. Le roi de Suède voulait s'assurer de la Poméranie, et mettre un pied dans l'Allemagne. L'électeur palatin, alors protestant et chef de la confession d'Augsbourg, avait des vues sur la Bohême, et entrait dans toutes celles du roi d'Angleterre. Les princes d'Allemagne avaient à réprimer les usurpations de la maison d'Autriche. Le duc de Savoie obtenait Milan et la couronne de Lombardie, qu'il désirait avec ardeur. Le pape même, fatigué de la tyrannie

---

[1] Hachette reads *ses*. MS. and Ed. 1782, as in the text.

espagnole, était de la partie, au moyen du royaume de Naples qu'on lui avait promis. Les Hollandais, mieux payés que tous les autres, gagnaient l'assurance de leur liberté. Enfin, outre l'intérêt commun d'abaisser une Puissance orgueilleuse qui voulait dominer partout, chacun en avait un particulier, très vif, très sensible, et qui n'était point balancé par la crainte de substituer un tyran à l'autre, puisqu'il était convenu que les conquêtes seraient partagées entre tous les alliés, excepté la France et l'Angleterre, qui ne pouvaient rien garder pour elles. C'en était assez pour calmer les plus inquiets sur l'ambition de Henri IV. Mais ce sage prince n'ignorait pas qu'en ne se réservant rien par ce traité il y gagnait pourtant plus qu'aucun autre. Car, sans rien ajouter à son patrimoine, il lui suffisait de diviser celui du seul plus puissant que lui, pour devenir le plus puissant lui-même ; et l'on voit très clairement qu'en prenant toutes les précautions qui pouvaient assurer le succès de l'entreprise, il ne négligeait pas celles qui devaient[1] lui donner la primauté dans le Corps qu'il voulait instituer.

De plus : ses apprêts ne se bornaient point à former au dehors des ligues redoutables, ni à contracter alliance avec ses voisins et ceux de son ennemi. En intéressant tant de peuples à l'abaissement du premier potentat de l'Europe, il n'oubliait pas de se mettre en état par lui-même de le devenir à son tour. Il employa quinze ans de paix à faire des préparatifs dignes de l'entreprise qu'il méditait. Il remplit d'argent ses coffres, ses arsenaux d'artillerie, d'armes, de munitions ; il ménagea de loin des ressources pour les besoins imprévus. Mais il fit plus que tout cela sans doute, en gouvernant sagement ses peuples, en déracinant insensiblement toutes les semences de divisions, et en mettant un si bon ordre à ses finances qu'elles pussent fournir à tout sans fouler ses sujets. De sorte que, tranquille au dedans et redoutable au dehors, il se vit en état d'armer et d'entretenir soixante mille hommes et vingt vaisseaux de guerre, de quitter son royaume sans y laisser la moindre source de désordre, et de faire la guerre durant six ans sans toucher à ses revenus ordinaires, ni mettre un sou de nouvelles impositions.

À tant de préparatifs ajoutez, pour la conduite de l'entreprise, le même zèle et la même prudence qui l'avaient formée, tant de la part de son ministre que de la sienne. Enfin, à la tête des expéditions militaires, un capitaine tel que lui, tandis que son adversaire n'en avait plus à lui opposer : et vous jugerez si rien

[1] MS. has *celles qui devait*; it is possible that this is a slip for *celle qui devait*. Ed. 1782, as in the text.

de ce qui peut annoncer un heureux succès manquait à l'espoir du sien. Sans avoir pénétré ses vues, l'Europe attentive à ses immenses préparatifs en attendait l'effet avec une sorte de frayeur. Un léger prétexte allait commencer cette grande révolution ; une guerre, qui devait être la dernière, préparait une paix immortelle, quand un événement, [1]dont l'horrible mystère doit augmenter l'effroi[1], vint bannir à jamais le dernier espoir du monde. Le même coup qui trancha les jours de ce bon roi replongea l'Europe dans d'éternelles guerres qu'elle ne doit plus espérer de voir finir. Quoi qu'il en soit, voilà les moyens que Henri IV avait rassemblés pour former le même établissement que l'abbé de Saint-Pierre prétendait faire avec un livre.

Qu'on ne dise donc point que, si son système n'a pas été adopté, c'est qu'il n'était pas bon ; qu'on dise au contraire qu'il était trop bon pour être adopté. Car le mal et les abus, dont tant de gens profitent, s'introduisent d'eux-mêmes ; mais ce qui est utile au public ne s'introduit guère que par la force, attendu que les intérêts particuliers y sont presque toujours opposés. Sans doute la paix perpétuelle est à présent un projet bien absurde ; mais qu'on nous rende un Henri IV et un Sully, la paix perpétuelle redeviendra un projet raisonnable. Ou plutôt, admirons un si beau plan, mais consolons-nous de ne pas le voir exécuter ; car cela ne peut se faire que par des moyens violents et redoutables à l'humanité.

On ne voit point de ligues fédératives s'établir autrement que par des révolutions : et, sur ce principe, qui de nous oserait dire si cette ligue européenne est à désirer, ou à craindre ? Elle ferait peut-être plus de mal tout d'un coup qu'elle n'en préviendrait pour des siècles[2].

---

[1] [dont il faut laisser le mystère infernal dans les ténèbres].

[2] Mercier tells the following anecdote:—Sortant de l'Académie française en 1775, si je ne me trompe, j'allai le trouver et je lui dis: 'On vient de parler de vous dans la séance publique.' 'Qui ? d'Alembert ? oh ! quelque méchanceté, pour servir son Voltaire.' 'Non; il a dit que vous étiez un homme éloquent, mais qu'en voulant faire revivre le projet de Paix perpétuelle de Saint-Pierre, malgré tout l'éclat de votre style, vous ne séduiriez pas les souverains.' 'Pas moi; mais ils y seront forcés un jour; car peut-être les hommes se lasseront-ils de verser leur sang pour leurs menus plaisirs.' 'Mais, au défaut des souverains, les nations ne se battraient-elles pas ?' 'Beaucoup moins, je l'espère: les nations ne se battent que pour un grand et véritable intérêt; tandis que les princes agissent par orgueil, ont autour d'eux des gens qui aiment la guerre et abusent toujours du pouvoir qui leur est confié.' Puis il ajouta ce mot piquant: 'Au reste, les auteurs se battront encore que les rois ne se battront plus.' Mercier, *J.-J. Rousseau*, Vol. II. pp. 210—1.

POLYSYNODIE DE L'ABBÉ DE SAINT-PIERRE

[Written 1756; published 1782. MS. Neuchâtel, 7829.]

CHAPITRE I.

Nécessité, dans la monarchie, d'une forme de gouvernement subordonnée au prince.

Si les princes regardaient les fonctions du Gouvernement comme des devoirs indispensables, les plus capables s'en trouveraient les plus surchargés ; leurs travaux, comparés à leurs forces, leur paraîtraient toujours excessifs ; on les verrait[1] aussi ardents à resserrer leurs États ou leurs droits qu'ils sont avides d'étendre les uns et les autres ; et le poids de la couronne écraserait bientôt la plus forte tête qui voudrait sérieusement la porter. Mais, loin d'envisager leur pouvoir par ce qu'il a de pénible et d'obligatoire, ils n'y voient que le plaisir de commander ; et, comme le peuple n'est à leurs yeux que l'instrument de leurs fantaisies, plus ils ont de fantaisies à contenter, plus le besoin d'usurper augmente ; et plus ils sont bornés et petits d'entendement, plus ils veulent être grands et puissants en autorité.

Cependant, le plus absolu despotisme exige encore un travail pour se soutenir. Quelques maximes qu'il établisse à son avantage, il faut toujours qu'il les couvre d'un leurre d'utilité publique ; qu'employant la force des peuples contre eux-mêmes il les empêche de la réunir contre lui ; qu'il étouffe continuellement la voix de la nature et le cri de la liberté, toujours prêt à sortir de l'extrême oppression. Enfin, quand le peuple ne serait qu'un vil troupeau sans raison, encore faudrait-il des soins pour le conduire ; et le prince qui ne songe point à rendre heureux ses sujets n'oublie pas au moins, s'il n'est insensé, de conserver son patrimoine.

Qu'a-t-il donc à faire pour concilier l'indolence avec l'ambition,

---

[1] Ed. 1782 (12mo) and Hachette read *et on les verrait*. MS. and Ed. 1782 (4º), as in the text.

la puissance avec les plaisirs, et l'empire des dieux avec la vie animale ? Choisir pour soi les vains honneurs, l'oisiveté, et remettre à d'autres les fonctions pénibles du Gouvernement, en se réservant tout au plus de chasser ou changer ceux qui s'en acquittent trop mal ou trop bien. Par cette méthode, le dernier des hommes tiendra paisiblement et commodément le sceptre de l'univers ; plongé dans d'insipides voluptés, il promènera, s'il veut, de fête en fête son ignorance et son ennui. Cependant on le traitera de *conquérant*, d'*invincible*, de *roi des rois*, d'*empereur auguste*, de *monarque du monde* et de *majesté sacrée*. Oublié sur le trône, nul aux yeux de ses voisins et même à ceux de ses sujets, encensé de tous sans être obéi de personne, faible instrument de la tyrannie des courtisans et de l'esclavage du peuple, on lui dira qu'il règne, et il croira régner. Voilà le tableau général du gouvernement de toute monarchie trop étendue. Qui veut soutenir le monde, et n'a pas les épaules d'Hercule, doit s'attendre d'être écrasé.

Le souverain d'un grand empire n'est guère au fond que le ministre de ses ministres, ou le représentant de ceux qui gouvernent sous lui. Ils sont obéis en son nom ; et quand il croit leur faire exécuter sa volonté, c'est lui qui, sans le savoir, exécute la leur. Cela ne saurait être autrement ; car, comme il ne peut voir que par leurs yeux, il faut nécessairement qu'il les laisse agir par ses mains. Forcé d'abandonner à d'autres ce qu'on appelle le détail[1], et que j'appellerais, moi, l'essentiel du gouvernement, il se réserve les grandes affaires, le verbiage des ambassadeurs, les tracasseries de ses favoris, et tout au plus le choix de ses maîtres ; car il en faut avoir malgré soi, sitôt qu'on a tant d'esclaves. Que lui importe, au reste, une bonne ou une mauvaise administration ? Comment son bonheur serait-il troublé[2] par la misère du peuple, qu'il ne peut voir ? par ses plaintes, qu'il ne peut entendre ? et par les désordres publics, dont il ne saura jamais rien[2] ? Il en est

---

[1] Ce qui importe aux citoyens, c'est d'être gouvernés justement et paisiblement. Au surplus, que l'État soit grand, puissant et florissant, c'est l'affaire particulière du prince ; et les sujets n'y ont aucun intérêt. Le monarque doit donc premièrement s'occuper du détail, en quoi consiste la liberté civile, la sûreté du peuple, et même la sienne à bien des égards. Après cela, s'il lui reste du temps à perdre, il peut le donner à toutes ces grandes affaires qui n'intéressent personne, qui ne naissent jamais que des vices du Gouvernement, qui par conséquent ne sont rien pour un peuple heureux, et sont peu de chose pour un roi sage*. [Note de J.-J. R.]

* Originally 'qui par conséquent sont des riens...et peu de chose' etc.

[2] [par la misère du peuple et par les désordres publics etc.]

de la gloire des princes comme des trésors de cet insensé, propriétaire en idée de tous les vaisseaux qui arrivaient au port : l'opinion de jouir de tout l'empêchait de rien désirer; et il n'était pas moins heureux des richesses qu'il n'avait point, que s'il les eût possédées.

Que ferait de mieux le plus juste prince avec les meilleures intentions, sitôt qu'il entreprend un travail que la nature a mis au-dessus de ses forces ? Il est homme, et se charge des fonctions d'un Dieu : comment peut-il espérer de les remplir ? Le sage, s'il en peut être sur le trône, renonce à l'empire, ou le partage. Il consulte ses forces ; il mesure sur elles les fonctions qu'il veut remplir ; et, pour être un roi vraiment grand, il ne se charge point d'un grand royaume. Mais ce que ferait le sage a peu de rapport à ce que feront les princes. Ce qu'ils feront toujours, cherchons au moins comment ils peuvent le faire le moins mal qu'il soit possible.

Avant que d'entrer en matière, il est bon d'observer que si, par miracle[1], quelque grande âme peut suffire à la pénible charge de la royauté, l'ordre héréditaire établi dans les successions, et l'extravagante éducation des héritiers du trône, fourniront toujours cent imbéciles pour un vrai roi ; qu'il y aura des minorités, des maladies, des temps de délire et de passion[2], qui ne laisseront souvent à la tête de l'État qu'un simulacre de prince. Il faut cependant que les affaires se fassent. Chez tous les peuples qui ont un roi, il est donc absolument nécessaire d'établir une forme de Gouvernement qui se puisse passer du roi ; et, dès qu'il est posé qu'un souverain peut rarement gouverner par lui-même, il ne s'agit plus que de savoir comment il peut gouverner par autrui. C'est à résoudre cette question qu'est destiné le *Discours sur la Polysynodie*[3].

CHAPITRE II.

Trois formes spécifiques de gouvernement subordonné.

Un monarque, dit l'abbé de Saint-Pierre, peut n'écouter qu'un seul homme dans toutes ses affaires, et lui confier toute son autorité; comme autrefois les rois de France la donnaient aux maires du palais, et comme les princes orientaux la confient encore aujourd'hui à celui qu'on nomme grand vizir en Turquie. Pour abréger, j'appellerai *vizirat* cette sorte de ministère.

[1] [par extraordinaire.]
[2] Ed. 1801 and Hachette read *passions*. MS. and Ed. 1782, *passion*.
[3] The title of Saint-Pierre's work (1719).

Ce monarque peut aussi partager son autorité entre deux ou plusieurs hommes qu'il écoute, chacun séparément, sur la sorte d'affaire qui leur est commise, à peu près comme faisait Louis XIV avec Colbert et Louvois. C'est cette forme que je nommerai dans la suite *demi-vizirat*.

Enfin, ce monarque peut faire discuter dans des assemblées les affaires du Gouvernement, et former à cet effet autant de Conseils qu'il y a de genres d'affaires à traiter. Cette forme de ministère, que l'abbé de Saint-Pierre appelle pluralité des conseils ou *polysynodie*, est à peu près, selon lui, celle que le régent, duc d'Orléans, avait établie sous son administration; et, ce qui lui donne un plus grand poids encore, c'était aussi celle qu'avait adoptée l'élève du vertueux Fénélon[1].

Pour choisir entre ces trois formes, et juger de celle qui mérite la préférence, il ne suffit pas de les considérer en gros et par la première face qu'elles présentent; il ne faut pas non plus opposer les abus de l'une à la perfection de l'autre, ni s'arrêter seulement à certains moments passagers de désordre ou d'éclat; mais les supposer toutes aussi parfaites qu'elles peuvent l'être dans leur durée, et chercher en cet état leurs rapports et leurs différences. Voilà de quelle manière on peut en faire un parallèle exact.

CHAPITRE III.

Rapport de ces formes à celles du Gouvernement suprême.

Les maximes élémentaires de la politique peuvent déjà trouver ici leur application. Car le vizirat, le demi-vizirat et la polysynodie se rapportent manifestement, dans l'économie du Gouvernement subalterne, aux trois formes spécifiques du Gouvernement suprême; et plusieurs des principes qui conviennent à l'administration souveraine peuvent aisément s'appliquer au ministère. Ainsi, le vizirat doit avoir généralement plus de vigueur et de célérité, le demi-vizirat plus d'exactitude et de soin, et la polysynodie plus de justice et de constance. Il est

---

[1] *i.e.* le duc de Bourgoigne. See Saint-Simon, *Mémoires*, Vol. x. pp. 210—2 (ed. Paris, 1829). Also *Écrits inédits de Saint-Simon* (ed. Faugère): 'Il était ami des États Généraux, des Conseils, des remontrances, des examens et de tout ce qu'il y a de meilleur, quoique de moins savoureux.' Vol. ii. p. 419 (*Collections sur feu M. le Dauphin*). Also Saint-Pierre, *Pol.* p. 106.

sûr encore que, comme la démocratie tend naturellement à l'aristocratie, et l'aristocratie à la monarchie, de même la polysynodie tend au demi-vizirat, et le demi-vizirat au vizirat. Ce progrès de la force publique vers le relâchement, qui oblige de renforcer les ressorts, se retarde ou s'accélère à proportion que toutes les parties de l'État sont bien ou mal constituées ; et, comme on ne parvient au despotisme et au vizirat que quand tous les autres ressorts sont usés, c'est, à mon avis, un projet mal conçu de prétendre abandonner cette forme pour en prendre une des précédentes ; car nulle autre ne peut plus suffire à tout un peuple qui a pu supporter celle-là. Mais, sans vouloir quitter l'une pour l'autre, il est cependant utile de connaître celle des trois qui vaut le mieux. Nous venons de voir que, par une analogie assez naturelle, la polysynodie mérite déjà la préférence ; il reste à rechercher si l'examen des choses mêmes pourra la lui confirmer. Mais, avant que d'entrer dans cet examen, commençons par une idée plus précise de la forme que, selon notre auteur, doit avoir la polysynodie.

CHAPITRE IV.

Partage et départements des conseils.

Le Gouvernement d'un grand État, tel que la France, renferme en soi huit objets principaux qui doivent former autant de départements, et par conséquent avoir chacun leur Conseil particulier. Ces huit parties sont la justice, la police, les finances, le commerce, la marine, la guerre, les affaires étrangères, et celles de la religion. Il doit y avoir encore un neuvième Conseil, qui, formant la liaison de tous les autres, unisse toutes les parties du Gouvernement ; où les grandes affaires, traitées et discutées en dernier ressort, n'attendent plus que de la volonté du prince leur entière décision ; et qui, pensant et travaillant au besoin pour lui, supplée à son défaut, lorsque les maladies, la minorité, la vieillesse, ou l'aversion du travail, empêchent le roi de faire ses fonctions. Ainsi ce Conseil général doit toujours être sur pied, ou pour la nécessité présente, ou par précaution pour le besoin à venir.

CHAPITRE V.

Manière de les composer.

À l'égard de la manière de composer ces Conseils, la plus avantageuse qu'on y puisse employer paraît être la méthode du scrutin. Car, par toute autre voie, il est évident que la synodie ne sera qu'apparente; que, les Conseils n'étant remplis que des créatures des favoris, il n'y aura point de liberté réelle dans les suffrages; et qu'on n'aura, sous d'autres noms, qu'un véritable vizirat ou demi-vizirat. Je ne m'étendrai point ici sur la méthode et les avantages du scrutin; comme il fait un des points capitaux du système de gouvernement de l'abbé de Saint-Pierre, j'en traite ailleurs plus au long[1]. Je me contenterai de remarquer que, quelque forme de ministère qu'on admette, il n'y a point d'autre méthode par laquelle on puisse être assuré de donner toujours la préférence au plus vrai mérite : raison qui montre plutôt l'avantage, que la facilité, de faire adopter le scrutin dans les cours des rois.

Cette première précaution en suppose d'autres qui la rendent utile. Car il le serait peu de choisir au scrutin entre des sujets qu'on ne connaîtrait pas; et l'on ne saurait connaître la capacité de ceux qu'on n'a point vus[2] travailler dans le genre auquel on les destine. Si donc il faut des grades dans le militaire, depuis l'enseigne jusqu'au maréchal de France, pour former les jeunes officiers et les rendre capables des fonctions qu'ils doivent remplir un jour, n'est-il pas plus important encore d'établir des grades semblables dans l'administration civile, depuis les commis jusqu'aux présidents des Conseils ? Faut-il moins de temps et d'expérience, pour apprendre à conduire un peuple que pour commander une armée ? Les connaissances de l'homme d'État sont-elles plus faciles à acquérir que celles de l'homme de guerre ? ou le bon ordre est-il moins nécessaire dans l'économie politique que dans la discipline militaire ? [3]Les grades scrupuleusement observés ont été l'école de tant de grands hommes qu'a produits la République de Venise; et pourquoi ne commencerait-on pas d'aussi loin à Paris, pour servir le prince, qu'à Venise, pour servir l'État[3] ?

---

[1] Rousseau partially carries out this design in his *Jugement* (pp. 415—6).
[2] MS. and Ed. 1782 read *vu*, by an oversight.
[3] This sentence is added, as an afterthought, in the margin. It is not in the *brouillon*, which forms part of MS. 7829.

Je n'ignore pas que l'intérêt des Vizirs s'oppose à cette nouvelle police : je sais bien qu'ils ne veulent point être assujettis à des formes qui gênent leur despotisme ; qu'ils ne veulent employer que des créatures qui leur soient entièrement dévouées, et qu'ils puissent d'un mot replonger dans la poussière d'où ils les tirent. Un homme de naissance, de son côté, qui n'a pour cette foule de valets que le mépris qu'ils méritent, dédaigne d'entrer en concurrence avec eux dans la même carrière ; et le Gouvernement de l'État est toujours prêt à devenir la proie du rebut de ses citoyens. Aussi n'est-ce point sous le vizirat, mais sous la seule polysynodie, qu'on peut espérer d'établir dans l'administration civile des grades honnêtes, qui ne supposent pas la bassesse, mais le mérite, et qui puissent rapprocher la noblesse des affaires, dont on affecte de l'éloigner, et qu'elle affecte de mépriser à son tour.

CHAPITRE VI.

Circulation des départements.

De l'établissement des grades s'ensuit la nécessité de faire circuler les départements entre les membres de chaque Conseil, et même d'un Conseil à l'autre, afin que chaque membre, éclairé successivement sur toutes les parties du Gouvernement, devienne un jour capable d'opiner dans le Conseil général, et de participer à la grande administration.

Cette vue de faire circuler les départements est due au Régent, qui l'établit dans le Conseil des finances ; et si l'autorité d'un homme qui connaissait si bien les ressorts du Gouvernement ne suffit pas pour la faire adopter, on ne peut disconvenir au moins des avantages sensibles qui naîtraient de cette méthode. Sans doute, il peut y avoir des cas où cette circulation paraîtrait peu utile, ou difficile à établir, dans la polysynodie ; mais elle n'y est jamais impossible, et jamais praticable dans le vizirat ni dans le demi-vizirat. Or, il est important, par beaucoup de très fortes raisons, d'établir une forme d'administration où cette circulation puisse avoir lieu.

1. Premièrement, pour prévenir les malversations des commis qui, changeant de bureaux avec leurs maîtres, n'auront pas le temps de s'arranger pour leurs friponneries aussi commodément qu'ils le font aujourd'hui. Ajoutez qu'étant, pour ainsi dire, à la discrétion de leurs successeurs, ils seront plus réservés, en changeant

de département, à laisser les affaires de celui qu'ils quittent dans un état qui pourrait les perdre, si par hasard leur successeur se trouvait honnête homme, ou leur ennemi. 2. En second lieu, pour obliger les conseillers même à mieux veiller sur leur conduite ou sur celle de leurs commis, de peur d'être taxés de négligence et de pis encore, quand leur gestion changera d'objet sans cesse, et chaque fois sera connue de leur successeur. 3. Pour exciter entre les membres d'un même corps une émulation louable, à qui passera son prédécesseur dans le même travail. 4. Pour corriger par ces fréquents changements les abus que les erreurs, les préjugés et les passions de chaque sujet auront introduits dans son administration. Car, parmi tant de caractères différents qui régiront successivement la même partie, leurs fautes se corrigeront mutuellement, et tout ira plus constamment à l'objet commun. 5. Pour donner à chaque membre d'un Conseil des connaissances plus nettes et plus étendues des affaires et de leurs divers rapports : en sorte qu'ayant manié les autres parties il voie distinctement ce que la sienne est au tout ; qu'il ne se croie pas toujours le plus important personnage de l'État, et ne nuise pas au bien général pour mieux faire celui de son département. 6. Pour que tous les avis soient mieux portés en connaissance de cause ; que chacun entende toutes les matières sur lesquelles il doit opiner ; et qu'une plus grande uniformité de lumières mette plus de concorde et de raison dans les délibérations communes. 7. Pour exercer l'esprit et les talents des ministres : car, portés à se reposer et s'appesantir sur un même travail, ils ne s'en font enfin qu'une routine qui resserre et circonscrit pour ainsi dire le génie par l'habitude. Or, l'attention est à l'esprit ce que l'exercice est au corps ; c'est elle qui lui donne de la vigueur, de l'adresse, et qui le rend propre à supporter le travail. Ainsi l'on peut dire que chaque conseiller d'État, en revenant après quelques années de circulation à l'exercice de son premier département, s'en trouvera réellement plus capable que s'il n'en eût point du tout changé. Je ne nie pas que, s'il fût demeuré dans le même, il n'eût acquis plus de facilité à expédier les affaires qui en dépendent. Mais je dis qu'elles eussent été moins bien faites, parce qu'il eût eu des vues plus bornées, et qu'il n'eût pas acquis une connaissance aussi exacte des rapports qu'ont ces affaires avec celles des autres départements : de sorte qu'il ne perd, d'un côté, dans la circulation que pour gagner, d'un autre, beaucoup davantage. 8. Enfin, pour ménager plus d'égalité dans le pouvoir, plus d'indépendance entre les conseillers d'État, et par conséquent plus de liberté dans les suffrages. Autrement, dans un Conseil nombreux en apparence, on n'aurait réellement que deux ou trois opinants, auxquels tous les autres seraient assujettis ; [1]à peu près comme ceux qu'on appelait autrefois à Rome *senatores pedarii*, qui pour l'ordinaire regardaient moins à l'avis qu'à l'auteur[1] : inconvénient d'autant plus dangereux, que ce n'est jamais en faveur du meilleur parti qu'on a besoin de gêner les voix.

On pourrait pousser encore plus loin cette circulation des départements, en l'étendant jusqu'à la présidence même. Car, s'il était de l'avantage de la République romaine que les Consuls redevinssent au bout de l'an simples sénateurs, en attendant un nouveau consulat, pourquoi ne serait-il pas de l'avantage du royaume que les Présidents redevinssent, après deux ou trois ans, simples conseillers, en attendant une nouvelle présidence ? Ne serait-ce pas, pour ainsi dire, proposer un prix tous les trois ans à ceux de la compagnie qui, durant cet intervalle, se distingueraient dans leur corps ? ne serait-ce pas un nouveau ressort très propre à entretenir dans une continuelle activité le mouvement de la machine publique ? et le vrai secret d'animer le travail commun n'est-il pas d'y proportionner toujours le salaire ?

CHAPITRE VII.

Autres avantages de cette circulation.

Je n'entrerai point dans le détail des avantages de la circulation portée à ce dernier degré. Chacun doit voir que les déplacements, devenus nécessaires par la décrépitude ou l'affaiblissement des Présidents, se feront ainsi sans dureté et sans effort[2] ; que les ex-présidents des Conseils particuliers auront encore un objet d'élévation, qui sera de siéger dans le Conseil général, et les membres de ce Conseil celui d'y pouvoir présider à leur tour ; que cette alternative de subordination et d'autorité rendra l'une et l'autre en même temps plus parfaite et plus douce ; que cette circulation de la présidence est le plus sûr moyen d'empêcher la polysynodie de pouvoir dégénérer en vizirat ; et qu'en général, la circulation

---

[1] This clause added, as an afterthought, in the margin. It is not in the *brouillon*.

[2] Hachette reads *efforts*. MS. and Ed. 1782, as in the text. After *effort* Rousseau had originally inserted the quotation : *est enim sua, sicut corpori, sic et menti senectus*, and then cancelled it. It is not in the *brouillon*.

répartissant avec plus d'égalité les [1] lumières et le pouvoir du ministère entre plusieurs membres, l'autorité royale domine plus aisément sur chacun d'eux. Tout cela doit sauter aux yeux d'un lecteur intelligent ; et s'il fallait tout dire, il ne faudrait rien abréger.

CHAPITRE VIII.

QUE LA POLYSYNODIE EST L'ADMINISTRATION EN SOUS-ORDRE LA PLUS NATURELLE.

Je m'arrête ici par la même raison sur la forme de la polysynodie, après avoir établi les principes généraux sur lesquels on la doit ordonner pour la rendre utile et durable. S'il s'y présente d'abord quelque embarras, c'est qu'il est toujours difficile de maintenir longtemps ensemble deux Gouvernements aussi différents dans leurs maximes que le monarchique et le républicain, quoique au fond cette union produisît peut-être un tout parfait, et le chef-d'œuvre de la politique. Il faut donc bien distinguer la forme apparente, qui règne partout, de la forme réelle, dont il est ici question : car on peut dire en un sens que la polysynodie est la première et la plus naturelle de toutes les administrations en sous-ordre, même dans la monarchie.

En effet, comme les premières lois nationales furent faites par la nation assemblée en corps, de même les premières délibérations du prince furent faites avec les principaux de la nation assemblés en Conseil. Le prince a des conseillers avant que d'avoir des vizirs ; il trouve les uns, et fait les autres. L'ordre le plus élevé de l'État en forme naturellement le synode, ou Conseil général. Quand le monarque est élu, il n'a qu'à présider ; et tout est fait. Mais quand il faut choisir un ministre, ou des favoris, on commence à introduire une forme arbitraire, où la brigue et l'inclination naturelle ont bien plus de part que la raison, ni la voix du peuple. Il n'est pas moins simple que, dans autant d'affaires de différentes natures qu'en offre le Gouvernement, le Parlement national se divise en divers comités, toujours sous la présidence du roi, qui leur assigne à chacun les matières sur lesquelles ils doivent délibérer. Et voilà les Conseils particuliers nés du Conseil général, dont ils sont les membres naturels, et la synodie changée en polysynodie : forme que je ne dis pas être, en cet état, la meilleure, mais bien la première et la plus naturelle.

---

[1] Hachette reads *des*. MS. and Ed. 1782, as in the text.

CHAPITRE IX.

Et la plus utile.

Considérons maintenant la droite fin du Gouvernement et les obstacles qui l'en éloignent. Cette fin est sans contredit le plus grand intérêt de l'État et du roi; ces obstacles sont, [1]outre le défaut de lumières[1], l'intérêt particulier des administrateurs. D'où il suit que, plus ces intérêts particuliers trouvent de gêne et d'opposition, moins ils balancent l'intérêt public; de sorte que, s'ils pouvaient se heurter et se détruire mutuellement, quelque vifs qu'on les supposât, ils deviendraient nuls dans la délibération, et l'intérêt public serait seul écouté. Quel moyen plus sûr peut-on donc avoir d'anéantir tous ces intérêts particuliers que de les opposer entre eux par la multiplication des opinants? Ce qui fait les intérêts particuliers, c'est qu'ils ne s'accordent point; car s'ils s'accordaient, ce ne serait plus un intérêt particulier, mais commun. Or, en détruisant tous ces intérêts l'un par l'autre, reste l'intérêt public, qui doit gagner dans la délibération tout ce que perdent les intérêts particuliers.

Quand un Vizir opine sans témoins devant son maître, qu'est-ce qui gêne alors son intérêt personnel? A-t-il besoin de beaucoup d'adresse pour en imposer à un homme aussi borné que doivent l'être ordinairement les rois, circonscrits [2] par tout ce qui les environne dans un si petit cercle de lumières? Sur des exposés falsifiés, sur des prétextes spécieux, sur des raisonnements sophistiques, qui l'empêche de déterminer le prince, avec ces grands mots d'*honneur de la couronne* et[3] de *bien de l'État*, aux entreprises les plus funestes, quand elles lui sont personnellement avantageuses? Certes, c'est grand hasard si deux intérêts particuliers, aussi actifs que celui du Vizir et celui du prince, laissent quelque influence à l'intérêt public dans les délibérations du cabinet.

Je sais bien que les Conseillers de l'État seront des hommes, comme les Vizirs; je ne doute pas qu'ils n'aient souvent, ainsi

---

[1] This clause is an afterthought, written between the lines. It is not in the *brouillon*.

[2] Originally *resserrés*. The whole clause, *circonscrits...lumières*, is wanting in the *brouillon*.

[3] d'*honneur de la couronne* et, an afterthought, written between the lines. It is not in the *brouillon*, which has *ce grand mot*.

qu'eux, des intérêts particuliers opposés à ceux de la nation, et qu'ils ne préférassent volontiers les premiers aux autres en opinant. Mais, dans une assemblée dont tous les membres sont clairvoyants et n'ont pas les mêmes intérêts, chacun entreprendrait vainement d'amener les autres à ce qui lui convient exclusivement : sans persuader personne, il ne ferait que se rendre suspect de corruption et d'infidélité. Il aura beau vouloir manquer à son devoir, il n'osera le tenter, ou le tentera vainement, au milieu de tant d'observateurs. Il fera donc de nécessité vertu, en sacrifiant publiquement[1] son intérêt particulier au bien de la patrie; et, soit réalité, soit hypocrisie, l'effet sera le même en cette occasion pour le bien de la société. C'est qu'alors un intérêt particulier très fort, qui est celui de sa réputation, concourt avec l'intérêt public. Au lieu qu'un Vizir qui sait, à la faveur des ténèbres du cabinet, dérober à tous les yeux le secret de l'État, se flatte toujours qu'on ne pourra distinguer ce qu'il fait en apparence[2] pour l'intérêt public de ce qu'il fait réellement pour le sien ; et comme, après tout, ce Vizir ne dépend que de son maître, qu'il trompe aisément, il s'embarrasse fort peu des murmures de tout le reste.

CHAPITRE X.

Autres avantages.

De ce premier avantage on en voit découler une foule d'autres qui ne peuvent avoir lieu sans lui. Premièrement, les résolutions de l'État seront moins souvent fondées sur des erreurs de fait; parce qu'il ne sera pas aussi aisé à ceux qui feront le rapport des faits de les déguiser devant une assemblée éclairée, où se trouveront presque toujours d'autres témoins de l'affaire, que devant un prince qui n'a rien vu que par les yeux de son Vizir. Or, il est certain que la plupart des résolutions d'État dépendent de la connaissance des faits ; et l'on peut dire même en général qu'on ne prend guère d'opinions fausses qu'en supposant vrais des faits qui sont faux, ou faux des faits qui sont vrais. En second lieu, les impôts seront portés à un excès moins insupportable, lorsque le prince pourra être éclairé sur la véritable situation de ses peuples et sur ses véritables besoins. Mais ces lumières, ne les trouvera-t-il pas plus aisément dans un Conseil dont plusieurs membres n'auront

---

[1] *publiquement*, an afterthought.   [2] *en apparence*, an afterthought.

aucun maniement de finances, ni aucun ménagement à garder, que dans un vizir qui veut fomenter les passions de son maître, ménager les fripons en faveur, enrichir ses créatures, et faire sa main pour lui-même ? On voit encore que les femmes auront moins de pouvoir, et que par conséquent l'État en ira mieux : car il est plus aisé à une femme intrigante de placer un vizir que cinquante Conseillers, et de séduire un homme que tout un collége. On voit que les affaires ne seront plus suspendues ou bouleversées par le déplacement d'un Vizir; qu'elles seront plus exactement expédiées, quand, liées par une commune délibération, l'exécution sera cependant partagée entre plusieurs Conseillers, qui auront chacun leur département, que lorsqu'il faut que tout sorte d'un même bureau ; que les systèmes politiques seront mieux suivis et les règlements beaucoup mieux observés, quand il n'y aura plus de révolution[1] dans le ministère, et que chaque Vizir ne se fera plus un point d'honneur de détruire tous les établissements utiles de celui qui l'aura précédé : de sorte qu'on sera sûr qu'un projet une fois formé ne sera plus abandonné, que lorsque l'exécution en aura été reconnue impossible ou mauvaise.

À toutes ces conséquences ajoutez-en deux non moins certaines, mais plus importantes encore, qui n'en sont que le dernier résultat, et doivent leur donner un prix que rien ne balance aux yeux du vrai citoyen. La première, que, dans un travail commun, le mérite, les talents, l'intégrité, se feront plus aisément connaître et récompenser: soit dans les membres des Conseils, qui seront sans cesse sous les yeux les uns des autres et de tout l'État ; soit dans le royaume entier, où nulles actions remarquables, nuls hommes dignes d'être distingués, ne peuvent se dérober longtemps aux regards d'une assemblée qui veut et peut tout voir, et où la jalousie et l'émulation des membres les porteront souvent à se faire des créatures qui effacent en mérite celles de leurs rivaux. La seconde et dernière conséquence est que les honneurs et les emplois distribués avec plus d'équité et de raison, l'intérêt de l'État et du prince mieux écouté dans les délibérations, les affaires mieux expédiées, et le mérite plus honoré, doivent nécessairement réveiller dans le cœur du peuple cet amour de la patrie qui est le plus puissant ressort d'un sage Gouvernement, et qui ne s'éteint jamais chez les citoyens que par la faute des chefs.

Tels sont les effets nécessaires d'une forme de Gouvernement qui force l'intérêt particulier à céder à l'intérêt général. La polysynodie offre encore d'autres avantages qui donnent un

---

[1] Ed. 1801 and Hachette read *révolutions*. MS. and Ed. 1782, *revolution*.

nouveau prix à ceux-là. Des assemblées nombreuses et éclairées fourniront plus de lumières sur les expédients; et l'expérience confirme que les délibérations d'un Sénat sont en général plus sages et mieux digérées que celles d'un Vizir[1]. Les rois seront plus instruits de leurs affaires; ils ne sauraient assister aux Conseils sans s'en instruire, [2]car c'est là qu'on ose dire la vérité[2]; et les membres de chaque Conseil auront le plus grand intérêt que le prince y assiste assidûment, pour en soutenir le pouvoir ou pour en autoriser les résolutions. Il y aura moins de vexations et d'injustices de la part des plus forts; car un Conseil sera plus accessible que le trône aux opprimés; ils courront moins de risque[3] à y porter leurs plaintes, et ils y trouveront toujours dans quelques membres plus de protecteurs contre les violences des autres, que sous le vizirat contre un seul homme qui peut tout, ou contre un demi-vizir d'accord avec ses collègues pour faire renvoyer à chacun d'eux le jugement des plaintes qu'on fait contre lui. L'État souffrira moins de la minorité, de la faiblesse ou de la caducité du prince. Il n'y aura jamais de ministre assez puissant pour se rendre, s'il est de grande naissance, redoutable à son maître même, ou pour écarter et mécontenter les grands, s'il est né de bas lieu; par conséquent, il y aura d'un côté moins de levain[4] de guerres civiles, et de l'autre plus de sûreté pour la conservation des droits de la maison royale. Il y aura moins aussi de guerres étrangères, parce qu'il y aura moins de gens intéressés à les susciter, et qu'ils auront moins de pouvoir[5] pour en venir à bout. Enfin, le trône en sera mieux affermi de toutes manières; la volonté du prince, qui n'est ou ne doit être que la volonté publique, mieux exécutée; et par conséquent la nation plus heureuse.

[1] Il y a plus de ruse et de secret dans le vizirat, mais il y a plus de lumières et de droiture dans la synodie. This note is neither in the MS. nor in the *brouillon*. It appears first in Ed. 1782. It was taken by du Peyrou from MS. Neuchâtel, 7842 (p. 52 v°), which contains, under the heading *Pour la Grande Édition*, a few additions to the *Contrat social* and other works. This entry is introduced by the word *Polysynodie*, with no specific reference. It was appended by du Peyrou as a note to the end of the preceding paragraph. I have ventured to shift it to the place in the text, where it seems more relevant.

[2] This clause is written, as an afterthought, in the margin. It is not in the *brouillon*.

[3] Ed. 1801 and Hachette read *risques*. MS. and Ed. 1782, as in the text.

[4] Ed. 1782 reads *levains*. MS. and *brouillon*, as in the text.

[5] Hachette reads *pouvoirs*, against MS., *brouillon* and Ed. 1782.

[1]Au reste, mon auteur convient lui-même que l'exécution de son plan ne serait pas également avantageuse en tous[2] temps; et qu'il y a des moments de crise et de trouble, où il faut substituer aux Conseils permanents des commissions extraordinaires; et que, quand les finances, par exemple, sont dans un certain désordre, il faut nécessairement les donner à débrouiller à un seul homme, comme Henri IV fit à Rosny, et Louis XIV à Colbert: ce qui signifierait que les Conseils ne sont bons, pour faire aller les affaires, que quand elles vont toutes seules. [3]En effet, pour ne rien dire de la polysynodie même du Régent[3], l'on sait les risées qu'excita, dans des circonstances épineuses, ce ridicule *Conseil de raison*, étourdiment demandé par les Notables de l'assemblée de Rouen, et adroitement accordé par Henri IV[4]. Mais, comme les finances des Républiques sont en général mieux administrées que celles des Monarchies, il est à croire qu'elles le seront mieux, ou du moins plus fidèlement, par un Conseil que par un ministre; et que, si peut-être un Conseil est d'abord moins capable de l'activité nécessaire pour les tirer d'un état de désordre, il est aussi moins sujet à la négligence ou à l'infidélité qui les y font tomber : ce qui ne doit pas s'entendre d'une assemblée passagère et subordonnée, mais d'une véritable polysynodie, où les Conseils aient réellement le pouvoir qu'ils paraissent avoir; où l'administration des affaires ne leur soit pas enlevée par des demi-vizirs; et où, sous les noms spécieux de *Conseil d'État* ou de *Conseil des finances*, ces Corps ne soient pas seulement des Tribunaux de justice ou des Chambres des comptes.

CHAPITRE XI.

Conclusion.

Quoique les avantages de la polysynodie ne soient pas sans inconvénients, et que les inconvénients des autres formes d'administration ne soient pas sans avantages, du moins apparents, quiconque fera sans partialité le parallèle des uns et des autres trouvera que la polysynodie n'a point d'inconvénients essentiels qu'un bon Gouvernement ne puisse aisément supporter: au lieu

---

[1] This paragraph is wanting in the *brouillon*.
[2] Hachette reads *en tout temps*. MS. and Ed. 1782, as in the text.
[3] This clause is an afterthought, written in the margin of the MS.
[4] See below, p. 415.

que tous ceux du vizirat et du demi-vizirat attaquent les fondements mêmes de la constitution ; qu'une administration non interrompue peut se perfectionner sans cesse, progrès impossible[1] dans les intervalles et révolutions du vizirat ; que la marche égale et unie d'une polysynodie, comparée avec quelques moments brillants du vizirat, est un sophisme grossier qui n'en saurait imposer au vrai politique, parce que ce sont deux choses fort différentes que l'administration rare et passagère d'un bon Vizir, et la forme générale du vizirat, où l'on a toujours des siècles de désordre sur quelques années de bonne conduite ; que la diligence et le secret, les seuls vrais avantages du vizirat, beaucoup plus nécessaires dans les mauvais Gouvernements que dans les bons, sont de faibles suppléments au bon ordre, à la justice et à la prévoyance, qui préviennent les maux au lieu de les réparer ; qu'on peut encore se procurer ces suppléments au besoin dans la polysynodie par des commissions extraordinaires, sans que le vizirat ait jamais pareille ressource pour les avantages dont il est privé ; que même l'exemple de l'ancien Sénat de Rome et de celui de Venise prouve que des commissions ne sont pas toujours nécessaires dans un Conseil pour expédier les plus importantes affaires promptement et secrètement ; que le vizirat et le demi-vizirat, avilissant, corrompant, dégradant les ordres inférieurs, exigeraient pourtant des hommes parfaits dans ce premier rang ; qu'on n'y peut guère monter ou s'y maintenir qu'à force de crimes, ni s'y bien comporter qu'à force de vertus ; qu'ainsi, toujours en obstacle à lui-même, le Gouvernement engendre continuellement les vices qui le dépravent, et, consumant l'État pour se renforcer, périt enfin comme un édifice qu'on voudrait élever sans cesse avec des matériaux tirés de ses fondements. C'est ici la considération la plus importante aux yeux de l'homme d'État, et celle à laquelle je vais m'arrêter. La meilleure forme de Gouvernement, [2]ou du moins la plus durable[2], est celle qui fait les hommes tels qu'elle a besoin qu'ils soient. Laissons les lecteurs réfléchir sur cet axiome, ils en feront aisément l'application.

[1] Ed. 1782 reads *progrès impossibles*. MS., as in the text.
[2] This clause is an afterthought, written between the lines of the MS.

JUGEMENT SUR LA POLYSYNODIE

[Written 1756 ; published 1782. MS. Neuchâtel, 7830.]

De tous les ouvrages de l'abbé de Saint-Pierre, le *Discours sur la Polysynodie* est, à mon avis, le plus approfondi, le mieux raisonné, celui où l'on trouve le moins de répétitions, et même le mieux écrit : éloge dont le sage auteur se serait fort peu soucié, mais qui n'est pas indifférent aux lecteurs superficiels. Aussi cet écrit n'était-il qu'une ébauche, qu'il prétendait n'avoir pas eu le temps d'abréger ; mais qu'en effet il n'avait pas eu le temps de gâter, pour vouloir tout dire : [1]et Dieu garde un lecteur impatient des abrégés de sa façon[1] !

Il a su même éviter dans ce Discours le reproche si commode aux ignorants qui ne savent mesurer le possible que sur l'existant, ou aux méchants qui ne trouvent bon que ce qui sert à leur méchanceté, lorsqu'on montre aux uns et aux autres que ce qui est pourrait être mieux. Il a, dis-je, évité cette grande prise que la sottise routinée a presque toujours sur les nouvelles vues de la raison, avec ces mots tranchants de *projets en l'air* et de *rêveries* ; car, quand il écrivait en faveur de la polysynodie, il la trouvait établie dans son pays. Toujours paisible et sensé, il se plaisait à montrer à ses compatriotes les avantages du Gouvernement auquel ils étaient soumis ; il en faisait une comparaison raisonnable et discrète avec celui dont ils venaient d'éprouver la rigueur. Il louait le système du prince régnant, il en déduisait les avantages ; il montrait ceux qu'on y pouvait ajouter ; et les additions même qu'il demandait consistaient moins, selon lui, dans des changements à faire que dans l'art de perfectionner ce qui était fait. Une partie de ses vues lui étaient venues sous le règne de Louis XIV ; mais il avait eu la sagesse de les taire jusqu'à ce que l'intérêt de l'État, celui du Gouvernement, et le sien, lui permissent de les publier.

Il faut convenir cependant que, sous un même nom, il y avait une extrême différence entre la polysynodie qui existait et celle que proposait l'abbé de Saint-Pierre ; et, pour peu qu'on y réfléchisse, on trouvera que l'administration qu'il citait en exemple lui servait bien plus de prétexte, que de modèle, pour celle qu'il avait imaginée. Il tournait même avec assez d'adresse en objections

[1] Afterthought.

contre son propre système les défauts à relever dans celui du Régent; et, sous le nom de réponses à ses[1] objections, il montrait sans danger et ces défauts et leurs remèdes. Il n'est pas impossible que le Régent, [2]quoique souvent loué dans cet écrit par des tours qui ne manquent pas d'adresse[2], ait pénétré la finesse de cette critique, et qu'il ait abandonné l'abbé de Saint-Pierre par pique autant que par faiblesse; plus offensé peut-être des défauts qu'on trouvait dans son ouvrage que flatté des avantages qu'on y faisait remarquer. [3]Peut-être aussi lui sut-il mauvais gré d'avoir, en quelque manière, dévoilé ses vues secrètes, en montrant que son établissement n'était rien moins que ce qu'il devait être pour devenir avantageux à l'État et prendre une assiette fixe et durable[3]. En effet, on voit clairement que c'était la forme de polysynodie établie sous la régence que l'abbé de Saint-Pierre accusait de pouvoir trop aisément dégénérer en demi-vizirat, et même en vizirat ; d'être susceptible, aussi bien que l'un et l'autre, de corruption dans ses membres, et de concert entre eux contre l'intérêt public ; de n'avoir jamais d'autre sûreté pour sa durée que la volonté du monarque régnant; enfin, de n'être propre que pour les princes laborieux, et d'être, par conséquent, plus souvent contraire que favorable au bon ordre et à l'expédition des affaires. C'était l'espoir de remédier à ces divers inconvénients qui l'engageait à proposer une autre polysynodie entièrement différente de celle qu'il feignait de ne vouloir que perfectionner.

[4]Il ne faut donc pas que la conformité des noms fasse confondre son projet avec cette ridicule polysynodie dont il voulait autoriser la sienne, mais qu'on appelait dès lors par dérision les soixante et dix ministres, et qui fut réformée au bout de quelques[5] mois sans avoir rien fait qu'achever de tout gâter[6]. Car la manière dont cette administration avait été établie fait assez voir qu'on ne s'était pas beaucoup soucié qu'elle allât mieux, et qu'on avait bien plus songé à rendre le Parlement méprisable au peuple qu'à donner réellement à ses membres l'autorité qu'on feignait de leur confier. C'était un piége aux pouvoirs intermédiaires, semblable

---

[1] Or *ces*. Ed. 1782 has *ses*.

[2] Afterthought. For *d'adresse*, Rousseau had originally written *de délicatesse et d'énergie*.

[3] Afterthought.

[4] This paragraph, an afterthought, written on the left margin.

[5] [trois.] Rousseau has understated the duration of the Councils. They were established in 1715, and abolished in 1718. See *Mémoires de la Régence* (la Haye, 1729), Vol. I. pp. 13—5 and II. pp. 134—8.

[6] [bouleverser.]

à celui que leur avait déjà tendu Henri IV à l'assemblée de Rouen : piége dans lequel la vanité les fera toujours donner, et qui les humiliera toujours[1]. L'ordre politique et l'ordre civil ont, dans les monarchies, des principes si différents et des règles si contraires, qu'il est presque impossible d'allier les deux administrations, et qu'en général les membres des Tribunaux sont peu propres pour les Conseils : soit que l'habitude des formalités nuise à l'expédition des affaires qui n'en veulent point ; soit qu'il y ait une incompatibilité naturelle entre ce qu'on appelle maximes[2] d'État et la justice et les lois.

Au reste, laissant les faits à part, je croirais, quant à moi, que le prince et le philosophe pouvaient avoir tous deux raison sans s'accorder dans leur système ; car autre chose est l'administration passagère et souvent orageuse d'une régence, et autre chose une forme de Gouvernement durable et constante qui doit faire partie de la constitution de l'État. C'est ici, ce me semble, qu'on retrouve le défaut ordinaire à l'abbé de Saint-Pierre, qui est de n'appliquer jamais assez bien ses vues aux hommes, aux temps, aux circonstances, et d'offrir toujours, comme des facilités pour l'exécution d'un projet, des avantages qui lui servent souvent d'obstacles. Dans le plan dont il s'agit, il voulait modifier un Gouvernement que sa longue durée a rendu déclinant, par des moyens tout à fait étrangers à sa constitution présente ; il voulait lui rendre cette vigueur universelle qui met, pour ainsi dire, toute la personne en action. C'était comme s'il eût dit à un vieillard décrépit et goutteux : 'Marchez, travaillez, servez-vous de vos bras et de vos jambes ; car l'exercice est bon à la santé.'

[3]En effet, ce n'est rien moins qu'une révolution dont il est question dans la *Polysynodie*, et il ne faut pas croire, parce qu'on voit actuellement des Conseils dans les cours des princes, et que ce sont des Conseils qu'on propose, qu'il y ait peu de différence d'un système à l'autre. La différence est telle, qu'il faudrait commencer par détruire tout ce qui existe pour donner au Gouvernement la forme imaginée par l'abbé de Saint-Pierre ; et nul n'ignore combien est dangereux, dans un grand État, le moment d'anarchie et de crise qui précède nécessairement un établissement nouveau. La seule introduction du scrutin devait faire un renversement épouvantable, et donner plutôt un mouvement convulsif et

---

[1] See *Mémoires de Sully*, Liv. VIII. (ed. 1788, Paris, II. pp. 307—317).
[2] Hachette reads *maxime*. Both MS. and Ed. 1782, as in the text.
[3] This paragraph and the next are an afterthought, written in the margin.

continuel à chaque partie qu'une nouvelle vigueur au corps. Qu'on juge du danger d'émouvoir une fois les masses énormes qui composent la monarchie française. Qui pourra retenir l'ébranlement donné, ou prévoir tous les effets qu'il peut produire ? Quand tous les avantages du nouveau plan seraient incontestables, quel homme de sens oserait entreprendre d'abolir les vieilles coutumes, de changer les vieilles maximes, et de donner une autre forme à l'État que celle où l'a successivement amené une durée de treize cents ans ? Que le Gouvernement actuel soit encore celui d'autrefois, ou que, durant tant de siècles, il ait changé de nature insensiblement, il est également imprudent d'y toucher. Si c'est le même, il le faut respecter[1] ; s'il a dégénéré, c'est par la force du temps et des choses, et la sagesse humaine n'y peut rien. Il ne suffit pas de considérer les moyens qu'on veut employer, si l'on ne regarde encore les hommes dont on se veut servir[2]. Or, quand toute une nation ne sait plus s'occuper que de niaiseries, quelle attention peut-elle donner aux grandes choses ? et dans un pays où la musique est devenue une affaire d'État, que seront les affaires d'État, sinon des chansons ? Quand on voit tout Paris en fermentation pour une place de baladin ou de bel esprit, et les affaires de l'Académie ou de l'Opéra faire oublier l'intérêt du prince et la gloire de la nation, que doit-on espérer des affaires publiques rapprochées d'un tel peuple, et transportées de la cour à la ville ? Quelle confiance peut-on avoir au scrutin des Conseils, quand on voit celui d'une académie au pouvoir des femmes ? Seront-elles moins empressées à placer des ministres que des savants ? ou se connaîtront-elles mieux en politique qu'en éloquence ? Il est bien à craindre que de tels établissements, dans un pays où les mœurs sont en dérision, ne se fissent peu[3] tranquillement, ne se maintinssent guère sans troubles, et ne donnassent pas les meilleurs sujets.

D'ailleurs, sans entrer dans cette vieille question de la vénalité des charges, qu'on ne peut agiter que chez des gens mieux pourvus d'argent que de mérite, imagine-t-on quelque moyen praticable d'abolir en France cette vénalité ? ou penserait-on qu'elle pût subsister dans une partie du Gouvernement, et le scrutin dans l'autre ? l'une dans les Tribunaux, l'autre dans les Conseils ? et que les seules places qui restent à la faveur seraient abandonnées aux élections ? Il faudrait avoir des vues bien courtes et bien

---

[1] Ed. 1782 has *il faut le respecter*. MS., as in the text.
[2] Rousseau had originally written *dont on veut se servir*.
[3] Ed. 1782 has *ne se fissent pas tranquillement*. MS., as in the text.

fausses pour vouloir allier des choses si dissemblables, et fonder un même système sur des principes si différents. [1]Mais laissons ces applications, et considérons la chose en elle-même[1].

Quelles sont les circonstances dans lesquelles une monarchie[2] héréditaire peut, sans révolutions, être tempérée par des formes qui la rapprochent de l'aristocratie ? Les corps intermédiaires entre le prince et le peuple peuvent-ils, doivent-ils, avoir une juridiction indépendante de l'un et de l'autre[3] ? ou, s'ils sont précaires et dépendants du prince, peuvent-ils jamais entrer comme parties intégrantes dans la constitution de l'État, et même avoir une influence réelle dans les affaires ? Questions préliminaires qu'il fallait discuter, et qui ne semblent pas faciles à résoudre : car, s'il est vrai que la pente naturelle est toujours vers la corruption et par conséquent vers le despotisme, il est difficile de voir par quelles ressources de politique le prince, même quand il le voudrait, pourrait donner à cette pente une direction contraire, qui ne pût être changée par ses successeurs, ni par leurs ministres. L'abbé de Saint-Pierre ne prétendait pas, à la vérité, que sa nouvelle forme ôtât rien à l'autorité royale ; car il donne au Conseil la délibération des matières, et laisse au roi seul la décision. Ces différents Conseils, dit-il, sans empêcher le roi de faire tout ce qu'il voudra, le préserveront souvent de vouloir des choses nuisibles à sa gloire et à son bonheur ; ils porteront devant lui le flambeau de la vérité, pour lui montrer le meilleur chemin et le garantir des piéges. Mais cet homme éclairé[4] pouvait-il se payer lui-même de si mauvaises raisons ? espérait-il que les yeux des rois pussent voir les objets à travers les lunettes des sages ? Ne sentait-il pas qu'il fallait nécessairement que la délibération[5] des Conseils devînt bientôt[5] un vain formulaire, ou que l'autorité royale en fût altérée ? et n'avouait-il pas lui-même que c'était introduire un Gouvernement mixte, où la forme républicaine s'alliait à la monarchique ? En effet, des Corps nombreux, dont le choix ne dépendrait pas entièrement du prince, et qui n'auraient par eux-mêmes aucun pouvoir, deviendraient bientôt un fardeau inutile à l'État. Sans mieux faire aller les affaires, ils ne feraient qu'en retarder

---

[1] Originally : *Voilà ce qu'il fallait d'abord considérer par rapport au temps et au lieu. Passons à la chose même.* The same connecting link (with the variations, *aux temps et aux lieux* and *Passons aux observations sur la nature des choses*) was placed originally at the end of the preceding paragraph.

[2] Originally, *une grande monarchie héréditaire.*

[3] Ed. 1782 has *indépendante l'un de l'autre.* MS., as in the text.

[4] Originally, *sage.*

[5] Originally, *l'établissement des conseils. Bientôt* is an afterthought.

l'expédition par de longues formalités, et, pour me servir de ses propres termes, ne seraient que des Conseils de parade. Les favoris du prince, qui le sont rarement du public, et qui, par conséquent, auraient peu d'influence dans les Conseils formés au scrutin, décideraient seuls toutes les affaires ; le prince n'assisterait jamais aux Conseils, sans avoir déjà pris son parti sur tout ce qu'on y devrait agiter, ou n'en sortirait jamais, sans consulter de nouveau dans son cabinet avec ses favoris[1] sur les résolutions qu'on y aurait prises. Enfin, il faudrait nécessairement que les Conseils devinssent méprisables, ridicules, et tout à fait inutiles, ou que les rois perdissent de leur pouvoir : alternative [2]à laquelle ceux-ci ne s'exposeront certainement pas[2], quand même il en devrait résulter le plus grand bien de l'État et le leur.

[3]Voilà, ce me semble, à peu près les côtés par lesquels l'abbé de Saint-Pierre eût dû considérer le fond de son système pour en bien établir les principes. Mais il s'amuse, au lieu de cela, à résoudre cinquante mauvaises objections qui ne valaient pas la peine d'être examinées ; ou, qui pis est, à faire lui-même de mauvaises réponses quand les bonnes se présentent naturellement ; comme s'il cherchait à prendre plutôt le tour d'esprit de ses opposants pour les ramener à la raison, que le langage de la raison pour convaincre les sages.

Par exemple, après s'être objecté que, dans la polysynodie, chacun des Conseillers a son plan général, que cette diversité produit nécessairement des décisions qui se contredisent, et des embarras dans le mouvement total, il répond à cela qu'il ne peut y avoir d'autre plan général que de chercher à perfectionner les règlements qui roulent sur toutes les parties du Gouvernement. Le meilleur plan général, n'est-ce pas, dit-il, celui qui va le plus droit au plus grand bien de l'État dans chaque affaire particulière ? D'où il tire cette conclusion très fausse, que les divers plans généraux, ni par conséquent les règlements et les affaires qui s'y rapportent, ne peuvent jamais se croiser ou se nuire mutuellement.

En effet, le plus grand bien de l'État n'est pas toujours une chose si claire, ni qui dépende, autant qu'on le croirait, du plus grand bien de chaque partie ; comme si les mêmes affaires

---

[1] *avec ses favoris*, an afterthought. Hachette has *on n'en sortirait*, against the MS. and Ed. 1782.

[2] Originally, *à laquelle ils ne s'exposeront pas, quoiqu'ils pussent le faire sans danger*.

[3] This paragraph, and the two next, are an afterthought, written in the margin.

ne pouvaient pas avoir entre elles une infinité d'ordres divers et de liaisons plus ou moins fortes, qui forment autant de différences dans les plans généraux. Ces plans bien digérés sont toujours doubles, et renferment, dans un système comparé, la forme actuelle de l'État et sa forme perfectionnée selon les vues de l'auteur. Or, cette perfection, dans un tout aussi composé que le Corps politique, ne dépend pas seulement de celle de chaque partie; comme pour ordonner un palais il ne suffit pas d'en bien disposer chaque pièce, mais il faut de plus considérer les rapports du tout, les liaisons les plus convenables, l'ordre le plus commode, la plus facile communication, le plus parfait ensemble, et la symétrie la plus régulière. Ces objets généraux sont si importants, que l'habile architecte sacrifie au mieux du tout mille avantages particuliers, qu'il aurait pu conserver dans une ordonnance moins parfaite et moins simple. De même, le politique ne regarde en particulier ni les finances, ni la guerre, ni le commerce; mais il rapporte toutes ces parties à un objet commun. Et des proportions qui leur conviennent le mieux résultent les plans généraux dont les dimensions peuvent varier de mille manières, selon les idées et les vues de ceux qui les ont formés; soit en cherchant la plus grande perfection du tout, soit en cherchant la plus facile exécution, sans qu'il soit aisé quelquefois de démêler celui de ces plans qui mérite la préférence. Or, c'est de ces plans qu'on peut dire que, si chaque Conseil et chaque Conseiller a le sien, il n'y aura que contradictions dans les affaires et qu'embarras dans le mouvement commun. Mais le plan général, au lieu d'être celui d'un homme ou d'un autre, ne doit être et n'est en effet, dans la polysynodie, que celui du Gouvernement; et c'est à ce grand modèle que se rapportent nécessairement les délibérations communes de chaque Conseil, et le travail particulier de chaque membre. Il est certain même qu'un pareil plan se médite et se conserve mieux dans le dépôt d'un Conseil que dans la tête d'un ministre et même d'un prince; car chaque Vizir a son plan, qui n'est jamais celui de son devancier; et chaque demi-vizir a aussi le sien, qui n'est ni celui de son devancier, ni celui de son collègue: aussi voit-on généralement les Républiques changer moins de systèmes que les Monarchies. D'où je conclus avec l'abbé de Saint-Pierre, mais par d'autres raisons, que la polysynodie est plus favorable que le vizirat et le demi-vizirat à l'unité du plan général.

À l'égard de la forme particulière de sa polysynodie et des détails dans lesquels il entre pour la déterminer, tout cela est très bien vu et fort bon séparément pour prévenir les inconvénients auxquels chaque chose doit remédier. Mais, quand on en viendrait à l'exécution, je ne sais s'il régnerait assez d'harmonie dans le tout ensemble : car il paraît que l'établissement des grades s'accorde mal avec celui de la circulation, et le scrutin plus mal encore avec l'un et l'autre. D'ailleurs, [1]si l'établissement est dangereux à faire[1], il est à craindre que, [2]même après l'établissement fait[2], ces différents ressorts ne causent mille embarras et mille dérangements dans le jeu de la machine, quand il s'agira de la faire marcher.

La circulation de la présidence en particulier serait un excellent moyen pour empêcher la polysynodie de dégénérer bientôt en vizirat, si cette circulation pouvait durer, et qu'elle ne fût pas arrêtée par la volonté du prince, en faveur du premier des présidents qui aura l'art, toujours[3] recherché, de lui plaire. C'est-à-dire que la polysynodie durera jusqu'à ce que le roi trouve un Vizir à son gré ; mais, sous le vizirat même, on n'a pas un Vizir plus tôt que cela. Faible remède que celui, dont la vertu s'éteint à l'approche du mal qu'il devrait guérir.

N'est-ce pas encore un mauvais expédient de nous donner la nécessité d'obtenir les suffrages une seconde fois, comme un frein pour empêcher les présidents d'abuser de leur crédit la première ? ne sera-t-il pas plus court et plus sûr d'en abuser au point de n'avoir plus que faire de suffrages ? et notre auteur lui-même n'accorde-t-il pas au prince le droit de prolonger au besoin les présidents à sa volonté, c'est-à-dire d'en faire de véritables Vizirs ? Comment n'a-t-il pas aperçu mille fois, dans le cours de sa vie et de ses écrits, combien c'est une vaine occupation de rechercher des formes durables pour un état de choses, qui dépend toujours de la volonté d'un seul homme ?

[4]Ces difficultés n'ont pas échappé à l'abbé de Saint-Pierre ; mais peut-être lui convenait-il mieux de les dissimuler que de les résoudre. Quand il parle de ces contradictions et qu'il feint de les concilier, c'est par des moyens si absurdes et des raisons si peu raisonnables, qu'on voit bien qu'il est embarrassé, ou qu'il ne procède pas de bonne foi. Serait-il croyable qu'il eût mis en avant si hors de propos, et compté parmi ces moyens, l'amour de la patrie, le bien public, le désir de la vraie gloire, et d'autres

---

[1] An afterthought. [2] An afterthought.
[3] *toujours*, an afterthought.
[4] This paragraph, and the two next (down to *semblables expédients*), are an afterthought, written in the margin.

chimères évanouies depuis longtemps, ou dont il ne reste plus de traces que dans quelques petites Républiques ? Pensait-il[1] sérieusement que rien de tout cela pût réellement influer dans la forme d'un Gouvernement monarchique ? et, après avoir cité les Grecs, les Romains, et même quelques modernes qui avaient des âmes anciennes, n'avoue-t-il pas lui-même qu'il serait ridicule de fonder la constitution de l'État sur des maximes éteintes ? Que fait-il donc pour suppléer à ces moyens étrangers dont il reconnaît l'insuffisance ? Il lève une difficulté par une autre, établit un système sur un système, et fonde sa Polysynodie sur sa République européenne. 'Cette République, dit-il, étant garante de l'exécution des capitulations impériales pour l'Allemagne, des capitulations parlementaires pour l'Angleterre, des *pacta conventa* pour la Pologne, ne pourrait-elle pas l'être aussi des capitulations royales signées au sacre des rois pour la forme du Gouvernement, lorsque cette forme serait passée en loi fondamentale ? et, après tout, garantir les rois de tomber dans la tyrannie des Nérons, n'est-ce pas les garantir, eux et leur postérité, de leur ruine totale ?

'On peut, dit-il encore, faire passer le règlement de la polysynodie en forme de loi fondamentale dans les États généraux du royaume, la faire jurer au sacre des rois, et lui donner ainsi la même autorité qu'à la loi salique[2].'

La plume tombe des mains, quand on voit un homme sensé proposer sérieusement de semblables expédients.

Ne quittons point cette matière sans jeter un coup d'œil général sur les trois formes de ministère, comparées dans cet ouvrage.

Le vizirat est la dernière ressource d'un État défaillant ; c'est un palliatif quelquefois nécessaire qui peut lui rendre pour un temps une certaine vigueur apparente. Mais il y a dans cette forme d'administration une multiplication de forces tout à fait superflue dans un Gouvernement sain. Le monarque et le Vizir sont deux machines exactement semblables, dont l'une devient inutile sitôt que l'autre est en mouvement ; car en effet, selon le mot de Grotius : *qui regit, rex est*[2]. Ainsi l'État supporte un double poids qui ne produit qu'un effet simple. Ajoutez à cela qu'une grande partie de la force du vizirat, étant employée à rendre le Vizir nécessaire et à le maintenir en place, est inutile ou nuisible à l'État. Aussi l'abbé de Saint-Pierre appelle-t-il avec raison le

---

[1] Ed. 1782 has *Penserait-il*. MS., as in the text.

[2] A note in the *brouillon* explains this : 'Mot de Grotius, allant toujours chez le Cardinal de Richelieu et négligeant Louis XIII : *Qui regit, rex est*.' It is quoted by Saint-Pierre, p. 134. The previous quotation, *ib.* p. 190.

vizirat 'une forme de Gouvernement grossière, barbare, pernicieuse aux peuples, dangereuse pour les rois, funeste aux maisons royales'; et l'on peut dire qu'il n'y a point de Gouvernement plus déplorable au monde que celui où le peuple est réduit à désirer un Vizir. Quant au demi-vizirat, il est avantageux sous un roi qui sait gouverner et réunir dans ses mains toutes les rênes de l'État; mais, sous un prince faible ou peu laborieux, cette administration est mauvaise, embarrassée, sans système et sans vues, faute de liaison entre ses parties[1] et d'accord entre les ministres; surtout, si quelqu'un d'entre eux, plus adroit ou plus méchant que les autres, tend en secret au vizirat. Alors tout se passe en intrigues de cour; l'État demeure en langueur; et pour trouver la raison de tout ce qui se fait sous un semblable Gouvernement, il ne faut pas demander à quoi cela sert, mais à qui cela nuit[2].

Pour la Polysynodie de l'abbé de Saint-Pierre, je ne saurais voir qu'elle puisse être utile ni praticable dans aucune véritable monarchie; mais seulement dans une sorte de Gouvernement mixte, où le chef ne soit que le président des Conseils, n'ait que la puissance exécutive, et ne puisse rien par lui-même. Encore ne saurais-je croire qu'une pareille administration pût durer longtemps sans abus. Car les intérêts des sociétés partielles ne sont pas moins séparés de ceux de l'État, ni moins pernicieux à la République, que ceux des particuliers; et ils ont même cet inconvénient de plus, qu'on se fait gloire de soutenir, [3]à quelque prix que ce soit[3], les droits ou les prétentions du corps dont on est membre; et que, ce qu'il y a de malhonnête à se préférer aux autres s'évanouissant à la faveur d'une société nombreuse dont on fait partie, à force d'être bon sénateur on devient enfin mauvais citoyen. C'est ce qui rend l'Aristocratie la pire des souverainetés[4]; c'est ce qui rendrait peut-être la Polysynodie le pire de tous les ministères.

[1] Ed. 1782 has *les parties*. MS., as in the text.
[2] Ed. 1782 has *à quoi cela nuit*, which spoils the point; the error is repeated in all the subsequent Editions which I have seen. MS., as in the text.
[3] This clause is an afterthought.
[4] Je parierais que mille gens trouveront encore ici une contradiction avec le *Contrat social**. Cela prouve qu'il y a encore plus de lecteurs qui devraient apprendre à lire, que d'auteurs qui devraient apprendre à être conséquents. [Note de J.-J. R.] This note is written in blacker ink and in a slightly different hand. It must have been added after the completion of the *Contrat social* (1761—2).

* *C. S.* III. v. and x. Compare 'Le meilleur des Gouvernements est l'aristocratique; la pire des souverainités est l'aristocratique' (*Lettres de la Montagne*, vi.; Vol. II. p. 202).

DROIT NATUREL

Article de Diderot (1755).

THE following piece was published in Vol. v. of the *Encyclopédie* (Nov. 1755). It was undoubtedly written by Diderot. But the references to it both in the *Économie politique*[1], which appeared in the same volume of the *Encyclopédie*, and in an important chapter of the first draft of the *Contrat social*[2], which was clearly written about the same time, are so close that their meaning is hardly to be understood, unless the words of Diderot are before the eyes of the reader. That is why it is reprinted in this Collection.

The question at once suggests itself: How far can we suppose that the article of Diderot was prompted by suggestions from Rousseau? It is obvious that no certain answer can be given. All that can be done is to note the points in which the two men agree, and those in which they differ.

The allusions to the evolutionary theory of species, with which some play is made towards the end of the article (9. § 7), are clearly of Diderot's devising. Such beliefs, or half-beliefs, had already found utterance in his early work, *L'interprétation de la nature* (1754)[3]. They were to reappear in the *Rêve de d'Alembert* (1769) and the *Voyage de Bougainville* (1772), which represent the settled convictions of his later years. Under a modified form, and without the materialist conclusions which Diderot drew from them, Rousseau was prepared to accept them, whenever stronger evidence should be forthcoming[4]. But the whole bent of his mind was against such speculations; and it is safe to assume that he had no part nor lot in their introduction.

On the conception of Natural Law, which underlies the whole

---

[1] *Éc. pol.*; above, pp. 242, 244. The former is the reference discussed below (p. 427); the latter is a half quotation of the words: 'Hélas! la vertu est si belle que les voleurs en respectent l'image dans le fond même de leurs cavernes.'

[2] Geneva MS. I. ii. See below, pp. 450—4.

[3] In particular, §§ XII. and L.

[4] See *Discours sur l'inégalité*, Vol. I. pp. 142—3 and pp. 207—212 (Note J).

Article, we can speak with much more assurance. It is a conception which Rousseau found himself compelled to reject. He had done so implicitly in the *Discours sur l'inégalité*, which was written at least a year before this article can have been composed[1]. He was to do so explicitly and with unanswerable cogency, in a passage of the first draft of the *Contrat social* (I. ii.), which must have been written very shortly after its publication; or indeed at any time after its original composition. So far then as Diderot accepts the idea of Natural Law—it is never easy to gauge the depth, or even the sincerity, of his convictions[2]—he must be regarded as arguing in conscious opposition to Rousseau. Rousseau, on his side, good-humouredly accepts the position, and fits the cap of the 'violent reasoner' without demur upon his own head; rejecting the arguments of Diderot, but setting other, and far more cogent, arguments against individualist anarchy triumphantly in their place. In later years, however, as we shall see directly, he became convinced, rightly or wrongly, that the main fire of the argument was directed not only against his opinions, but even against his character; that he was himself the red-handed anarchist whom Diderot desired to 'stifle,' the 'enemy of the human race,' who was to be hunted down 'like a wild beast.' It is not necessary to take this conclusion for gospel. But the mere fact that Rousseau drew it is enough to prove how profoundly he disagreed with the belief in Natural Law which Diderot here invokes against the 'individualism' of the second *Discourse*.

The only other point that calls for notice is the doctrine of the 'general will,' which here—so far as I know, for the first time—makes its appearance in political speculation. This, it need hardly be said, is an idea which lies at the very root of Rousseau's theory of the State. It would be a strange irony, if it could be shewn that he had drawn the first hint of it from the armoury of his arch-enemy, Diderot. And it may well be that this was the case. Nothing is, in itself, more likely than that Diderot, most inventive of men, should have thrown out the idea in the heat of argument, made play with it for the purposes of the moment and then left it, as he left so many other happy improvisations, to take its chance in the struggle for existence.

[1] Vol. I. pp. 136—8.
[2] See *Droit naturel*, § I. It will be observed that Diderot expressly—and justly—admits the idea of Right to be valid only on the assumption that the will is free. And it is more than doubtful whether, in his heart, he believed the will to be so.

On the other hand, it is no less likely that the idea—in germ, no less than in its subsequent developments—had its origin with Rousseau; that Diderot, who had the keenest eye for an effective argument, saw at a glance how readily it might be pressed into the defence of Natural Law, built his hypothesis accordingly, and then dismissed both hypothesis and argument from his mind. And as he had manifestly thought about these matters far less deeply than Rousseau—as, moreover, it is certain that, at the time in question, the two men were in daily communication with each other—there is much to be said for this supposition. Where the truth may lie, it is, and will most likely always remain, impossible to determine. We must be content with probabilities.

In favour of the former supposition is the fact that, when for the first time Rousseau introduces the conception of the 'general will,' he speaks of it as 'that great and luminous principle' of which some use had already been made in the article *Droit naturel* with reference to the state of nature, and which he is now about to 'develope' further, in its application to the State[1]. The most natural interpretation of this passage, it may fairly be argued, is to take it as an acknowledgment of a debt to the author of the *Droit naturel*: a fairly explicit avowal that the idea of the *volonté générale* was originally due to Diderot.

On the other hand, it may be pleaded that this, though a possible, is not the necessary construction to be put upon Rousseau's words; and that, in the particular circumstances of the case, there are good reasons for rejecting it. For, if Diderot were really the author of an idea which played so great a part in Rousseau's theory of politics, it must be admitted that he shewed unwonted forbearance in not proclaiming the fact when, in after years, he went about picking up every missile, fair or foul, deadly or frivolous, which might serve to belittle the genius, and blacken the character, of Rousseau[2]. He invented an absurd story that Rousseau was in debt to him for the leading idea of the first *Discourse*, and consequently of the many-headed indictment against Society which followed[3]. Is it likely that he would have kept silence if Rousseau had really borrowed from him one of the

[1] Voyez au mot *Droit* la source de ce grand et lumineux principe, dont cet article n'est que le développement: above, p. 242.

[2] These are embodied, above all, in his *Vie de Sénèque* (1778 and 1781) and in the *Mémoires* of Mme d'Épinay, to which he is now known to have largely contributed. See Mrs Macdonald's *Jean-Jacques Rousseau*.

[3] *Mémoires de Marmontel*, Liv. VII. (Vol. II. pp. 240—1. Ed. Paris, 1804).

seminal principles of the *Contrat social* and the *Économie politique*? Once again, it is impossible to be certain. The reader must judge for himself.

In any case, it is important to notice that Diderot does not apply the idea of the 'general will' in the same way as Rousseau; and that his use of it, if it is to be justified at all, must be justified on quite different grounds. Rousseau applies it solely to the civil state; Diderot, primarily if not solely, to the state of nature. To Rousseau, none but an organised body—a body organised at least as fully as the more primitive forms of the State—is to be credited with a general will. To Diderot, a loose and casual aggregate is sufficient. On the latter theory, animals, if they could only make their voice heard, would be entitled to an equal share with man in the formation of the general will[1]. On the former, not even all men are capable of this function. They become so only when they have lost their personal identity in the corporate unity of the State.

It is manifest that the whole advantage rests with the 'development' devised by Rousseau. As applied to the state of nature, the idea of the general will is nothing more than an ingenious fancy; a freak thrown out on the spur of the moment, or caught up to buttress a theory—that of Natural Right—of which, in his heart of hearts, the author was profoundly sceptical. It is only in the organised State that such an idea has any validity; or, indeed, any meaning whatsoever. Apply the idea to the state of nature, and we are at once driven to ask: What is the organ of the general will of the human race? where are we to look for its pronouncements? by what sanction are its decrees to be enforced? To the first and third of these questions Diderot does not even attempt an answer. To the second he offers one which is manifestly irrelevant. What have the writings of philosophers and jurists upon Natural Law, what have even the 'social actions of savage and barbarous nations' to do with a state of things in which, *ex hypothesi*, nations have not yet come into being, and philosophers and jurists are unknown[2]? It is clear that the author of *Droit naturel* had not taken the pains to weave a consistent theory, that he had never thought out the question as a whole.

[1] Si les animaux étaient d'un ordre à peu près égal au nôtre,...en un mot, s'ils pouvaient voter dans une assemblée générale, il faudrait les y appeler; et la cause du *droit naturel* ne se plaiderait plus par devant *l'humanité*, mais par devant *l'animalité*. *Droit naturel*, § 6.

[2] *Ib.* § 8.

On the other hand, when applied to the civil state, the idea of the general will is not only perfectly intelligible, but it explains difficulties which otherwise have no solution. If it be once admitted that the State has a corporate life apart from the separate lives of its individual members—and all the facts of the case drive us to this admission—then the conception which Rousseau first formulated as the 'general will' of the community necessarily follows. This, and not the 'general will of humanity,' was the conception which had the seeds of life in it. And it was the contribution of Rousseau. All that Diderot did was either to throw out a hint which, inadmissible in itself, at least served to put Rousseau on the scent; or, by refining upon a truth already discovered by Rousseau, purely and simply to confuse the issue. The former is the more charitable supposition. It may well be that it is also the more probable.

There remains one point of purely personal interest. No one who reads the *Droit naturel* can fail to be struck by the vehemence, not to say the bitterness, with which the author speaks of his imaginary opponent. He is 'an unnatural being who, having renounced his human character, ought to be treated as a wild beast'; a wretch who, unless he can be made to listen to reason, ought to be summarily 'stifled[1].' The last phrase, which is thrice repeated, clearly made a deep impression upon Rousseau. He takes it up in the unanswerable reply to Diderot's arguments which is to be found in a cancelled chapter of the *Contrat social*[2]. And in his later years he obviously came to think that it was aimed, deliberately and treacherously, against himself. Twice over he recurs to it with indignant protest; and each time with manifest reference to the slanders which, as he well knew, Diderot was sowing in men's ears. The first time he does so is in the letter to Saint-Germain of Feb. 26, 1770; and it occurs in a context where Diderot is mentioned by name[3]. The second

[1] Celui qui refuse de chercher la vérité renonce à la qualité d'homme, et doit être traité par le reste de son espèce comme une bête farouche... comme un être dénaturé. Que répondrons-nous donc à notre raisonneur violent, avant que de l'étouffer ?... Sans quoi, il faudrait l'étouffer sans lui répondre. *Droit naturel*, §§ 4, 5, 9.

[2] 'Je sens que je porte l'épouvante et le trouble au milieu de l'espèce humaine,' dit l'homme indépendant que le sage étouffe. Geneva MS. I. ii.; Vol. I. p. 450. See also the last paragraph of the chapter. *Ib.* pp. 453—4. It will be observed that the words of the 'violent interlocutor' are a quotation from the *Droit naturel*.

[3] Si jamais pareille contradiction, pareille extravagance, pareille absurdité, pouvaient réellement trouver foi dans l'esprit d'un homme, oui,

is in the closing words of the *Confessions* : a paragraph which appears to have been added as an Epilogue, for the benefit of the audience which gathered to hear the book read at the end of the same year or the beginning of the next (1770—1)[1]. The occasion was critical. It is manifest that he intended to speak daggers, and that the words he used were the deadliest he could find. In each case, he hurls back the charge of 'inhumanity' in the teeth of his opponent. In each he declares plainly that it is not he, but the slanderer, who should be 'stifled[2].' Nothing could shew more clearly how bitterly the words of Diderot had rankled in his mind. Nothing, we may add, could prove more conclusively the depth of the gulf which separated his views from those of the *Droit naturel*.

j'ose le dire sans crainte, il faudrait étouffer cet homme-là. *Œuvres*, XII. p. 182. The reference here is clearly to Diderot. And, later in the letter, Rousseau states his grievances against Diderot by name. *Ib.* pp. 187—8.

[1] Pour moi, je le déclare hautement et sans crainte : quiconque, même sans avoir lu mes écrits, examinera par ses propres yeux mon naturel, mon caractère, mes mœurs, mes penchants, mes plaisirs, mes habitudes, et pourra me croire un malhonnête homme, est lui-même un homme à étouffer. *Confessions*, Liv. XII.; *Œuvres*, VIII. p. 82.

[2] I am not sure that the following passage, which is certainly aimed at the person of Diderot, does not also contain a reference to his phrase : Quoi ! c'est par bonté qu'on rend cet infortuné (*i.e.* Rousseau) le jouet du public, la risée de la canaille, l'horreur de l'univers ; qu'on le prive de toute société humaine ; qu'on l'étouffe à plaisir dans la fange ; qu'on s'amuse à l'enterrer tout vivant ! *Dialogues*, I.; *Œuvres*, IX. p. 156 (compare *ib.* p. 248). The reference in this passage (written between 1772 and 1776) is not certain. About the other passages there can be no mistake. I do not remember to have seen this anywhere noticed.

DROIT NATUREL

Encyclopédie, T. v. pp. 115—116.

L'usage de ce mot est si familier qu'il n'y a presque personne qui ne soit convaincu au-dedans de soi-même que la chose lui est évidemment connue. Ce sentiment intérieur est commun au philosophe et à l'homme qui n'a point réfléchi ; avec cette seule différence qu'à la question, *Qu'est-ce que le droit ?* celui-ci, manquant aussitôt et de termes et d'idées, vous renvoie au tribunal de la conscience et reste muet ; et que le premier n'est réduit au silence et à des réflexions plus profondes qu'après avoir tourné dans un cercle vicieux, qui le ramène au point même d'où il était parti, ou le jette dans quelqu'autre question non moins difficile à résoudre que celle dont il se croyait débarrassé par sa définition.

Le philosophe interrogé dit : ' Le droit est le fondement, ou la raison première, de la justice.' Mais qu'est-ce que c'est la justice ? ' C'est l'obligation de rendre à chacun ce qui lui appartient.' Mais qu'est-ce qui appartient à l'un plutôt qu'à l'autre, dans un état de choses où tout serait à tous, et où peut-être l'idée distincte d'obligation n'existerait pas encore ? et que devrait aux autres celui qui leur permettrait tout, et ne leur demanderait rien ? C'est ici que le philosophe commence à sentir que, de toutes les notions de la morale, celle du *droit naturel* est une des plus importantes et des plus difficiles à déterminer. Aussi croirions-nous avoir fait beaucoup dans cet article si nous réussissions à établir clairement quelques principes, à l'aide desquels on pût résoudre les difficultés les plus considérables qu'on a coutume de proposer contre la notion du *droit naturel*.

Pour cet effet, il est nécessaire de reprendre les choses de haut, et de ne rien avancer qui ne soit évident : du moins de cette évidence dont les questions morales sont susceptibles et qui satisfait tout homme sensé.

i. Il est évident que, si l'homme n'est pas libre ou que si, ses déterminations instantanées, ou même ses oscillations, naissant de quelque chose de matériel qui soit extérieur à son âme, son choix n'est point l'acte pur d'une substance incorporelle et d'une faculté simple de cette substance, il n'y aura ni bonté ni méchanceté raisonnées, quoiqu'il puisse y avoir bonté et méchanceté animales ; il n'y aura ni bien ni mal moral, ni juste ni injuste, ni obligation, ni droit. D'où l'on voit, pour le dire en passant, combien il importe d'établir solidement la réalité, je ne dis pas du *volontaire*, mais de la *liberté*, qu'on ne confond que trop ordinairement avec le *volontaire*.

ii. Nous existons d'une existence pauvre, contentieuse, inquiète. Nous avons des passions et des besoins. Nous voulons être heureux ; et à tout moment l'homme injuste et passionné se sent porter à faire à autrui ce qu'il ne voudrait pas qu'on lui fît à lui-même. C'est un jugement qu'il prononce au fond de son âme et qu'il ne peut se dérober. Il voit sa méchanceté ; et il faut qu'il se l'avoue, ou qu'il accorde à chacun la même autorité qu'il s'arroge.

iii. Mais quels reproches pourrons-nous faire à l'homme tourmenté par des passions si violentes que la vie même lui devient un poids onéreux, s'il ne les satisfait, et qui, pour acquérir le droit de disposer de l'existence des autres, leur abandonne la sienne ? Que lui répondrons-nous, s'il dit intrépidement : [1] 'Je sens que je porte l'épouvante et le trouble au milieu de l'espèce humaine ; mais il faut ou que je sois malheureux, ou que je fasse le malheur des autres ; et personne ne m'est plus cher que je ne[2] le suis à moi-même[1]. Qu'on ne me reproche point cette abominable prédilection ; elle n'est pas libre. C'est la voix de la nature, qui ne s'explique jamais plus fortement en moi que quand elle me parle en ma faveur. Mais n'est-ce que dans mon cœur qu'elle se fait entendre avec la même violence ? O hommes, c'est à vous que j'en appelle. Quel est celui d'entre vous qui, sur le point de mourir, ne rachèterait pas sa vie aux dépens de la plus grande partie du genre humain, s'il était sûr de l'impunité et du secret ? Mais, continuera-t-il, je suis équitable et sincère. Si mon bonheur demande que je me défasse de toutes les existences qui me seront importunes, il faut aussi qu'un individu, quel qu'il soit, puisse se défaire de la mienne, s'il en est importuné. La raison le veut, et j'y souscris. Je ne suis pas assez injuste pour exiger d'un autre un sacrifice que je ne veux point lui faire.'

iv. J'aperçois d'abord une chose qui me semble avoué par le bon et par le méchant ; c'est qu'il faut raisonner en tout, parce

---

[1] This passage reappears in the first draft of *C. S.* (i. ii.), where Rousseau, assuming the part of the 'violent reasoner,' gives his reply. See below, p. 450.

[2] In the *Encyclopédie, ne* is misprinted *me*.

que l'homme n'est pas seulement un animal, mais un animal qui raisonne ; qu'il y a par conséquent, dans la question dont il s'agit, des moyens de découvrir la vérité ; que celui qui refuse de la chercher renonce à la qualité d'homme, et doit être traité par le reste de son espèce comme une bête farouche ; et que, la vérité une fois découverte, quiconque refuse de s'y conformer est insensé ou méchant d'une méchanceté morale.

v. Que répondrons-nous donc à notre raisonneur violent avant que de l'étouffer ? Que tout son discours se réduit à savoir s'il acquiert un droit sur l'existence des autres en leur abandonnant la sienne : car il ne veut pas seulement être heureux ; il veut encore être équitable, et par son équité écarter loin de lui l'épithète de *méchant* ; sans quoi il faudrait l'étouffer sans lui répondre. Nous lui ferons donc remarquer que, quand bien même ce qu'il abandonne lui appartiendrait si parfaitement qu'il en pût disposer à son gré, et que la condition qu'il propose aux autres leur serait encore avantageuse, il n'a aucune autorité légitime pour la leur faire accepter ; que celui qui dit, *je veux vivre*, a autant de raison que celui qui dit, *je veux mourir* ; que celui-ci n'a qu'une vie et qu'en l'abandonnant il se rend maître d'une infinité de vies ; que son échange serait à peine équitable, quand il n'y aurait que lui et un autre méchant sur toute la surface de la terre ; qu'il est absurde de faire vouloir à d'autres ce qu'on veut ; qu'il est incertain que le péril qu'il fait courir à son semblable soit égal à celui auquel il veut bien s'exposer ; que ce qu'il permet au hasard peut n'être pas d'un prix proportionné à ce qu'il me force de hasarder ; que la question du *droit naturel* est beaucoup plus compliquée qu'elle ne lui paraît ; qu'il se constitue juge et partie, et que son tribunal pourrait bien n'avoir pas la compétence dans cette affaire.

vi. Mais si nous ôtons à l'individu le droit de décider de la nature du juste et de l'injuste, où porterons-nous cette grande question ? Où ? Devant le genre humain ; c'est à lui seul qu'il appartient de la décider, parce que le bien de tous est la seule passion qu'il ait. Les volontés particulières sont suspectes ; elles peuvent être bonnes ou méchantes ; mais la volonté générale est toujours bonne ; elle n'a jamais trompé, elle ne trompera jamais. Si les animaux étaient d'un ordre à peu près égal au nôtre ; s'il y avait des moyens sûrs de communication entre eux et nous ; s'ils pouvaient nous transmettre évidemment leurs sentiments et leurs pensées et connaître les nôtres avec la même évidence : en un mot, s'ils pouvaient voter dans une assemblée générale, il faudrait les y appeler, et la cause du droit naturel ne se plaiderait plus par-devant *l'humanité*, mais par-devant *l'animalité*. Mais les animaux sont séparés de nous par des barrières invariables et éternelles ; et il s'agit ici d'un ordre de connaissances et d'idées particulières à l'espèce humaine, qui émanent de sa dignité et la constituent.

vii. C'est à la volonté générale que l'individu doit s'adresser pour savoir jusqu'où il doit être homme, citoyen, sujet, père, enfant, et quand il lui convient de vivre ou de mourir. C'est à elle à fixer les limites de tous les devoirs. Vous avez le *droit naturel* le plus sacré à tout ce qui ne vous est point contesté par l'espèce entière. C'est elle qui vous éclairera sur la nature de vos pensées et de vos désirs. Tout ce que vous concevrez, tout ce que vous méditerez, sera bon, grand, élevé, sublime, s'il est de l'intérêt général et commun. Il n'y a de qualité essentielle à votre espèce que celle que vous exigez dans tous vos semblables, pour votre bonheur et pour le leur. C'est cette conformité de vous à eux tous et d'eux tous à vous qui vous marquera quand vous sortirez de votre espèce, et quand vous y resterez. Ne la perdez donc jamais de vue : sans quoi vous verrez les notions de la bonté, de la justice, de l'humanité, de la vertu, chanceler dans votre entendement. Dites-vous souvent : Je suis homme, et je n'ai d'autres *droits naturels* véritablement inaliénables que ceux de l'humanité.

viii. Mais me direz-vous : Où est le dépôt de cette volonté générale ? Où pourrai-je la consulter ? Dans les principes du Droit écrit de toutes les nations policées ; dans les actions sociales des peuples sauvages et barbares ; dans les conventions tacites des ennemis du genre humain entre eux ; et même dans l'indignation et le ressentiment, ces deux passions que la nature semble avoir placées jusque dans les animaux, pour suppléer au défaut des lois sociales et de la vengeance publique.

ix. Si vous méditez donc attentivement tout ce qui précède, vous resterez convaincu : 1° que l'homme qui n'écoute que son volonté particulière est l'ennemi du genre humain ; 2° que la volonté générale est dans chaque individu un acte pur de l'entendement, qui raisonne dans le silence des passions sur ce que l'homme peut exiger de son semblable et sur ce que son semblable est en droit d'exiger de lui ; 3° que cette considération de la volonté générale de l'espèce et du désir commun est la règle de la conduite relative d'un particulier à un particulier, dans la même société, d'un particulier envers la société dont il est membre, et de la société dont il est membre envers les autres sociétés ; 4° que la soumission à la volonté générale est le lien de toutes les sociétés, sans en excepter celles qui sont formées par le crime. Hélas ! la vertu est si belle que les voleurs en respectent l'image dans le fond même de leurs cavernes[1] ; 5° que les lois doivent être faites pour tous, et non pour un ; autrement cet être solitaire ressemblerait au raisonneur violent que nous avons étouffé dans le paragraphe v. ; 6° que, puisque des deux volontés, l'une générale et l'autre particulière, la volonté générale n'erre jamais, il n'est pas difficile de voir à laquelle il faudrait, pour le bonheur du genre humain, que la puissance législative appartînt et quelle vénération on doit aux mortels augustes, dont la volonté particulière réunit et l'autorité et l'infaillibilité de la volonté générale ; 7° que, quand on supposerait la notion des espèces dans un flux perpétuel, la nature du *droit naturel* ne changerait pas, puisqu'elle serait toujours relative à la volonté générale et au désir commun de l'espèce entière ; 8° que l'équité est à la justice comme la cause est à son effet, ou que la justice ne peut être autre chose que l'équité déclarée ; 9° enfin, que toutes ces conséquences sont évidentes pour celui qui raisonne, et que celui qui ne veut pas raisonner, renonçant à la qualité d'homme, doit être traité comme un être dénaturé.

[1] This sentence is quoted by Rousseau in *Éc. pol.* See above, p. 244

CONTRAT SOCIAL, FIRST DRAFT

[Geneva, MS. français, 225.]

OF all the Rousseau Manuscripts which have come down to us, this is perhaps the most important. Its only rivals are that containing *L'état de guerre* (Neuchâtel, 7856); the *Projet de Constitution pour la Corse* (Geneva MS. f. 229); the early draft of the *Confessions* (Neuchâtel, 7841); above all the note-book containing the rough draft of the *Économie politique* and the last five of the *Lettres de la Montagne* (Neuchâtel, 7840). It was presented to the Library of Geneva in 1882 by Mme Amélie Moultou, widow of M. Streckeisen-Moultou. It must have been presented to Paul Moultou by Rousseau himself: but at what time, it is impossible to determine.

It consists of 72 pages in large quarto, each of which is framed in a faint red line drawn by Rousseau himself, according to the fashion which, as he tells us in the *Dialogues*, he also employed to decorate his collection of dried plants[1]. It was manifestly intended for the copy to be sent to press. Owing, however, to a sudden change of plan, the motives of which will be discussed later, this copy was thrown aside, in the course of 1761; and another, distinguished by many additions, omissions and alterations, was sent in its stead. The latter, that actually used for the first edition, has unfortunately vanished. But, to judge from Rousseau's correspondence with the publisher[2], it can hardly have differed materially from the text as we have it (Rey, Amsterdam, 1762).

Our manuscript, which had apparently lost its interest for Rousseau, was subsequently torn in two; the latter part is lost; and the part which has come down to us represents somewhat less than half of the whole work. It contains Books I. and II. entire, and the first few paragraphs of Book III. These are written in

---

[1] *Dialogue* II.; *Œuvres*, IX. p. 188.
[2] *Lettres inedites de J.-J. Rousseau à M. M. Rey*, Bosscha (1858).

Rousseau's fairest hand, which is hardly to be surpassed for clearness and beauty. On the back, however, of certain pages (46—51) is scribbled, in a hand often almost indecipherable, the rough copy of the chapter on *La religion civile* (IV. viii. of the existing text). This was obviously added as an afterthought. Rousseau himself tells us that it was done after his arrangements with the publisher had been completed[1]; probably about the time when he determined to recast the whole text. The rough copy presents several marked differences from the chapter as finally given to the world.

The manuscript was reviewed by M. Eugène Ritter in the *Journal de Genève*, shortly after its donation to the Library (1882). It has been twice published: by M. Alexeieff (Moscow, 1887), and by M. Dreyfus-Brisac in his edition of the *Contrat social* (Paris, 1896). The most important chapter, that on *La Société Générale du genre humain* (I. ii.), has also been published, and with more complete accuracy, by M. Windenberger, as an appendix to *La République confédérative des petits États* (Paris, 1900).

The main ideas of the *Contrat social* have been fully discussed in the General Introduction. Neither here, nor in connection with the definitive text, need anything be added to what was there said as to their bearing and significance. There are, however, several points in which the two versions differ more or less completely from each other. And these call for further examination.

There has been some difference of opinion as to the importance of the variations between the two texts. I agree with M. Windenberger in rating it very high. Broadly speaking, it may be said that the earlier draft represents a sounder, as well as a more

[1] He seems to have begun his negotiations with Rey, when the latter visited him at Montmorency in December, 1760 (Bosscha, p. 111), and to have completed them in August, 1761 (*ib.* p. 114). The MS. was despatched at the beginning of November (*ib.* p. 121); and it is in his letter of Dec. 23 that he informs Rey that the chapter on Civil Religion had been added since he saw the 'rough draft' twelve months earlier (*ib.* p. 126). I incline to think that what he there calls the 'rough draft' (*brouillon*), and describes as written on 'le plus fort papier d'Hollande' (*ib.* p. 116), is to be identified with the Geneva MS., which answers to that description; whereas the MS. actually sent to Rey, 'écrit en menu caractère, était fort petit' (*Confessions*, Liv. XI.; *Œuvres*, XI. p. 12). In that case the recasting of the whole MS. must have been carried through between the middle of August and the end of October, 1761. On the other assumption, the book may have been recast at any time in the course of 1761.

consistent view than the later. There are several indications that Rousseau is here more ready to distinguish between abstract principles and the qualifications to which they must submit in practical working; that he is less under the sway of the former; that, on the whole, he is considerably nearer to purging his theory of its alien elements—the state of nature and the social contract—than he was when, apparently at the last moment, he revised the whole treatise for its passage through the press.

Few things have caused more perplexity to those who read the final version of the *Contrat social* than Rousseau's failure to distinguish between the abstract and the concrete elements of his theory; between what is absolute in it and what is merely conditional; between what is true only under certain circumstances, given from within or from without, and what is true always, everywhere and for all. How is the 'empire of climate' to be reconciled with the assertion that 'all men are born free'? Is the Contract, which *ex hypothesi* lies at the root of the whole system, a historical fact? or is it no more than a 'tacit understanding'? And does the latter alternative mean no more than that no Government is to be reckoned rational which does not rest upon the free, unbroken consent of the governed? and that this truth is so obvious that it is unconsciously acted upon by all communities which have risen above barbarism, and would be universally admitted by all their members, the moment it was put before them either for challenge or acceptance? It may be doubted whether Rousseau himself would have always given— whether the *Contrat social*, in either of its forms, always gives— the same answer to these questions. But in both cases—on the more general, as well as on the more particular point—the first version comes nearer to a consistent account of the matter than the second.

Take first the more general of the two questions: that raised by the passage from the abstract, unqualified doctrine of the opening chapters to the allowance for circumstances of soil, climate and communal character which, as we have seen, is unexpectedly, but none the less decisively, made by Rousseau in the sequel. In the final text this transition is carried through without a word of warning. There is nothing to shew that the author was in the least aware of the difficulties in which it entangled him. In the earlier version, it may be admitted that we are no nearer to a reasoned justification of what, to say the least, appears to be a contradiction. But it must, in fairness, be allowed that

Rousseau strikes the note of warning. The passage where the transition occurs in the final text begins abruptly: 'Before putting up a large building, the architect observes and tests the ground, to see if it will bear the weight. In the same way, the Lawgiver begins not by drawing up the code which is the best in itself, but by examining whether the people for whom it is destined are capable of standing it[1].' In the earlier version these trenchant words are introduced by the following preface: 'Although my subject here is not expediency but right, still I cannot refrain from casting a glance, by the way, upon those demands of expediency which must be obeyed in all sound forms of political institution[2].' And the same warning is repeated—it is true, with a slightly different intention—in at least one other passage of the earlier version[3]. It would be difficult to produce a parallel from the text, as finally published. And it is certain that the final text, while retaining in each case the rest of the passage, deliberately omits the caution with which, in the earlier text, it was accompanied. It would almost seem as though, on second thoughts, Rousseau desired to hide from his readers the nature of the step—from the sphere of right to that of expediency—which all the time he was calling on them to take.

A possible reason for the difference is that the *Contrat social*—so Rousseau himself tells us—was originally written as part of a larger work, the *Institutions politiques*[4]; that this larger work must have been, in great measure, concerned with questions of expediency and historical fact; and that the author, naturally and rightly, felt himself bound to warn the readers from the first that, sooner or later, the passage from the sphere of right to that of expediency and of fact must necessarily be taken. It is even conceivable—though, one would suppose, hardly likely—that in the *Institutions politiques* he had attempted to define the relation between the two spheres, and thus to meet the difficulties which,

[1] *C. S.* II. viii.
[2] Geneva MS. II. iii. Below, p. 483.
[3] After stating, as he does also in the final text, that 'le souverain ne peut charger les sujets d'aucune chaîne inutile à la communauté,' Rousseau adds in the Geneva MS.: 'Mais il ne faut pas confondre ce qui est convenable avec ce qui est nécessaire, le simple devoir avec le droit étroit.' *Ib.* II. vi. Below, p. 471. It may be observed that, in the preceding paragraph, Rousseau omits the words: 'mais il faut convenir aussi que le souverain seul est juge de cette importance.'
[4] See, in particular, *Confessions*, Liv. x.; *Œuvres*, VIII. p. 270.

as we have seen, the *Contrat social*, in both versions, inevitably suggests.

In the earlier version it is natural enough that clearer traces of the original design should survive than in the later. And it is no unlikely supposition that when, a few months before publication, he submitted all that he was willing to publish to a final revision, he should have sought, if not to remove them, at least to strike out all that called unnecessary attention to their presence. In any case, it is fair to remember that, in the *Contrat social*, we have no more than a fragment of the treatise, as originally conceived by the author; and that, if the whole design had been executed, or had come down to us, many of the difficulties which now present themselves might have been either diminished, or altogether removed[1].

On the narrower question, that of the character of the Contract as presented in the two versions, there is less to say. The later version hovers uncomfortably between representing it as a historical fact and representing it as an idea of right. On the whole, it would appear to settle down on the 'tacit understanding,' which embodies a compromise between the two views, with a cant in favour of the former[2]. The earlier text offers no trace of the

[1] There is no reason to doubt Rousseau's statement that he had actually written considerable parts of the larger work, and destroyed them on publication of the *Contrat social*. It is made twice, and explicitly: 'Je résolus de brûler tout le reste' (*Confessions*; *Œuvres*, VIII. p. 370); and 'Le reste n'est déjà plus' (*C. S. Avertissement*). The motive for this destruction may have been either caution—the work probably contained much criticism of existing Governments—or simply a great author's discouragement. If d'Antraigues' story is true, he actually preserved sixteen chapters on Federation and gave them to d'Antraigues, who destroyed them in a panic (1790). Some of the Fragments, printed in this Collection, may represent notes for the *Institutions*. But it is certain that much, perhaps most, of what Streckeisen-Moultou prints as such is nothing of the kind. See prefatory note to Fragments, B (1). For d'Antraigues' story, see Vol. II. pp. 135—6.

[2] The general effect of the crucial chapter in the final version (I. vi.) is to persuade us that the Contract was a historical fact. The same effect is given by *Émile*, Liv. v.: 'Le contrat social est donc la base de toute société civile'; and by *Lettres de la Montagne*, VI.: 'Les fondements de l'État sont les mêmes dans tous les Gouvernements.' But in the opening paragraph of the final version it is clear that most existing Governments are treated as 'illegitimate'—and, consequently, as *not* based upon Contract. Finally, in the crucial chapter itself, the phrase 'partout *tacitement* admises et reconnues' is slipped in, as if by accident. It reappears in a cancelled sentence of *Lettres de la Montagne*, VI.: 'La société civile est fondée sur un contrat entre ses membres: tacite ou forme, n'importe; il existe toujours virtuellement' (MS.

compromise. It explicitly rejects the historical character of the Contract, and treats it purely as an idea of right. 'There are a thousand ways of herding men together; there is only one way of uniting them. That is why, in this work, I offer only one method for the formation of political societies; although, among the multitude of aggregations actually existing under that name, there are perhaps no two which have been formed in the same manner, and not one which has been formed after the model I lay down. But I am in search of right and reason, and am not concerned to wrangle over facts[1].'

Taken in this sense, the Contract—or rather, the principle of civic unity for which it stands—becomes little more than an ideal: an ideal which may never have been realised in fact, but which all communities, not utterly disqualified by adverse circumstances, ought to hold before their eyes, and which some of them may one day be able to attain. It may be attained by a sudden effort; or it may be attained by the way of slow changes and of gradual advance. In the former case we shall have a revolution; in the latter, a lingering process of development and transformation. Rousseau does not commit himself to a preference for either. But, in view of the words, 'Man was born free, but everywhere he is in chains'—words which appear in the earlier as well as the later text—we may suspect that, at this time at any rate, his instinctive choice would have been for revolution[2]. For our present purpose, however, that is a matter of small importance. The main point is that the question of right is much more completely separated from the question of fact in the earlier than in the later version; and consequently that the earlier presentment of the Contract is both more consistent and intrinsically sounder than that which the later text has made familiar to the world.

There are two further points in the earlier version of which it

Neuchâtel, 7840, v° of p. 24). It must be added that, except for its position, the opening paragraph of the final version is the same in the earlier version; that the earlier version entirely omits the 'tacit understanding' (I. iii.); and that the whole business of the Contract is hurriedly slurred over (*ib.*). Moreover, as will be seen above, it is only in the earlier version that the passage occurs in which the 'historical fact' is entirely thrown overboard.

[1] Geneva MS. I. v. Below, p. 462.
[2] Compare, however, the following: 'Il n'y a plus de remède, à moins de quelque grande révolution, presque aussi à craindre que le mal qu'elle pourrait guérir, et qu'il est blâmable de désirer et impossible à prévoir.' *Réponse au Roi de Pologne* (1752). See also the close of *Jugement sur la Paix perpétuelle* (1756); above, p. 396.

is necessary to take notice. The first has already been mentioned in the General Introduction. And there is no need to add anything to what was there said of the light it throws on the direction in which the political thought of Rousseau was, perhaps unconsciously, tending. It is the passage in which he speaks of expediency, the 'common interest,' as being the true base of civil society[1]. If he had followed up the vista here opened, it is hard not to believe that he would have seen the necessity of abandoning the Contract, even in the attenuated form to which, as was pointed out in the last paragraph, it is, throughout the earlier version, commonly to be reduced.

The other—attention has often been called to it before—is the refutation of the idea of natural law[2]. The effect of this, as has already been urged, is to destroy the sanction without which the Contract, as described in the following chapter, could have no force—we may almost say, no meaning—whatsoever. By the rejection of natural law, by the assertion that, in the state of nature, there is no such thing as moral obligation, the Contract is, in fact, discredited in advance. It is reduced, in the phrase of Hobbes, to nothing more than 'words, without strength to secure any man at all.' From this conclusion it is impossible to escape. And the only question remaining is, whether Rousseau himself was aware of its necessity.

Why was this chapter, one of the most convincing pieces of argument ever written, struck out of the definitive text? M. Dreyfus-Brisac suggests two reasons, both of which it is worth while to examine. The first is that Rousseau felt its rhetorical form to be out of keeping with the dogmatic mould in which the remainder of the treatise is consistently cast. The second, that, in a treatise on the *Contrat social*, he came to see that a discussion of natural law—of the conditions which prevailed in the state of nature—was 'out of place[3].'

In the former suggestion there is considerable force. The difference of style between this chapter and the rest of the work, even as it stands in the earlier version, is certainly glaring. The objection, however, is not so serious as it looks. For what was to prevent Rousseau from recasting his argument in the dogmatic form which he adopts through the remainder of the work? He

---

[1] Geneva MS. I. v. and vi. Below, p. 470. See Introduction, pp. 46—7.
[2] Geneva MS. I. ii. Below, pp. 447—454. See Introduction, pp. 42—4.
[3] Dreyfus-Brisac, *Contrat social*, Introduction, p. x.

did this with the Fragments constituting *L'état de guerre*, which reappear, with sweeping alterations of form, in the opening chapters of th *Contrat social*, as finally published: those devoted to the refutation of Grotius and Hobbes. Why should he not have dealt with the refutation of natural law in the same manner?

But, if the first explanation is unconvincing, the second must be rejected altogether. What could be more relevant to an account of the Social Contract than a discussion of the conditions out of which it was universally supposed to have sprung? And what more disconcerting than to be thrown head foremost into the Contract, which forms the entrance to civil society, without one word to tell us by what motives this *salto mortale* was brought about? Yet the latter is precisely the method adopted in the final version of the *Contrat social*. And it is precisely this gap in the argument which the cancelled chapter of the earlier version is intended to fill up.

In the definitive text, the state of nature, which forms the necessary preliminary to the Contract, is dismissed in a few phrases which leave us no wiser than we were before. The transition from the state of nature to the civil state is despatched in a sentence which tells us no more than that it took place when it took place[1]. In the earlier version both omissions are carefully made good. Proofs in hand, Rousseau there argues that, directly the isolation, which was the primitive mark of the natural state, gave way, through natural causes, to a state of forced contact and lawless collision, the life of man became intolerable; and that it was as an escape from these miseries that the Social Contract was devised. The assumption on which the argument is based may not be justified. But, as an argument, it is sound. And, what is more, it is not only relevant but, for the author's purpose, absolutely essential. Why then, we ask once more, was it eventually suppressed?

It is hard to resist the suspicion that Rousseau suppressed the peccant chapter, not because it was irrelevant, but because it was fatally relevant, to his argument; because he became aware that, in refuting the idea of natural law, he had unwittingly made a deadly breach in the binding force of the Contract; and because, having no other principle to put in place of the Contract as the foundation of civil society, he felt that his only course was to silence the battery which he had incautiously unmasked against

[1] *C. S.* I. vi.

it: in one word, to strike out the refutation, and to let the Social Contract stand. The explanation is not certain. But it is surely more probable than any which has been suggested hitherto.

And if that be the true account of the matter, we are once more brought to see how slight were the bands which bound Rousseau to the doctrine of the Social Contract; how near he was at one moment to severing them altogether. The doctrine of Contract was devised to serve a double purpose. It strove to account for the first formation of civil society. And it strove to provide a pledge for its subsequent continuance. The former was found in the free choice of the original members. The latter, in the sanctity of an oath which, once taken, could never justly be revoked.

On the latter of these two purposes Rousseau had never laid much stress. He had always denied that the Contract was irrevocable. He had always refused to bind the future action of those who came within its scope[1]. It was to carry this refusal only one step further, when he expressly repudiated the moral sanction by which alone the Contract could be made binding; when he proved that, at the moment of its making, there neither was, nor could be, any such thing as a sense of moral obligation among those who made it. To suppose that there could be, he had argued elsewhere, is to put the effect before the cause; to assume ideas and motives to have operated before the formation of civil society, which could only have been brought to birth by civil society itself[2]. On its moral side, the whole work of the Contract is thus reduced to a miracle. And, for a miracle, there are too many explanatory circumstances. We are impelled to ask the author: Why all these feints of explaining the inexplicable? why not table your miracle at once, and have done with it?

The other purpose served by the Contract is twofold. It is firstly to furnish a purely natural explanation of the origin of civil society: an explanation, that is, from which all moral considerations—and, with them, all moral sanctions—are excluded. It is secondly to insist that no State is legitimate which is not founded upon the free consent of its members. It is upon the latter point that the main stress of Rousseau is invariably laid.

[1] *C. S.* III. xviii.; *Émile*, Liv. v.; *Œuvres*, II. p. 427: 'Par un droit que rien ne peut abroger, chaque homme, en devenant majeur et maître de lui-même, devient maître aussi de renoncer au Contrat par lequel il tient à la communauté, en quittant le pays dans lequel elle est établie.'
[2] *C. S.* II. vii.

Now it is clear that, on Rousseau's principles, neither of the two ends here in question is affected by the stability, or instability, of the Contract which they both assume; that each of them, considered purely in abstraction, might conceivably be pursued by men to whom the sense of moral obligation, of a Contract as binding upon those who make it, is a thing utterly unknown. In the former of the two cases, that will hardly be disputed. The very words 'natural explanation' obviously imply it. A little reflection will shew that it is equally true of the latter also. All that, by the strict necessities of the case, is demanded—in particular, all that Rousseau himself demands— is that, at the moment of making the Contract, the individuals concerned shall be acting with perfect freedom. And even though the Contract should result in placing severe restrictions on that freedom—as Rousseau would say, in replacing the 'natural freedom' of the primitive state by the 'moral freedom' of the civil state[1]—this can never do away with the fact that, in the first instance, the step was taken spontaneously, and that it was prompted not by moral, but by purely natural, motives.

Logically, the argument is valid. And it would be hard to shew that Rousseau ever departs from the narrow limits of the premisses on which it rests. Yet, when all is said, it is strangely unconvincing. The premisses are, in fact, far too narrow. They are a chain of pure abstractions. They have no relation to the mixed motives of human nature; none to the creatures of flesh and blood—whether we think of them as half-formed men, or as 'stupid and limited animals'—whose place they usurp in the shadowy world of Rousseau. And if we have dwelt for a moment upon such fine-spun subtleties, it is not for their own sake, but for the light they throw upon the turn—so unexpected, so seldom understood—which he gave to the well-worn theory of Contract.

That theory, it may be well to repeat once more, contains two distinct, if not conflicting elements: the element of freedom, of individual independence, which asserts itself until the moment when the Contract is made; and the element of collective compulsion, of obligation to abide by the pledged word, which becomes the dominant factor the moment the Contract is concluded. Both elements are necessary to the life of the State. And it is because the same two elements are present in the familiar transaction called a Contract that the analogy between it and civil society took such persistent hold of men's imagination. If the

[1] *C. S.* I. viii.

two elements could be united in an affair of such every-day occurrence as a lease, it seemed easy to account for their union in a thing so apparently complex as the life of the community or the State. The fortune of the theory was made by the coincidence. And in their delight at the discovery, men failed to remember that neither lease, nor any other form of bargain, is possible except in civil society; that to use them as an explanation of that society is to bring forward the effect as an explanation of its own cause; that the whole theory is consequently, in the strictest sense, preposterous; that, in plain English, it is to put the cart before the horse. It affects to provide a sanction for the duties of civil society. But, when closely sifted, it is seen to do nothing of the kind.

This objection is as fatal to Rousseau's as to all other forms of the theory of Contract. The only difference is that all the other champions of Contract, Spinoza excepted, betray no suspicion of the difficulty; and that Rousseau—at any rate, in the earlier version of his political masterpiece—is alive to it in the highest degree. His uneasiness reveals itself in a curious variety of ways. He vacillates over the very title of the treatise; and it is only after much hesitation that he consents to let the misleading word *Contract* remain[1]. He mocks at the practice of exacting promises from children, on the ground, which is equally fatal to the social pact or promise, that they are still in the state of nature and cannot know, therefore, what they are about[2]. He is willing to replace the idea of Contract by that of expediency, *l'utilité commune*, as the foundation of the State[3]. He leaves a Fragment in which he asks himself the awkward question: 'How can we count on the promises which nothing can force the contracting parties to make good, and which, when the interest that makes them acceptable changes, they will inevitably desire to break[4]?' Finally, in the very forefront of a treatise, which its title proclaims to be based on the idea of Contract, he places a crushing assault upon the idea of natural law, without which no Contract is worth a moment's purchase. And when, at the last minute, he sets himself to remove all these traces of doubt or unbelief, it is not to replace them by any arguments to the contrary, but simply to leave a gap which, but for the blindness of his readers, could never have passed without notice and without challenge.

[1] See Introduction, p. 22.   [2] *Ib.* p. 43.
[3] *Ib.* p. 46.
[4] See Fragments, A (above, p. 324); MS. Neuchâtel, 7858.

Dussaulx tells us that, in after years, he saw Rousseau take up the volume and heard him say: That is a book which needs to be rewritten[1]. What was it that wrung from him this strange admission? Was it the consciousness that, as he laboured over the writing of it, he had struck veins of thought which he had never had the courage to follow out? that he had caught glimpses of a truth which others, if they had but the will and genius, must now be left to make their own? It is impossible to say. We cannot stifle the regret that he himself shrank from the task which, by his own avowal, he knew was to be done afresh. But it is well to remember that there is no surer sign of greatness than to be discontented with achievement; and that no thinker deserves our gratitude so deeply as the man whose work prompts others to raise questions which he himself is either unable or unwilling to solve[2].

[1] 'C'est un livre à refaire; mais je n'en ai plus la force ni le temps.' The story must refer to 1770 or 1771. Dussaulx, *De mes rapports avec J.-J. Rousseau*, p. 102 (ed. Paris, 1798).

[2] Is it possible to date the Geneva MS. with any precision? The more the subject is considered, the less certain seem the conclusions to be drawn. The one fixed point is that the bulk of the second chapter (*De la société générale du genre humain*) must have been written after Diderot had composed his article on *Droit naturel* for the fifth volume of the *Encyclopédie*. This volume was published in November, 1755. And, as Diderot was principal contributor as well as editor, it would seem hardly probable that the article was written long before. Probably 1754 is as far back as it can reasonably be put. And this would throw Rousseau's reply, which is given by the chapter in question, as late as 1754 or 1755. We know from a Fragment (above, p. 322) that this was originally designed for the opening chapter of the treatise. But, considering Rousseau's known habits of composition, it would be hazardous to assume that it was necessarily the first written. It may have been, or it may not. Again, who can say whether the passages (I. v. and I. vii.), which reappear in *Éc. pol.*, were copied from *C. S.*, or the reverse? Is Rousseau likely to have copied passages from a published work into one which he intended to publish hereafter?

On the whole, the most natural assumption—but it is no more than an assumption—would seem to be that the *Contrat social*, in the form represented by the Geneva MS., was begun in 1754 or 1755; that the greater part of it, including the portion torn off from the existing manuscript, was composed between the spring of 1756 and the early months of 1759 (*Confessions*; *Œuvres*, VIII. pp. 289, 370); and that the whole treatise was recast into its final shape during the latter half of 1761. The closing chapter, that on Civil Religion, was undoubtedly added in that year. The Fragments— *L'état de guerre* and those contained in MS. Neuchâtel, 7840—*may* go back into the two or three years before 1754; but on this point we are left entirely to conjecture.

DU CONTRACT SOCIAL, OU ESSAI SUR LA FORME DE LA RÉPUBLIQUE

[Geneva, MS. f. 225.]

LIVRE I.

Premières notions du corps social.

CHAPITRE I.

Sujet de cet ouvrage.

Tant d'auteurs célèbres ont traité des maximes du Gouvernement et des règles du droit civil qu'il n'y a rien d'utile à dire sur ce sujet qui n'ait été déjà dit. Mais peut-être serait-on mieux d'accord, peut-être les meilleurs rapports du Corps social auraient-ils[1] été plus clairement établis, si l'on eût commencé par mieux déterminer sa nature. C'est ce que j'ai tenté de faire dans cet écrit. Il n'est donc point ici question de l'administration de ce Corps, mais de sa constitution[2]; [3]je le fais vivre, et non pas agir[3]. Je décris ses ressorts et ses pièces, je les arrange à leur place. Je mets la machine[4] en état d'aller[5]. D'autres plus sages en régleront les mouvements.

Que la souveraineté est indivisible[6].

---

[1] [seraient-ils mieux.]
[2] [son établissement.]
[3] [je dis ce qu'il est, et non ce qu'il fait.]
[4] [le tout.]
[5] [de se mouvoir.]
[6] This heading comes at the bottom of the page and leads nowhere. It is immediately followed by these words (which occur in the chapter on Civil Religion):—'et quand il y aurait de la philosophie à n'avoir point de religion, je trouverais la supposition d'un peuple de vrais philosophes encore plus chimérique que celle d'un peuple de vrais chrétiens.'

CHAPITRE II.

DE LA SOCIÉTÉ GÉNÉRALE DU GENRE HUMAIN[1].

Commençons par rechercher[2] d'où naît la nécessité des institutions politiques[3].

[4]La force de l'homme[4] est tellement proportionnée à ses besoins naturels et à son état primitif que, pour peu que cet état change et que ces besoins augmentent, l'assistance de ses semblables lui devient nécessaire; et quand[5] enfin ses désirs embrassent toute la nature, le concours de tout le genre humain suffit à peine pour les assouvir. C'est ainsi que les mêmes causes qui nous rendent méchants nous rendent encore esclaves, et nous asservissent[6] en nous dépravant. Le sentiment de notre faiblesse vient moins de notre nature que de notre cupidité : nos besoins nous rapprochent à mesure que nos passions nous divisent; et plus nous devenons ennemis de nos semblables, moins nous pouvons nous passer d'eux[7]. Tels sont les premiers liens de la société générale; tels sont les fondements de cette bienveillance universelle dont la nécessité reconnue semble étouffer le sentiment, et dont chacun voudrait recueillir le fruit sans être obligé de la cultiver. Car, quant à l'identité de nature, son effet est nul en cela; parce qu'elle est autant pour les hommes un sujet de querelle que d'union, et met aussi souvent entre eux la concurrence et la jalousie que la bonne intelligence et l'accord.

De ce nouvel ordre de choses naissent des multitudes de

---

[1] [Originally 'Qu'il n'y a point naturellement de société générale entre les hommes.'] The primitive title of this chapter, as appears from a Fragment in MS. (Neuchâtel) 7854, was *Du droit naturel et de la société générale*. This marks still more clearly the connection between it and Diderot's article, *Droit naturel*. For the Fragment in question, see p. 322.

[2] [examiner.]

[3] Written on v° of p. 1 : Les signes moraux sont incertains, difficiles à soumettre au calcul.

La sûreté, la tranquillité, la liberté même.

Plusieurs peuples au milieu des guerres et des dissensions intestines ne laissent pas de multiplier extrêmement. Dans d'autres Gouvernements, au contraire, la paix même est dévorante et consume les citoyens.

[4] [L'homme isolé est un être si faible, ou du moins dont la force.] This paragraph, with the foregoing variant, appears also in MS. Neuchâtel, 7840. See above, p. 323. D. B. reads *ses besoins*. MS. has *ces*.

[5] [à force de progrès.]

[6] [assujettissent.]   [7] [d'être ensemble—les uns des autres.]

rapports sans mesure, sans règle, sans consistance, que les hommes altèrent et changent continuellement, cent travaillant à les détruire pour un qui travaille à les fixer. Et comme l'existence relative d'un homme dans l'état de nature dépend de mille autres rapports[1] qui sont dans un flux continuel, il ne peut jamais s'assurer d'être le même durant deux instants de sa vie; la paix et le bonheur ne sont pour lui qu'un éclair; rien n'est permanent que la misère qui résulte de toutes ces vicissitudes. Quand ses sentiments et ses idées pourraient s'élever jusqu'à l'amour de l'ordre et aux notions sublimes de la vertu, il lui serait impossible de faire jamais une application sûre de ses principes dans un état de choses qui ne lui laisserait discerner ni le bien ni le mal, ni l'honnête homme ni le méchant.

La société générale, telle que nos besoins mutuels peuvent l'engendrer, n'offre donc point une assistance efficace à l'homme devenu misérable; ou du moins elle ne donne de nouvelles forces qu'à celui qui en a déjà trop, tandis que le faible, perdu, étouffé, écrasé dans la multitude, ne trouve nul asile où se réfugier, nul support à sa faiblesse, et périt enfin victime de cette union trompeuse, dont il attendait son bonheur.

[²Si l'on est une fois convaincu que, dans les motifs qui portent les hommes à s'unir entre eux par des liens volontaires, il n'y a rien qui se rapporte au point de réunion; que, loin de se proposer un objet de félicité commune d'où chacun pût[3] tirer la sienne, le bonheur de l'un fait le malheur d'un autre; si l'on voit enfin qu'au lieu de tendre tous au bien général ils ne se rapprochent entre eux que parce que tous s'en éloignent; on doit sentir aussi que, quand même un tel état pourrait subsister, il ne serait qu'une source de crimes et de misères pour des hommes dont chacun ne verrait que son intérêt, ne suivrait que ses penchants et n'écouterait que ses passions[2].]

Ainsi, la douce voix de la nature n'est plus pour nous un guide infaillible, ni l'indépendance, que nous avons reçue d'elle, un état désirable; la paix et l'innocence nous ont échappé pour jamais, avant que nous en eussions goûté les délices. Insensible aux stupides hommes des premiers temps, échappée aux hommes éclairés des temps postérieurs, l'heureuse vie de l'âge d'or fut toujours un état étranger à la race humaine, ou pour l'avoir

---

[1] [relations.]
[2] All this paragraph is cancelled and replaced by 'ainsi.'
[3] D. B. reads *puisse*, against the MS.; and *ces* (for *les*) *motifs*, three lines above.

méconnu quand elle en pouvait jouir, ou pour l'avoir perdu[1] quand elle aurait pu le connaître.

Il y a plus encore : cette parfaite indépendance et cette liberté sans règle, fût-elle même demeurée jointe à l'antique innocence, aurait eu toujours un vice essentiel, et nuisible au progrès de nos plus excellentes facultés : savoir, le défaut de cette liaison des parties qui constitue le tout. La terre serait couverte d'hommes, entre lesquels il n'y aurait presque aucune communication[2] ; nous nous toucherions par quelques points, sans être unis par aucun ; chacun resterait isolé parmi les autres, chacun ne songerait qu'à soi ; notre entendement ne saurait se développer ; nous vivrions sans rien sentir, nous mourrions sans avoir vécu ; tout notre bonheur consisterait à ne pas connaître notre misère ; il n'y aurait ni bonté dans nos cœurs ni moralité dans nos actions, et nous n'aurions jamais goûté le plus délicieux sentiment de l'âme, qui est l'amour de la vertu.

[[3]Il est certain que le mot de *genre humain* n'offre à l'esprit qu'une idée purement collective, qui ne suppose aucune union réelle entre les individus qui le constituent. Ajoutons-y, si l'on veut, cette supposition : concevons[4] le genre humain comme une personne morale ayant, avec un sentiment d'existence commune[5] qui lui donne l'individualité et la constitue une, un mobile universel qui fasse agir chaque partie pour une fin générale[6] et relative au tout. Concevons que ce sentiment commun soit celui de l'humanité, et que la loi naturelle soit le principe actif de toute la machine. Observons ensuite ce qui résulte de la constitution de l'homme dans ses rapports avec ses semblables : et, tout au contraire de ce que nous avons supposé, nous trouverons que le progrès de la société étouffe l'humanité dans les cœurs, en éveillant l'intérêt personnel, et que les notions de la loi naturelle, qu'il faudrait plutôt appeler la loi de raison, ne commencent à se développer que quand le développement antérieur des passions rend impuissants tous ses préceptes. Par où l'on voit que ce prétendu traité social, dicté par la nature, est une véritable chimère ; puisque les conditions en sont toujours inconnues ou impraticables, et qu'il faut nécessairement les ignorer ou les enfreindre.

Si la société générale existait ailleurs que dans les systèmes des philosophes, elle serait, comme je l'ai dit, un être moral qui aurait

---

[1] D. B. and W. read *méconnue, perdue*, against the MS.   [2] [liaison.]
[3] Two next paragraphs, in brackets, cancelled.
[4] D. B. reads *concevoir*.   [5] D. B. omits *commune*.
[6] [commune.]

des qualités propres, et distinctes de celles des êtres particuliers qui la constituent ; à peu près comme les composés chimiques ont des propriétés qu'ils ne tiennent d'aucun des mixtes qui les composent. Il y aurait une langue universelle que la nature apprendrait à tous les hommes, et qui serait le premier instrument de leur mutuelle communication. Il y aurait une sorte de sensorium commun qui servirait[1] à la correspondance de toutes les parties. Le bien ou le mal[2] public ne serait pas seulement la somme des biens ou des maux particuliers, comme dans une simple agrégation, mais il résiderait dans la liaison[3] qui les unit ; il serait plus grand que cette somme ; et, loin que la félicité publique fût établie sur le bonheur des particuliers[4], c'est elle qui en serait la source.]

[5]Il est faux que, dans l'état d'indépendance, la raison nous porte[5] à concourir au bien commun[6] par la vue de notre propre intérêt. Loin[7] que l'intérêt particulier s'allie au bien général, ils s'excluent l'un l'autre dans l'ordre naturel des choses ; et les lois sociales sont un joug que chacun veut bien imposer aux autres, mais non pas s'en charger lui-même. '[8]Je sens que je porte l'épouvante et le trouble au milieu de l'espèce humaine,' dit l'homme indépendant que le sage étouffe ; ' mais il faut que je sois malheureux, ou que je fasse le malheur des autres, et personne ne m'est plus cher que moi[8]. C'est vainement,' pourra-t-il ajouter, ' que je voudrais concilier mon intérêt avec celui d'autrui ; tout ce que vous me dites des avantages de la loi sociale pourrait être bon, si, tandis que je l'observerais scrupuleusement envers les autres, j'étais sûr qu'ils l'observeraient tous envers moi. Mais quelle sûreté pouvez-vous me donner là-dessus ? et ma situation peut-elle être pire que de me voir exposé à tous les maux que les plus forts voudront me faire, sans oser me dédommager sur les faibles[9] ? Ou donnez-moi des garants[10] contre toute entreprise injuste, ou n'espérez pas que je m'en abstienne à mon tour. Vous avez beau me dire qu'en renonçant aux devoirs

---

[1] D. B. reads *survivrait*, wrongly. MS. has *commune*, by a slip.
[2] D. B. reads *le bien et le mal*.
[3] D. B. and W. read *dans la raison*.
[4] ['et à leurs dépens' written between the lines and then cancelled.]
[5] [Il faudrait que chacun fût porté.]
[6] [ou par une force coactive qui l'y contraignît, ou par la vue.]
[7] [mais loin.]
[8] This sentence is quoted from article 'Droit naturel' of *Encyclopédie*, with the small variant *ou que je sois malheureux*. See above, p. 430. The rest of the chapter is one long reply to Diderot.
[9] [sur de plus faibles que moi.]
[10] D. B. reads *garanties*.

que m'impose la loi naturelle je me prive en même temps de ses droits, et que mes violences autoriseront toutes celles dont on voudra user envers moi. J'y consens d'autant plus volontiers que je ne vois point comment ma modération pourrait m'en garantir. Au surplus, ce sera mon affaire [1]de mettre les forts dans mes intérêts, en partageant avec eux les dépouilles des faibles; cela vaudra mieux que la justice pour mon avantage et pour ma sûreté.' La preuve que c'est ainsi qu'eût raisonné l'homme éclairé[2] et indépendant est que c'est ainsi que raisonne toute société souveraine qui ne rend compte[3] de sa conduite qu'à elle-même.

Que répondre de solide à de pareils discours, si l'on ne veut amener la religion à l'aide de la morale, et faire intervenir immédiatement la volonté de Dieu pour lier la société des hommes? Mais les notions sublimes du Dieu des sages, les douces lois de la fraternité qu'il nous impose, les vertus sociales des âmes pures, qui sont le vrai culte qu'il veut de nous, échapperont toujours à la multitude. On lui fera toujours des Dieux insensés comme elle, auxquels elle sacrifiera de legères commodités pour se livrer en leur honneur à mille passions horribles et destructives. La terre entière regorgerait de sang, et le genre humain périrait bientôt, si la philosophie et les lois ne retenaient les fureurs du fanatisme, et si la voix des hommes n'était plus forte que celle des Dieux.

En effet, si[4] les notions du grand Être et de la loi naturelle étaient innées dans tous les cœurs, ce fut un soin bien superflu d'enseigner expressément l'une et l'autre. C'était nous apprendre ce que nous savions déjà, et la manière dont on s'y est pris eût été bien plus propre à nous le[5] faire oublier. Si elles ne l'étaient pas, tous ceux à qui Dieu ne les a point données sont dispensés de les savoir. Dès qu'il a fallu pour cela des instructions particulières, chaque peuple a les siennes qu'on lui prouve être les seules bonnes, et d'où dérivent plus souvent le carnage et les meurtres que la concorde et la paix.

Laissons donc à part les préceptes sacrés des religions diverses, dont l'abus cause autant de crimes que leur usage en peut épargner; et rendons au philosophe l'examen d'une question que le théologien n'a jamais traitée qu'au préjudice du genre humain.

Mais[6] le premier me renverra par devant le genre humain même, à qui seul il appartient de décider, parce que le plus grand

---

[1] [de mettre dans mes intérêts ceux qui seront plus forts que moi.]
[2] It is not clear whether *éclairé et* is cancelled or not.
[3] [répond.]   [4] [comme je le crois.]
[5] [les; a reading retained by D. B.]   [6] *Droit naturel*, § vi.

bien de tous est la seule passion qu'il ait. C'est, me dira-t-il, à la volonté générale que l'individu doit s'adresser pour savoir jusqu'où il doit être homme, citoyen, sujet, père, enfant, et quand il lui convient de vivre et de mourir. 'Je vois bien là, je l'avoue, la règle que je puis consulter; mais je ne vois pas encore,' dira notre homme indépendant, 'la raison qui doit m'assujettir à cette règle. [1]Il ne s'agit pas de m'apprendre ce que c'est que justice[2]; il s'agit de me montrer quel intérêt j'ai d'être juste.' [3]En effet, que la volonté générale soit dans chaque individu un acte pur de l'entendement qui raisonne dans le silence des passions sur ce que l'homme peut exiger de son semblable, et sur ce que son semblable est en droit d'exiger de lui, [4]nul n'en disconviendra[4]. Mais où est l'homme qui puisse ainsi se séparer de lui-même? et, si le soin de sa propre conservation est le premier précepte de la nature, peut-on le forcer de regarder ainsi l'espèce[5] en général pour s'imposer, à lui, des devoirs dont il ne voit point la liaison avec sa constitution particulière? Les objections précédentes ne subsistent-elles pas toujours? et ne reste-t-il pas encore à voir comment son intérêt personnel exige qu'il se soumette à la volonté générale?

De plus; comme l'art de généraliser ainsi ses idées est un des exercices les plus difficiles et les plus tardifs de l'entendement humain, le commun des hommes sera-t-il jamais en état de tirer de cette manière de raisonner les règles de sa conduite? et quand il faudrait consulter la volonté générale sur un acte particulier, combien de fois n'arriverait-il pas à un homme bien intentionné de se tromper sur la règle ou sur l'application, et de ne suivre que son penchant en pensant obéir à la loi? Que fera-t-il donc pour se garantir de l'erreur? Écoutera-t-il la voix intérieure? Mais cette voix n'est, dit-on, formée que par l'habitude de juger et de sentir dans le sein de la société, et selon ses lois; elle ne peut donc servir à les établir. [6]Et puis il faudrait qu'il ne se fût élevé dans son cœur aucune de ces passions qui parlent plus haut que la conscience, couvrent sa timide voix, et font soutenir aux philosophes que cette voix n'existe pas[6]. Consultera-t-il[7] les principes du Droit écrit, les actions sociales de tous les peuples, les conventions tacites des ennemis mêmes du genre humain? La première difficulté revient toujours, et ce n'est que de l'ordre social, établi parmi nous, que

---

[1] This sentence added on opposite blank, to *En effet* inclusive.
[2] [je le sais aussi bien que vous.]   [3] [car.]
[4] [je n'en disconviens pas.]   [5] [l'homme.]
[6] This sentence written on the opposite blank.
[7] See *Droit naturel*, § viii.

nous tirons les idées de celui que nous imaginons. Nous concevons la société générale d'après nos sociétés particulières ; l'établissement des petites Républiques nous fait songer à la grande ; et nous ne commençons proprement à devenir hommes qu'après avoir été citoyens. Par où l'on voit ce qu'il faut penser de ces prétendus cosmopolites qui, justifiant leur amour pour la patrie par leur amour pour le genre humain, se vantent d'aimer tout le monde, pour avoir droit de n'aimer personne.

Ce que le raisonnement nous démontre à cet égard est parfaitement confirmé par les faits ; et pour peu qu'on remonte dans les hautes antiquités, on voit aisément que les saines idées du droit naturel et de la fraternité commune de[1] tous les hommes se sont répandues assez tard, et ont fait des progrès si lents dans le monde qu'il n'y a que le Christianisme qui les ait suffisamment généralisées. Encore trouve-t-on dans les lois mêmes de Justinien les anciennes violences autorisées à bien des égards, non seulement sur les ennemis déclarés, mais sur tout ce qui n'était pas sujet de l'Empire ; en sorte que l'humanité des Romains ne s'étendait pas plus loin que leur domination.

En effet, on a cru longtemps, comme l'observe Grotius, qu'il était permis de voler, piller, maltraiter les étrangers et surtout les barbares, jusqu'à les réduire en esclavage. De là vient qu'on demandait à des inconnus, sans les choquer, s'ils étaient brigands ou pirates ; parce que le métier, loin d'être ignominieux, passait alors pour honorable. Les premiers héros[2], comme Hercule et Thésée, qui faisaient la guerre aux brigands ne laissaient pas[3] d'exercer le brigandage eux-mêmes[3] ; et les Grecs appelaient souvent traités de paix ceux qui se faisaient entre des peuples qui n'étaient point en guerre. Les mots d'étrangers et d'ennemis ont été longtemps synonymes chez plusieurs anciens peuples, même chez les Latins. *Hostis enim*, dit Cicéron, *apud majores nostros dicebatur, quem nunc peregrinum dicimus.* L'erreur de Hobbes n'est donc pas d'avoir établi l'état de guerre entre les hommes indépendants et devenus sociables ; mais d'avoir supposé cet état naturel à l'espèce, et de l'avoir donné pour cause aux vices dont il est l'effet[4].

[5]Mais quoiqu'il n'y ait point de société naturelle et générale

---

[1] [à.] D. B. retains this reading, in spite of the correction.
[2] [Aussi voit-on que les héros.]
[3] [de l'être eux-mêmes dans d'autres occasions.]   [4] [l'ouvrage.]
[5] The rough draft of this paragraph is found in MS. Neuchâtel, 7840. See above, p. 323.

entre les hommes, quoiqu'ils deviennent malheureux et méchants en devenant sociables, quoique les lois de la justice et de l'égalité ne soient rien pour ceux qui vivent à la fois dans la liberté de l'état de nature et soumis aux besoins de l'état social; loin de penser qu'il n'y ait ni vertu ni bonheur pour nous, et que le ciel nous ait abandonnés sans ressource à la dépravation de l'espèce, efforçons nous de tirer du mal même le remède qui doit le guérir. Par de nouvelles associations, corrigeons[1], s'il se peut, le défaut de l'association générale. Que notre violent interlocuteur[2] juge lui-même du succès. Montrons-lui, dans l'art perfectionné, la réparation des maux que l'art commencé fit à la nature; montrons-lui toute la misère de l'état qu'il croyait heureux, tout le faux du raisonnement qu'il croyait solide. Qu'il voie dans une meilleure constitution de[3] choses le prix des bonnes actions, le châtiment des mauvaises et l'accord aimable de la justice et du bonheur. Éclairons sa raison de nouvelles lumières, échauffons son cœur de nouveaux sentiments[4], et qu'il apprenne à multiplier son être et sa félicité, en les partageant avec ses semblables. Si mon zèle ne m'aveugle pas dans cette entreprise, ne doutons point qu'avec une âme forte et un sens droit cet ennemi du genre humain n'abjure enfin sa haine, avec ses erreurs; que la raison qui l'égarait ne le ramène à l'humanité; qu'il n'apprenne à préférer à son intérêt apparent son intérêt bien entendu; qu'il ne devienne bon, vertueux, sensible, et pour tout dire enfin, d'un brigand féroce, qu'il voulait être, le plus ferme appui d'une société bien ordonnée.

CHAPITRE III.

Du pacte fondamental.

L'homme est né libre, et cependant partout il est dans les fers. Tel se croit le maître des autres qui ne laisse pas d'être plus esclave qu'eux. Comment ce changement s'est-il fait? On n'en sait rien. Qu'est-ce qui peut le rendre légitime? Il n'est pas impossible de le dire. Si je ne considérais que la force, ainsi que les autres, je dirais: tant que le peuple est contraint d'obéir et qu'il obéit, il fait bien; sitôt qu'il peut secouer le joug et qu'il le secoue, il fait

---

[1] [réparons.]
[2] A reference to Diderot's phrase: 'Que répondrons-nous donc à notre raisonneur violent, avant que de l'étouffer?' *Droit naturel*, § v.
[3] D. B. reads *des*.   [4] [feux.]

encore mieux ; car, recouvrant sa liberté par le même droit qui la lui a ravie, ou il est bien fondé à la reprendre, ou l'on ne l'était point à la lui ôter. Mais l'ordre social est un droit sacré qui sert de base à tous les autres; cependant ce droit n'a point sa source dans la nature ; il est donc fondé sur une convention. Il s'agit de savoir quelle est cette convention, et comment elle a pu se former[1].

Sitôt que les besoins de l'homme passent ses facultés et que les objets de ses désirs[2] s'étendent et se multiplient, il faut qu'il reste éternellement malheureux[3], ou qu'il cherche à se donner un nouvel être duquel il tire les ressources qu'il ne trouve plus en lui-même. Sitôt que les obstacles qui nuisent à notre conservation l'emportent par leur resistance sur les forces que chaque individu peut employer à les vaincre, l'état primitif ne peut plus subsister ; et le genre humain périrait, si l'art ne venait au secours de la nature. Or, comme l'homme ne peut pas engendrer de nouvelles forces, mais seulement unir et diriger celles qui existent, il n'a plus d'autre moyen pour se conserver que de former par agrégation une somme de forces qui puisse l'emporter sur la résistance, de les mettre en jeu par un seul mobile, de les faire agir conjointement et de les diriger sur un seul objet. Tel est le problème fondamental dont l'institution de l'État donne la solution.

Si donc on rassemble ces conditions, et qu'on écarte du pacte social ce qui n'est pas de son essence, on trouvera qu'il se réduit aux termes suivants. 'Chacun de nous met en commun sa volonté, ses biens, sa force et[4] sa personne, sous la direction de la volonté générale, et nous recevons tous en corps chaque membre comme partie inaliénable du tout.'

À l'instant, au lieu de la personne particulière de chaque contractant, cet acte d'association produit un corps moral et collectif, composé d'autant de membres que l'assemblée a de voix, et auquel le moi commun donne l'unité formelle, la vie et la volonté. Cette personne publique, qui se forme ainsi par l'union de toutes les autres, prend en général le nom de Corps politique : lequel est appelé par ses membres *État* quand il est passif, *Souverain* quand il est actif, *Puissance* en le comparant à ses semblables.

---

[1] [pour être légitime.]
[2] D. B. reads *dessins*.
[3] The phrase seems to be deliberately quoted from Diderot's *Droit naturel* (§ iii.), and turned against the author. It may be that Rousseau intended to cancel this sentence (which he has not done in the MS.) and to replace it by the following: *Sitôt que les obstacles*, etc.
[4] [toute.]

À l'égard des membres eux-mêmes, ils prennent le nom de *Peuple* collectivement, et s'appellent en particulier *Citoyens*, comme membres de la *Cité* ou participants à l'autorité souveraine, et *Sujets*, comme soumis aux lois de l'État. Mais ces termes, rarement employés dans toute leur précision, se prennent souvent l'un pour l'autre; et il suffit de les savoir distinguer, quand le sens du discours le demande.

On voit par cette formule que l'acte de la confédération primitive renferme un engagement réciproque du public avec les particuliers, et que chaque individu, contractant pour ainsi dire avec lui-même, se trouve engagé sous un double rapport: savoir, comme membre du Souverain envers les particuliers, et comme membre de l'État envers le Souverain. Mais il faut remarquer qu'on ne peut pas appliquer ici la maxime du Droit Civil que nul n'est tenu aux engagements pris avec lui-même; car il y a bien de la différence entre s'obliger envers soi, ou envers un tout dont on fait partie. Il faut remarquer encore que la déliberation publique, qui peut obliger tous les sujets[1] envers le souverain à cause des deux différents rapports sous lesquels chacun d'eux est envisagé, ne peut, par la raison contraire, obliger le souverain[2] envers lui-même; et que par conséquent il est contre la nature du Corps politique que le souverain impose[3] une loi qu'il ne puisse enfreindre. Ne pouvant se considérer que sous un seul et même rapport, il est alors[4] dans le cas d'un particulier contractant avec soi-même. Par où l'on voit qu'il n'y a, ni ne peut y avoir, nulle espèce de loi fondamentale obligatoire pour le Corps du peuple: ce qui ne signifie pas que ce Corps ne puisse fort bien s'engager envers autrui, du moins en ce qui n'est pas contraire à sa nature; car[5], à l'égard de l'étranger, il devient[5] un être simple ou un individu.

Sitôt que cette multitude est ainsi réunie en un corps, on ne saurait offenser un des membres sans attaquer le corps dans une partie de son existence, encore moins offenser le corps sans que les membres s'en ressentent; puisqu'outre la vie commune, dont il s'agit, tous risquent[6] encore la partie d'eux-mêmes [7]dont le souverain n'a pas actuellement disposé, et dont ils ne jouissent en sûreté que sous la[7] protection publique. Ainsi le devoir et l'intérêt obligent également les deux parties contractantes à s'entr'aider mutuellement; [8]et les mêmes personnes doivent chercher à réunir sous ce

---

[1] [citoyens envers l'État.] [2] [engager l'État.]
[3] [se prescrive.] [4] [exactement.]
[5] [alors il n'est considéré que comme.] [6] [chacun risque.]
[7] [dont il ne jouit que sous la.] [8] [c'est à dire que.]

double rapport tous les avantages qui en dépendent. Mais il y a quelques distinctions à faire en ce que le souverain, [1]n'étant formé que[1] des particuliers qui le composent, n'a jamais d'intérêt contraire au leur; et que par conséquent la puissance[2] souveraine ne saurait jamais avoir besoin de garant envers les particuliers, parce qu'il est impossible que le corps veuille jamais nuire à ses membres. Il n'en est pas de même[3] des particuliers vis-à-vis du souverain; à qui, malgré l'intérêt commun, rien ne répondrait de leurs engagements, s'il ne trouvait des moyens de s'assurer de leur fidélité. En effet, chaque individu peut, comme homme, avoir une volonté particulière contraire ou dissemblable à la volonté générale, qu'il a comme citoyen. Son existence absolue et indépendante peut lui faire envisager ce qu'il doit à la cause commune comme une contribution gratuite dont la perte sera moins nuisible[4] aux autres que le payement n'en[5] est onéreux pour lui; et regardant la personne morale qui constitue l'État comme un être de raison, parce que ce n'est pas un homme, il jouirait des droits du citoyen sans vouloir remplir les devoirs du sujet: injustice dont le progrès causerait bientôt la ruine du Corps politique.

Afin donc que le Contrat social ne soit pas un vain formulaire, il faut qu'indépendamment du consentement des particuliers le souverain ait quelques garants le leurs engagements envers la cause commune. Le serment est ordinairement le premier de ces garants: mais, comme il est tiré d'un ordre de choses tout à fait différent et que chacun selon ses maximes internes modifie à son gré l'obligation qu'il lui impose, on y compte peu dans les institutions politiques; et l'on préfère avec raison les sûretés plus réelles qui se tirent de la chose même. Ainsi le pacte fondamental renferme tacitement cet engagement, qui seul peut donner de la force à tous les autres, que quiconque refusera d'obéir à la volonté générale y sera contraint par tout le Corps. Mais il importe ici de se bien souvenir que le caractère propre et distinctif de ce pacte[6] est que le peuple ne contracte qu'avec lui-même; c'est à dire, le peuple en corps, comme souverain, avec les particuliers qui le composent, comme sujets: condition qui fait tout l'artifice et le jeu de la machine politique, et qui seul rend légitimes, raisonnables et sans danger, des engagements qui sans cela seraient absurdes, tyranniques et sujets aux plus énormes abus.

[1] [ne tirant son existence que.]   [2] [souveraineté.]
[3] *de même* not cancelled; *ainsi* written above. D. B. omits *parce qu'il est ...des particuliers*.
[4] [sensible.]   [5] D. B. omits *en*.   [6] [du pacte social.]

Ce passage de l'état de nature à l'état social produit dans l'homme un changement très[1] remarquable, en substituant dans sa conduite la justice à l'instinct, et donnant à ses actions des rapports moraux qu'elles n'avaient point auparavant. C'est alors seulement que, la voix du devoir succédant à l'impulsion physique et le droit à l'appétit, l'homme, qui jusque là n'avait regardé que lui-même, se voit forcé d'agir sur d'autres principes, et de consulter sa raison avant d'écouter ses penchants. Mais, quoiqu'il se prive dans cet état de plusieurs avantages qu'il tient de la nature, il en regagne de si grands, ses facultés s'exercent et se développent, ses idées s'étendent, ses sentiments s'ennoblissent et son âme toute entière s'élève à tel point que, si les abus de cette nouvelle condition ne le dégradaient point souvent au-dessous même de celle dont il est sorti, il devrait bénir sans cesse l'instant heureux qui l'en arracha pour jamais et qui, d'un animal stupide et borné, fit un être intelligent et un homme.

Réduisons toute cette balance à des termes faciles à comparer. Ce que l'homme perd par le Contrat social, c'est la liberté naturelle et un droit illimité a tout ce qui lui est nécessaire ; ce qu'il gagne, c'est la liberté civile et la propriété de tout ce qu'il possède. Pour ne pas se tromper dans ces estimations, il faut bien distinguer la liberté naturelle, qui n'a pour bornes que la force de l'individu, de[2] la liberté civile, qui est limitée par la volonté générale ; et la possession, [3]qui n'est que l'effet de la force ou le droit du premier occupant[3], de la propriété, qui ne peut être fondée que sur un titre juridique.

Du domaine réel[4].

Chaque membre de la communauté se donne à elle au moment qu'elle se forme, tel qu'il se trouve actuellement, lui et toutes ses forces, dont les biens qu'il occupe font partie. Ce n'est pas que, par cet acte, la possession change de nature en changeant de mains, et devienne propriété dans celles du souverain. Mais, comme les forces de l'État sont incomparablement plus grandes que celles de chaque[5] particulier, la possession publique est aussi, dans le fait, plus forte et plus irrévocable, sans en être plus légitime, au moins par rapport aux étrangers. Car l'État, par rapport à ses membres, est maître de tous leurs biens par une convention solennelle : droit le plus sacré

---

[1] D. B. omits *très*.   [2] [d'avec.]
[3] [qui n'est que le droit du plus fort.]
[4] This written in between the lines.   [5] [d'un.]

qui soit connu des hommes. Mais il ne l'est, à l'égard des autres États, que par le droit de[1] premier occupant qu'il tient des particuliers : droit moins absurde, moins odieux que celui de conquêtes[2], et qui pourtant, bien examiné, n'est guère plus légitime.

Voilà comment les terres des particuliers réunies et contiguës deviennent le territoire public, et comment le [3]droit de souveraineté, s'étendant des sujets au terrain qu'ils occupent, devient à la fois réel et personnel : ce qui met les possesseurs dans une plus grande dépendance, et fait de leurs forces mêmes les cautions de leur fidélité. Avantage qui ne paraît pas avoir été bien connu des anciens monarques, lesquels semblaient se regarder comme les chefs des hommes plutôt que comme les maîtres du pays. Aussi ne s'appelaient-ils que Rois des Perses, des Scythes, des Macédoniens ; mais les nôtres s'appellent plus habilement Rois de France, d'Espagne, d'Angleterre. En tenant ainsi le terrain, ils sont bien sûrs d'en tenir les habitants.

Ce qu'il y a d'admirable dans cette aliénation, c'est que, loin qu'en acceptant les biens des particuliers la communauté les en dépouille, elle ne fait que leur en assurer la légitime disposition, changer l'usurpation en un véritable droit, et la jouissance en propriété. Alors, leur titre étant respecté de tous les membres de l'État et maintenu de toutes ses forces contre l'étranger, par une cession avantageuse à la communauté et plus encore à eux-mêmes, ils ont, pour ainsi dire, acquis tout ce qu'ils ont donné : énigme qui s'explique aisément par la distinction des droits que le souverain et le propriétaire ont sur le même fonds.

Il peut arriver aussi que les hommes commencent à s'unir, avant que de rien posséder ; et que, s'emparant ensuite d'un terrain suffisant pour tous, ils en jouissent en commun, ou bien le partagent entre eux, soit également, soit selon certaines proportions établies par le souverain. Mais, de quelque manière que se fasse cette acquisition, le droit que chaque particulier a sur son propre bien est toujours subordonné au droit que la communauté a sur tous ; sans quoi, il n'y aurait ni solidité dans le lien social, ni force réelle dans l'exercice de la souveraineté.

Je terminerai ce chapitre par une remarque[4] qui doit servir de base à tout le système social. C'est qu'au lieu de détruire l'égalité naturelle le pacte fondamental substitue au contraire une égalité morale et légitime à ce que la nature avait pu mettre d'inégalité

---

[1] D. B. reads *du premier occupant*.   [2] D. B. reads *celui de conquête*.
[3] [le terrain qu'ils....]
[4] [importante en matière de droit politique.]

physique entre les hommes; et que, pouvant naturellement être inégaux en force ou en génie, ils deviennent tous égaux par convention et de droit.

CHAPITRE IV.

En quoi consiste la souveraineté, et ce qui la rend inaliénable[1].

Il y a donc dans l'État une force commune qui le soutient, une volonté générale qui dirige cette force, et c'est l'application de l'une à l'autre qui constitue la souveraineté. Par où l'on voit que le souverain n'est par sa nature qu'une personne morale, qu'il n'a qu'une existence abstraite et collective, et que l'idée qu'on attache à ce mot ne peut être unie à celle d'un simple individu. Mais, comme c'est ici une proposition des plus importantes en matière de droit politique, tâchons de la mieux éclaircir.

Je crois pouvoir poser pour une maxime incontestable, que la volonté générale peut seule diriger les forces de l'État selon la fin de son institution, qui est le bien commun. Car, si l'opposition des intérêts particuliers a rendu nécessaire l'établissement des sociétés civiles, c'est l'accord de ces mêmes intérêts qui l'a rendu possible. C'est ce qu'il y a de commun dans ces différents intérêts qui forme le lien social; et s'il n'y avait pas quelque point dans lequel tous les intérêts s'accordent, la société ne saurait exister. Or, comme la volonté tend toujours au bien de l'être qui veut, que la volonté particulière a toujours pour objet l'intérêt privé, et la volonté générale l'intérêt commun, il s'ensuit que cette dernière est, ou doit être, seule le vrai mobile du Corps social.

Je conviens qu'on peut mettre en doute si quelque volonté particulière ne saurait s'accorder en tout avec la volonté générale; et par conséquent, supposé qu'une telle volonté particulière existât, si l'on ne pourrait pas sans inconvénient lui confier l'entière direction des forces publiques. Mais, sans prévenir sur cette question les solutions que j'en donnerai ci-après, chacun doit voir dès à présent qu'une volonté particulière, substituée à la volonté générale, est un instrument superflu quand elles sont d'accord, et nuisible quand elles sont opposées. On doit voir encore qu'une pareille supposition est absurde et impossible par la nature des choses; car l'intérêt privé tend toujours aux préférences, et l'intérêt public à l'égalité.

[1] [Ce que c'est que la souveraineté et qu'elle est inaliénable.]

CH. III, IV] *La volonté générale et la force publique* 461

De plus ; quand on aurait trouvé pour un moment l'accord des deux volontés, on ne pourrait jamais s'assurer que cet accord durerait encore le moment d'après[1], et qu'il ne naîtrait jamais d'opposition entre elles. [2]L'ordre des choses humaines est sujet à tant de révolutions, et les manières de penser, ainsi que les manières d'être, changent avec tant de facilité, que ce serait une témerité d'affirmer qu'on voudra demain ce qu'on veut aujourd'hui ; et, si la volonté générale est moins sujette à cette inconstance, rien n'en peut mettre à couvert la volonté particulière. Ainsi, quand même le Corps social pourrait dire une fois : 'je veux maintenant tout ce que veut un tel homme,' jamais il ne pourrait dire en parlant du même homme : 'ce qu'il voudra demain, je le voudrai encore.' Or, la volonté générale, qui doit diriger l'État, n'est pas celle d'un temps passé, mais celle du moment présent ; et le vrai caractère de la souveraineté est qu'il y ait toujours accord de temps, de lieu, d'effet, entre [3]la direction de la volonté générale et l'emploi de la force publique[3] : [4]accord sur lequel on ne peut plus compter[4], sitôt qu'une autre volonté, telle qu'elle puisse être, dispose de cette force. Il est vrai que, dans un État bien réglé, l'on peut toujours inférer[5] la durée[6] d'un acte de la volonté du peuple, de ce qu'il ne le détruit pas par un acte contraire. Mais c'est toujours en vertu [7]d'un consentement présent[7] et tacite que l'acte antérieur peut continuer d'avoir son effet ; [8]dans la suite, on verra[8] quelles conditions sont nécessaires pour faire présumer ce consentement.

Comme dans la constitution de l'homme l'action de l'âme sur le corps est l'abîme de la philosophie, de même l'action de la volonté générale sur la force publique est l'abîme de la politique dans la constitution de l'État. C'est là que tous les Législateurs [9]se sont perdus[9]. J'exposerai dans la suite les meilleurs moyens [10]qu'on ait employés à cet effet[10], et [11]je ne me fierai pour les apprécier au raisonnement qu'autant qu'il sera justifié par l'expérience[11]. Si[12] vouloir et faire sont la même chose pour tout être libre, et

---

[1] D. B. reads *le moment après*.
[2] [Car.] [3] In reverse order originally.
[4] [ce qu'on ne peut plus affirmer ; accord dont on ne peut plus s'assurer.]
[5] [inférer quelquefois.] [6] [continuation.]
[7] [de ce consentement actuel.]
[8] [et je ferai voir [je dirai] dans la suite.]
[9] [sont échoués.]
[10] [qui semblent pouvoir être employés pour cela.]
[11] [je me fierai moins pour en juger au raisonnement qu'à l'expérience.] In the text, D. B. omits *ne* before *me fierai*, by a slip.
[12] [Cependant.]

si la volonté d'un tel être mesure exactement la quantité de ses forces, qu'il emploie à l'accomplir, il est évident que, dans tout ce qui n'excède pas la puissance publique, l'État exécuterait toujours fidèlement tout ce que veut le souverain et comme il le veut, si la volonté était un acte aussi simple, et l'action un effet aussi immédiat, de cette même volonté, dans le corps civil que dans le corps humain.

Mais, quand même la liaison dont je parle serait établie [1]aussi bien qu'elle peut l'être[1], toutes les difficultés ne seraient pas levées. Les ouvrages des hommes, toujours moins parfaits que ceux de la nature, ne vont jamais si directement à leur fin. L'on ne peut éviter en politique, non plus qu'en mécanique, d'agir plus faiblement ou moins vite, et de perdre de la force ou du temps. La volonté générale est rarement celle de tous, et la force publique est toujours moindre que la somme des forces particulières; de sorte qu'il y a dans les ressorts de l'État un équivalent aux frottements des machines, qu'il faut savoir réduire à la moindre quantité possible, et qu'il faut du moins calculer et déduire d'avance de la force totale, pour proportionner exactement les moyens qu'on emploie à l'effet qu'on veut obtenir. Mais, sans entrer dans ces pénibles recherches qui font la science du Législateur, achevons de fixer l'idée de l'état civil.

CHAPITRE V.

Fausses notions du lien social.

Il y a mille manières de rassembler les hommes, il n'y en a qu'une de les unir. C'est pour cela que je ne donne dans cet ouvrage qu'une méthode pour la formation des sociétés politiques; quoique, dans la multitude d'agrégations qui existent actuellement sous ce nom, il n'y en ait peut-être pas deux qui aient été formées de la même[2] manière, et pas une qui l'ait été selon celle que j'établis. Mais je cherche le droit et la raison, et ne dispute pas des faits. Cherchons[3] sur ces règles quels jugements on doit porter des autres voies d'association civile, telles que les supposent la plupart[4] nos écrivains.

1. Que l'autorité naturelle d'un père de famille s'étende sur ses enfants au delà même de leur faiblesse et de leur besoin, et qu'en continuant de lui obéir ils fassent à la fin par habitude et

---

[1] Added in margin.   [2] [cette.]   [3] [Voyons.]
[4] Added. D. B. reads *la plupart de nos écrivains*, against the MS.

par reconnaissance ce qu'ils faisaient d'abord par nécessité, cela se conçoit sans peine ; et les liens qui peuvent unir la famille sont faciles à voir. Mais que, le père venant à mourir, un des enfants usurpe sur ses frères, dans un âge approchant du sien, et même sur des étrangers le pouvoir que le père avait sur tous, voilà ce qui n'a plus de raison ni de fondement. Car les droits naturels de l'âge, de la force, de la tendresse paternelle, les devoirs de la gratitude[1] filiale, tout manque à la fois dans ce nouvel ordre ; et les frères sont imbéciles ou dénaturés de soumettre leurs enfants au joug d'un homme qui, selon la loi naturelle, doit donner toute préférence aux siens. On ne voit plus ici dans les choses de nœuds qui unissent le chef et les membres. La force agit seule, et la nature ne dit plus rien.

Arrêtons-nous un instant à ce parallèle fait avec emphase par tant d'auteurs. Premièrement, [2]quand il y aurait entre l'État et la famille autant de rapports qu'ils le prétendent, il ne s'ensuivrait pas pour cela que les règles de conduite propres à l'une de ces deux sociétés convinssent[3] à l'autre. Elles diffèrent trop en grandeur pour pouvoir être administrées de la même manière ; et il y aura toujours une extrême différence entre le gouvernement domestique, où le pere voit tout par lui-même, et le gouvernement civil, où le chef ne voit presque rien que par les yeux d'autrui. Pour que les choses devinssent égales à cet égard, il faudrait que les talents, la force, et toutes les facultés du père augmentassent en raison de la grandeur de la famille ; et que l'âme d'un puissant monarque fût à celle d'un homme ordinaire comme l'étendue de son empire est à l'héritage d'un particulier.

Mais comment le gouvernement de l'État pourrait-il être semblable à celui de la famille, dont le principe est si différent ? Le père étant physiquement plus fort que ses enfants, aussi long-temps que son secours leur est nécessaire le pouvoir paternel passe avec raison pour être établi par la nature. Dans la grande famille, dont tous les membres sont naturellement égaux, l'autorité politique, purement arbitraire quant à son institution, ne peut être fondée que sur des conventions, ni le magistrat commander au citoyen qu'en vertu des lois[4]. Les devoirs du père lui sont dictés par des

[1] [reconnaissance.]
[2] The remainder of this paragraph, and the four following paragraphs— down to 'a jamais fait un bon roi'—reappear, with some variations, in the *Économie politique*. See above, pp. 237—240.
[3] [fussent convenables.]
[4] A sentence concerning the Right of life and death is inserted here in the 1782 Ed. of the *Économie politique*.

sentiments naturels, et d'un ton qui lui permet rarement de désobéir. Les chefs n'ont point de semblable règle, et ne sont réellement tenus envers le peuple qu'à ce qu'ils lui ont promis de faire, et dont il est en droit d'exiger l'exécution. Une autre différence plus importante encore est[1] que, les enfants n'ayant rien que ce qu'ils reçoivent du père, il est évident que tous les droits de propriété lui appartiennent ou émanent de lui. C'est tout le contraire dans la grande famille, où l'administration générale n'est établie que pour assurer la possession particulière, qui lui est antérieure. Le principal objet des travaux de toute la maison est de conserver et d'accroître le patrimoine du père, afin qu'il puisse un jour le partager entre ses enfants sans les appauvrir; au lieu que la richesse [2]du prince, loin de rien ajouter au bien-être des particuliers, leur coûte presque toujours la paix et l'abondance[2]. Enfin la petite famille est destinée à s'éteindre et à se résoudre un jour en plusieurs autres familles semblables. Mais, la grande étant faite pour durer toujours dans le même état, il faut que la première s'augmente pour se multiplier; et non seulement il suffit que l'autre se conserve, on peut prouver même[3] que toute augmentation lui est plus préjudiciable qu'utile.

Par plusieurs raisons tirées de la nature de la chose, le père doit commander dans la famille. Premièrement, l'autorité ne doit pas être égale entre le père et la mère; mais il faut que le gouvernement soit un, et que, dans les partages d'avis, il y ait une voix prépondérante qui décide. 2°. Quelques légères qu'on veuille supposer les incommodités particulières à la femme, comme elles sont toujours pour elle un intervalle d'inaction, c'est une raison suffisante pour l'exclure de cette primauté; car, quand la balance est parfaitement égale, un rien[4] suffit pour la faire pencher. De plus, le mari doit avoir inspection sur la conduite de la femme, parce qu'il lui importe que les enfants qu'il est forcé de reconnaître n'appartiennent pas à d'autres qu'à lui. La femme, qui n'a rien de semblable à craindre, n'a pas le même droit sur le mari. 3°. Les enfants doivent obéir au père, d'abord par nécessité, ensuite par reconnaissance; après avoir reçu de lui leurs besoins durant la moitié de leur vie, ils doivent consacrer l'autre à pourvoir aux siens.

[1] D. B. reads *c'est*.
[2] [du publique n'est *souvent* (written in margin) qu'un moyen, souvent fort mal entendu, pour conserver les particuliers dans la paix et [dans] l'abondance.] The text of *Éc. pol.* is considerably different here.
[3] [mais on peut prouver aisément.]
[4] *Éc. pol.* has *une paille*.

4°. À l'égard des domestiques, ils lui[1] doivent aussi leurs services en échange de l'entretien qu'il leur donne ; sauf à rompre le marché dès qu'il cesse de leur convenir. Je ne parle point de l'esclavage, parce qu'il est contraire à la nature, et que rien ne peut l'autoriser.

Il n'y a rien de tout cela dans la société politique. Loin que le chef ait un intérêt naturel au bonheur des particuliers, il ne lui est pas rare de chercher le sien dans leur misère. La couronne est-elle héréditaire ? C'est souvent un enfant qui commande à des hommes[2]. Est-elle élective ? Mille inconvénients se font sentir dans les élections ; et l'on perd, dans l'un et dans l'autre cas, tous les avantages de la paternité. Si vous n'avez qu'un seul chef, vous êtes à la discretion d'un maître qui n'a nulle raison[3] de vous aimer ; si vous en avez plusieurs, il faut supporter à la fois leur tyrannie et leurs divisions. En un mot ; les abus sont inévitables et leurs suites funestes dans toute société, où l'intérêt public et les lois n'ont aucune force naturelle et sont sans cesse attaqués par l'intérêt personnel et les passions du chef et des membres.

Quoique les fonctions du père de famille et du prince doivent tendre au même but, c'est par des voies si différentes, leurs devoirs et leur droits sont tellement distingués, qu'on ne peut les confondre sans se former les plus fausses idées des principes de la société, et sans tomber dans des erreurs fatales au genre humain. En effet, si la voix de la nature est le meilleur conseil que doive écouter un bon père pour bien remplir ses devoirs, elle n'est pour le magistrat qu'un faux guide qui travaille sans cesse à l'écarter des siens, et qui l'entraîne tôt ou tard à sa perte ou à celle de l'État, s'il n'est retenu par la prudence ou par la vertu. La seule précaution nécessaire au père de famille est de se garantir de la dépravation, et d'empêcher que les inclinations naturelles ne se corrompent en lui ; mais ce sont elles qui corrompent le magistrat. Pour bien faire, le premier n'a qu'à consulter son cœur ; l'autre devient un traître, au moment qu'il écoute le sien ; sa raison même lui doit être suspecte, et il ne doit suivre que la raison publique, qui est la Loi. Aussi la nature a-t-elle fait une multitude de bons pères de famille ; [4]mais j'ignore si la sagesse humaine a jamais fait un bon roi. Qu'on voie dans le *Civilis* de Platon[5] les qualités

---

[1] D. B. omits *lui*.

[2] [Note de J.-J. R.] La loi française sur la majorité des Rois prouve que des hommes très sensés et une longue expérience ont appris aux peuples que c'est un plus grand malheur encore d'être gouvernés par des Régences que par des enfants.

[3] [nul intérêt.]   [4] From this point the MS. differs from *Éc. pol.*

[5] *Politicus* 293 A.

que cet homme royal doit avoir, et qu'on cite quelqu'un qui les ait eues. Quand on supposerait[1] même que cet homme ait existé et qu'il ait porté la couronne, la raison permet-elle d'établir[2] sur un prodige la règle des Gouvernements humains[3] ? Il est donc certain que le lien social de la Cité n'a pu ni dû se former par l'extension de celui de la famille, ni sur le même modèle[4].

2. Qu'un homme riche et puissant, ayant acquis d'immenses possessions en terres, imposât des lois à ceux qui s'y voulaient établir; qu'il ne le leur permît qu'à condition de reconnaître son autorité suprême et d'obéir à toutes ses volontés; je puis encore concevoir cela. Mais comment concevrai-je qu'un traité, qui suppose des droits antérieurs, soit le premier fondement du Droit, et qu'il n'y ait pas dans cet acte tyrannique double usurpation : savoir, sur la propriété de la terre et sur la liberté des habitants ? Comment un particulier peut-il s'emparer d'un territoire immense et en priver le genre humain, autrement que par une usurpation punissable, puisqu'elle ôte au reste des habitants du monde le séjour et les aliments que la nature[5] leur donne en commun ? Accordons au besoin et au travail le droit de premier occupant; pourrons-nous ne pas donner des bornes à ce droit[6] ? Suffira-t-il de mettre le pied sur un terrain commun pour s'en prétendre aussitôt propriétaire exclusif[7] ? Suffira-t-il d'avoir la force d'en chasser tous les autres pour leur ôter le droit d'y revenir ? Jusqu'où l'acte de prise de possession peut-il fonder la propriété ? Quand Nuñez Balbao prenait sur le rivage possession de la mer du Sud et de toute l'Amérique méridionale au nom de la couronne de Castille, était-ce assez pour en deposséder tous les habitants et en exclure tous les princes du monde ? Sur ce pied-là ces cérémonies se multipliaient assez vainement. Car le Roi Catholique n'avait tout d'un coup qu'à prendre de son cabinet possession de tout l'univers : sauf à

---

[1] [pourrait supposer.]

[2] [établirait-on.]

[3] 'Quand...humains,' written on v° of p. 28.

[4] Contrast the opinion expressed in the final version of the treatise (I. ii.): *La famille est donc, si l'on veut, le premier modèle des sociétés politiques.*

[5] [qu'elle.]

[6] D. B. reads *pourrions-nous donner des bornes*, in defiance of the MS., the sense and the final version (I. ix.). Also, *le droit du premier occupant*.

[7] [Note de J.-J. R.] J'ai vu dans je ne sais quel écrit, intitulé, je crois, *l'Observateur Hollandais*, un principe assez plaisant : c'est que tout terrain qui n'est habité que par les sauvages doit être censé vacant, et qu'on peut légitimement s'en emparer et en chasser les habitants, sans leur faire aucun tort selon le droit naturel. D. B. omits *légitimement*.

retrancher ensuite de son empire ce qui était auparavant possédé par les autres princes.

Quelles sont donc les conditions nécessaires pour autoriser sur un terrain quelconque le droit de premier occupant ? Premièrement, qu'il ne soit encore habité par personne ; secondement, qu'on n'en occupe que la quantité dont on a besoin pour sa subsistance ; en troisième lieu, qu'on en prenne possession non par une vaine cérémonie, mais par le travail et la culture : seul signe[1] de propriété qui doive être respecté d'autrui. Les droits d'un homme avant l'état de société ne peuvent aller plus loin[2] ; et tout le reste, n'étant que violence et usurpation contre le droit de nature, ne peut servir de fondement au droit social.

Or, [3]quand je n'ai pas plus de terrain qu'il n'en faut pour mon entretien, et assez de bras pour le cultiver[4], si j'en aliène encore, il m'en restera moins qu'il ne m'en faudra. Que puis-je donc[5] céder aux autres sans m'ôter ma subsistance ? ou quel accord ferai-je avec eux, pour les [6]mettre en possession[6] de ce qui ne m'appartient pas ? Quant aux conditions de cet accord, il est très évident qu'elles sont illégitimes et nulles pour ceux qu'elles soumettent sans réserve à la volonté d'un autre. Car, outre qu'une telle soumission est incompatible avec la nature de l'homme, et que c'est ôter toute moralité à ses actions que d'ôter toute liberté à sa volonté, c'est une convention vaine, absurde, impossible, de stipuler d'un côté une autorité absolue, et de l'autre une obéissance sans bornes. N'est-il pas clair qu'on n'est engagé à rien envers celui dont on a droit de tout exiger ? et cette seule condition, incompatible avec toute autre, n'entraîne-t-elle pas nécessairement la nullité de l'acte ? Car, comment mon esclave pourrait-il avoir des droits contre moi, puisque tout ce qu'il a m'appartient, et que, son droit étant le mien, ce droit de moi contre moi-même est un mot qui n'a aucun sens ?

3. Que par le droit de guerre le vainqueur, au lieu de tuer ses captifs, les réduise en une servitude éternelle ; sans doute il fait bien pour son profit. Mais puisqu'il n'en use ainsi que par le droit de la guerre, l'état de guerre ne cesse point entre les vaincus[7] et lui ; car il ne peut cesser que par une convention libre et volontaire, comme il a commencé. Que s'il [8]ne les tue pas tous, cette prétendue[9]

---

[1] D. B. reads *seuls signes qui doivent*, against the MS.
[2] D. B. reads *bien loin*, against the MS.   [3] [si.]
[4] [et que j'aie assez de bras pour le cultiver] [ou j'en aurai tiop pour son produit.] D. B. omits *et assez de bras pour le cultiver*.
[5] [me reste-t-il donc à.]   [6] [laisser jouir.]   [7] [eux.]
[8] [leur fait grâce de la vie] [les laisse vivre.]
[9] 'prétendue' added in margin.

grâce n'en est point une, quand il faut la payer de sa liberté[1], qui seule peut donner un prix à la vie. Comme ces captifs[2] lui sont plus utiles vivants que morts, il les laisse[3] vivre pour son intérêt et non pas pour le leur; ils ne lui doivent donc rien que l'obéissance aussi longtemps qu'ils sont forcés de lui obéir. Mais à l'instant que le peuple subjugué peut [4]secouer un joug imposé par force et[4] se défaire de son maître, c'est à dire de son ennemi, s'il[5] le peut, il le doit; et recouvrant sa liberté légitime, il ne fait qu'user du droit de guerre, qui ne cesse point[6] tant que la violence qu'il autorise a lieu. Or, comment l'état de guerre servirait-il de base à un traité d'union qui n'a pour objet que la justice et la paix ? Peut-on rien concevoir de plus absurde que de dire : 'nous sommes unis en un seul corps, attendu que la guerre subsiste entre nous ?' Mais la fausseté de ce prétendu droit de tuer les captifs a été si bien reconnue qu'il n'y a plus d'homme civilisé qui ose exercer ou réclamer ce chimérique et barbare droit, ni même de sophiste payé qui l'ose soutenir.

Je dis donc, premièrement, que, le vainqueur n'ayant pas le droit de mettre à mort les vaincus sitôt qu'ils rendent les armes, il ne peut fonder leur esclavage sur un droit qui n'existe point. Secondement, que, quand même le vainqueur aurait ce droit [7]et ne s'en prévaudrait pas[7], il [8]ne résulterait jamais de là[8] un état civil, mais seulement un état de guerre modifié.

Ajoutons que, si par ce mot de *guerre* on entend la guerre publique, on suppose des sociétés antérieures, dont on n'explique point l'origine. Si l'on entend la guerre privée et d'homme à homme, on n'aura par là qu'un maître et des esclaves, jamais un chef et des citoyens; et, pour distinguer ce dernier rapport, il faudra toujours supposer quelque convention sociale qui fasse un Corps de peuple et unisse les membres entre eux, ainsi qu'à leur chef.

Tel est, en effet, le véritable caractère de l'état civil; un peuple est un peuple indépendamment de son chef; et, si le prince vient à périr, il existe encore entre les sujets des liens qui les maintiennent en Corps de nation. Vous ne trouvez rien de pareil dans les principes de la tyrannie. Sitôt que le tyran cesse d'exister, tout se sépare et tombe en poussière, comme un chêne en un tas de cendres, quand le feu s'éteint après l'avoir dévoré.

4. Que par le laps de temps une violente usurpation devienne enfin un pouvoir légitime; que la prescription seule puisse changer

---

[1] [s'il leur ôte la liberté.]
[2] [mais ils lui sont.]
[3] [cons[erve].]
[4] Added.
[5] ' s ' ' added before ' il le peut.'
[6] [n'a point cessé.]
[7] Added.
[8] [n'en résulterait jamais.]

un usurpateur en magistrat suprême, et un troupeau d'esclaves en Corps de nation ; c'est ce que beaucoup de savants hommes ont osé soutenir, et à quoi il ne manque d'autre autorité que celle de la raison. Bien loin qu'une longue violence puisse, à force de temps, se transformer en un Gouvernement juste, il est incontestable au contraire que, quand un peuple serait assez insensé pour accorder volontairement à son chef un pouvoir arbitraire, ce pouvoir ne saurait être transmis sur d'autres générations, et que sa durée seule est capable de le rendre illégitime. Car on ne peut présumer que les enfants à naître approuveront l'extravagance de leurs pères, ni [1]leur faire[1] porter justement la peine d'une faute qu'ils n'ont pas commise.

On nous dira, je le sais, que comme ce qui n'existe point n'a aucune qualité, l'enfant qui est encore à naître n'a aucun droit ; de sorte que ses parents peuvent renoncer aux leurs, pour eux et pour lui, sans qu'il ait à s'en plaindre. Mais pour détruire un si [2]grossier sophisme, il suffit de distinguer les droits que le fils tient uniquement de son père, comme la propriété de ses biens, des droits qu'il ne tient que de la nature et de sa qualité d'homme, comme la liberté. Il n'est pas douteux que par la loi de raison le père ne puisse aliéner les premiers, dont il est seul propriétaire, et en priver ses enfants. Mais il n'en est pas de même des autres, qui sont des dons immédiats de la nature, et dont par conséquent nul homme ne les peut dépouiller. Supposons qu'un conquérant habile et zélé pour le bonheur de ses sujets leur eût persuadé qu'avec un bras de moins ils en seraient plus tranquilles et plus heureux : en serait-ce assez pour obliger tous les enfants à perpétuité de se faire couper un bras, pour remplir les engagements de leurs pères ?

À l'égard du consentement tacite par lequel on veut légitimer la tyrannie, il est aisé de voir qu'on ne peut le présumer du plus long silence ; parce qu'outre la crainte, qui empêche les particuliers de protester contre un homme qui dispose de la force publique, le peuple, qui ne peut [3]manifester sa volonté qu'en Corps, n'a pas le pouvoir de s'assembler pour la déclarer. Au contraire, le silence des citoyens suffit pour rejeter un chef non reconnu : il faut qu'ils parlent pour l'autoriser et qu'ils parlent en pleine liberté. Au reste, tout ce que disent là-dessus les jurisconsultes, et autres gens payés pour cela, ne prouve point que le peuple n'ait pas le droit de reprendre sa liberté usurpée, mais qu'il est dangereux de le tenter. C'est aussi ce qu'il ne faut jamais faire, quand on connaît de plus grands maux que celui de l'avoir perdue.

[1] [les obliger d'en.]   [2] [léger.]   [3] [déclarer.]

Toute cette dispute du pacte social me semble se réduire à une question très simple. Qu'est-ce qui peut avoir engagé les hommes à se réunir volontairement en corps de société, si ce n'est leur utilité commune ? L'utilité commune est donc le fondement de la société civile. Cela posé, qu'y a-t-il à faire pour distinguer les États légitimes des attroupements forcés, que rien n'autorise, sinon de considérer l'objet ou la fin des uns et des autres ? Si la forme de la société tend au bien commun, elle suit[1] l'esprit de son institution; si elle n'a en vue que l'intérêt des chefs, elle est illégitime par droit de raison et d'humanité; car, quand même l'intérêt public s'accorderait quelquefois avec celui de la tyrannie, cet accord passager ne saurait suffire pour autoriser un Gouvernement dont il ne serait pas le principe. Quand Grotius nie que tout pouvoir soit établi en faveur de ceux qui sont gouvernés, il n'a que trop raison dans le fait; mais c'est du droit qu'il est question. Sa preuve unique est singulière; il la tire du pouvoir d'un maître sur son esclave, comme si l'on autorisait un fait par un fait, et que l'esclavage lui-même[2] fût moins inique que la tyrannie. C'est précisément le droit d'esclavage qu'il fallait établir. Il n'est pas question de ce qui est, mais de ce qui est [3]convenable et[3] juste; ni du pouvoir auquel on est forcé d'obéir, mais de celui qu'on est obligé de reconnaître.

CHAPITRE VI.

Des droits respectifs du souverain et[4] du citoyen.

Si l'intérêt commun est l'objet de l'association, il est clair que la volonté générale doit être la règle des actions du Corps social. C'est le principe fondamental que j'ai tâché d'établir. Voyons maintenant quel doit être l'empire de cette volonté sur les particuliers, et comment elle se manifeste à tous.

L'État ou la Cité faisant une personne morale, dont la vie consiste dans le concours et l'union de ses membres, le premier et le plus important de ses soins est celui de sa propre conservation : soin qui demande une force universelle et compulsive, pour mouvoir et disposer chaque partie de la manière la plus convenable au tout. Ainsi, comme la nature donne à chaque homme un pouvoir absolu

---

[1] [marche selon.]   [2] Added.
[3] Added. D. B. reads *Il n'est pas question de ce qui est convenable, mais de ce qui est juste*, against MS. and sense.
[4] [de ceux.]

CH. V, VI] *Droits du souverain et du citoyen* 471

sur ses membres, le pacte social donne au Corps politique un pouvoir absolu sur les siens; et c'est ce même pouvoir dont l'exercice, dirigé par la volonté générale, porte, comme je l'ai dit, le nom de souveraineté.

Mais comme, outre la personne publique, nous avons à considérer les personnes privées qui la composent, et dont la vie et l'existence est naturellement indépendante de la sienne, cette matière demande quelque discussion.

Tout consiste à bien distinguer les droits que le souverain a sur les citoyens de ceux qu'il doit respecter en eux[1]; et les devoirs qu'ils ont à remplir en qualité de sujets du droit naturel [2]dont ils doivent jouir en qualité d'hommes. Il est certain[3] que tout ce que chacun aliène par le pacte social de ses facultés naturelles, de ses biens, de sa liberté, c'est seulement la partie de tout cela dont la possession importe à la société[4].

Ainsi tous les services qu'un citoyen peut rendre à l'État, il les lui doit; et le souverain de son côté ne peut charger les sujets d'aucune chaîne inutile [5]à la communauté[5]: car sous la loi de raison rien ne se fait sans cause, non plus que sous la loi de nature. Mais il ne faut pas confondre ce qui est convenable avec ce qui est nécessaire, le simple devoir avec le droit étroit, [6]et ce qu'on peut exiger de nous avec ce que nous devons faire[6] volontairement[7].

Les engagements qui nous lient au Corps social ne sont obligatoires que parce qu'ils sont mutuels, et leur nature est telle qu'on ne peut travailler pour autrui sans travailler en même temps pour soi. Pourquoi la volonté générale est-elle toujours droite, et pourquoi tous veulent-ils constamment le bonheur de chacun d'eux, si ce n'est parce qu'il n'y a personne qui ne s'approprie en secret ce mot *chacun*, et qui ne songe à lui-même en votant pour tous ? Ce qui prouve que l'égalité de droit et la notion de justice, qui en [8]découle, dérive[8] de la préférence que chacun se donne, et par conséquent

---

[1] ' en eux ' added.

[2] There is a slight variant of this page (v° of p. 37) on a cancelled sheet, numbered 38, in Rousseau's hand (like all the rest). When it was cancelled the new page was written on the back of 37, and in a hurried hand.

[3] [incontestable.]

[4] [au Corps social.] In the final version (II. iv.), Rousseau added the qualification: Mais il faut convenir aussi que le souverain seul est juge de cet importance.   [5] Added.

[6] ' ni ce qu'on peut nous forcer à faire...librement et....'

[7] Variant adds: Ces distinctions, qui se développeront en leur lieu, jetteront un nouveau jour sur ce chapitre, après la lecture des suivants.

[8] [dérive, tire sa source.]

de la nature de l'homme; que la volonté générale, pour être vraiment telle, doit être générale dans son[1] objet ainsi que dans son essence; qu'elle doit partir de tous pour retourner à tous; et qu'elle perd sa rectitude naturelle, sitôt qu'elle tombe sur un sujet individuel et déterminé; parce qu'alors, jugeant de ce qui n'est pas nous, nous n'avons aucun vrai principe d'équité qui nous guide.

En effet, sitôt qu'il s'agit d'un fait ou d'un droit particulier sur un point qui n'a pas été réglé par une convention générale et antérieure, l'affaire devient contentieuse; c'est un procès où les particuliers intéressés sont une des parties, et le public l'autre, mais où je ne vois ni la loi qu'il faut suivre, ni le juge qui doit prononcer. Il serait ridicule de vouloir alors s'en rapporter à une expresse décision de la volonté générale, qui ne peut être que la conclusion de l'une des parties, et qui par conséquent n'est pour l'autre qu'une volonté particulière, sujette en cette occasion à l'injustice ou à l'erreur. Ainsi, de même qu'une volonté particulière ne peut représenter la volonté générale, la volonté générale, à son tour, ne peut, sans changer de nature, devenir une volonté particulière; elle ne peut prononcer nommément ni sur un homme, ni sur un fait. Quand le peuple d'Athènes, par exemple, nommait ou cassait ses chefs, décernait une recompense à l'un, imposait une amende à l'autre, et par des multitudes de décrets particuliers exerçait indistinctement tous les actes du Gouvernement, le peuple alors n'avait plus de volonté générale, proprement dit; il n'agissait plus comme souverain, mais comme magistrat.

On doit concevoir par là que ce qui généralise la volonté publique n'est pas la quantité des votants, mais l'intérêt commun qui les unit. Car, [2]dans cette institution[2], chacun se soumet nécessairement aux conditions qu'il impose aux autres: accord admirable de l'intérêt et de la justice, qui donne aux délibérations communes un caractère d'équité qu'on voit évanouir dans la discussion de toute affaire particulière, faute d'un intérêt[3] commun qui unisse et identifie la volonté[4] du juge avec celle de la partie.

Par quelque côté qu'on remonte au principe, on arrive toujours à la même conclusion: savoir, que le pacte social établit entre les citoyens une telle égalité de droit qu'ils s'engagent tous sous les mêmes conditions, et doivent jouir tous des mêmes avantages. Ainsi, par la nature du pacte, tout acte de souveraineté, c'est à dire, tout acte authentique de volonté générale[5], oblige ou favorise également tous les citoyens; de sorte que le souverain connaît

---

[1] Here ends the cancelled page.   [2] Added.
[3] [principe.]   [4] [l'intérêt.]   [5] D. B. reads *de la volonté générale*.

seulement le Corps de la nation, et ne distingue aucun de ceux qui le composent. Qu'est-ce donc proprement qu'un acte de souveraineté ? Ce n'est pas un ordre du supérieur à l'inférieur, ni un commandement du maître à l'esclave ; mais une convention du Corps de l'État avec chacun de ses membres : convention légitime, parce qu'elle a pour base le Contrat social ; équitable, parce qu'elle est volontaire et générale ; utile, parce qu'elle ne peut avoir d'autre objet que le bien de tous ; et solide, parce qu'elle a pour garants la force publique et le pouvoir suprême. Tant que les sujets ne sont soumis qu'à de telles conventions, ils n'obéissent à personne, mais seulement à leur propre volonté ; et demander jusqu'où s'étendent les droits respectifs du souverain et des particuliers, c'est demander jusqu'à quel point ceux-ci peuvent s'engager avec eux-mêmes : chacun envers tous, et tous envers chacun d'eux.

Il s'ensuit de là[1] que le pouvoir souverain, tout absolu, tout sacré, tout inviolable qu'il est, ne passe ni ne peut passer les bornes des conventions générales, et que tout homme peut disposer pleinement[2] de ce qui lui a été laissé de ses biens et de sa liberté par ces conventions ; de sorte que le souverain n'est jamais en droit de charger un particulier plus qu'un autre ; parce qu'alors, l'affaire devenant particulière, son pouvoir n'est plus compétent.

Ces distinctions une fois admises, il est si faux que dans le Contrat social il y ait de la part des particuliers aucune renonciation véritable, que leur situation, par l'effet de ce Contrat, se trouve réellement préférable à ce qu'elle était auparavant ; et qu'au lieu d'une simple aliénation ils n'ont fait qu'un échange avantageux d'une manière d'être [3]incertaine et précaire[3] contre une autre meilleure et plus sûre : de l'indépendance naturelle contre la liberté civile ; de leur pouvoir de nuire à autrui contre leur sûreté personnelle ; et de leur force, que d'autres pouvaient surmonter, contre un droit que l'union sociale rend invincible. Leur vie même, qu'ils ont dévouée à l'État, en est continuellement protégée ; et lorsqu'ils l'exposent ou la perdent pour sa défense, que font-ils alors qu'ils ne fissent[4] plus fréquemment et avec plus de danger dans l'état de nature, lorsque, livrant des combats inévitables[5], ils défendraient au péril de la vie ce qui leur sert à la conserver ? Tous ont à combattre au besoin pour la patrie, il est vrai ; mais aussi nul n'a jamais à combattre pour soi. [6]Ne gagne-t-on pas encore à courir, pour ce qui fait notre sûreté, une partie des risques

---

[1] [tout ceci.]   [2] Added.   [3] Added.
[4] [fassent—a reading retained by D. B.]   [5] [qu'ils pourraient éviter.]
[6] [n'est-il pas simple.]

qu'il faudrait courir pour nous-mêmes, sitôt ¹qu'elle nous serait ôtée¹.

CHAPITRE VII.

Nécessité des lois positives.

Voilà, ce me semble, les plus justes idées qu'on puisse avoir du pacte fondamental qui est la base de tout vrai Corps politique : idées qu'il importait d'autant plus de développer que, faute de les avoir bien conçues, tous ceux qui ont traité de cette matière² ont toujours fondé le gouvernement civil sur des principes arbitraires, qui ne découlent point de la nature de ce pacte. On verra dans la suite³ avec quelle facilité tout le système politique se déduit de ceux que je viens d'établir⁴, et combien les conséquences en sont naturelles et lumineuses. Mais achevons de poser les fondements de notre⁵ édifice.

L'union sociale ayant un objet déterminé, sitôt qu'elle est formée, il faut chercher à le remplir. Pour que chacun veuille ce qu'il doit faire selon l'engagement du Contrat social, il faut que chacun sache⁶ ce qu'il doit vouloir. Ce qu'il doit vouloir, c'est le bien commun ; ce qu'il doit fuir, c'est le mal public. Mais, l'État n'ayant qu'une existence idéale et conventionnelle, ses membres n'ont aucune sensibilité naturelle et commune, par laquelle ⁷immédiatement avertis⁷ ils reçoivent une impression agréable de ce qui lui est utile⁸, et une impression douleureuse sitôt qu'il est offensé. Loin de prévenir les maux qui l'attaquent, rarement sont-ils à temps⁹ d'y remédier quand ils commencent à les sentir ; il faut les prévoir de loin pour les détourner¹⁰ ou les guérir¹¹. Comment donc les particuliers garantiraient-ils la communauté des maux qu'ils ne peuvent ni voir ni sentir qu'après coup ? comment lui procureraient-ils des biens dont ils ne peuvent juger qu'après leur effet ? Comment s'assurer d'ailleurs que, sans cesse rappelés par la nature à leur condition primitive, ils ne négligeront jamais cette autre condition artificielle, dont l'avantage ne leur est sensible que par des conséquences souvent fort éloignées ? Supposons-les

---

[1] [que nous ne l'aurions plus.]
[2] D. B. reads *travaillé de cette manière.*
[3] [de cet ouvrage.]   [4] [de poser.]
[5] [ce grand.]   [6] [voie.]
[7] Added.   [8] [bon.]
[9] D. B. reads *ont-ils le temps.*
[10] [s'en garantir.]   [11] [s'en délivrer.]

toujours soumis à la volonté générale, comment cette volonté pourra-t-elle se manifester dans toutes les occasions ? Sera-t-elle toujours évidente ? L'intérêt particulier ne l'offusquera-t-il jamais de ses illusions ? Le peuple restera-t-il toujours assemblé pour la déclarer, ou s'en remettra à des particuliers toujours prêts à lui substituer la leur ? Enfin, comment tous agiront-ils de concert, quel ordre mettront-ils dans leurs affaires, quels moyens auront-ils de s'entendre, et comment feront-ils entre eux la répartition des travaux communs ?

Ces [1]difficultés, qui devaient paraître insurmontables, ont [2]été levées par la plus sublime de toutes les institutions humaines, ou plutôt par une inspiration céleste qui apprit au peuple à imiter ici-bas les décrets immuables de la divinité. Par quel art inconcevable a-t-on pu trouver le moyen[3] d'assujettir les hommes pour les rendre libres ? d'employer au service de l'État les biens, les bras, la vie même de ses membres[4], sans les contraindre et sans les consulter ? d'enchaîner leur volonté de leur propre aveu ? de faire valoir leur consentement contre leur refus ? et de les forcer à se punir eux-mêmes, quand ils font ce qu'ils n'ont pas voulu ? Comment se peut-il faire que[5] tous obéissent et que nul[6] ne commande ? qu'ils servent et n'aient point de maître ? d'autant plus libres en effet que, sous une apparente sujétion, nul ne perd de sa liberté que ce qui peut nuire à celle d'un autre ? Ces prodiges sont l'ouvrage de la Loi. C'est à la Loi seule que les hommes doivent la justice et la liberté. C'est cet organe salutaire de la volonté de tous qui rétablit dans le droit l'egalité naturelle entre les hommes. C'est cette voix céleste qui dicte à chaque citoyen les préceptes de la raison publique, et lui apprend à se conduire sur les maximes de son propre jugement, et à n'être pas sans cesse en contradiction avec lui-même. Les lois sont l'unique mobile du Corps politique ; il n'est actif et sensible que par elles[7]. Sans les lois, l'État formé n'est qu'un corps sans âme ; il existe et ne peut agir. Car ce n'est pas assez que[8] chacun soit soumis à la volonté générale ; pour la suivre, il la faut connaître[9]. Voilà d'où naît la nécessité d'une législation.

[1] This paragraph, down to *en contradiction avec lui-même*, reappears in *Éc. pol.* See above, p. 245.   [2] [semblent avoir.]
[3] [l'art.]   [4] D. B. reads *de ses semblables*.
[5] [qu'ils.]   [6] [personne.]
[7] [mais d'où viennent-elles ? quelle est leur nature ? à quel caractère est-on sûr de les reconnaître ?]
[8] 'que' omitted in MS. by error.   [9] [ce qu'il importe de bien expliquer.]

Les lois ne sont proprement que les conditions de l'association civile. Le peuple soumis aux lois en doit donc être l'auteur; car il n'appartient qu'à ceux qui s'associent de déclarer[1] les conditions sous lesquelles ils veulent s'associer. Mais comment les déclareront[2]-ils? Sera-ce [3]d'un commun accord, et[3] par une inspiration subite? Le Corps politique a-t-il un organe pour énoncer ses volontés? Qui lui donnera la prévoyance nécessaire pour[4] en former les actes[4] et les publier[5] d'avance? ou comment[6] les prononcera-t-il au moment du besoin? Comment voudrait-on qu'une multitude aveugle qui souvent ne sait ce qu'elle veut, parce qu'elle sait rarement ce qui lui est bon, pût former et exécuter d'elle-même une entreprise aussi difficile qu'un système de législation, qui est le plus sublime effort de la sagesse et de la prévoyance humaine? De lui-même, le peuple veut toujours le bien; mais, de lui-même, il ne le voit pas toujours. La volonté générale est toujours droite, il n'est jamais question de la rectifier; mais il faut savoir l'interroger à propos[7]. Il faut lui présenter les objets tels qu'ils sont, quelquefois tels qu'ils doivent lui paraître; lui montrer le bon chemin qu'elle veut suivre; la garantir de la séduction des volontés particulières[8]; rapprocher à ses yeux les lieux et les temps; balancer l'illusion des avantages[9] présents [10]et sensibles[10] par le danger des maux éloignés [10]et cachés[10]. Les particuliers voient le bien qu'ils rejettent; le public veut le bien qu'il ne voit pas. Tous ont également besoin de guides; il faut obliger les uns à conformer leurs volontés à leur raison; il faut apprendre à l'autre à connaître[11] ce qu'il veut. Alors des lumières publiques résultera la vertu des particuliers; et de cette union de l'entendement et de la volonté dans le Corps social, l'exact[12] concours des parties et la plus grande force du tout. Voilà d'où naît la nécessité d'un Législateur.

---

[1] [déterminer.]   [2] [détermineront.]   [3] Added.
[4] [les former en actes.]   [5] [déclarer.] D. B. reads *calculer*.
[6] [le moyen de les déterminer.]
[7] In the final version (II. vi.) the words, *il n'est jamais question...à propos*, are replaced by *mais le jugement qui la guide n'est pas toujours éclairé*.
[8] [qui tâchent d'emprunter son ton.]
[9] [biens.]   [10] Added in both cases.   [11] [faire.]
[12] [parfait, vrai.]

LIVRE II.

Établissement des lois.

CHAPITRE I.
Fin de la législation.

Par le Pacte social nous avons donné l'existence et la vie au Corps politique; il s'agit maintenant de lui donner le mouvement et la volonté par la législation. Car l'acte primitif, par lequel ce Corps se forme et s'unit, ne détermine rien encore de ce qu'il doit faire pour se conserver. C'est à ce grand objet que tend la science de la législation. Mais quelle est cette science? où trouver un génie qui la possède? et quelles vertus sont nécessaires à celui qui l'ose exercer? Cette recherche est grande et difficile; elle est même décourageante pour qui se flatterait de voir naître un État bien institué.

CHAPITRE II.
Du Législateur.

En effet, pour découvrir[1] les meilleurs règles de société qui conviennent aux nations, il faudrait une intelligence supérieure qui connût tous les besoins des hommes, et n'en éprouvât aucun; qui n'eût nul rapport avec notre nature, et qui vît tous ceux qui lui conviennent; dont le bonheur fût indépendant de nous, et qui pourtant voulût bien s'occuper du nôtre. En un mot, il faudrait un Dieu pour donner de bonnes lois au genre humain; et comme les pâtres sont d'une espèce supérieure au bétail qu'ils conduisent, les pasteurs d'hommes, qui sont leurs chefs, devraient être d'une espèce plus excellente que[2] les peuples.

Ce raisonnement que Platon faisait, quant au droit, pour définir l'homme civil ou royal qu'il cherche dans son livre *du Règne*, Caligula s'en servait dans le fait, au rapport de Philon, pour prouver que les maîtres du monde étaient d'une nature supérieure au reste des hommes[3]. Mais, s'il est vrai qu'un grand prince est un

---

[1] [trouver.]   [2] [supérieure au.]
[3] The curious passage of Philo is as follows : καθάπερ οἱ τῶν ἄλλων ζῴων ἀγελάρχαι, βουκόλοι καὶ αἰπόλοι καὶ νομεῖς, οὔτε βόες εἰσὶν οὔτε αἶγες οὔτε ἄρνες, ἀλλ' ἄνθρωποι, κρείττονος μοίρας καὶ παρασκευῆς ἐπιλαχόντες· τὸν αὐτὸν τρόπον

homme rare, que sera-ce d'un grand Législateur ? Car le premier n'a qu'à suivre le modèle, que l'autre doit proposer. Celui-ci est le méchanicien qui invente la machine ; celui-là[1] n'est que l'ouvrier qui la monte ou la fait marcher. Dans la naissance des sociétés, dit Montesquieu, ce sont les chefs des Républiques qui font l'institution ; et c'est ensuite l'institution qui forme les chefs des Républiques[2].

[3]Celui qui se croit capable de former un peuple doit se sentir en état, pour ainsi dire, de changer la nature humaine. Il faut qu'il transforme chaque individu, qui par lui-même est un tout parfait et solitaire, en partie d'un plus grand tout, dont cet individu reçoive en quelque sorte sa vie et son être ; qu'il mutile en quelque sorte la constitution[4] de l'homme pour[5] la renforcer ; qu'il substitue une existence partielle et morale à l'existence [5]physique et[5] indépendante que nous avons tous reçue de la nature. Il faut, en un mot, qu'il ôte à l'homme toutes ses forces propres et innées[6], pour lui en donner qui lui soient étrangères, et dont il ne puisse faire usage sans le secours d'autrui. Or, plus ces forces naturelles sont mortes et anéanties, et plus les acquises sont grandes et durables, plus aussi l'institution est solide et parfaite. En sorte que, si chaque citoyen ne peut rien que par tous les autres, et que la force acquise par le tout soit égale ou supérieure à la somme des forces naturelles de tous les individus[7], on peut dire que la législation est au plus haut point de perfection qu'elle puisse atteindre.

Le Législateur est de toutes manières[8] un homme extraordinaire dans l'État. S'il doit l'être par ses talents, il ne l'est pas moins par son emploi. Ce n'est point magistrature ; ce n'est point souveraineté. Cet emploi, qui constitue la République, n'entre point dans sa constitution. C'est, en quelque manière, une fonction particulière et presque divine, qui n'a rien en commun avec l'empire humain. Car, si celui qui commande aux hommes ne doit point commander aux lois, celui qui commande aux lois ne doit pas non

ἀγελαρχοῦντα κἀμὲ τῆς ἀρίστης ἀνθρώπων γένους ἀγέλης νομιστέον διαφέρειν καὶ μὴ κατ' ἄνθρωπον εἶναι, μείζονος δὲ καὶ θειοτέρας μοίρας τετυχηκέναι. *De Virtutibus et Legatione ad Caium*, p. 1002 (ed. Mangey, London, 1742, II. 556—7). Rousseau may have read it in the accompanying Latin translation. The other reference seems to be to Plato's *Politicus* ; in particular, Chaps. III.—XVII.

[1] [l'autre.]   [2] *Considérations sur la grandeur des Romains*, Chap. I.

[3] The rough draft of the opening of this paragraph is preserved in MS. Neuchâtel, 7830. It agrees almost word for word with the above. In the final version (II. vii.) *qu'il mutile* is softened into *d'altérer*.

[4] [condition.]   [5] Added.   [6] [les forces dont il a le sentiment naturel.]
[7] [particuliers.]   [8] D. B. reads *de toute manière*.

plus commander aux hommes : autrement ses[1] lois, faites pour servir ses passions, ne feraient souvent que perpétuer ses injustices, et jamais il ne pourrait éviter que des vues particulières n'altérassent la sainteté de son ouvrage. C'est ainsi que les variations du Droit écrit prouvent les motifs particuliers qui en ont dicté les décisions : compilation immense, informe, contradictoire ; ouvrage d'un empereur imbécile, d'une femme perdue et d'un magistrat corrompu qui, à chaque violence qu'il voulait faire, publiait une loi pour l'autoriser[2].

Quand Lycurgue voulut donner des lois à sa patrie, il commença par abdiquer la souveraineté. C'était la coutume de la plupart des villes grecques de confier à des étrangers la rédaction des leurs. Rome, dans son plus bel âge, fit renaître en son sein tous les crimes de la tyrannie et se vit prête a périr, pour avoir réuni sur les mêmes têtes l'autorité législative et le pouvoir souverain.

Ce n'est pas qu'on ait jamais imaginé que la volonté d'un homme pût passer en loi sans le consentement du peuple. Mais comment refuser ce consentement à celui qu'on sait être le maître, et qui réunit en lui la confiance et la force publique ? Les gens raisonnables ont[3] peine à se faire entendre ; les gens faibles n'osent[4] parler ; et le silence forcé des sujets a tellement passé pour une approbation tacite que depuis les empereurs romains, qui sous le nom de Tribuns s'arrogèrent tous les droits du peuple, on a osé mettre au-dessus de la Loi la volonté du prince, qui ne tire que d'elle son autorité. Mais nous traitons des droits et non pas des abus.

Celui qui rédige les lois n'a donc, ou ne doit avoir, aucun pouvoir législatif ; et le peuple même ne peut se dépouiller de ce droit suprême, parce que selon le pacte fondamental il n'y a que la volonté générale qui oblige les particuliers, et qu'on ne peut jamais s'assurer qu'une volonté particulière est conforme à la volonté générale, à moins de la soumettre aux suffrages libres du peuple.

[5]Si l'on dit[5] que, tout le peuple s'étant une fois soumis volontairement, solennellement et sans contrainte à un homme, toutes les volontés de cet homme doivent, en vertu de cette soumission, être censées autant d'actes de la volonté générale, on dit un sophisme auquel j'ai déjà répondu. J'ajouterai que la soumission volontaire et supposée du peuple est toujours conditionnelle ; qu'il ne se donne point pour l'avantage du prince, mais pour le sien ; que,

---

[1] D. B. reads *ces*, against the MS.
[2] See the Fragment, *Des Lois* (MS. Neuchâtel, 7867), above, p. 331.
[3] [avaient.]   [4] [osaient.]   [5] [On pourra dire.]

si chaque particulier promet d'obéir sans réserve, c'est pour le bien de tous; que le prince en pareil cas prend aussi des engagements, auxquels tiennent ceux du peuple; et que, même sous le plus absolu despotisme, il ne peut violer son serment sans relever à l'instant ses sujets du leur.

[1]Quand un peuple serait assez stupide pour ne rien stipuler[2], en échange de son obéissance, sinon le droit de lui commander, encore ce droit serait-il conditionnel par sa nature. Pour éclaircir cette vérité, il faut bien remarquer que ceux qui prétendent qu'une promesse gratuite oblige rigoureusement le promettant distinguent pourtant avec soin les promesses purement gratuites de celles qui renferment quelques conditions tacites, mais évidentes: car, en ce dernier cas, ils conviennent tous que la validité des promesses dépend de l'exécution de la condition sous-entendue; comme, quand[3] un homme s'engage au service d'un autre, il suppose évidemment que cet autre le nourrira. De même, un peuple, qui se choisit [4]un ou plusieurs[4] chefs et promet de leur obéir, suppose évidemment qu'ils ne feront de sa liberté, qu'il leur aliène, qu'un usage avantageux pour lui-même; sans quoi, ce peuple étant insensé, ses engagements seraient nuls. À l'égard de la même aliénation extorquée par force[5], j'ai montré ci-devant qu'elle est nulle, et qu'on n'est obligé d'obéir à la force qu'aussi longtemps qu'on y est contraint.

Il reste donc toujours à savoir si les conditions sont remplies, et par conséquent si la volonté du prince est bien la volonté générale: question dont le peuple est le seul juge. Ainsi, les lois sont comme l'or pur, qu'il est impossible de dénaturer par aucune opération, et que la première épreuve[6] rétablit aussitôt sous sa forme naturelle[7]. De plus: il est contre la nature de la volonté, qui n'a point d'empire sur elle-même, de s'engager pour l'avenir; [8]on peut bien s'obliger à faire, mais non pas à vouloir; et il y a bien de la différence entre exécuter ce qu'on a promis, [9]à cause qu'on l'a promis[9], et le vouloir encore, quand même on ne l'aurait pas promis auparavant. Or, la Loi d'aujourd'hui ne doit pas être un acte de la volonté générale d'hier, mais de celle d'aujourd'hui; et nous nous[10] sommes engagés à faire non pas ce que tous ont voulu, mais ce que

---

[1] [Pour éclaircir cette vérité, il faut.] [Quand même.]
[2] [se soumettre sans (phrase unfinished).]   [3] [si.]   [4] Added.
[5] D. B. makes the clause, *à l'égard...par force*, part of the preceding sentence; against the sense.
[6] [opération.]   [7] [première forme.]   [8] [et l'on.]
[9] Added.   [10] Added. D. B. omits it.

CH. II] *Le Législateur et la volonté générale* 481

tous veulent: attendu que, les résolutions du souverain, comme souverain, ne regardant que lui-même[1], il est toujours libre d'en changer. D'où il suit que, quand la Loi parle au nom du peuple, c'est[2] au nom du peuple d'à présent, et non de celui d'autrefois. Les lois, quoique reçues, n'ont une autorité durable qu'autant que le peuple, étant libre de les révoquer, ne le fait pourtant pas : ce qui prouve le consentement actuel. Il n'est pas douteux non plus que, dans le cas supposé, les volontés publiques du prince légitime n'obligent les particuliers aussi longtemps[3] que la nation, pouvant s'assembler et s'y opposer sans obstacle, ne donne aucun signe de désaveu.

Ces éclaircissements montrent que, la volonté générale étant le lien continuel du Corps politique[4], il n'est jamais permis au Législateur, quelque autorisation antérieure qu'il puisse avoir, d'agir autrement qu'en dirigeant cette même volonté par la persuasion, ni de rien prescrire aux particuliers qui n'ait reçu premièrement la sanction du consentement général ; de peur de détruire, dès la première opération, l'essence[5] de la chose même qu'on veut former, et de rompre[6] le nœud social en croyant affermir la société.

Je vois donc à la fois, dans l'ouvrage de la législation, deux choses qui semblent s'exclure mutuellement : une entreprise au-dessus de toute force humaine et, pour l'exécuter, une autorité qui n'est rien.

Autre difficulté qui mérite attention. Ce fut souvent l'erreur des[7] sages de parler au vulgaire leur langage, au lieu du sien ; aussi n'en furent-ils jamais entendus. Il est mille sortes d'idées qui n'ont qu'une langue, et qu'il est impossible de traduire au peuple. Les vues trop générales et les objets trop éloignés sont également hors de sa portée ; et chaque individu, ne voyant, par exemple, d'autre plan de gouvernement que son bonheur[8] particulier, aperçoit difficilement les avantages qu'il doit retirer des privations continuelles qu'imposent les bonnes lois. Pour qu'un peuple naissant pût sentir les grandes maximes de la justice et les règles fondamentales de la raison d'État, il faudrait que l'effet pût devenir la cause ; que l'esprit social, qui doit être l'ouvrage de l'institution, présidât à l'institution même ; et que les hommes fussent, avant les lois, ce qu'ils doivent devenir par elles. Ainsi, le Législateur ne pouvant employer la force ni le raisonnement, c'est une nécessité

---

[1] [ne peuvent l'obliger envers autrui.]   [2] [ce doit être.]
[3] D. B. reads *qu'aussi longtemps*, which wrecks the sense.
[4] [social.]   [5] [même.]   [6] [d'anéantir.] D. B. omits *social*.
[7] [faux.]   [8] [que les objets.]

qu'il recourre à une autorité d'un autre ordre, qui puisse entraîner sans violence et persuader sans convaincre.

Voilà ce qui força de tout temps[1] les pères des nations de recourir à l'intervention céleste et d'honorer les Dieux de leur propre sagesse, afin que les peuples, soumis aux lois [2]de l'État[2] comme à [2]celles de[2] la nature, et reconnaissant le même pouvoir dans la formation du corps physique et dans celle du corps moral, obéissent avec liberté et portassent docilement le joug de la félicité publique. Cette raison sublime, qui s'élève au-dessus de la portée des hommes vulgaires, est celle dont le Législateur met les décisions dans la bouche des immortels[3], pour subjuguer par l'autorité divine ceux que ne pourrait ébranler la prudence[4] humaine. Mais il n'appartient pas à tout homme de faire parler les Dieux, ni d'en être cru quand il s'annonce pour leur interprète. La grandeur des choses dites en leur nom doit être soutenue par une éloquence et une fermeté plus qu'humaine. Il faut que le feu de l'enthousiasme se joigne aux profondeurs de la sagesse et à la constance de la vertu. En un mot, la grande âme[5] du Législateur est le vrai miracle qui doit prouver sa mission. Tout homme peut graver des tables de pierre, ou acheter un oracle, ou feindre un secret commerce avec quelque divinité, ou dresser un oiseau pour lui parler à l'oreille, ou trouver quelque autre moyen grossier[6] d'en imposer au peuple. Celui qui ne saura que cela pourra même assembler par hasard une troupe d'insensés; mais il ne fondera jamais un empire, et son extravagant ouvrage périra bientôt avec lui. Car, si de vains prestiges forment un lien passager, il n'y a que la sagesse qui le rende durable. La Loi judaïque toujours subsistante, celle de l'enfant d'Ismaël qui depuis onze siècles régit la moitié du monde, annoncent encore aujourd'hui les grands hommes qui les ont dictées; et tandis que l'orgueilleuse[7] philosophie, ou l'aveugle esprit de parti, ne voit en eux que d'heureux imposteurs, le vrai politique admire dans leurs institutions ce grand et puissant génie qui préside aux établissements[8] durables.

Il ne faut pas [9]de tout ceci conclure[9], avec Warburton[10], que la politique et la Religion puissent avoir un objet commun; mais que l'une sert quelquefois d'instrument à l'autre[11]. [Chacun[12] sent assez

---

[1] D. B. reads *de tous temps*. [2] Added—both. [3] [Dieux.]
[4] [sagesse.] [5] [le génie.] [6] Added.
[7] Added. [8] [législations.]
[9] [conclure de tout ceci.] [10] Added. MS. has *Waburton*.
[11] The remainder of chapter cancelled in MS.
[12] [Je reviendrai ci-après sur; J'en parlerai ci-après.]

l'utilité de l'union politique, pour rendre certaines opinions permanentes et les maintenir en corps de doctrine et de secte ; et quant au concours de la religion dans l'établissement civil[1], on voit aussi qu'il n'est pas moins utile de pouvoir donner au lien moral une force intérieure qui pénètre jusqu'à l'âme et soit toujours indépendante[2] des biens, des maux, de la vie même et de tous les événements humains.

Je ne crois pas contredire dans ce chapitre ce que j'ai dit ci-devant sur le peu d'utilité du serment dans le contrat de société ; car il y a bien de la différence entre demeurer fidèle à l'État seulement parce qu'on a juré de l'être, ou parce qu'on [3]tient son institution pour[3] céleste et indestructible[4].]

CHAPITRE III.

Du peuple à instituer.

[5]Quoique je traite ici du Droit et non des convenances, je ne puis m'empêcher de jeter en passant quelques coups d'œil sur celles qui sont indispensables dans toute bonne institution[5].

Comme, avant d'élever un édifice, l'habile architecte observe et sonde le sol pour voir s'il en peut soutenir le poids, le sage Instituteur ne commence pas par rédiger des lois au hasard ; mais il examine auparavant si le peuple, auquel il les destine, est propre à les supporter. C'est pour cela que Platon refusa de donner des lois aux Arcadiens [6]et aux Cyréniens[6], sachant[7] que[8] les uns et les autres étaient riches et ne pouvaient souffrir l'égalité. C'est pour cela qu'on vit en Crète de bonnes lois et de méchants hommes, parce que Minos n'avait discipliné qu'un peuple chargé de vices. Mille nations ont longtemps brillé sur la terre, qui n'auraient jamais pu souffrir[9] de bonnes lois ; et celles même qui l'auraient pu n'ont eu dans toute leur durée[10] qu'un temps fort court pour cela. Les peuples, ainsi que les hommes, ne sont maniables que dans leur jeunesse ; ils deviennent incorrigibles en vieillissant. Quand une fois les coutumes sont établies et les préjugés enracinés, c'est une entreprise dangereuse et vaine de vouloir y toucher. Ils ne peuvent

---

[1] [outre ce que j'en ai déjà dit, on [chacun].]   [2] [indépendamment.]
[3] [regarde...comme.]   [4] [inébranlable.]
[5] This paragraph written on v° of p. 53. See Introduction, p. 437.
[6] Added.   [7] [appre..., unfinished.]
[8] [qu'ils.]   [9] [supporter.]   [10] [vie.]

pas même souffrir qu'on parle de les rendre heureux, comme ces malades stupides et sans courage qui frémissent à la vue du médecin. Il y a peu de nations aviles sous la tyrannie qui fassent le moindre cas de la liberté ; et[1] celles même qui en voudraient encore ne sont plus en état de la supporter.

Ce n'est pas que, comme certaines maladies bouleversent la tête des hommes et leur ôtent le souvenir du passé, il ne se trouve quelquefois dans la durée des États des époques violentes où les révolutions font sur les peuples ce que certaines crises font sur les individus : où l'horreur du passé tient lieu d'oubli, et où l'État, embrasé par des guerres civiles, renaît pour ainsi dire de sa cendre, et reprend la vigueur de la jeunesse en sortant des bras de la mort. Telle fut Sparte au temps de Lycurgue ; telle fut Rome après les Tarquins ; et telles ont été parmi nous la Suisse et la Hollande, après l'expulsion des tyrans.

Mais ces événements sont rares ; ce sont des exceptions, dont la raison se trouve toujours dans la constitution particulière de l'État excepté[2]. En général, les peuples, énervés par un long esclavage et par les vices qui en sont le cortége, perdent à la fois l'amour de la patrie et le sentiment du bonheur ; ils se consolent d'être mal, en s'imaginant qu'on ne peut mieux être ; ils vivent ensemble sans aucune véritable union, comme des gens rassemblés sur un même terrain, mais séparés par des précipices. Leur misère ne les frappe point, parce que l'ambition les aveugle, et que nul ne voit[3] la place où il est, mais celle à laquelle il aspire.

Un peuple dans cet état n'est plus capable d'une institution saine, parce que sa volonté n'est pas moins corrompue que sa constitution. Il n'a plus rien à perdre, il ne peut plus rien gagner ; hébété par l'esclavage, il méprise les biens qu'il ne connaît pas[4]. Les troubles peuvent le détruire, sans que les révolutions puissent le rétablir ; et sitôt que ses fers sont brisés, il tombe épars et n'existe plus. Ainsi il lui faut désormais un maître, et jamais de libérateur.

Un peuple non encore corrompu peut avoir dans ses dimensions les vices qui ne sont pas dans sa substance. Je m'explique.

Comme la nature a donné des termes à la stature d'un homme bien conformé, au delà desquels elle ne fait plus que des géants ou des nains, il y a de même, eu égard à la meilleure constitution d'un

---

[1] Added.
[2] D. B. inserts here two sentences (*Elles ne sauraient même...ressort civil est usé*) from the final version (II. viii.). They are not in the MS.
[3] [regarde.]   [4] [plus.]

État, des bornes à l'étendue qu'il doit avoir, afin qu'il ne soit ni trop grand pour pouvoir être bien gouverné, ni trop petit pour pouvoir se maintenir par lui-même. Il est difficile de rien imaginer de plus insensé que les maximes de ces nations conquérantes qui croyaient augmenter toujours leur puissance, en étendant sans mesure leur territoire. On commence à sentir qu'il y a dans tout Corps politique un *maximum* de forces qu'il ne saurait passer, et duquel il s'éloigne souvent à force de s'agrandir. Mais on ne sent peut-être pas encore assez que, plus le lien social s'étend, plus il se relâche ; et qu'en général un petit État est toujours proportionnellement plus puissant qu'un grand.

Il ne faut qu'ouvrir l'histoire pour se convaincre de cette maxime par l'expérience, et mille raisons peuvent la démontrer[1]. Premièrement, l'administration devient plus pénible dans les grandes distances, comme un poids devient plus lourd au bout d'un grand levier. Elle devient aussi plus onéreuse, à mesure que les degrés se multiplient ; car chaque ville a la sienne que le peuple paye ; chaque district la sienne, encore payée par le peuple ; ensuite chaque province, puis les grands gouvernements, les satrapies, les viceroyautés, qu'il faut toujours payer plus cher à mesure qu'on monte. Enfin vient l'administration suprême, qui écrase tout. À peine reste-t-il des ressources pour les cas extraordinaires ; et quand il y faut recourir, l'État est toujours à la veille de sa ruine. Le Gouvernement a moins de vigueur et de célérité pour faire observer les lois, prévenir les vexations, corriger[2] les abus, et réprimer les entreprises séditieuses qui peuvent se faire dans des lieux éloignés. Le peuple a moins d'affection pour ses chefs, qu'il ne voit jamais ; pour la patrie, qui est [3]à ses yeux[3] comme le monde ; et pour ses concitoyens, dont la plupart lui sont étrangers. Les mêmes lois ne peuvent convenir à tant de nations diverses, qui ont des mœurs différentes, qui vivent sous[4] des climats opposés et qui ne peuvent souffrir la même forme de Gouvernement. Des lois différentes n'engendrent que trouble et confusion parmi des peuples qui, vivant sous les mêmes chefs et dans une communication continuelle, passent sans cesse les uns chez les autres et, soumis à d'autres coutumes, ne sont jamais sûrs que leur patrimoine soit bien à eux. Les talents sont enfouis, les vertus ignorées, le vice impuni, dans cette multitude d'hommes inconnus les uns aux autres, que le siège de l'administration rassemble dans un même lieu. Les chefs, accablés d'affaires, ne voient rien par eux-mêmes. Enfin, les mesures

---

[1] [confirmer.]   [2] [et réprimer.]   [3] [pour lui.]
[4] D. B. reads *dans*, against the MS.

qu'il faut prendre pour maintenir partout l'autorité générale, à laquelle tant d'officiers éloignés veulent toujours se soustraire ou en imposer, absorbent[1] tous les soins publics; il n'en reste plus pour le bonheur du peuple; à peine en reste-t-il pour sa défense au besoin; et c'est ainsi qu'un État, trop grand pour sa constitution, périt toujours écrasé sous son propre poids.

D'un autre côté, l'État doit se donner[2] une certaine base, pour avoir de la solidité et résister aux secousses[3], qu'il ne manquera pas d'éprouver, [4]et aux efforts[5], qu'il sera contraint de soutenir[4]; car tous les peuples ont une espèce de force centrifuge, par laquelle ils agissent continuellement les uns contre[6] les autres et tendent à s'agrandir aux dépens de leurs voisins[7]. .Ainsi les faibles risquent d'être bientôt engloutis; et l'on ne peut guère se conserver qu'en se mettant avec tous dans une sorte d'équilibre, qui rende la compression à peu près égale.

On voit par là qu'il y a des raisons de s'étendre et des raisons de se resserrer; et ce n'est[8] pas le moindre talent du politique de trouver, entre les unes et les autres, la proportion la plus avantageuse à la conservation de l'État. On peut dire en général que les premières, étant purement extérieures et relatives, doivent toujours être subordonnées aux autres, qui sont intérieures et absolues. Car une forte et saine constitution est la première chose qu'il faut rechercher; et l'on doit plus compter sur la vigueur qui naît d'un bon Gouvernement que sur les ressources que fournit un grand territoire.

Au reste, on a vu des États tellement constitués que la nécessité des conquêtes était dans leur constitution même; et que, pour se maintenir, ils étaient forcés de s'agrandir sans cesse. Peut-être se félicitaient-ils beaucoup de cette heureuse nécessité, qui leur montrait pourtant, avec le terme de leur grandeur, l'inévitable moment de leur chute.

Pour que l'État puisse être bien gouverné, il faudrait que sa grandeur, ou pour mieux dire son étendue, fût mesurée aux facultés de ceux qui la gouvernent; et l'impossibilité que de grands génies[9] se succèdent sans cesse dans le Gouvernement veut qu'on se règle sur la portée commune. Voilà ce qui fait que les nations, agrandies sous des chefs illustres, dépérissent nécessairement entre les mains des

---

[1] MS. *absorbe*. It is retained by D. B., against the grammar.
[2] [il est nécessaire que l'État ait.] [3] [externes.]
[4] Added over the line. [5] or *assauts*.
[6] [sur.] [7] [comme les tourbillons de Descartes.] D. B. retains it.
[8] [peut-être.] [9] D. B. reads *de grands hommes*.

imbéciles qui ne manquent pas de leur succéder; et que, pour peu qu'un État soit grand, le prince est presque toujours trop petit. Quand, au contraire, il arrive que l'État est trop petit pour son chef, ce qui est très rare, il est encore mal gouverné; parce que le chef, suivant toujours la grandeur de ses vues et les projets de l'ambition, oublie les intérêts du peuple et ne le rend pas moins malheureux par l'abus des talents qu'il a de trop, qu'un chef borné par le défaut de ceux qui lui manquent. Cet inconvénient de l'administration d'une monarchie, même bien réglée, se fait surtout sentir quand elle est héréditaire, et que le chef n'est point choisi par le peuple, mais donné par la naissance. Il faudrait, pour ainsi dire, que le royaume s'étendît ou se resserrât à chaque règne, selon la portée du prince; au lieu que, les talents d'un Sénat ayant des mesures plus fixes, l'État peut avoir des bornes constantes sans que l'administration en souffre.

Au reste, une règle fondamentale pour toute société, bien constituée et gouvernée légitimement, serait qu'on en pût assembler aisément[1] tous les membres toutes les fois qu'il serait nécessaire; car on verra[2] ci-après que les assemblées par députation ne peuvent ni représenter le Corps, ni recevoir de lui des pouvoirs suffisants pour statuer en son nom comme souverain. Il suit de là que l'État devrait se borner à une seule ville, tout au plus. Que s'il en a plusieurs, la capitale aura toujours de fait la souveraineté, [3]et les autres seront sujettes[3]: sorte de constitution où la tyrannie et l'abus sont inévitables.

Il faut remarquer qu'on peut mesurer un Corps politique de deux manières: savoir, par l'étendue du territoire ou par le nombre du peuple; et qu'il y a entre l'une et l'autre de ces mesures un rapport nécessaire pour donner à l'État sa véritable grandeur; car ce sont les hommes qui font l'État, et c'est le terrain qui nourrit les hommes. Ce rapport est que la terre suffise à l'entretien de ses habitants, et qu'il y ait autant d'habitants que la terre en peut nourrir. C'est dans cette proportion que se trouve le *maximum* de forces d'un nombre[4] donné de peuple; car, s'il y a du terrain de trop, la garde [5]en est onéreuse[5], la culture insuffisante, et le produit superflu; s'il n'y en a pas assez, l'État se trouve, pour le supplément, dans la dépendance de ses voisins[6].

Les considérations que fournit cette importante matière nous mèneraient trop loin, s'il fallait ici nous y arrêter. Il est certain, par

[1] [facilement.]
[2] [je ferai voir.]
[3] Added.
[4] [peuple.]
[5] [et la culture en sont onéreuses.]
[6] [ou contraint de s'affaiblir par des colonies.]

exemple, qu'on ne saurait donner en calcul un rapport fixe entre la mesure de terre[1] et le nombre d'hommes qui se suffisent l'un à l'autre; tant à cause des différences qui se trouvent dans les qualités du terrain, dans ses degrés de fertilité, dans la nature de ses productions, dans l'influence des climats, que de celles qu'on remarque dans les tempéraments des hommes qui les habitent, dont les uns consomment peu dans un pays fertile, les autres beaucoup sur un sol plus ingrat. De plus: il faut avoir égard à la plus grande ou moindre fécondité des femmes, à ce que le pays peut avoir de plus ou moins favorable à la population, à la quantité dont le Législateur peut espérer d'y concourir par ses établissements; de sorte qu'il ne doit pas toujours fonder son jugement sur ce qu'il voit, mais sur ce qu'il prévoit, ni s'arrêter autant à l'état actuel de la population qu'à celui où elle doit naturellement parvenir. Enfin, il y a mille occasions où les accidents particuliers du lieu exigent, ou permettent, d'embrasser plus ou moins[2] de terrain qu'il ne paraît nécessaire. Ainsi, l'on s'étendra beaucoup dans un pays de montagnes, où les productions naturelles, savoir les bois et les pâturages, exigent moins le travail humain[3]; où l'expérience apprend que les femmes sont plus fécondes que dans les plaines; et où un grand sol incliné ne donne qu'une petite base horizontale, la seule qu'il faut compter pour la végétation. Au contraire, on peut se resserrer au bord de la mer, même dans des rochers et des sables presque stériles; parce que la pêche y peut suppléer en grande partie aux productions de la terre; que les hommes doivent être plus rassemblés pour repousser les corsaires et coureurs de mer; et qu'on a d'ailleurs plus de facilité pour[4] décharger le pays, par le commerce et les colonies, des habitants dont il serait surchargé.

À ces conditions il en faut ajouter une qui ne peut suppléer à nulle autre, mais sans laquelle elles sont toutes inutiles: c'est qu'on jouisse de l'abondance et d'une profonde paix. Car le temps où s'ordonne un État est, comme celui où se forme un bataillon, l'instant où le Corps est le plus faible, le moins capable de résistance et le plus facile à détruire. On résisterait mieux dans un désordre

---

[1] [du terrain.]   [2] In the final version, *ou moins* is omitted.
[3] [des hommes.] D. B. reads *moins de travail* (as in the final version).
[4] [fournir, au moyen du commerce et des colonies, à la subsistance des habitants dont [le pays] il serait surchargé.] It looks as though Rousseau hesitated whether to retain from *des habitants*, as part of the version in the text: but *des* is, for that purpose, corrected into *les*, which seems strange. He seems to have vacillated between (1) éloigner par le commerce et les colonies les habitants, etc. (2) décharger le pays...des habitants.

CH. III] *Conditions propres à l'institution* 489

absolu que dans un moment de fermentation, où chacun s'occupe[1] de son rang et non du péril. Qu'une guerre, une famine, une sédition survienne en ce temps de crise ; l'État est infailliblement renversé[2]. Ce n'est pas qu'il n'y ait beaucoup de Gouvernements établis durant ces orages[3] ; mais alors ce sont ces Gouvernements mêmes qui détruisent l'État. Les usurpateurs amènent ou choisissent toujours ces temps de trouble pour faire passer, à la faveur de l'effroi public, des lois destructives que le peuple n'adopterait jamais de sang-froid[4] ; et l'on peut dire que le moment[5] de l'institution est un des caractères les plus sûrs, par lesquels on peut distinguer l'ouvrage du Législateur de celui du tyran.

Au[6] risque de quelques répétitions, récapitulons les considérations qu'un Législateur doit faire avant d'entreprendre l'institution d'un peuple ; car ces considérations sont importantes pour ne pas user vainement le temps et l'autorité. D'abord, il ne doit pas tenter de changer celle d'un peuple déjà policé, encore moins d'en rétablir une qui soit abolie, ni de ranimer des ressorts usés ; car il en est de la force des lois, comme de la saveur du sel[7]. Ainsi, l'on peut donner de la vigueur à un peuple qui n'en eut jamais, mais[8] non pas en rendre à celui qui l'a perdue ; je regarde cette maxime comme fondamentale. Agis essaya[9] de remettre en vigueur à Sparte la discipline de Lycurgue ; les Maccabées voulaient rétablir à Jérusalem la théocratie de Moïse ; Brutus voulut rendre[10] à Rome son ancienne[11] liberté ; Rienzi tenta la même chose dans la suite. Tous étaient des héros ; le dernier même le fut un moment de sa vie. Tous périrent dans leur entreprise[12].

Toute grande nation est incapable de discipline ; un État trop petit n'a point de consistance ; la médiocrité même ne fait quelquefois qu'unir les deux défauts.

Il faut encore avoir égard au voisinage. Ce qui fit subsister les petits États de la Grèce, c'est qu'ils étaient eux-mêmes environnés

---

[1] [doit s'occuper.] [2] [détruit.]
[3] [dans ces moments dangereux.] [4] MS. *sens froid*. [5] [temps.]
[6] This paragraph originally began with the following sentence : 'Il importe de ne pas perdre le temps et l'autorité à former des entreprises [toujours dangereuses sitôt qu'elles sont] chimériques.' This, however, appears to be cancelled and to be replaced lower by the subsequent sentence : 'car ces considérations,' etc. D. B. omits *Au risque de quelques répétitions*.
[7] [qui ne vient que d'elle-même, et à laquelle rien ne peut suppléer.]
[8] [il est impossi (word unfinished).] [9] [voulut.]
[10] [rétablir.] [11] Added. 'la' cancelled before 'liberté.'
[12] D. B. has *leurs entreprises*.

d'autres[1] petits États, et qu'ils en valaient tous ensemble un fort grand, quand ils étaient unis pour l'intérêt commun. [2]C'est une triste[3] position que d'être entre deux puissants voisins, jaloux l'un de l'autre; on évitera difficilement d'entrer dans leurs querelles, et d'être écrasé avec le plus faible[2]. Tout État enclavé dans un autre doit être compté pour rien. Tout État trop grand pour ses habitants, ou trop peuplé pour son territoire, ne vaut guère mieux, à moins que ce mauvais rapport[4] ne soit accidentel, et qu'il n'y ait une force naturelle qui ramène les choses à leur juste proportion.

Enfin, il faut avoir égard aux circonstances; car, par exemple, on ne doit point parler de règle au peuple quand il a faim, [5]ni de raison à des fanatiques[5]; et la guerre qui fait taire les lois existantes ne permet guère d'en établir. [6]Mais la famine, la fureur, la guerre ne durent pas toujours. Il n'y a presque[7] ni homme ni peuple qui n'ait quelque intervalle meilleur[7] et quelque moment de sa vie à donner à la raison: voilà l'instant qu'il faut savoir saisir.

Quel peuple est donc propre à la législation? Celui qui n'a jamais encore porté le joug des lois; celui qui n'a [8]ni coutumes ni superstitions enracinées, et qui pourtant se trouve déjà lié par quelque union d'origine ou d'intérêt; celui qui ne craint pas d'être écrasé par une invasion subite, et qui, sans entrer dans les querelles de ses voisins, peut résister [9]à chacun[9] par lui-même, ou s'aider de l'un pour repousser l'autre[10]; celui dont tous les membres peuvent être connus de chacun d'eux, et où l'on n'est point forcé de charger un homme d'un plus grand fardeau qu'un homme ne peut porter; celui qui peut se passer des autres peuples et dont tout autre peuple peut se passer[11]; celui qui n'est ni riche ni pauvre, [12]et se suffit à lui-même[12]: [13]en un mot, celui qui réunit la consistance

---

[1] Added.
[2] Added on opposite page. It is not clear whether it is intended for the text or for a note.   [3] [mauvaise.]   [4] [ce dérangement.]
[5] Added.   [6] Down to end of paragraph added.
[7] D. B. reads *même*. MS. *may* have *intervalles*, etc.   [8] [point de.]
[9] Added.   [10] [d'un voisin pour en repousser un autre.]
[11] Si de deux peuples voisins l'un ne pouvait [v.l. peut] se passer de l'autre, ce serait une situation très dure pour le premier, mais très dangereuse pour le second. Toute nation sage, en pareil cas, s'efforcera bien vite de délivrer l'autre de cette dépendance. [Note de J.-J. R.] Contrast the Fragment, *Le Bonheur public*; above, p. 327. D. B. embodies this note in the text, wrongly.

[v.l. si dangereuse pour le second que je ne sais [v.l. doute] si celle du premier n'est pas encore préférable.]

[12] Added. Compare Buttafuoco's first letter (Vol. II. pp. 365—7).
[13] [celui qui, sortant d'une révolution, jouit [pourtant] d'une profonde paix.]

d'un ancien peuple avec la docilité d'un peuple nouveau. Ce qui rend pénible l'ouvrage de la législation, c'est moins ce qu'il faut établir que ce qu'il faut détruire ; et ce qui rend le succès si rare, c'est l'impossibilité de trouver la simplicité de la nature jointe aux besoins de la société. Toutes ces conditions se trouvent difficilement rassemblées, je l'avoue; aussi voit-on ¹peu d'États bien constitués¹.

CHAPITRE IV.

DE LA NATURE DES LOIS ET DU PRINCIPE DE LA JUSTICE CIVILE.

Ce² qui est bien et conforme à l'ordre est tel par la nature des choses, et indépendamment de toute convention humaine.

Toute justice vient de Dieu, lui seul en est la source ; mais si nous savions la recevoir de si haut, nous n'aurions besoin ni de Gouvernement ni de lois. ³Sans doute, il est pour l'homme une justice universelle, émanée de la raison seule et fondée sur le simple droit de l'humanité⁴. Mais cette justice, pour être admise, doit être réciproque : à considérer humainement les choses, faute de sanction naturelle, les lois de la justice sont vaines entre les hommes ; elles ne font⁵ que le profit des méchants et la charge du juste, quand celui-ci les observerait avec tous les hommes, sans qu'aucun d'eux les observe avec lui. Il faut donc des conventions et des lois, pour unir les droits aux devoirs et ⁶ramener la justice à son objet⁶. ⁷Dans l'état de nature, où tout⁸ est commun, je ne dois rien à ceux à qui je n'ai rien promis ; je ne reconnais rien pour être à autrui que ce qui m'est inutile.

Mais il importe d'expliquer ici ce que j'entends par ce mot de *loi*. Car, tant qu'on se contentera d'attacher à ce mot des idées vagues et métaphysiques, on pourra savoir ce que c'est qu'une loi de la nature, ⁹et l'on continuera d'ignorer ce que c'est qu'une loi dans¹⁰ l'État¹¹.

---

[1] 'rarement un État bien constitué'—variant on opposite page.
[2] This and the next two paragraphs are written hurriedly, with many corrections, on v° of p. 63.
[3] [Quant à ceux qui reconnaissent.]
[4] [ils se trompent. Ôtez la voix de la conscience, et la raison se tait à l'instant.]
[5] D. B. reads *elles ne feraient*.
[6] [rendre la justice utile au juste.]   [7] [Autrement.]
[8] [rien (phrase unfinished).]   [9] [mais on n'en saura rien.]   [10] [de.]
[11] This sentence seems to be aimed at Montesquieu : *Esprit des lois*, I. i.

Nous avons dit que la Loi est un acte public et solennel de la volonté générale; et comme par le pacte fondamental chacun s'est soumis à cette volonté, c'est de ce pacte seul que toute loi tire sa force. Mais tâchons de donner une idée plus nette de ce mot *loi*, pris dans le sens propre et resserré dont il est question dans cet écrit.

La matière et la forme des lois sont ce qui constitue leur nature: la forme est dans l'autorité qui statue[1]; la matière est dans la chose statuée[2]. Cette partie, la seule [3] dont il s'agit dans ce chapitre, semble avoir été mal entendue de tous ceux qui ont traité des lois.

Comme la chose statuée se rapporte nécessairement au bien commun, il s'ensuit que l'objet de la Loi doit être général, ainsi que la volonté qui la dicte; et c'est[4] cette double universalité qui fait le vrai caractère de la Loi. [5]En effet, quand un[5] objet particulier a des relations diverses avec divers individus, [6]chacun ayant sur cet objet une volonté propre, il n'y a point de volonté générale parfaitement une sur cet objet individuel[7].

Que signifient ces mots *universalité* ou *généralité*, qui sont ici la même chose ? Le genre considéré par abstraction, ou ce qui convient au tout dont il s'agit[8]: et le tout n'est tel qu'à l'égard de ses parties. Voilà pourquoi la volonté générale de tout un peuple n'est point générale pour un particulier étranger; car ce particulier n'est pas membre de ce peuple. Or, à l'instant qu'un peuple considère un objet particulier, fût-ce un de ses propres membres, il se forme[9] entre le tout et sa partie une relation qui en fait deux êtres séparés, dont la partie est l'un, et le tout, moins cette même partie, est l'autre. Mais le tout, moins une partie, n'est point le tout; et tant que ce rapport subsiste, il n'y a plus de tout, mais deux parties inégales.

---

[1] [et dans l'organe qui prononce.] [2] [et dans l'objet qu'on s'y propose.]
[3] Added. [4] [dans.]
[5] [Pour le prouver, je pourrais dire que tout...a nécessairement des relations.]
[6] [d'où il suit que chacun.]
[7] [Mais ceci demanderait beaucoup d'éclaircissements; essayons de me faire entendre d'une autre manière.]
[8] [il est question.]
[9] J'ai dit qu'il n'y avait point de volonté genérale sur un objet particulier. Car cet objet particulier est dans l'État, ou hors de l'État. S'il est hors de l'État, une volonté qui lui est étrangère n'est point générale par rapport à lui; et si ce même objet est dans l'État, il en fait partie. Alors il se forme, etc. This note, or variant (MS. p. 64), appears in the text of the final version (II. vi.).

Au contraire, quand tout le peuple statue sur tout le peuple, il ne considère que lui-même; et s'il se forme alors un rapport, c'est de l'objet entier, sous un point de vue, à l'objet entier sous un autre point de vue, sans aucune division du tout. Alors l'objet sur lequel on statue est général comme la volonté qui statue; et[1] c'est cet acte que j'appelle une loi.

Quand je dis que l'objet des lois est toujours général, j'entends que la Loi considère [2]les sujets[3] en corps et[2] les actions par leurs genres ou par leurs espèces; jamais [4]un homme en particulier, ni[4] une action unique et individuelle. Ainsi, la Loi peut bien statuer qu'il y aura des priviléges, mais elle n'en peut donner nommément à personne; elle peut faire plusieurs classes de citoyens, assigner même les qualités qui donneront droit à chacune de ces classes, mais elle ne peut spécifier tels et tels pour y être admis; elle peut établir un Gouvernement royal et une succession héréditaire, mais elle ne peut élire un roi, ni nommer une famille royale. En un mot, toute fonction qui se rapporte à un objet individuel n'appartient point à la puissance législative[5].

Sur cette idée, on voit aisément qu'il ne faut plus demander à qui il appartient de faire des lois, puisqu'elles sont des actes de la volonté générale; ni si le Prince est au-dessus les lois, puisqu'il est membre de l'État; ni si la Loi peut être injuste, puisque nul n'est injuste envers lui-même; ni comment on est libre et soumis aux lois, puisqu'elles ne sont que les registres de nos volontés.

On voit encore que, la Loi réunissant l'universalité de la volonté et de l'objet, ce qu'un homme, quel qu'il puisse être, ordonne de son chef n'est point une loi; ce qu'ordonne même le souverain sur un objet particulier n'est pas[6] non plus une loi, mais un décret; ni un acte de souveraineté, mais de magistrature, comme je [7]l'expliquerai ci-après[7].

Le plus grand avantage qui résulte de cette notion est de nous montrer clairement les vrais fondements de la justice et du droit naturel. En effet la première loi, la seule véritable loi fondamentale qui découle immédiatement du pacte social, est que chacun préfère en toute chose le plus grand bien de tous.

---

[1] D. B. omits *et*. [2] Added. [3] [citoyens.] [4] Added.
[5] [Et c'est une des raisons pourquoi la Loi ne saurait avoir d'effet rétroactif; car elle aurait statué sur un fait particulier, au lieu de statuer généralement sur une espèce d'actions qui, n'étant encore celles de personne, n'ont rien d'individuel qu'après la publication de la loi, et par la volonté de ceux qui les commettent.] This cancelled passage is not reproduced by D. B.
[6] D. B. omits *pas*. [7] [l'ai déjà dit ci-devant.]

Or, la spécification des actions qui concourent à ce plus grand bien, par autant de lois particulières, est ce qui constitue le droit étroit et positif. Tout ce qu'on voit concourir à ce plus grand bien, mais que les lois n'ont point spécifié, constitue les actes de civilité[1], de bienfaisance; et l'habitude qui nous dispose à pratiquer ces actes, même à notre préjudice, est ce qu'on nomme force, ou vertu.

Étendez cette maxime à la société générale dont l'État nous donne l'idée. [2]Protégés par cette société dont nous sommes membres ou par celle où nous[3] vivons[2], la répugnance naturelle à faire du mal n'étant plus balancée en nous par la crainte d'en recevoir, nous sommes portés à la fois par la nature, par l'habitude, par la raison, à en user avec les autres hommes à peu près comme avec nos concitoyens; et de cette disposition[4], réduite en actes, naissent les règles du droit naturel raisonné, différent du droit naturel proprement dit, qui n'est fondé que sur un sentiment [5]vrai, mais[5] très vague et souvent étouffé par l'amour de nous-mêmes.

C'est ainsi que se forment en nous[6] les premières notions distinctes[6] du juste et de l'injuste. Car la Loi est antérieure à la justice, et non pas la justice à la Loi. Et si la Loi ne peut être injuste, ce n'est pas que la justice en soit la base, ce qui pourrait n'être pas toujours vrai; mais parce qu'il est contre la nature qu'on veuille se nuire à soi-même, ce qui est sans exception.

C'est un beau et sublime précepte de faire à autrui comme nous voudrions qu'il nous fût fait. Mais n'est-il pas évident que, loin de servir de fondement à la justice, il a besoin de fondement lui-même? car où est la raison claire et solide de me conduire, étant moi, sur la volonté que j'aurais, si j'étais un autre? Il est clair encore que ce précepte est sujet à mille exceptions, dont on n'a jamais donné que des explications sophistiques. [7]Un juge qui condamne un criminel ne voudrait-il pas[7] être absous, s'il était criminel lui-même? [8]Où est l'homme qui voudrait qu'on lui refusât jamais rien[8]? s'ensuit-il qu'il faille accorder tout ce qu'on

---

[1] Je n'ai point besoin d'avertir, je crois, qu'il ne faut pas entendre ce mot à la française. [Note de J.-J. R.] For *civilité*, Rousseau had at first written *humanité*. [2] Added.

[3] [sommes établis.] When he wrote this, Rousseau was himself 'established' in France. D. B. reads *Protégés par la société*.

[4] [générale.] [5] Added. [6] *en nous* and *distinctes*. Added.

[7] [Peut-on douter par exemple qu'] [voulût].

[8] [Où est le riche qui ne voudrait pas, s'il était pauvre, qu'un riche lui donnât son bien?] D. B. reads *Où est l'homme qui ne voudrait qu'on lui refusât jamais?* against MS., sense and grammar.

nous[1] demande ? Cet autre axiome, *cuique suum*, qui sert de base à tout le droit de propriété, sur quoi se fonde-t-il que sur le droit de propriété même ? Et si je ne dis pas avec Hobbes : *tout est à moi*, pourquoi du moins ne reconnaîtrais-je pas pour mien, dans l'état de nature, tout ce qui m'est utile et dont je puis m'emparer ?

C'est donc dans la loi fondamentale et universelle du plus grand bien de tous, et non dans les relations particulières d'homme à homme, qu'il faut chercher les vrais principes du juste et de l'injuste ; et il n'y a point de règle particulière de justice qu'on ne déduise aisément de cette première loi. Ainsi, *cuique suum* ; parce que la propriété particulière et la liberté civile sont les fondements de la communauté. Ainsi, *que ton frère te soit comme toi-même* ; parce que le moi particulier répandu sur le tout est le plus fort lien de la société générale, et que l'État a le plus haut degré de force et de vie qu'il puisse avoir, quand toutes nos passions[2] particulières se réunissent en lui. En un mot, il y a mille cas où c'est un acte de justice de nuire à son prochain, au lieu que toute action juste a nécessairement pour règle la plus grande utilité commune : cela est sans exception.

CHAPITRE V.

Division des lois.

Pour ordonner le tout[3], ou donner la meilleure forme possible à la chose publique, il y a diverses relations à considérer. Premièrement, l'action du Corps entier agissant sur lui-même : c'est à dire, le rapport du tout au tout, ou du souverain à l'État ; et ce rapport est[4] composé de celui des forces intermédiaires, comme nous verrons ci-après. Les lois qui règlent ce rapport portent le nom de *lois politiques*, et s'appellent aussi *lois fondamentales* : non sans quelque raison si ces lois sont sages[5]. Car, s'il n'y a dans chaque État[6] qu'une bonne manière de l'ordonner, le peuple qui l'a trouvée n'y doit jamais rien changer. Mais, si l'ordre établi[7] est mauvais, pourquoi prendrait-on pour fondamentales des lois qui l'empêchent d'être bon ? D'ailleurs, en tout état de cause, le peuple a toujours le pouvoir de changer ses lois, même les

---

[1] D. B. reads *vous*. [2] [sensations.]
[3] [un corps composé le mieux qu'il est possible] [le Corps politique.]
[4] [doit être.] [5] [bonnes.]
[6] [qu'un bon Gouvernement possible.] [7] [le Gouvernement.]

meilleures; car, s'il plaît à un homme de se faire mal à lui-même, qui est-ce qui a droit de l'en empêcher?

La seconde relation est celle des membres entr'eux, ou avec le Corps entier; et ce rapport doit être au premier égard aussi petit, et au second aussi grand, qu'il est possible; de sorte que chaque citoyen soit dans une parfaite indépendance de tous les autres, et dans une excessive dépendance de la Cité: ce qui se fait toujours par les mêmes moyens; car il n'y a que la force de l'État qui fasse la liberté de ses membres. [1]C'est de ce deuxième rapport que naissent les lois civiles[1].

Les lois qui règlent l'exercice et la forme de l'autorité souveraine par rapport aux particuliers s'appelaient à Rome *lois de majesté*: telle que celle qui défendait d'appeler au Sénat des jugements du peuple, et celle qui rendait sacrée et inviolable la personne des Tribuns.

Quant aux lois particulières qui règlent les devoirs et les droits respectifs des citoyens, elles s'appellent *lois civiles*, en ce qui regarde les relations domestiques et la propriété des biens; *police*, en ce qui regarde le bon ordre public et la sûreté des personnes [2]et des choses[2].

On peut considérer une troisième sorte de relation entre l'homme et la Loi: savoir, celle de la désobéissance à la peine; et celle-ci donne lieu à l'établissement des *lois criminelles*, qui dans le fond sont moins une espèce particulière de lois que la sanction de toutes les autres.

À ces trois sortes de lois il s'en joint une quatrième, la plus importante de toutes, qui ne se grave [3]ni sur le marbre, ni[3] sur l'airain, mais dans les cœurs des citoyens; qui fait la véritable constitution de l'État; qui prend tous les jours de nouvelles forces; qui, lorsque[4] les autres lois vieillissent ou s'éteignent[5], les ranime ou les supplée, conserve un peuple dans l'esprit de son institution, et substitue insensiblement la force de l'habitude à celle de l'autorité. Je parle des mœurs et des coutumes: partie inconnue à nos politiques, mais de laquelle dépend le succès de toutes les autres; partie dont le grand Législateur s'occupe en secret, tandis qu'il paraît se borner à des règlements particuliers qui ne sont que le cintre de la voûte, dont les mœurs, plus lentes à naître, forment enfin l'inébranlable clef. Entre ces diverses sortes de lois, je me borne[6] dans cet écrit à traiter des lois politiques.

---

[1] Added. [2] Added. [3] D. B. omits, and replaces by *pas*.
[4] [tandis que toutes.]
[5] [insensiblement.] [6] [suis proposé (?)...de ne traiter que.]

CHAPITRE VI.

DES DIVERSES SYSTÈMES DE LÉGISLATION.

Si l'on recherche en quoi consiste précisément ce plus grand bien de tous, qui doit être la base de tout système de législation, on trouvera qu'il se réduit à ces deux objets principaux, la *liberté* et l'*égalité*. La liberté, parce que toute dépendance particulière est autant de force ôtée au corps de l'État; l'égalité, parce que la liberté ne peut subsister sans elle.

J'ai déjà dit ce que c'est que la liberté civile. À l'égard de l'égalité, il ne faut pas entendre par ce mot [1]que les degrés de puissance et de richesse soient exactement les mêmes[1]; mais que, quant à la puissance, elle soit au-dessous de toute violence et ne s'exerce jamais qu'en vertu du rang et des lois; et, quant à la richesse, que nul citoyen ne soit assez opulent pour en pouvoir acheter un autre, et nul assez pauvre pour être contraint de se vendre. Ce qui suppose, du côté des grands, modération de biens et de crédit, et, du côté des petits, modération d'avarice et de convoitise[2].

Mais ces objets généraux de toute bonne institution doivent être modifiés dans chaque pays par les rapports qui naissent tant de la situation locale que du caractère des habitants; et c'est sur ces rapports qu'il faut assigner à chaque peuple un système particulier de législation qui soit le meilleur, non peut-être en lui-même, mais pour l'État auquel il est destiné[3]. Par exemple, le sol[4] est-il ingrat et stérile, ou le pays trop serré pour les habitants?

---

[1] [une régularité (?) géométrique.]

[2] At the bottom of the page: Cette égalité, disent-ils, est une chimère de spéculation qui ne peut exister dans la pratique. Mais quoi? parce que l'effet est inévitable, s'ensuit-il qu'il ne faille pas au moins le régler? C'est parce que la force des choses tend toujours à détruire l'égalité que la force de la législation doit toujours tendre à la maintenir [v.l. rétablir] [c'est précisément parce que la force des choses tend à détruire cette égalité que]. This passage may have been intended for the text, where indeed it appears in the final version (II. xi.).

[3] On v° of p. 69: Mais il ne faut pas croire qu'on puisse établir partout des Cités. [Je ne vois dans toute l'Europe plus de peuple en état de supporter l'honorable fardeau de la liberté: ils ne savent plus soulever que des chaînes.] Le fardeau de la liberté n'est pas fait pour de faibles épaules. [Il faut de fortes épaules pour porter l'honorable fardeau de la liberté.] Neither this note, nor the one before, has any reference in the MS.

[4] [la terre.] D. B. reads *le sol en est-il*, against the MS.

tournez-vous du côté de l'industrie et des arts, dont vous échangerez les productions contre les denrées qui vous manquent. Au contraire, occupez-vous de riches plaines et des coteaux fertiles[1]? dans un bon terrain manquez-vous d'habitants? donnez tous vos soins à l'agriculture, et chassez les arts, de peur qu'ils n'achèvent de dépeupler le pays en attroupant sur quelques points du territoire le peu d'habitants qu'il a: car on sait que, toute proportion gardée, les villes peuplent moins que la campagne. Occupez-vous des rivages étendus et commodes? couvrez les mers de vaisseaux, cultivez le commerce et la navigation. La mer ne baigne-t-elle sur vos côtes que des rochers presque inaccessibles? restez barbares et ichthyophages; vous en vivrez[2] plus tranquilles, meilleurs peut-être, et sûrement plus heureux. En un mot, outre les maximes communes à tous, chaque peuple renferme en soi quelque cause qui les ordonne d'une manière particulière, et rend sa législation propre à lui seul. C'est ainsi qu'autrefois les Hébreux et récemment les Arabes ont eu pour principal objet la religion, les Athéniens les lettres, Carthage et Tyr le commerce, Rhodes la marine, Sparte la guerre, et Rome la vertu. L'auteur de l'*Esprit des lois* a montré dans une foule d'exemples par quel art le Législateur dirige l'institution sur chacun de ces[3] objets.

Ce qui rend la constitution d'un État véritablement solide et durable, c'est quand les convenances sont tellement observées que les rapports naturels et les lois tombent toujours de concert sur les mêmes points, et que celles-ci ne font pour ainsi dire qu'assurer, accompagner, rectifier[4] les autres. Mais, si le Législateur, se trompant dans son objet, prend un principe différent de celui qui naît de la nature des choses; que l'un tende à la servitude et l'autre à la liberté; l'un aux richesses, l'autre à la population; l'un à la paix et l'autre aux conquêtes; on verra les lois s'affaiblir insensiblement, la constitution s'altérer; et l'État ne cessera d'être agité, jusqu'à ce qu'il soit détruit ou changé, et que l'invincible nature ait repris son empire.

[1] D. B. omits *fertiles*. [2] [serez.]
[3] D. B. reads *ses*. [4] [la marche des autres.]

LIVRE III.

Des lois politiques
ou de l'institution du gouvernement.

Avant de parler des diverses formes de Gouvernement, il sera bon de déterminer le sens précis qu'il faut donner à ce mot dans une Société[1] légitime.

CHAPITRE I.
Ce que c'est que le gouvernement d'un état.

J'avertis les lecteurs que ce chapitre demande quelque attention, et que je ne sais pas l'art d'être clair pour qui ne veut pas être attentif.

Toute action libre a deux causes qui concourent à la produire : l'une morale, savoir la volonté qui détermine l'acte ; l'autre physique, savoir la puissance qui l'exécute. Quand je marche vers un objet, il faut, premièrement, que j'y veuille aller ; en second lieu, que mes pieds m'y portent. Qu'un paralytique veuille courir, qu'un homme agile ne le veuille pas, tous deux resteront en place. Le Corps politique a les mêmes mobiles. On y distingue de même la force et la volonté : celle-ci, sous le nom de puissance législative[2] ; l'autre, sous le nom de puissance exécutive. Rien ne s'y fait, ou ne s'y doit faire, sans leur concours.

Nous avons vu que la puissance législative appartient au peuple, et ne peut appartenir qu'à lui. Il est aisé de voir de même que la puissance exécutive ne peut appartenir au peuple. * * *

De la religion civile[3].

Sitôt que les hommes vivent en société, il leur faut une religion qui les y maintienne. Jamais peuple n'a subsisté, ni ne subsistera, sans religion ; et si on ne lui en donnait point, de

---

[1] [Cité regulière.]

[2] Je dis *exécutive* et *législative*, non *exécutrice* ni *législatrice*, par ce que je prends ces deux mots adjectivement. En général, je ne fais pas grand cas de toutes ces vétilles de grammaire : mais je crois que dans les écrits didactiques on doit souvent avoir moins d'égards à l'usage qu'à l'analogie, quand elle rend le sens plus exact [discours plus clair]. [Note de J.-J. R.]

[3] The following is written on verso of pp. 46—51 (also on the margin, side and bottom, of p. 51 r°), hurriedly and with many corrections. It is the rough draft of the closing chapter of the *Contrat social* (iv. viii.).

lui-même[1] il s'en ferait une, ou serait bientôt détruit. Dans tout État qui peut exiger de ses membres le sacrifice de leur vie, celui qui ne croit point[2] de vie à venir est nécessairement un lâche[3], ou un fou. Mais on ne sait que trop à quel point l'espoir de la vie[4] à venir peut engager un fanatique à mépriser celle-ci. Ôtez ses visions à ce fanatique, et donnez lui ce même espoir pour prix de la vertu, vous en ferez un vrai citoyen[5].

La religion considérée par rapport à la société peut se diviser en deux espèces: savoir, la religion de l'homme, et celle du citoyen. La première[6], sans temple, sans autels, sans rites[7], bornée au culte purement spirituel du Dieu suprême et aux devoirs éternels de la morale, est la [8]pure et simple[8] religion de l'Évangile, ou le vrai théisme. L'autre, renfermée[9] pour ainsi dire dans [10]un seul pays[10], lui donne ses Dieux propres et tutélaires[11]; elle a ses cérémonies, ses rites, son culte extérieur, prescrit par les lois; hors de la seule nation qui la suit, tout le reste est pour elle infidèle, étranger, barbare; elle n'étend les devoirs et les droits de l'homme qu'aussi loin que ses Dieux et ses lois[12]. Telles étaient[13] les religions de tous les anciens peuples[14], sans aucune exception[15].

Il y a une troisième sorte de religion, plus bizarre, qui donne aux hommes[16] deux chefs, deux lois, deux patries, les soumet à des devoirs contradictoires[17], et les empêche de pouvoir jamais être à la fois pieux et citoyens. Telle est la religion des Lamas[18], telle est celle des Japonais, tel est le Christianisme romain. On peut appeler[19] celle-ci la religion du prêtre.

---

[1] D. B. omits *de lui-même*.   [2] [pas l'immortalité de l'âme.]
[3] [mauvais citoyen.]   [4] [du bonheur.]
[5] [le plus grand [v.l. vertueux] des hommes.] It is possible that *vrai* is cancelled. D. B. omits it.
[6] [bornée aux lois.]   [7] [cérémonies.]   [8] Added.
[9] [circonscrite.]   [10] [la patrie.]
[11] [y borne, pour ainsi dire, son culte à ses Dieux tutélaires et ses devoirs à ses concitoyens.]
[12] [elle restreint à un peuple particulier les devoirs qu'elle impose; elle fait que chaque nation regarde tous les autres comme infidèles; hors de la seule nation qui la suit, tout le reste est pour elle infidèle, étranger: celle-ci fut la Religion et donne à ce peuple et à ses lois de quelque origine; elle fait que chaque nation regarde toutes les autres comme infidèles, n'a pas de frères, ne re...et ne connaît aucun devoir; tout ce qui ne reconnaît pas ses Dieux et ses lois est infidèle.]   [13] [la plupart des.]
[14] [du paganisme et celle du peuple juif.] D. B. omits *peuples*.
[15] *sans aucune exception*, added.   [16] [citoyens.]
[17] [qu'il leur est impossible de concilier.]
[18] [catholique.]   [19] [j'appellerai.]

CH. VIII]   *Trois sortes de religions*   501

À considérer politiquement ces trois sortes de religions, elles ont toutes ¹leurs défauts¹. La troisième est si évidemment mauvaise, que c'est perdre le temps de s'amuser à le démontrer.

La seconde est bonne en ce qu'elle réunit² le culte divin et l'amour des lois et que, faisant de la patrie³ l'objet de l'adoration des citoyens, elle leur apprend que servir l'État c'est servir Dieu. C'est une espèce de théocratie, dans laquelle l'État ne doit point avoir⁴ d'autres prêtres que ses magistrats. Alors, mourir pour son pays, c'est⁵ aller au martyre ; désobéir aux lois, c'est être impie et sacrilége ; et ⁶soumettre un criminel à l'exécration publique, c'est le dévouer au courroux céleste des Dieux : *Sacer estod*⁶.

Mais elle est mauvaise, en ce qu'étant fondée⁷ sur l'erreur et sur le mensonge elle trompe les hommes, les rend crédules et superstitieux, et noie le vrai culte de la Divinité dans⁸ un vain cérémonial. Elle est mauvaise encore, quand, devenant exclusive et tyrannique, elle rend un peuple sanguinaire et intolérant ; en sorte qu'il ne respire que meurtre et massacre, et croit faire une action sainte de tuer quiconque n'admet pas ses Dieux et ses lois. ⁹Il n'est pas permis de serrer le nœud d'une société particulière aux dépens du reste du genre humain⁹.

¹⁰Que si dans le paganisme, où chaque État avait son culte ¹¹et ses Dieux tutélaires, il n'y avait point de guerres de religion, c'était par cela même que chaque État, ayant son culte particulier aussi bien que son Gouvernement¹², ne distinguait point ses Dieux de ses lois. La guerre, étant purement civile, était tout ce qu'elle pouvait être. Les départements des Dieux étaient, pour ainsi dire,

¹ or *bien de fautes*.   ² [sur les mêmes points.]
³ [donnant à la patrie, pour ainsi dire.]
⁴ [Dans cette religion l'État ne doit point avoir.]
⁵ [pour eux.]
⁶ [il n'y a que dans un tel État que la malédiction des Dieux peut être imposée pour peine aux criminels. *Sacer estod* : disaient les lois romains. C'est une (*sic*) beau mot que ce *sacer estod*.]
⁷ [à fond.]
⁸ [de vains rites qui ne peuvent honorer Dieu ; les attacher à la patrie, mais.]
⁹ [Il faut bien serrer le nœud social, mais non pas aux dépens du reste des hommes.]
¹⁰ [Si chaque État était, pour ainsi dire.] D. B. inserts *l'on demande comment*, after *si* ; and *je réponds que*, before *c'était par cela* ; in both cases, against the MS.
¹¹ [son culte et sa religion particulière.]
¹² [ayant ses Dieux et sa religion, combattait pour ses Dieux en combattant pour ses lois.]

fixés par les bornes des nations. Le Dieu d'un peuple n'avait aucun droit sur un autre peuple. Les Dieux des païens n'étaient point des Dieux jaloux ; ils partageaient paisiblement entr'eux l'empire du monde[1], et en suivaient sans souci les partages des mortels ; l'obligation d'embrasser une religion ne venait que de celle d'être soumis aux lois qui la prescrivaient. [2]Comme il n'y avait donc point d'autre manière de convertir un peuple que de l'asservir[3], c'eût été un discours ridicule de lui dire : *adore mes Dieux, ou je t'attaque* ; l'obligation de [4]changer de culte étant attachée à la victoire[4], il fallait commencer par vaincre, avant d'en parler. En un mot, loin que les hommes combattissent pour les Dieux, c'était, comme dans Homère, les Dieux qui combattaient pour les hommes. Les Romains, avant de prendre[5] une place, sommaient[6] ses Dieux de l'abandonner[7] ; et quand ils laissaient aux Tarentins leurs Dieux irrités, c'est qu'ils les regardaient alors[8] comme soumis aux leurs et forcés[9] à leur faire hommage. Ils laissaient aux vaincus leurs Dieux, comme ils leur laissaient leurs lois. Une couronne d'or au Jupiter du Capitole était souvent le seul tribut qu'ils en[10] exigeaient.

Or, si, malgré cette mutuelle tolérance, la superstition païenne[11], au milieu des lettres et de mille vertus, engendra tant de cruautés, je ne vois point qu'il soit possible de séparer ces mêmes cruautés du même zèle et de concilier les droits[12] d'une religion nationale avec ceux de l'humanité. Il vaut donc mieux attacher les citoyens à l'État par des liens moins forts et plus doux, et n'avoir ni héros, ni fanatiques.

Reste donc[13] la religion de l'homme, ou le Christianisme : non pas celui d'aujourd'hui, mais celui de l'Évangile[14]. Par cette religion[15], sainte, sublime, véritable, les hommes, enfants du même Dieu, se reconnaissent tous pour frères ; et la société qui les unit est d'autant plus étroite qu'elle ne se dissout pas même à la mort.

---

[1] [et ne le disputaient que quand il plaisait aux mortels.] D. B. omits the clause ' et en suivaient…des mortels.'

[2] [Loin que les hommes combattissent pour les Dieux, c'étaient, comme dans Homère, les Dieux qui combattaient pour les hommes.]

[3] [le conquérir.]

[4] [servir les Dieux des vainqueurs ne venant que de la victoire.]

[5] [en attaquant.]   [6] [priaient.]   [7] [la quitter.]

[8] [Ces Dieux.]   [9] [pour ainsi dire.]   [10] D. B. omits *en*.

[11] Three or four words illegible before or after this.

[12] [de l'humanité avec ceux d'une religion nationale.]

[13] D. B. omits *donc*.   [14] [qui est un peu différent.]

[15] [la seule.]

CH. VIII] *Le Christianisme n'est pas de ce monde* 503

Cependant, cette même religion, n'ayant [1]nulle relation particulière[1] à la constitution de l'État[2], laisse aux lois politiques et civiles la seule force que leur donne le droit naturel, sans leur en ajouter aucune autre ; et par là, un des plus grands soutiens de la société reste sans effet dans l'État.

On nous dit qu'un peuple[3] de vrais chrétiens formerait la plus parfaite société qu'on puisse imaginer. La plus parfaite, en un sens[4] purement moral, cela peut être ; mais non pas certainement la plus forte, ni la plus durable. Le peuple serait soumis aux lois, les chefs seraient équitables, les soldats[5] mépriseraient la mort : j'en conviens. Mais ce n'est pas là tout.

Le[6] Christianisme[7] est une religion toute spirituelle, qui détache[8] les hommes des choses de la terre. La patrie du chrétien n'est pas de ce monde. Il fait son devoir, il est vrai : mais il le fait avec une profonde indifférence sur le succès des soins qu'il se donne. Peu lui importe que tout aille bien ou mal ici bas[9] : si l'État est florissant, il jouit modestement[10] de la félicité publique ; si l'État dépérit, il bénit la main de Dieu qui s'appesantit sur son peuple. Pour que la société fût paisible et que l'harmonie se maintînt, il faudrait que tous les citoyens sans exception fussent également bons chrétiens ; mais si malheureusement il s'y trouvait quelque ambitieux ou quelque hypocrite, un Catilina, par exemple, ou un Cromwell, celui-là très certainement aurait bon marché de ses pieux compatriotes[11]. Dès qu'il aurait trouvé par quelque ruse le secret de les tromper et de s'emparer d'une partie de l'autorité publique, aussitôt voilà une puissance. Dieu veut qu'on lui obéisse ; c'est la verge dont il punit ses enfants ; on se ferait conscience de chasser l'usurpateur ; il faudrait verser du

---

[1] [pas une force [parti—broken off] exclusive et particulière, relative.]
[2] [cette même religion ne donne aucune force nouvelle au Contrat social et laisse, etc.]
[3] [une société.]   [4] [en un certain sens.]
[5] [les soldats, chacun toujours prêt à mourir pour son devoir, feraient.]
[6] Written at top of p. 48 v° : La religion n'empêche pas les scélérats de commettre des crimes, mais elle empêche beaucoup de gens de devenir des scélérats : and, detached : On eût eu bien de la peine à donner aux anciens l'idée de ces hommes brouillons et séditieux qu'on appelle missionnaires.
[7] [n'inspire qu'indifférence pour les (broken off).]
[8] [Le Christianisme déjà détache trop les hommes des soins terrestres pour les rendre fort attentifs à ce qui s'y passe.]
[9] [pourvu que lui personnellement fasse son devoir, peu lui importe, au surplus, que tout aille, etc.]
[10] [modérément.]   [11] [concitoyens.]

sang, user de violence, troubler le repos public. Tout cela ne s'accorde point avec la douceur du chrétien ; et après tout, qu'importe qu'on soit libre, ou dans les fers, dans cette vallée de misère ? L'essentiel est d'aller en paradis, et la résignation n'est qu'un moyen de plus pour cela. On peut être tout aussi bien sauvé esclave qu'homme libre.

Survient-il quelque guerre étrangère ? les citoyens marchent au combat ; nul d'eux ne songe à fuir ; ils font leur devoir[1], mais ils ont peu de passion pour la victoire ; ils savent plutôt mourir que vaincre. Qu'ils soient vainqueurs ou vaincus, qu'importe ? La providence sait mieux qu'eux ce qu'il leur faut. Qu'on imagine quel parti un ennemi impétueux[2], actif, passionné[3], peut tirer de leur stoicisme. Mettez vis-à-vis d'eux ces peuples généreux et fiers que dévorait l'ardent amour de la gloire et de la patrie. Supposez votre République chrétienne vis-à-vis de Sparte ou de Rome : les chrétiens seront battus, écrasés, détruits avant d'avoir eu le temps de se reconnaître ; ou ne devront leur salut qu'au mépris que leur ennemi concevra pour eux. [4]C'était un beau serment, ce me semble, que celui des soldats de Fabius : ils ne jurèrent pas de vaincre ou de mourir ; ils jurèrent de revenir vainqueurs, et ils revinrent tels. Jamais des chrétiens ne s'aviseront[5] d'un pareil serment ; car ils croiraient tenter Dieu[6].

Mais je me trompe en disant une *République chrétienne*[7] : chacun de ces deux[8] mots exclut l'autre. Le Christianisme ne prêche que servitude et dépendance. [9]L'esprit du Christianisme est trop favorable à la tyrannie pour qu'elle n'en profite pas toujours. Les vrais chrétiens sont faits pour être esclaves[10]. Ils le savent et ne s'en émeuvent guère ; cette courte vie a trop peu de prix pour eux.

Les troupes chrétiennes sont excellentes[11], me dira-t-on. Je

---

[1] [ils sont braves mais.]   [2] [ardent.]
[3] [et déterminé à vaincre ou mourir.]
[4] Added as afterthought, in very black ink.   [5] or *s'aviseraient*.
[6] Written at bottom of p. 49 r⁰ : Sous les empereurs païens, les soldats chrétiens étaient braves : je le crois bien. C'était une espèce de guerre d'honneur entre eux et les troupes païennes. Sitôt que les empereurs furent chrétiens, cette émulation ne subsista plus, et leurs troupes ne firent plus rien qui vaille. Ce n'était pas tant, alors, une affaire de religion qu'une espèce.... The last sentence is written on the left margin of the same page. D. B. omits *je le crois bien* ; and reads *ne furent plus rien*, omitting *qui vaille*.
[7] [il est impossible qu'il y en ait de telle.]
[8] [excellents.]   [9] [il est [sa doctrine est].]
[10] [dans ce monde.]   [11] [braves.]

CH. VIII]   *Profession de foi civile*   505

le nie. Qu'on m'en montre de telles. Quant à moi, je ne connais point de troupes chrétiennes[1]. On me citera les croisades. Sans disputer sur la valeur des croisés, je me contenterai de remarquer que, bien loin d'être des chrétiens, c'étaient des soldats du prêtre[2]; c'étaient des citoyens de l'Église; ils se battaient pour leur pays spirituel. À le bien prendre[3], ceci rentre dans le paganisme[4]. Comme l'Évangile n'est point une religion civile, toute guerre de religion est impossible parmi les chrétiens.

Revenons au droit, et fixons les principes. Le droit [5]que le pacte social donne au souverain sur les sujets ne passe point[5], comme je l'ai dit, les bornes de l'utilité publique. [6]Les sujets ne doivent donc compte au souverain de leurs opinions qu'autant que ces opinions importent à la communauté. [7]Or, il importe bien à l'État que chaque citoyen ait une religion; mais les dogmes de cette religion ne lui importent qu'autant qu'ils se rapportent à la morale; tous les autres ne sont point de sa compétence; et chacun peut avoir au surplus telles opinions qu'il lui plaît, sans qu'il appartienne au souverain d'en connaître[8].

[9]Il y a des dogmes positifs que le citoyen doit admettre comme avantageux à la société, et des dogmes négatifs qu'il doit rejeter comme nuisibles[9].

Ces dogmes divers composent une profession de foi purement civile qu'il appartient à la Loi de prescrire, non pas précisément comme dogmes de religion, mais comme sentiments de sociabilité, sans lesquels il est impossible d'être bon citoyen ni sujet fidèle. Elle ne peut obliger personne à les croire, mais elle peut bannir de l'État quiconque ne les croit pas[10]; elle peut le bannir non comme impie, mais comme insociable; comme incapable d'aimer

---

[1] [Je ne connais pas même de chrétiens en Europe. S'il y en a, j'ignore où ils sont.]

[2] [pape.]   [3] D. B. reads *À le comprendre.*

[4] [C'est la religion du prêtre.]

[5] [Nous avons dit que ce que chacun aliène donne, etc.]

[6] [Le souverain n'est [n'a] (broken off).]

[7] [ce qui se rapporte (broken off).]

[8] [de s'en mêler.]

[9] [Il y a donc une Religion purement civile: c'est à dire, dont les dogmes, uniquement relatifs à la morale, donnent une nouvelle force aux lois. Cette Religion consiste en dogmes positifs et en dogmes négatifs: c'est à dire, en dogmes que le citoyen doit admettre comme avantageux à la société, et d'autres [négatifs] qu'il doit rejeter comme nuisibles. D'où il suit qu'on doit établir dans l'État.]

[10] [parce qu'alors il est impossible.]

32—5

sincèrement les lois, la justice, la patrie, et d'immoler[1] au besoin sa vie à ses devoirs[2].

Tout citoyen doit être tenu de prononcer cette profession de foi par devant le magistrat et d'en reconnaître expressément tous les dogmes. Si quelqu'un[3] ne les reconnaît pas, qu'il soit retranché[4] de la Cité, mais qu'il emporte paisiblement tous ses biens. Si quelqu'un, après avoir reconnu ces dogmes, se conduit comme ne les croyant pas, qu'il soit puni de mort[5]. Il a commis le plus grand des crimes : il a menti devant les lois.

Les dogmes de la religion civile seront[6] simples et en petit nombre[7] ; énoncés avec précision et sans explication ni commentaire. L'existence de la Divinité[8], bienfaisante, puissante, intelligente, prévoyante et pourvoyante ; la vie à venir ; le bonheur des justes et le châtiment des méchants ; la sainteté du Contrat social et des lois : voilà les dogmes positifs[9]. Quant aux dogmes négatifs, je les borne à un seul : c'est l'intolérance[10].

Ceux qui distinguent l'intolérance civile et l'intolérance ecclésiastique se trompent. L'une mène nécessairement à l'autre ; ces deux intolérances sont inséparables. Il est impossible de vivre en paix avec des gens qu'on croit damnés. Les aimer, ce serait haïr Dieu qui les punit. Il faut nécessairement qu'on les convertisse, ou qu'on les persécute[11]. Un article nécessaire et indispensable dans la profession de foi civile est donc celui-ci : Je ne crois point que personne soit coupable devant Dieu, pour n'avoir pas pensé comme moi sur son culte[12].

Je dirai plus[13] : il est impossible que les intolérants, réunis sous les mêmes dogmes, vivront jamais en paix entre eux. Dès qu'ils

---

[1] [de vouloir mourir pour.] D. B. inserts *et* before *la patrie*.
[2] [au devoir et à la vertu.]
[3] [quiconque.] [4] [il ne doit point être puni.]
[5] [il doit être puni de mort.] [6] [sont.]
[7] [Les dogmes positifs, l'existence de la Divinité, etc.]
[8] [sa toute puissance, sa justice, sa providence, la vie à venir, les punitions.]
[9] [le sommaire des dogmes positifs.]
[10] [Mais il faut expliquer ce mot.]
[11] [L'intolérance n'est donc pas dans ce dogme : *il faut contraindre ou punir les incrédules* ; elle est dans cet autre : *Hors de l'Église, point de salut*. Quiconque damne ainsi libéralement son frère au diable dans l'autre monde ne se fera jamais un grand scrupule de le tourmenter dans celui-ci.]
[12] [je ne crois point que Dieu punisse personne dans l'autre vie, pour n'avoir pas pensé comme moi dans celle-ci.]
[13] [Il y a plus ; c'est qu'il est impossible, etc.] D. B. reads *Je dirai qu'il est impossible*.

ont inspection sur la foi les uns des autres[1], ils deviennent tous[2] ennemis, alternativement persécutés et persécuteurs, chacun sur tous et tous sur chacun. L'intolérant est l'homme de Hobbes ; l'intolérance est la guerre de l'humanité. [3]La société des intolérants est semblable à celle des démons; ils ne s'accordent que pour se tourmenter. Les horreurs[4] de l'inquisition n'ont jamais régné que dans les pays où tout le monde était intolérant[5]; dans ces pays, il ne tient qu'à la fortune que les victimes ne soient les bourreaux.

[6]Il faut penser comme moi pour être sauvé: voilà[7] le dogme affreux[8] qui désole la terre. Vous n'aurez jamais rien fait pour la paix publique si vous n'ôtez de la Cité ce dogme infernal. Quiconque ne le trouve pas exécrable ne peut être ni chrétien, ni citoyen, ni homme ; c'est un monstre qu'il faut immoler au repos du genre humain.

[9]Cette profession de foi une fois établie, qu'elle se renouvelle tous les ans avec solennité, et que cette solennité[10] soit accompagnée d'un culte auguste[11] et simple dont les magistrats soient seuls les ministres[12] et qui réchauffe dans les cœurs l'amour de la patrie[12]. Voilà tout ce qui est permis au souverain de prescrire quant à la religion. Qu'au surplus on laisse introduire toutes les opinions qui ne sont point contraires à la profession de foi civile, tous les cultes qui peuvent compatir avec le culte public ; et qu'on ne craigne ni disputes de religion, ni guerres sacrées ! Personne ne s'avisera de subtiliser sur les dogmes, quand on aura

---

[1] [la religion sert [ils feront servir la religion d'] d'instrument à leurs passions.]

[2] [réciproquement.]

[3] [Il n'y a pas plus (broken off).]

[4] D. B. reads *hommes* ; he may possibly be right.

[5] [l'intolérance était la plus universelle.]

[6] [Ne souffrez donc jamais dans l'État aucun homme.] [Quiconque ne pense pas comme moi ne peut être sauvé.]

[7] [voici.] D. B. reads *dévore la terre* ; he may possibly be right.

[8] [négatif qu'il faut rejeter. Quiconque ne trouve pas ce dogme exécrable, les guerres de religion, les discordes civiles, tout qui porte le fer et le feu dans les États, qui arme les pères et les enfants les uns contre les autres devrait s'ôter de la Cité.]

[9] [Telle est la [véritable] religion civile qui donne aux lois la sanction intérieure de la conscience et du droit divin, qui attache les citoyens à leurs devoirs plus qu'à leur vie, qui n'a pas besoin de les tromper pour leur faire aimer la patrie, ni de les détacher de la terre.]

[10] [ce renouvellement.]   [11] [touchant.]

[12] [et qui ramène les cœurs [les âmes] pieux à l'amour de la patrie.]

si peu d'intérêt à les discuter. [1]Nul apôtre ou missionnaire n'aura droit de venir taxer d'erreur une religion, qui sert de base à toutes les religions du monde et qui n'en condamne aucune. Et si quelqu'un vient prêcher son horrible intolérance[2], il sera puni sans disputer contre lui. On le punira[3] comme séditieux et rebelle aux lois, sauf à aller, s'il lui plaît, narrer son martyre dans son pays. Ainsi l'on réunira les avantages de la religion de l'homme et de celle du citoyen. L'État aura son culte et ne sera ennemi de celui d'aucune autre[4]. Les lois divine et humaine se réunissant toujours sur le même objet, les plus pieux théistes seront[5] aussi les plus zélés citoyens, et la défense des saintes lois sera la gloire du Dieu des hommes[6].

[7]Maintenant qu'il n'y a plus, et qu'il ne peut plus y avoir, de religion nationale exclusive, on doit tolérer toutes celles qui tolèrent les autres, pourvu que leurs dogmes n'ayent[8] rien de contraire aux devoirs du citoyen. [9]Mais quiconque dit : *Hors de l'Église, point de salut*, doit être chassé de l'État, à moins que l'État ne soit l'Église[9]. Ce dogme intolérant ne doit être admis que dans un Gouvernement théocratique ; dans tout autre il est absurde et pernicieux[10].

Il est clair que l'acte civil doit avoir tous les effets civils,

---

[1] [Tout apôtre sera (broken off)—tout missionnaire sera puni du dernier supplice, non comme un fourbe ou un faux prophète, mais comme un séditieux et un perturbateur de la société.] With this attack upon the missionaries, compare Bayle, *Ce que c'est que la France toute catholique* (ed. Rotterdam, Vol. I. pp. 66—72).

[2] [ses dogmes comme nécessaires à croire.]

[3] [qu'il soit puni. v.l. mis à mort.] D. B. omits *On le punira*, and *sauf à aller...son pays*.

[4] [Le citoyen mourant pour sa patrie mourra pour sa religion.]

[5] [ne seront point indifférents pour le bien public, et le meilleur chrétien sera le plus zélé citoyen.] It is not absolutely certain that this is cancelled.

[6] [le bien public et la gloire de Dieu (la liberté publique).]

[Quand je ne ferais pas ici la meilleure police religieuse, elle est la seule que le souverain peut prescrire ; [tout le reste], il ne peut aller plus loin sans usurper un droit qu'il n'a pas.]

[7] This paragraph (in different ink) was probably meant for the close of the chapter ; the next two (MS. p. 51, r° and v°) for a note.

[8] [ne faisent point (unfinished).]

[9] [Mais l'intolérance ne convient qu'à la théocratie ; dans tout autre Gouvernement, ce dogme est pernicieux. Tout homme qui dit *Hors de l'Église, point de salut*, est nécessairement un mauvais citoyen et doit être chassé de l'État, à moins que l'État ne soit l'Église et que le Prince ne soit le Pontife.] This on lower margin of p. 51 (recto). [Le dogme de l'intolérance.]

[10] [il ôte le glaive au Prince, pour le donner au prêtre.] D. B. has *Le dogme*.

CH. VIII] *L'état civil des Protestants* 509

comme l'état ¹et le nom¹ des enfants, la succession des biens, etc. Les effets du sacrement doivent être purement spirituels. Or, point du tout : ils ont tellement confondu tout cela que l'état des citoyens et la succession des biens dépendent uniquement des prêtres. Il dépend absolument du clergé qu'il ne naisse pas dans tout le royaume de France un seul enfant légitime, ²qu'aucun citoyen n'ait droit au bien de son père², et que dans trente ans d'ici la France entière³ ne soit peuplée que de bâtards. Tant que les fonctions des prêtres auront des effets civils, les prêtres seront les vrais magistrats⁴. Les assemblées du clergé de France sont, à mes yeux, les vrais États de la nation⁵.

Je ne vois pas pourquoi le clergé de France n'étendrait pas à tous les citoyens, quand il lui plaira, le droit⁶ dont il use⁷ actuellement sur les Protestants français⁸. ⁹L'expérience ayant fait sentir à quel point la révocation de l'Édit de Nantes avait affaibli la monarchie, on a voulu retenir dans le Royaume, avec les débris¹⁰ de la secte persécutée, la seule pépinière de sujets qui lui reste. ¹¹Depuis lors¹², ces infortunés, réduits à la plus horrible situation où jamais peuple se soit vu depuis que le monde existe, ne peuvent ni rester ni fuir. ¹³Il leur est permis d'être ni étrangers, ni citoyens, ni hommes. Les droits même de la nature leur sont ôtés ; ¹⁴le mariage leur est interdit ; et dépouillés à la fois de la patrie, de la famille et des biens, ils sont réduits à l'état des bêtes¹⁵.

Voyez¹⁶ comment ce traitement¹⁷ inouï suit d'une chaîne de

¹ Added.   ² Added.   ³ Added.
⁴ [D'où je conclus que.]
⁵ [et que les Parlements ne sont que des magistrats subalternes.]
[On voit de ceci un exemple bien remarquable dans la conduite qu'on tient avec les Protestants du Royaume.] [Voulez-vous de ceci un exemple attesté [authentique] mais presque incroyable ? Vous n'avez qu'à considérer la conduite. On s'est aperçu [v.l. senti] ce qu'on aurait…(unfinished).]
⁶ [pouvoir.]   ⁷ [exerce.]
⁸ [du royaume.]
⁹ [Depuis la ré (broken) de N. il semble que le plus simple bon sens aurait annoncé [a dû faire prévoir] le tort.]   N. = l'édit de Nantes.
¹⁰ [restes des protestants.]
¹¹ [Le Gouvernement a donc se trouvé (*sic*) dans la plus horrible, etc.]
¹² [ce temps.]
¹³ [Le plus saint des droits.]   D. B. inserts *ne* between *Il* and *leur est permis*.
¹⁴ [le seul qu'on les prive—du seul.]   D. B. omits *leur* before *est interdit*.
¹⁵ [et c'est fait dans ce siècle de lumières et d'humanité.]
¹⁶ [Voici comment.]
¹⁷ [si peu compatible avec l'humanité.]

principes mal entendus. Les lois du Royaume ont prescrit les formes solennelles que doivent avoir les mariages légitimes; et cela est très bien. Mais elles ont attribué au clergé l'administration de ces formes, et les ont confondues avec le prétendu sacrement. Le clergé, de son côté, refuse d'administrer le sacrement à qui n'est pas enfant de l'Église, et l'on ne saurait taxer le refus d'injustice. Le Protestant donc ne peut pas se marier selon les formes prescrites par les lois, sans renoncer à sa religion; et le magistrat ne reconnaît de mariages légitimes que ceux qui sont faits selon les formes prescrites par les lois. Ainsi l'on tolère et l'on proscrit à la fois le peuple protestant: on veut à la fois qu'il vive et qu'il meure[1]. Le malheureux a beau se marier, et respecter dans sa misère la pureté du lien qu'il a formé; il se voit condamné par les magistrats; il voit dépouiller sa famille de ses biens, traiter sa femme en concubine et ses enfants en bâtards; le tout, comme vous voyez, juridiquement et conséquemment aux lois.

Cette situation est unique, et je me hâte de poser la plume, de peur de céder au cri de la nature, qui s'élève et gémit devant son auteur.

[The remainder of the text is made up of Fragments.]

[2]L'expérience apprend que, de toutes les sectes du Christianisme, la protestante, comme la plus sage et la plus douce, est aussi la plus pacifique et la plus sociale. C'est la seule où les lois puissent garder leur empire, et les chefs[3] leur autorité.

[4]Mais il est clair que ce prétendu droit de tuer les vaincus ne résulte en aucune manière de l'état de guerre. La guerre n'est point une relation entre les hommes[5], mais entre les Puissances[6], dans laquelle les particuliers ne sont ennemis qu'accidentellement[7], et moins comme citoyens que comme soldats. [8]L'étranger qui vole, pille et détient les sujets, sans déclarer la guerre au prince, n'est pas un ennemi, c'est un brigand[8]. Et même en pleine guerre,

---

[1] [Les Protestants français se marient pourtant, parce que le droit de la nature est le (broken off); mais ils voient enlever leurs biens à leurs familles. Cette situation est unique.]

[2] At bottom of p. 51 (verso).   [3] [magistrats.]

[4] This Fragment (p. 72 v°) is a variant on *C. S.* I. iv. Compare also *L'état de guerre.*

[5] [d'homme à homme.]

[6] [qui a pour fin la destruction de l'État ennemi et.]

[7] [et autant qu'ils prennent les armes comme soldats.]

[8] [Ceux qui volent...ne sont pas des ennemis, ce sont des brigands.]

un prince juste[1] s'empare en pays ennemi de tout ce qui appartient au public[2], mais il respecte la personne et les biens des particuliers; il respecte les droits sur lesquels est fondé son propre pouvoir. La fin de la guerre est la destruction de l'État ennemi ; on a droit d'en tuer les défenseurs, tant qu'ils ont les armes à la main. Mais, sitôt qu'ils les posent et se rendent, ils cessent[3] d'être ennemis, ou plutôt instruments de l'ennemi ; et l'on n'a plus droit sur leur vie. On peut[4] tuer l'État sans tuer[5] un seul de ses membres. Or la guerre ne donne[6] aucun droit qui ne soit nécessaire à sa fin.

Le Pape est le vrai roi des rois [7]dans l'Église romaine. Toute la division des peuples en États et Gouvernements n'est qu'apparente et illusoire. Dans le fond, il n'y a qu'un État dans l'Église romaine. Les vrais magistrats sont les Évêques ; le clergé est le souverain ; les citoyens sont les prêtres : les laïques ne sont rien du tout[8]. Il doit... (broken off).

On verso of p. 1, the following:

Les signes moraux sont incertains, difficiles à soumettre au calcul.

La sûreté, la tranquillité, la liberté même.

Plusieurs peuples, au milieu des guerres et des dissensions intestines, ne laissent pas de multiplier extrêmement. Dans d'autres Gouvernements, au contraire, la paix même est dévorante et consume les citoyens.

Dans un État libre, les hommes, souvent rassemblés entr'eux, vivent peu avec les femmes.

Les lois de Sparte, au lieu d'assurer la propriété, la détruisent. Où les lois étaient les mœurs, les mœurs devenaient des lois[9].

---

[1] [on.]   [2] [prince.]
[3] [ne sont plus ennemis, ils sont hommes.]
[4] [pour ainsi dire.]   [5] [qu'il coutât la vie à.]
[6] [peut donner.]
[7] D. B. omits *dans l'Église romaine*.
[8] [D'où il suit que la division des États et des Gouvernements catholiques n'est qu'apparente et illusoire.]
[9] [devaient être des lois.] The last two Fragments are written on r⁰ of p. 47.

APPENDIX I

A REPLY TO CRITICISMS ON THE *DISCOURS SUR L'INÉGALITÉ*.

In MS. Neuchâtel 7872 is a folio sheet, folded as quarto and written on all four sides. It contains the criticisms of a naturalist (unnamed) upon the biological arguments of the *Discours sur l'inégalité*, with Rousseau's answers subjoined in autograph.

(a) *Criticism on Note* (d). Il est vrai que la terre abandonnée à elle-même est très fertile: mais qu'en conclure? Il n'en est point moins certain que l'homme, s'il était frugivore et errant, mourrait de faim pendant cinq ou six mois de l'année. Les fruits farineux, comme le gland, la châtaigne etc., sont ceux qui se conservent le plus longtemps. Mais tout cela est pourri ou germé au mois d'avril, à moins qu'on n'en ait eu un grand soin. Alors, il faudrait admettre des amas et une habitation fixe. Il n'y a d'animaux uniquement frugivores que ceux qui peuvent paître et se nourrir de boutons ou d'écorce d'arbre. Les sangliers, qui vivent ordinairement des racines etc., sont contraints au printemps de dévorer de jeunes animaux, lapins etc. Il faut convenir que nous ressemblons aux sangliers à beaucoup d'égards.

**Rousseau's rejoinder*. Je ne sais qu'il en est de cette ressemblance; et je ne sais pas non plus pourquoi l'homme, faute de fruits, ne brouterait pas l'herbe, les bourgeons, et ne se servirait pas de ses mains ou de ses griffes pour déterrer des racines, comme ont fait souvent même plusieurs des nôtres dans des lieux déserts. De plus, on me cite toujours les longs hivers: et l'on ne veut pas faire attention que, pour plus de la moitié de la terre, il n'y a presque point d'hiver; que les arbres ne se dépouillent point, et qu'il y a des fruits toute l'année. Les raisons qu'on m'oppose sont toujours tirées de Paris, de Londres, ou de quelque autre petit coin du monde. Je tâche de ne tirer les miennes que du monde même.

(b) *Criticism on Note* (h). Les lièvres, les lapins et beaucoup d'autres animaux frugivores font jusqu'à sept ou huit petits; et les carnassiers qui les mangent, comme belettes etc., n'en font pas davantage. Parmi les oiseaux, les perdrix en font beaucoup plus que les éperviers. Le crapaud-volant, qui ne vit que de mouches et ne mange aucune graine, ne fait que deux petits, comme la tourterelle. Il n'est pas vrai qu'il faille plus de temps aux frugivores qu'aux carnassiers pour chercher leur nourriture. Les bêtes sauvages qui paissent sortent pour la plupart tous les soirs à la même heure, et rentrent avant le jour. Les bêtes carnassières emploient le même temps à chercher, mais la chasse est journalière. Quelquefois c'est l'affaire d'un instant; plus souvent c'est celle de toute la nuit. On s'assure aisément de tout le chemin qu'un loup a été obligé de faire. Il arrive même que le jour les surprend encore à jeun; c'est dans ce cas-là que les loups attaquent les enfants. Ce n'est donc pas la facilité de vivre qui détermine le nombre d'enfants. On suppose toujours que tout est bien réglé dans la nature. Assurez-vous des faits, et vous verrez peut-être que tout n'est pas bien réglé.

Rousseau's rejoinder. La difficulté qu'ont les bêtes carnassières de trouver leur proie dans les pays défrichés et cultivés par les hommes ne serait peut-être pas la même, si toute la terre était en friche. Il est certain que vous pouvez mettre un chat ou un loup dans cette position que le soin de sa nourriture ne lui coûtera pas vingt minutes dans les six heures. Mais quelque supposition que vous fassiez, il faudra toujours qu'un cheval ou un bœuf emploient plusieurs heures à paître. Ainsi le désavantage en général sera toujours pour ceux-ci. Au reste, quelque observation qu'on puisse faire sur les faits particuliers, la preuve que tout est bien réglé se tire d'un fait général et incontestable: c'est que toutes les espèces subsistent. Mais je comprends que nous pouvons souvent nous tromper, et moi surtout, sur le choix et l'application des règles.

(c) *Criticism on Note* (l). Le fait que cite M. Locke est vrai, et on ne peut pas le lui contester. La société entre le mâle et la femelle du loup subsiste d'une manière très constante, jusqu'à ce que les petits n'aient plus besoin de secours. * * * * Il ne paraît pas que tous ces détails de mœurs aient aucune relation avec la manière de se nourrir.

On this Rousseau makes no comment.

[It may be noted that the quotations from the *Histoire des voyages* in Notes (*f*) ('Les Hottentots entendent mieux...une main invisible'), (*j*) ('On trouve dans le royaume de Congo...des femmes sauvages') and (*p*) ('Tous les efforts...on ne le revit au Cap') are to be found copied out in MS. Neuchâtel 7842. See above, pp. 200—1, 208—9, 219.]

APPENDIX II

CONTENTS OF MS. NEUCHÂTEL, 7840.

The MS. is a smallish Folio book (pp. 86), with a limp vellum cover.
Cover: (a) Fragments: (i) Qu'est-ce qui rend les lois... [see p. 320].
        (ii) De cette maxime, s'il est vrai... [*ib.*].
        (iii) Le peuple ne peut contracter... [*ib.*].
  (b) Washing-bills, Dec. 1758—April, 1759.

Pages	
1—3	*Comparison between Rome and Sparta* [see pp. 314—20].
3 v°	Fragments: (i) Si Carthage eût été... [see p. 312].
	(ii) Mais il ne voyait pas... [see p. 318].
4	Washing-bill, June, 1758.
4 and 5 v°	Fragment: Quand toutes les parties de l'État... [see p. 321].
5 v°	Fragments: (i) on theory of Music.
	(ii) L'homme isolé [see pp. 323, 447].
6	Fragments: (i) Concluons que le cœur des citoyens... [see p. 321].
	(ii) Mais, quoiqu'il n'y ait pas... [see p. 323].
6 v°	Fragments: (i) Ils sacrifient leur liberté... [see p. 321].
	(ii) Two, on theory of Music.
7 and 8 v°	List of Saint-Pierre's MSS. (6 Cartons).
9, 9 v°, 10	List of Saint-Pierre's printed Works (17 vols.).
10 v°	Fragments: (i) En examinant la constitution... [see p. 321].
	(ii) La Loi n'agit qu'en dehors... [*ib.*].
	(iii) Ce grand ressort de l'opinion... [*ib.*].
	(iv) Birth-rate etc. of Paris, 1758 [*ib.*].
11	Extracts from Strabo (Homère le premier géographe; Tragedy; Comedy).
11 v° and 12	Washing-bills, Jan.—April, 1761.
13—55	Rough draft of *Lettres de la Montagne*, v.—ix. [see Vol. II. pp. 197—291, and 527—32].
52 v°	Second part of *Comparison between Rome and Sparta* [Vol. I. pp. 319—20].
56—8	Blank.

The remainder is written from the other end of the MS.
Cover: Fragments: (i) Ayant à parler du Gouvernement... [see pp. 274—5].
       (ii) Les impôts sont une sorte de revenu... [see p. 275].
       (iii) Après avoir longtemps puisé... [*ib.*].
       (iv) Note of debt (3 f.) to M. d'Épinay.
Two pages next Cover torn out: the first entirely; the second (p. 86) as to $\frac{2}{3}$.

Appendix II

Pages	
86—78	Rough draft of *Économie politique*.
78 v°	(a) Washing-bill (hand of Thérèse).
	(b) Fragments: (i) Il est certain que les habitants sont à la longue... [see p. 248].
	(ii) Vous pourriez peut-être prévenir... [see p. 277].
	(iii) Pouvoir de commander pour conserver la liberté.
	(iv) Ce n'est donc pas en proportion des biens que la taxe personnelle doit être établie.
	(v) Jamais Jésus-Christ... [see p. 277].
	(c) Washing-bill, Dec. 1757 (hand of Thérèse).
77	(a) Fragment: Si les citoyens tirent d'elle... [see pp. 277—8].
	(b) Washing-bill, Oct. 1757.
77 v°, 76, 76 v°	Washing-bills, Jan.—Nov. 1758; Dec. 1758; Feb. 1761.
75	Blank.
75 v°—73	Rough draft of *Économie politique* (continued).
73 v°	Fragments: (i) Il n'y a que des peuples... [see pp. 308—9].
	(ii) Le temps des plus honteux dérèglements... [see p. 309].
72	Fragments: (i) Et quant à moi... [see p. 319, note].
	(ii) Remarks on the use of *danger, risque, péril*.
72 v°	Fragments: (i) Grâce à Dieu, on ne voit plus... [see p. 309].
	(ii) Pour peu qu'on marche... [*ib.*].
	(iii) Il y a plus... [see pp. 310—1].
71	Fragment: Quand mille peuples féroces... [see p. 311].
71 v°	Rough draft of a letter about the *Lettre à d'Alembert* (to M. Leroy, Nov. 4, 1758; see *Œuvres*, x. p. 197).
70	Fragment (1755): Si tout est bien comme il est... [see pp. 224, 308].
69	Three notes on theory of Music.
69 v°	Fragment on theory of Art [see Vol. II. Appendix I. D (b)].
68	Three Fragments, possibly intended for the sequel to *Émile*.
67—4	Blank.
63 v°	Fragments: (i) Maintenant que l'état de nature... [see p. 313].
	(ii) Premièrement, le vainqueur... [see pp. 313—4].
63	Fragment: Pour connaître exactement... [see pp. 312—3].
62 v°	Fragments: (i) Il paraît par divers traits... [see pp. 311—12].
	(ii) Car, que des hommes effrénés [see p. 312].
62	(a) Three literary Fragments: (i) O Grecs, rassurez-vous....
	(ii) J'errais dans d'épaisses ténèbres....
	(iii) *Les Philènes* (title only).
	(b) Fragment: On aurait beau dire... [see p. 320].

Pages		
61 v°	Fragments:	(i) Dans le sein de la superstition... [see p. 322].
		(ii) Sans doute, il fallait dire de bonnes choses... [*ib.*].
		(iii) Les deux sexes en vaudront mieux, s'en estimeront davantage; et soyez sûr que le véritable amour n'y perdra rien [*ib.*].
		(iv) Il n'y a guère que des fous... [*ib.*].
		(v) C'est le défaut de fer... [*ib.*].
61	Fragments:	(i) Sur quoi, l'on doit se garder [see p. 311].
		(ii) Plusieurs, sans doute, aimeraient mieux [*ib.*].
60	Baker's bill ('avec Mme Lefebvre, ma boulangère'), undated.	
60 v°	Fragment: Si sous le chêne où reposera ma cendre... [broken off].	
59	Fragment: *De la solitude*: Êtres inanimés que j'ai préférés à la société des hommes...[broken off].	
59 v°	List of addresses (Mme de Chenonceaux, Comte de Zinzendorf, M. Boswell, etc.), probably 1764—5.	
84	(in pencil): Après que quelques années auront effacé mon nom des fastes littéraires, puisse-t-il vivre encore chez quelque nation pauvre et ignorée, mais juste, sage et heureuse, qui, préférant la paix et l'innocence à la gloire et aux conquêtes, lira quelquefois avec plaisir... [broken off].	

[From the above it will be seen that the earliest dateable entry in this MS. is the Rough Draft of the *Économie politique*, which cannot have been written later than the first half of 1755 (seeing that the Volume of the *Encyclopédie*, in which it was published, appeared in November of that year) and which may go back to the latter part of 1754. The Fragment of the *Lettre à Philopolis* must have been written in October or November, 1755 (see above, pp. 221, 227). The entry concerning the writings of Saint-Pierre was probably made in 1754 or 1755 (see above, p. 360). The earliest dated washing-bill is that of Oct. 1757. The latest entry is probably either the Rough Draft of *Lettres de la Montagne* (1764; see Vol. II. p. 173); or, more probably, the list of addresses (p. 59 v°), which includes that of Boswell, hardly to be dated earlier than December, 1764 (see Vol. II. p. 293).]

END OF VOLUME I.